CorelDRA...
for Beginners

Gary David Bouton

NRP
NEW RIDERS PUBLISHING

New Riders Publishing, Indianapolis, Indiana

CorelDRAW! 5 for Beginners

By Gary David Bouton

Published by:
New Riders Publishing
201 West 103rd Street
Indianapolis, IN 46290-1097 USA

All rights reserved. No part of this book may be reproduced or transmitted in any form or by any means, electronic or mechanical, including photocopying, recording, or by any information storage and retrieval system, without written permission from the publisher, except for the inclusion of brief quotations in a review.

Copyright © 1994 by New Riders Publishing

Printed in the United States of America   3 4 5 6 7 8 9 0

```
Bouton, Gary David, 1953-
   CorelDRAW! for beginners / Gary David Bouton.
         p.        cm

   Includes index.
   ISBN 1-56205-327-2 : $24.99
   1. CorelDRAW! 2. Computer graphics.
T385.B6828 1994
006.6' 869-dc20                                    94-13141
                                                   CIP
```

Publisher
  Lloyd J. Short

Associate Publisher
  Tim Huddleston

Managing Editor
  Matthew Morrill

Product Development Manager
  Rob Tidrow

Marketing Manager
  Ray Robinson

Director of Special Projects
  Cheri Robinson

Product Director
  Cheri Robinson

Aquisitions Editor
  Alicia Krakovitz

Senior Editor
  Tad Ringo

Production Editor
  Steve Weiss

Editor
  Sarah Kearns

Technical Editor
  Lisa Agnes Windham

Acquisitions Coordinator
  Stacey Beheler

Editorial Assistant
  Karen Opal

Publisher's Assistant
  Melissa Lynch

Cover Designer
  Jay Corpus

Book Designer
  Kevin Spear

Production Imprint Manager
  Juli Cook

Production Imprint Team Leader
  Katy Bodenmiller

Graphics Image Specialists
  Tim Montgomery
  Dennis Sheehan
  Susan VanDeWalle

Production Analysts
  Mary Beth Wakefield
  Dennis Clay Hager

Production Team
  Carol Bowers
  Elaine Brush
  Stephanie Davis
  Kimberly K. Hannell
  Greg Kemp
  Jenny Kucera
  Wendy Ott
  Shelly Palma
  Ryan Rader
  Kim Scott
  Tonya R. Simpson
  SA Springer
  Marcella Thompson
  Scott Tullis
  Dennis Wesner

Indexer
  Bront Davis

About the Author

Gary David Bouton is a computer graphics artist who documents programs like CorelDRAW version 5 with a sensitivity to artists (and others) who have used traditional tools and are finally adding the PC to their collection. He is the author of *Adobe Photoshop NOW!* and *Inside Adobe Photoshop version 2.5 for Windows*, and a contributing author to *CorelDRAW! Special Effects*, all published by New Riders Publishing. After a 20-year career in advertising, the author turned to the IBM-PC to give his ideas the complex graphical shape that only a computer can assist in bringing to life.

With his partner and wife Barbara, the two concentrate on the core elements of software programs like CorelDRAW! and Adobe Photoshop in their books. Partners at Exclamat!ons, a company that polishes rough ideas, Gary and Barbara spend as much time educating clients in the how-tos as they do creating brochures, logos, computer screen shows, and other collateral material companies need to maintain a fresh, thought-provoking corporate image.

Gary was a finalist in the Second Annual CorelDRAW International Design Contest and an Award of Excellence winner in the Third Annual CorelDRAW International Design Contest. As editor of *NewsBytes*, the newsletter of The Central New York PC Users Group, Gary won First Prize in the 1993 Intergalactic Newsletter Competition, an international competition sponsored by Lotus, InfoWorld, and NYPC.

According to Gary, "CorelDRAW version 5 is a bit of a surprise to both the novice and experienced user. Folks who have been working with it since its first version have said the same thing every year: 'this program *can't* get any larger.' But it does! Happily, both the seasoned professional and the new user can quickly get down to business with version 5, because Corel Corporation has put a lot of effort into making the effects that used to be hard to accomplish very automatic."

It is the author's wish that the reader will feel at home with the author's informal method of conveying an idea, a trick, or a profound realization about CorelDRAW. A book can be a barrier, or it can be a conduit, depending on how it's written, and if you learn things quicker than you imagine and still have fun while learning, then the author hopes you'll continue to share in the same spirit and tell everyone this is an art book, and not simply another book about PCs.

Gary can be reached at:

CompuServe 74512,230

Dedication

This one is for my grandmother, Effie Hill Bouton. If she were alive today, she'd intuitively understand that I've ported my design skills to the personal computer, that it's a good thing, and tell me that I shouldn't sit too so close to my monitor. Grandmothers like mine, yours, and everyone's, are an important natural resource and an endangered species. If you can still visit yours, make it a good visit real soon.

Acknowledgements

How does an author release a truckload of CorelDRAW version 5 information specifically tailored for the beginner the moment Corel Corporation releases version 5? Simple. He doesn't. The book you're holding is the result of teamwork by editors, Corel employees, and human resources who, as the author, I simply can't begin thank enough.

Here's my best try at letting you know who makes the fella onstage look good from behind the scenes. Thanks to:

- Cheri Robinson, at New Riders Publishing. Although Cheri's official title is Director of Special Projects, Cheri played Reader, Pupil, Assistant Technical Editor, and Novice Designer on this book. Cheri actually did the assignments as I've outlined them, and mailed me her chess piece from Chapter 5. And I put a gold star on her laser print as any good art teacher would. Cheri, thanks for understanding my need to communicate the way I do about art, computer or physical, and thanks for letting me do it without compromise.

- Steve Weiss, lead editor on the CorelDRAW book, and a buddy o' mine on the Corel version 4 beginner's book last year. Steve's clarity, focus, succinctness, and tell-it-like-it-is spirit helped my work on this book beyond measure, and I thank him for sharing his Word-a-Day calendar with me. Steve is actually a very provoking author *disguised* as an editor at NRP, and I'm grateful that he approaches my manuscripts with skill, craft, and a gentleman's hand. Peer-to-peer, Steve. Peer-to-peer.

- New Riders Editor Sarah Kearns, who guided me back to communicating in English after spending what seemed like 40 or 50 years compressed into a few months with CorelDRAW 5. After a while, you sort of start thinking that everyone intuitively knows what and where an Envelope Roll-Up is, and Sarah gently prodded me back to reality. Sarah? Turn around quick! There's an Outline Roll-Up on your shoulder! Onnnnly kidding. And thanks again.

- Technical Editor Lisa Agnes Windham, who shared the same triumphs and frustrations as I did experimenting with the numerous Beta versions of CorelDRAW months before the commercial release. Lisa made certain our readers get the full command menu references as well as the shortcut keys, and holds the same belief as I do that new users will have a blast with Corel's new Lens Roll-Up. Thanks, Lisa!

- Alicia Krakovitz, NRP's acquisitions editor, who helped get this whole ball rolling. Alicia, my thanks for letting me work with my friends again and the rest of the gang.

- Karen Opal, for being Karen Opal, a one-of-a-kind, wonderful editorial assistant.

- My friend Stacey Beheler, NRP acquisitions coordinator, for making sure the chapters and accompanying candy is always parceled out in a fair and prudent fashion for the editorial staff.

- Spousal Editor Barbara Bouton, my better half, for her technical and copy editing far beyond the call of duty. My name's on the cover, but so is hers. Thanks, Barbara, and I hope if I'm good, you'll let me work on one of your books.

- Corel Corporation's Michael Bellefeuille, and Kelly Grieg, Beta coordinator for the version 5 build. If we hadn't been given the chance to explore the inner workings of Corel 5 through product development, our readers wouldn't now have the thorough documentation of the wonderful things you can do with it. Everyone at Corel has treated me like a friend since I was first introduced to them, and they've been gracious providers to us even when a book had nothing to do with their software. Kelly, Michael, and the software developers at Corel should be very proud of what's surely the greatest version of CorelDRAW! yet.

- Brete Root, who assisted in scanning many of the original images used in this book. CorelDRAW was the design program used for 90 percent of the illustrations you'll see between these covers, but as a traditional designer, I frequently relied on my trusty drafting table for preliminary sketches, and as some of you are already well aware, pictures on paper don't go into a PC too well without digitizing them first. Thank you, Brete.

- My folks, Jack and Eileen; and my brother Dave. I moved from Madison Avenue back to my hometown three years ago so I could see them a little more as years go by. As it turns out, I talk to Cheri and Steve more often, and my family actually understands and accepts this. More than that, they're proud and truly believe what I'm doing eight days a week, 28 hours a day benefits people. Simple love is the best kind, and to be able to continue doing this with your blessings means the world to me.

Trademarks and Copyrights

In Chapter 7, the TIF file 056.tif, from the Majestic Places CD, is used here with the permission of Aris Entertainment. Copyright © Aris Entertainment, 1992. Photo by Tom Atwood.

New Riders Publishing has made every attempt to supply trademark information about company names, products, and services mentioned in this book. Trademarks indicated here were derived from various sources. New Riders Publishing cannot attest to the accuracy of this information.

Ami Pro is a trademark of Lotus Development Corp.

CorelDRAW! and other Corel products are trademarks of Corel Systems Corporation.

Fonter is by George Campbell and OSOSOFT.

FontSee is by Alan Reeve.

Gill Sans Ultra is a trademark of The Monotype Corporation.

Hewlett-Packard and LaserJet are trademarks of Hewlett Packard, Inc.

Norton Desktop is a trademark of Symantec.

PCTools is a trademark of Central Point Software.

PostScript, ATM, Adobe Type Manager are trademarks or registered trademarks of Adobe Systems, Inc.

TrueType is a registered trademark of Apple Computer Company.

Word for Windows is a trademark of Microsoft Corporation.

WordPerfect is a trademark of Novell, Inc.

Trademarks of other products mentioned in this book are held by the companies producing them.

Warning and Disclaimer

This book is designed to provide information about the CorelDRAW! 5 computer program. Every effort has been made to make this book as complete and as accurate as possible, but no warranty or fitness is implied.

The information is provided on an "as is" basis. The author and New Riders Publishing shall have neither liability nor responsibility to any person or entity with respect to any loss or damages arising from the information contained in this book or from the use of the disks or programs that may accompany it.

Contents at a Glance

Introduction

Chapter 1   The CorelDRAW! Test Drive

Chapter 2   Installing the Corel Bundle

Chapter 3   Customizing CorelDRAW!/Finding the Features

Chapter 4   Drawing the Line Somewhere

Chapter 5   Creating Shading with Shapes

Chapter 6   Making a Scene

Chapter 7   Working with Bitmap Images

Chapter 8   Serving Up a Page Layout

Chapter 9   Creating a Custom Typeface

Chapter 10   Clip Art Can Save Your Life!

Chapter 11   CorelPHOTO-PAINT!

Chapter 12   The Many Hats of CorelDRAW

Chapter 13   Very Special CorelDRAW Effects

Appendix A: A CorelDRAW! Glossary

Index

Contents

	Introduction	**1**
	Drawing and Painting Aren't the Same	2
	What Is Vector Art?	2
	Other *Noms de Plume* for Vector Art	4
	But Designers Never Get into Vector Math!	5
	The CorelDRAW Advantage	5
	The Game Plan	5
	Stepping Through the Chapters	6
	The Icons	8
	New Riders Publishing	9
	A Word about the Figures in This Book	11
	Ready To Hit the Ground Running?	12
1	**The CorelDRAW! Test Drive**	**13**
	Creating a Vector Art Greeting Card	14
	Launching the Good Ship CorelDRAW!	14
	The Corel Workspace	15
	Your First Pick of Tools	15
	Shaping Up for the Test Drive	16
	On Your Marquee, Get Set, Go!	16
	Using a Fountain Fill To Imitate Lighting	18
	Creating a Surface Shadow for the Ball	19
	Using the Contour Roll-Up Menu	20
	Enhancing the Contour Shadow	22
	The Order of CorelDRAWn Shapes	24
	Creating a Unique Shape To Bend Text With	26
	Creating Type and Adjusting Your View	29
	Zooming In	30
	Making the Type Bigger	31
	Picking a Better Typeface	32
	Bending the Type	33
	Positioning the Text	35
	Cruising on Past the Test Drive	36
2	**Installing the Corel Bundle**	**39**
	What To Do After You Get the CorelDRAW Box	40
	Pre-Flight Planning for the CorelDRAW Installation	40
	Making Backup Disks	41

Your Rights To Copy Corel's Disks	41
Copying Disks from Windows Program Manager	42
Checking Your Hard Disk for Corel Space	46
The Custom CorelDRAW Install	47
Should You Install All Five Programs?	50
CorelDRAW	51
CorelCHART	51
CorelSHOW	51
CorelPHOTO-PAINT	52
CorelMOVE	52
Corel's Utilities	52
Clip Art	52
Customizing a Single Application for Installation	53
Taking Stock of Your Peripheral Needs	55
Choosing Which Filters To Install	55
Installing TrueType Fonts	56
Use Business Sense When Choosing Your Fonts	58
Installing Only the Fonts You Need	59
Scanner Drivers	60
Installing Animation Run-Time Modules	61
The Necessity of Temp File Space	62
The Importance of Temporary Files	62
Considerations When Selecting a Temp Drive Location	63
The Last Dialog Box Before Installing	64
Removing Unwanted TrueType Fonts From Your System	67
Removing Unwanted Corel Files (Advanced Users Only)	68
Making Corel's Workspace Your Own	69
3 Customizing CorelDRAW!/Finding the Features	**71**
Leave The Drawing to Us	72
Keeping Your Work in One Place	72
Saving Your Work	73
Annotating and Creating a Preview of Your Corel File	74
Creating a Template for Similar Assignments	76
Assigning and Creating a Graphic Style	78
Saving a Design as a Template	79
Opening a New File Based on Your Template	80
An Alternative Method for Applying Styles	83
Preferences for the Way You Work	86
Creating a Do Not Disturb Sign	89

Nudging a Duplicate Shape	91
Getting a Better View of Your Work	93
Making a Preset Special Effect	96
Applying Your Preset to a Different Shape	99
Creating Drawings of a Grander Scale	101
The Uses For Drawing Scale	102
Picking Custom Colors for Your Designs	103
The Many Color Models of CorelDRAW	104
How Professional Do You Want Your Hard Copy?	107
Printing from CorelDRAW	109
Putting Your New Wisdom To Work	111

4 Drawing the Line Somewhere — 113

Shaping Up for Your Corel Design Work	114
Making the First Mark	114
The Freehand Style of CorelDRAWing	116
Changing the Properties of Line Segments	119
Editing an Object	119
Controlling Line Segments	120
Working with Curved Line Segments	121
Smoothing Out a Freehand Curve	122
Assembling the Pieces of a Drawing	124
Using the Bézier Tool	126
Creating the Duck's Body	126
Defining the Right Number of Nodes	129
Adding Tail Feathers to the Duck	131
Modifying the Duck Shape	133
Adding Dimension Lines and Callouts	136
Setting Up the Dimension Lines	136
Creating Duck Callouts	141
Repositioning Callout Text	142
Moving From Lines to Shading Fills	144

5 Creating Shading with Shapes — 145

Customizing the Workspace for an Assignment	146
Displaying Rulers and Grids	146
Changing the Ruler's Zero Point	147
Using the Snap To Mode	149
Simplifying the Geometry of a Rectangle	150
Creating the Neckpiece for the Pawn	152

Designing a Base for the Pawn	154
Modifying a Rectangle	154
Finishing the Profiles of the Pawn	155
Aligning the Shapes	156
Welding Shapes Together	157
Shading the Chess Piece with Blends	160
Preparing the First Control Object	161
Creating the Second Control Object	161
Aligning the Two Control Objects	161
Editing the Control Objects	162
Topping Off the Second Control Object	164
Making a Backgound for the Pawn	166
Using the Blend Command	166
Using Layers To Protect Your Work	169
Adding a New Layer	169
Secret Powers of Blending Lines	171
Giving the Wireframe Some Outline Characteristics	172
Creating the Second Control Segment	174
Using the Break Apart Command To Separate Segment Parts	176
Realizing the Blend Effect	178
Duplicating Your Blending Work	179
Summary	180
Digging Deeper Into the Bag of Tricks	180
6 Making a Scene	**181**
Working with the Multi-Page Feature	181
Deleting the Guidelines	183
Duplicating and Mirroring Objects	183
Adding Perspective to Objects	186
Rotating Objects	186
Changing Perspective	188
Understanding Vanishing Points	190
Adding a Third Dimension	190
Adding Dimensional Lighting	192
Creating a Background	194
Moving Layers, Moving Pages	198
Working the Pawns into the Background	201
Adding Background Ornaments	203
Adding Order to the Universe	204
Summary	206

7	**Working with Bitmap Images**	**207**
	Constructing a Picture Postcard	208
	Finding a Stock Image	208
	Opening an Image in PHOTO-PAINT	208
	Tilting the Image	210
	Saving the TIF Image	212
	Creating an Airbrush Effect with Fountain Fills	212
	Gathering the Background Materials	212
	Understanding the Intersection Command	215
	Using the Fill Roll-Up To Speed Up Your Work	217
	Tightening Up the Background Design	220
	Using the Snap To Objects Command	220
	Removing Unnecessary Objects	222
	Grouping Objects	222
	Adding A Pre-Built Symbol as a Design Element	223
	Using the Break Apart and Fill Commands	225
	Adding Artistic Text to the Postcard	228
	Editing Artistic Text	230
	Aligning Artistic Text	231
	Manually Kerning Artistic Text	233
	Precision Rotating the Text	235
	Making the Artistic Text the Star	236
	Importing the Beach	236
	The Power of the Clip	236
	Tricks on Repositioning Contents	238
	Summary	239
8	**Serving Up a Page Layout**	**241**
	Modifying an Ellipse with the Shape Tool	242
	Drawing the Pizza	242
	Drawing a Pie Wedge	242
	Adding Artistic Text to the Pizza Slice	244
	Entering Artistic Text	245
	Sizing the Type	246
	Shaping Artistic Text with the Envelope Effect	246
	Creating the Envelope	247
	Applying the Envelope	248
	Creative Design and the Intersection Command	251
	Adding a New Artistic Text Element	254
	Adding Toppings to the Pizza	255

CorelDRAW! 5 for Beginners

	Using Symbol Art	257
	Adding Artificial Coloring to Pizza	258
	Grouping the Pizza Ingredients	261
	Setting Up Guidelines for the Paragraph Text	262
	The Special Properties of Paragraph Text	263
	Working with Paragraph Text	266
	Typesetting a Story in CorelDRAW	268
	The Strange Things Rulers Do in Paragraph Mode	269
	Pouring Paragraph Text into an Envelope	271
	Where Does the Rest of the Text Go?	272
	Summary	275
9	**Creating a Custom Typeface**	**277**
	Beginning with a Typeface Template	277
	Understanding Typeface Measurements	279
	The Architecture of a Font	281
	Creating Your Own Font	283
	Describing a Typeface	284
	When Is a Font a Typeface?	284
	The Beginning of Your Alphabet	284
	Finalizing a Font Outline	286
	Refining Your Character	288
	Using Open Paths To Create Your Alphabet	290
	An "Outline" for the Rest of the Alphabet	293
	Exporting Your Typeface	294
	Tackling the Lowercase Letters	299
	Installing Your Custom Font	300
	Using Fonts as Symbols	302
	Creating a Mini-Art Collection	304
	Adding a Corporate Logo to an Existing Font	307
	Sizing the Logo for the Typeface	309
	Renaming a Now-Customized Font	312
	Summary	312
10	**Clip Art Can Save Your Life!**	**315**
	The Origins of Clip Art	315
	What You Can (and Can't) Do with Clip Art	316
	The 5-Minute Professional Design (Using Clip Art)	317
	Copying Attributes	319
	CorelMOSAIC and Previewing Collections	321

	MOSAIC and Your Clip Art Collection	322
	Recoloring Clip Art	325
	Re-Using Clip Art	327
	Creating Props To Enhance Clip Art	329
	Rotating and Resizing the Text	331
	Cosmetic Alteration of Corel Clip Art	334
	Changing a Character's Facial Appearance	335
	Adding a Graphic Prop to Clip Art	337
	Comparing Your Editing Work to Clip Art Work	338
	Switching from the Pencil to a Brush	340
11	**CorelPHOTO-PAINT!**	**341**
	Assembling Your Imaging Essentials	342
	Making a Splashy Movie Title	343
	Enveloped Text as a Design Element	344
	Exporting Vector Art to Bitmap Format	347
	Selecting Colors PHOTO-PAINT-Style	351
	Setting Up a Paintbrush Tip	353
	Selecting an Area Based on Color	355
	Considerations for a New Background Image	359
	A Brief Orientation on Objects	360
	The "Paint" Part of PHOTO-PAINT	362
	Adding Custom Text to the Poster	366
	Using a Mask as a Design Template	367
	Creating PHOTO-PAINT Text	371
	Merging Your Image Areas	373
	Summary	374
12	**The Many Hats of CorelDRAW**	**377**
	Charts Can Be Cool Business	378
	Matching a Chart to Your Needs	378
	Navigating a CorelCHART Spreadsheet	380
	Tagging a Range of Cells	381
	Creating Row Headers	383
	Entering a Data Range for Your Chart	384
	Auto-Positioning Your Data on the Chart	385
	Customizing Your CorelCHART	388
	Changing a Chart Color Scheme	389
	Changing Linked Group Sizes	390
	Further Customizing the CorelCHART	392

Removing Labels from the Chart		392
Adding a Manual Label		394
Reducing the Amount of Z2 Axis Entries		395
Changing Your View of Your Chart		397
Saving Your Custom Chart		399
Making an Animation Object		400
What's an Actor?		400
Choosing How You Create the Actor		401
Converting and Animating a Graphic		404
Adding a Cycle to an Actor		406
Playing Your CorelMOVE Movie		408
Timing Is Everything with Actors		409
Changing a Timeline		411
The Greatest (Slide)Show on Earth		412
Adding a CorelCHART to a Show		415
Adding a Pre-Drawn Background		416
Adding/Coloring a Text Selection		417
Adding Bullets to Lists		419
Removing the Background from Frames		421
Sorting This Whole Show Out		422
Did Someone say "Transition Effects?"		423
Playing Your CorelSHOW		424
Summary		425
13	**Very Special CorelDRAW Effects**	**427**
	Creating a Stained Glass Effect	428
	Making Frames for the Stained Glass Elements	429
	Combining Shapes To Create A Subpath for Caming	431
	Using the Blend Command To Make Lots of Tubes	433
	Applying a Blend to the Heart	436
	Making Stained Glass with Texture Fills	438
	Adding Texture to the Background	440
	Adding Stained Glass Text	443
	Refining Love as a Compositional Element	445
	Working with the Custom Fountain Fill	448
	Creating Effects with the Lens Roll-Up	451

Rules for the Lens Roll-Up	452
Making an Attention-Getting Announcement	452
Fitting a Lens into the Magnifying Glass	454
Behind the Scenes with a Finished Illustration	456
What Do You Want To Magnify?	457
Getting the Big Picture on the Lens Roll-Up	458
Reflections on a Lens	460
Summary	460
Next Steps to Other Voyages	461
A A CorelDRAW! Glossary	**463**
A	464
B	464
C	465
D	467
E	468
F	468
G	470
H	470
I	470
J	471
K	471
L	471
M	472
N	473
O	473
P	474
Q	475
R	476
S	476
T	477
U	479
V	479
W	479
X	480
Y	480
Z	480
Index	**483**

INTRODUCTION

Art Expressed as Little Ones and Zeros

My college art history instructor gave a one-question midterm exam all too many years ago. The puzzler was, "What is art?" And he flunked anyone who attempted to give a definitive answer, because he was making a point about the all-embracing, universal quality about art that defies simple explanation. I got an A (unlike my many other courses) because I wrote, "Art is an event," let him read my statement, then tore up the exam paper in his face.

Today, art is known by a fancier name if it is created by using a PC. It's called *computer graphics*. The change in name, however, doesn't alter the scope, the aesthetics, or the reasons why you're attracted to art. The computer is merely an enhancement, a magnifying glass of the artist's skills. With the right software, you can build impossible mountains of art that would take thousands of hours if created with just a pencil and paper.

A good place to begin earning your title of Computer Graphics-type Person is with a beginner's book—specifically *CorelDRAW! 5 for Beginners*.

In this chapter, you will:

- Learn how CorelDRAW is similar to conventional drawing, and where that similarity ends
- Learn this book's conventions and what's in store in the following chapters
- See how art fits into your business life
- Get a better understanding of the many ways CorelDRAW can help you create excellent art

Drawing and Painting Aren't the Same

Corel Corporation bundles several design modules around its star attraction, CorelDRAW. These modules address different business applications that you will explore in *CorelDRAW! 5 for Beginners*, but the core program, and the focus of this book, is on DRAW-ing.

Think of the two most common artist's tools—the pencil (or charcoals, pastels, and crayons) and the brush (house paint, oil, watercolor, and tooth). The digital equivalents of these two tools belong to two different categories of computer graphics: *vector* and *raster*.

You've probably heard of paint-type software programs that produce *bitmap* artwork. These programs *raster*-ize pixels (units of light) to your screen, to a printer, and to a file format as information written to your hard disk. At their worst, bitmap designs display harsh, jagged, stairsteppy edges. At their best, bitmaps produce soft, fuzzy-edged images. This inability of bitmaps to display smooth, crisp edges is due to the way in which a bitmap is composed—little squares of color representing *bits* of digital information that are *mapped* to an imaginary grid; a bitmap.

Let's leave bitmaps and painting alone for a while because CorelDRAW doesn't paint. Rather, CorelDRAW lets you draw, as in with a "virtual pencil," to create *vector* information. Your finished illustrations can display some remarkable qualities, which we'll get into a little here...

What Is Vector Art?

If you own Microsoft Office products, such as Word for Windows or Publisher, you've already had a taste of vector graphics. The clip art, in Computer Graphics Metafile (CGM) or WMF (Windows MetaFile) format, can be resized smoothly without displaying jagged (bitmap) qualities. They display quickly on your screen, and the vector image files don't take up a lot of space on your hard drive.

The reason why vector art, the art you can create in CorelDRAW, is so compact and smooth is because vector information about a design *describes* geometric shapes as mathematical formulas rather than plotting (or mapping) designs. A square designed in a painting program, for example, must contain all the pixels that make up the square. The same shape designed with CorelDRAW, however, contains information about what degree the angle lines meet, whether the square has a colored fill or not, its position on the page, and what size you've presently specified for the square. It is rasterized (mapped) to your monitor so that you can view your work, but the design *file* and the way it *prints* are always smooth and clean because the math behind a square's or an ellipse's construction contains only pure geometric equations.

Figure i.1 is of a bitmap image, created in a paint-type program like CorelPHOTO-PAINT. Notice the flowing washes of shading, and how there's no distinct edge to image areas.

Figure i.1
Bitmap images are easily distinguished from CorelDRAW art by soft edges in image areas.

In contrast, vector images, the ones you'll learn to design in CorelDRAW, consist of objects that have distinct edges, and the art produced with vectors reminds the viewer of pencil, and pen and ink, renderings: clean in their execution, and precise in the presentation of graphical content.

Introduction

Figure i.2 is an example of a CorelDRAW vector design.

Figure i.2
Vector computer graphics typically display clear, clean edges around image areas.

Other Noms de Plume for Vector Art

Because of the unique outline/fill/math information nature of vector artwork, it's acquired one or two nicknames that are descriptive of the qualities vector art exhibits. *Object-oriented* art is the same as vector art, for instance, because you draw discrete objects that can be grouped into more complex shapes. Each object (a part of a torso, a piece of clothing, and so on) can exist as its own entity, and you can move each entity independently of other objects, unlike bitmap design areas, which are fused and blended together.

Vector-based art also is called *resolution-independent*, because a piece can be scaled as small as an ant or as large as a Winnebago without loss of image detail or quality. This capability is possible because the information about a drawing exists as perfect math. If you want a graphical object twice its original size, you perform the operation that causes this in CorelDRAW (usually clicking and dragging on an image selection handle), and the underlying math that represents the image is multiplied by two.

But Designers Never Get into Vector Math!

For as complicated as vector design sounds, CorelDRAW manages to insulate you from the wealth of behind-the-scenes, mind-boggling mathematics. Most designers don't question the physics behind their mechanical pencils; they only rest assured that it works when they click on the tip.

Similarly, you have enough to preoccupy yourself with in learning the functions of CorelDRAW's workspace and how they can be best used to create outstanding designs. You can leave the intricacies of why a vector arc arcs and how come you can't smudge a CorelDRAWn line to the technical forums on CompuServe.

The CorelDRAW Advantage

There are a lot of distinct advantages an artist who has adopted CorelDRAW and computer technology has over conventional designing. You can zoom in and out of your design to get perspective, an activity that would otherwise cause bodily harm and/or irritate your co-workers in real life. You can make different versions of the same graphical idea, all of which have an identical element to one found in your original. But the most compelling reason why many designers choose CorelDRAW is that it has an *integrated environment* in which text, graphics, and other types of data are handled similarly.

You can design art that contains a chart, some body copy, a headline, photos, and an illustration or two all on the same virtual page. No actual cutting or pasting is required to create a seamlessly composed assignment that you can print or modify ad infinitum! I can't remember the last time X-Acto blades or Band-Aids went along with an assignment. Nor do I *care* to.

The Game Plan

Because CorelDRAW's tools closely match the design tools you'd use in real life, and this is an art book as well as a CorelDRAW beginners book, I've organized the information accordingly. You'll start with the simple feats, then combine these feats to create more substantial work. Along the way, you'll take excursions to Corel's other modules, such as CHART and MOVE, to discover the possibilities of combining different media to create a business presentation.

But if all this sounds a tad dry, you'll be pleasantly surprised when you dig into our non-tutorials. Besides being a powerful professional design tool, CorelDRAW is *fun*, and it's a drag for everyone concerned when your accomplishments consist of a box, a stick figure, or a pattern. Your real-life assignments are goal-oriented, and so are the larger-than-life examples I'll guide you through.

Stepping Through the Chapters

To get your experience with CorelDRAW off to a quick start, **Chapter 1** is a taxi driver's tour of CorelDRAW's workspace. You see how to get graphical results from the program from the word go. Is it a complete education? Nope—that's what the *rest* of the book is for. But when asked, an awful lot of readers have said that they immediately turn to the middle of computer books to get to the "good stuff," so I've put a healthy helping right up front to accommodate your curiosity!

In **Chapter 2**, you learn to install CorelDRAW. The entire Corel bundle can gobble over 50MB of hard drive space, and a lot of people don't realize they have a choice whether to go for the whole nine yards, or to be a little more selective. Is CorelMOVE or CorelCHART part of your own business graphics solution? Are there some of Corel's 830 typefaces you can live without? If you don't have these answers on the tip of your tongue, pay a visit to Chapter 2, and I'll make some very thoughtful recommendations.

CorelDRAW's Setup program installs every tool, option, palette, gizmo, and doodad in its default setting. What's a default setting? In **Chapter 3**, I explain how to access the inaccessible, reset factory presets, and show what you can do to customize CorelDRAW and make it a virtual workspace in which you feel at home as a designer. And as a bonus, you'll learn how to create an embossing effect, set up styles and templates, and create drawings to scale so that your maps, machine parts, and six-foot submarine sandwich illustrations will be accurate right down to the olive loaf.

With **Chapter 4**, you'll gain a lot of experience using the Freehand Pencil tool, and take a look at this tool's modes. Bézier, Dimension, and Callout tools are also powerful variations on a drawing tool, and I'll show you how to use them, and give you a few situations where you may want to call on them. Again, this is an assignment-oriented book, so by the end of Chapter 4, you'll actually be able to draw stuff; our focus is on how tools can help you to produce real, live work in addition to understanding CorelDRAW features.

Chapters 5 and 6 take you through the complete process of designing in Corel to wind up with a finished illustration: background design, composition, lighting... all the elements of a great commercial piece are put together step-by-step for you to follow.

Chapter 7 takes you into a world of graphical multimedia. You'll find out how to combine a photographic image with an airbrush background, add a vector graphic or two, and add Artistic Text to make a very smart-looking digital collage.

CorelDRAW handles text the same way it handles graphics—superbly. Once you get a firm foothold on graphical design, you'll elevate your sights in **Chapter 8** to creating a flyer with special effects, wrap-around body text, and everything! CorelDRAW is a powerful visual communications tool, and you'll learn how text and graphics can be melded together to produce stunning graphical messages.

Guess what? In **Chapter 9**, you'll learn not only how to use CorelDRAW to export a design as a Type 1 or TrueType font, but you'll also learn some of the tricks to *creating* a typeface, Corel-style. You'll also see how to add your own creations to CorelDRAW's Symbols Roll-Up, and how to add your company's logo to an existing typeface.

Chapter 10 is a creative guide to using Corel clip art. Corel ships with over 22,000 pieces of professionally rendered artwork. You're free to edit, add to, and incorporate these designs into your own work. Don't settle for simply plopping clip art on a page! Instead, you can customize clip art to suit your own needs, and here's the starting place.

Chapter 11 is a departure from drawing; in this chapter you'll focus on painting, retouching, and creating splendid bitmap artwork in CorelPHOTO-PAINT. It's the "other side of the fence" as far as computer graphics go, and you'll go further than you imagine toward your design goals when you understand the tricks, tips, and enhancements *image editing* brings to your work.

Chapter 12 is split into three parts, each introducing you to the latest versions of CorelMOVE, CorelCHART, and CorelSHOW. You'll take an assignment all the way to completion through Corel's "other" modules. First, you'll see how CHART makes an instant dimensional graph from data you enter in a spreadsheet. Then it's back to art lessons in the spirit of Fleischer and

Disney as you learn how to create a small computer animation. Finally, you'll add the animation and the chart you create to a CorelSHOW, along with a fancy title, and special-effect dissolves between slides.

Before the party ends, it's a good time for some fireworks, and in **Chapter 13** you'll get hands-on experience *creating* effects, not push-buttoning them. Learn how to make a photorealistic design and get your feet wet with the Lens Roll-Up, a new feature to CorelDRAW 5 that can turn a single drawing into a multitude of exotic variations. You'll take *control* of the effects, and by adding your creative input, you'll achieve something *exceptionally* special as a newcomer to CorelDRAW 5.

The Icons

Along the road to discovering the secrets of CorelDRAW with this book, you'll occasionally see signposts. They're an indication that you should stop and ponder the accompanying point for a moment.

Note

Notes are simply extra info about the subject at hand (without diverting the main discussion). Sometimes they just add detail to stuff in the main text. And sometimes they're a Great Truth about Windows, your operating system, CorelDRAW, or other things that indirectly relate to your designing experiences. They may not lead you to a design solution, but there's an element of putting two and two together to arrive at better, more advanced solutions in your work.

Stop

These markers are the inverse of the aforementioned Notes. In other words, don't apply these little gems to your computer graphics experience. Sidestepping these pitfalls will keep you on the easiest course to hassle-free PC work and CorelDRAW.

Tip

Tricks, tips, and shortcuts are peppered throughout our discussions to make doing things in CorelDRAW a little easier, and quite often, a more inspired effort. Check out these various points to work smarter and more quickly in CorelDRAW.

Closer Look

No one is a beginner for very long in the world of PCs. And from time to time, you may want the inside scoop on a CorelDRAW technique—the physics behind what's happening on-screen, or what's the real, as opposed to the design, purpose for an item. Closer Look pointers are asides that give the straight facts about stuff you ordinarily wouldn't find in a beginner's book.

New Riders Publishing

The staff of New Riders Publishing is committed to bringing you the very best in computer reference material. Each New Riders book is the result of months of work by authors and staff who research and refine the information contained within its covers.

As part of this commitment to you, the NRP reader, New Riders invites your input. Please let us know if you enjoy this book, if you have trouble with the information and examples presented, or if you have a suggestion for the next edition.

Please note, though: New Riders staff cannot serve as a technical resource for CorelDRAW! 5 or for related questions about software- or hardware-related problems. Please refer to the documentation that accompanies CorelDRAW! 5 or to the application's Help systems.

If you have a question or comment about any New Riders book, there are several ways to contact New Riders Publishing. We will respond to as many readers as we can. Your name, address, or phone number will never become part of a mailing list or be used for any purpose other than to help us continue to bring you the best books possible. You can write us at the following address:

New Riders Publishing
Attn: Associate Publisher
201 W. 103rd Street
Indianapolis, IN 46290

If you prefer, you can fax New Riders Publishing at (317) 581-4670.

You can send electronic mail to New Riders from a variety of sources. NRP maintains several mailboxes organized by topic area. Mail in these mailboxes will be forwarded to the staff member who is best able to address your concerns. Substitute the appropriate mailbox name from the following list when addressing your e-mail. The mailboxes are as follows:

ADMIN	Comments and complaints for NRP's publisher
APPS	Word, Excel, WordPerfect, other office applications
ACQ	Book proposals, inquiries by potential authors
CAD	AutoCAD, 3D Studio, AutoSketch, and CAD products
DATABASE	Access, dBASE, Paradox, and other database products
GRAPHICS	CorelDRAW!, Photoshop, and other graphics products
INTERNET	Internet
NETWORK	NetWare, LANtastic, and other network-related topics
OS	MS-DOS, OS/2, and all other operating systems except UNIX and Windows
UNIX	UNIX
WINDOWS	Microsoft Windows (all versions)
OTHER	Anything that doesn't fit the preceding categories

If you use an MHS e-mail system that routes through CompuServe, send your messages to:

mailbox @ NEWRIDER

To send NRP mail from CompuServe, use the following address:

MHS: *mailbox* @ NEWRIDER

We also welcome your electronic mail to Cheri Robinson at the following CompuServe number:

75250, 1431

To send mail from the Internet, use the following address format:

mailbox@newrider.mhs.compuserve.com

NRP is an imprint of Macmillan Computer Publishing. To obtain a catalog or information, or to purchase any Macmillan Computer Publishing book, call (800)428-5331.

Thank you for selecting *CorelDRAW! 5 for Beginners*!

A Word about the Figures in This Book

You'll be wondering about the non-standard figures in this book shortly, and all sorts of questions will fill your head, like, "Hey, my screen doesn't have speed lines on it. And how'd they get drop-shadows on the text? The author must've surely hoked up his screen captures!"

And if you think this later on, you'd be mostly right. Screen captures of a program as "eventful" as CorelDRAW miss a lot of things. Try explaining Corel's flipping hourglass to someone who's never seen the program. Even if you did press PrintScreen to capture the custom hourglass, it would still be hard to explain it in one single image, right?

I felt the same way about the figures you'll see in this book. They've been carefully annotated and enhanced to give you more information than a simple snapshot of your screen would. Treat them without the literal interpretation; they're a guide and they're illustrations. Hey, this is what this book and CorelDRAW are all about!

Ready To Hit the Ground Running?

Okay, you're probably as fond of lingering introductions as I am about writing them, so I think we're all set to jump into our CorelDRAW "test drive" next. We'll cover what you do in more detail throughout the book, but Chapter 1 will give you the immediate hands-on experience every owner of new software craves.

If you don't have Corel installed on your hard disk yet, skip Chapter 1 for the moment, and proceed to Chapter 2. Then come back to Chapter 1 if you like. That's the great thing about books! Instant rewind!

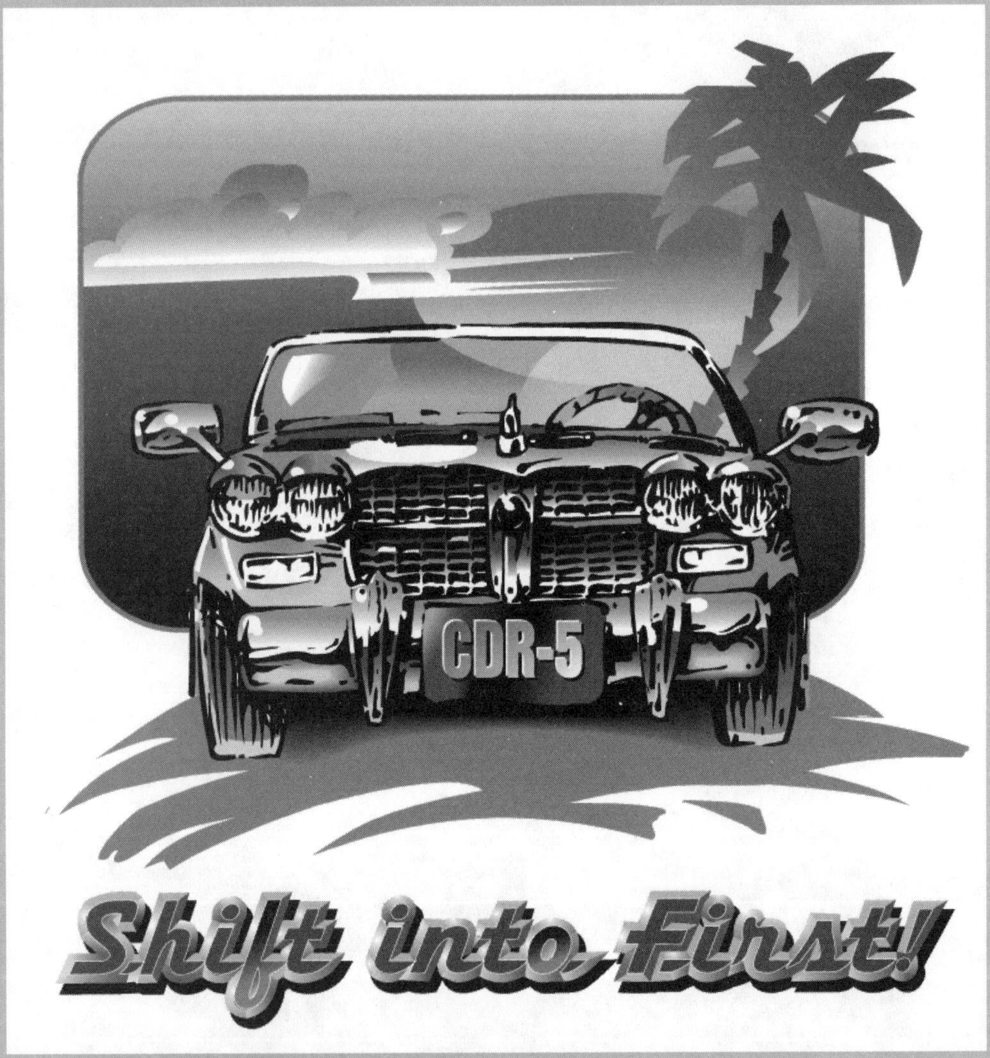
CDR-5
Shift into First!

CHAPTER 1

The CorelDRAW! Test Drive

When I began designing stuff with a computer, CorelDRAW version 2 was the *au courant* software design package. Today version 5 features a lot more advanced functions and tools, but the potential for frustration while you're learning remains a constant. The trick to leaping over the initial hurdle is to make it a fun and productive one. This is what Chapter 1 addresses—how to get the personal satisfaction of designing a CorelDRAW image right from the beginning, without a thorough review of what the application features are.

Let's abandon the "big picture" that follows in future chapters, and instead design a small one right now.

In this chapter, you will:

- Use cool fills
- Marquee-select on-screen elements
- Trim an object with another object
- Manipulate text
- Create realistic shadows
- Explore CorelDRAW's Ribbon Bar
- Learn the secrets of the "X" button
- Work over your creation like so much digital Silly Putty

Creating a Vector Art Greeting Card

Like any test drive, it helps to have a destination in mind before firing up the engine. To get a better feel for CorelDRAW's amazing power, your first venture into vector art tools and effects will be to create a greeting card. "Have a Ball" is an alternative expression to "Bon Voyage" (also timely advice to Cinderella), and this is the theme of the greeting card you will create.

Launching the Good Ship CorelDRAW!

To begin at the beginning, you must have CorelDRAW running before you can create anything. Find the Corel group in Windows Program Manager (or whatever "shell" you may use for Windows, e.g. Norton Desktop, PCTools), and find the group Corel created when it was installed. If you don't have Corel installed yet, make a pit stop at Chapters 2, "Installing the Corel Bundle," and 3, "Customizing Corel." Then circle back here for the test drive.

In figure 1.1, you can see Program Manager, some icon groups, and more Corel balloons than you can shake a stick at! The one you're looking for is the plain, single balloon; no camera, no funny little guy running, just a balloon with the CorelDRAW! title beneath it. Double-click on it and let's set sail!

Figure 1.1
The Corel group in Program Manager is easily identified by all the hot-air balloon icons.

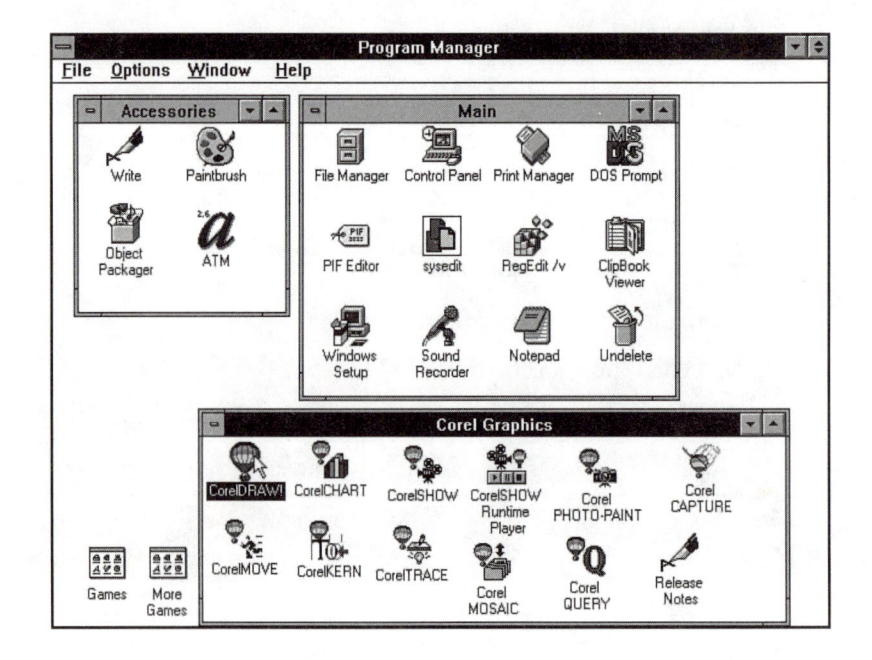

Launching the Good Ship CorelDRAW!

Note

Double-clicking is actually a combination event in the Windows environment. It selects and simultaneously runs the executable file associated with the icon. If you don't have the hang of double-clicking with a mouse yet, you'll get plenty of experience learning CorelDRAW.

Windows also provides an alternative way to launch an application. You can click once on the CorelDRAW (or any other Windows) icon, and then press the Enter key. This keyboard-mouse combination provides the same results as double-clicking.

The Corel Workspace

Once the "splash screen" (the title most programs flash while the program is loading) is gone, you'll see the CorelDRAW workspace. You'll learn more about the workspace's menus and tools in future chapters, and how to customize them to your own work preferences. But for now, you're going to use some things that don't change in the workspace, namely CorelDRAW's tools.

Remembering all the tool names and what they do isn't really necessary to work in the Corel modules. Pop-Up Help is turned on by default when you install Corel. All you need to do is let your cursor "linger" for a second or two over a tool or a button on the Ribbon Bar, and a yellow Pop-Up Help box will appear.

These Help boxes identify the tool or command that your cursor is hovering over and sometimes even tell you what the keyboard shortcut is for the command. Additionally, the status line at the bottom of the Corel screen expands on the Pop-Up Help box's explanation. The inside front and back covers of this book have a complete listing of the tools and their Pop-Ups for easy reference.

Your First Pick of Tools

When you first open CorelDRAW, a couple assumptions are made for you. First, a new Printable page is displayed each time you launch CorelDRAW. The document is called UNTITLED.CDR, and you can design to your heart's content on it, then save it with your own file name.

Also, by default, a tool is selected for you upon opening. CorelDRAW's Pick tool is used to select shapes or groups of shapes that you draw. Use this tool to select shapes to which you want to move, stretch, or apply an effect. It's only when something's selected that it can be edited, and most of the time you'll want to use the Pick tool.

Don't confuse the Pick tool with the Windows arrow cursor, however. Any Corel tool that's over a non-drawing area of your screen (outside of the Drawing Window) will sport a white, black-outlined arrow cursor. When you move inside the Drawing Window with the Pick tool chosen, the arrow turns completely black and that's when your cursor's ready for editing work.

Shaping Up for the Test Drive

There are four categories of tools on the Toolbox that produce shapes; the Pencil tool, the Rectangle tool, the Ellipse tool, and the Text tool. They're all pretty clearly illustrated on their respective button faces.

As the adage goes, "The right tool for the right job" applies to CorelDRAW's virtual tools. You'll "draw" heavily on the Text and Ellipse tools to create your greeting card.

On Your Marquee, Get Set, Go!

First, you create the ball by drawing with the Ellipse tool in a motion called a *marquee*. You click, hold the left mouse button down, and then diagonally drag the mouse. You have four possible directions in which to make a marquee with the Ellipse tool, and where you start and wind up has a direct effect on where the resulting ellipse is placed within Corel's Drawing Window. I personally like working from upper left to lower right, but if you don't feel like echoing my sentiments in places along this test drive, you can certainly mirror them!

To create a ball, follow these steps:

1. Click on the Ellipse tool on the Toolbox. Run your cursor slowly down the Toolbox, and a Pop-Up will inform you that the button with an Ellipse shape is indeed the right tool.

2. Place your cursor (now a crosshair) toward the upper left of CorelDRAW's Printable page (the drop-shadowed rectangle dead-center on the screen).

Shaping Up for the Test Drive

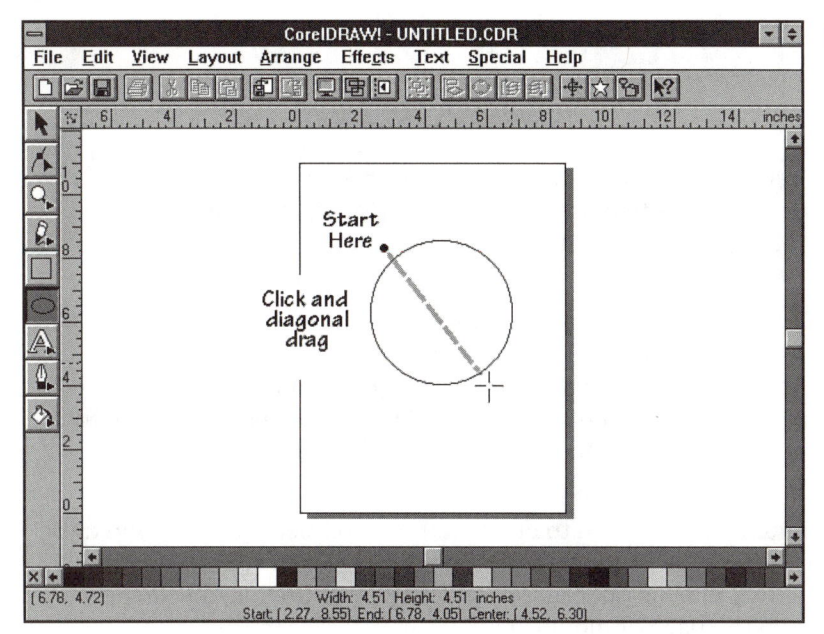

Figure 1.2

The Ctrl key constrains CorelDRAW ellipses to perfect circles.

3. Hold down the Ctrl key while you click+diagonal-drag (marquee) down and to the right with the mouse, as shown in figure 1.2.

4. Release the mouse button, and your finished circle is selected and ready to be filled in.

Tip

CorelDRAW's status line provides a wealth of information about what's happening as you design. Look at the status line in the last figure. You'll see that the circle is 4.51" by 4.51", indicating that the circle is indeed perfectly round.

After you release the mouse button, the information on the status line rearranges itself slightly. The top line of information tells you what sort of shape is presently selected (in this case, an ellipse), and the outermost dimensions of the shape move to the second line of the status line.

Using a Fountain Fill To Imitate Lighting

A closed CorelDRAW shape has only two properties: an outline and a fill. What adds to the diversity of the shapes you create is your selection of fill for a closed shape, and Corel offers a ton of them, one of the fancier ones being the Fountain Fill.

Fountain Fills are sometimes called gradient fills, stepped fills, or color ramps in other programs, but they all refer to the same computer graphics phenomenon of filling an enclosed area with a series of colors to produce a smooth transition from one color to another. Fountain Fills in CorelDRAW are terrific for adding resonance and motion to the most static of graphical shapes.

When a Fountain Fill is defined to create a transition between light and dark, you can take advantage of the fill's property to suggest a source of lighting cast on a flat, two-dimensional shape. And when you do this, the shape "pops" right off the page or monitor!

Let's see how to make that flat circle you drew in the last few steps practically roll off your monitor. CorelDRAW offers many different kinds of Fountain Fills, but the best choice to get the ball rolling is the Radial Fill. It produces a fill pattern of concentric rings that change in steps from one color to another.

To apply a Radial Fill, follow these steps:

1. Click on the Fill tool to reveal its fly-out menu.

2. Choose the Fountain Fill button, which is the third button from the left. Whoa! The Fountain Fill dialog box is a lot bigger than most programs, and some department stores, huh?

3. In the Type box, click on the down arrow to see the Type drop-down list. Then choose Radial.

4. Place your cursor in the center of the preview box (the large square in the upper right corner of the dialog box). You can change the center of the Radial Fill by clicking and dragging within the preview box.

    Move the center of the Radial Fill so that a highlight will appear toward the upper left of the circle (see fig. 1.3). Notice that a transition to black occurs toward the bottom right.

Using a Fountain Fill to Imitate Lighting

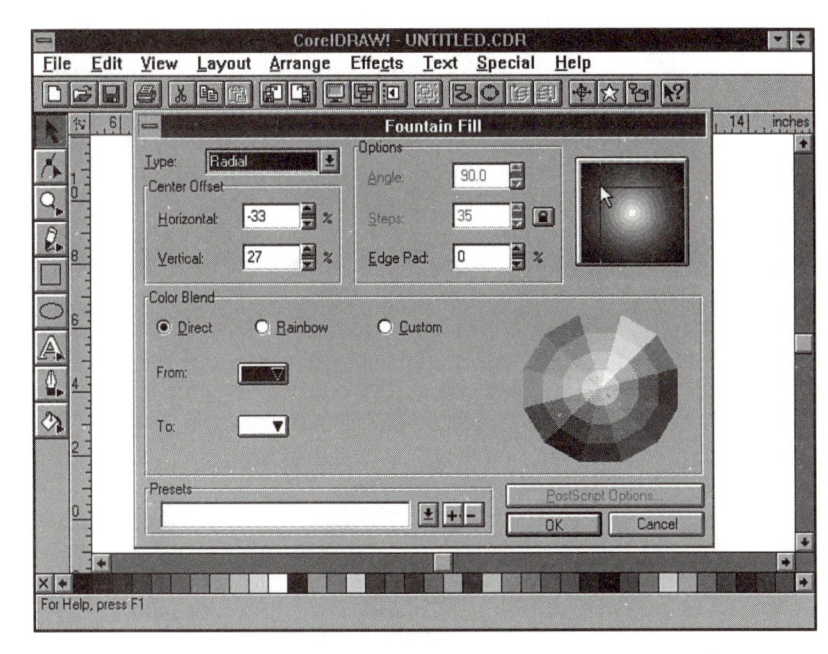

Figure 1.3
Change the highlight in the preview box within the Fountain Fill dialog box.

5. Click on OK to return to a gloriously shaded, 3D ball on your workspace!

Creating a Surface Shadow for the Ball

Shading can be accomplished in a number of ways in CorelDRAW, and now it's time to check out a different technique. Most three-dimensional objects have highlights reflected from a light source, as our ball presently does. And most highlighted objects have a darker side on the face that's turned away from a light source. Ditto our ball.

But *nowhere* in real life does a ball with a highlight and shaded side fail to observe light and color theory by neglecting to cast a shadow in the opposing direction from the light source! In essence, the ball is incomplete.

The following steps show you how to make a different sort of rounded, closed shape that can be the basis of the ball's shadow.

Chapter 1: The CorelDRAW! Test Drive

1. With the Ellipse tool still selected, click+diagonally drag (marquee) to create ellipse beneath the ball, but don't hold down the Ctrl key this time. As you can see in figure 1.4, you're striving for a squashed, circular shape. This ellipse represents the shadow that would be produced by the ball if the light shining on it was cast from a steep angle.

Figure 1.4

Drawing an ellipse to represent the ball's shadow.

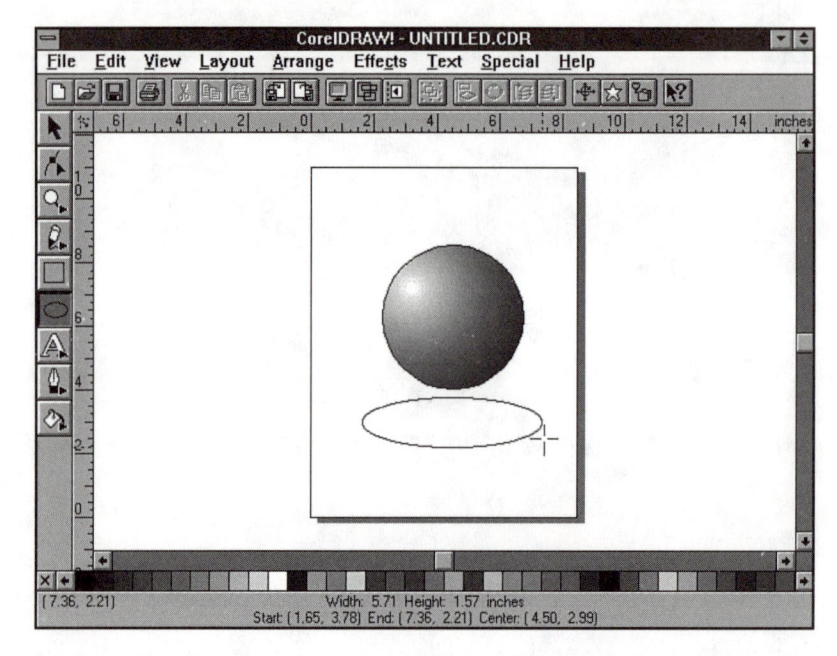

2. Let go of the mouse button after you draw the flattened ellipse. Note that the last-drawn object is automatically selected. The ball isn't selected any more, which means no changes can be applied to it at present.

3. Press Ctrl+F9, or choose Effects, Contour Roll-Up, and bang—the Contour Roll-Up menu is displayed.

Using the Contour Roll-Up Menu

Roll-Ups are mini-menus, much like the fly-out menu you accessed to produce the Fountain Fill. Roll-Ups, however, linger ad infinitum; they stay on your workspace, eager to provide you with specific tools and effects until you get sick of them and roll them up.

Creating a Surface Shadow for the Ball

The Contour Roll-Up offers an effect similar to the Fountain Fill, except it produces a transition to both color and shape when applied to an object. Simply put, it perfectly outlines a shape, either to the inside or the outside of a closed object. Here's where the Contour Effect provides a more lifelike lighting effect than the Radial Fountain Fill. The Radial Fill is always perfectly round like our circle, but a contour can be applied to an ellipse (or other shapes) to provide a smooth, *irregularly shaped* transition.

Let's do some basic math before twiddling with the knobs and controls on the Contour Roll-Up, okay? The status bar says that the ellipse in the last figure measures 1.57" on its narrowest side. The contour can be applied to the inside of the ellipse in evenly spaced increments known as the Offset value. And the number of times you want CorelDRAW to automatically create a shape that "contours" around its neighboring shape can be entered in the Steps field on the Roll-Up. Ten contour steps will make a nice color transition in a space this size. Since the color inside each shape will represent a transitional step from white to black, 10 steps will create a tonally smooth contour, each component displaying no more than 10-percent variation from its neighbor. Fewer than 10 will produce visible (unwanted) banding in your shadow.

So to figure out what the size of the Offset should be, take the narrowest side of the ellipse (1.57") and divide it in half. Take that figure (.78") and divide it by the number of steps (10) and round down your answer to get an Offset value of 0.07. If you're like me, it's easier to visualize the math when applied to something meaningful, like shadowmaking. So let's do it!

1. Place your cursor inside the Offset entry field on the Contour Roll-Up, and type **0.07**. Don't worry about the ellipse. It's still active and selected.

2. In the Steps box, enter **10** (or use the elevator button to the right of the entry field).

Note

Whenever you have an amount that's greater than will mathematically fit in Steps × Offset, versus available space, CorelDRAW drops the number of steps down to the maximum allowable.

Chapter 1: The CorelDRAW! Test Drive

3. Click on Apply. As you can see in figure 1.5, you have a dizzying amount of concentric ellipses nestled within the original ellipse shape. Actually, it only *looks* dizzying; it's only 10, but the outline on the ellipse and its contour offspring buzz your eyes a little.

Figure 1.5

The Contour Roll-Up menu lets you create progressively larger shapes outside an original, or smaller ones inside.

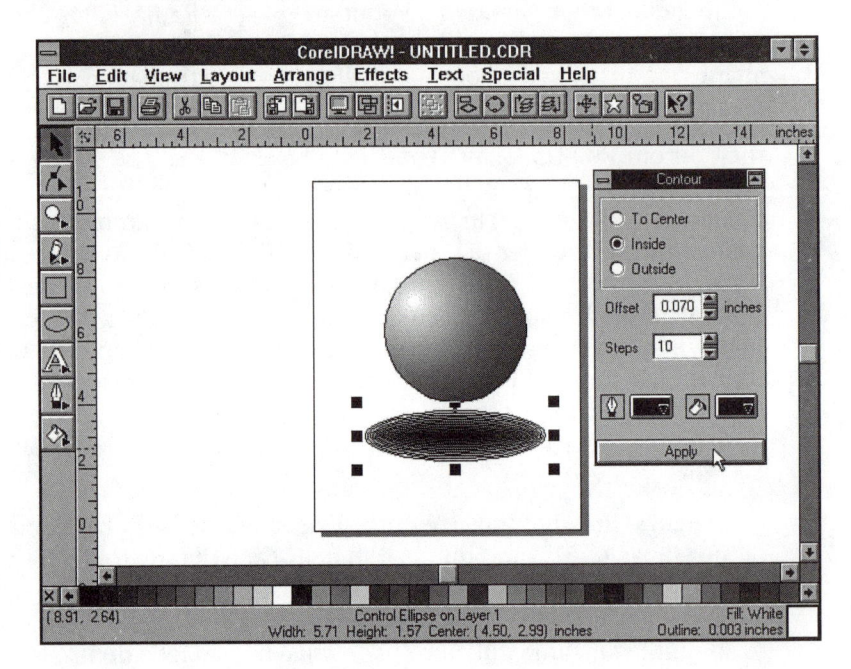

Enhancing the Contour Shadow

Impressive effect, this contour, except in the last example it didn't create the soft shadow we hoped for. This is not so much a deliberate mistake I let you make as the creation of an opportunity to correct it by exploring more of CorelDRAW's workspace.

Corel's default assigns every freshly-drawn object the attributes of no fill and a 0.003" outline. In Corel-Land, "no fill" does *not* mean a white fill—it's empty, the Drawing Window and Printable page (both white) are peeking through the ellipse and its contour, and they must be filled with white to complete this shadow-making task.

Fortunately, you're only a mouse click or two away from a solution, because all 10 of the inside contours are linked to the "parent" object, the ellipse. The fill will make a transition shortly, between the fill of the parent ellipse and whatever contour fill color is specified on the Contour Roll-Up.

Creating a Surface Shadow for the Ball

The setting for the last contour color (in this case, the innermost shape) is, by default, black, shown on the face of the color selection button next to the tiny paint bucket symbol on the Contour Roll-Up menu. No fill doesn't make too swift a contour transition to black, but let's see what happens when you assign a color to fill the original ellipse you drew.

To assign a color to fill the original ellipse, follow these steps:

1. Click on the white color on the on-screen color palette that runs across the bottom of the Drawing Window. Your ellipse and contour objects should immediately display more verve.

2. Place your cursor at the far left of the on-screen color palette, directly over the box that has an "x" on it, and right-mouse click, as shown in figure 1.6.

Note

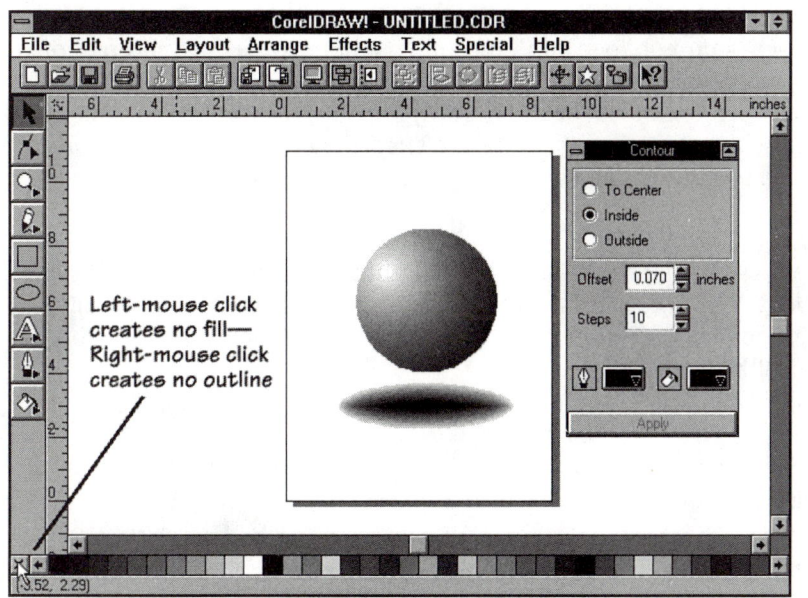

CorelDRAW is one of the Windows programs that actually takes advantage of the right mouse button. When working with the color palette, the left mouse button assigns object fill color, and the right mouse button assigns outline color.

Figure 1.6
The "x" on the on-screen color palette issues either a no-fill or no-outline command.

You changed the outline and fill attributes of the original ellipse you designed, and the Contour effect was automatically updated because it was created with a dynamic relationship to the original. The no-fill attribute prevented the contour from blending colors to black in an inward direction, but as soon as you colored the original ellipse white, the transition to black was allowed to happen. The opposite is true of the outline attribute of the ellipse; removing the outline from the original removed the outline capability from the "child" contour shapes.

The Order of CorelDRAWn Shapes

Vector-drawn shapes never intermingle with other vector-drawn shapes because each object is an entity unto itself. The ball you designed is not part of the contour, which in turn is not part of the ellipse you drew to base the contour upon. They're all discrete shapes, free to be selected and repositioned.

If you've followed the figures so far, you now have a ball apparently hovering above its shadow. This is an interesting effect, but people usually use the word "interesting" with a sense of irony, and say this about bizarre art which needs toning down a little. Because Corel art can be repositioned, you can bring the ball "down-to-earth" quite easily.

This means overlapping one object (the ball) over another (the shadow), however, since vector shapes don't intermingle but instead lay on top of or behind one another. How do you tell the hierarchy of shapes in Corel's Drawing Window? The most recently drawn object is always on top, unless you *change* the order of objects. Since the shadow is the most recent shape, it would be on top of the ball when you position the two to meet.

Here's how to move your shapes around and lay them on top of each other:

1. Press the spacebar to activate the Pick tool (the tool on the top of the Toolbox). You only use this tool for selecting and assisting in modifying shapes; you can't draw with it, but you can't easily move shapes you've drawn without it!

Note

Newly drawn shapes frequently aren't in the exact position you'd like in Corel's Drawing Window, and the preceding step is a shortcut for switching between a drawing tool and a selection tool. You can also switch between the Ellipse and Pick tools by clicking on the Pick tool button on the Toolbox, but it's a good idea to reinforce all the shortcuts you'll find in this book as early in your CorelDRAW adventures as possible!

2. When something's selected in CorelDRAW, eight selection corner handles appear around the outskirts of the shape. Don't click and drag on them, though. That stretches the selection, and you merely want to move it! To do so, first click on the ball.

3. Place your cursor on a part of the ball, and drag it down so it starts sitting behind the shadow.

4. You now need to place the ball on top of the shadow. The Ribbon Bar places the most common menu items within easy reach. One such item is the To Front command, which places a selection, or multiple selections, at the top of the stack of shapes you've created. As you can see in figure 1.7, while the ball shape is selected, clicking on the button that has the drawing of a stack of sheets (with an arrow pointing to the topmost) puts the ball on top of the shadow!

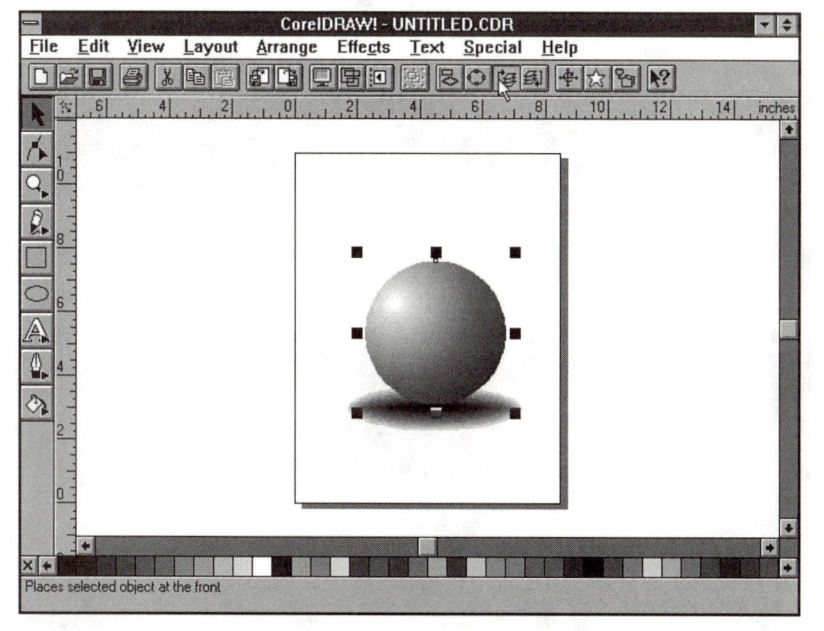

Figure 1.7

Click the To Front button on the Ribbon Bar to move a selected shape to the top of every other shape.

Creating a Unique Shape To Bend Text With

If you're getting a little impatient for some "gee-whiz" fireworks along the vista of this CorelDRAW test drive, buckle up now. You're going to plunge into some high-order reshaping of Artistic Text. In CorelDRAW, Artistic Text is the kind of text that you enter on-screen with the Text tool.

The game plan is to arc the phrase "Have a Ball!" over the ball you designed. But to perform this feat, you need to create the shape of the arc that the text should take. All this begins with two different geometric shapes and the Trim command. As you'll see shortly, the Trim command treats one object as a pair of scissors, and the other shape as the object you trim away with the scissors. Here's how you create a custom-designed arc:

1. Choose the Rectangle tool from the Toolbox.
2. Start above and to the left of the ball, and draw a rectangle so that it's centered and the bottom edge intersects the ball, as shown in figure 1.8.

Figure 1.8
Use the same designing conventions with the Rectangle tool as you would with the Ellipse tool.

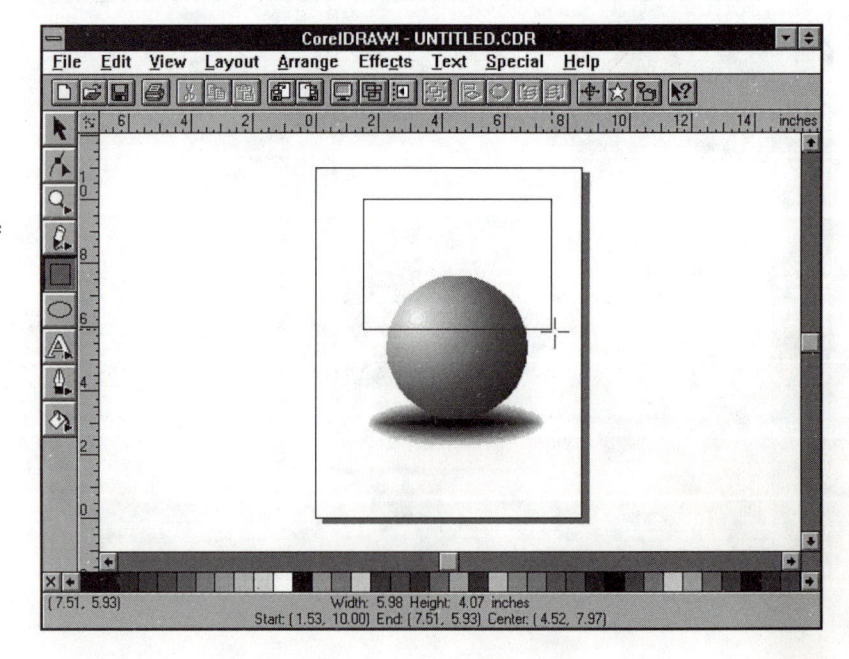

Creating a Unique Shape to Bend Text With

27

Tip: Double-click on the control button (the upper-left corner minus sign) on any Roll-Up to close it. When you don't need a Roll-Up in an assignment any longer, clear the view in your Drawing Window for more important things!

3. Choose the Ellipse tool and place the crosshair cursor in roughly the center of the ball. Accuracy is unimportant here; you're only discovering techniques in this test drive chapter.

4. Press and hold down the Shift and Ctrl keys and drag away from the center of the ball. The Shift key changes the Ellipse tool's function to design a circle from the center outward.

5. Release the mouse button when your new circle's diameter meets the bottom two corners of the rectangle shape, as shown in figure 1.9.

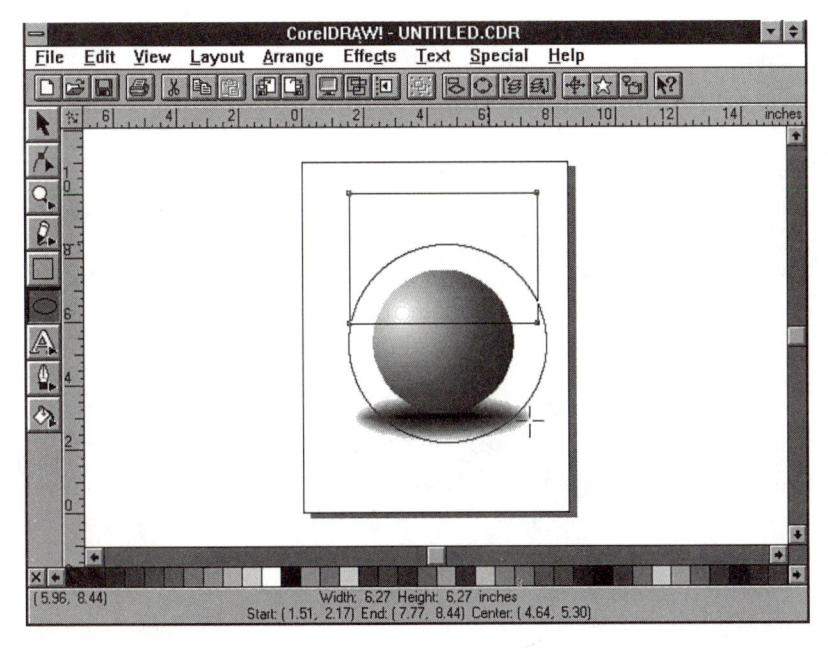

Figure 1.9
The Shift key changes the properties of the Rectangle and Ellipse tools to draw from the center outward.

6. Press the spacebar. This toggles the active Toolbox tool to the Pick tool.

7. Press and hold down the Shift key, and click on one of the sides of the rectangle. The Shift key (used when the Pick tool is active) lets you additively select stuff. You now have the circle and the rectangle selected, the selection handles change to encompass both objects, and your status bar no longer reports the shape of what you have selected. Instead, it reports two objects selected.

8. Choose **A**rrange, **T**rim from the menu, as shown in figure 1.10. I scrolled the view over a little so you could see what's happening. On your own screen, you'll see a very subtle action performed; the circle carves its profile out of the rectangle.

Figure 1.10
Trim, Intersect, Combine, and Weld are variations on the same theme—creating new shapes out of two other ones.

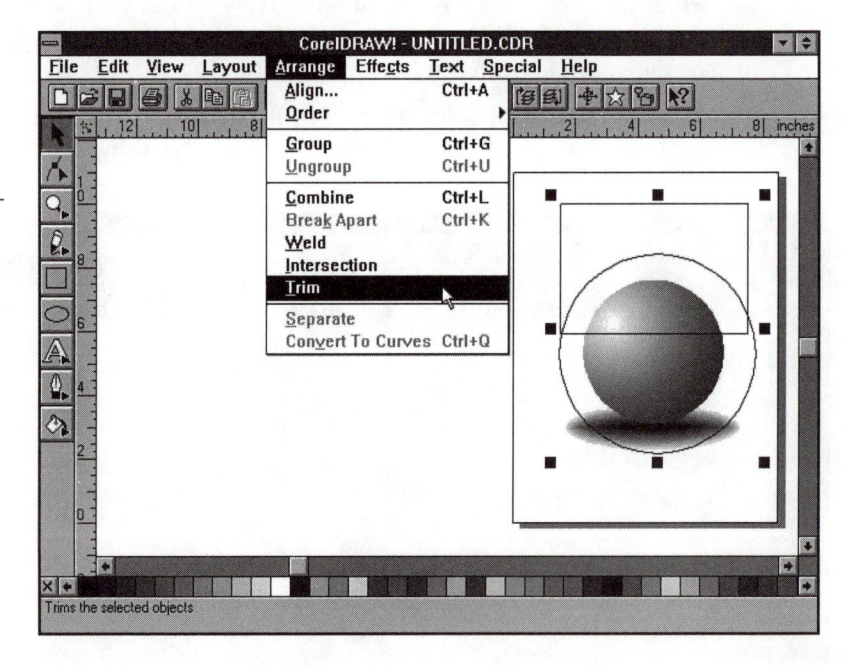

Tip

The order in which you select a *trimming object* and an *object to be trimmed* matters a lot. If you have two overlapping shapes, pick one object, then the other, and then choose Trim. The first one selected is the trimming shape, and the second one gets trimmed. However, if you marquee-select two shapes (click and diagonal drag with the Pick tool), the most recently drawn shape is the trimmer, and the first-drawn shape in the Drawing Window is the trimmee.

Creating a Unique Shape to Bend Text With

In the event that you marquee-select *multiple* overlapping shapes, all the most recent ones gang up on the *first* drawn shape, and they all go to work on the least-recently drawn one.

As a rule, you always have to have shapes overlapping to perform the Trim function.

As a default of CorelDRAW, a shape that's been trimmed (the rectangle here) is now the selected shape in the Drawing Window. But you want to get rid of the circle now, because it's served its purpose. Click on the border of the circle (not the ball!), and press the Del key.

You can't select a shape with no fill, like the circle in the last step, without clicking on its border. Clicking inside the circle will avail you not, because there's only empty space defined inside, with no relationship to the circle shape.

If you find selecting a border the size of a human hair a little hard, try this trick. No matter what's selected in the Drawing Window, you can "cycle" between selecting objects by pressing the Tab key. Watch how the selection handles bounce from object to object as you Tab among them! This works well if you have a *limited* number of objects drawn; it'll drive you nuts trying to Tab to one object out of 500, though.

Creating Type and Adjusting Your View

It's time to create the snappy phrase for our greeting card, and also time to zoom into our work a little. Hey, two more tools to cover, to add to the four we've already had a test drive with!

Adding Text is as simple as one, two, three, which coincidentally happen to be our following step numbers:

1. Choose the text tool (the one with the "A" on it), and click an insertion point (exactly like you do in word processing programs) inside the trimmed shape you created last. Exact location is unimportant, since we now know how to reposition stuff.

2. Type **Have a Ball!**, as shown in figure 1.11.

Chapter 1: The CorelDRAW! Test Drive

3. Click on the Pick tool, and the text is now selected, ready for repositioning.

Figure 1.11
By default, inserted text always flows to the right of the insertion point, and has the same typeface and size.

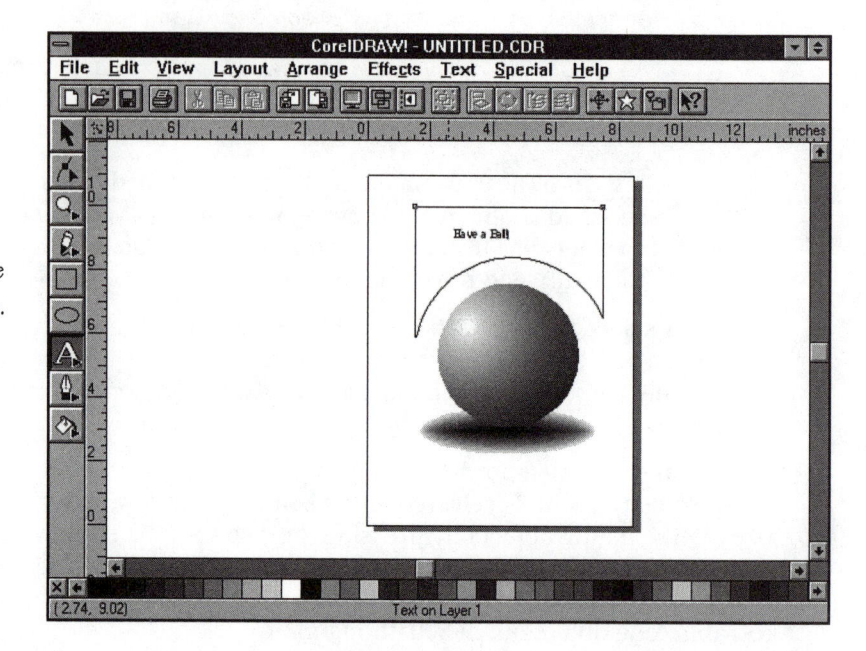

Zooming In

Next, let's zoom into our masterpiece so we can see what we're doing, and reposition the text. To zoom in on the text, follow these steps:

1. Click on the Zoom tool (the button with the magnifying glass on it). You get fly-out menus in CorelDRAW everywhere you see a button with a triangle etched on it.

2. Click on the first fly-out button—the magnifying glass with the plus sign in the center of it. The Zoom In tool is the proper CorelDRAW name for it.

3. Use the same marquee technique you learned before with the Zoom In tool. As shown in figure 1.12, click above and to the left of the area you want to zoom into, then diagonally drag the cursor to the bottom right boundary of the desired field of zoomishness.

Creating Type and Adjusting Your View

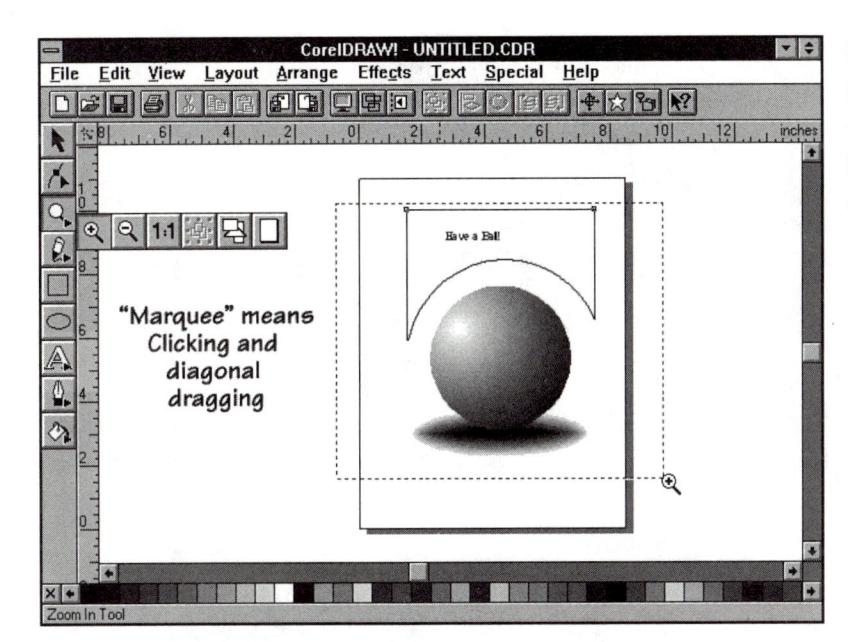

Figure 1.12
Use the Zoom In tool to get a better view of designs.

Making the Type Bigger

Remember I mentioned not to touch the corner selection handles when repositioning an object? Well, it's okay now, because you don't want to move the type, you need to make it bigger. To do so, follow these steps:

1. Select the type with the Pick tool.

2. Place your cursor over the bottom right corner selection handle, and click and drag in a four o'clock direction. As you can see in figure 1.13, when the cursor changes shape, it allows the object to be stretched in various directions.

3. Stop when the status bar says you have 60-point type, or around there.

Figure 1.13
Corner handles of an object scale a selection; tugging on a middle handle stretches the selection.

Stop

What if you clicked on the text in the last example and didn't get selection handles, but a bunch of arrows on the corners instead?

This means the text was already selected. Clicking a second time on a selected shape changes CorelDRAW functions—click once with the Pick tool to select something, click a second time to offer up special handles for skewing and rotating the selection.

If your selection has arrows for corners, click once again and the object will have normal selection handles; you can then proceed.

Picking a Better Typeface

In addition to the Type 1 and TrueType fonts you may already own, CorelDRAW offers a gazillion more body copy and display (headline) typefaces. So there's no reason why your "Have a Ball" greeting card must be cast in Avant Garde (or whatever comes first in your list of system-installed fonts). Let's pay a visit to your system's type foundry and pick something with a little more meat on it.

Picking a Better Typeface

1. Assuming the text is still selected, press Ctrl+T. This is a valuable shortcut to the Te**x**t, **C**haracter... command, which displays the Character Attributes dialog box in CorelDRAW. If your text is not selected, click on it with the Pick tool now.

2. Select a font that's bold and clean from the **F**onts list. Figure 1.14 shows Kabel Ultra. You're going to stretch and twist this phrase shortly; therefore, don't select a wimpy font, because it might break. Try Ad Lib or Gill Sans Ultra as alternatives to Kabel.

3. Click on OK, and you're returned to the illustration.

Figure 1.14
Pick a bold typeface from those available on your installed fonts list.

Bending the Type

The Envelope Roll-Up is only one of many ultra-sophisticated menus CorelDRAW offers, but it's perhaps the most exciting one to test drive. When you designate a selection as the target for the Envelope effect, Corel then shapes the piece to conform to a pre-existing different shape. Your labors in trimming the rectangle pay off, because you use it as the defining boundary for the "Have a Ball" text.

Watch how you achieve an effect that would take a designer using conventional tools all afternoon to execute, by following these steps:

Chapter 1: The CorelDRAW! Test Drive

1. Press Ctrl+F7 (or take the scenic route, Effe**c**ts, **E**nvelope Roll-Up).
2. With the text selected, click on the Create From button on the Envelope Roll-Up.
3. Your cursor turns into a huge arrow. This is an indicator, in several instances on many Roll-Ups in Corel, that you should click on a shape or a word to pick up its properties and apply them to your present selection. Click on the shape you want the text selection to be enveloped into, as shown in figure 1.15.
4. As with all Roll-Ups, you have to click on the Apply button to execute the effect. Do this, and check out figure 1.16. Is this cool, or what?

Figure 1.15
The Create From button lets you click on a shape to be the "container" for a selection.

Figure 1.16

Selected objects conform to the shape you specify for an Envelope effect.

Positioning the Text

A dotted outline with little handles on it envelopes the selected text. The dotted line envelope is not positioned directly over the trimmed rectangle shape you specified for the envelope shape. Why not?

The text selection was not exactly centered relative to the trimmed rectangle, but that's okay. To reposition the enveloped text and have the trimmed rectangle as a visual guide for precise placement, follow these steps:

1. Press the spacebar to regain the Pick tool as the active tool in Corel.

2. Click and drag the text so that it is neatly positioned inside the trimmed rectangle, as shown in figure 1.17.

3. You're finished with the trimmed rectangle, so click on it to select it, and press the Del key.

4. Double-click on the control button on the Envelope Roll-Up to close it. People who drop by to admire your handiwork will be amazed at your tidiness.

5. Choose File, Save, and call your card HAVABALL.CDR. Choose a directory that you can easily locate later to store your work in.

Figure 1.17

Use the shape you defined as an envelope as a guideline for the positioning of the text.

6. Press the Full-Screen Preview button on the Ribbon Bar (or press F9) to see your creation without all the buttons and tools cluttering your view!

As you can see in figure 1.18, you have a pretty handsome reward for a little time spent test-driving CorelDRAW!

Cruising on Past the Test Drive

In the following chapters, you'll learn how to get more functionality out of the tools, the other 17 Roll-Ups (yes, Envelope and Contour were only two), exotic fills, and other stuff that's only been foreshadowed in this chapter.

If you now have a stunning greeting card on your monitor, it was designed by an ambitious, eager soul, and you should give the card to *yourself*, because you *will* have a ball with this program and this book.

And if you're only browsing this chapter and don't have Corel installed yet, flip the page quick, and you'll learn the leanest, slickest way to install the "toys" you'll want the chance to tinker with the most.

Let's take this road trip around the world!

Cruising on Past the Test Drive

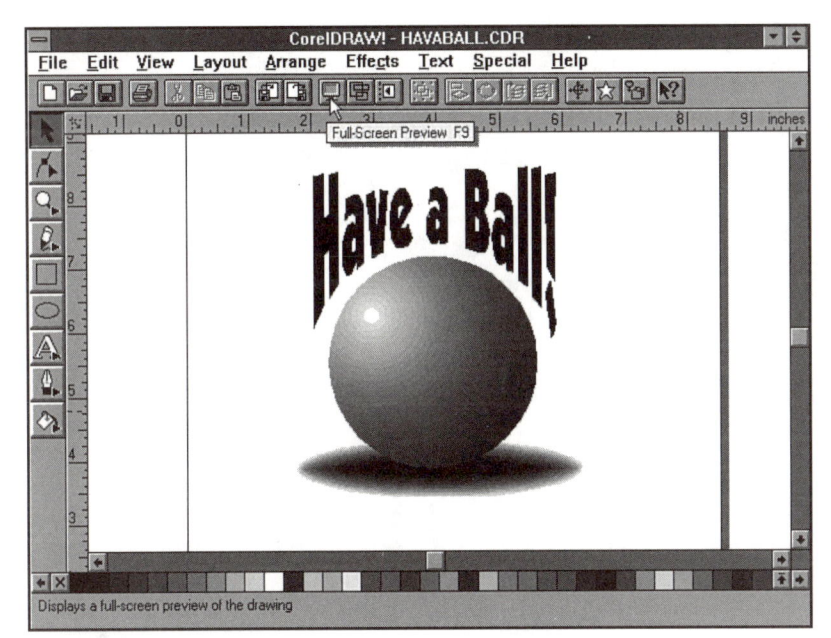

Figure 1.18
The finished greeting card.

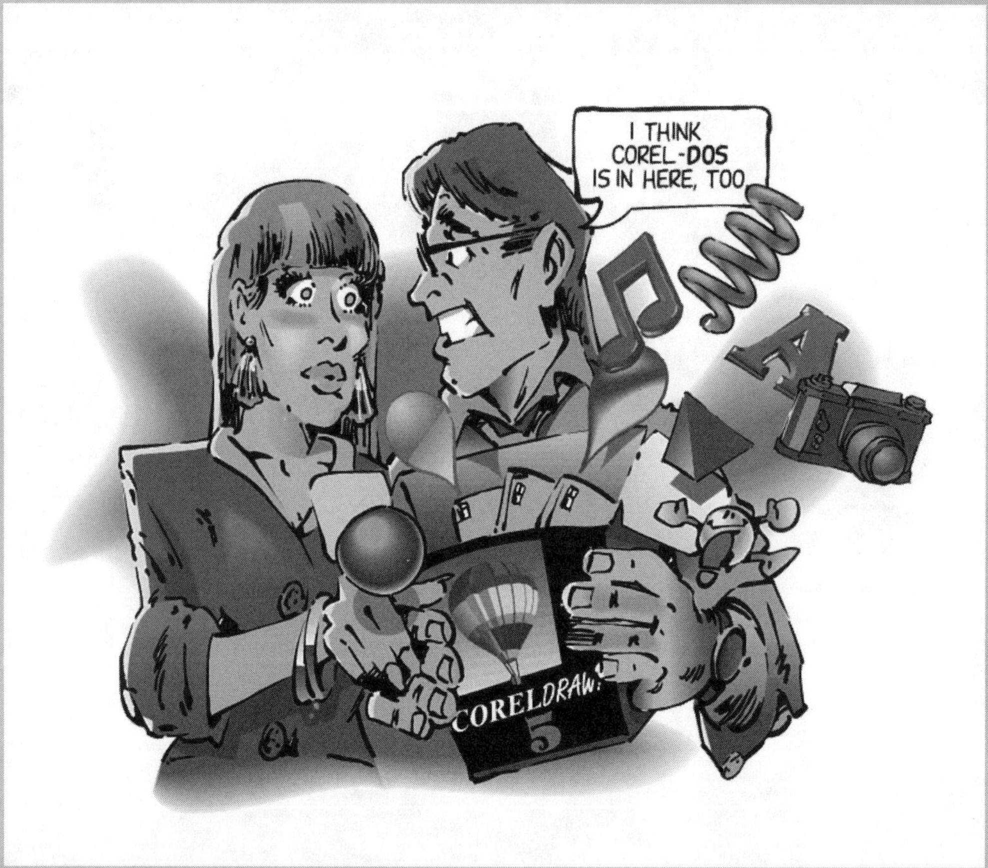
I THINK COREL-DOS IS IN HERE, TOO.
CORELDRAW!
5

CHAPTER 2

Installing the Corel Bundle

A very wise MIS Director once told me that, "For every solution, there is a problem." Corel Corporation bills its star product as *The Complete Graphics and Desktop Publishing Solution,* and the only problem anyone could have with this accurate claim is where to begin installing the programs (plural!), utilities, clip art, samples, symbols, fonts, and quite possibly CorelKITCHEN-SINK!

The solution is in this chapter. If you haven't installed the CorelDRAW bundle yet, pull up a chair, lend an ear, and take heed of some very solid advice about what you need, what you don't need, and what you should find on CorelDRAW's installation disks.

In this chapter, you:

- Make some decisions about your hard disk needs versus the Corel bundle's needs
- Learn how to back up a very precious investment—the Corel installation disks
- Perform a custom installation of Corel
- Get an explanation of what you're installing
- Discover a safe way or two to pare back Corel's installation after it's been installed

What To Do After You Get the CorelDRAW Box

You should probably thank the person who delivered it to you, be it UPS or your boss. You're going to have the time of your life with this software. However, you'd be well-advised to keep every shred of paper that came with Corel: the receipt, the registration card, the shipping box, and everything that came inside, even if it looks unimportant.

Why?

Because, presumably, if you're reading this chapter, you haven't installed Corel yet, and unless Corel seeped into your PC because you put the Corel box on top of it (this almost never happens), you can't be sure the program *works* yet! Yes, slipups do occur at shipping and manufacturing plants, and if you have one bum disk, or one of the CDs looks like a taco shell, your negotiating power with a sales representative will be severely challenged if you toss anything away. Let's assemble a list of things you'll need for installation before allowing Corel to assemble its programs in Windows Program Manager.

Pre-Flight Planning for the CorelDRAW Installation

For installation, basically you'll need two books:

- The one you're holding right now
- The Corel catalog of symbols, fonts, and clip art

It's a good idea to keep all the other stuff that came with the Corel package together in one safe place in the unlikely event you find something defective. Why not keep everything except the disks (and/or the CDs) and the Corel catalog (the 300+ page book) in the Corel box, then put it on your bookshelf?

Write your registration number from the owner's manual on a piece of paper and put it right next to your PC. Corel won't install unless you feed it a valid registration number during installation.

Do not open the disk envelope or break a seal on the CD case yet. We're not up to this phase, and there's important information we'll cover concerning some legal stuff you agree to when you break the seal on the commercial program's container.

Pre-Flight Planning for the CorelDRAW Installation

If you purchased the disk version of Corel, you'll want to scare up at least 20 blank, formatted 3 1/2-inch high-density disks for the purpose of making a backup copy of your investment. Preformatted disks can be purchased from any number of places. You could also ask someone at work if they have any unwanted or used 3 1/2-inch high-density disks they don't mind showing you how to format. The size and capacity is important for these disks, because digital copies of disk information are *perfect* copies, and must have the same capacity and size as the Corel originals. Disk labels are important, too, because one blank disk tends to look like another without a tag on it.

Making Backup Disks

Backing up the data on the Corel disks isn't necessary for owners of the CD version, and purchasers of the CD version may want to wander off through this next section. Don't go too far away, though, because Corel has a litany of dialog boxes for you to answer before the installation program arranges the Corel files on your hard disk.

Experienced users and novices alike should adopt the practice of making a backup copy of program disks, then installing the program from the back-ups, not the original disk set. The reasons for this are:

- In the event of a cataclysmic situation, like a coffee spill near your machine, your original program disks are off-site in a box and are unaffected.

- By installing from backup disks, you automatically ensure that the backup set works, and that the copies of the originals are flawless. It's a real tragedy to lose your original set only to discover months later that your backup set isn't perfect.

Get a sandwich and a beverage of your choice, more than 20 high-density 3 1/2-inch disks, the envelope your Corel disks are in, and the paper with your serial number—you're on your way to installation.

Your Rights To Copy Corel's Disks

As odd as it may seem, you own the box that CorelDRAW came in, the catalog of fonts and clip art, the disks, even the tape holding the box together, but you are not the owner of CorelDRAW. What you've purchased is a *license* to use CorelDRAW version 5. You can use it to create award-winning art, to produce work that makes you a million bucks, or simply to make a more attractive garage sale sign. But this CorelDRAW program (and all its other modules) is the *intellectual property* of the Corel Corporation, and you are not allowed to resell the fonts or the clip art, or make unauthorized copies of the program disks.

The "mice type" (which no one on Earth reads, admittedly) on the envelope containing the program disks makes a long, legalistic, important point of what I've just summed up for you. You are permitted to make one backup set of Corel installation disks for your personal use (in case your originals get damaged or broken), but your glorious adventures with this wonderful design program will be dampened if you're caught distributing copies of Corel.

In work situations, companies can be fined $100,000 and up if the Software Protection Association discovers multiple copies of the same Corel license running. Careers have been ruined, relationships destroyed, and offenders' pleas of ignorance denied by unsympathetic courts.

Programmers who create CorelDRAW and other applications work for a living the same as we all do, and when you illegally copy and distribute their work to another person, in a very real way you've cut their earnings in half.

If it seems like an important action you're embarking on, the point's been well made—we now can start the party.

Copying Disks from Windows Program Manager

If you're new to Windows as well as CorelDRAW, the following set of steps will help you through a lot of situations. If you want to copy a disk of reports a co-worker handed you, or back up a set of installation disks, the procedure's the same—you open File Manager from Windows' Program Manager.

Tear open the envelope that contains the installation disks, and you've accepted Corel's license agreement. Put the disks in a convenient location that's *not* on top of the unmarked, blank backup disks. And *never* put disks with data on them next to a source of magnetism, like your monitor, TV set, or refrigerator magnets! Data is stored on disk as a collection of magnetic impulses, and other magnetic sources will make sushi out of your data.

Follow these steps to back up the Corel installation disks:

1. Make sure the Corel installation disks have the write-protection tabs in their locked positions. You do not want to accidentally copy data back onto an original disk, or your Corel installation will abruptly end. Figure 2.1 is of the back of a 3 1/2-inch disk. When you can see the sun peek through both holes, the disk is write-protected. When one's covered, the disk is writable, and your PC can copy to it.

Figure 2.1

Your original Corel disks should be write-protected; the disks you'll copy to should not.

Can't write on

Can write on

2. In Windows Program Manager, double-click on the **F**ile Manager icon in the Main Group.

3. Choose **D**isk, **C**opy Disk... from the Menu Bar.

4. The Copy Disk dialog box appears, as shown in figure 2.2. Select the drive letter (B usually, but sometimes it's A with newer PCs) that's your 3 1/2-inch drive in both the Source In and Destination In fields by clicking on the down arrows, then click on OK.

5. You'll then be advised in the Confirm Copy Disk dialog box that whatever you stick in your 3 1/2-inch floppy drive will be erased and replaced by the data on your source disk (the Corel disk). Click on **Y**es to accept this responsibility.

6. Take a moment to get the labels and the blank disks.

7. Place the Corel disk labeled Disk 1 in your 3 1/2-inch drive, with the metal shutter heading in first, and the metal circle facing down.

Figure 2.2

Choose the floppy drive for 3 1/2-inch disks on your PC.

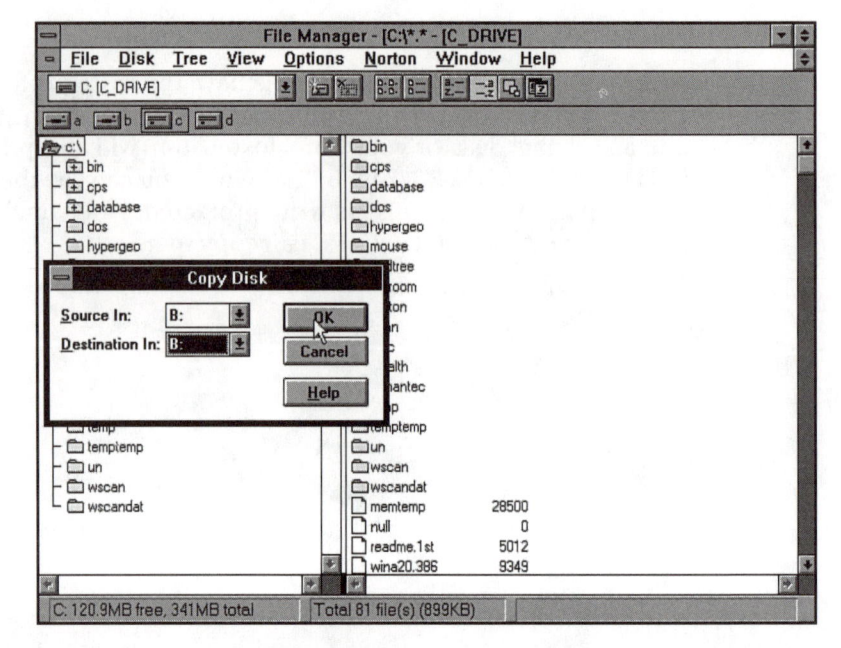

8. Click on OK in the Copy Disk dialog box.

9. File Manager will report the percentage of the copying process in a dialog box on-screen. Use this time to write **Corel version 5 backup disk #1 of 20** on a disk label. Don't put the label on a blank disk yet.

10. When the Copy Disk dialog box hits 50%, your copying process is half done, and you'll be prompted to insert the destination disk (a blank disk).

11. Take the Corel disk out of the floppy drive and put it in a safe place, then insert the blank disk in the drive, and click on OK.

12. In figure 2.3, you see a stylized summary of the dialog boxes you'll encounter, in order, while copying a disk.

13. When the dialog box reports that copying is 100% complete, remove the disk, affix the label you've written onto it, and push the write-protection slider into its up position to protect your copy from accidental erasure in the future. See figure 2.4 for a good example of your CorelDRAW 5 backup disk number 1.

Copying Disks from Windows Program Manager

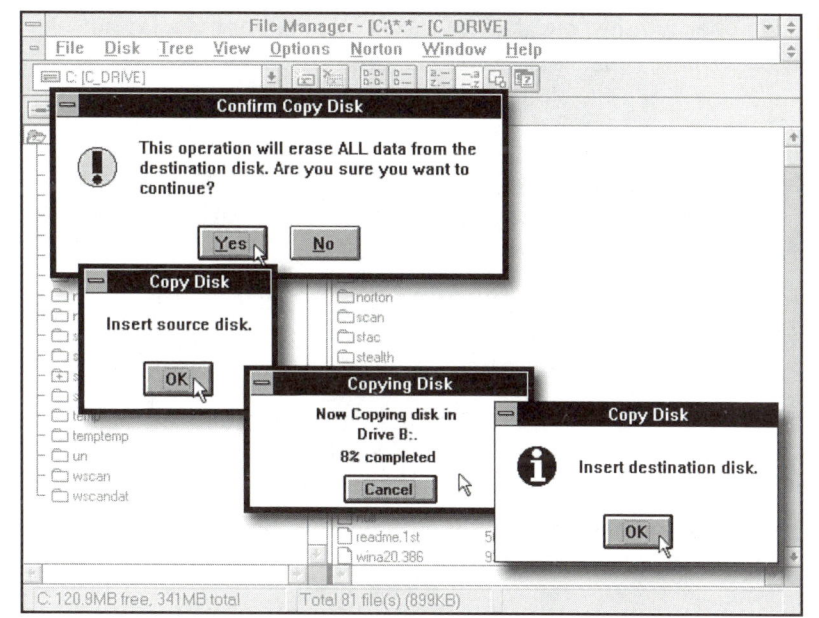

45

Figure 2.3
Answer the dialog boxes to copy your CorelDRAW disks.

Figure 2.4
Put this info on each backup disk: program name, version number, date made, and disk number.

Stop

All disks share the potential for failing to copy, for manufacturing or physical reasons. If File Manager is unable to make a copy of a disk, it'll tell you that the destination disk contains an error.

What you do in this instance is to use another blank disk, and take the clunker out of the drive and toss it. This is why labeling a disk prior to copying to it isn't a good idea; you lose your label in addition to the bum disk.

This is also why you want to bring more than 20 disks with you when backing up CorelDRAW.

Repeat steps 3-13 for the other Corel disks. When you have your complete backup set, put the originals in an exceptionally safe, non-magnetic climate that's always room temperature (i.e. not on the back seat of your car).

Owners of the CD version of Corel should perk up now, because the tricks and tips for the smartest installation of CorelDRAW await everyone, regardless of media type!

Checking Your Hard Disk for Corel Space

CorelDRAW! 5 for Beginners' recommendations for a successful installation aren't the same as Corel Corporation's. In general, when you have a large hard drive (at least 240MB), system RAM to spare (at least 8MB; Windows *alone* likes 8MB to play with), and a co-processor on your motherboard (as found on i486 IBM/PCs and compatibles), Corel will run effortlessly, and your explorations will be satisfying.

Before beginning the installation process, use File Manager to see if you have enough open hard disk space. You want to have more than 50MB free on the drive on which you want to install CorelDRAW, and at least 10MB free on the drive where Windows is located. Additionally, you need some "elbow room" for Corel's temp file location. CorelDRAW requires empty space on your drive where it can swap pieces of your work in and out of system RAM while you work; my recommendation is that in addition to the 50MB for Corel program files, tack on another 30MB, and CorelDRAW will operate smoothly and quickly.

Checking Your Hard Disk for Corel Space

Stop

Do not continue to run Corel Setup if you don't have enough hard disk space, as previously recommended. As you are guided through the Setup routine, you'll come to the temp file setup section of the installation (covered later in this chapter), and you'll have to exit the setup if you don't have enough space. At the very least, you'll have to click on Back, and choose not to install some of the modules—that would be a shame.

In Windows File Manager, click on the drive on which you now want to install CorelDRAW 5. If you have more than, say, 70MB free (look at the status bar on the bottom of File Manager), you can proceed with Corel setup. If not, you may want to move some files onto floppy disks or backup tape. Engage the help of an experienced user if you're in doubt as to backing up your hard drive.

In theory, CorelDRAW can be run directly from the CD, in which case you need about 10MB open on your Windows drive for fonts and Corel links to Windows. Running Corel from a CD may conserve hard drive space, but it's not really recommended, because it will run like molasses in January. Even the fastest triple- or quad-speed CD-ROM drive can't compete with the 8 to 12 millisecond access time of today's hard disks.

The Custom CorelDRAW Install

Take a deep breath. You're going to have options galore as the install procedure commences, but take heart—you can pause in the installation at a number of points to check your options, your hard drive space, or to take an aspirin!

Get the Corel catalog handy, because you'll be selecting which fonts, symbols, and clip art you want on your drive. I'll make some recommendations and explain the consequences of others along the way.

Stop

Turn off screen savers and any other active applications (especially fax/modem programs), before you run the installation program. Other programs steal from system processor cycles, and can actually result in an abrupt, unexpected end to the CorelDRAW installation process.

Chapter 2: Installing the Corel Bundle

Here's how to take the plunge, and add the world's greatest graphics package to your collection of artist's tools:

1. From CD or from disk, Choose File, Run... from Program Manager (Norton Desktop, or other third party Windows shells).

2. Disk installers: place backup disk 1 in your floppy drive. CD installers have to have the CorelDRAW CD number 1 inserted in the CD-ROM drive now.

3. In the Command Line: field, type the drive letter you want to install from, semicolon, backslash, then type SETUP.EXE (Example: **B:\SETUP.EXE**). You may want to choose Browse at this point, and find the SETUP.EXE file on the floppy or CD-ROM drive by choosing the correct Drives drop-down, and clicking on the File Name.

4. Click on OK once the command line has been entered, and you're off!

5. The Corel installation executable file will take a moment or two to load into system RAM, and then you are greeted by the version 5 Setup screen, as shown in figure 2.5. Click on Continue.

Figure 2.5
Clicking on Continue will take you to registering CorelDRAW.

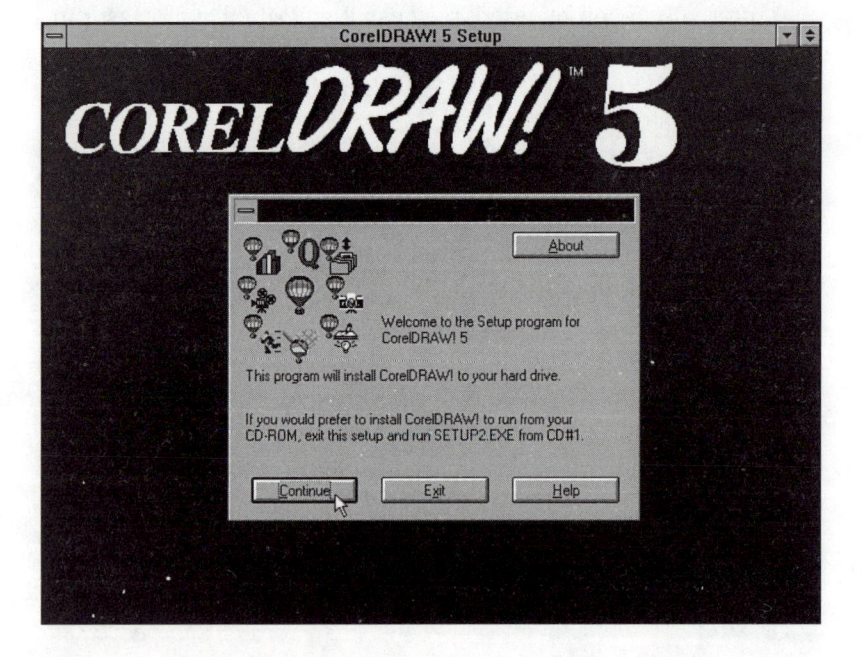

The Custom CorelDRAW Install

6. Pick up the piece of paper with your registration number written on it that you left near the PC earlier. In figure 2.6, you can see that Corel wants User Information, namely your name, and evidence that you actually paid for the product. Type in your unique registration number, or Corel Setup will pester you for it, delaying the installation. Click on **C**ontinue to advance to the next field.

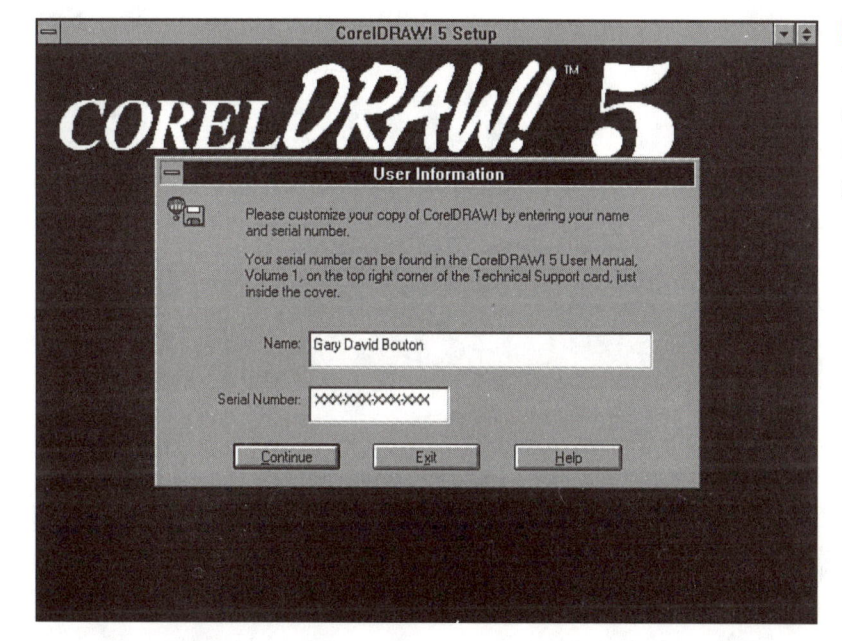

Figure 2.6
This is not my serial number; it's been disguised, but you get the idea.

7. In figure 2.7, you see that you have two ways to go: Full Installation or Custom. Choose the Custom Install.

8. The Destination directory dialog box appears, with a suggestion as to where Setup can install the Corel program files, and a name for the Corel subdirectory under which it will put the files on your hard disk. If you don't have more than 50MB free on the drive Corel suggests, type the path to the drive and subdirectory where you want Corel to reside in the **D**irectory field—for example, **D:\COREL50**. Corel will create the directory for you if it doesn't already exist.

9. Click on **C**ontinue. In the next section, you'll review the options that you will be presented with during the installation. By following along, you'll save on both hard disk space and aspirin.

Chapter 2: Installing the Corel Bundle

Figure 2.7
You've got the option to install only the features you really need by choosing Custom Install.

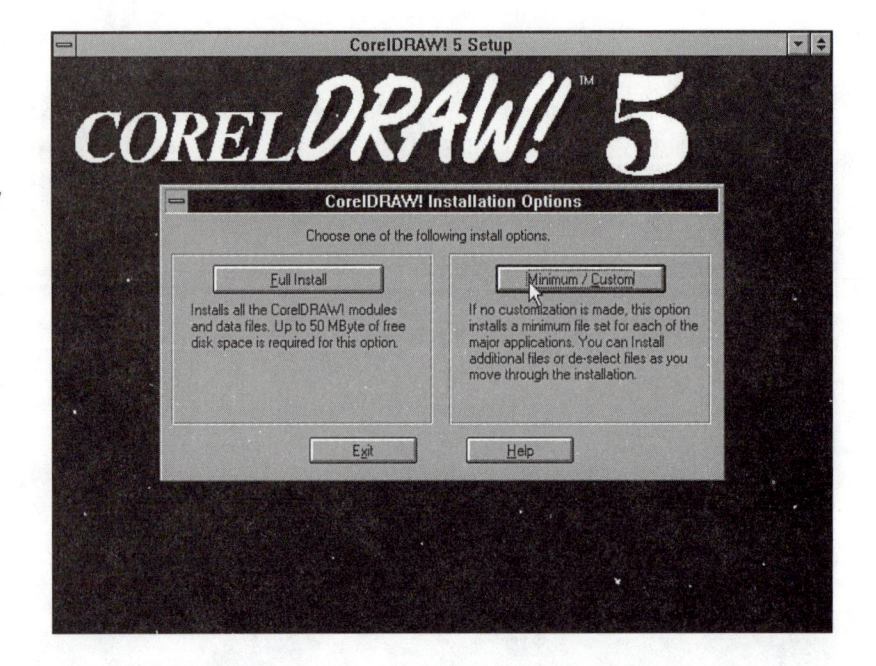

Should You Install All Five Programs?

Since you bought the package, you're entitled to install all, some, or none of Corel's five program modules, as well as the three utilities that offer even more graphics and database features.

In figure 2.8, you can see that Corel gives you the option to individually customize the installation of the modules. If you uncheck the box to the left of a module, none of it will install. Also worthy of some thought is the "tally" the Custom Install dialog box shows you. Check to see your available space versus the space required on your hard disk. The top number should be *way* less than the bottom!

As you saw in the last figure, the author has plenty of room to go the whole nine yards. It's not so much a question of whether you can install all of Corel, but rather, what do you *need* from the package?

This and the following are questions all Corel users must ask themselves. Are you familiar with what each module can do? Do you deal with a lot of statistics at work? Do you work with a photographer who's involved in scanning photos? Before continuing, here's a list of brief descriptions about what the Corel modules do, and on what occasions they are useful. Take a look at the list that follows to determine the modules you're interested in.

Should You Install All Five Programs?

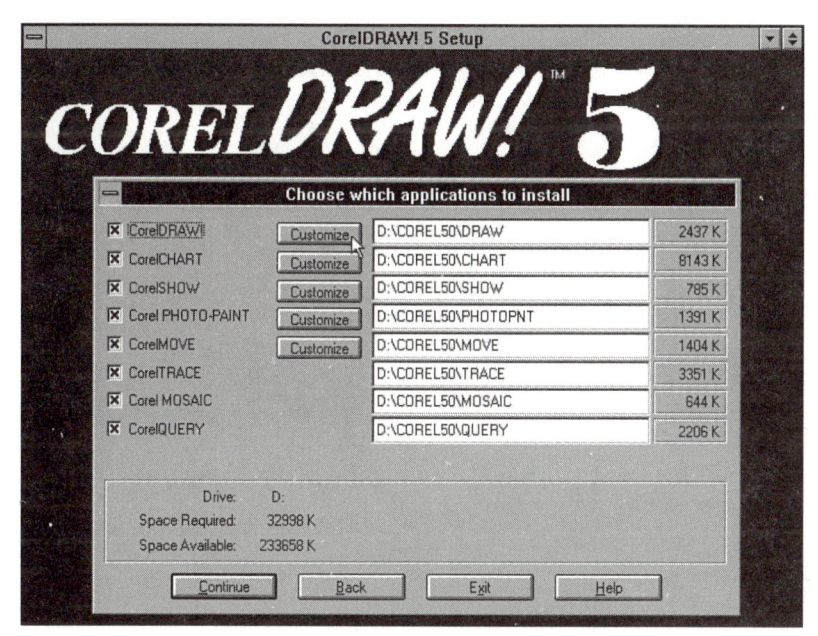

Figure 2.8
Customizing a Corel module can reduce or increase the required space on your hard disk.

CorelDRAW

CorelDRAW is needed by just about every other module to build titles, designs, and other graphics, so you'll surely want to install it.

CorelCHART

CorelCHART is a ridiculously full-featured charting program that'll take data from popular database and spreadsheet programs, or manual entry of data. If your career depends on snappy charts, you'll want to install CorelCHART. If you only do an occasional chart and your word processor or spreadsheet program's charting utility meets your needs, don't install CorelCHART now. You can always install it in the future if your needs change.

CorelSHOW

CorelSHOW is a presentation program that enables you to assemble a multimedia event out of charts, sound files, animations, bitmap designs, and CorelDRAW graphics. You can run a slide show on-screen, or send a CorelSHOW document to a service bureau to have 35mm slides made from your work. It's a middle-of-the-road business tool. If your main attraction to

Corel is for its artistic and design capabilities, you may not want to install CorelSHOW. But if you need to produce presentations that keep a room full of people awake, CorelSHOW definitely earns its keep, and you should install it.

CorelPHOTO-PAINT

CorelPHOTO-PAINT works with bitmap graphics and scanned photo images. This paint program is a natural companion to the vector graphic-based CorelDRAW. You can use PHOTO-PAINT to retouch, or add special effects to, new or existing bitmapped images such as photographs or scanned images. You can create new images in PHOTO-PAINT, or you can edit existing ones by adding textures, text, CorelDRAW designs, or by using special effects filters. CorelPHOTO-PAINT is the only Corel module that will take direct input from a scanner via the File, Acquire command on its Menu Bar. You should strongly consider installing this module.

CorelMOVE

CorelMOVE is an awful lot of fun to use—you could get fired if you play with it too much. But I give it a thumbs-up based on its usefulness in creating limited animations for use in CorelSHOW documents.

Corel's Utilities

The rest of the hit list consists of Corel utilities, and you only have the option of installing all or none of them. CorelTRACE is a useful utility for converting a bitmap graphic to a file format on which CorelDRAW can work. Install it. CorelMOSAIC is an image cataloging utility. Install it, and you can make thumbnail collections of many different image types, which is handy when you want to quickly refer to something or print an image. CorelQUERY is a utility for extracting specific data from large databases, like those built by public utilities and Fortune 500 companies. There's no compelling reason to install it if you don't work with data, but if you do, install both QUERY and CHART.

Clip Art

Disk installers can choose whether to install the clip art, but if you're installing from a CD, you'll have no clip art on your hard drive. Instead, you load clip art directly from the second CD in the Corel bundle. I recommend disk owners install the clip art. It's in Corel's CMX (Corel Presentation Exchange) format, very similar to CorelDRAW's native *.CDR, and you'll see how to use it in your design work in Chapter 10.

Should You Install All Five Programs? 53

Tip

If you don't have the space required to install your Corel programs on a single drive, you can change the drive and location of any of the programs without exiting Setup. Simply type a different name and directory in the field to the right of the program you want to install to another drive.

Customizing a Single Application for Installation

In each program module, you have your choice of which components you want on your hard drive. The procedure for whittling down or beefing up each module is shown in the next steps, using CorelDRAW as an example. Here's how to install exactly what you want:

1. Start with CorelDRAW. Click on the Customize button to the right of the CorelDRAW check box on the applications install screen.

2. In figure 2.9, you can see the options available. You can also see that installing each component affects the space required to install. You definitely want the Online Help, so check this box. If you'd like a gander at CorelDRAW Samples, check this one also, but it'll add about 1/2MB to your hard drive. Finally, you can decide which symbols you want to be available for use in CorelDRAW. Click on the Customize button next to Symbols and take a look at the available symbol categories.

3. Symbols are prebuilt CorelDRAW illustrations you can simply drag into CorelDRAW for instant use. They come in categories, some of which are more useful than others. As shown in figure 2.10, I have no professional use for Morse Code symbols, Plants, or Plants that communicate using Morse Code. Find any category you think you don't need, click on it, then click on the Delete button. The Weather and Food categories are good ones to install, and they are used in several chapter assignments in this book.

Chapter 2: Installing the Corel Bundle

Figure 2.9
Choose to install the Online Help for fingertip information about this new version of CorelDRAW.

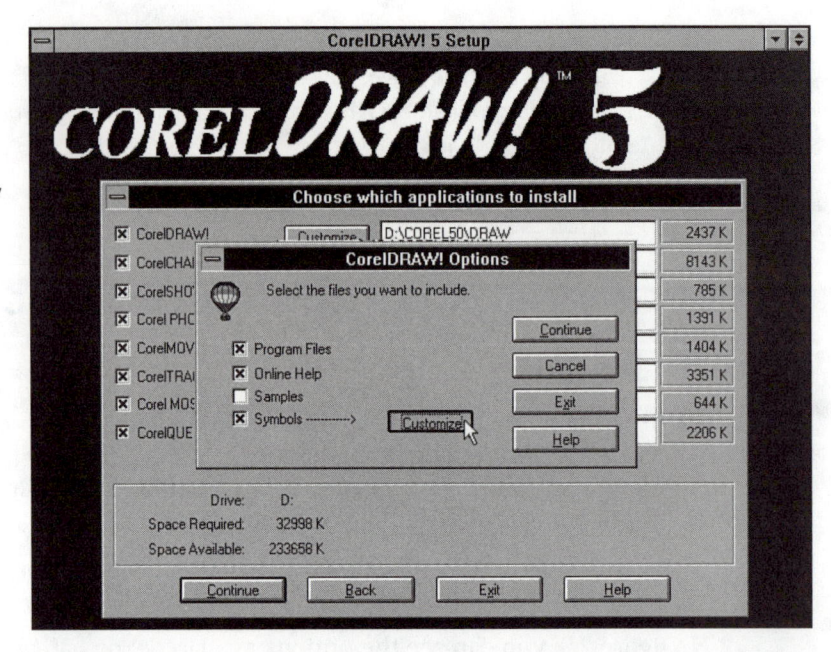

Figure 2.10
Add or remove specific symbol categories, depending on your specific design needs.

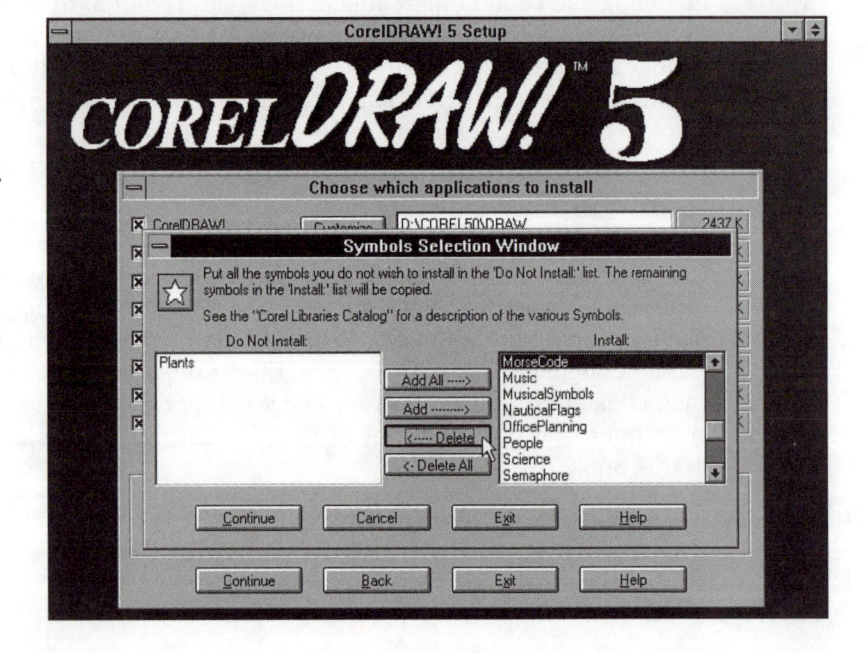

Customizing a Single Application for Installation

Stop

Corel means "Don't Install" when it says Delete in any of the installation dialog boxes. You won't delete anything from your disks or hard drive when you press the Delete button during the installation procedure. Besides, your disks are write-protected now, aren't they? And CD-ROMs are always read-only, anyway.

4. Click on **C**ontinue, and you'll return to the Choose which applications to install dialog box.

5. Proceed through the rest of the applications, choosing to install the Online Help files; if you're really curious about the sample images, data, or animations, choose to install the Samples by checking the box.

6. Press **C**ontinue after you've made your selections. You'll then see another dialog box about which auxiliary files you want installed. This is discussed in the next section.

Taking Stock of Your Peripheral Needs

The Choose which files to install dialog box contains a range of categories that cover additional filters for importing and exporting your documents to and from different formats (very useful), scanner drivers (not useful at all if you have a scanner that came with a TWAIN interface of its own), and enough fonts to choke a professional type foundry.

Choosing Which Filters To Install

The first category of files from which you have to choose are Corel's import and export filters. If you install all of them, they will take up almost 2MB of hard disk space. That's not bad considering that once the word gets out that you're a graphics guru, you'll sometimes be asked to work assignments involving files *other* than those in a CorelDRAW format. This means that the more import and export filters you have available to you, the easier it will be to handle requests with grace and ease.

Here's how to choose which filters will be installed:

1. In the Choose which files to install dialog box, click on the **C**ustomize button (next to Filters).

2. Take a look through the scroll boxes on the left side of the dialog box. These filters will not be installed unless you add them to the Install: list

Chapter 2: Installing the Corel Bundle

on the right side of the dialog box. I recommend that you add *all* of the import and export filters. To do this, click on the Add All button for Export filters and then click on the Add All button for Import Filters. This puts all of the filters into the Install boxes on the right, as seen in figure 2.11.

Figure 2.11
Install filters to Import and Export between Corel and your other applications.

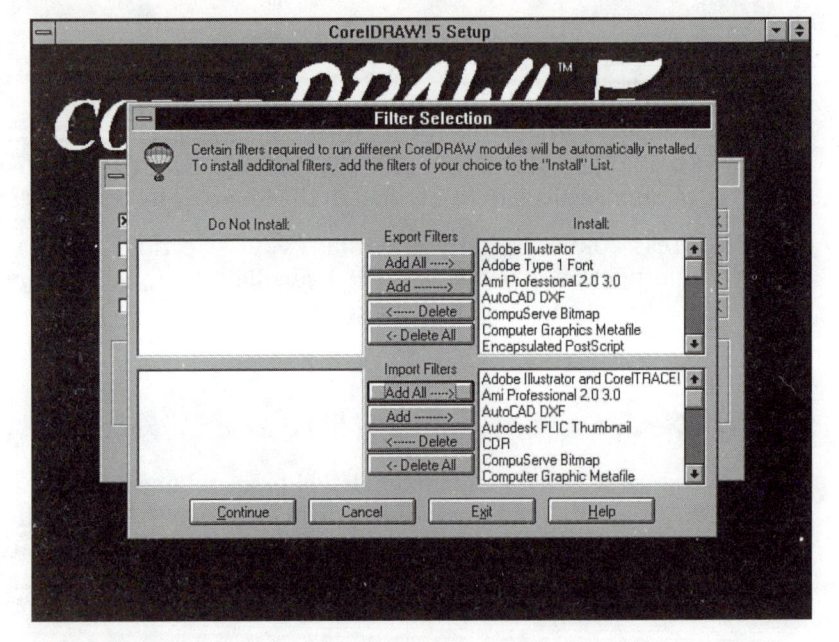

3. Now all of the filters are set to be installed. If you know for sure that you will never use a particular filter, you can highlight it and press the Delete button. This will move it to the Do Not Install side of the dialog box.

4. When you're done with your selections, press the Continue button to return to the Choose which files to install dialog box.

Installing TrueType Fonts

Everyone who works in Windows can be accused of being a font addict at one time or another. Fonts are fun to collect; folks use them once or twice to make a greeting card or poster, then they stick around forever on your ever-shrinking hard disk. I know. I've been there, and I have some advice: the

CD-ROM have 830 fonts in both the TrueType and Type1 format available any time you want to fetch them using the Control Panel Fonts utility (explained in Chapter 9), so there's no need to dive face-forward into Corel's fonts during installation.

If you're installing from disk, you have less fonts to choose from, but Corel and New Riders Publishing will tell you the same thing—adding more than 100 Corel fonts will slow down Windows (and Corel) noticeably, because each font has to be immediately available to the user in every application. Having too many (over 250) installed fonts can be a heavy drain on your system resources. In addition, every TrueType font has to be registered in your WIN.INI file, which can make your WIN.INI file expand tremendously. If your WIN.INI file reaches its 64K size limit, Windows will cease to work, and then so will you!

Tip

To learn more about strange Windows stuff that can have a bearing on Corel's performance without you even realizing it, check out *Windows for Non-Nerds* by Rob Tidrow and Jim Boyce, a very popular and user-friendly tome by New Riders Publishing.

Here's how to make the most sensible use of Corel's font bounty:

1. Pick up the Corel catalog, and find the section where the fonts are listed, illustrated with small examples of each font.

2. Prop up the book somewhere where you can leaf through the fonts section while you choose their names from the installation program on-screen.

3. Click on the Customize button next to the TrueType Fonts check box.

4. In figure 2.12, you can see that the TrueType Fonts Selection dialog box offers collections of fonts grouped into categories. If there's a group of particular interest you've found in the Corel catalog, check the box next to it. But if you want more control over which fonts are loaded, check the Assorted check box, and read on.

Chapter 2: Installing the Corel Bundle

Figure 2.12
Click on a collection of TrueType fonts you want installed.

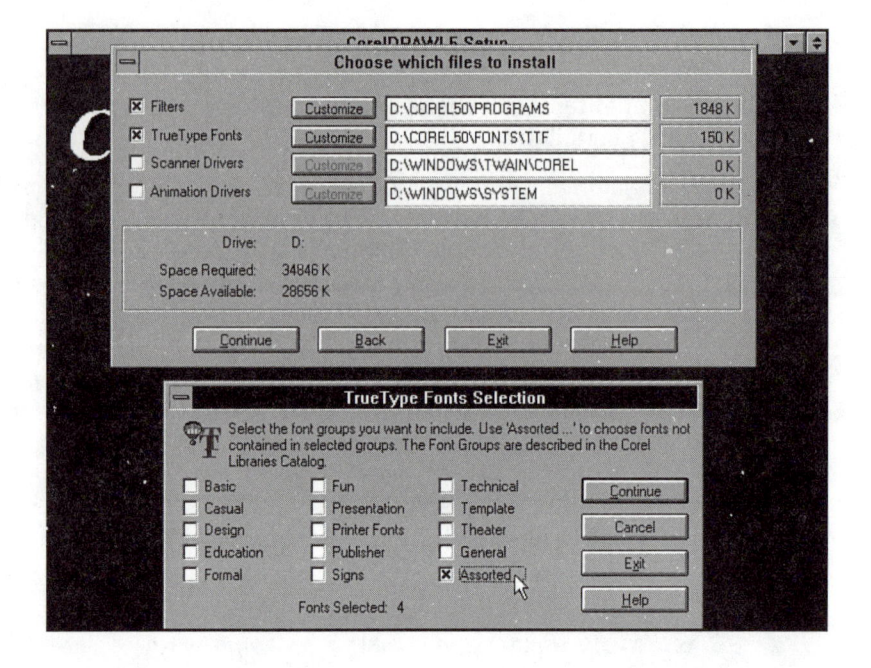

Even if you don't check any category of fonts, Corel will still install four that it uses as the default font in the Corel programs. Avant GardeBT, bold, italic, and regular should *not* be uninstalled from Windows after you install Corel. When Corel fails to find Avant Garde installed, Corel is forced to use another typeface as its default, and sometimes it's one you don't expect or want.

Note

Use Business Sense When Choosing Your Fonts

Corel puts the user in a position not unlike a kid in a candy store with all these font selections. Now is a good time to take a good, long look at the fonts in the Corel catalog, and reflect for a moment on your business/professional needs. This doesn't mean you can't be a designer anymore—a handful of splashy display fonts (like Tiffany, Compacta, Snell, and other ornamental fonts) can liven up even your dullest design project.

But installing a font is a lot like buying a car—it's (hopefully) going to be around a long while, so you should show a little discrimination and balance everyday functionality against flash. For instance, if you pick more than 100

Taking Stock of Your Peripheral Needs

fonts from the Assorted list, Corel Setup will warn you that you're going to degrade Windows and Corel's performance, so set 100 typefaces as your personal limit before selecting fonts.

If you want to play it safe, look at the categories (like Basic and Casual) in the Corel catalog, decide on a maximum of three categories that will fill your professional needs, and then you'll have less than 100 fonts installed.

Stop

Even before you install Corel, there are probably other fonts you've installed from other applications, or perhaps you've bought a collection from a digital type foundry. Whether they are TrueType or Adobe Type Manager Type 1 fonts, keep their number in mind as you tally up your entire system font collection.

On a typically fast 386 or 486 machine with 8MB RAM and a 240MB hard disk, you will notice a system slowdown after more than a total of 250 fonts have been installed on it.

Font Minder is a good utility you should familiarize yourself with; it automatically groups a collection of fonts, and removes them if the need arises. A limited edition of Font Minder is on one of Corel's CD-ROM disks, and as a Corel owner, you can purchase the full-featured edition at a substantial savings.

Installing Only the Fonts You Need

Figure 2.13 is an example of the world's worst interoffice memo. It's illegible because Amelia, Stop, and Buster are esoteric display fonts not in big demand in a corporate environment. If you are producing a lot of official-looking documents at work, choose the plainer, more practical, everyday kinds of typefaces. Baskerville, Helvetica, and the Futura family of fonts aren't splashy, but designers use them almost daily for a wide range of assignments.

Here's how to pick only the typefaces you need from the Assorted list:

1. Click on the Assorted check box in the TrueType Fonts Selection dialog box.

2. By default, all the fonts on the CD are in the Do Not Install list box, except for Avant Garde. Scroll down the Do Not Install list until you find a font you'd like installed, and double-check what the font looks like in the Corel catalog.

Figure 2.13
Evaluate your professional need for the specific font you install.

3. To select a bunch of fonts at one time, hold the Ctrl key while you make your selections.

4. As shown in figure 2.14, American Typewriter, Bold, and Medium have been selected in the Do Not Install list. When you have your choices selected, press the Add button.

5. When you're done selecting fonts, press **C**ontinue.

Scanner Drivers

If your scanner is one that is directly supported by Corel scanner drivers, or if it is one of the newer TWAIN-compliant scanners, you'll then be able to scan source images and documents directly into CorelPHOTO-PAINT for immediate use. Scanners create bitmap images, and PHOTO-PAINT is the only Corel module that supports bitmap editing. If you plan to use a scanner with PHOTO-PAINT, you may need to install one of Corel's scanner drivers.

To install a scanner driver, do the following:

1. Click on the Scanner Drivers check box and then click on the Customize button next to it.

Taking Stock of Your Peripheral Needs

2. Click on the down arrow next to the Scanner drop-down list box. If you see your scanner listed, click on it and then make any Option or Value settings your scanner may require. Check your scanner documentation for the information you'll need to make the right choices in these boxes. If your scanner does not require any special settings, these boxes will be dimmed.

3. Click on OK.

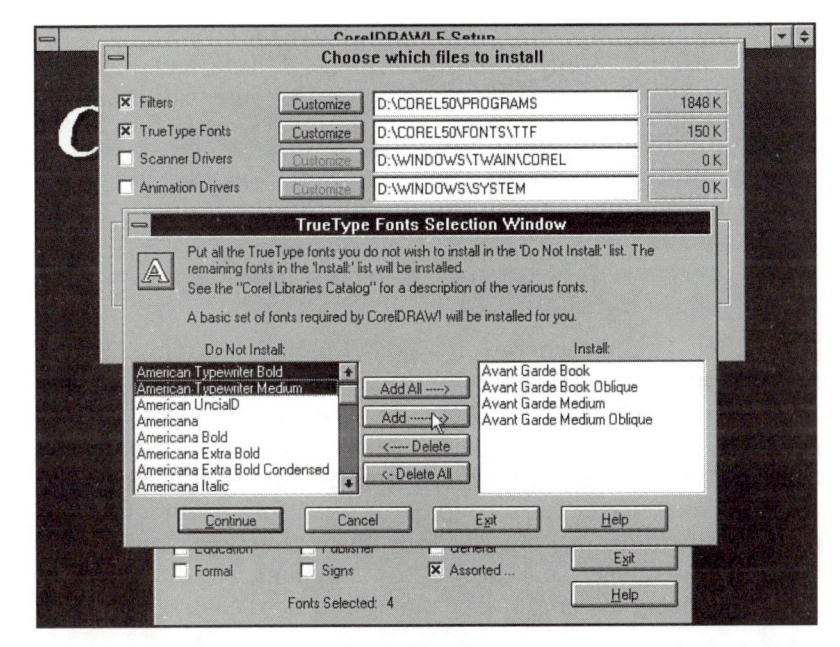

Figure 2.14
You can delete or add as many times as you like before pressing the Continue button.

If your scanner is not specifically listed in Corel's list of scanners but is a TWAIN standard scanner (that came with TWAIN interface software), you will still be able to use your scanner with PHOTO-PAINT. Check with your scanner manufacturer, or the scanner's owners manual, to see how to install the TWAIN software if it has not already been installed on your computer.

If you don't have a scanner, installing Corel's scanner software is a useless effort and you'll lose hard drive space.

Installing Animation Run-Time Modules

Animation drivers is the last category of options from which you can select before CorelDRAW installs its program files. Animation drivers are actually run-time modules that enable you to play animation and motion picture clips from your screen.

Autodesk Animator *.FLI and *.FLC files can't be created by the Corel modules, but this is a handy utility—the Autodesk format is the oldest of PC animation standards, and you may come across files in this format in business.

Both the QuickTime for Windows and the AVI formats are supported by CorelMOVE, and you may export animations you create in MOVE to be played using these run-time modules. I don't recommend installing them if you choose not to install CorelMOVE, however. Additionally, the AVI and QuickTime modules may already be on your PC if you've purchased other new software in the last year. Many word-processing, database, and graphics programs can embed AVI and QuickTime files into the documents that they produce.

CorelMOVE animations can be played within CorelMOVE; you'll see in Chapter 12 how to insert an animation into a CorelSHOW document.

The Necessity of Temp File Space

CorelDRAW next wants to know where you want Setup to define temp file space on your hard disk. A temp file directory (an empty space on your hard disk) enables Corel to run smoothly. Part of your hard disk needs to be reserved for Corel to put in pieces of the program and file information as you work. When you're finished, the temp files are cleaned from your hard disk and, in theory, you should never see a temp file as you browse Windows File Manager. You need to have some hard disk free most of the time, however, for no other reason than being a "parking lot" for temp files. The dialog box Corel presents you with is the Temp Drives dialog box, as seen in figure 2.15.

The Importance of Temporary Files

Corel and other Windows programs need *at least* 5 to 10MB of free hard disk space to store temporary files. If you don't have enough free space, Corel will install and you'll be able to run it—sort of. Eventually, you'll get a warning message (if you're lucky) while you're working, or your system will crash and you may lose your work.

Corel's Temp Drives dialog box prompts you for information regarding which hard drive (or drives) Corel should use to store temporary files. Corel will create a temp subdirectory for you on the drive(s) you choose if a temp directory doesn't already exist. Chances are you already have a temp directory on your hard drive that was made when you installed Windows; it's most commonly found on your C drive. This temp directory is already being used by Windows and other Windows programs to store their temporary files. If you have other programs running while you are using Corel (not a recommended practice), there may not be enough room on the drive that holds your current temp subdirectory for Corel's temporary files, plus your other programs' temporary files.

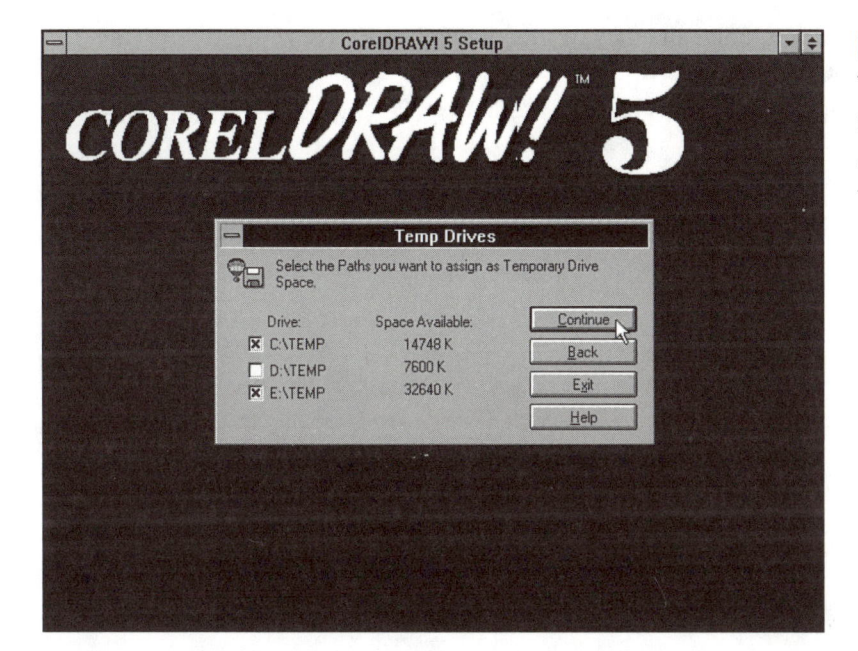

Figure 2.15
You can choose more than one drive to hold temporary files.

Considerations When Selecting a Temp Drive Location

Read the following recommendations, and keep them in mind when you make your choices in the Temp Drives dialog box.

- Put a checkmark next to the drive that has the most open space in the Setup dialog box. Do your addition carefully; if you're installing CorelDRAW and other Corel programs to the same drive as the one you choose for the temp location, tag at least 10MB onto what the required space on the Setup dialog box tells you to arrive at a total.

- If you have more than one hard drive installed in your computer (you can't use network drives for temporary file storage), checkmark two (or more) of the suggested drive boxes.

- If you have a choice between using a drive that has been compressed (like with Stacker or DoubleSpace) and one that is not compressed, choose the uncompressed drive(s).

- If you choose two drive locations for temp locations, make sure the total space on both drives adds up to more than 10MB.

- If you don't make an entry in this dialog box, Corel will use or create a temp subdirectory on your C drive.

When you have made your selections, click on the Continue button on the Temp Drives dialog box.

Tip

The Temp Drives dialog box is the last place you make selections before Corel actually assembles the programs on your hard disk. If you think you've missed something or made an unwise decision about anything, you can always review your selections by clicking on the Back button on the bottom of each dialog box. This will move you one dialog box back. If you keep choosing Back on each dialog box, you can go as far back as the first dialog box in which you made entries.

The Last Dialog Box Before Installing

Once you've pressed Continue in the Temp Drives dialog box, it's on to the Corel 5 Setup dialog box. As you can see in figure 2.16, this is the very last place you get to make decisions before the installation process actually begins. If you want to go back and make any changes to anything you've told Corel to do, press the Back button. The Back button on each dialog box will take you one step back through the dialog boxes, so it's not too late to make changes. If you're satisfied with all of your selections, and you're ready to go, the procedure you'll follow is slightly different if you are installing from CD or from disk.

For CD installation of CorelDRAW, the process is automatic. For disk owners, follow these simple steps to install:

1. Click on the Install button. Corel Setup will then give you an on-screen status report of how much of the program's bundle has been installed, as shown in figure 2.17.

The Last Dialog Box Before Installing

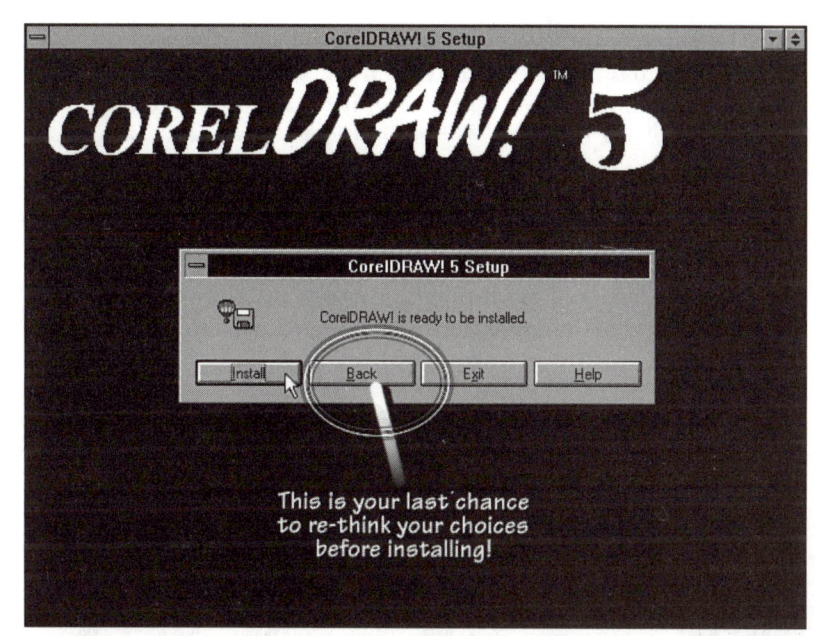

Figure 2.16
Press Back if you're not absolutely certain about your custom options!

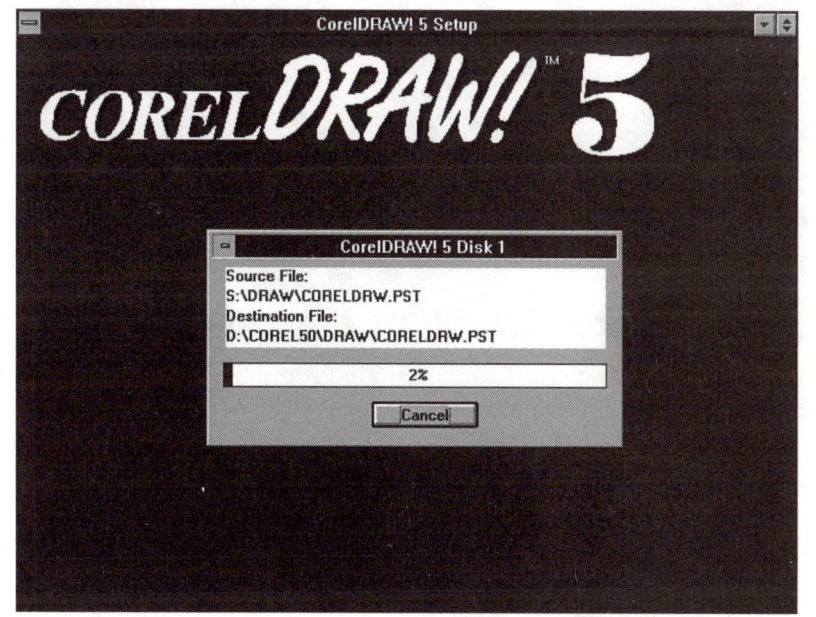

Figure 2.17
Corel tells you which disk is in your floppy drive, and how much of the program has been installed.

2. When Setup has completed transferring disk 1's information to your hard drive, Setup will tell you to put in the next disk. Pay careful attention to the disk number Setup asks for. It's possible you'll leap from disk 4 to disk 9, for instance, depending on which installation components you selected in your custom Setup.

3. Be patient. Disk installation takes about three or four minutes per disk.

4. For both CD and disk installers, figure 2.18 is the last stop! Corel has successfully transferred and assembled the program files you asked for, and your TrueType is immediately available for use after clicking on OK.

Figure 2.18
Corel likes to feature winning artwork from the annual World Design contest in Setup, and in the clip art collection.

5. Take a moment to arrange the Corel group in Program Manager. Resize and reposition the group so it doesn't hinder your view of other application icons. It's larger than the Windows Main group!

6. Read the Release Notes by double-clicking on the icon in the Corel group. This contains last-minute information that didn't make it into your owner's manual. It could contain vital material, like a warning not to use a certain brand of video driver you own.

The Last Dialog Box Before Installing

7. Go fill out your registration card, put a stamp on it, and whistle for your local mail carrier. Completing the action in one fell swoop avoids procrastination, which will delay your rights to Corel tech support.

Congratulations! You've successfully completed a custom installation of a very large suite of applications. After all this you probably want to get started. You're rightfully anxious to get your feet wet and play with this program a little, but before you double-click on CorelDRAW's icon and go back to Chapter 1's assignment, take a moment to look over the following notes.

Removing Unwanted TrueType Fonts From Your System

You may find down the road that you've installed a font you have no further use for. Typically, TrueType fonts are around 55KB (55,000 bytes) in size, although Ice Age is a whopping 140KB. Perhaps your boss or administrative assistant at work did you the favor of running Corel Setup, and they chose to install every font on earth on the PC, mistakenly believing this would assist you in your work.

In either case, when you want to remove a TrueType font from your hard disk, the steps are taken in Windows, not CorelDRAW. Here's how to reduce the number of fonts available to you in CorelDRAW and other Windows applications:

1. Double-click on Control Panel in the Windows Main group. If you moved Control Panel out of this group, find it in another location; if someone else did this favor for you, yell at them.

2. Double-click on the Fonts icon. As you can see in figure 2.19, this action offers you a dialog box listing which fonts are installed and available for use. Clicking on a font's name in the Installed Fonts list displays a sample of what the typeface looks like. Click on the name of the font you want to delete from the List of Installed fonts, then click on **Re**move.

Figure 2.19
Hold the Ctrl key and click on multiple font titles if you want to remove several at a time.

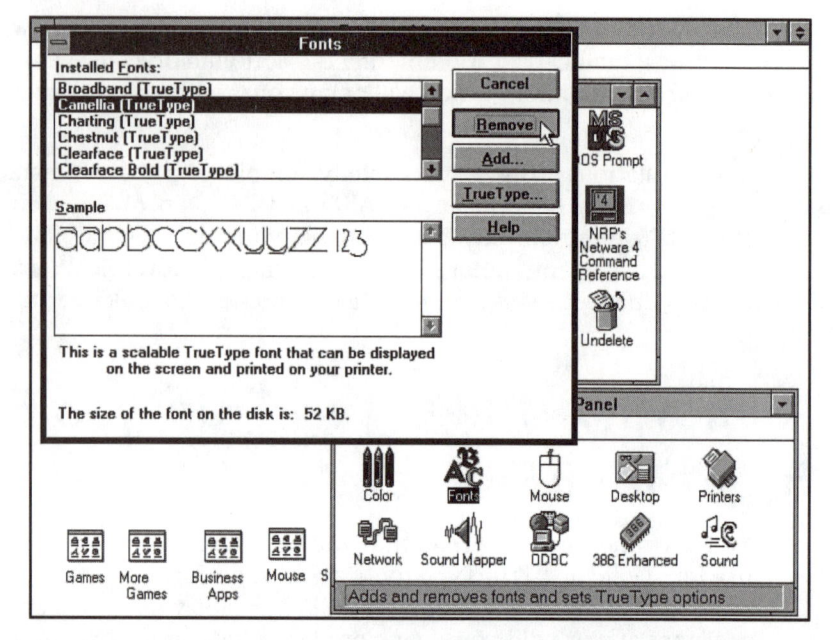

3. In the Remove Font dialog box, you'll make a very important decision if you check the Delete Font File From Disk box. Checking this box before clicking on Yes will cause Windows to erase the font from your hard drive.

   If you leave this box *un*checked and click on Yes, the font will still be on your hard disk, but it won't be recognized by Windows, Corel, or any other Windows program. Either way, the less fonts you have installed, the quicker Corel and Windows will run. Click on Yes (or Yes to All, depending on whether you selected multiple fonts to remove).

4. Click on Close to return to Program Manager.

Removing Unwanted Corel Files (Advanced Users Only)

This is for experienced Windows users only—you can get into a world of trouble deleting files if you're new to Windows File Manager.

If you change your mind about clip art or Corel samples and don't want them on your hard disk, you stand to gain 1 or 2MB by deleting them. Sometimes, this small gain is exactly what you need, though, because Corel, Microsoft, and other manufacturers are creating absolutely huge programs this year!

Files in the SAMPLES subdirectory, located under the DRAW subdirectory, all bear the *.CDR extension associated with CorelDRAW. If you click on them to select them in File Manager, and choose **D**elete from the **F**ile menu, File Manager may or may not ask you for a confirmation (depending on how your Options for Confirmation is set up), then poof—the CDR files go away and you have more hard disk space.

Stay away from program directories, however, and don't delete anything other than *.CDR files. If you accidentally delete a program file, such as the ones in the DRAW, CHART, PROGRAMS, or CONFIG subdirectories (bearing *.PAT, *.DLL, *.EXE and other extensions), you'll ruin the program and have to reinstall it.

This is *not* a trick for the inexperienced Windows user.

Making Corel's Workspace Your Own

If you've completed Chapters 1 and 2, you probably have more questions than answers about CorelDRAW's workspace. The workspace is as flexible as the objects you draw in it, and can be tailored to meet your exact designing needs. In Chapter 3, you'll explore the preferences you can exhibit, the best way to print a CorelDRAW design, and how to whip CorelDRAW into shape so it's a sleeker place to draw in!

Let's do some virtual interior decorating next!

CORELDRAW! 5
Special
Preferences
Menu
Onions
Cheese
Tomato
Pickles
Alt+C
Ctrl+P
BUILD YOUR OWN SPECIAL

CHAPTER 3

Customizing CorelDRAW!/Finding the Features

Many professional designers agree that using CorelDRAW to complete an assignment is the best way to get something done. And although Corel installs a lot of helpful default settings for the new user, there's a better way to accomplish your design goal, if you know where Corel's options are and how to fine-tune them.

Every option you imagine (and a few you can't possibly!) is twistable, refinable, and has a setting you can call your own in CorelDRAW. In this chapter, you'll see who's really in charge after you install this multi-megabyte, digital Swiss army knife of a program!

In this chapter, you:

- Set up a Windows working directory for your artwork
- See how styles and templates can make your work fly
- Program your right mouse button for CorelDRAW sessions
- Learn how to create virtual embossing
- Make your own preset
- Discover how to add PANTONE colors to the color palette
- Get an introduction to printing, Corel-style

Leave the Drawing to Us

Plenty of examples of CorelDRAW artwork are in this chapter's figures, but since this is primarily a chapter on customizing, *not* drawing, we don't expect you to intuitively re-create the examples. Learning some of the tricks and tips about the *workspace* will be the very first part of your CorelDRAW education. *Before* you get the hang of designing intricate shapes, backgrounds, and compositions, you need to know how to save your work and find the options that'll make CorelDRAW feel more like home to the artist or businessperson.

So let the illustrations here serve as some visual relief and treat 'em as an "Idea Book" collection. By the end of this book, you *will* learn how to create the designs, but for now, simply peruse them—I'll guide you through creating a specific shape or entering text if it's key to learning about a Corel option.

Keeping Your Work in One Place

The best time to create a working directory, one in which you store documents you create, is before you've generated too many documents. Programs, including CorelDRAW, are all too often prone to saving a piece of work to the root of your hard drive or to a directory that contains program files (a bad practice!).

The solution to this is to create a user-defined subdirectory on your hard disk to which you can always direct CorelDRAW when it's time to save a new file.

Here's how to make a special place on your hard disk for your CorelDRAW work:

1. Double-click on the File Manager icon in Windows Program Manager's Main group to launch it.

2. Click on the drive icon of your choice (the buttons beneath the drive label drop-down list) to reveal the directory structure of it. Make sure the icon is a hard drive, and not A: or B: (your floppy drives).

3. Double-click on the open folder icon at the top of the directory tree with the drive letter next to it. Now you're in the root of your hard drive.

4. Choose File, Create Directory... from the Menu Bar.

Keeping Your Work in One Place

73

5. Type an eight-character-or-less name in the Create Directory Name field, as shown in figure 3.1. Use of an underscore or hyphen is permitted, but spaces, or special punctuation like question marks, aren't!

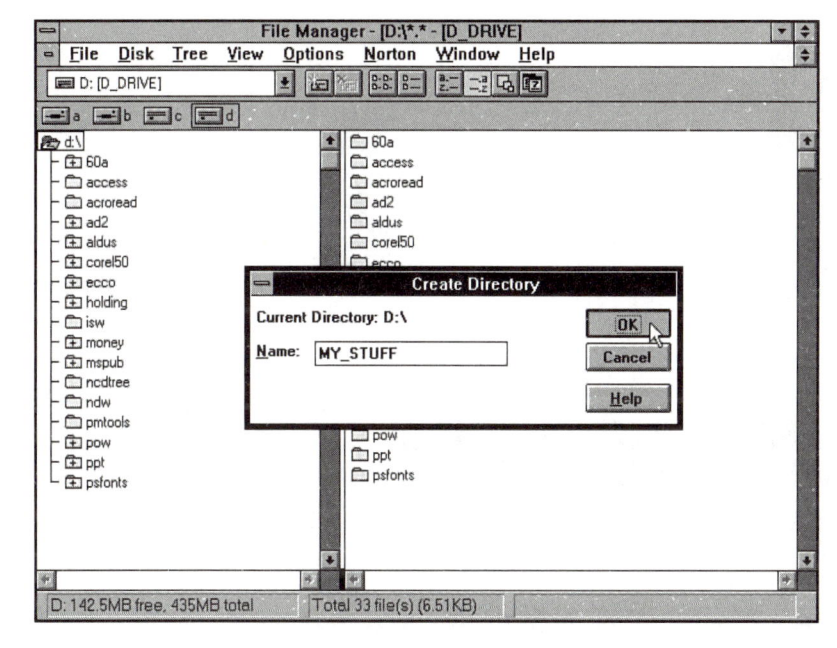

Figure 3.1

Create a working directory in the root of a hard drive (or partition) that has enough room for plenty of work!

6. Click on OK, and you're through. Simpler and less painful than a company audit, right? Close File Manager (either Alt+F4 or double-click on the Control Menu box in the upper left of the window), and you're off to customize CorelDRAW.

Saving Your Work

Anything you design in CorelDRAW is a candidate for a plain *.CDR document, a Corel template, or a pattern with which you can fill another closed CorelDRAW shape. You'll cover pattern fills in Chapter 6, and for the moment, concentrate on a "plain" save of a Corel design. Plain is in quotes here, because even the most rote task in Corel offers options!

Follow these steps to save your work as a standard CorelDRAW file:

1. Create something. In figure 3.2, the Ellipse tool malfunctioned, and we have a cartoon character. You don't have to be this ambitious; you only need to draw a circle or a square so there's something on the Printable page to save. Click on the Save button on the Ribbon Bar.

Figure 3.2
Let your cursor linger over the Ribbon Bar to display pop-up help about the button's function.

2. Click on the Dri**v**es drop-down list in the Save Drawing dialog box, then select the drive your working directory is on. For the example here, I'm using D:\MY_STUFF as the drive and directory, but you should substitute your own name if you've been inventive.

3. Choose the directory in the **D**irectories scrolling box, and name your file in the File **N**ame field in the top left of the dialog box. *Don't* click on OK after doing this—you have more exploring to do in the dialog box.

Annotating and Creating a Preview of Your Corel File

If you intend to use CorelDRAW extensively for designing similar-looking industrial parts, variations on corporate logos, or septuplets, Corel has two options to explore so you can benefit from the Save Drawing's cataloging feature.

By default, Corel places a tiny bitmap of your illustration in the saved document, so you can preview it in the future. This "snapshot" of your drawing can be in color or monochrome, or you can decide not to "have your picture taken" at all. These graphical headers can add one to eight kilobytes to your CorelDRAW file; remember that using this on many illustrations will eat up file space.

Additionally, you can make notes about the document that you can preview. This comes in handy when you have a rough draft and a finished sketch of something, and the two documents look almost identical. Don't click on the Save **P**resentation Exchange Data checkbox unless you understand what Presentation Data is or you've peeked at Chapter 10.

Here's how to put a visual and text header in a file you intend to save to disk:

1. Click on the down arrow in the **I**mage Header field. A list of different graphics types from None to 8KB (Color) are available. Generally, a 2KB (mono) header will suffice to distinguish a graphic you preview later. Select 2KB (mono) for this assignment.

2. In the Notes field, type something like, "This is a test. Definitely delete this file at a future date." See figure 3.3 to see how your Save Drawing dialog box should appear.

3. Click on OK, and click on the New button on the Ribbon Bar (or choose **F**ile, **N**ew; Ctrl+N).

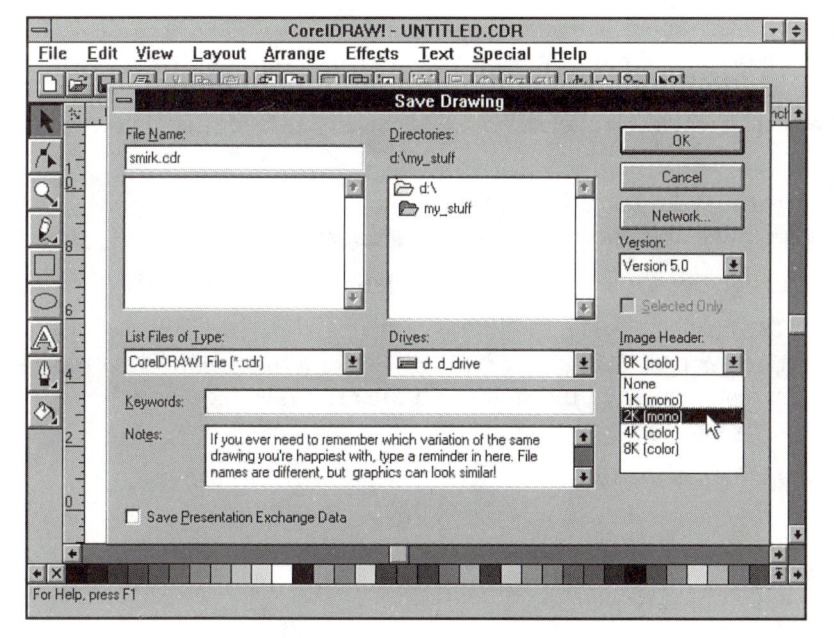

Figure 3.3

You can type a note to yourself and save a low-resolution bitmap of your file when you save your CorelDRAWing.

By default, CorelDRAW saves your work as a *.CDR file. You can change this to other options, and you'll see them in the next section. When you name a file, you don't have to type the dot and CDR after entering an eight-character (or less) name in the File Name field; if you forget it, Corel will automatically tag the file with a CDR extension.

Corel will also remember the location of the last four files you've created or opened under the File menu command. You can click on one of the underscored numbers under File to retrieve a file you've just worked on without going to the File, Open dialog box.

If you're really in a hurry and want your very last file, press Alt+F, and then press 1. This is the hot key combo for your last file, providing you didn't move it since you last saved it.

Creating a Template for Similar Assignments

Stretch your imagination a little for this next assignment and pretend you're the chief graphics designer and pin boy for Pindrop Alleys in beautiful Tully, New York. Your assignment between league nights is to design a special menu for the restaurant at Pindrop where week-in and week-out the specials change. When you save a Corel design as a template, all you have to do is retype a few words when the chef substitutes cheese curls for Cornish game hen.

Rather than wearing your felt tip pen to the bone, here's how to design a template with a blank area for non-reoccurring foodstuffs:

1. For this assignment, draw a box (click and diagonal-drag with the Rectangle tool) to enter the bowling alley specials later.

2. To add some Artistic Text to your design, click on the Artistic Text tool, choose an insertion point by clicking on the Printable page, and then do the following:

   Type **400 Lanes, Shoe Rentals,**
   Press Enter
   Type **Fine Dining in a**
   Press Enter
   Type **Quiet Atmosphere.**

3. Press Ctrl+spacebar to toggle to the Pick tool, then click and drag on the bottom right selection handle of the Artistic Text in a four o'clock direction to make it larger. When the status line tells you the text is about 40 points, you've click+dragged enough.

4. Press Ctrl+T (or choose Te*x*t, *C*haracter...), and choose a bold italic display face (Bodoni Poster works well) from the *F*onts list. Click on the *C*enter Alignment radio button, then click on OK.

5. With the Artistic Text tool, click another insertion point and type **Today's Specials**, then repeat steps 3 and 4, except choose a typeface other than the one you used last. (Mona Lisa or Mistral are eye-catching choices.)

6. Figure 3.4 shows the fictitious bowling alley template. The embellishments aren't necessary; you just need some Artistic Text and a rectangle on the page. When you have them, you're all set to explore Corel's Styles feature in the next section.

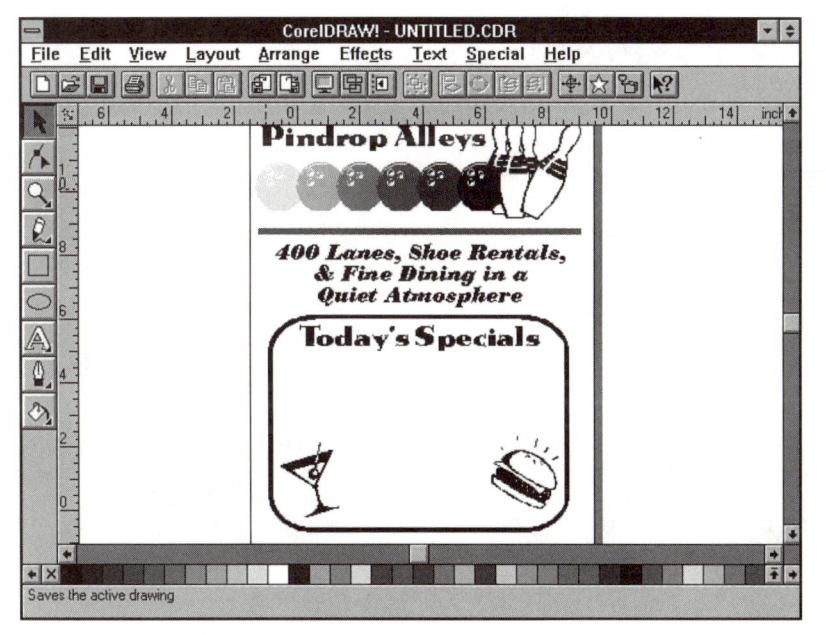

Figure 3.4

Templates should have elements that you want to repeat in a different document later.

Tip

CorelDRAW installs a wide variety of premade templates; you can open and copy elements from them and then place the elements in your own designs. To load a copy of one into Corel, choose New From Template from the File menu, hunt down the TEMPLATE subdirectory under COREL50\DRAW in the dialog box, and you have a visual preview of the types of templates as you click on their file names.

The value of learning how to create your own template, however, shouldn't be underestimated—with all the new Corel users out there, there are only so many premade templates a person can use before your design looks like someone else's who uses Corel predesigned templates, too.

Assigning and Creating a Graphic Style

If you've made an investment of time and effort in creating a symbol or "spec-ing" type so it's the right size and font, you can extend the investment and use the same style of graphical or text treatment in other documents by using the Corel Style feature. Styles operate independently of templates (you can use one without the other), but the two are a natural together, and an assignment like Pindrop Alley's is a perfect opportunity to explore the inner workings of Styles.

By default, Corel makes Artistic Text you type in the Drawing Window 24 points using Avant Garde BT. Unless your day-to-day assignments make regular use of these settings, here's how to create a style you can quickly apply to default text to make whatever you type conform to your own, custom specs:

1. With the Pick tool, right-mouse click over the 400 Lanes (etc.) Artistic Text, and hold the mouse button.

2. In one or two seconds, CorelDRAW's Object menu will pop up. Pop-up menus are a common occurrence in all the Corel modules, and they pertain to the specific object (shape or text) on which you've right-mouse clicked. Click on Save As Style, as shown in figure 3.5.

Assigning and Creating a Graphic Style

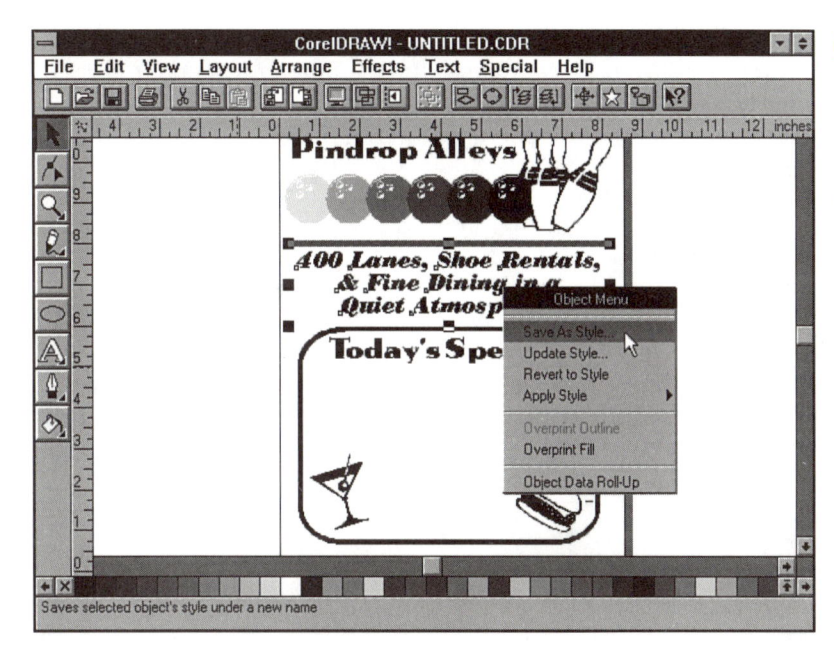

Figure 3.5
Styles can be created by selecting an object with the properties you want to use later.

3. Corel is intelligent about this style-saving process, and only offers you style options that are relevant to the object you've selected. In figure 3.6, you can see that the Artistic Text selected has outline and fill attributes, but no bullet, effects, or hyphenation characteristics, so Corel dims these options. Type **Text for Pindrop Alleys** in the Name field in the Save As dialog box, and click on OK.

Saving a Design as a Template

In this assignment-oriented example, you have a template and a style of Artistic Text for reuse later. You can save the style of a shape, Artistic Text, and Paragraph Text; the steps you went through last to set up a style of text for Pindrop Alleys can be used whether the design is in a CDR document format, a template format, or an unsaved document as you did last.

While the style you've set up has been saved, this Specials flyer is still untitled. Follow these steps for saving your art as a template that can be used over and over again, as Pindrop's chef stirs up exotic meal combos in the future:

1. Click on the Save button on the Ribbon Bar (File, Save, or Ctrl+S).

2. In the Save Drawing dialog box, click on the List Files of Type

Chapter 3: Customizing CorelDRAW!/Finding the Features

drop-down list, and choose the CorelDRAW! template. You'll notice that Corel "remembers" your preference for Image Header from your last save, which should be 2KB (mono), and again, you have the opportunity to annotate the template document in the Not<u>e</u>s field, as shown in figure 3.7.

Figure 3.6

When you save an object's style, many characteristics of the host object can be recalled later for applying to other objects.

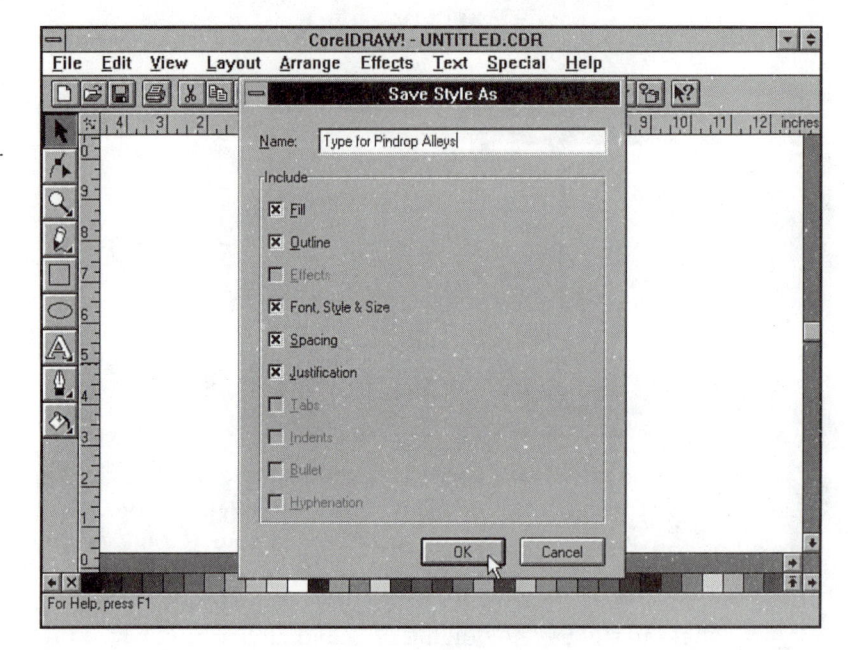

3. Name your template PINDROP.CDT, and click on OK.

Opening a New File Based on Your Template

Templates, as defined by CorelDRAW, are duplicates of a document you've defined as a template. You never need to touch an original template; Corel generates a copy, with all the elements you've created in the original, that can be modified, extruded, blended, and edited to your satisfaction.

By opening a new file based on the Pindrop template, you're almost done with the Today's Specials before you begin. Let's say it's Wednesday, and Armand the chef has whipped up his legendary BowlBurger for customers.

Opening a New File Based on Your Template

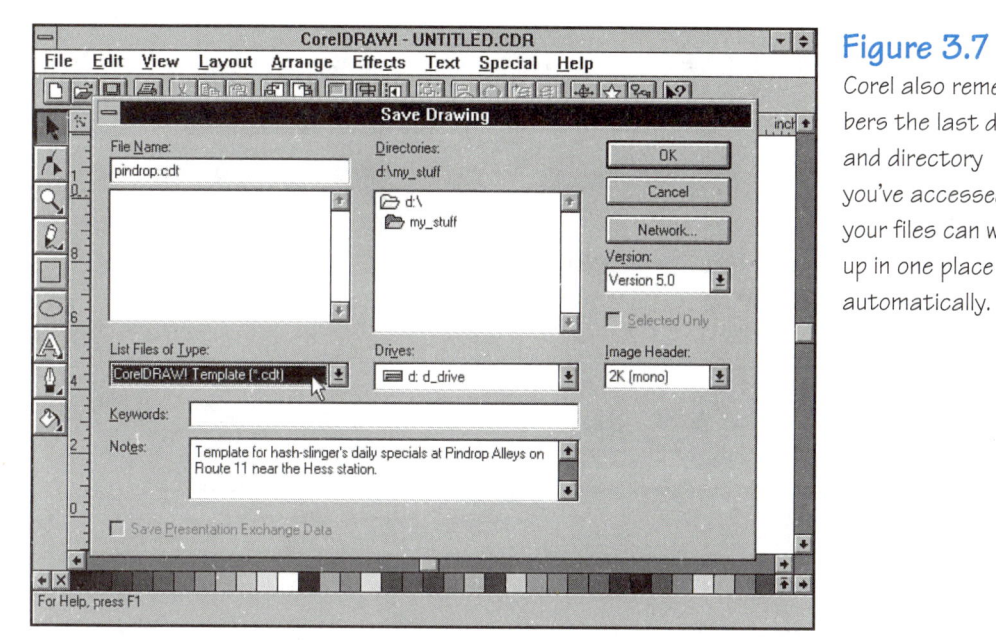

Figure 3.7

Corel also remembers the last drive and directory you've accessed, so your files can wind up in one place automatically.

Here's how to make a complete sign for this gastronomic event in less than ten minutes:

1. From **F**ile, choose New **F**rom Template.

2. As you can see in figure 3.8, the New From Template dialog box offers a low-resolution bitmap preview of the design, and you have the option of opening a copy of the template with or without its contents. Definitely check the **W**ith Contents box. Without the template's contents, your New From Template page would have the right dimensions and any guidelines you might have, but no objects.

3. Choose PINDROP.CDT from your working directory, then click on OK.

4. Choose the Text tool, then pretend you're Pindrop's chef and type the specials within the rectangle you drew in the template earlier. In figure 3.9, you can see the text entered in default Avant Garde BT in 24-point size. This will be changed shortly with Corel's Style feature.

Chapter 3: Customizing CorelDRAW!/Finding the Features

Figure 3.8
Preview a template, and decide whether you want the contents along with a copy of the template here.

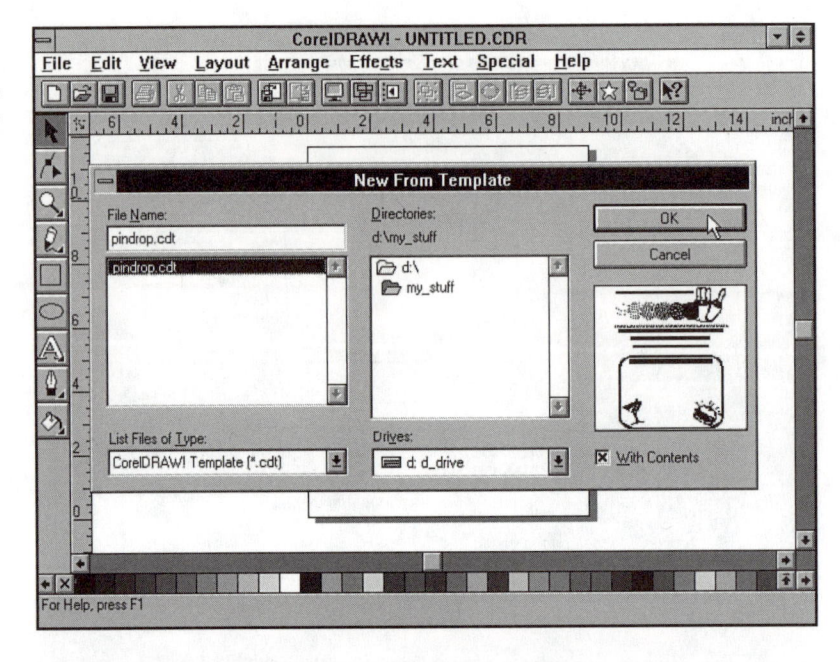

Figure 3.9
Type some of Pindrop's specials using the Text tool. And hold the onions.

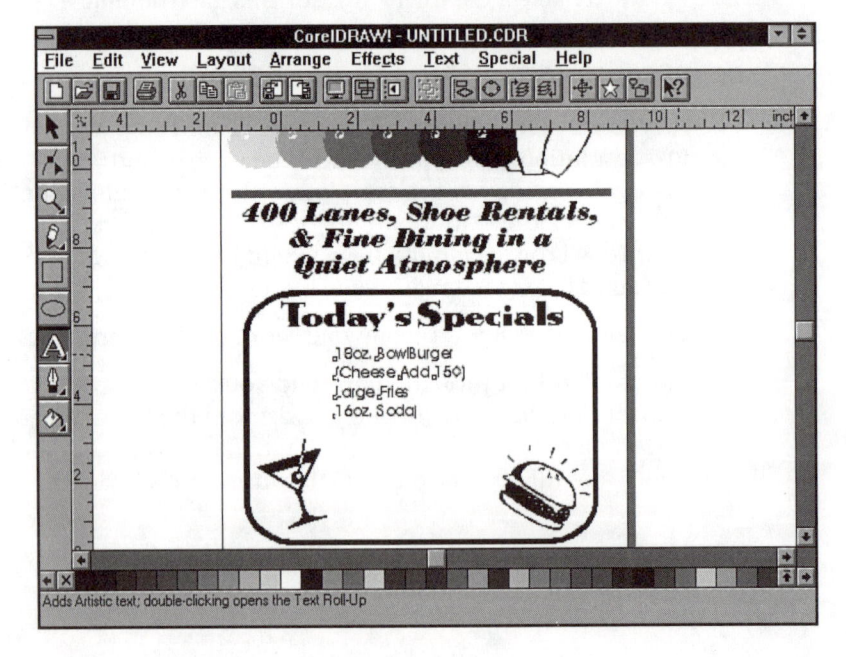

Opening a New File Based on Your Template

5. Press Ctrl+F5 (or choose <u>L</u>ayout, S<u>t</u>yles Roll-Up) to display the Styles Roll-Up. This Roll-Up has options for Corel's own default styles of shapes and text, but as you can see in figure 3.10, it now contains your user-defined style for Pindrop Alley's Text. With the Pick tool, click on the Artistic Text you just typed, click on the Pindrop Alley Style, and press Apply.

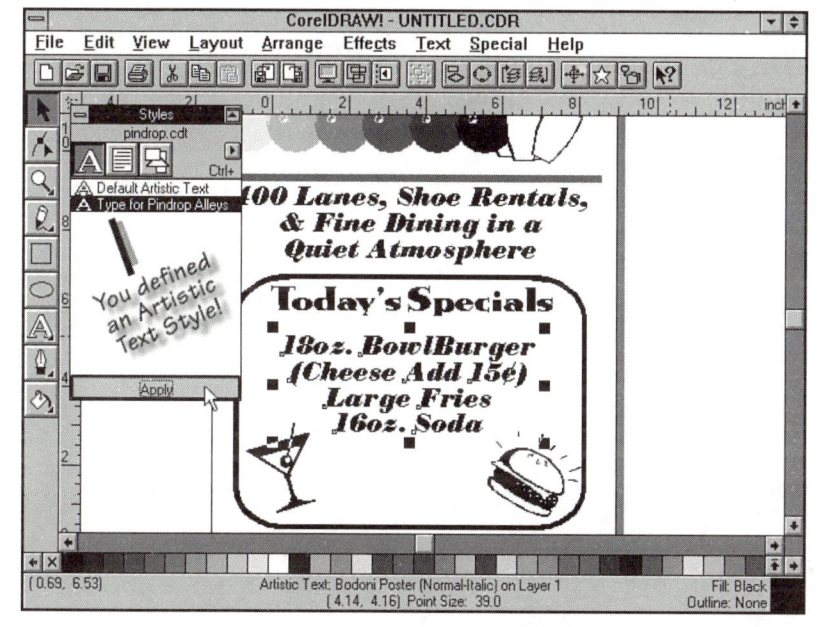

Figure 3.10
All the text attributes you defined as a style are applied to other Artistic Text objects using the Styles Roll-Up.

6. Click and drag the specials so they're centered in the rectangle, but leave room for the price of the feast beneath the specials.

An Alternative Method for Applying Styles

There's rarely an instance in CorelDRAW when you can't perform the same task a number of different ways. In the next example, you'll type an Artistic Text string for the price of Today's Specials, then apply the same style you defined earlier without a trip to the Menu Bar for the Roll-Up.

Here's a handy way of applying a style by using the menu pop-up feature in Corel:

Chapter 3: Customizing CorelDRAW!/Finding the Features

1. Use the Text tool, and type **$4.28**, press Enter, and then type **Tax Incl.** beneath the specials to which you applied the style. Pindrop thinks of everything, huh? See figure 3.11.

Figure 3.11

Type the price for the meal using the Artistic Text tool.

2. Press Ctrl+spacebar to toggle to the Pick tool. The price text should be selected now.

3. Click and hold the right mouse button on the price text, and a pop-up Object Menu appears.

4. Choose Apply Style. As you can see in figure 3.12, a menu fly-out appears with Corel's default style for Artistic Text, but also the style you defined earlier. Click on your style.

An Alternative Method for Applying Styles

Figure 3.12
Object Menus have style options, too.

Closer Look

The Object Menu has many more features that we simply don't have room in this book to document, but of particular interest to you might be the Object Data Roll-Up. If you select this command from the pop-up, you can tag individual objects in a document for easy reference later.

Sometimes, you want more explicit instructions about a component of a drawing, and while the Notes feature in the Save Drawing dialog box is good for overall comments, you may want to tag a comment like, "this is the undercarriage restraint bolt on the Diffractional Wave Accelerator Assembly" or something. Who knows?

5. In figure 3.13, I've increased the size of the price because it should be larger than the style of the text applied to it. You can do this by click+dragging a corner selection handle away from the selected object using the Pick tool.

Chapter 3: Customizing CorelDRAW!/Finding the Features

Figure 3.13

When you click+drag on a corner selection handle, the cursor changes shape to indicate you're scaling something.

6. When you're done, save your drawing as a CDR type file from the Save Drawing dialog box, and call it TEST2.CDR. You can then easily find (and delete) your tryout with styles and templates at a future time.

Think about the applicability of both styles and templates in your own work. This was a meager example of the power you can use in "assembly line" production of similar documents with similar text formatting. Begin to think of CorelDRAW as a power tool that you can streamline for any task once you understand what the options offer.

Preferences for the Way You Work

There are many settings that control your workspace in CorelDRAW that have to do with your input devices. The two most useful ones you can tweak are the options for your right mouse button and for how your nudge keys work.

In this section, you'll explore and evaluate the usefulness of the **S**pecial, **P**references dialog boxes, and learn how to increase your productivity through the options that can be set here in Corel.

First, your keyboard arrow keys have a special purpose in CorelDRAW, and that's to nudge a selection in a direction without ever moving the selection with the cursor. It's a precision feature that works along with the Place Duplicate preference. Here's the trick: if you prefer to have a duplicate of a selection land directly on the original, you can then accurately move the copy fractions of an inch away from it, and the two overlapping shapes can create a wonderful effect.

As you explore the Preference menu where you can set the nudge option, you'll also notice that you can program your right-mouse clicks to perform a specific function. Selecting a specific function from the drop-down list for right-mouse clicking won't affect the ability to display the Object Data pop-up menu; the pop-up is displayed by clicking and holding the right mouse button, whereas a single, quick right-mouse click can provide a zoom in, a full-screen preview, or lots of other custom features.

Here's how to select general preferences for your session in CorelDRAW:

1. Choose File, New first to clear your TEST2 document from Corel's Drawing Window. After you set some options, you have an "assignment" that calls for a fresh Printable page.

2. Press Ctrl+J (or choose Special, then Preferences).

3. The first index dialog box is General Preferences. You'll explore the View dialog box a little later, but you should check out all the dialog boxes for a special need you might have. Type **0.0000** in the Horizontal field in the Place Duplicates and Clones area, then do the same in the Vertical field. From now on, all duplicate objects will land exactly on top of the original.

4. Type **0.02** to the left of the inches drop-down for the Nudge option in the field below the Place Duplicates stuff. You may frequently want to reset this option, but for the assignment coming up, it's a good value.

5. Additionally, you can set the number of undos in Corel up to 99 moves. By default, Corel gives you 4 "gimme backs," but as a beginner, you may want more levels of backpedaling your design work. I recommend you increase this number to 8—see the Stop note about this after these steps. (Ctrl+Z is the shortcut to Edit, Undo.)

6. Last stop is what you want the right mouse button Action to be. Click on the drop-down list in this field to see your choices. Full-screen preview is a good choice, because you can instantly view your work coming together without distracting Roll-Ups, guidelines, and grids thwarting your view. This is another option you may have a preference to reset after you become more familiar with CorelDRAW features, but for now, your General Preferences menu should look like figure 3.14.

Chapter 3: Customizing CorelDRAW!/Finding the Features

Figure 3.14
Configure how your right mouse button and keyboard work in CorelDRAW using the General Preferences menu.

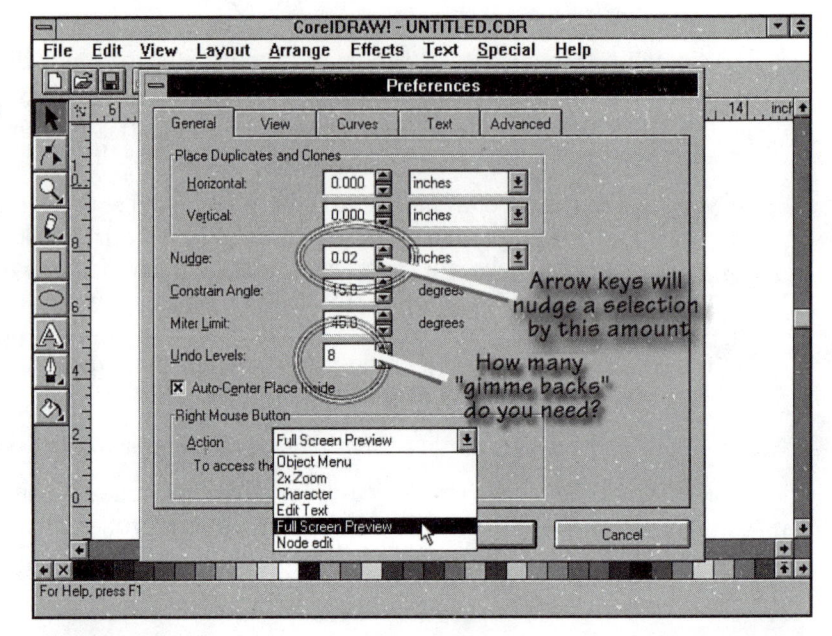

7. Click on OK to confirm your preferences and return to the workspace. Corel will recall the settings you've made in all subsequent sessions in the application.

Although you can back up the steps you've taken by choosing a number in the Undo Levels field, be aware that the higher the number, the more system RAM you're encouraging CorelDRAW to use to perform this memorization feat. Corel stores previous versions of your work in order to Undo a move you don't like, and the more information CorelDRAW has to remember, the more system RAM it takes. On a slower 386 machine, setting the Undo Levels to 99 will slow down your PC and your CorelDRAW work. A number less than 10 steps is always a wise preference.

P.S.—Zooming into a view and selecting nodes or shapes doesn't count as a move, so you can't undo these actions.

Creating a Do Not Disturb Sign

It's time to reap some rewards from the customizing work you did in the Preferences dialog box. Now that you have the duplicate and nudge features set to a specific assignment, it's time to get to work on the assignment!

Embossing involves multiple copies of the same graphic or text, slightly offset from each other, with each copy colored differently to suggest dimensional lighting. So your embossing adventure in CorelDRAW begins with making a background, and then a shape you want to emboss on the background.

Here's how to create a classy Do Not Disturb sign (in case you move from the restaurant business to hotels):

1. Choose the Zoom tool, then select the Zoom In tool from the menu flyout.

2. Marquee-zoom (click+diagonal drag) an area about 7" wide by 5" tall on the Printable page. Working at a Zoomed in view is a good CorelDRAW work practice to get into, so you can extend an illustration later without rescaling it.

3. Choose the Rectangle tool, then click+diagonal-drag (marquee) a rectangle that fairly fills your view. You need a background against which you can emboss the Do Not Disturb Artistic Text.

4. Click on the 30% black swatch on the color palette with your left mouse button. This fills the rectangle with a light fill, perfect for embossing.

5. Click on the x on the color palette with the right mouse button. This removes the outline from your rectangle. See the Stop note that follows these steps for more about this process.

6. With the Text tool, type **DO NOT**, press Enter, and type **DISTURB**.

7. Press Ctrl+spacebar to toggle to the Pick tool, then press Ctrl+T (or choose Te**x**t, **C**haracter from the menu) to display the Character Attributes dialog box.

8. Choose an ornamental typeface (Davida is used in this example, but Mistral, Motter Fem, or Gallia also work well) from the scrolling **F**onts list.

9. Click on the **C**enter radio button in the Alignment field, then click on OK.

10. Enter 60 in the Size spin box. Click on OK to return to your design. Once your Artistic Text appears in the font of your selection, press the Plus key on your keypad to duplicate it, as shown in figure 3.15.

You'll eventually want to work out some proportions for future reference, but for now, the 0.02" nudge setting is good for moving 60-point text to create embossing.

Figure 3.15
Use the Plus key, or choose Edit, Duplicate (Ctrl+D) to place a copy of the text directly on top of the original.

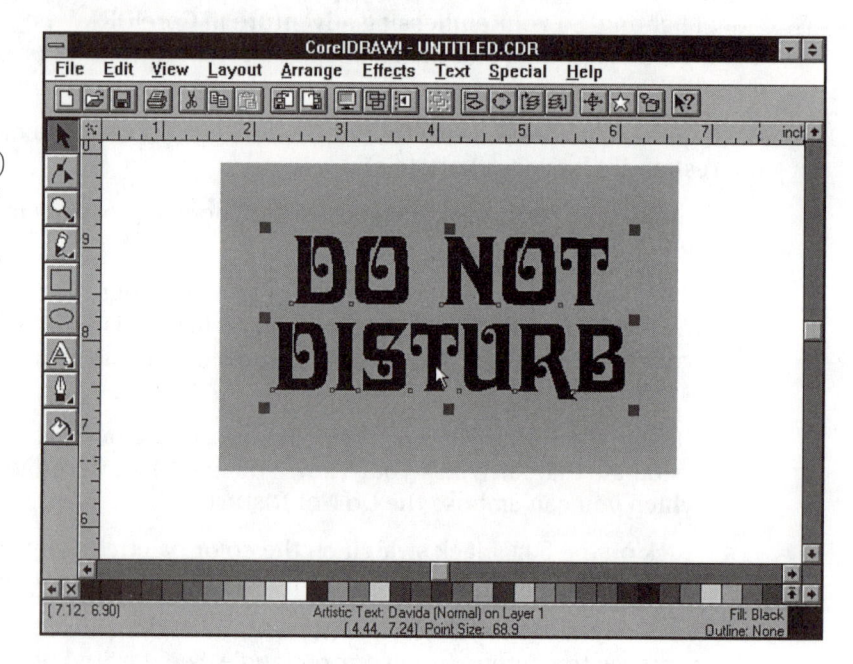

Stop

There is another, potentially dangerous, way of customizing the fills, outlines, and text attributes of anything you create in the Drawing Window. When you have no shape or text actively selected, click on the Fill tool or Outline tool, or double-click on the Artistic Text tool to display the Text Roll-Up; Corel will question you about all future objects being assigned the color or font you chose.

If you answer this dialog box, you'll change the default settings in CorelDRAW for text, outlines, and/or fills. By default, shapes have a 0.003" black outline, and text has a black fill with no outline. Corel gave careful consideration to what would be the best attributes for new objects you create, and if you change this, you'll most likely mess up your future work by accident. At the very least, you'll have a hard time following this book, which was written presuming you didn't change object attribute defaults.

If you *ever* get a dialog box that reads, "Nothing has been selected...", with check boxes For Graphic, Artistic, and Paragraph Text, press Cancel, and save yourself the ensuing headaches.

Nudging a Duplicate Shape

Frequently, I'll reset the Nudge feature to either really small amounts (like 0.004") or the maximum of two inches, depending on what I'm trying to accomplish. At two inches, you can move a shape you're drawing clear out of view on the Printable page to reveal another shape you're tracing. By selecting the nudged shape and pressing an arrow key, you then can precisely align it with the other shape again.

Two one-hundreds of an inch is a good setting for the Nudge feature when creating an embossing effect in Corel.

In the next example, you'll master the art of embossing a shape, text, or anything you dream up, and it's all because you know where to customize the nudge and place duplicate options.

1. With the duplicate of the black DO NOT DISTURB lettering selected, press the up arrow twice, then press the left arrow twice. This moves the duplicate on top of the original up and to the left .04". Click on the white color swatch on the color palette to get a graphic like the one in figure 3.16.

2. Press the Plus key to duplicate the present selection (the white lettering), then press the down key once, and the right key once.

3. Click on the 30% black swatch on the color palette. In figure 3.17, you can see that a convincing embossing effect can be easily achieved by simply customizing CorelDRAW's Preferences. Why not right-mouse click now and get an instant full-screen preview of your work?

4. Save your work. Click on the Save button on the Ribbon Bar, name the document EMBOSS.CDR, and choose your working directory for its home.

Chapter 3: Customizing CorelDRAW!/Finding the Features

Figure 3.16
There's still a copy yet to be added for the embossed effect, but for now, you've created drop-shadow lettering!

Figure 3.17
Embossing is achieved by overlapping identical shapes of different colors, then offsetting them using the nudge keys.

Getting a Better View of Your Work

Let's take another trip to the Preferences menu to see what can be done in the way of customizing your view of Corel's Drawing Window. Fountain Fills (like the one you applied to the ball in Chapter 1) can be viewed at low or high resolution, the status line can be positioned, and a few more niceties have been made available for you by Corel. If you think you can arrange screen stuff better than Corel, you have the right, and Corel obliges you in this.

Follow these steps to customize your screen elements, and discover what they do:

1. Click on the New button on the Ribbon Bar (or Press Ctrl+N; File, New) because you're going to experiment again, and you don't want to mess up your embossing work.

2. Choose Special, then Preferences.

3. Click on the View tab to display the View index dialog box.

Here's a point-by-point description of what each feature does to your view of the Drawing Window and the screen elements. You can decide to leave options alone, or change them based on your personal preferences:

- Auto-Panning will move your screen view of the Drawing Window if you ever decide to draw or edit a shape that would normally go off the monitor. Try clicking and dragging an object really far to the left or right, and you'll see this is a valuable alternative to scrolling all the time.

- Interruptable Refresh. Every time you make a change to a drawing, CorelDRAW wants to update your display to reflect the change. This can get to be a hassle when you have 5,000 individual shapes on the page, so by leaving this option on, Corel butts out of your work until you're finished drawing. When you pause for two seconds or so in your work, Corel will then redraw the scene when Interruptable Refresh is chosen.

- Manual Refresh isn't really necessary if you choose right-mouse click assigned to full-screen preview. Previewing a design automatically refreshes your display and removes "screen trash."

Chapter 3: Customizing CorelDRAW!/Finding the Features

- Don't choose Cross H<u>a</u>ir Cursor. This turns your Freehand tool into a gigantic crosshair that extends the length and width of the Drawing Window. Unless you're into science fiction movies, this is a technologic, irritating feature best reserved for nerds.

- The Status Line field is pretty self-explanatory. You can choose where the status line goes, and the size of it.

- Don't check the Draw When Mo<u>v</u>ing box under the Moving Objects field. This tends to result in screen trash, and its purpose is for "eyeballing" the relative position of shapes while you move them. We have better ways of aligning things that you'll read about in other chapters.

- The choice of showing or hiding the Ribb<u>o</u>n Bar and Pop-Up <u>H</u>elp is up to you. The Ribbon Bar is a terrific feature, and a first for Corel in version 5. Many users of versions 3 and 4 may not like it, but this book constantly reinforces its purposefulness. After you get familiar with the Ribbon Bar buttons, you may no longer want Pop-Up Help displaying when you linger your cursor on top of the buttons. You can shut the help "balloons" off, but I recommend you leave them on for the first month or two with Corel. Additionally, by right-mouse clicking over any tool or button on the Ribbon Bar, a context-sensitive Help topic will appear in front of the Drawing Window to elaborate on what you clicked over.

- Finally, here's an option you can make work for you or against you—the P<u>r</u>eview Fountain Steps preference. In figure 3.18, you'll see the whole layout of the View Preferences menu, with the author tuning the number of steps way down to four. This is a stupid action, and you should not do this. Lesson one is to learn from the misteaks of others.

Fountain Fills display and print as smooth, airbrush-like gradations between two or more colors. In reality, they're a collection of solid fills with closely-matched shading butted together. Preview Fountain Steps won't affect your printed design, but the higher the amount you set in this preference, the slower they'll redraw on-screen when you preview them. Conversely, setting the number below 20 gives you an inaccurate view of your design, which can spell trouble later, as shown in figure 3.19. Below 20=fast screen redraws, poor image quality; higher than 20=gorgeous Fountain Fills that take an eternity to display.

Getting a Better View of Your Work

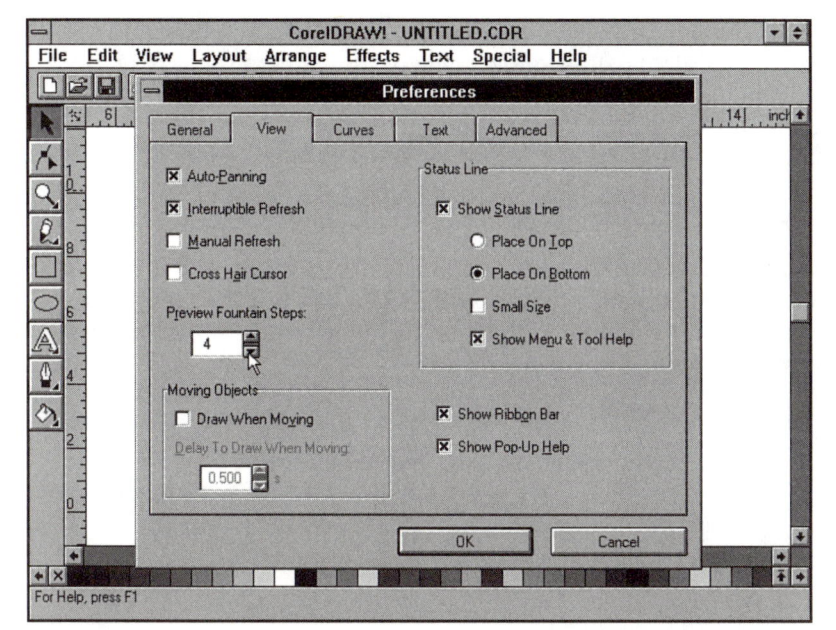

Figure 3.18
Fountain Steps can be previewed on-screen with a varying amount of "banding."

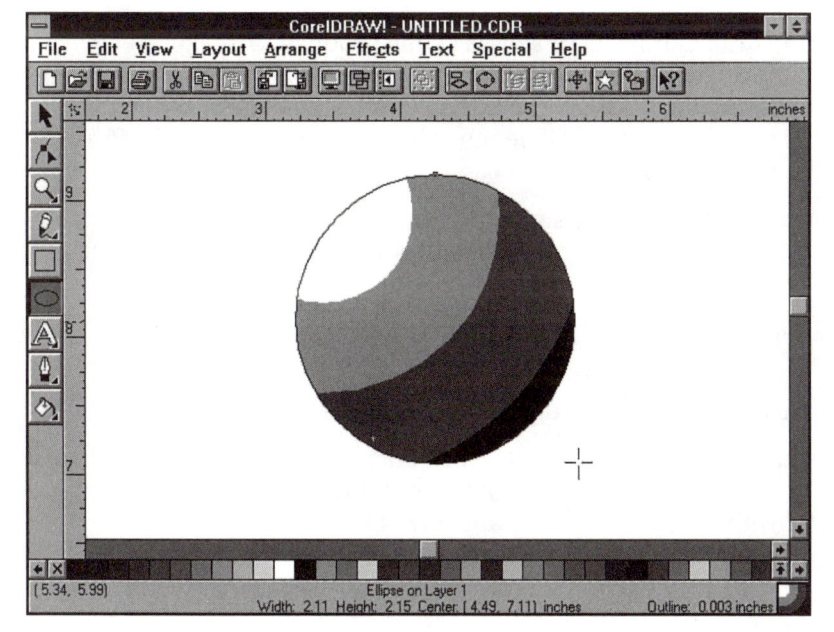

Figure 3.19
This low-quality Fountain Fill Preview will print fine, but looks awful on the monitor.

Make your selections in the View Preferences menu based on how you need the screen elements displayed—follow some of the hints in the last section, and then click on OK. Next, you have a date with the Presets Roll-Up to discover how you can create and save special effects.

Making a Preset Special Effect

Like the templates, CorelDRAW installs some factory Preset effects you can apply to shapes and text, and wind up with instant art. But the soul of a designer yearns to innovate, not imitate, and shortly you'll see how to stock your own vending machine of special effects.

Note

In addition to the preset Roll-Up, you can invent custom calligraphic pen tips through the PowerLine Roll-Up and the Extrude Roll-Up. The procedure for adding user-defined macros is identical to the procedures covered in the Preset Roll-Up steps.

Creating a mirror of a drawing or simple shape produces a design element you and other designers can frequently tap into to make everything from an ornament to a stunning effect. In the next section, you'll learn how to mirror a shape, but there's a twist: you'll be recording your moves with the Presets Roll-Up to be named as an effect you can later apply to anything you draw.

Adding a custom preset is very similar to adding a style to Corel. Here's how you "work the controls" to invent, save, and get a special effect ready for instant reuse:

1. Press Alt+F5, or choose **S**pecial, P**r**esets Roll-Up from the menu.

2. Type a word with the Artistic Text tool, then pick a fancy typeface for it using the commands and steps you learned earlier (Ctrl+T is the key).

3. In the example in figure 3.20, the word Looking Glass has been assigned the MotterFem font; regardless of the font you choose, you should select it with the Pick tool first, and press the Start Recording button on the Preset Roll-Up before you perform the following fancy mirroring effect.

Figure 3.20

Decide the effect you want to record, select the subject for the effect, and then press the Start Recording button.

4. Place your cursor on the top selection handle of your text.

5. Hold the Ctrl key and drag the cursor down until you see a dotted line boundary box beneath the text.

6. While still holding the left mouse button, click on the right mouse button, then release both buttons, as shown in figure 3.21. This performs a duplication and a vertical mirroring of a selection.

7. Click on the 40% black swatch on the color palette with the left mouse button, then click on Stop Recording on the Presets Roll-Up, as shown in figure 3.22. You've recorded this "reflection" effect, and you'll be asked by Corel to give the effect a title next.

8. In the Edit Preset dialog box, give your effect a name in the top field, and a brief description of what the effect does, as shown in figure 3.23.

Chapter 3: Customizing CorelDRAW!/Finding the Features

Figure 3.21
Hold the Ctrl key while you drag on a middle selection handle to flip a selection.

Figure 3.22
Stop recording your set of actions to produce an effect immediately after you're done.

Making a Preset Special Effect

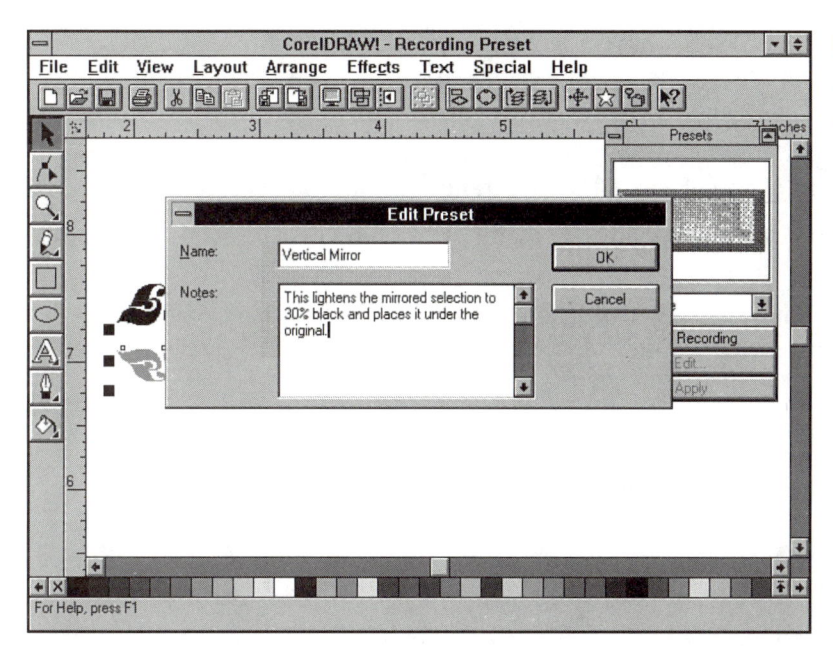

Figure 3.23
Get the description of a Preset effect by clicking and holding on its name in the drop-down list.

Note

Corel and Beta site testers of CorelDRAW 5 came up with a lot of nifty effects built right into the Preset Roll-Up. You should take a little time to read the descriptions of each effect by clicking and holding on a preset title after clicking on the down arrow next to the drop-down list.

You can edit the Corel presets, but make sure you save an edited preset under a different title, or you'll mess up some fairly complicated, beautiful preset macros.

Applying Your Preset to a Different Shape

This is the gratifying part of creating a custom preset. You can watch as it's applied to any shape you like, and in the future you may want to record more complex presets to make quick work out of an effect.

Chapter 3: Customizing CorelDRAW!/Finding the Features

In the next example, you have a mock book cover design for Arthur Schtrüdelklømpfnür's best-seller *Reflections on a Pretzel*. While Arthur and the novel are a figment, here's how to get some very real results from your recorded preset:

1. Design a shape like an ellipse, rectangle, or other closed shape.

2. Click on the black swatch (actually, any color will do) on the color palette to fill the shape.

3. Right-mouse clicking over the x on the color palette isn't really necessary here, but why not remove the outline of your closed shape to get into the swing of it anyway?

4. In figure 3.24, the shape has been selected with the Pick tool, and you can see that the Vertical Mirror Preset has been chosen from the drop-down list of effects. Do the same with your custom preset.

Figure 3.24
Select a shape, then pick your custom preset from the Presets drop-down list.

5. Click on the Apply button. As shown in figure 3.25, a mirror of the selected object (the pretzel drawing) automatically appears and colors itself in 30% black.

Applying Your Preset to a Different Shape

Figure 3.25
The Apply command will play back the steps you originally recorded to create the custom effect.

Closer Look

Check Corel's owner's manual and the Online Help for further information about which objects can be changed by presets, and which you shouldn't use when recording your own. Certain moves and effects are not considered "legal" by CorelDRAW, and you might get an error message to this effect.

Creating Drawings of a Grander Scale

You may want to skip ahead to Chapter 4 and get a peek at how dimension lines are created, because this next set of options has a bearing on them, and also on how you can customize Corel to design in miles or kilometers instead of inches.

If your work calls for architectural scaling of floor plans, or if you'd simply like to create a map for people who want to attend Chip's graduation party, here's how to set the Drawing Scale in CorelDRAW:

1. Double-click on either ruler. This is the shortcut to the Layout, Grid & Scale Setup.

2. Check the Use **D**rawing Scale box, then click on the drop-down list for **W**orld Distance, and set the increments to Miles, as shown in figure 3.26. More of the Grid & Scale Setup options are discussed in Chapter 9.

Figure 3.26
Page Distance in inches will now equal a World Distance in Miles.

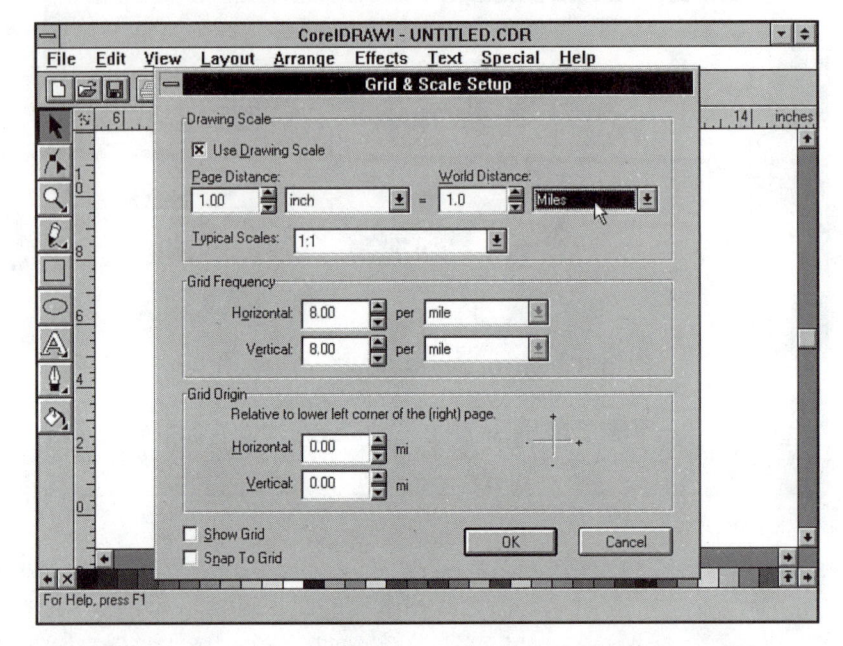

3. Click on OK, then take a look at the rulers bordering the Drawing Window. Weird and awesome, huh?

The Uses for Drawing Scale

Besides simply messing with your ruler increments, you've performed a useful customization of CorelDRAW that can be used as much as you need for conveying physical dimensions that won't fit on a printed page.

Figure 3.27 was created after customizing the Drawing Scale in Corel. The buildings are from the Buildings Symbol category, which you'll learn how to use in Chapter 7, and the dimension lines were drawn using the dimension line tools in the Pencil tool menu fly-out, which you'll experiment with in the next chapter.

The distances between locations in the last figure are accurate, and it didn't take a whit of mathematics on the author's part, because Corel's dimension lines respond to the settings you determine in the Grid & Scale Setup dialog box.

Creating Drawings of a Grander Scale

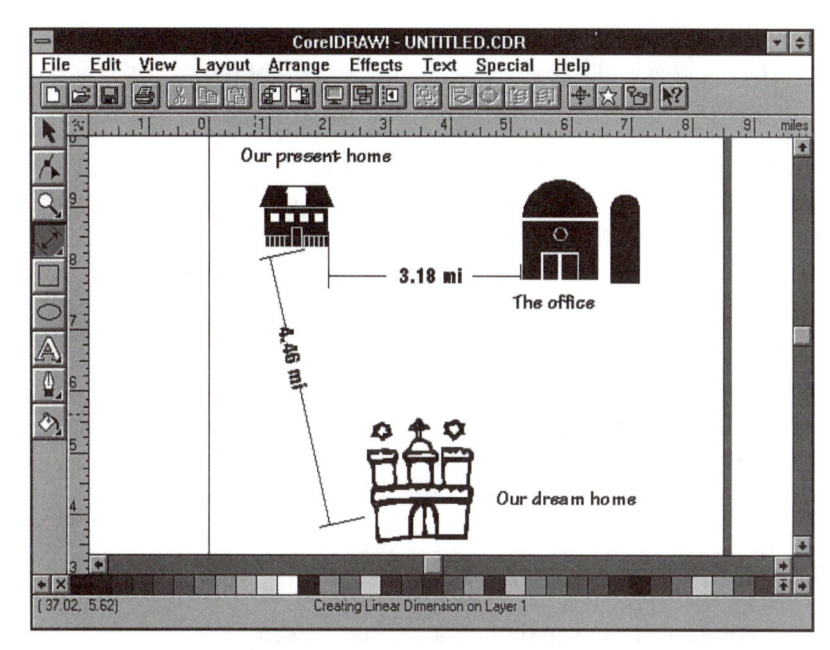

Figure 3.27
Express miles on an 8 1/2" by 11" page by customizing Corel's Drawing Scale.

While this is useful information and you now know how to change the scale with which you draw, none of the rest of this book uses scaling for designs, so you'd best revert to regular increments on your ruler. Here's how to set the rulers and other features that depend on drawing scale back to 1:1:

1. Double-click on a ruler, then uncheck the Use **D**rawing Scale box, and the **W**orld Distance drop-down arrow will dim; this means regardless of whether it says Miles or Chickens in the box, Corel won't read the Distance increment.

2. Click on OK, and you've learned a few new valuable customizing options!

Picking Custom Colors for Your Designs

You'll get a client every so often who is a pain in the derrière about using "their" corporate colors in a design piece. Like they invented light peach and dark green, right?

No matter. In this next section, you'll encounter a fictitious espresso house whose owner would like small paper beverage coasters embossed with the cafe's logo and a very exact set of colors specified. You would give them the document on disk and they can take it to their commercial printer, who also runs CorelDRAW on their PC. You can laugh about the first part of this tall tale, but before you realize it, you'll be interfacing with commercial print presses in your professional design career—color specification is part of this craft, and CorelDRAW makes it easy to match any color a customer decides on using.

Here's how to begin with two simple shapes that will be color-specked in your adventures with custom colors:

1. Draw a rectangle using the Rectangle tool, then click on the white swatch on the color palette. You'll eventually change this color, but by filling a shape while it's still selected, you make it easier to select the shape later. Unfilled outlines of shapes require precision and patience to select, because you have to click on the outline dead-on with the Pick tool, which is hard even for experienced CorelDRAW users.

2. Put some Artistic Text on the rectangle, using the same techniques you've learned in this chapter with the bowling alley.

3. Your napkin design should look nothing like figure 3.28 because you haven't read Chapters 6 and 10 yet on using symbols and rotating selections. But you do need at least two separate elements here to continue; a rectangle for the background shape, and some text (or a different shape) for a foreground element.

The Many Color Models of CorelDRAW

Sometime in history, folks who used color in their product decided it would be nice to come up with an indexing method by which a specific color value could be written down or telephoned across a continent, to be duplicated by other folks who couldn't physically receive a color swatch to match.

Computer colors aren't physical, but rather are displayed on your monitor as illuminated pixels of red, green, and blue; it's been up to Corel and a lot of other companies to standardize custom colors on-screen so they bear an approximation to printed colors, photographic colors, and so on.

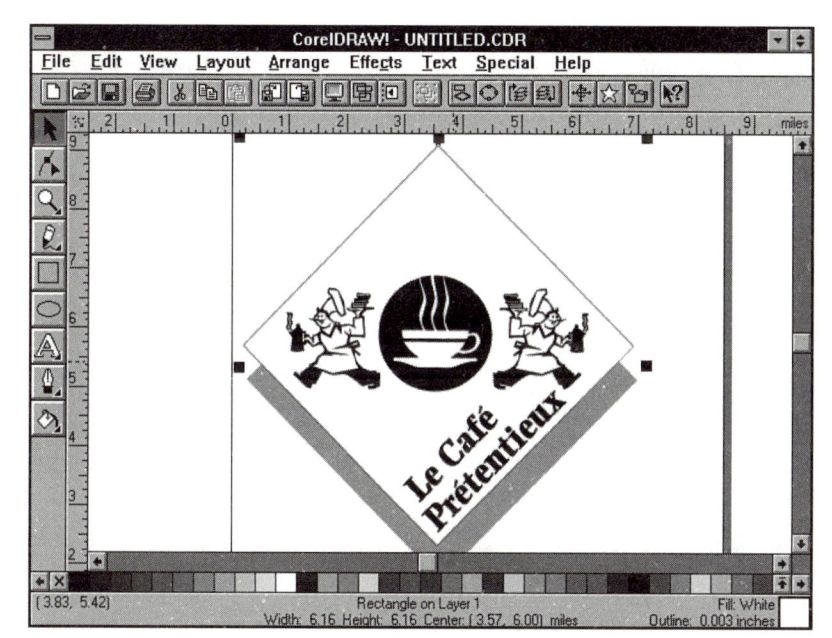

Figure 3.28

Create a filled background shape and a foreground shape, then "spec" custom colors within.

The range, or *gamut*, of colors available for use on your PC is presently 24 bit, or a total of 16 million unique color values. These 16 million possibilities are organized into color spaces, or color models, that are organized according to their purpose. For instance, by default, Corel displays a CMYK color model in the Fill and Outline dialog boxes, which describes how much cyan, magenta, yellow, and black a commercial printer should use to represent a color you see on-screen in a printed page of your work.

PANTONE is both the name of a company and the name of a highly accurate color matching system (the PMS, or PANTONE Matching System) that, when specified in Corel as the color model used in filling a shape, appears on-screen as pretty close to what a printer or textile manufacturer can reproduce with inks and dyes.

PANTONE number 1495 CV is a meaningless phrase until you see the color sample it represents. Likewise, 1495 is meaningless to a textile manufacturer or commercial printer until they look it up in their PANTONE book, see the swatch on a page, and get the recipe for duplicating this color with pigments.

Let's see what all the fuss about PANTONE 1495 CV is about, and discover how to specify this and other PANTONE colors next:

Chapter 3: Customizing CorelDRAW!/Finding the Features

1. So the espresso house owner wants PANTONE 1495 CV as the background color for the coaster design. Additionally, the foreground design calls for PANTONE 3435. Select the background rectangle first with the Pick tool and get to it.

2. Click on the Fill tool (the paint bucket icon), then select the Uniform Fill Color tool (the button with the color wheel drawing on it).

3. In the Show: field, by default, CorelDRAW displays the CMYK color model. Click and drag in the color space to define a new color or one you'd like to approximate. Click on the down arrow to display the drop-down list, then select PANTONE Spot Colors, and click on the Show Color Names box below the list.

4. Scroll the name and swatch list until you find PANTONE 1495. Click on it to select it. Alternatively, you can type **1495** in the Search for: field, and Corel will pop you right to that color.

5. You don't really want to go hunting for this color again, so the sensible thing to do is to add it to your CorelDRAW color palette, where it's in easy reach while you design. In the Custom Palettes field, click on the right arrow next to coreldrw.cpl.

6. Choose Add Color from the drop-down list, as shown in figure 3.29.

Figure 3.29

Choose to add a color from a different color model to Corel's color palette.

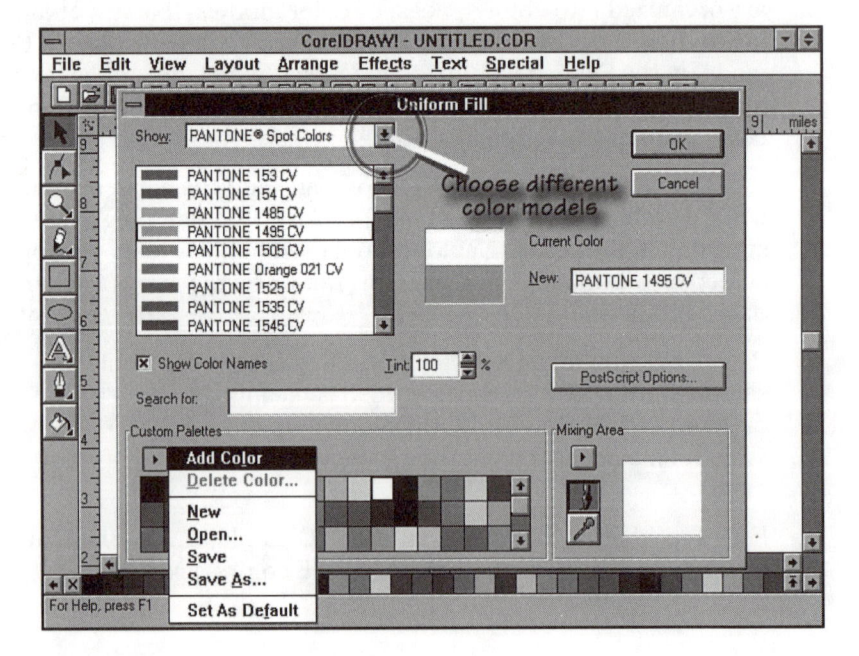

Note

The changes you make to Corel's color palette aren't permanent ones unless you choose **S**ave or Save **A**s in addition to adding a color or two. This means colors aren't written to the CORELDRW.CPL file on your disk, and can be removed as easily as they're added by selecting the color from the Drawing Window view of the color palette, then choosing **D**elete Color from the Uniform Fill menu.

Don't delete a default color, however, or you'll lose 30# black, green, or some other color you'll expect to find in other sessions using the color palette!

7. Make this one-stop shopping with these custom PANTONE colors. Type **3435** in the S**e**arch for box, and click on Add Co**l**or. This is the *wrong* color for the selected rectangle background shape, but creates an opportunity to change it using the color palette now that the PANTONE colors have been added. Click on OK to return to the assignment.

8. The color palette is scrolled back and forth to display all the colors by clicking on the arrow buttons on either end of it. But do this instead (it's a shortcut): click on the *up* arrow on the right of the color palette.

9. Surprise! The color palette expands, and by moving to the last two colors on the full set of swatches, you'll notice what would appear as a peach and a dark green color if this book was printed in four-color, as shown in figure 3.30. Move your cursor over the light peach, and notice that the status line tells you this is indeed PANTONE 1495. Click on the swatch, and the color palette retracts.

10. Repeat steps 8 and 9, but click on your foreground text or design, and select PANTONE 3435. By this point, you probably have more solutions than problems awaiting your future with CorelDRAW!

How Professional Do You Want Your Hard Copy?

Most places of business, and many homes, have laser printers. The models may vary, but you can get pretty decent prints of your CorelDRAW work with a 300 dot-per-inch (dpi) printer. If you want to take your work to unparalleled heights of commercial printing or transparencies, this desire will

Chapter 3: Customizing CorelDRAW!/Finding the Features

take you outdoors and down the block, away from your <u>F</u>ile, <u>P</u>rint menu command. You should definitely become familiar with:

- The art of copying to a disk or other removable media
- The telephone numbers of commercial printers, imaging centers, and service bureaus that do IBM/PC work
- Writing checks

But if you're starting slow and procedurally, there's a wealth of design tips and helpful hints for the new user of CorelDRAW 5 in the next chapters. You wouldn't want the pleasure of flashing a hard copy of your first design stifled because you don't know how to print from CorelDRAW, so the final section shows you a few of the options for printing to a laser printer. You can improve the way a hard copy print from CorelDRAW looks with a mere handful of pointers.

Figure 3.30
Additions to the default color palette are located on the far right. Click on the up arrow on the right to expand the palette.

Printing from CorelDRAW

The command to print from Corel is the same as most Windows applications—choose File, Print from the menu (or press Ctrl+P). Once more, Corel gives you options for printing that you may want to customize. You'd be best advised to create your artwork only using grayscale fills and outlines if a laser printer is your output device, because color values are weighted. This means blues come out too light when printed from a black and white printer, and reds and greens may turn out darker than you anticipate. Here's how to set up the options for printing a CorelDRAWing to a laser printer:

1. Corel's not going to do much if you haven't any graphic on the Printable page, so you might want to search your SAMPLES subdirectory on your hard disk for any CorelDRAW art Corel Setup installs, and open it (or you can always print the HAVE A BALL! greeting card, if you did the assignment in Chapter 1).

2. When you have something on the Printable page, Press Ctrl+P (File, Print).

3. The first thing you want to do is check your printer setup by clicking on the Setup... button. This is not a CorelDRAW option, but it instead has to do with the setting Windows has as a default for the printer you're connected to. Is your paper size correct? Do you have the correct printer defined? A lot of people forget when they have fax software installed, and wind up faxing their art rather than printing it! If your printer is in good shape, click on OK to return to Corel's Print menu.

4. Most of the laser printer options are calculated by CorelDRAW—how many steps are used to render a Fountain Fill to a PCL printer (45) or to a PostScript Printer (120) are intelligent decisions based on mathematical principals. Although you can change them, you won't come up with a better way to print. Click on the Layout tab in the Print menu to see some options you do have input about—the following are the options you may want to consider:

- Click on Preview Image to see what your artwork looks like from the laser printer's point of view. Notice in the Preview box that dotted lines surround the Printable page. These are the trim dimensions, and anything outside these lines will be lost because printers cannot render an 8 1/2" by 11" page border to border.

- If you've designed outside of the Printable page, press Cancel, reposition your artwork within the page, and rescale it if it simply won't fit. Use the Pick tool for either of these operations. If your art appears clipped on one side, that's the way it'll print.

- The Position and Size field gives you the option of precisely placing your design on the Printable page. If your design is too close to one edge, type a new value in the Top or Left field and you'll be able to preview the new position for your art. None of these options change your design in any way. Position and Size don't move your artwork; they only affect the way it prints.

- The Center check box enables you to center a design. Perhaps you started a piece in the upper left of the Printable page. Without repositioning your design (which means exiting the Print menu), you can create an even border of white space around your design.

- The Fit to Page option maximizes your design for printing. If you drew a peanut and want it printed as the size of a melon, check this box, and see what Corel proposes to print in the Preview window.

- Print Tiled Pages is an option only to use when you've defined a page larger than 8 1/2" by 11" in the Layout, Page Setup command on the Menu Bar. If you've designed a 20-foot wide Welcome Home banner, Corel will print it on more than 20 pages you can then tape together (right after you buy a new toner cartridge!) when you pick Print Tiled Pages.

- Don't uncheck the Maintain Aspect box. This scales the height and width of your design disproportionately, and will turn your design into a funhouse mirror reflection. No one knows the purpose of this option.

- Finally, if you're printing to a laser printer, only two buttons beneath the Preview window are of interest to you. The others pertain to color separations and printing to film, not paper. The button with the "i" on it will print document (file) information on the same sheet as your design. When you push this button, you

Printing from CorelDRAW

have the additional option of printing the info within the page (next to your design), or near the page margin away from your artwork. The button with the lines on it to the right of the info button is for crop marks. If you want to trim a print right next to where the "live" image area begins in your Corel design, the crop marks will appear on your printed page when you press this button.

In figure 3.31, I've checked all my options, and the by-product of a faulty Corel Ellipse tool is all set to print.

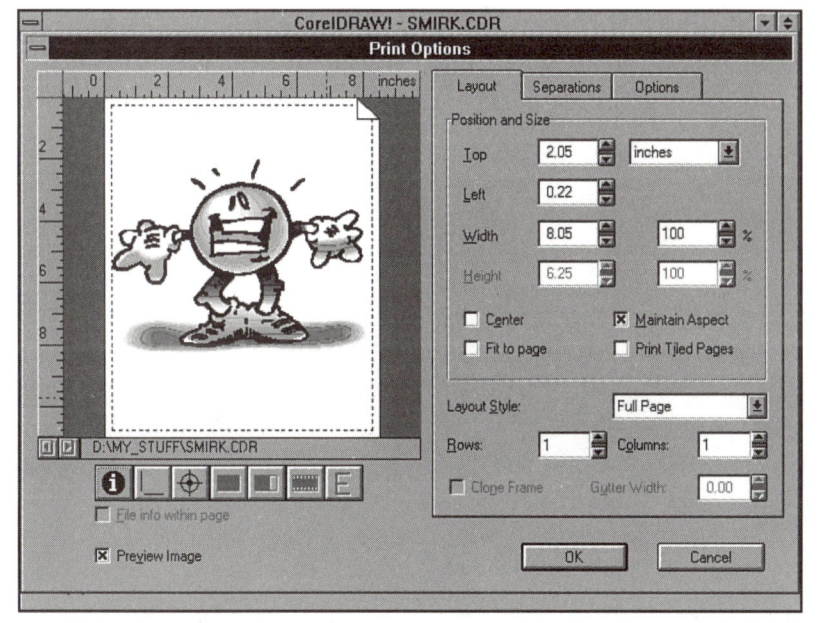

Figure 3.31
Set your options, and click on OK to return to the Print menu. Press OK to print your work.

Vector graphics, the ones you produce using CorelDRAW, print quickly and smoothly. Vector designs can be scaled to fill a page, and because they're a mathematical description of arcs, lines, and fills, you'll get consistent printed results in no time.

Putting Your New Wisdom To Work

Half the secret to success in using CorelDRAW, however you may measure it, lies in the chapter you've just read. You have a lot of options for the smartest way to work in CorelDRAW safely tucked away in your mind, and if you forget one or two in your travels, the information will always be right here.

The other half of the secret is in the use of Corel's tools—knowing how to set a dimension line isn't very meaningful if you don't know how to draw one! I believe that by presenting you with options before you learn to draw, you'll learn quicker and have less questions that'll bring fun design work to a halt. You'll also develop a broadened scope of possible uses for Corel tools that may not be mentioned here.

The proof's in the pudding and the fun is in the designing—what do you say to a mega-art lesson in the next chapter? You're going to learn everything there is to know about the Freehand Pencil tool, and then some. You'll then put this wisdom to excellent use as you design a shape intermediate to advanced CorelDRAW users wouldn't have thought possible!

A challenge, yes. But one you don't want to bet against. Read on!

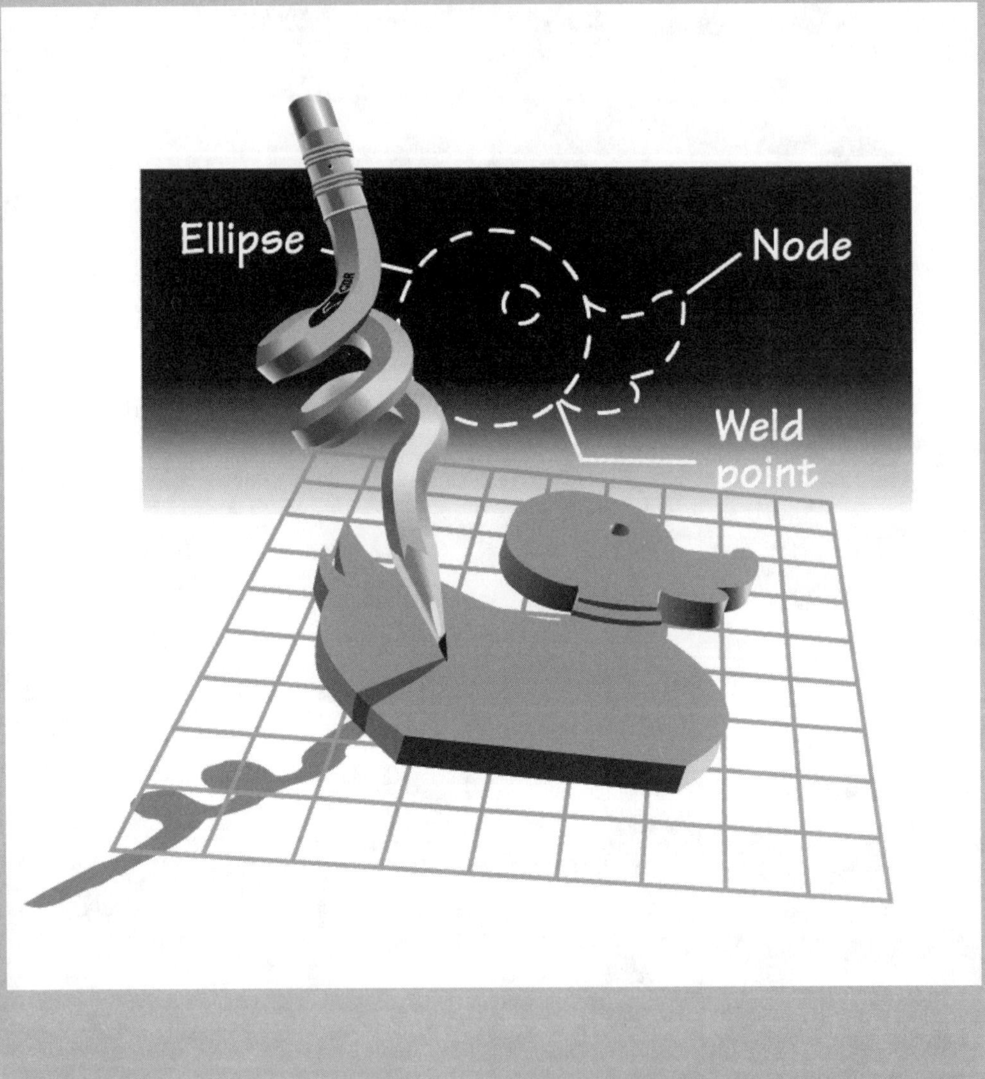
Ellipse
Node
Weld
point

CHAPTER 4

Drawing the Line Somewhere

The contemporary abstract painter Ralph Rauchenberg said once that his most terrifying professional moments come when he stares at a fresh, new, *blank* canvas. Many artists of all skill levels fear the first, decisive stroke, because of its permanence and because it dominates the flow and mood of the resulting art.

Lesson number one with computer graphics, however, is that nothing is permanent—you can press the Undo button, rescale an area, and rearrange stuff ad infinitum.

Lesson number two begins right here with using the Freehand Pencil tool. While it's true you still have to draw that first line to create an illustration, CorelDRAW's tools work *in concert*, with many of them designed to supplement uncomplicated lines to build impressive renderings.

In this chapter, you will:

- Bend lines and discover the powers of node editing
- Use different varieties of Pencil tools
- Take up welding as a profession
- Design a duck
- Measure and provide callouts for a duck

Shaping Up for Your Corel Design Work

If you're old enough to remember John Nagey on television (before TV was in color, okay?), you might recall how his synopsized art lessons went. You started with a few geometric "primitives" (a square or an ellipse) to rough out your design. Then in a few steps of refining and adding some lines, you had a portrait of a sailor, a house, or a fuzzy animal.

While the same technique of going from a general outline to the specific shape of a design still holds true, CorelDRAW adds a twist. The geometric primitives you create are actually *incorporated in* the final design; no pencil sketches, only definitive shapes you refine to perfection with Corel's wonderful tools.

The assignment in this chapter is to build a stencil of a duck. If the subject matter sounds simplistic, the techniques, while easy to execute, are quite sophisticated. Creating this simple duck will reveal many of Corel's features and capabilities that you can apply to your own work.

Making the First Mark

Let's begin duck-making in Corel by zooming into a comfortable view of the Printable page in Corel's Drawing Window. Although you can design anywhere you please in the Drawing Window, get into the habit of staying within the boundary defined by the virtual sheet of paper in the center of the window. Anything outside of the Printable page border does not print.

Zooming into a specific area where you begin designing is a good tactic to use, for several reasons. When you confine yourself to a visible area of the Printable page, you naturally allow yourself some room to add to a design later. Also, it's important to learn how to scale a design, especially for those who are coming to CorelDRAW from a traditional, physical art background. A simple design, like the duck in this chapter, wouldn't normally be designed with a pencil on paper using the entire page, so let's begin by "focusing" on an area of the 8 1/2" by 11" virtual page.

To draw the duck's head, follow these steps:

1. Click on the Zoom tool on the Toolbox, and select the Zoom in tool (the one with the plus sign inside the magnifying glass).

2. Marquee-zoom into the page by starting inside the Printable page's upper left corner and dragging down to just inside the page's bottom left corner.

Making the First Mark

3. The Ellipse tool is a good choice to define the rough shape of the duck's cranium. You'll work on the beak later. Click on the Ellipse tool, and place the crosshair cursor in a two o'clock location on the Printable page.

4. Press and hold down the Ctrl key (to make the ellipse a perfect circle), and make a marquee-motion with your cursor (click+diagonal drag) in a four o'clock direction until the Status Line reports that your circle is about 2" in diameter.

5. Release the mouse button and release the Ctrl key.

Now that the duck's head has been defined, you need to decide where the bottom of its body will end. This will be a sitting duck, as it were, so don't consider where the webbed feet will end or anything. You'll use CorelDRAW's Guidelines feature to mark the top and bottom of the duck.

■ Click in the center of the top (horizontal) ruler, then hold and drag down into the Drawing Window until you have a dotted blue guideline at about the 5" mark on the vertical ruler.

■ Click in the center of the horizontal ruler again, and drag a guideline down until it touches the top of the circle/duck head, as shown in figure 4.1.

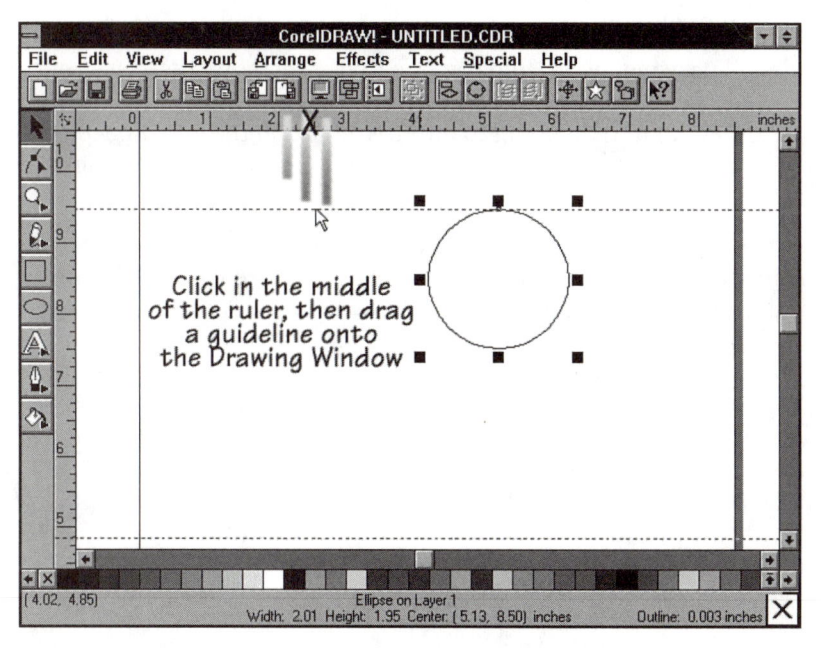

Figure 4.1

Guidelines are a helpful visual key to placing and designing objects.

Tip

You can't pull guidelines out of the rulers if you don't have rulers displayed! Select <u>V</u>iew, and if <u>R</u>ulers isn't checked, check this menu item. Alternatively, you can simply press Ctrl+R if you can't see any rulers on the edges of the Drawing Window. Ctrl+R is a "toggling" function; do it once, and it removes the rulers, Ctrl+R a second time to restore them.

Because guidelines are placement guides on your screen and don't print, you can't delete them as you would an object that you've drawn. When a guideline is no longer useful, you have two options: you can put it back in the ruler (use the inverse process of taking them out), or you can double-click on the guideline to display the Guideline Setup box, which enables you to delete a single guideline or all of them.

The Freehand Style of CorelDRAWing

Unfortunately, there aren't any Beak tools on Corel's Toolbox, so the next set of steps use the next best thing—the Pencil tool. You'll notice that the Pencil tool button on the Toolbox has a triangle in its lower corner. This means that, like the Fill, Outline, and Text tools, the Pencil tool has a fly-out menu that offers more functions.

The default Pencil drawing mode (and the one that's currently displayed on the Toolbox) is the Freehand tool. With the Freehand tool, lines can be made by clicking an initial point, then going to another point on the workspace and clicking again. As you'll see, this produces straight lines between the points you clicked.

The trick to freehand drawing is knowing where to click to come up with a *path* that roughly describes the shape you desire. Paths are connected line segments, and what connects the line segments are *nodes*. A node is produced whenever you click the Freehand tool cursor, and a straight line segment is produced automatically between the nodes you create. Figure 4.2 shows a light gray outline of the ideal path of the duck beak, with a black outline representing the lines you'll use to define the beak. *Points of inflection* (changes in the path's course) are marked where each line ends and a node should be placed.

The Freehand Style of CorelDRAWing

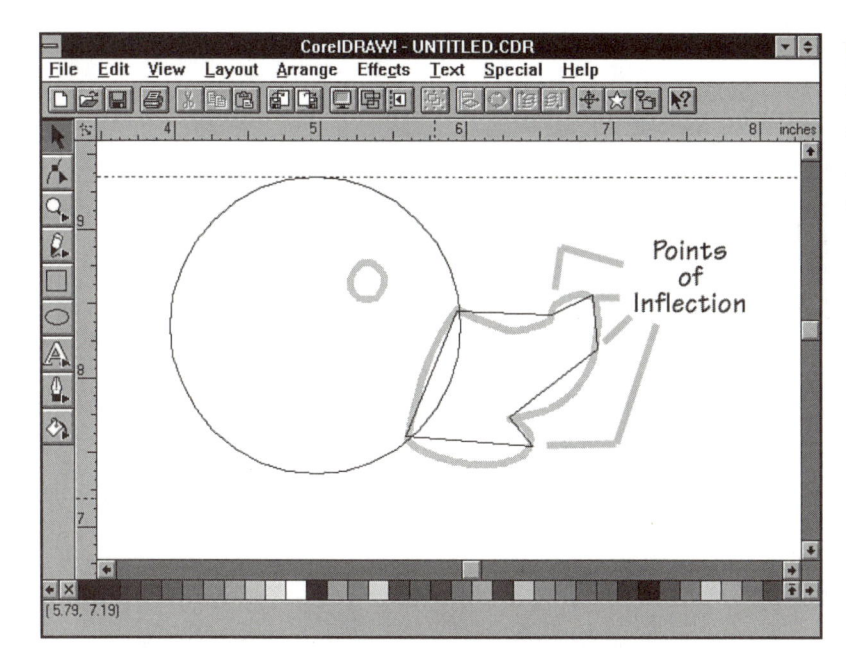

117

Figure 4.2
Wherever there's a change in path direction, there should be a node.

A vector path is similar to a path around a geographical location; it has a distance between points and a *direction*. It's important that you go clockwise or counterclockwise to create a path that returns to its beginning point. By doing so, you close a path—closed paths are the only type CorelDRAW can fill with color and texture.

With this in mind, let's give this duck a beak. Follow these steps:

1. Click on the Zoom tool to get the Zoom In tool again, and marquee-zoom in. You want about a 3" vertical view of the duck head circle, with room to view it right where you'll draw the beak. (Hint: use the scroll bar at the bottom of the window to scroll right if your zoom is a little off.)

2. Select the Freehand tool. Using the last figure as a reference, click once (at about three o'clock) where the top of the duck's beak will meet its head.

3. Move your cursor to the right and slightly down about three-fourths of a screen inch and double-click.

   Continue clockwise and double-click at each point, as shown in figure 4.3. Do this everywhere there is a change in the direction that the lines take to form the beak outline.

Chapter 4: Drawing the Line Somewhere

Figure 4.3
Double-clicking ends a line and begins a new one, with a single node connecting the two lines.

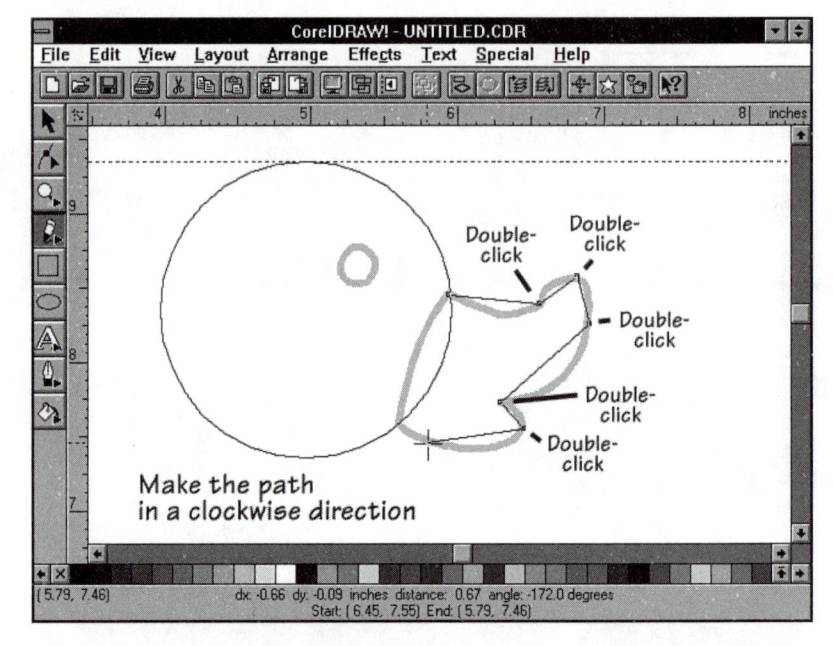

4. When you get to where the bottom of the beak meets the circle, you're only one line away from completing the path that's a rough outline of the duck's beak. Place the cursor over the first node you created and click *once*. This closes the path, and no lines trail behind the Freehand tool cursor when you move it.

Note

A second, but imprecise, method of pathmaking with the Pencil tool's Freehand tool selected is performed by clicking and holding down the mouse button, and dragging the cursor in much the same way you move a pencil on paper. CorelDRAW tracks the cursor's movement across the screen and places nodes at seemingly arbitrary points along the path you are drawing. You achieve instant curved segments between nodes, but will understand less about the properties of nodes by doing this.

Reserve click+hold+dragging for bitmap-based painting programs like CorelPHOTOPAINT (discussed later in the book). CorelDRAW offers the designer a lot of precision; this freehand technique doesn't.

Changing the Properties of Line Segments

Now that the closed path has been rendered, it's time to make it more duckbill-like by making the straight line segments curved.

Tip

Corel is a little misleading in terms of the information it places on the Status Line display when you select an irregularly shaped object. It'll tell you this object is a curve, even though you know darn well it's composed of straight lines.

Closer Look

Presumably, Corel does this to distinguish between the prebuilt geometry of rectangles and ellipses created with the other drawing tools. These prebuilt shapes have a "special" kind of node that defines construction points. Because these special nodes are less malleable, rectangles and ellipses can't be manipulated in the same way as objects that are drawn in Freehand mode. You'll learn how to edit prebuilt shapes in Chapter 5.

Editing an Object

The first step to converting all the straight lines to curved ones is to select all the nodes that connect them. You can only make changes to stuff you've designed by selecting it; since nodes aren't objects, but rather components of objects, you need a special editing tool for the task—the Shape tool.

Follow these steps to select the nodes:

1. Select the Shape tool (the one between the Pick and the Zoom tools).

2. Click once on the outline of the duckbill path to make it an active selection (if it isn't already), then marquee-select the entire shape. The nodes in the path become black as a visual indicator that they're all selected.

3. Double-click on a single node (don't click on a line segment or you'll deselect all the nodes). The Node Edit Roll-Up appears.

Chapter 4: Drawing the Line Somewhere

4. Click on the To Curve button on the Node Edit Roll-Up, as shown in figure 4.4. You won't see a dramatic difference in the duckbill path, but you've just changed the properties of the nodes, which in turn control the segments they connect.

Figure 4.4
The Node Edit Roll-Up is used to assign different properties to nodes you select.

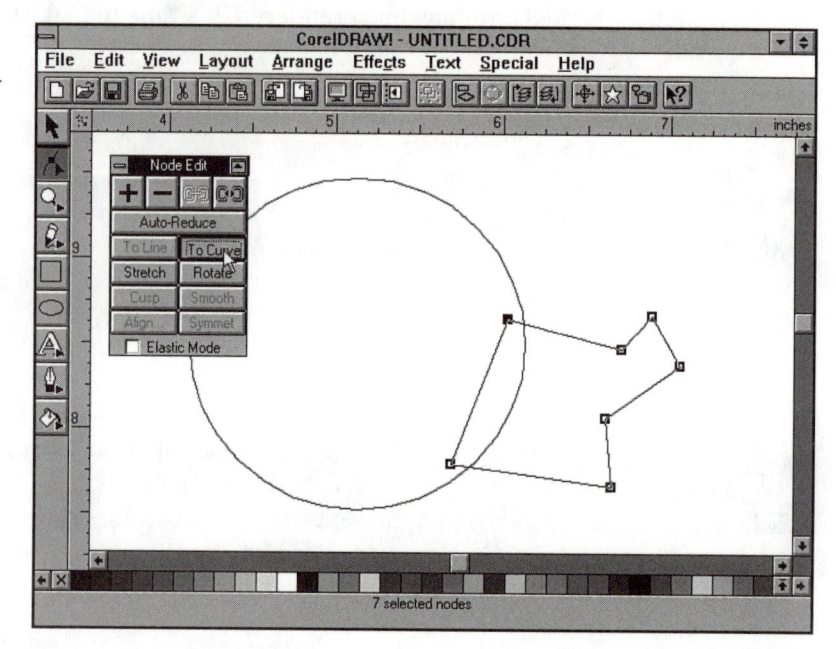

Controlling Line Segments

A logical question arises from the concept that nodes control line segment properties: Which node is responsible for which segment?

The line (path segment) that's formed between two nodes is governed by the most recently created node. To change the property of a single segment, click on the node that comes *after* the segment you want to change. Which node is "after" depends on which direction you drew the path—clockwise or counterclockwise.

Stop

You also can click on a line segment to change its attributes (curved, straight, etc.), but be aware that a curve in an object always runs through a node. By reshaping a segment only, you won't take control of the segment's neighboring segment.

Working with Curved Line Segments

CorelDRAW provides two ways to reshape the path now that it's composed of curved segments. The first is to reshape a line segment directly, which you'll do to make the top of the duckbill a little more swoopy. Then you'll work with *control points*. Control points are little handles you can manipulate that sprout off a node when it has curve properties, as the nodes in this path now have.

To reshape a curved line segment directly, follow these steps:

1. Click and drag down on the top line segment in the path that represents the top of the duck's bill.

2. Quit dragging when the vertical distance, the y-axis distance [dy] on the Status Bar reads about -0.07, as shown in figure 4.5. The slope of the curved segment now looks more waterfowl-like.

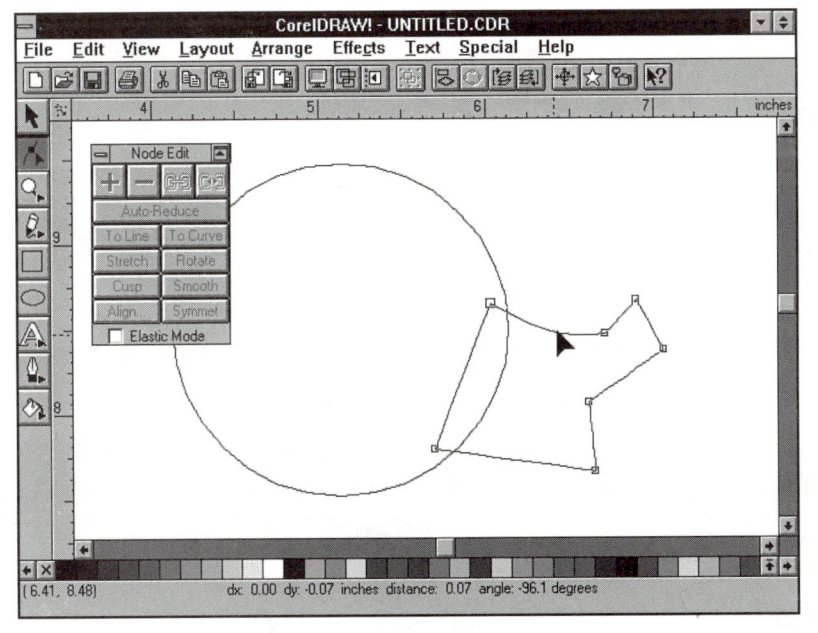

Figure 4.5

Only line segments that have a Curve attribute can be bent by clicking and dragging them.

3. Click on the top, far-right node. You'll see two control points lying flush with the line segments they govern. The initial location of control points (the *launch point*) is established when a node (or several nodes) assumes the To Curve properties.

4. Pull in an eleven o'clock direction with the left control point. The segment it governs begins to arc in the direction you're pulling, and related control points at the end of the segment become visible.

Chapter 4: Drawing the Line Somewhere

5. Click on the control point to the right of the same node, then drag in a 5 o'clock direction, as shown in figure 4.6. Congratulations! You are shaping a curved path! Refer back to the outline of the duck's bill in figures 4.2 and 4.3 as you continue modifying the path.

Figure 4.6

The farther you drag a control point from a node, the more the curve sweeps away from it.

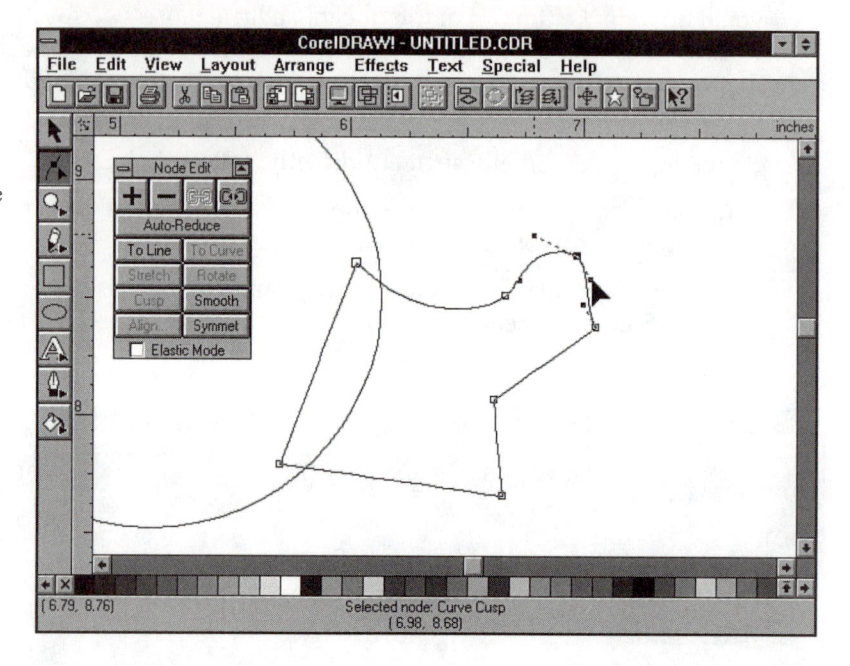

Note

You also can click and drag on a node itself to shape a curved line segment. The node's control points move along with it, and readjust the angles between the node and line segment. The method you choose depends on the amount of precision you need. Moving a node is the coarsest adjustment, dragging on a segment is more precise, and moving a node's control points offers the most control over shaping a curved line segment.

Smoothing Out a Freehand Curve

As mentioned before, curves actually run through nodes, and a complete arc is determined by the angle at which two curved line segments meet. By default, when you convert nodes and their associated line segments to curves as we did last, the properties of these nodes are that of *cusps*—the angle at which the line segments meet can be anywhere between 0 and 360°.

Next, you're going to *change* the cusp property of a node to make it smooth; the control points will be opposed at a fixed 180° angle. The reason why is purely for aesthetics. Smooth curves in a path are graceful and print cleanly, and make for a more professional illustration.

To smooth out the line, follow these steps:

1. Click on the node that defines the tip of the duck's top bill, the node *after* the one in the path you adjusted in the last steps. The lines associated with this node should meet at a smooth angle.

2. Click on the Smooth button on the Node Edit Roll-Up. As you can see in figure 4.7, the line and node properties associated with smooth, flowing curved lines are on the right of the Roll-Up, and ones for sharper, steeper path angles are on the left.

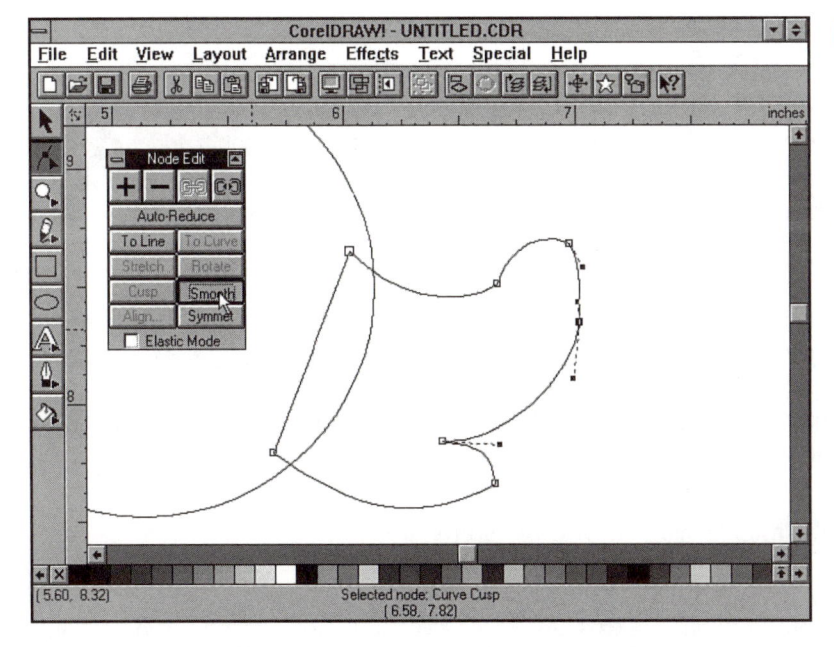

Figure 4.7

One or several selected nodes can be assigned different angles at which line segments meet.

3. Next, click and drag on a control point. The opposite control point mirrors the angle in which you drag. Smooth the tip of the duck's bill now by "playing" with either control point.

Control points affect the characteristics of their related line segment in two ways; the angle at which the control point meets the node affects the angle at which a line passes through the node, and the distance the control point is from the node affects how wide or shallow an arc the line makes when approaching the node.

With a smooth attributed node, independent distances may be set for opposing control points, but their angles are always fixed at 180° from each other.

Tip: If you click the Symmet(rical) button while a node is selected and already attributed a Smooth quality, the node's control points will always be equidistant; you pull away from the node with one, and the opposing control point moves away identically. The angle is also fixed between opposing control points at 180°.

Additionally, you cannot attribute a symmetrical or smooth property to a node between a straight line and a curve. Straight lines have no control points, and smooth and symmetrical nodes, by definition, must have opposing control points (plural!).

Symmetrical nodes are used to build elliptical shapes. The Ellipse tool actually produces closed paths consisting of symmetrical geometry; ellipses created using this tool simply don't appear to have symmetrical nodes because their geometry is pre-built and hidden from users until the Convert to Curves command is applied to them.

Assembling the Pieces of a Drawing

Once you have a shape for the bill that you and the duck are comfortable with, it's time to add the duck's eye, and then assemble the three pieces to form the complete duck head.

To create the duck's eye, follow these steps:

1. Select the Ellipse tool.

2. As you hold down the Ctrl key, create a small circle at a position within the duck head similar to that shown back in figure 4.2. Stop when the Status Bar says the diameter of the circle is about 0.125".

3. Press the spacebar to toggle to the Pick tool on the Toolbox; click and drag on the circle's outline to reposition it, if necessary.

4. Click on the Zoom tool. You need to zoom out a little to get a perspective on the duck design. Click on the Zoom out tool (the magnifying glass with the minus sign). This returns you to your previous, looser field of zoom.

Assembling the Pieces of a Drawing

125

Tip

The Zoom In tool is the only Zoom mode that requires your input; you don't have to perform a marquee with any of the other zoom modes, and after clicking on one, you are switched back to whatever tool you were using last.

5. Marquee-select both the duck head and duck eye circles, but not the beak.

   Unless you completely marquee a shape, it's not selected; you can skim into the beak object as you select both circles, and it won't be selected.

6. Choose Arrange, Combine. The duck head and eye are now one object, with two subpaths. In other words, the head is now a big donut, with a hole where the eye shape created an empty space within the head shape. This will become more apparent when you fill the completed duck shape with color.

7. Now marquee-select the combined circles and the duck beak.

8. Choose Arrange, Weld, as shown in figure 4.8. The Weld command removes lines from within two or more overlapping shapes and creates a composite outline of the shapes involved.

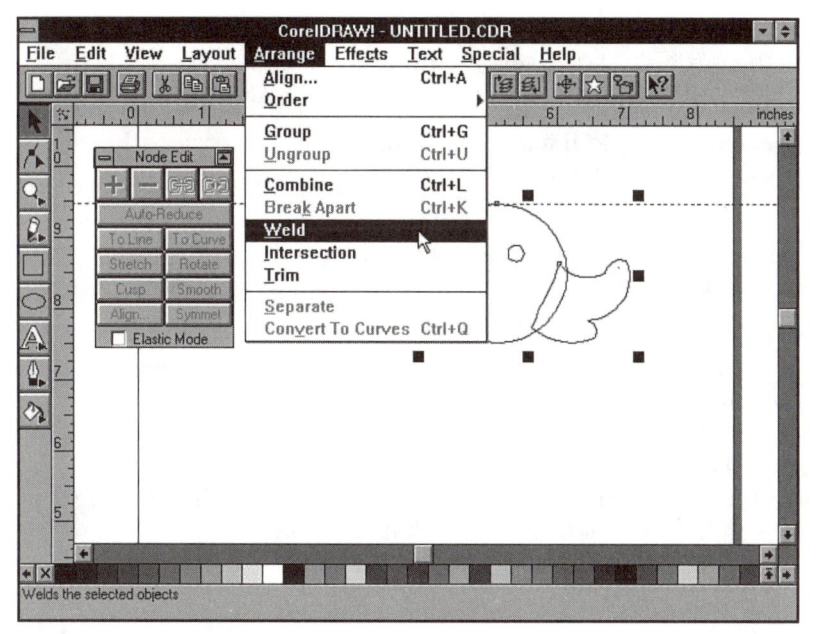

Figure 4.8

The Weld command acts like a hot summer day does on a bag of candy.

Using the Bézier Tool

The Bézier mode of drawing is quite different from the double-clicking technique of freehand design. Bézier drawing produces curved line segments that infrequently require the assistance of the Node Edit Roll-Up options to modify. You simultaneously draw and modify the control points of nodes when you use the Bézier tool. You single-click, instead of double-clicking, to connect segments; single-clicks between segments without dragging the cursor produce straight lines.

Drawing Bézier curves requires patience and practice. You'll tackle the design of the duck's body in this next section using the Bézier drawing mode, so you can make a decision about the way you prefer to design lines in CorelDRAW.

Creating the Duck's Body

The duck's body should be a squat, oval shape. You'll begin by starting a (neck)line down from the duck's head to the bottom guideline you pulled from the ruler in an earlier set of steps.

Follow these steps:

1. Click and hold on the Pencil tool icon on the Toolbox. A fly-out menu appears.

2. Click on the Bézier tool (the second from the left).

3. Place your cursor slightly inside the duck head in a 5 o'clock position. You will eventually weld the duck body to the head; therefore, head and body must be overlapping shapes.

4. Click and drag downward for a distance of about one-half screen inch. Surprise! You haven't even clicked two nodes yet, but you now have a control point sprouting from your initial click point, as shown in figure 4.9. Don't release the mouse button yet.

5. Click again, but don't drag that far yet. If you move your cursor now, you're actually moving a control point that governs the curve of the line between the first and second node. Move your cursor slightly to the left, then drag downward toward the bottom guideline, as shown in figure 4.10. You're both drawing a second segment and determining the curvature of the first segment. How's that for multitasking?

Using the Bézier Tool

Figure 4.9
Bézier drawing sets a control point (an angle for the ensuing curve) from the beginning of clicking a point.

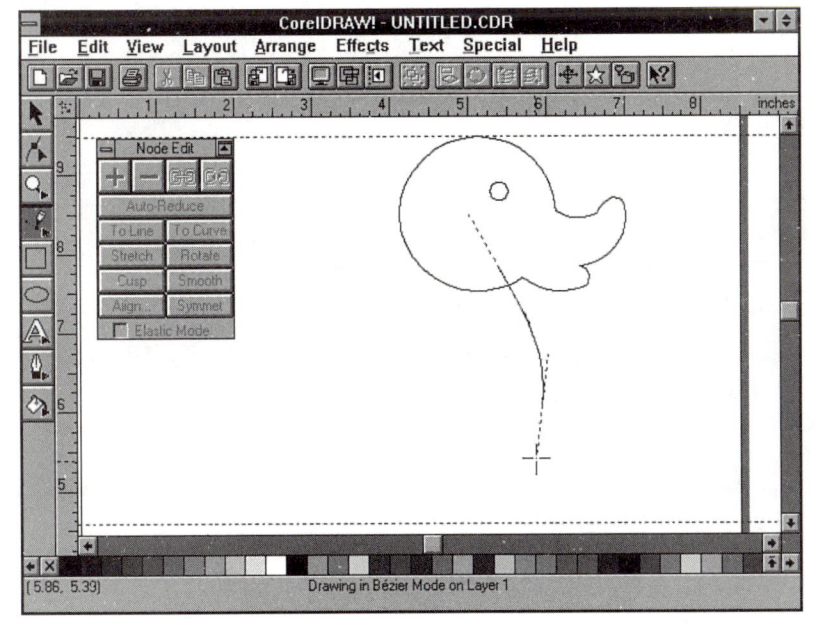

Figure 4.10
Bézier curves are manipulated while you draw.

Chapter 4: Drawing the Line Somewhere

6. Give the duck a flat bottom, like those carved ducks that cost so much in New England antique shops. To do this, click another point when you reach the guideline, but don't drag the cursor. Release the mouse button, click again on this point, and continue left.

7. Move to about 2.5" horizontal measurement, then click a point. A straight segment will appear between the guideline nodes on your path. In figure 4.11, you'll see the "dance steps" for using the Bézier tool to complete the duck body. The points at which you click and drag, or simply click (to produce a straight segment after you click) with the Bézier tool, are shown by some "speed lines."

Figure 4.11
Follow these points clockwise, then single-click to close the path.

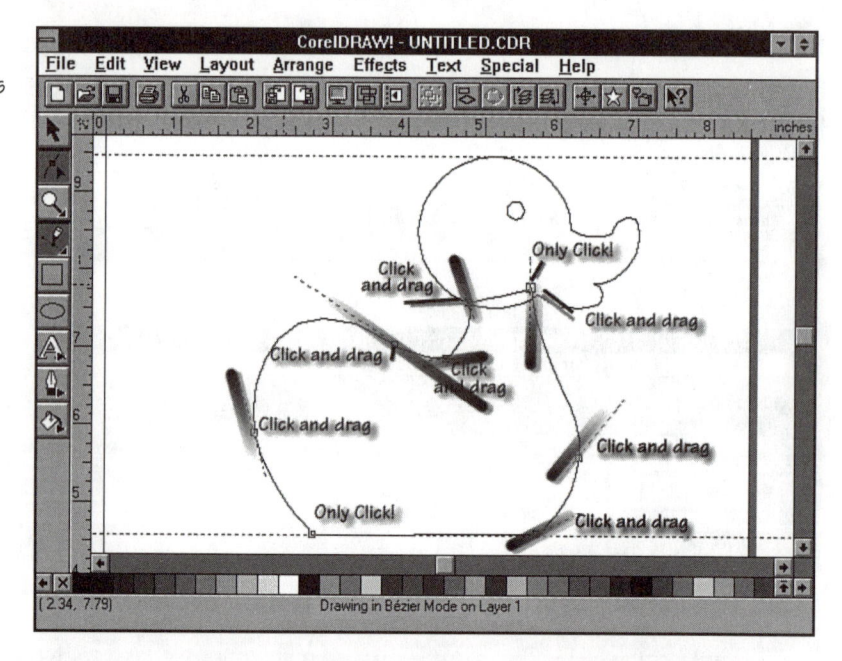

8. Skip ahead in your view of figures so you can see what the finished outline of the duck body looks like. In figure 4.12, you see that eight nodes define the duck's body. I've talked you through four of them; you need to make four more clicks to establish nodes, and drag the Bézier curves so they match the figure. Close the path at the first node you created by single-clicking on it.

Using the Bézier Tool

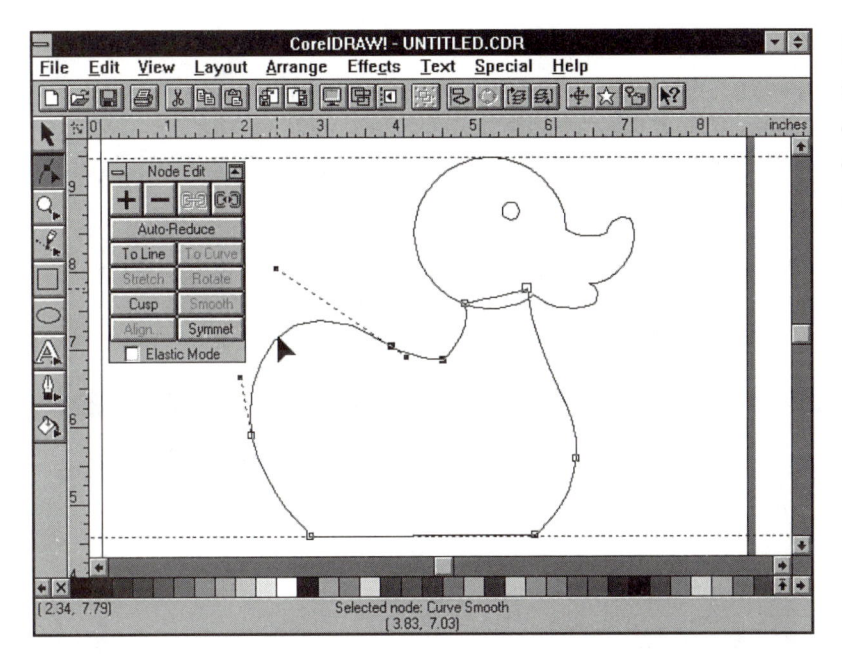

Figure 4.12
Straight lines and curved ones can be created in Bézier mode.

Defining the Right Number of Nodes

If you noticed in the last figure, the Shape tool has been clicked along the Bézier curve path to display the control points that govern the segment where you'd find tail feathers on an actual duck. There's a mistake in this picture, not having to do with the duck's likeness, but rather how many nodes were used to construct it. Corel's official position on curved paths is that there should be, at most, one node every 120°. If you followed the last figure, you presently have about 180° of curve to represent the duck's backside.

The problem this causes concerns how easy the control points are to handle. Nodes that connect two Bézier curves have a smooth property; when you adjust one control point, the other shifts equally in an opposing direction. This means that if you adjust the shorter control point to the right of the node, the left, opposing control point will wildly gyrate all over the place—its "spoke" to the center of its rotation (the node) is too far away.

Chapter 4: Drawing the Line Somewhere

Follow these steps to solve this problem:

1. Click the Shape tool cursor on the curved segment where the tail feathers on an actual duck would be. A dot appears on the segment to indicate where your point of placement is with the Shape tool.

2. Either press the + key on your *keypad* (the plus sign above your keyboard letters doesn't work), or press the plus sign button on the Node Edit Roll-Up. This creates a new node with its own control points, and takes the pressure off the node with the ponderously long control point, as shown in figure 4.13.

Figure 4.13

You can add nodes to a finished path by clicking and pressing the plus button or keypad key.

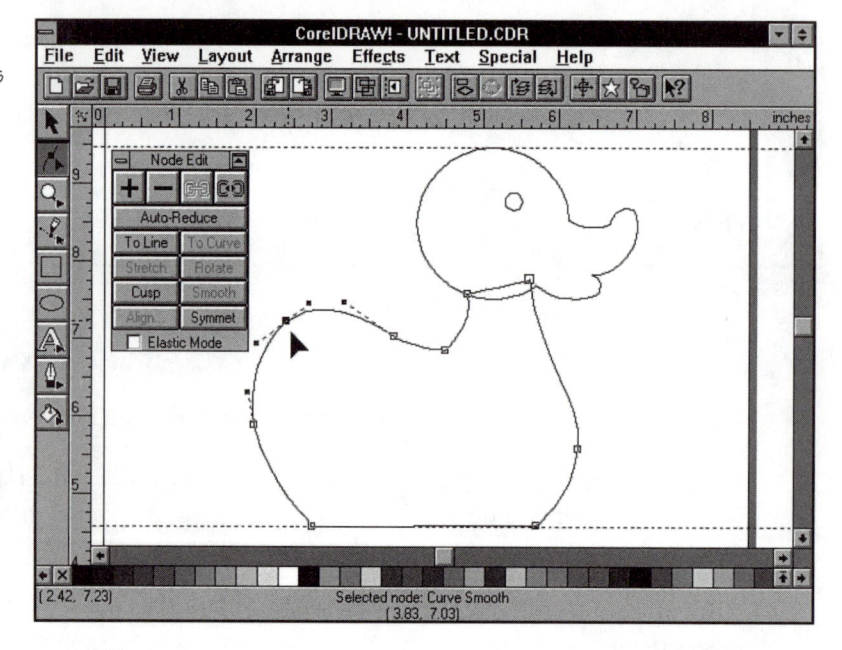

Tip

Added nodes share the properties of the line on which they're placed. If you click on a straight segment, the added node has no curved properties (and no control points). If you click on a curved segment whose parent nodes have smooth properties, the new node also has smooth properties, with control points set at 180° from each other.

Adding Tail Feathers to the Duck

Let's get back in the swing of standard freehand drawing to add tail feathers to your duck shape. You'll begin with straight segments that you'll modify to produce curved ones, and reshape the flow of the path.

To add the tail feathers, follow these steps:

1. Click and hold the Pencil tool. The fly-out menu appears; you should select the default, Freehand tool, by clicking on the picture of the pencil drawing the squiggle (if you linger over the picture a Pop-Up Help box will confirm the identity of the tool).

2. Click a counterclockwise path that suggests two tail feathers around the area where you added a node on the duck's backside, as shown in figure 4.14. Remember to double-click every time you stop a line, to continue building the next, and to end the path where you began it with a single click.

Figure 4.14

Corners (nodes) of straight line paths should suggest where the finished path takes directional changes.

3. I moved the Node Edit Roll-Up between figures so you could get a better view of the tail-feather area. You can also do this by clicking on the title bar of the Node Edit (or any other) Roll-up and dragging it out of the way.

Chapter 4: Drawing the Line Somewhere

4. Click on the top part of the path that represents the top tail feather, then click on the To Curve button on the Node Edit Roll-Up.

5. Click and drag the newly converted, curved segment toward an 8 o'clock position. You needn't drag it too far; simply put a bend in the segment.

6. Repeat the last two steps to the top and bottom of the other lines that represent the tail feathers, as shown in figure 4.15.

Figure 4.15
Directly manipulating a curved segment with the Shape tool is good for putting slight bends in a path.

7. Choose **E**dit, Select **A**ll (or double-click on the Pick Tool), then **A**rrange, **W**eld, and presto—the tail feathers become another part of the duck's outline! It would have been a lot harder to design the head, beak, body, and tail as one single outline. (P.S.—You could have marquee-selected the tail and duck, but you just learned another method!)

Tip

When you performed the Weld command, the node you added earlier to the backside of the duck disappeared, as did the segment on which it was placed. Nodes were automatically created at the Weld points of the two objects. This is another creative way to add nodes to an object outline to reduce the distance between points of inflection on a path.

Modifying the Duck Shape

The reason you're doing a lot of welding in this assignment is because designs or shapes that consist of one closed path can be filled in. You'll give this mere outline of a duck some substance when you fill it in later in this assignment.

Now it's time to modify the duck shape to represent a specific type of duck—the ring-necked mallard. It's fun, easy, and gives you the opportunity to experiment with another CorelDRAW Arrange command! You'll also see how a CorelDRAW shape, a rectangle, is converted to a simpler geometry where its nodes can be freely manipulated.

Follow these steps:

1. Choose the Rectangle tool, and marquee-drag a rectangle through the duck's neck. It should overlap the neck area completely, and be no wider than about one-quarter of a screen inch.

2. Just to experiment, select the Shape tool and try moving one of the corner nodes of the rectangle.

3. Aha! The rectangle's corners become arcs, and the rectangle takes on rounded corners! Press Ctrl+Z (Edit, Undo) to restore the rectangle to an undistorted shape with sharp, 90° corners.

4. You need to simplify the geometry of the rectangle to make it more malleable, so click on the Convert to Curves button on the Ribbon Bar, as shown in figure 4.16.

5. Click in the center of the top rectangle line, then click on the To Curve button on the Node Edit Roll-Up, and drag the curved segment down slightly. Then do the same thing to the bottom line of the rectangle, as shown in figure 4.17.

6. Press the spacebar to get the Pick tool back again, then hold the Shift key and click on the outline of the duck. The Status Line should say, 2 Objects selected on Layer 1.

Chapter 4: Drawing the Line Somewhere

Figure 4.16
You can take a shortcut by clicking on the Convert to Curves button on the Ribbon Bar.

Figure 4.17
Create a dimensional shape by changing the rectangle segment properties to curves.

Modifying the Duck Shape

7. Choose <u>A</u>rrange, <u>T</u>rim. The first object (the distorted rectangle) acts like scissors and trims its own shape out of the second selection, the duck, which will now be the active selection.

8. Click on the distorted rectangle, which has outlived its purpose, and press the Del key.

Now, you've marquee-selected object outlines a lot in this chapter and, admittedly, objects with no fill are hard to select by merely clicking on them. For the grand finale, then, select the duck the "hard" way and fill it, so it can easily be selected in your future work with it (if you decide to do any).

9. Click on the outline of the duck, either the head or the body—it doesn't matter since the two shapes still belong to one object.

10. Left-click on a green color swatch on the color palette located above the Status Line. As you can see in figure 4.18, the filled duck is more substantial in appearance, and can be selected with the Pick tool by clicking on either the outline or the fill.

11. Let's tidy up the workspace and close the Node Edit Roll-Up by double-clicking on the Control menu button in the upper left corner of the Roll-Up.

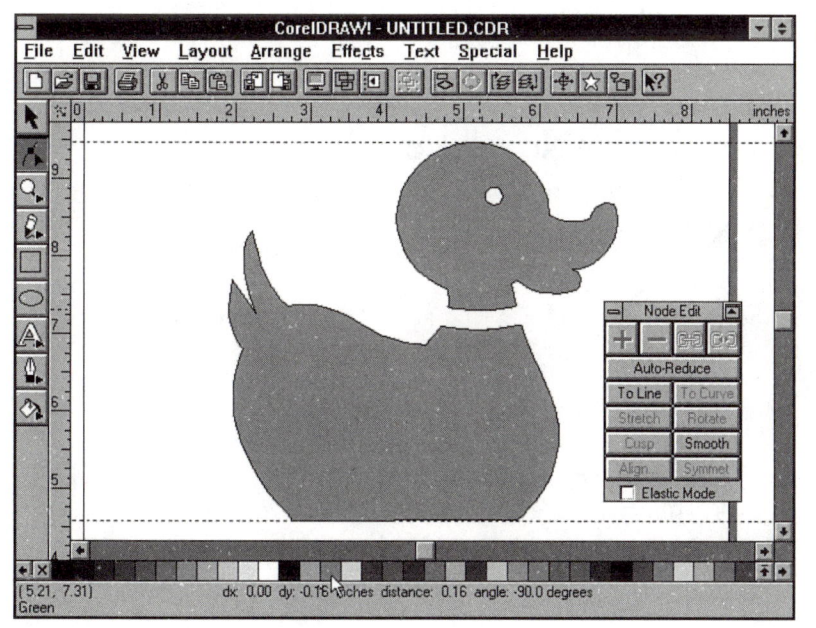

Figure 4.18

Closed-path CorelDRAW shapes can be selected by clicking on either the fill or their outlines.

Chapter 4: Drawing the Line Somewhere

Note

Unlike in the real world, when you trim across an object, the object doesn't fall apart into two pieces. As you saw in the last example, the duck's head and body are still treated as one object, except this new object now consists of two subpaths. Subpaths, like the eye added to the duck's head with the assistance of the Combine command, can be broken apart by using the Arrange, Break Apart Command. The Break Apart Command only works on an object that has two or more subpaths; welded objects don't break apart.

Adding Dimension Lines and Callouts

You can create some kinds of lines with Corel that don't have anything to do with aesthetics, but they're nevertheless very useful on assignments when you want to attach specifications to your artwork. Suppose that someone wanted the details about your duck creation; folks who work in manufacturing facilities, or who write documentation, love to have figures "specked out."

Now that you have your duck design completed, let's use the two other modes of the Pencil tool to clearly label and define the duck. Yes, this drawn-out chapter concludes with "Specking a Duck"!

Setting Up the Dimension Lines

First, let's tackle Corel's dimension lines. These are lines that place accurate measurements around a design. Think of the usefulness when you've drawn a gear, doodad, or frammitz, and you want the manufacturing department to build it to scale. Dimension lines are dynamic, too. As you'll soon see, when you resize a graphic, dimension lines that are attached to the graphic also reflect the scaling.

Follow these steps:

1. From the Layout menu, select Snap To, then choose Objects. Now, every line or shape you draw will be "attracted" to the node points of other objects. This step is necessary to create a dynamic link between the duck and the dimension lines, so the two can be resized later in tandem.

Adding Dimension Lines and Callouts

Tip

Like the Snap To Guidelines and Grid (covered in Chapter 5), the Snap To Objects mode is flagged on the Status Line when it's active. You'll want to shut off this mode after you're done using it—objects are harder to reposition with accuracy when they're preoccupied with snapping to everything else in sight! Check the Status Line for the Snap To mode the next time you get erratic behavior when repositioning stuff. For all its designing value, it's responsible for a lot of CorelDRAW tech support calls from frustrated users!

2. Click on and hold the Pencil tool to get the menu fly-out.

3. Click on the Vertical Dimension tool button (it has little up and down arrows on it).

4. Place your cursor at the bottom of the duck on the guideline, and click. You'll "feel" the cursor drawn to the bottom of the duck. The Snap To Object feature is actually guiding your cursor to a node point on the duck's bottom.

5. Move your cursor up to the top of the duck, and "feel" around for a Snap To Object point. When the cursor seems to lock into a location, click again. As you can see in figure 4.19, the dimension line has been drawn between the top and bottom of the duck.

Figure 4.19

Always activate Snap To Object when creating dimension lines.

6. You want the dimension line placed to one side of the duck; therefore, move the cursor to the right, and click a second time. This action moves the dimension line and creates *extension lines* that connect to the top and bottom of the object and to the dimension line.

7. The third and final click that's required to complete a dimension line will place the label for the dimension line, which uses Corel's default typeface (usually Avant Garde), and increments set in decimal values. Move your cursor to the center of the dimension line, as shown in figure 4.20. You'll see a box that can be positioned anyplace you choose with a final click.

Figure 4.20

The dimension line label can be positioned inside or outside of a dimension line.

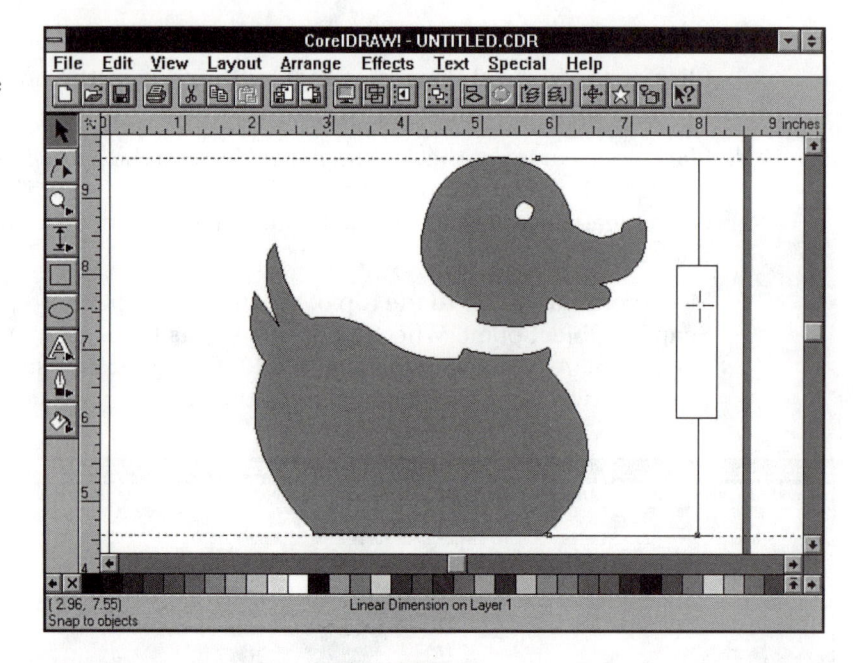

8. Click, and the measurement of the duck, from top to bottom, appears in the label box.

Tip

The two tools to the right of the Vertical Dimension tool on the Pencil tool menu fly-out are also dimension lines, except they are for diagonal and horizontal measuring. You'd use them exactly the same way you used the Vertical Dimension tool in this set of steps.

Adding Dimension Lines and Callouts

139

9. Suppose you don't want the measurements for this duck to be expressed in decimals, as seen in figure 4.21. Press the spacebar to regain the Pick tool, then double-click on the text, and the Dimension Roll-Up appears.

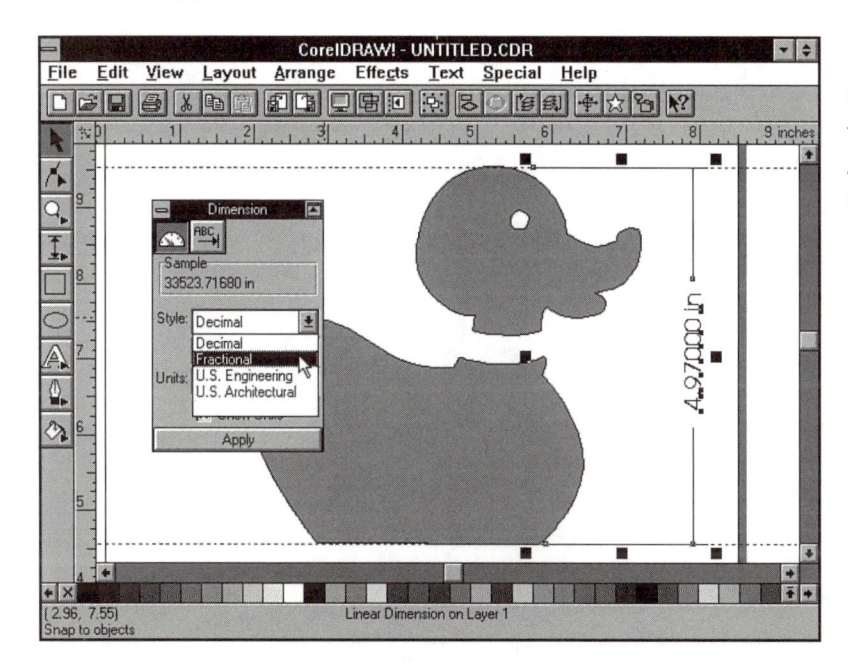

Figure 4.21
Double-clicking on the dimension text displays the Dimension Roll-Up.

Note

Dimension lines and text can be reassigned attributes the same way as you'd change Artistic Text or regular outlines of shapes. Highlight the dimension text and press Ctrl+T to change the dimension text font, or choose the Outline tool from the Toolbox to change the dimension line's color or width.

10. Click on the down arrow for the style of dimension measurement, and you'll see various increments. Choose Fractional, then choose eighths of an inch in the box beneath Style. You can be more specific in the increments (like thirty-seconds, or sixty-fourths), but, hey, this is only a duck illustration we're measuring!

11. Click on the Apply button, and presto—CorelDRAW automatically converts decimals to fractions!

Chapter 4: Drawing the Line Somewhere

12. Test the binding quality of a linked dimension line. Click on the duck, then click and drag a corner selection handle toward the center of the duck, as shown in figure 4.22. Surprise! The dimension line scaled along with the duck, and is keeping tabs on its new size!

Figure 4.22

As long as dimension lines are linked, they constantly update changes made to the parent object.

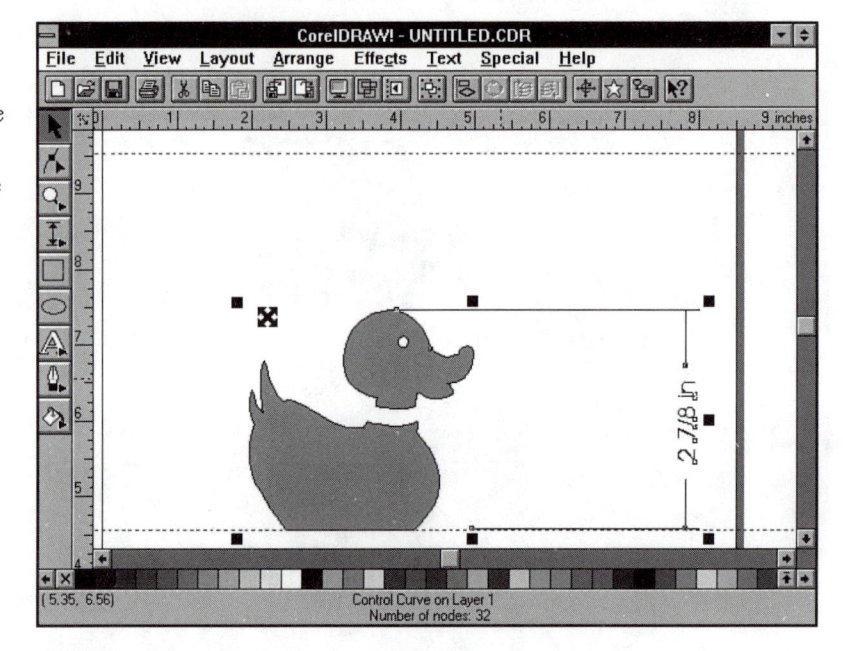

- Dimension lines can be deleted simply by clicking on them and pressing the Del key.

- Additionally, they can be broken away from the parent object by using the Arrange, Separate command. Dimension lines drawn without the Snap To Objects command active have no link to the object you measure, and therefore aren't very useful when you resize an object.

Tip

You can easily identify a shape linked to a dimension line by clicking on the shape and looking at the Status Line. A linked object displays the status of a *control object*.

Adding Dimension Lines and Callouts

141

Creating Duck Callouts

Besides specifying the height, width, or diagonal measurement of shapes you draw, you can also annotate various areas of interest in your drawing. Pretend this duck illustration is a highly technical one, and it's being published so that others can learn about this amazing new duck technology. You'd naturally want to label important innovations like the duck's tail feathers and head, and this is where CorelDRAW's Callout tool, found on the Pencil tool fly-out menu, comes in handy. Like the dimension lines, callouts are not "artistic" lines, but they do contain text and line attributes that can be changed just like any other graphic you design.

Follow these steps to add callouts:

1. Click and hold on the Pencil tool to access the menu fly-out.

2. Click on the far right button with the bent-arrow icon. This is the Callout tool. If you let your cursor linger over the button, a Pop-Up Help box will appear and confirm your suspicion as to the identity of the tool.

3. Click on the duck's head, then move the cursor up in an 11 o'clock direction. You'll see a label box appear, ready for you to finish the line, as shown in figure 4.23.

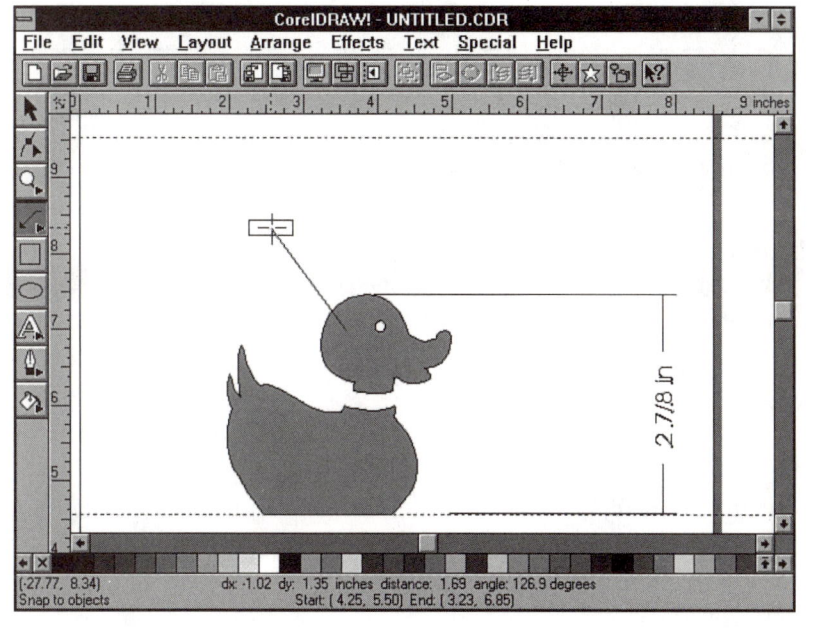

Figure 4.23

Callout lines behave like dimension lines when drawn and customized.

4. Double-click when you think the callout line is long enough. The line will end, and a text insertion point will appear at the end of the line. Start typing. As you can see in figure 4.24, I've created a callout to indicate where the duck's Intellect is located.

Figure 4.24

As soon as you finish a callout line, you can label it. No Text tool required!

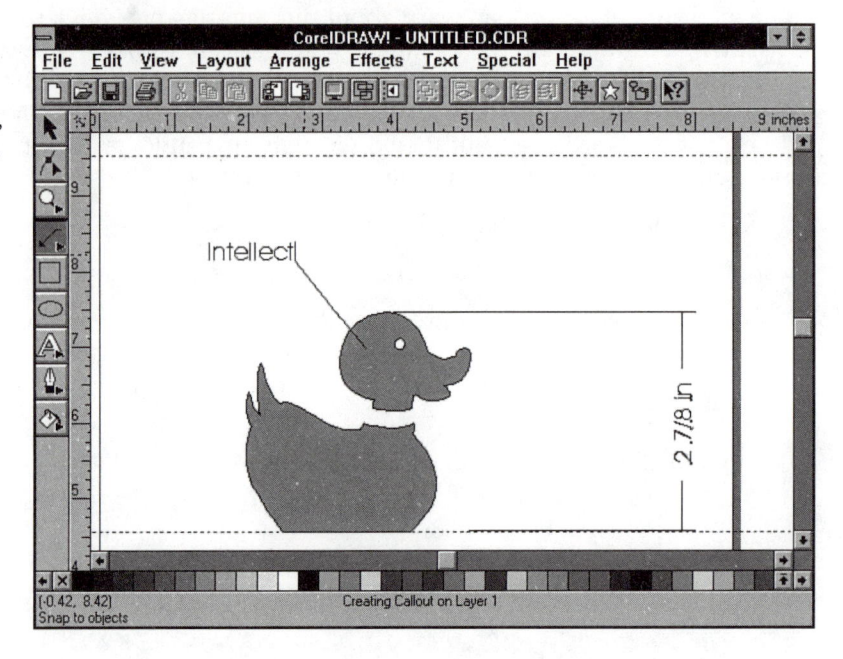

Tip

Like dimension lines, callout lines can have extensions. This is useful when you have a lot of callouts, and get cramped for space on the Printable page for long, detailed text labels.

To draw a callout with an extension, click an initial point, single-click a second time where you'd like the line to break, then click a final, single time to end the line and start typing a text label.

Double-clicks end a callout line, while single-clicks provide an extension to the callout line.

Repositioning Callout Text

As you can see in figure 4.25, I had some fun with my callouts, and there's no reason why you shouldn't too. Even the most droll of drafting acumen is automated in CorelDRAW!

Since the most frequent cause of ulcers among drafting, CAD, and technical illustrators is revising an illustration, CorelDRAW makes this simple with dynamically linked callouts. Once you've established a callout, you can move the text to the moon if you like, and the callout line will still connect the text and what it's pointing to.

Check this out as you conclude this chapter, and your duck-specking work. If you haven't added any callouts since the Intellect one, use this as your example next. If you've added callouts, you obviously take your ducks seriously and should be commended because you now have your pick of callouts to modify.

To reposition the text, follow these steps:

1. Click on callout text with the Pick tool. As you can see in figure 4.25, the callout indicating where a duck has communication capability has been selected.

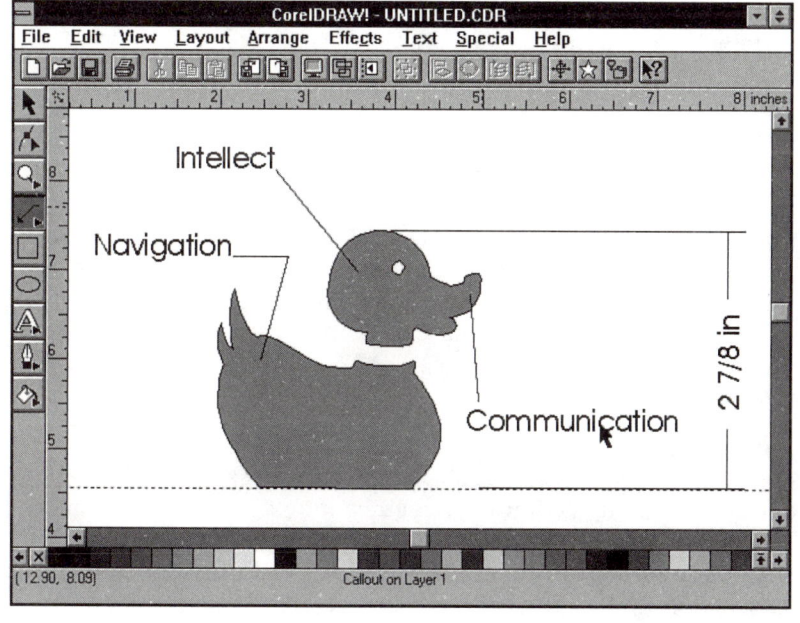

Figure 4.25

Check the Status Line for indicators that you've selected a normal line, a callout, or a dimension line.

2. Drag the callout to a different location on the Printable page. As you can see in figure 4.26, the Communications callout text moves, and the callout line takes on an elastic quality.

Figure 4.26
Callout lines are dynamically linked to the text and the location you begin the callout line.

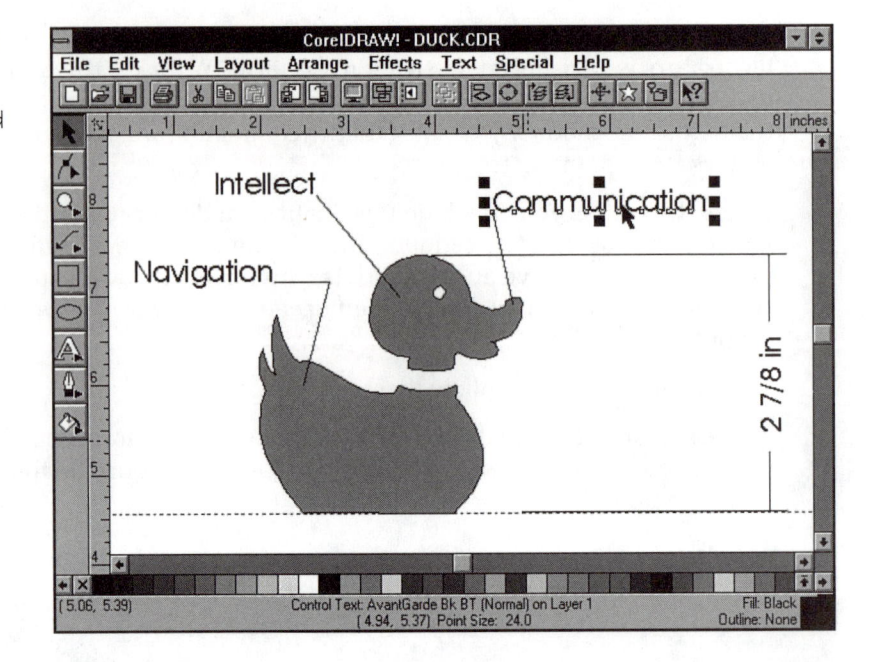

Moving From Lines to Shading Fills

There's obviously more than one way to draw a line in CorelDRAW. They can form closed paths, they can measure other lines, and they are an integral part of building complex, one-of-a-kind illustrations. Through this chapter, you've moved much further along in your CorelDRAW experience than you may realize. Many intermediate-to-advanced books use illustrations similar to the duck you created as an example.

Unlike the duck, however, you've hardly gotten your feet wet. In Chapter 5, you'll commence your investigation of shading the closed shapes you now know how to create. Although color fills, fractal and texture fills, and Fountain Fills are examined throughout *CorelDRAW 5! for Beginners*, there's a special technique for getting the exact shading in the right places within an object that makes it as dimensional and realistic as bitmap photographic images. It's called *blending* objects, and next you'll discover how to make your closed path shapes leap right off the page!

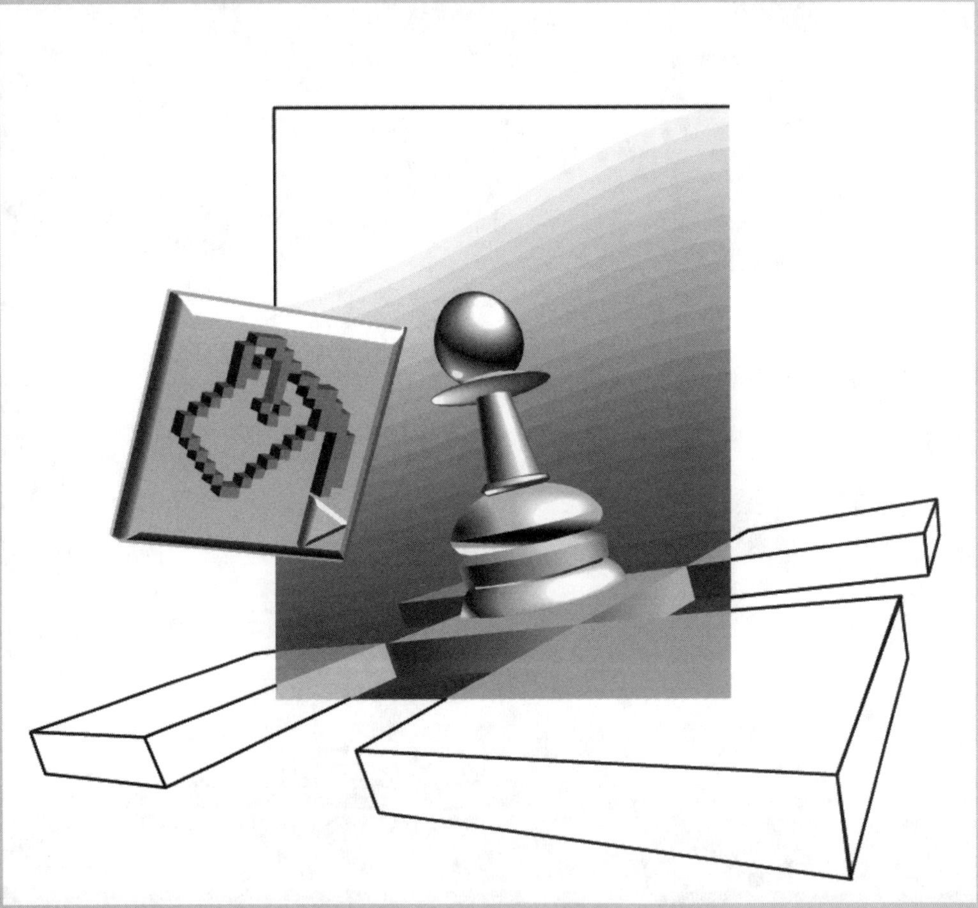

CHAPTER 5

Creating Shading with Shapes

My good friend Boris Spassky (who runs the corner deli, not the chess player) once confided in me that designing things in CorelDRAW was a lot harder than winning at chess (okay, so he plays a *little* chess). What Boris and a lot of other people new to Corel don't realize is that the name of the game is wireframe, outline, and fill—three simple components with which you can create anything you imagine.

When your imagination fuels your desire to take flat, 2D renderings into the next dimension, Corel's right there with you. Specifically, you'll see how to build and shade a chess piece. The techniques shown in this chapter can lead you to designing spires, 18-wheeler transaxle assemblies, and sausage links (like Boris would like to).

And as all spectacular things are done in CorelDRAW, shading is accomplished through the use of wireframes, outlines, and fills. So if your chess game is going to wind up a "draw," here's how to make it look good with CorelDRAW.

In this chapter, you:

- Work with CorelDRAW guidelines
- Customize CorelDRAW's rulers
- Build a realistic chess piece from several simple shapes
- Change the properties of rectangles
- Take advantage of the CorelDRAW Wireframe and Preview views of your work
- Create naturalistic lighting with the Blend command

Customizing the Workspace for an Assignment

Before you begin to build the star of this chapter, a lowly pawn, it's a good idea to set up the workspace to make the whole process easier. Whether you draw on paper or on a computer monitor, using grids (the electronic equivalant to graph paper), rulers, and guidelines makes it easier to produce a well-balanced, accurately scaled design. In Corel's digital workspace, the grid settings and guidelines are "stored" in the rulers, so they are always only a few mouse-clicks away. Take a better look at Corel's rulers and see what you can find to make drawing this chapter's assignment (or any assignment you have) easier.

Displaying Rulers and Grids

As you saw in Chapter 3, CorelDRAW has many settings that you can customize to make your workspace look and operate the way you want it to. Two of those settings determine whether or not the grid and the rulers should be displayed. When you installed CorelDRAW, they were both turned on by default. If by chance you don't see rulers or a gridwork of blue dots on your screen, it's easy enough to fix. Here's how in the next few steps:

1. From the View menu, select Rulers, and a set of horizontal and vertical rulers appear on-screen.

2. Double-click anywhere on the rulers to display the Grid & Scale Setup dialog box (or you can mouse your way there by choosing Layout, and then Grid & Scale Setup from the Menu Bar). In the lower left-hand corner of the Grid & Scale Setup dialog box, click on Show Grid. Then click on OK to return to the workspace.

Stop

When you were in the Grid & Scale Setup dialog box just a moment ago, you may have noticed that the default setting for the Grid Frequency (coarseness or fineness of the Grid's spacing) was set to display eight per inch in both the horizontal and vertical directions.

The visibility of all eight grid markers in the space of an inch can only be seen when you zoom in really close to the Drawing Window—greater than a 1:1 viewing resolution. At less than this resolution, you'll see grid markers at 1/4" increments, 1/2", or even at 1" points.

There's no way to increase the visibility of grid markers at various resolutions, but the markers are very useful, as you'll soon see, regardless of how frequently they appear.

With rulers on and a grid in place, you're all set to move on and find out what that wierd little box in the corner of the rulers is good for.

Changing the Ruler's Zero Point

You may notice that as you move around the workspace, the rulers change to reflect your position; when you zoom in and out, the increments on the rulers become finer or coarser. What doesn't change, however, is the point at which the rulers start measuring, also known as the *zero origin point*.

You may find it handy to have the zero origin point, the place at which the vertical and horizontal rulers meet, centered on the Printable page. With the zero origin point centered, you can easily measure to the left and to the right of the design to make certain that the piece is symmetrical.

It's easier to set the Zero Origin Point exactly where you need it if you've already zoomed into a view of the section of the page where you'll be working. Zooming into the center of the page where you'll draw the pawn is your first order of business in the steps that follow.

1. Click on the Zoom tool on the Toolbox to display the fly-out menu. Choose the Zoom In tool, and marquee-zoom into the center of the page by diagonally dragging the Zoom In tool cursor from a starting point of about 8" on the vertical rule and 2" on the horizontal rule, down to about 2" on the vertical rule and 7 " on the horizontal rule.

2. Click and drag a guideline from the center of the vertical rule to the 4 1/4" mark on the horizontal rule to set a reference point for adjusting the zero origin of the page.

3. Click and drag the symbol where the vertical and horizontal rulers meet (the zero origin box) down and across to the guideline at the 4 1/4" mark, as shown in figure 5.1. Don't worry about "zeroing" the vertical rule; you'll be concentrating only on widths (horizontal measurements) in this section.

Chapter 5: Creating Shading with Shapes

Figure 5.1
You can set the rulers to begin at any point in the Drawing Window by adjusting the zero origin point.

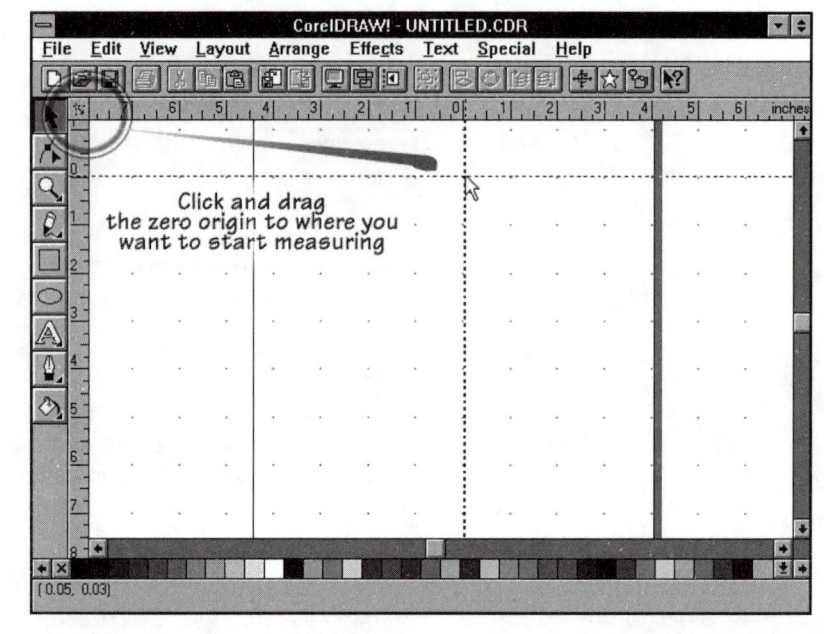

4. When the guideline at 4 1/4" vanishes (it's covered exactly by the new zero setting), release the mouse and you now have a zero point in the center of the page, with positive and negative horizontal rulers measurements.

If you let go of the mouse before you got the zero origin point exactly where you wanted it, just repeat steps 3 and 4. If you want to reset the zero origin point back to its default setting, double-click on the Zero Origin Point box where the two rulers meet.

Closer Look

Sometimes having the rulers at the edge of the screen is just not very handy. You might need to have them right next to what you are working on. If you hold down the Shift key and then double-click on a ruler, the ruler will pop away from the edge of the workspace.

Once you've released the ruler, you can position it anywhere within the Drawing Window by holding down the Shift key and dragging the ruler with your mouse. When you let go of the ruler, it locks into place where you've moved it. To return the ruler to the edge of the workspace, hold down the Shift key and double-click on the ruler.

Using the Snap To Mode

Although it's unlikely a viewer would criticize a drawing of a chess piece for being malproportioned, you'll frequently be called upon in professional circles to create designs with finesse and accuracy. From the beginning, you should think of this chapter's assignment as an example you can use to create other designs requiring precise measurements; a bolt, spindle, or peppermill can be drawn using techniques similar to those you use to create the pawn.

The pawn's head should be 2" in diameter, and using the Snap To Guideline feature makes this a snap to accomplish. Follow these steps:

1. Click and drag a vertical guideline to the −1" marker on the horizontal ruler, and place another guideline at the +1" marker.

2. Click on the Snap To button on the Ribbon Bar (the third of three buttons just above your present −1" vertical guideline). Nodes in lines, ellipses, and rectangles are now attracted to any guideline you have in the Drawing Window.

3. Select the Ellipse tool, and place your cursor at the zero" horizontal rule, about one screen inch from the top of the Drawing Window.

4. Press Ctrl+Shift, and click and drag in a 12 o'clock direction.

   Your cursor will offer some resistance when and if you try to end the ellipse beyond the Snap To Guidelines. Accept this magnetic attraction, and end the ellipse at the 1 inch marks.

5. Click and drag a horizontal guideline out of the horizontal rulers, and place it about 5" beneath the bottom of your circle. This forms the baseline for the pawn.

6. Choose the Rectangle tool, and place the cursor halfway down the circle's height on the left vertical guideline.

7. Click and drag in a 4 o'clock direction. The left, right, and bottom guidelines direct the cursor, and you should get a rectangle whose size and shape look like figure 5.2.

Figure 5.2
Guidelines attract your cursor and direct the flow of curves, ellipses, and rectangles.

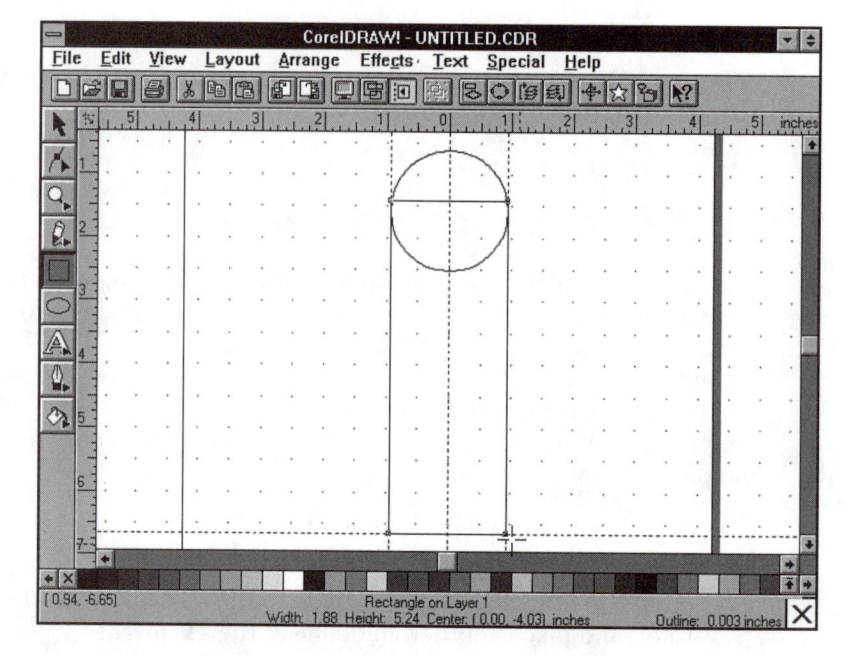

Simplifying the Geometry of a Rectangle

Most pawns I've seen in chess sets have necks that taper from their base up to the head. Although the Snap To mode of guidelines allows you to create complex geometric shapes like ellipses and rectangles, you'll sometimes want to modify these shapes to make closed paths whose corners do not meet with geometric perfection.

In the following steps, you'll simplify the geometry of the rectangle by using the Convert to Curves command. Corel refers to a set of segments connected by nodes as being a Curve shape. As you saw in the last chapter, however, curves can be composed of straight segments or contain control points that can be used to bend the segments.

In any event, the nodes that make up rectangle shapes have *special* properties. The segments that make up rectangles cannot be set at any other angle than 90° by tugging on their nodes. This is why the shape has to be converted to a simpler geometry.

Simplifying the Geometry of a Rectangle

To make the side of the rectangle shape slope inward toward the top, follow these steps:

1. Press the spacebar to toggle from the Rectangle tool to the Pick tool. The rectangle is still selected.

2. Click on the Convert to Curves button on the Ribbon Bar (the figure of a circle with little nodes, just above your +1" horizontal ruler mark). The status line confirms this action by telling you a closed curve (not a rectangle) is the present, active selection.

3. Click on the Snap To button on the Ribbon Bar. This, as with all the buttons here, toggles its function on and off. The guidelines aren't magnetic any more, and the top two nodes of your ex-rectangle can now move freely and be modified.

4. Click on the Shape tool on the Toolbox. Click on the upper left node of the closed curve, and drag straight right until it has the same vertical position, but horizontally it's placed one and a half gridmarks away from the zero horizontal rule.

5. Click and drag the upper right node an equal distance toward the horizontal zero rule. As you can see in figure 5.3, you've created a skinny rhomboid shape out of the rectangle—a perfect shape for a component of the pawn.

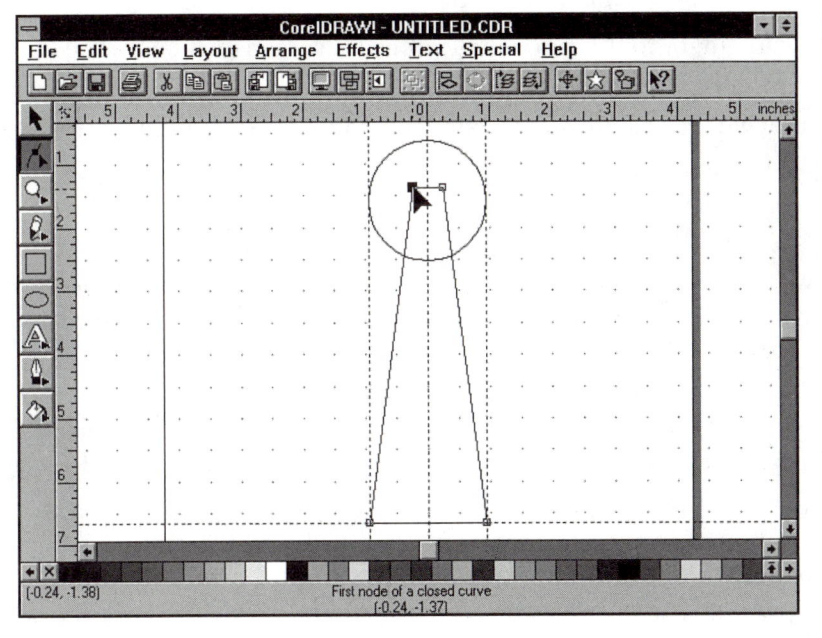

Figure 5.3

With the Snap To mode toggled off, nodes and line segments can be freely manipulated.

Stop: Don't worry if, in your rearranging of nodes, the top line they border is no longer perfectly vertical. This line will be sheared off later when you use the Weld command to bring the component shapes together to create the pawn. Just make sure the vertical sides slope toward each other.

Creating the Neckpiece for the Pawn

Many CorelDRAW users disassemble the sample images that come with CorelDRAW, and can't understand how a closed curve can be made up of only two nodes. You're going to learn a very useful trick in the next section that produces exactly this sort of mathematics-defying shape: you'll create an ellipse that ends in cusp corners. Besides representing a neckpiece for a pawn, you can also use this shape for many other assignments, such as drawing a convex lens viewed at an angle.

1. Click on the Freehand (Pencil) tool, and position your cursor to start a horizontal line where the former rectangle meets the circle, about half a gridmark from the –1" vertical guideline.

2. Click, and then drag to extend the line to half a gridmark beyond the right vertical guideline. Double-click the cursor at that point so that you can continue to extend the path.

3. Move your cursor to the zero point, about 1/4 screen inch below the horizontal line of your path, and double-click again.

4. Click a single time where you began the path to close the path.

5. Click on the Shape tool, and marquee-select all three nodes that make up the path. With all three nodes selected, double-click on one of the nodes.

6. The Node Edit Roll-Up is displayed. Click on the To Curve button, as shown in figure 5.4. The straight segments can now be curved using the Shape tool.

7. Click the Shape tool in a vacant area within the Drawing Window to deselect the three nodes. The nodes change in appearance from filled-in boxes (selected nodes) to hollow boxes (unselected).

8. Click on the bottom node of the triangle shape, and press the Del key (or the – button on the Node Edit Roll-Up). The bottom line arcs, and the nodes that border the two segments have cusp properties.

Creating the Neckpiece for the Pawn

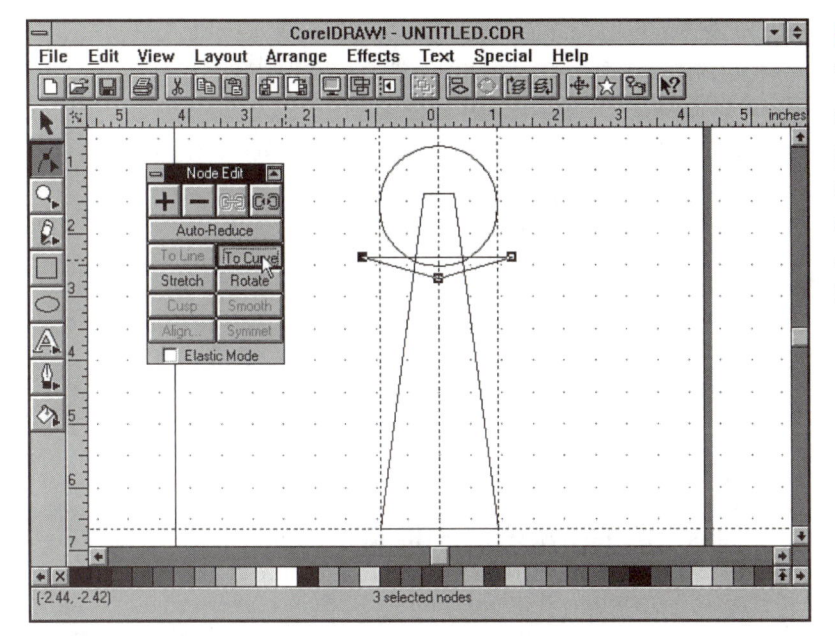

Figure 5.4

You can only change the properties of segments and nodes in a shape drawn with the Pencil tool.

9. Click and drag on the top and bottom segments until you get a neckpiece shape like that shown in figure 5.5. As you can see, you started with three nodes for the neckpiece shape, but only two are really necessary to finish it.

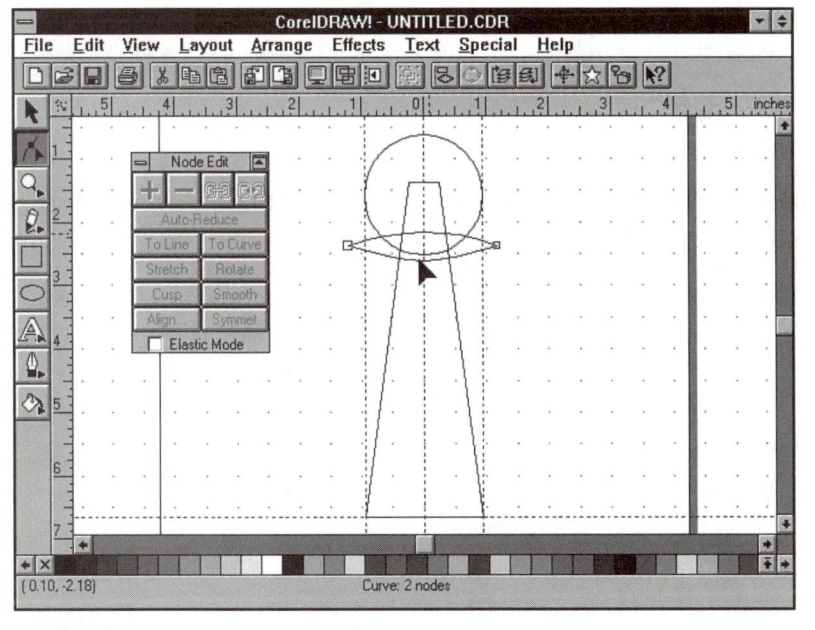

Figure 5.5

Segments can be easily reshaped when their surrounding nodes have cusp properties.

Tip

Each node you create in CorelDRAW adds one byte of information to the graphics file. This is additional information a printer must process to produce your design on the printed page.

There will soon come a time in your design work when you'll be creating complex CorelDRAW designs consisting of shapes with hundreds of nodes in them. PostScript printers (and even some PCL printers) have a problem digesting graphics information that contains too many nodes. If you can't print your CorelDRAW design, or it only partially prints, consider deleting nodes that aren't critical to your design, as you did with the pawn's neckpiece.

It's easy to wind up with a Drawing Window cluttered with tools, menus, and Roll-Ups. In this assignment, you don't use the Node Edit Roll-Up all the time, so click on the minimize triangle button on the Node Edit's upper right corner. The triangle will then turn upside-down to indicate that the next time you click on it, the Roll-Up will roll down. Also, you may choose to close the Node Edit Roll-Up at any time, and display it later by double-clicking on the Shape Tool.

Designing a Base for the Pawn

A traditionally designed chess piece has symmetrical ornamental tooling on its base. Since the profile of the pawn is the same on the left and right side, you can duplicate the symmetrical property of the base of the pawn by using the Rectangle and Ellipse tools.

Modifying a Rectangle

You are going to create a rectangle with rounded corners to add to the base. This is easy, because rectangles are made of complex geometry; when the Shape tool is used to modify rectangles, the angles where lines meet retain their 90° relationship to one another, but the corners become rounded. Test out this property while creating the first of four shapes that will comprise the base of the pawn.

1. Click and hold on the Zoom tool and choose the Zoom In tool from the fly-out menu.

2. Marquee-zoom in on the middle of the pawn's body.

Designing a Base for the Pawn

3. Choose the Rectangle tool, and marquee-drag a rectangle that's about 1/8" tall and a little less than 2" wide. The center of the rectangle should be at the zero mark. Don't worry if the rectangle is not perfectly centered now.

4. Choose the Shape tool, click on the upper left corner of the rectangle, and while still holding down on the left mouse button, drag to the right. As you can see in figure 5.6, this doesn't budge the node, but instead rounds all four corners of the rectangle.

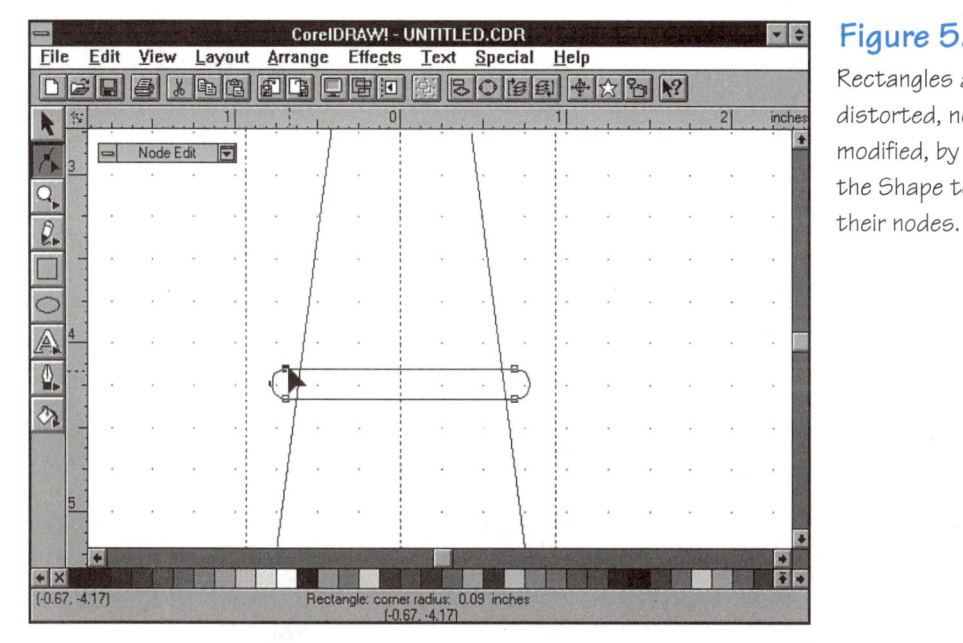

Figure 5.6
Rectangles are distorted, not modified, by using the Shape tool on their nodes.

Finishing the Profiles of the Pawn

Create and place two more ellipses and another rectangle by selecting the appropriate tools and clicking and dragging. Use figure 5.7 as a guide to the size and placement of the new ellipses and the rectangle.

Figure 5.7

Think of the outline of the pawn, not where the shapes intersect.

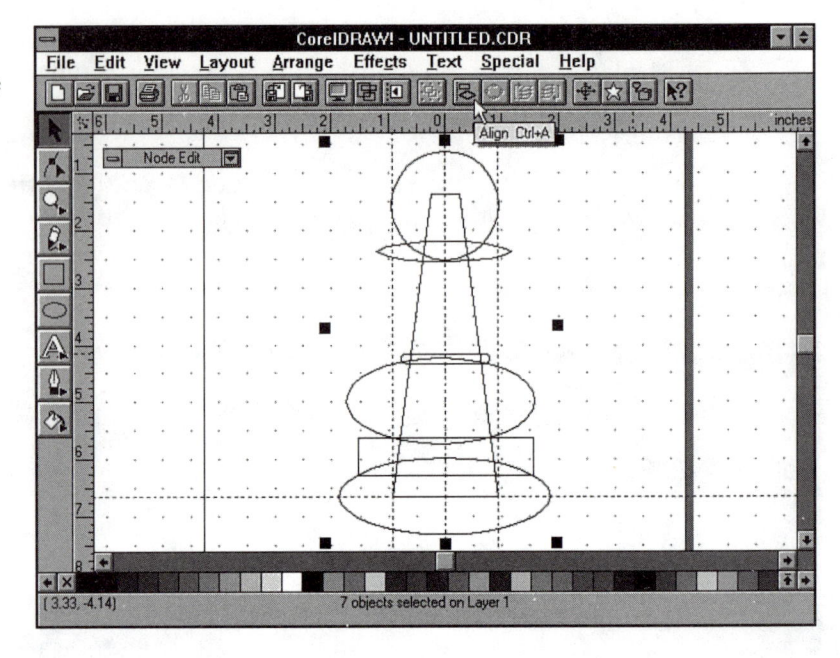

Aligning the Shapes

If you now have seven discrete objects on the Printable page, you're ready to align them and weld the shapes into the outline of the pawn.

To align the objects, follow these steps:

1. Click on the Zoom tool, and choose the Zoom To All Objects tool. This is the second button from the far right with all the geometric shapes on it. This tool automatically zooms you into (or out of) the Drawing Window to a view that includes all the shapes you've drawn.

2. Choose the Pick tool, and marquee-select all the objects (or choose Edit, Select All or simply double-click on the Pick Tool).

3. Click on the Align button on the Ribbon Bar (or press Ctrl+A). It's the one to the left of the Convert to Curves button you used earlier. If you are in doubt as to a button's purpose, let your cursor linger over the button, and a Pop-Up Help box will appear that displays the function of the button.

4. In the Align dialog box, click on the Center button in the field of choices marked Horizontally, as shown in figure 5.8.

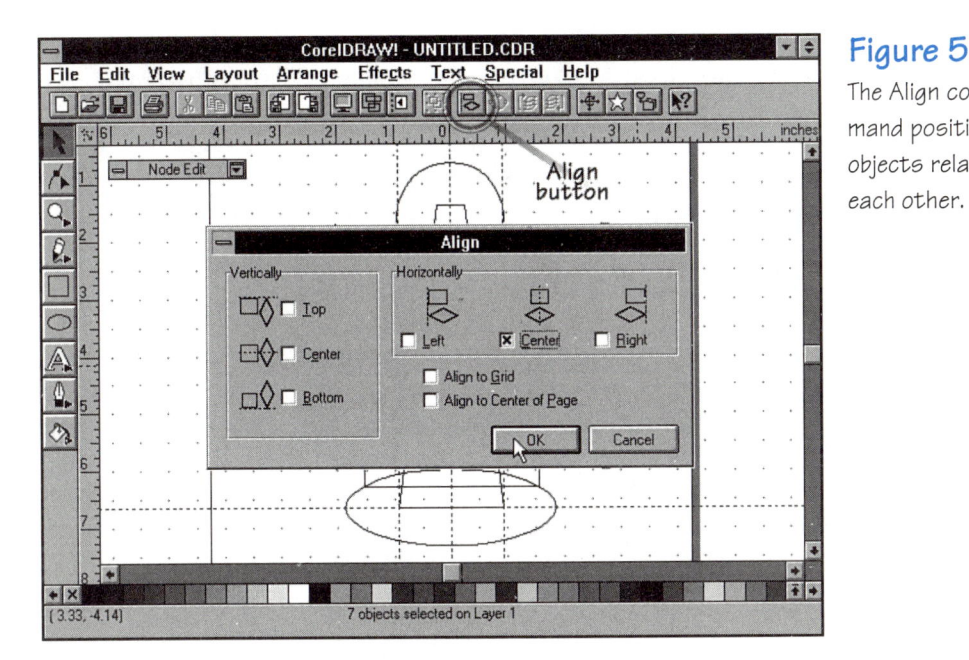

Figure 5.8
The Align command positions objects relative to each other.

Stop

The Align command's Align to Center of **P**age option is an *absolute* action, and therefore will not maintain the *relative* differences in position with multiple objects when it is performed.

Use the Align to Center of **P**age option only when you have grouped objects you want neatly centered for printing purposes, or when you want a single object perfectly centered in relation to the Printable page.

5. Click on OK, and every one of the shapes will be centered in relation to the first object drawn (the circle).

Welding Shapes Together

The Weld command was featured in the last chapter to add the outline of a hand-drawn shape to an ellipse. As you've seen, this command removes segments from the insides of intersecting objects to create a single closed path.

Chapter 5: Creating Shading with Shapes

Welding several objects, as you'll do next, also changes the properties of the ellipses and rectangles involved. The complex geometric structure of these shapes immediately becomes simpler. This means that after being welded, the resulting nodes and segments that are the remains of the rectangles and ellipses can easily be manipulated with the Shape tool without the additional step of converting them to curves first.

With all the shapes still selected, choose **A**rrange, and **W**eld. You'll get a profile of all the shapes, as shown in figure 5.9.

Figure 5.9
The Weld command converts geometry of all types to a single, simple, closed path.

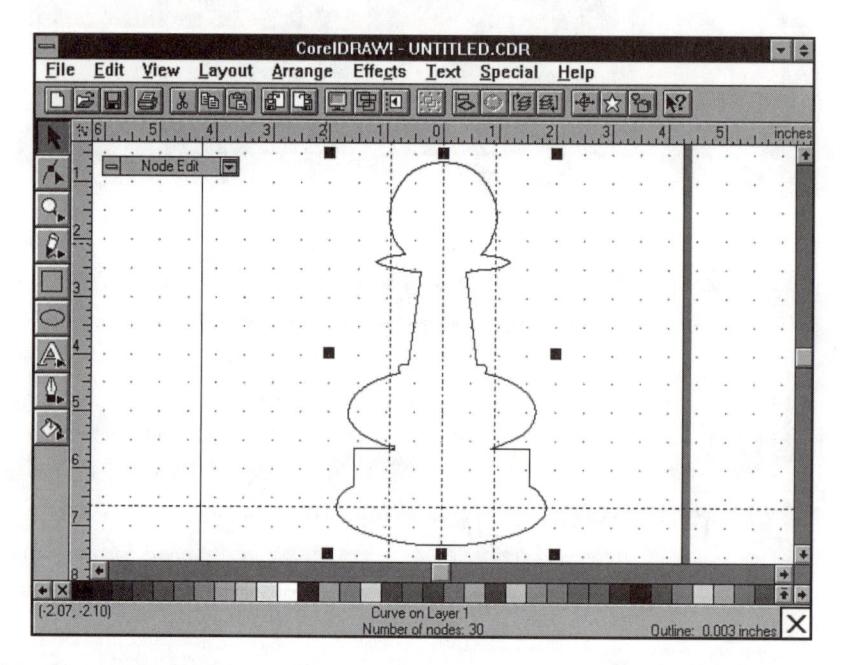

You should take into account that the pawn's bottom is wrong. It was a good move to use the ellipse because the top portion of the base should be symmetrically curved. The bulbous bottom needs work, however. It should be curved to suggest dimensionality, but not as severely curved as it is now.

Because this bottom curve consists of simple segments and nodes, touching up this area can be done by following these steps:

1. Choose the Shape tool, and marquee-select the bottom three nodes of the pawn outline, as shown in figure 5.10. When a node that has curve

properties is selected, its inside is filled. (When the node has line properties, it becomes a bold, hollow box when it's selected.) Double-click on the bottom, center node to spring the Node Edit Roll-Up back into action.

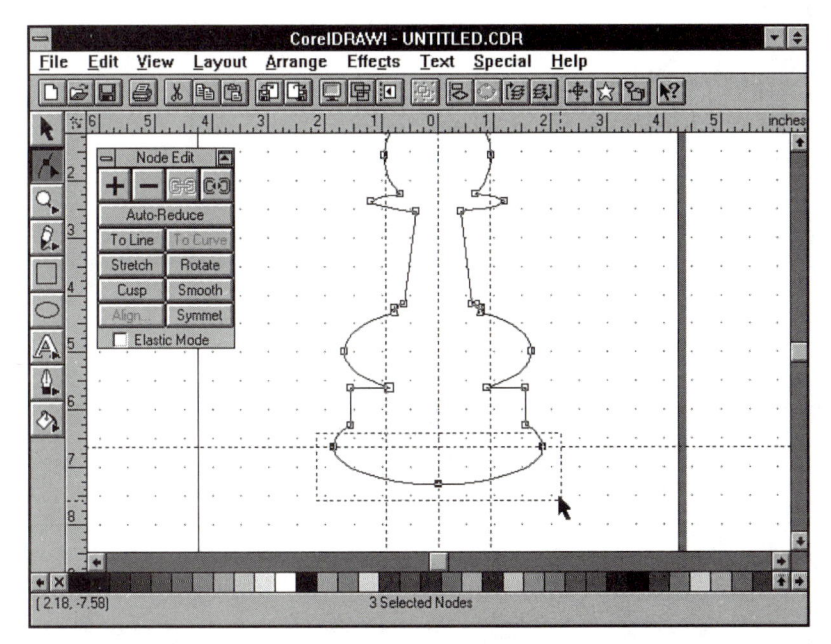

Figure 5.10

The Pick tool is for selecting complete objects, but the Shape tool can select only nodes within a shape.

2. Click on the Cusp button on the Node Edit Roll-Up. The three nodes selected will now have control points that can be independently manipulated.

3. You don't need the bottom, middle node. It sits in the middle of the curve you want to reshape. Click on the Printable page with the Shape tool to deselect the three cusp nodes. Click on only the bottom middle node, and press the Del key (or the – button on the Node Edit Roll-Up).

4. In an upward direction, click and drag on the single segment that makes up the pawn's bottom until it looks like a shallow convex shape, as shown in figure 5.11. Because the two nodes that define the segment are cusps, bending the segment has no effect on neighboring segments.

Figure 5.11
Make the cusp curve shallower by dragging it upwards.

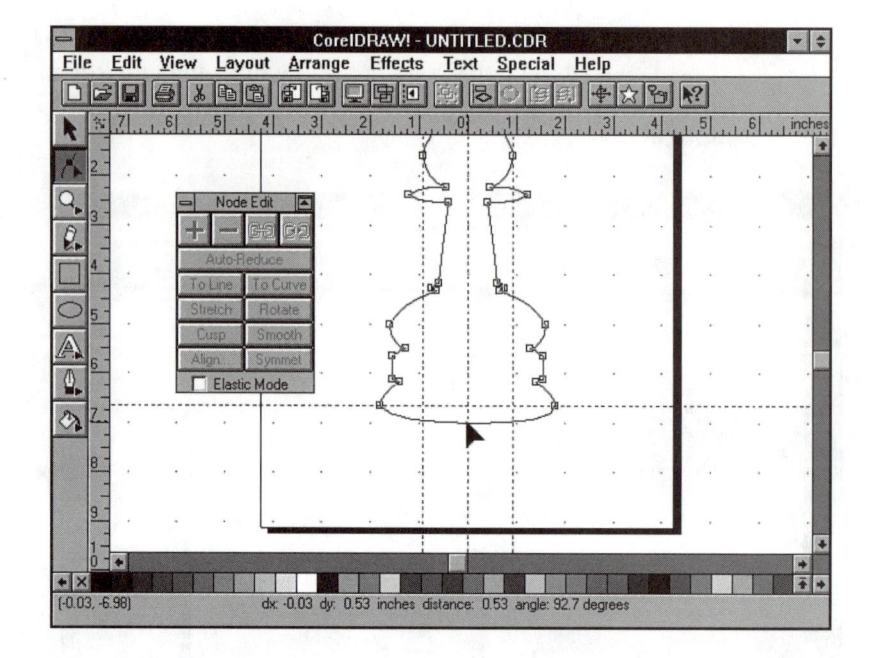

Shading the Chess Piece with Blends

Depending on how far apart two objects are, CorelDRAW's Blend effect can produce a series of slightly overlapping, nearly-identical shapes whose fills differ in color. The blend process is fairly automatic; CorelDRAW will calculate each of the blend steps between one object's shape and fill, and another object's shape and fill. The control objects (the original starting and ending objects) can be modified or moved even after the blend has been executed, with the blend obediently reflecting any changes. Like Contours and dimension lines, blends are dynamic.

In the following sections you'll use Corel's Blend command to turn your outline of a pawn into a gleaming black pawn with dramatic edge lighting. The edge lighting will be created by using the current drawing of the pawn as one of the two control objects. The second control object is made by duplicating the first (the original drawing), and modifying and recoloring the duplicate. When the Blend effect is applied using these two control objects, many transitional shapes will be added inside the original pawn shape to effectively represent lighting and shading.

Preparing the First Control Object

To create the dramatic edge lighting you have planned for this pawn, you'll need to create and fill the control objects for the blend. The pawn you have on-screen now will be your first control object. To make this outline of a pawn a suitable first control object, follow these steps:

1. With the pawn selected, choose the Pick tool and click on the white swatch on the color palette with your left mouse button. The pawn fills with white. This white pawn will be the first control object for the blend shading.

2. Click on the Wireframe button on the Ribbon Bar, which is next to the monitor icon at about the –2" mark, or press Shift+F9.

3. With the pawn selected, click with your right mouse button on the x in the lower left hand corner of the screen to remove the white pawn's outline.

Creating the Second Control Object

To create the second control object for the blend, you need to create another pawn and fill it with black. Instead of redrawing the pawn, you'll use Corel's Duplicate command in the following steps.

1. Press the plus key on your keypad (or press Ctrl+D) to duplicate the pawn. As the last created item, it automatically becomes the currently selected object.

2. Click with your left mouse button on the black swatch on the color palette. You won't *see* the second pawn filled with black, because you are in wireframe mode. The status line, however, does report that the object is filled with black.

Aligning the Two Control Objects

If you followed the advice back in Chapter 3 about setting the placement of Duplicates and Clones (under **S**pecial, **P**references) to the same value as the object you copy, you now have a black pawn exactly on top of a white one, and you're done with this section.

If you changed the settings and the two pawns are not on top of each other, choose **E**dit, Select **A**ll, and click on the Align button. Choose **C**enter for both **H**orizontal and **V**ertical alignment, and click on OK.

Editing the Control Objects

The black pawn, which is now on top of the white pawn, needs to have some nodes moved inward if there is to be any kind of noticeable Blend effect. This is because blends depend on there being a difference between the two control objects it uses to make the blend. You need some control over which areas will be different and which areas will contain no visible Blend effect; that's why the two pieces need to share the same space at present.

Think about where you'd like the lighting to show around the edges of the pawn. This is where you'll drag nodes (moving curve segments) inward.

But before you can edit the black pawn's nodes you have to be sure that you have it selected. In Wireframe the black and the white pawn look the same, so a quick trip to Preview mode is in order. To get there and back with the black pawn as the selected item, you should do the following:

- Click on the Wireframe button on the Ribbon Bar to return to Preview mode or press Shift+F9.

- Deselect everything by clicking on a blank portion of the Printable page.

- Click inside the black pawn, and return to Wireframe view by clicking on the Wireframe button on the Ribbon Bar or pressing Shift+F9. The Wireframe button is one of Corel's toggle buttons that take you back and forth from one state to another.

With the black pawn selected, you're ready to begin moving parts of the black pawn inward. Begin with the "straight" curve on the pawn's left side. You'll see how in the following steps:

1. Choose the Shape tool, and marquee-select the four nodes bordering the line between the neckpiece and the base on the left side of the black pawn. See figure 5.12 if you are uncertain about which four nodes you should select.

2. Click and drag the four nodes inwards about 1/8th-screen inch, as shown in figure 5.12. When the two shapes are blended, this part of the design will make a transition out from white, into black.

3. Continue "working" the black pawn profile inward, both on the left and right sides, until you get an illustration similar to that shown in figure 5.13.

Shading the Chess Piece with Blends

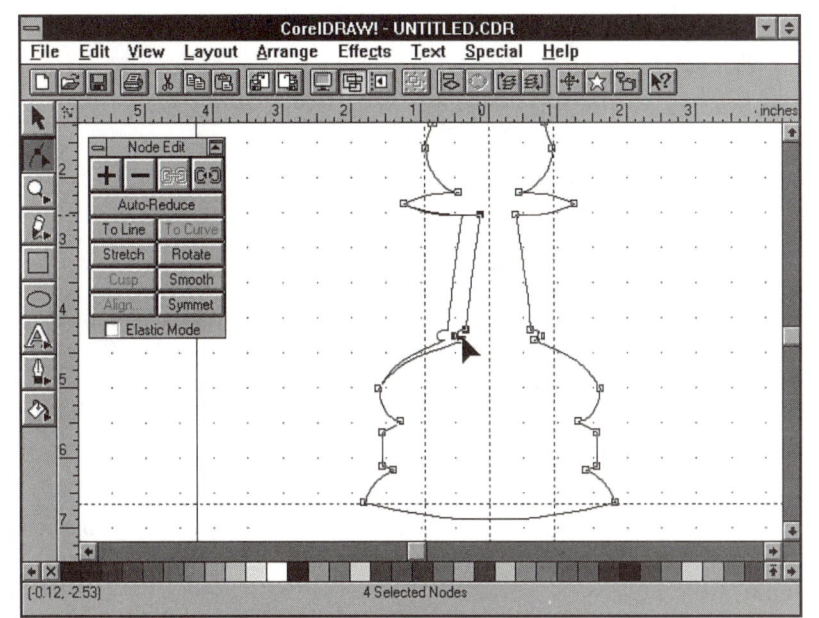

Figure 5.12

Marquee-selecting with the Shape tool selects nodes, not multiple objects.

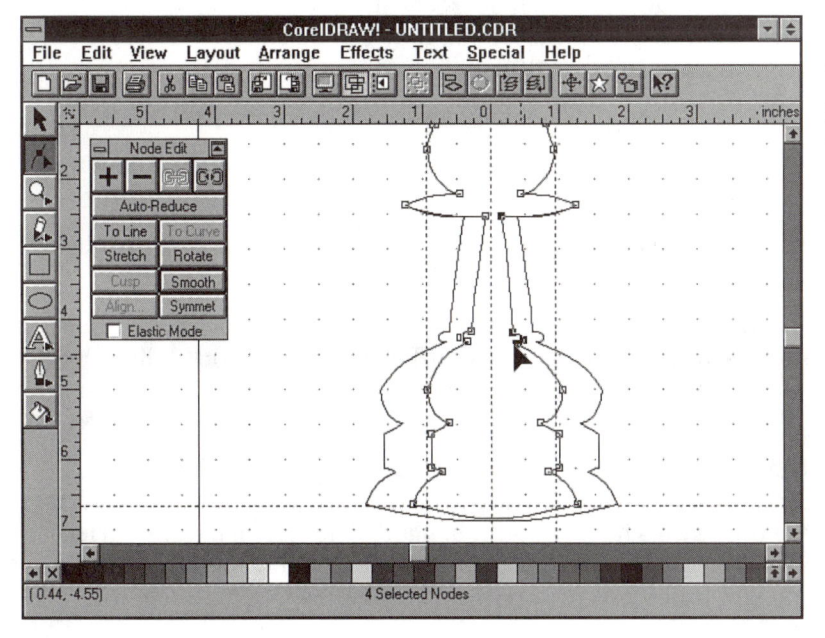

Figure 5.13

The inward profile you are modifying will determine the last control object of the blend.

Tip: Besides the marquee technique for selecting multiple nodes, you can also additively select them. Click on a single node; with the Shift key held down, click on others. This trick also works for selecting multiple objects with the Pick tool.

Topping Off the Second Control Object

The base and body of the black pawn should now be pushed inward. The differences between its present profile and the white pawn's profile will be spanned by the blend effect to produce hints of light around the edge of the pawn shape.

This leaves the head of the black pawn to modify. Ellipses that have been converted to curves via the Weld command take on cusp properties at the node points. Because the segments on each side of a node with cusp properties move independently of each other, making a smooth, matching curve on each side becomes difficult.

A quick solution is to convert the segments that make up the head into straight lines so the nodes may then be freely and precisely repositioned. Once the nodes are where you want them, they can be converted to smooth curves with segments neighboring them that are curved again.

To modify the head of your pawn, complete the following steps:

1. Scroll up to the pawn's head area. You don't have to use the Zoom tool here.

2. Marquee-select the three nodes that the curve segments pass through: left, right, and topmost.

3. You'll see the Cusp button go gray on the Node Edit Roll-Up, because the nodes are already cusps. Click on To Line on the Node Edit Roll-Up, as shown in figure 5.14. The properties of the curves will change from curved to straight line.

4. Now the nodes can be moved without having to cope with runaway control points and segments! Click and drag the three nodes toward the center of the pawn's head, as seen in figure 5.15. Then marquee-select the nodes, click on the To Curve Button, then on the Smooth button on the Node Edit Roll-Up to restore the shape.

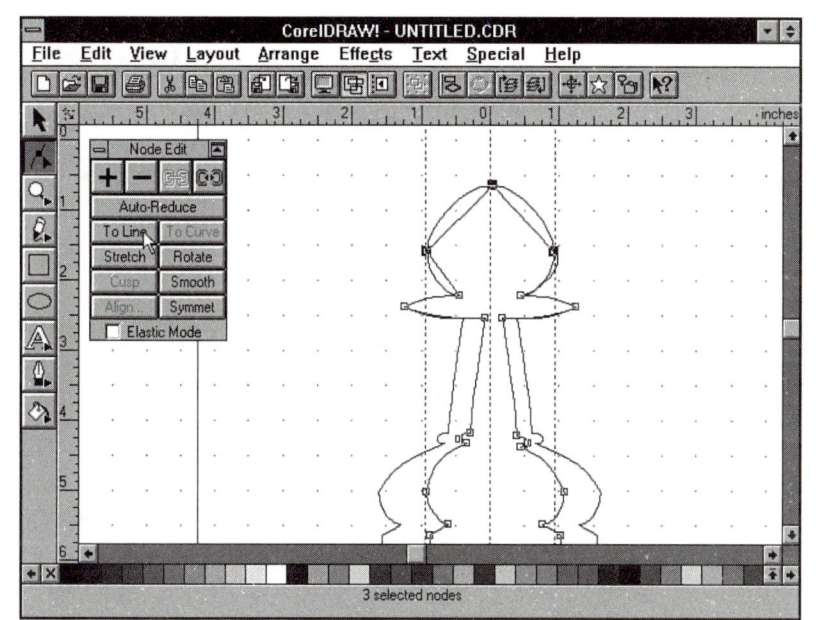

Figure 5.14

Node properties affect both the nodes and the segments they border.

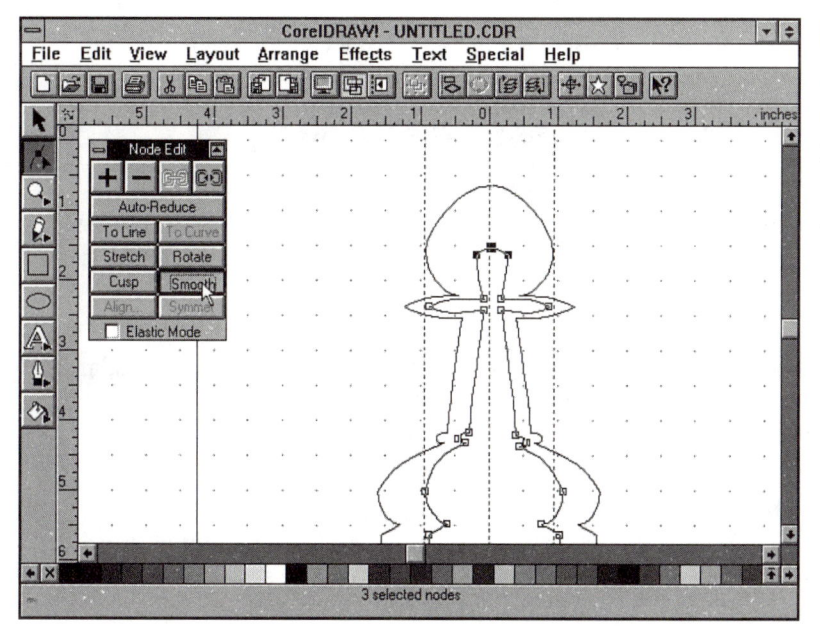

Figure 5.15

Nodes can be easily repositioned when you don't have to worry about altering curve segments.

Stop

What happens when a control object's node properties don't match the other's, and the Blend command is used? You wind up with a harsh, terrible-looking blend.

Smooth nodes make a gradual transition to cusp nodes, and the effect looks more like an afternoon spent with a Spirograph than even, natural shading.

Making a Backgound for the Pawn

You're almost ready now to use the Blend command. The effect will be great, but after all the preparation work you've done, you may find the act of performing it a little anticlimactic.

First of all, to get the most drama out of this piece, you need a black background, so the edges of the shaded pawn stand off from the Printable page. Complete the process by following these steps:

1. Choose the Rectangle tool, and marquee-drag a rectangle that surrounds the pawn on the page. You may want to zoom out at this point. The newly created rectangle becomes the currently selected object.

2. With your left mouse button, click on the black color swatch on the color palette at the bottom of the screen. Then click on the Wireframe button on the Ribbon Bar to toggle back to Preview mode so you can get a good look at the pawn with the background in place.

3. Click on the To Back button, as shown in figure 5.16, or press Shift+PgDn. This sends the selected object (the rectangle) to the back of the order of objects in the Drawing Window.

Using the Blend Command

The stage is set—you have your control objects created, filled, edited, and properly positioned. You've got a background in place so you can see the the effect of black shading to white. The moment you've been waiting for approaches. You'll "flick the switch" that lights up this pawn if you complete the following steps.

1. With the Pick tool, click on the white pawn and, while holding the Shift key down, click on the black pawn. The status line should say 2 Objects selected.

2. Click on the Wireframe button on the Ribbon Bar to return to Wireframe view. You'll want to get a good, behind-the-scenes look at what the Blend command does when you apply it. Choose Effects, Blend Roll-Up or press Ctrl+B to bring the Roll-Up on-screen.

Shading the Chess Piece wth Blends

Figure 5.16

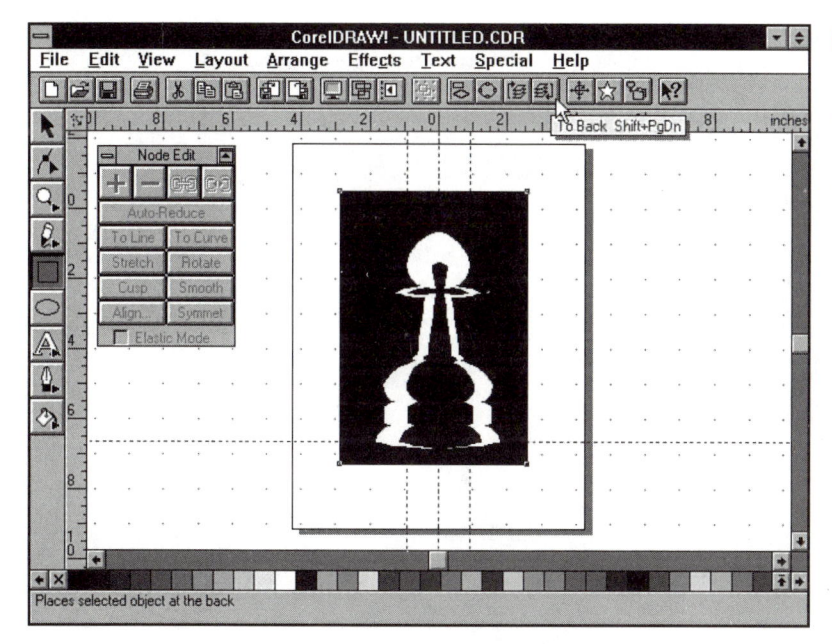

The To Back and To Front buttons can send a selection to the top or bottom of a collection of shapes.

3. Type **12** in the Steps entry field, and click on Apply. As you can see in figure 5.17, 12 blend steps produces a pretty impressive set of overlapping pawn pieces. To see what all these objects look like, return to the Preview mode, as seen in figure 5.18, by pressing the Wireframe button on the Ribbon Bar.

4. Press Ctrl+S (**F**ile, **S**ave), and name your work PAWN.CDR.

Stop

Depending on the complexity of the graphic you're creating, try to remember to limit the number of steps you assign to a blend. If you followed along in the last section, you now have 14 objects on the page, each consisting of many nodes and segments. The higher the number of blend steps, the smoother the shading you create, but the more taxing the illustration will be when your printer has to render the piece.

Strive for the minimum amount of graphical information to convey an idea. This doesn't mean skimp on your design work—just don't create excessively ornamental stuff that your printer may not be able to handle.

Chapter 5: Creating Shading with Shapes

Figure 5.17
The Blend command produces 12 transitional shapes and color fills between control objects.

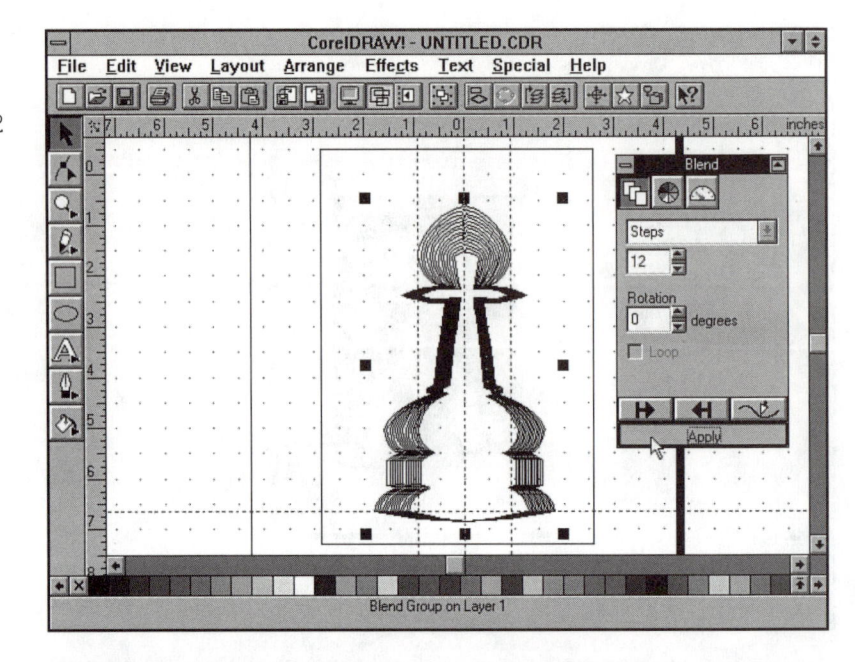

Figure 5.18
The fruits of your labor—a dimensional, dramatically lit pawn.

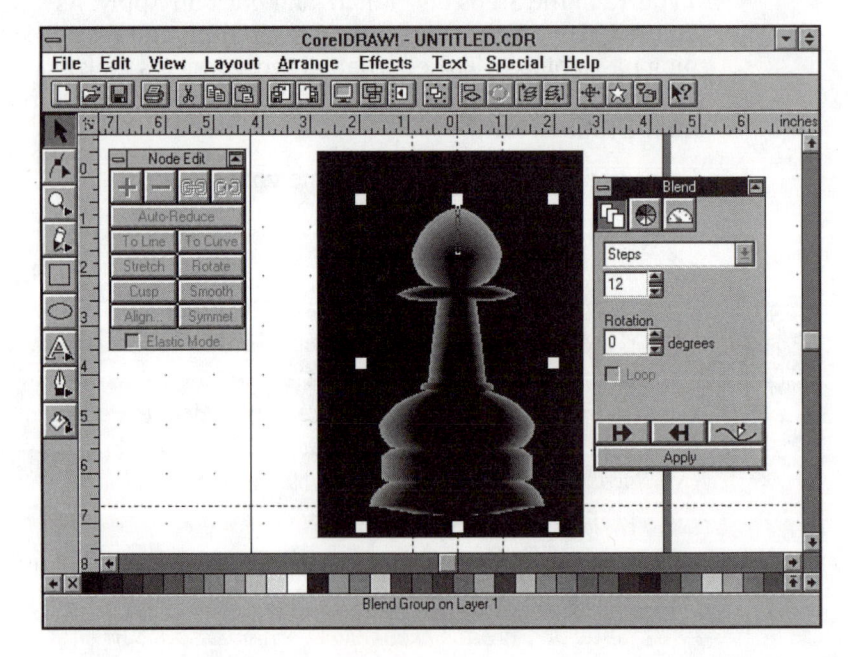

Using Layers To Protect Your Work

Because CorelDRAW objects can be modified independently of other objects, you have a rather loose collection of shapes that make up your pawn masterpiece at the moment. Also, because the blend is still modifiable, a wrong click on the piece can move a control object and send the blend spinning into a new, really ugly configuration.

One solution is always to group a collection of shapes, but a better one is to use CorelDRAW's Layer feature.

Adding a New Layer

Corel Layers are like sheets of transparent acetate piled one on top of another. You can work on a layer, open a new layer, and draw on the new one without disturbing what's on the other layers. And just like acetate, you can see what lies underneath your current layer. But Corel's Layers have additional properties that you'll get a chance to explore.

You have a twofold purpose here for working across layers: you'll lock Layer 1 (the default layer each time you open a new page) so the pawn is protected, and you'll place a new layer on top of Layer 1 where you can continue to design. You do this without having to worry about disturbing the work you've already done. Follow these steps:

1. Your workspace is going to get a little cluttered with three Roll-Ups extended, so click on the Blend Roll-Up's upper right corner triangle to retract it, and click and drag on its title bar to position it in an out-of-the-way place in the Drawing window.

2. Choose **L**ayout, and **L**ayers Roll-Up (or press Ctrl+F3).

   Each layer has different attributes or properties, most of which you can change. The icons represent a status for a layer: the grid is visible (tiny monitor icon), and locked (tiny lock icon), whereas Layer 1, which holds the pawn, is the only layer sporting a printer icon. This means only the pawn prints; no grids or guidelines will be rendered to paper by your printer.

3. Click on the fly-out menu arrow near the top of the Layers Roll-Up, and choose New.

4. Accept the defaults you see shown in figure 5.18. You want this new layer to be printable and visible. Although you can type in a name like Fred, **Layer 2** is a perfectly evocative and adequate name.

Chapter 5: Creating Shading with Shapes

Figure 5.19

The Layers Roll-Up is where you can add layers, or redefine the properties of existing ones.

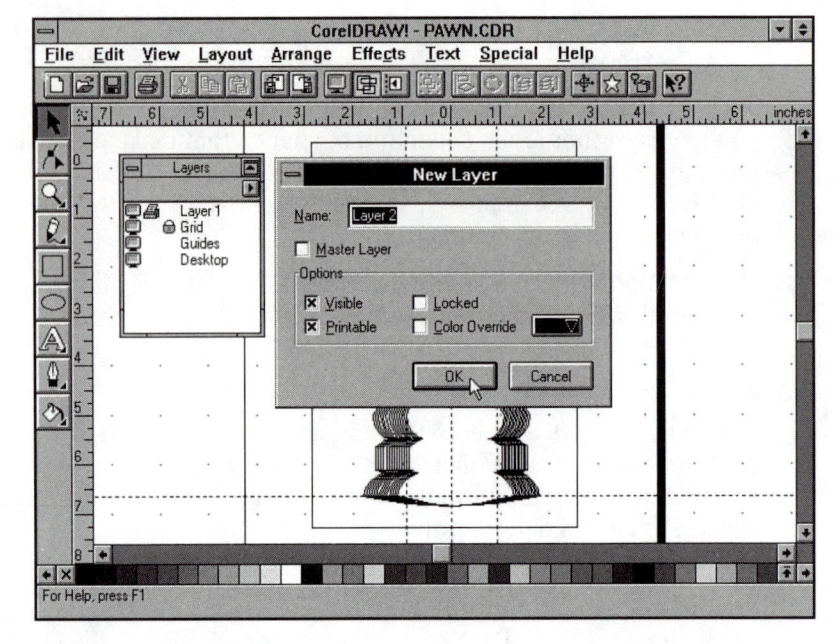

5. Click on OK.

6. Click on the Layer 1 title on the Layers Roll-Up, and choose Edit from the menu fly-out.

7. Click on the **L**ocked option, and click on OK. You can't draw on the layer selected on the Roll-Up if it's locked.

8. Click on the Layer 2 title on the Layers Roll-Up. By default, each new layer created is editable, visible, and printable.

Closer Look

Each new layer you create falls on top of the previous one, and Layer 1 (the one each new CorelDRAW session opens with) is beneath all the CorelDRAW-defined layers such as Grid and Desktop.

If you want to change the arrangement of layers, go to the Layers Roll-Up and click on the title of the layer you want to move. Drag the title up or down to the place in the stack you want it to be. In the following figures, Layers 1 and 2 have been dragged to the top of the "pile." Therefore, any guidelines in use will appear *behind* lines, rectangles, and other drawn stuff. With this arrangement of the layers, drawn objects can be clearly seen. Customizing Layer hierarchy is simply a matter of preference you should evaluate for your own work.

Secret Powers of Blending Lines

Lines that are not part of a closed path have their uses as design elements, too. Although you can't fill them, you can still color them, and even blend two open line paths together. This is a very special feature that yields fantastic results, and is one you'll cover next to add little glints of highlight to the pawn.

There are one or two areas on the pawn that can be made more dimensional with a well-designed highlight, in particular where the base meets the body of the pawn. Right now, it's a mass of black, and in real life, highlights would be evident where the shape makes a sharp dip inward.

Zoom into this area and draw a simple two-node line that you'll modify and dress up to create the highlight by following these steps:

1. Click on the Zoom tool and select the Zoom In tool.
2. Marquee-zoom into the area at about the 6" mark on the vertical ruler and zero on the horizontal ruler.
3. Click on the Wireframe button on the Ribbon Bar, because there's *no way* you're going to see a thin black line on top of the black area of the chess piece otherwise.
4. Choose the Freehand (Pencil) tool, and click a point on the black pawn where the left side has a cusp node (where the profile sharply dips inward).
5. Click another time to the right, where the mirror of the pawn profile dips in.
6. Choose the Shape tool, and double-click in the center of the line you created. Press the To Curve button on the node Edit Roll-Up.
7. Click and drag the center of the curve segment down very slightly, as seen in figure 5.20, so it arcs similarly to the curve that forms the base of the pawn.

Figure 5.20

A single segment has two control points, and is bordered by two nodes.

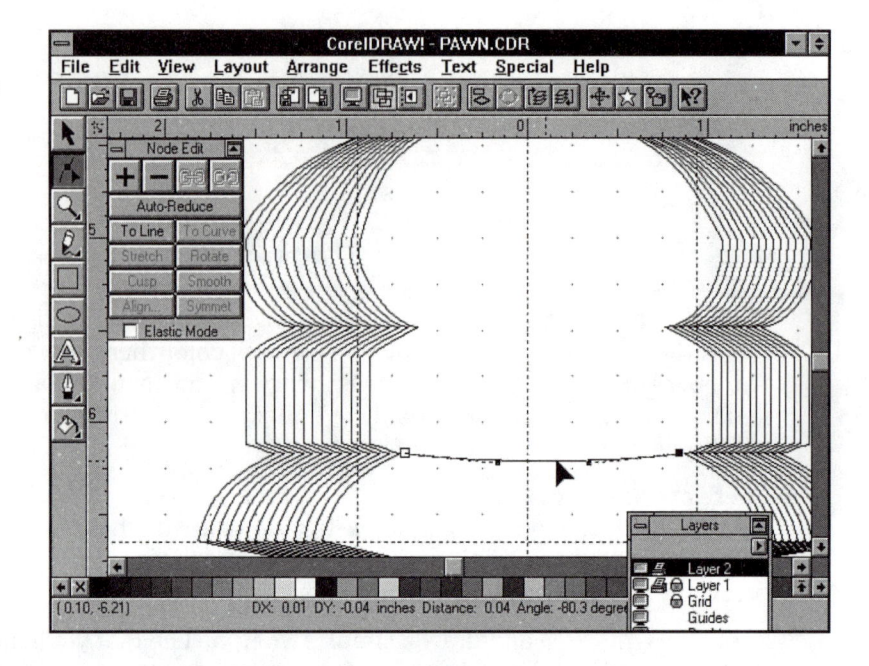

Giving the Wireframe Some Outline Characteristics

The segment you curved in the last section isn't exactly a shape yet. Strictly speaking, it's a wireframe; it can't be filled, but *outline* attributes can be assigned to it—here's your chance to explore the Outline menu fly-out.

The pawn highlights can also be created using the Blend effect. But unlike a blend between two slightly different shapes with different fills, the Blend technique using open line segments provides the most pleasant results when the two control objects have different thicknesses. Make the first control curve really wide by following these steps:

1. With the curve selected, click on the Outline tool (the fountain pen icon on the Toolbox).

2. Click on the Outline Dialog tool (the first button on the fly-out that has an identical icon to the Outline tool).

3. Type **.2** in the Width box. Two-tenths of an inch is a hefty outline for the curve segment, but it's necessary as the first control object in the blend.

Secret Powers of Blending Lines

173

4. Click on the middle Line Caps selection. This will give the segment a rounded end at each node.

5. Click on **S**cale With Image, and click on OK. Your settings in the Outline Pen dialog box should look like figure 5.21. In Preview mode, this appears as a wide black outline with blunt ends.

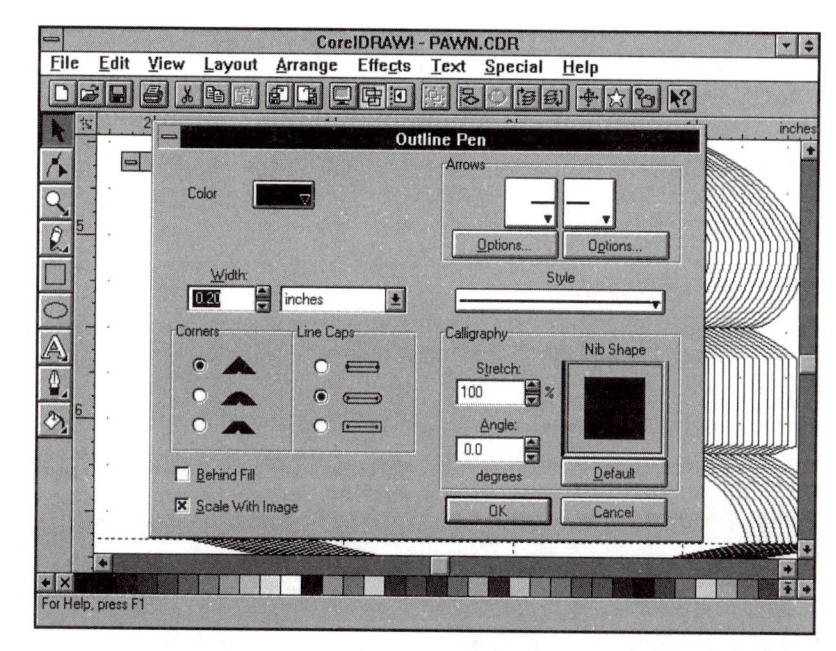

Figure 5.21
Set all the outline characteristics for your wireframe curve segment in the Outline Pen dialog box.

As the name suggests, the **S**cale with Image attribute will make your outline shrink in width if you ever decide to shrink this pawn illustration in overall size.

If you *don't* click this option, and scale the pawn down to ant-size, the outline of the segment would still be .2 inches wide, and out of proportion with the rest of the objects.

Tip

Coloring an outline can actually be performed five ways:

■ By clicking on a preset value on the Outline tool menu fly-out.

■ By right-mouse clicking on the color palette.

Chapter 5: Creating Shading with Shapes

- By selecting a color from a color model in the Outline Pen dialog box.
- By selecting a color from the Outline Color dialog box, which is accessed by pressing on the Outline Color tool (the color wheel button on the Outline tool menu fly-out).
- By selecting a color from the Pen Roll-Up.

Creating the Second Control Segment

Next, create a second control object segment and give it a different width and color. You accomplish this using almost the same method you used when you copied and modified the pawn shape earlier in the chapter:

1. The curved segment should still be selected; if not, click on it with the Pick tool. When you have the segment selected, press the + key on the keypad to duplicate the segment.

2. Click on the Outline tool, and select the Hairline Outline tool from the top row of buttons. The duplicate line segment will have an outline of only .003", but it will still have the same blunted ends and scale with image attributes that the original line had. Click on the Outline tool and choose the White Outline Color tool, as seen in figure 5.22.

Figure 5.22

You have seven preset grayscale values on the Outline tool fly-out menu.

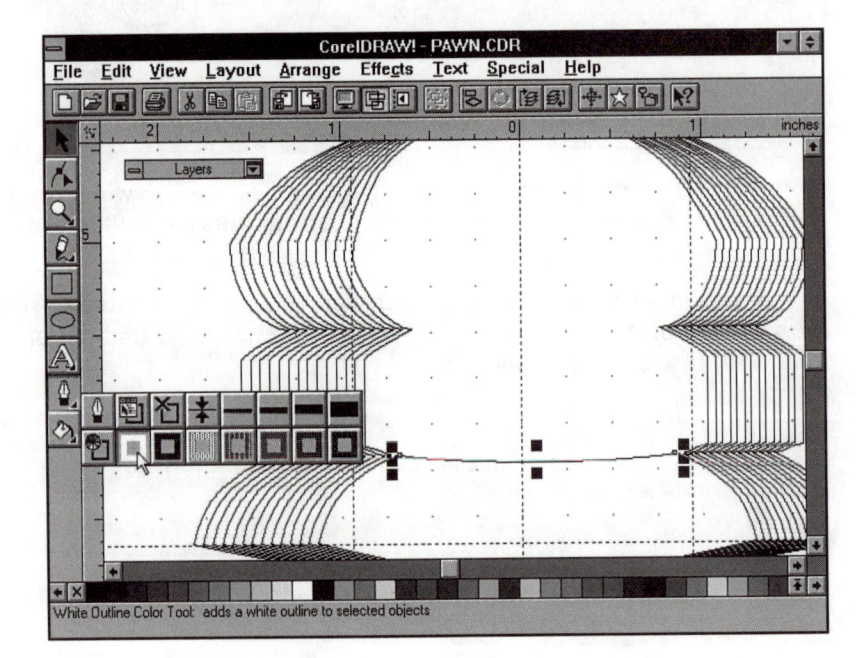

Secret Powers of Blending Lines

3. To align the two segments, follow these steps:

   a. Choose **E**dit.

   b. Select **A**ll.

   c. Press the Align button on the Ribbon Bar.

   d. Choose **C**enter in both the horizontal and vertical fields of the dialog box.

   e. Click on OK.

Note

The Select **A**ll command doesn't include the pawn piece on Layer 1 because that layer is locked.

4. Deselect both segments by clicking your cursor on a vacant area of the Printable page.

5. Click on the white, .003" segment with the Pick tool. It's hard to tell which one you've selected while viewing in Wireframe view, so check the status line to confirm your choice.

If you picked the white one, move on to the next section. If not, press the Tab key. In CorelDRAW, the Tab key moves you from one selectable object to another on an unlocked layer. Because there are only two possible choices at present, pressing the Tab key toggles between selecting the black segment and the white segment.

Closer Look

The Tab key maneuver only works if you have an object selected in the Drawing Window to begin with.

Using the Break Apart Command to Separate Segment Parts

Using the blend steps will make a transition between the wide black and narrow white segments. The effect produced can even be heightened by making the white segment shorter in addition to being narrower. The trick is to keep the shorter, white segment placed exactly over the wide black one; the blend will be pronounced at either end, but smooth when it reaches the middle of the segments.

To do this, break the white line at two points and delete each end. The remaining center portion of the line remains positioned in the same spot as the wide black line. You don't have to fuss with moving nodes that border a curved, uncooperative line.

1. With the white segment still selected (check the status line to make sure), choose the Shape tool, and click on a point that is right around the –3/16th" mark, as shown in figure 5.23. Click on the Break Apart button on the Node Edit Roll-Up (the little-chain-links-coming-apart icon in the upper right corner).

   There's a big difference between making a break in a path with the Shape tool and actually breaking the path into two separate objects. At present, you have one line that's an open path, with four nodes that define two segments that are still part of the same path. Now that you have a break point defined, separate and delete the part of the segment on the left.

2. Choose **A**rrange, **B**reak Apart (or press Ctrl+K). The status line will report that you have 2 Objects Selected.

3. Because you only want the left segment, press the spacebar to get the Pick tool. Place the Pick tool in the center of the line, and Shift+click once to deselect one of the two selected objects.

4. The left line segment is now selected. Press the Del key.

Note

Just as you can add to a selection by pressing the Shift key while clicking on different shapes, you can subtract from the bunch by pressing the Shift key while you click. This removes the object you're clicking on from the selection.

Secret Powers of Blending Lines

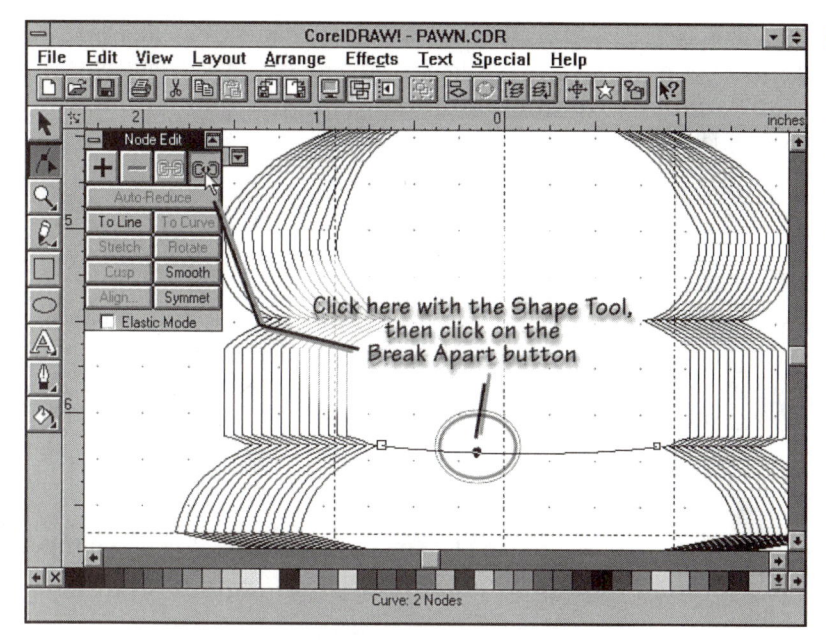

Figure 5.23
The Break Apart command separates parts of a segment from a path.

5. Repeat steps 1–4 to shorten the right side of the line segment. As you can see in figure 5.24, the white line is still perfectly positioned over the black line, but it measures about one third of its former length.

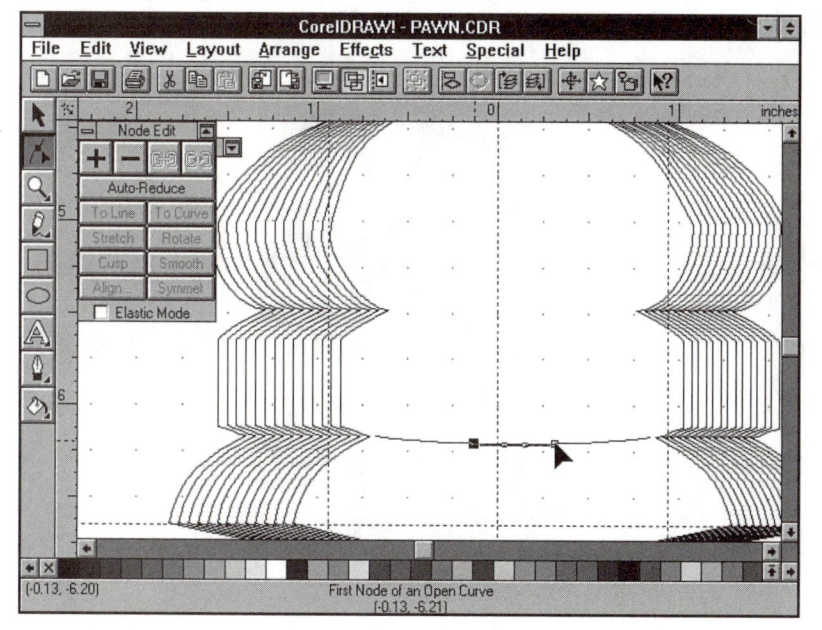

Figure 5.24
The white line is now shorter and narrower than the black line.

Even when you break off one line segment from another, each line still has the same outline attributes. In this case, the segment left on the Printable page has a .003" white outline with rounded ends and will shrink in scale if you resize it.

Tip

Realizing the Blend Effect

Your hard work pays off when you use the Blend command on these two segments. You'll work in Preview mode for this step. Selecting both objects within the pawn shape will be easy, because the pawn is locked on Layer 1 and can't accidentally be selected.

1. Click on the Wireframe mode button on the Ribbon Bar to return to the editable Preview view.

2. Choose Edit, Select All, or double-click on the Pick Tool. Roll down the Blend Roll-Up by pressing on the down-pointing arrow in the upper right corner.

3. Type **10** in the Steps field, and press Apply. You should get a dramatic highlight on the pawn like the one in figure 5.25.

Figure 5.25

The Blend effect creates ten transitional shapes whose differences in color create a soft highlight.

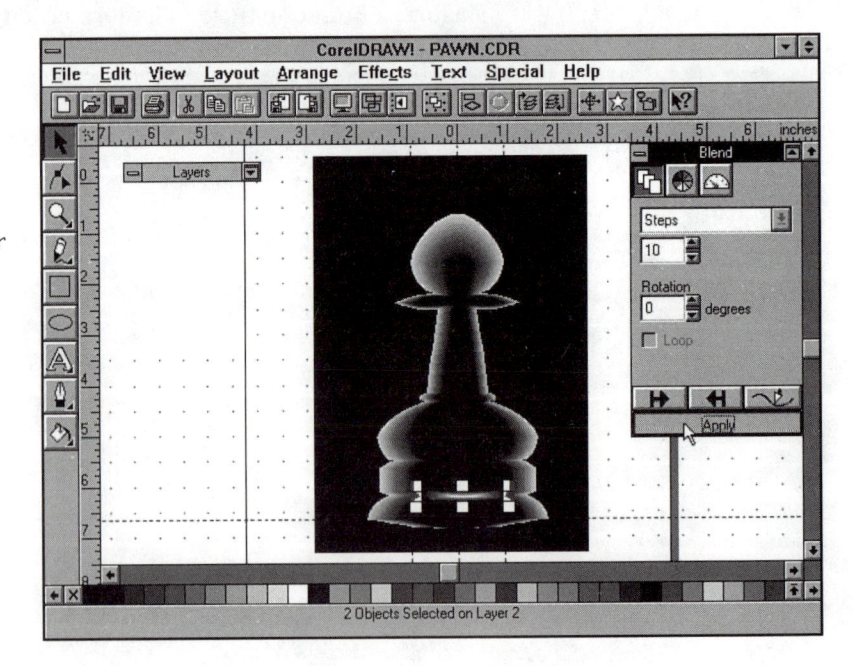

Duplicating Your Blending Work

CorelDRAW's capability to duplicate single objects, groups, or linked objects makes it nearly effortless to re-create effects like you've just done with only a mouse click or two. To conclude the pawn shading adventure, let's add a second highlight above the first by using a Duplicate command shortcut.

1. With the composite Blend still selected, click and drag upwards. You're moving the Blend objects away from their intended position, but bear with me here.

2. When the Blend objects are about 1/4" above their original location, press the right mouse button (both buttons are held down at the moment).

3. Release both buttons and *boing* (or some other sound effect)—you've performed a *manual* Duplicate command, as shown in figure 5.26.

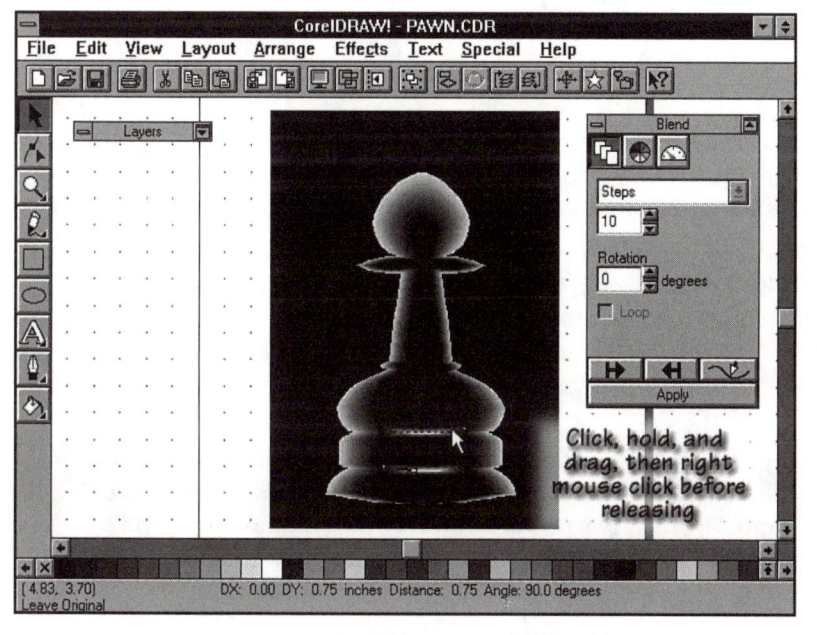

Figure 5.26

Duplicating the highlight is the last step to the finished design.

Tip

Duplicating objects can also be performed by choosing <u>E</u>dit, <u>D</u>uplicate, or simply by using the keyboard shortcut Ctrl+D. Duplicating should *not* be confused with copying, though. Duplicate is an internal CorelDRAW command, and the preferred method of making an extra, identical shape. Copying something (Ctrl+C) involves Windows' Clipboard, and if you have a precious item stored on it at any given moment, your Corel copy will replace it.

You now have a pretty smart piece of work before you! Congratulations are certainly in order. You should save your chess piece again, because you'll be using it in the next chapter as a subject in a much grander composition.

Don't worry that the segment blend is on a different layer than the pawn right now—you'll be using the Layers Roll-Up in Chapter 6, "Making a Scene," where you'll put the pieces together.

Summary

Although this chapter has been focused around the special effect of the Blend command, reflect on what you've learned about node editing, using Layers, and using Corel's unique Roll-Ups.

You've created a very lifelike chess piece, but more importantly you now own the skills to create a rook, bishop, industrial air conditioner part, or whatever you need to communicate a graphic idea with realistic lighting.

Digging Deeper Into the Bag of Tricks

With the exception of Gilligan, no man is an island, and no illustration of a foreground object (like the pawn) is complete without a supporting *background*. In Chapter 6 you'll learn some new techniques, more of Corel's automated features, and a terrific way to design a graphic that you can place the pawn within.

As your world of experience expands with CorelDRAW, you'll learn to create universes within your design work.

Getting the big Picture...

CHAPTER 6

Making a Scene

In art school, my Still Life professor would constantly lament that I spent too much time rendering a foreground object without paying attention to "supporting elements." It took me a while to realize that he meant a *background*.

Lack of background makes an element sit on a page rather than fit into it, and ruins the viewer's depth perception of even the most beautifully rendered object. Backgrounds help an audience put foreground images in a context, and keep the eye moving from area to area. This makes static geometry more dynamic and flowing and, most importantly, can improve your grade point average if you have Mr. Fricke for Basic Design I.

Let's use the chess piece you designed in Chapter 5 as the focus of this chapter, as you take a CorelDRAWing seminar on the design element called the background. This is the part of your work that will make the difference between designing an illustration and creating a piece of clip art.

In this chapter, you:

- Mirror objects to create a chessboard
- Dimensionalize stuff with the Extrude effect
- Work across pages and layers
- Create your own pattern fill

Working with the Multi-Page Feature

As you saw in the last chapter, the Layers command is great for building a stack of objects that, when drawn on separate layers, can be locked, or even invisible.

But there's another CorelDRAW feature you can use, when designing several compositional elements, to keep your Drawing Window fresh each time you want to build additional pieces (like the chess piece background discussed

Chapter 6: Making a Scene

in this chapter). CorelDRAW versions 4 and 5 have multi-page layout capabilities; this means you can draw a pawn (as you already have done) and begin a new page within the same CorelDRAW file. In this example, your access to the pawn is only a mouse click away. The multi-page feature can be used for a variety of purposes (such as designing a four-page flyer), but you'll use it in this assignment to build a background for the pawn, into which the chess piece can easily be moved later.

1. Open the PAWN.CDR file from your hard disk.

Tip

CorelDRAW has a recently used file list under the File command, listing the last four designs you've saved to disk. If you haven't been exceptionally experimental between Chapter 5 and this chapter, you can find PAWN.CDR at the bottom of the File menu. Click on the name to open the file, or hot key your way there by pressing Alt+F, and then 1, 2, 3, or 4.

2. Press either the Page Up or Page Down key (the long way around to adding a page is Layout, Insert Page...). The Insert Page dialog box is displayed (see fig. 6.1).

3. By default, Corel adds a single page after the current one. Click on OK to accept the default settings.

Figure 6.1

You can insert one or more pages before or after the current Printable page.

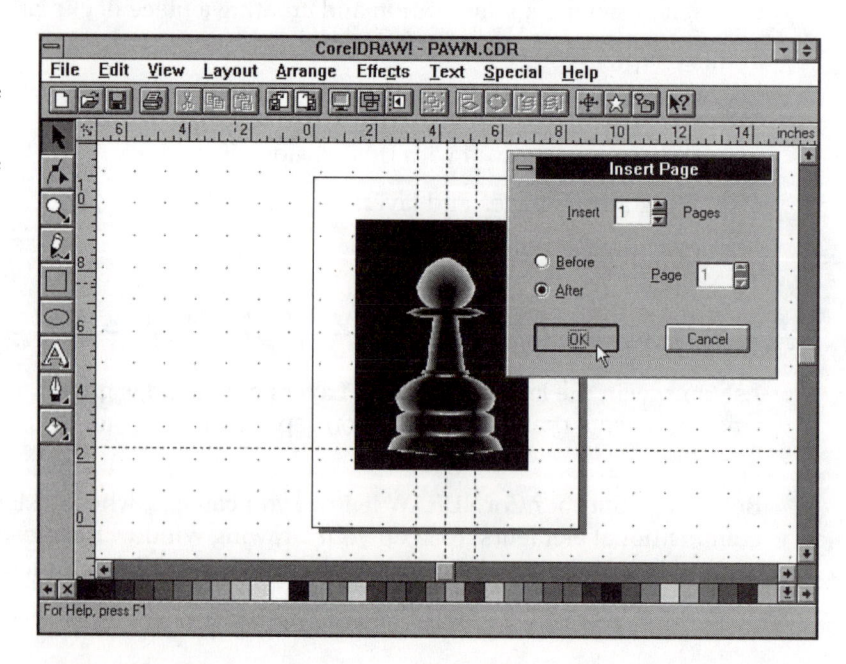

You're immediately moved to a view of the page you inserted; notice that Page Controls appear above the color palette on the left. They indicate that you are presently viewing page 2 of 2. Clicking on the left arrow moves you to the previous page, and clicking on the + button will move you ahead one page.

Deleting the Guidelines

If you followed the exercises in Chapter 5, your workspace contains vertical and horizontal guidelines. Although guidelines are helpful in many instances, the following exercise does not need them. The process for deleting guidelines is simple.

1. Double-click on a vertical guideline.
2. In the Guidelines setup dialog box, click Delete All.
3. In the View area, click on the Horizontal Guidelines radio button.
4. Press Delete All again, then click on OK. The guidelines are gone from all page views of PAWN.CDR.

Duplicating and Mirroring Objects

In the next steps, you'll use a CorelDRAW shortcut to design a mini-chessboard as a background element. You don't need to design a whole 64-square board (mostly because you don't have a whole chess set designed). You'll stylize the look of the mini-board you create so that the white squares aren't necessary.

You can mirror (horizontally and vertically flip) objects by holding the Ctrl key down while dragging a selection handle in a horizontal or vertical direction. The square you'll use to create the chessboard doesn't actually need to be mirrored because it's perfectly square. If you use the mirroring technique developed in this chapter, however, you can precisely reposition duplicates of the square at an identical distance from the original to create the chessboard without any measuring or math involved.

These next steps are a lot like a dime store game where you shuffle squares around in a frame. Since these squares aren't numbered, however, this assignment is more fun than frustrating!

Because you last designed on Layer 2 in PAWN.CDR in Chapter 5, Corel, by default, presents the new page to you with Layer 2 as the active layer.

Chapter 6: Making a Scene

To create the chessboard squares, follow these steps:

1. Choose the Rectangle tool. With the Ctrl key pressed, click and drag a square in the upper left of the Printable page. Stop when the status line tells you it's about 2 1/2".

2. Left-mouse click on the 40% black swatch on the color palette (hint: the status line will display the color name of the swatch you have your cursor over), then right-mouse click on the white swatch. Your square will now have a white 0.003" outline with a light gray fill, as shown in figure 6.2.

Figure 6.2

The white hairline around the square will help separate it from other objects you'll draw later.

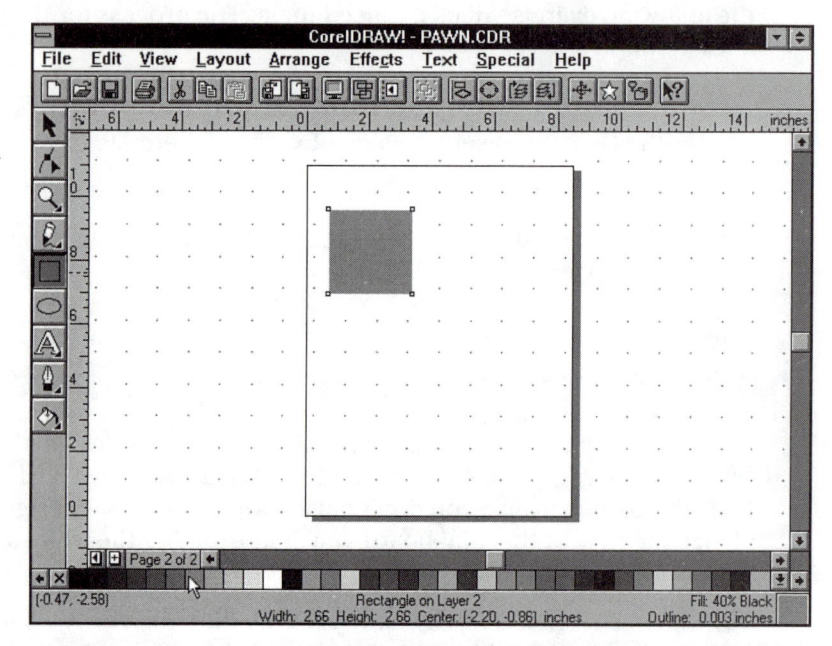

3. It's duplicating time! Press the spacebar to get the Pick tool, and move the crosshair cursor over the the 9 o'clock selection handle on the square. Press down the Ctrl key and hold it down until you are told to release it in step 5. Then click on the 9 o'clock selection handle and drag the selection handle across the square (to the right). Don't let go of the left mouse button or the Ctrl key yet.

4. When a dotted outline of the square appears, press down on the right mouse button, so both the left and right mouse buttons are pressed

down. Release both mouse buttons. Now you can release the Crtl key. You'll have duplicated (made an identical copy) and mirrored (flipped) the 2 1/2" square so it sits flush with the right of the original. This is a "visual" technique, so check out the dance steps in figure 6.3.

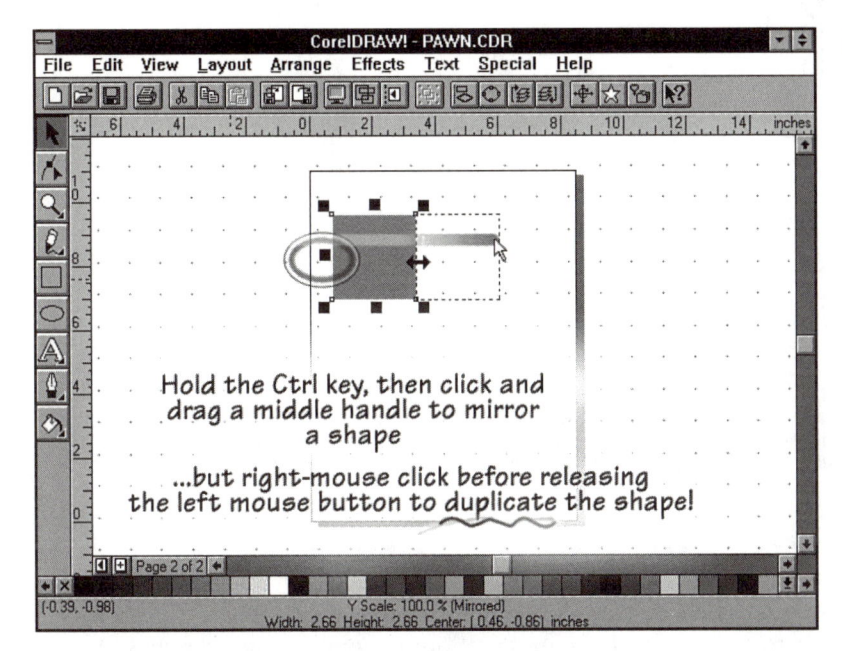

Figure 6.3

By duplicating and mirroring, you also precisely place the duplicate next to the original.

5. You want to move this duplicate square one "space" away to suggest a white square separating the two, so hold the Ctrl key and click+drag the duplicate's 9 o'clock selection handle to the right, the same as you did with the original. This time, however, don't right-mouse click to duplicate the square.

6. Fun, isn't it? Continue to duplicate squares. To duplicate downward, drag the 12 o'clock selection handle down across the square using this technique. In figure 6.4, I've duplicated and mirrored down one row, and am proceeding to create a three-row, three-column chessboard for the pawn. You should, too.

Figure 6.4
Use horizontal and vertical mirroring, then duplicating, to create five squares with equal spaces surrounding them.

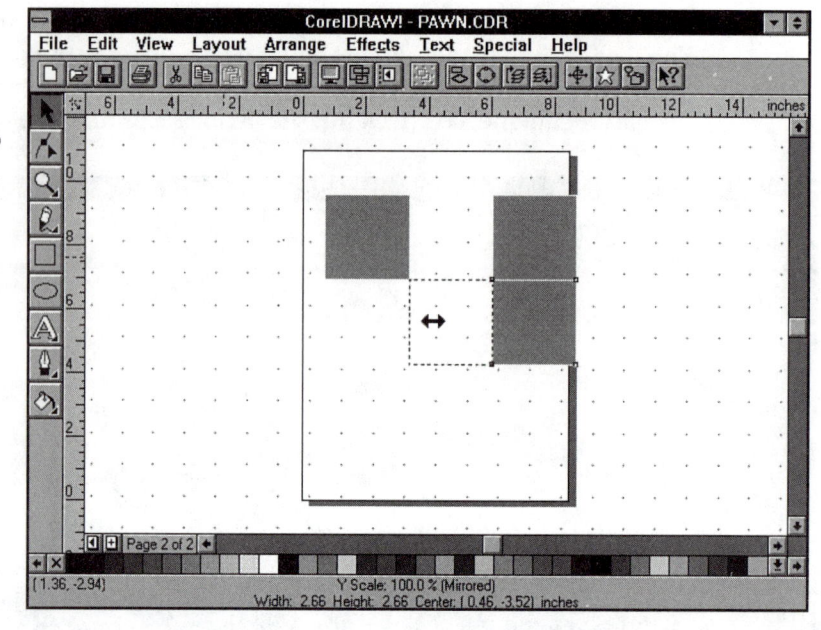

Adding Perspective to Objects

One of the nicest things designers discover when they start with CorelDRAW is that vector graphics can be rotated without producing jagged edges around their outlines. This ability to smoothly rotate and otherwise distort an object leads to exciting design possibilities. While artists still using Brand X produce staid, ho-hum, even-column-and-line layouts, Corel users can dimensionalize artwork by angling it in any direction to create eye-catching perspectives.

Rotating Objects

You may have noticed that if you double-click on an object that you've drawn, the first click produces eight selection handles around the object, but the second click surrounds the object with strange curved and straight double-headed arrows. The second click took you to Corel's Rotate and Skew mode. Rotation and skewing are related actions; access to these commands is found on the same Transformation Roll-Up or by double-clicking an object. They are, however, by no means interchangeable effects.

When you rotate an object, the object retains its shape, but it's tilted, as though you were viewing a horizon aboard a ship that's sailing choppy seas.

Adding Perspective to Objects

When you skew an object, the angles within the object itself change. The Leaning Tower of Pisa and italic type are skewed.

In Corel's Rotate and Skew mode, clicking and dragging curved double-headed arrows will rotate the object and dragging on the straight double-headed arrows will skew and object.

The chessboard at present looks a little flat, and is not as visually interesting as it could be. It also looks more like a place to frame a chess piece than where one could sit. Rotating the squares is your first stop in the process of making this chessboard a visually exciting dimensional design element. Here's how:

1. Choose **E**dit, Select **A**ll from the menu (or marquee-select the bunch with the Pick tool), then press Ctrl+L (or choose **A**rrange, **C**ombine from the menu). All five squares are now one object (with five subpaths), and none will drift away during the changes you'll put them through.

2. With the chessboard selected, click on it a second time (anywhere you see colored fill is a good place to click). Clicking on a selected object takes you to a different mode—Rotating and Skewing. Figure 6.5 shows what each screen element surrounding the selected object does.

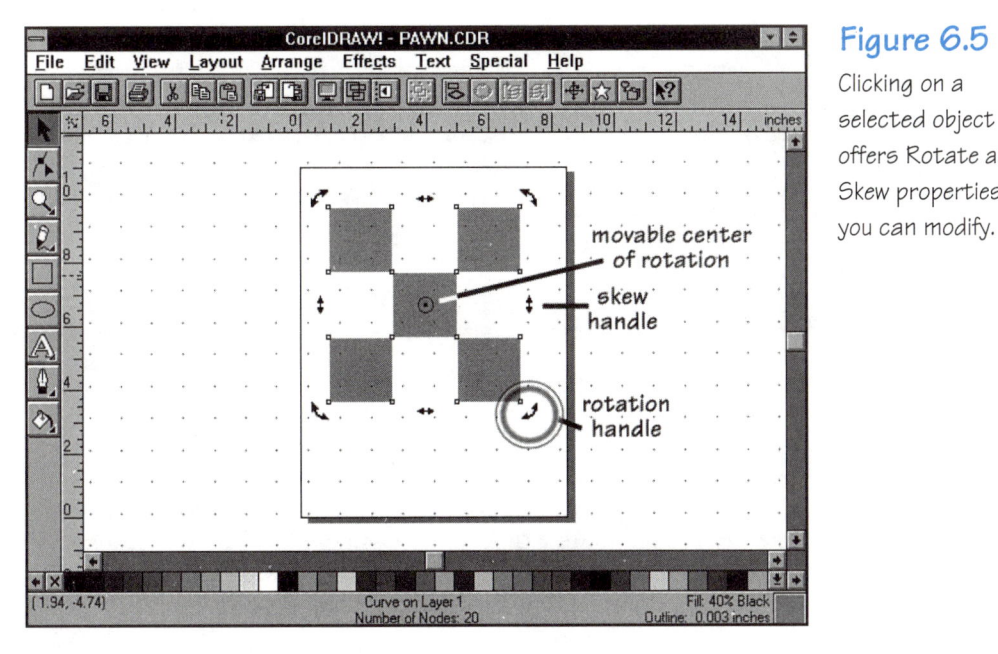

Figure 6.5

Clicking on a selected object offers Rotate and Skew properties you can modify.

3. Let's turn the chessboard slightly counterclockwise. Click on the bottom-right rotate handle (circled in the last figure), and drag it upwards until the status line says about 23–25°, as shown in figure 6.6. You may not see the effects of the rotation immediately, but instead see an outline of your proposed changes. Your cursor will turn into a special indicator of the function being performed.

Figure 6.6
Freeform-rotate an object by clicking and dragging on a corner rotation handle.

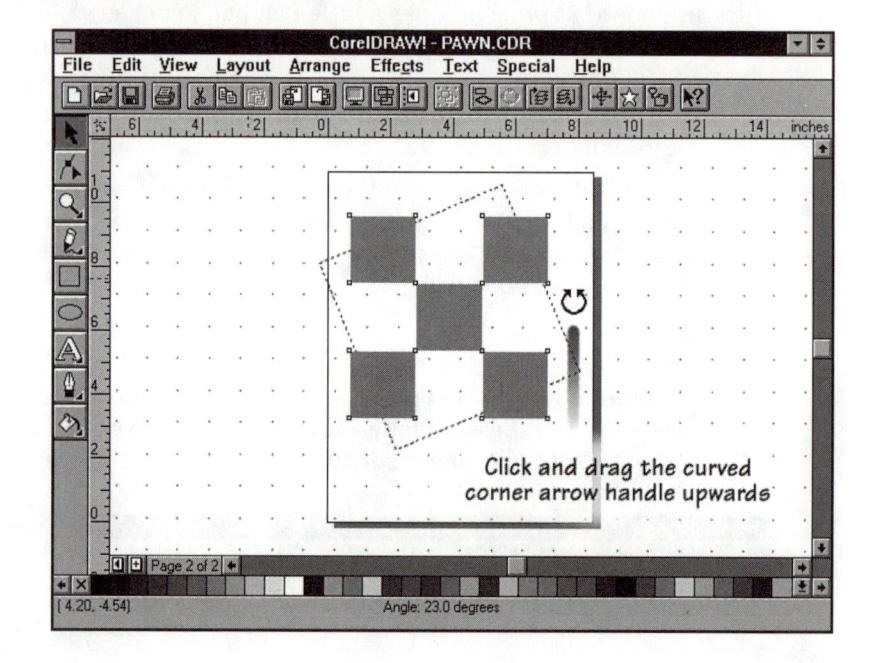

Click and drag the curved corner arrow handle upwards

Tip

For some reason no one understands, rotation is specified and reported on the status line as positive degrees when you rotate counterclockwise, and negative degrees in the clockwise direction in Corel.

Changing Perspective

The Perspective command in CorelDRAW is an invaluable feature for re-arranging a selection to simulate a different viewing angle. You're actually changing the object, not the view you're seeing of it in the Drawing Window. It's a very user-friendly command; when you use it next, you might be reminded of the perspective drawings seen in classical design books and taught in architectural school.

The idea here is to modify the chessboard so it takes on a look similar to that of the pawn. The pawn looks like it is being viewed from a perspective very near the ground.

To change the perspective of the chessboard, follow these steps:

1. Choose Effects, Add Perspective from the menu. Add Perspective is a self-contained command that offers no additional functionality through other tools or Roll-Ups.

   The dotted Perspective boundary box has four corner control handles on it, which you manipulate in the same way that you manipulate nodes that connect line segments. In fact, you'll notice the Shape tool automatically becomes the current editing tool while in the Perspective command.

2. Click on the bottom left Perspective handle, and drag it up and to the left. The front of the chessboard appears to come toward you, while the back steeply recedes.

3. Click and drag the bottom right Perspective handle up and to the right so the Perspective effect is symmetrical, as shown in figure 6.7.

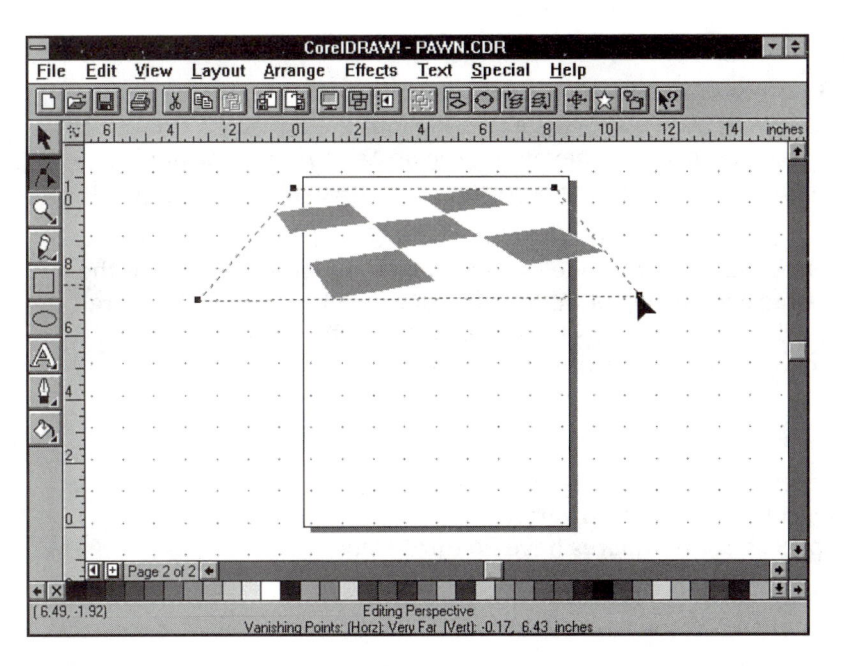

Figure 6.7

You create the impression something is viewed at an angle other than perpendicular to the page when you use Perspective.

4. Get the chessboard back on the Printable page, lest you forget and try printing this thing. Press the spacebar to switch to the Pick tool; click and drag on a corner selection handle to resize the chessboard so that the entire board will fit on the Printable page. Then position it anywhere you like within the page.

Note

Another helpful item under the Effe<u>c</u>ts menu is the <u>C</u>lear Transformations command. If you don't like the Perspective you've added to an object and want to remove the effect entirely, use this command. The Clear Transformations command removes any Perspective that has been applied to a selected shape, along with any other effects that have been applied to the object.

You can't edit the nodes of a shape that has a Perspective around it, but you can directly modify a Perspective by selecting the Shape tool and dragging on the Perspective corners.

The only way you can node-edit a shape that's experiencing a Perspective is by Converting to Cur<u>v</u>es (Ctrl+Q); this causes you to lose the ability to edit the Perspective any further.

Understanding Vanishing Points

You may have been taught the principle of vanishing points in grade school with an example of train tracks disappearing into the horizon. CorelDRAW sports vanishing points—whenever you see an "X" on-screen while Perspective editing, the "X" marks either a horizontal or vertical vanishing point.

You can click and drag on the vanishing point "X" to further automate the task of altering perspective while in this command. But be aware that the closer you drag a vanishing point toward your selected object, the more distorted it will get. It does this to suggest that the horizon of an image is extremely close, and that the object recedes to miles away.

Adding a Third Dimension

While the chessboard now leaps at the viewer at a very dramatic angle, its three-dimensionality is a bit thwarted by its lack of depth; the scene suggests 3D space, but the squares have no third plane.

This is easy to fix with the Extrude command. Version 5 of CorelDRAW has refined this feature to such an extent that it rivals the capability of some 3D

Adding Perspective to Objects

CAD modeling programs. Yet Corel's Extrude is push-button simple. Just select the proper option, and Corel will automatically shade an extruded shape while taking into account the viewing perspective.

Use the Extrude command to turn these squares into tiles.

1. With the chessboard selected, Press Ctrl+E (or from the menu, select Effe**c**ts, E**x**trude Roll-Up). Then click on the second button from the left, on the top row of the Extrude Roll-Up. It's the one with the picture of a 3D rectangle.

2. The Extrude Roll-Up is a beautifully laid-out visual guide to, well... *extruding* stuff! First, the Extrude command can be set to add front or back facets of a 3D shape to the original, flat-plane shape. Choose Back Parallel from the first drop-down list box, as shown in figure 6.8. Press the Edit button on the Roll-Up, and dotted outlines of which direction and dimension Corel proposes to extrude the chessboard appear around the chessboard.

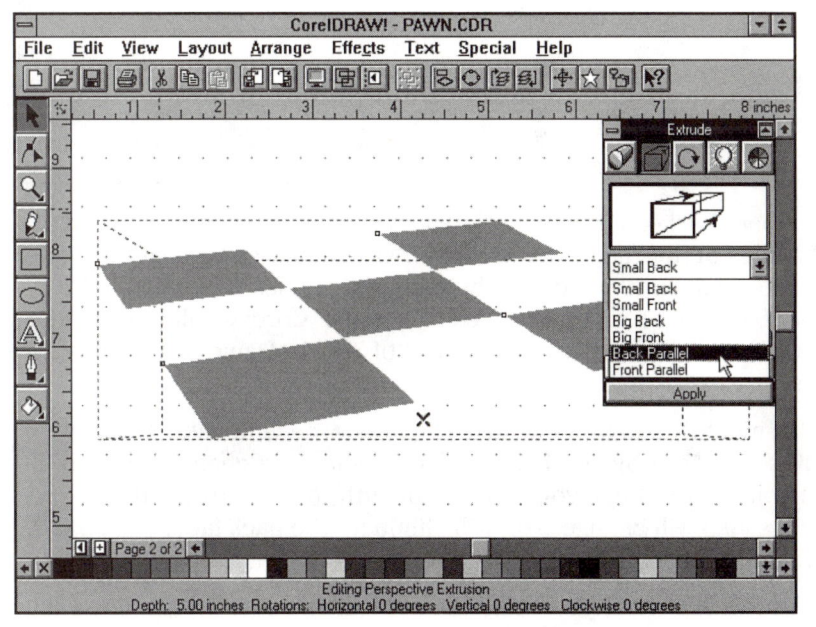

Figure 6.8
Visual explanations of parameters appear in a viewing window on the Extrude Roll-Up.

3. Notice that the dotted outline has an "X" within it. This is similar to the vanishing point "X" the Perspective command offers to users. Click and drag on this "X" to set the amount (depth) of the chessboard extrusion to about 1/4 screen inch.

Chapter 6: Making a Scene

4. Click on Apply, as shown in figure 6.9, and Corel adds the necessary facets to the flat chessboard surfaces to make them appear as 3D objects.

Figure 6.9
Extruding an object adds other sides (facets) to complete a 3D shape.

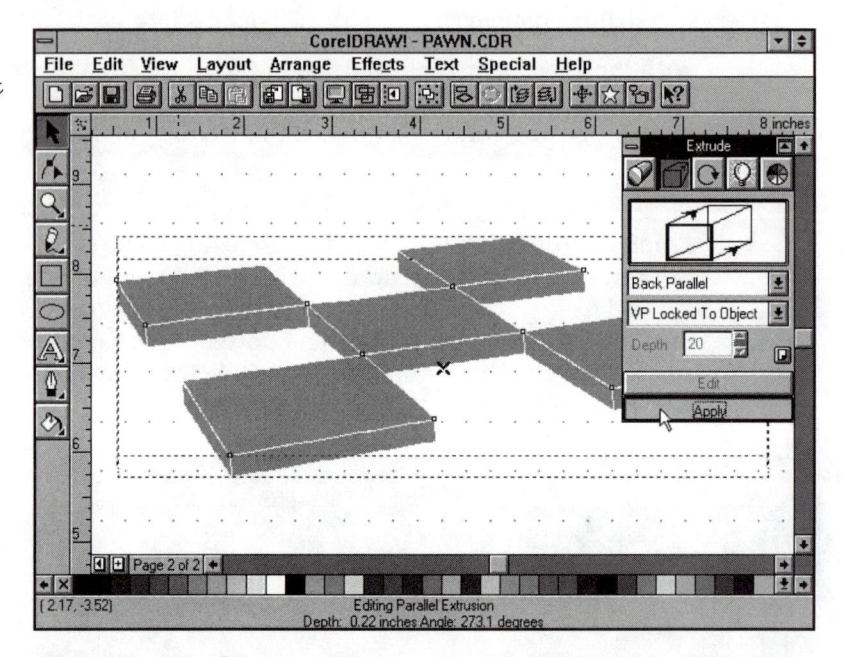

How these other sides of a 3D extrude are created depends on the fill and outline attributes of the shape you extrude. Because the chessboard is made up of filled, closed subpaths, Corel only renders the sides visible from the user's point of view. If no fill was applied to a shape, Corel would also render the back face of an extrude, displaying a sort of 3D wireframe of a cube or other shape.

Extrudes, like most effects in Corel, are editable because the effect is dynamically linked to the object. This means that when you change the fill of the control object (the shape you started out with) of an Extrude, the extruded sides also will change. You will eliminate the back facet of a no-fill extruded shape if you later add a fill to the control object.

Also, the 3D effect is actually a 2D simulation of an extruded shape; you can't rotate this 3D representation to get a more complete view of other facets.

Adding Dimensional Lighting

Dimensional lighting can also be added to your chessboard directly through the Extrude Roll-Up. This automatic shading was not used on the pawn in the

Adding Perspective to Objects

193

last chapter because you didn't extrude it; if you had, the pawn would have looked "boxy," as all extruded shapes in CorelDRAW do.

But whenever you use the Extrude command to dimensionalize a shape, you get an extra perk: Corel will automatically provide realistic shading. All you have to do is tell Corel where to set up the lights and how strong you want 'em!

To add lighting, follow these steps:

1. Click on the light bulb button on the Extrude Roll-Up. You get an entirely different set of visual controls.

2. You have three possible light sources. Using all three on this chessboard is overkill, so let's start with one. Click on the number 1 bulb.

3. You can click and drag the bulb on the test surface (the 3D ball) to reposition it. You'll notice it "sticks" to one of 14 positions for the light, relative to the chessboard. Click and drag to the front center area of the ball.

4. Click and drag the Intensity slider to 55%, and press Apply. Your chessboard comes alive, as shown in figure 6.10.

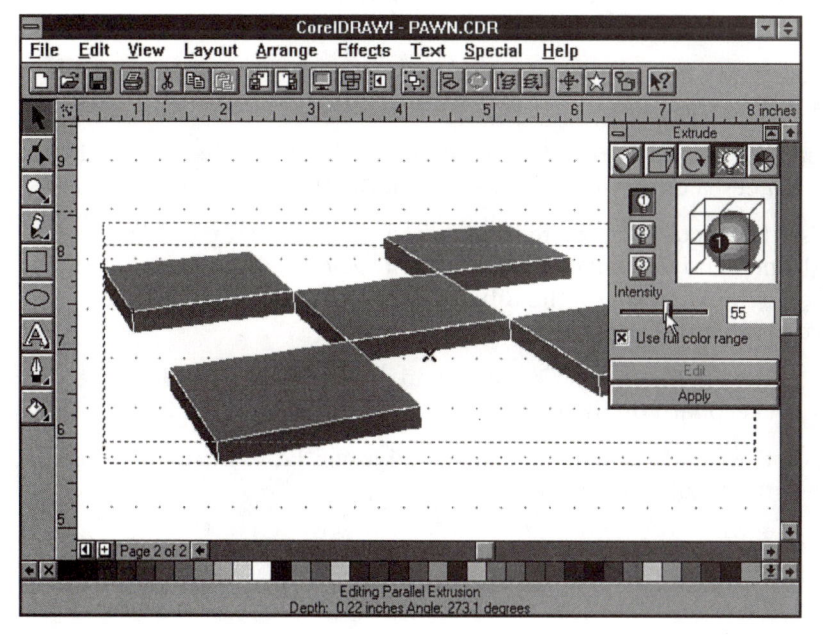

Figure 6.10

The Extrude lighting treats your selection just like the model of the ball on the Roll-Up.

Tip

Corel provides bazillions of combinations of lighting, rotating, and extruding images. I recommend you indulge yourself in some quality time with the Extrude Roll-Up with some independent investigating, as it will be time well spent.

Incidentally, the far top left button of the cylinder is for Preset Extrudes. If you achieve an Extrude effect you want to apply to other shapes, press the Save button, name the extrude, and use it again at any time.

Creating a Background

Most foreground shapes are supported by a background consisting of a floor and a wall. Let's think of the chessboard as the background floor for the pawn, and get started on a wall to complete the dimensionality of the whole illustration.

Most walls have ordinary patterns, but the one you'll create next will have stellar qualities, quite literally. A starry void can communicate the timeless quality of a chess game; it's a sport that's survived a millennia, and chess matches held in the park frequently take almost this long.

Here's the easy way to custom-design a simple pattern that will make an impressive wall in this piece.

1. Roll up (or click on the Control menu button to close) the Extrude Roll-Up. You need a clear view of the action in the Drawing Window.

2. Choose the Rectangle tool, marquee-drag a shape on top of the chessboard, and send this shape to the back of the chessboard by clicking on the To Back button on the Ribbon Bar (or press Shift+PgDn), as shown in figure 6.11.

3. Click on the Fill tool on the Toolbox and choose the Two-color Fill tool (the checkerboard on the top row).

4. Click on the Create button, as shown in figure 6.12, to bring the Two-Color Pattern Editor to the screen.

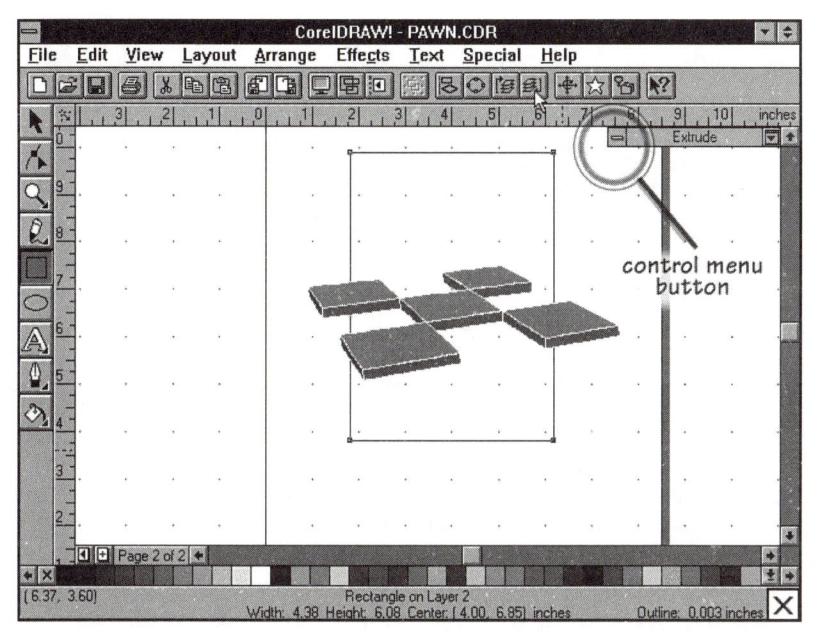

Figure 6.11

The To Back command is necessary every time you design something after an element you want to be in the foreground.

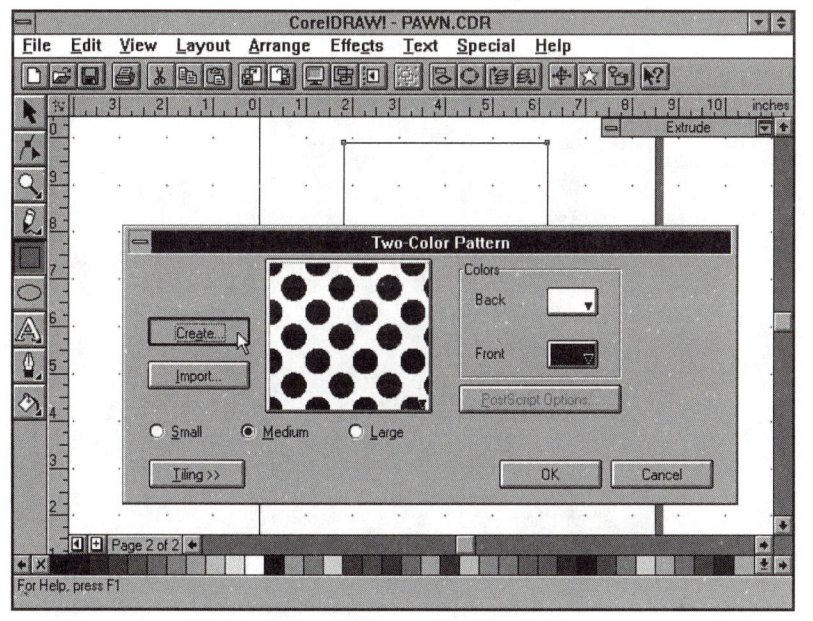

Figure 6.12

The Two-color Pattern dialog box contains preset patterns and the capability to design originals.

Chapter 6: Making a Scene

Tip

Although CorelDRAW is a vector design program, you'll find it can also handle a bitmap fill. You'll find bitmap fill options, like the Two-Color fill, in many of Corel's menus.

This is a *proprietary* handling of bitmap information, and you cannot copy a bitmap-filled shape to the Clipboard for other applications to use. You'll only get a 50-percent black shape if you try this.

You can, however, print a bitmap fill (textures, fractals, Two-Color, and Full-Color are all legitimate), and export a bitmap-filled object as a TIF, BMP, or other file type; the image will retain its special property. See Chapter 11 on exporting Corel designs.

5. The Two-Color Pattern Editor has a drawing surface composed of a gridwork of cells that are adjustable in size. The arrow cursor is used like a pen to fill in the cells with color. You can set the number of cells that will be filled with each click of the arrow cursor. In figure 6.13, I've created a field of stars to use as a pattern fill by clicking on cells with the foreground color to create the "star" pattern. You should create your own Milky Way.

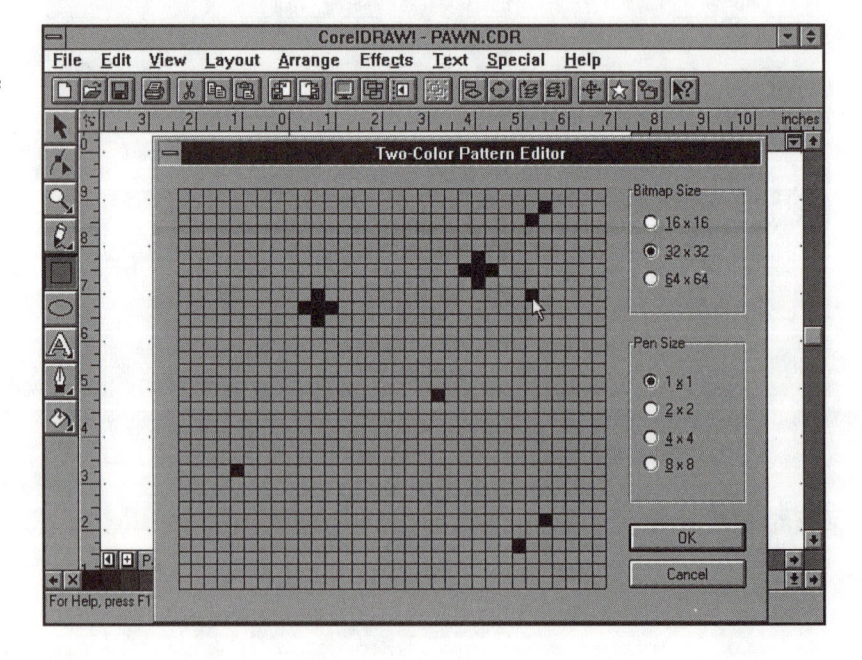

Figure 6.13
Use the Editor like any other paint-type application.

Creating a Background

197

Tip

Use the right mouse button to click over and erase any unintentional marks in the Two-Color Pattern Editor.

Also, keep the "stars" you design here sparse. This is a repeat pattern you're designing, so imagine how many stars you want in the entire rectangle, then divide by about 20.

6. Click on OK to return to the Pattern menu.//
7. Choose **L**arge as the size of the star Pattern tile.
8. To get white stars on a black background, you need to invert the colors used to make the pattern. Click on the Back button in the Colors field, and select black from the mini-palette. Then click on the Front button, and select white, as shown in figure 6.14.

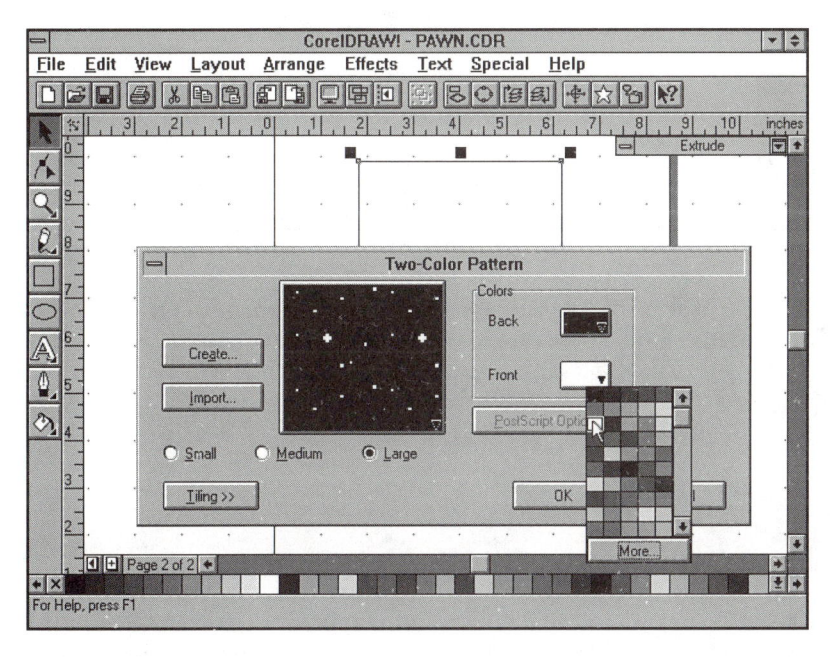

Figure 6.14
Any two colors can be used to make a Two-Color Pattern fill.

Tip

If small, medium, and large seem more suitable choices for popcorn than for Two-Color Patterns, click on the **T**iling button on the bottom of the menu, and you'll get a broad selection of options for pattern tiles, including the exact size of each bitmap pattern.

Chapter 6: Making a Scene

9. Click on OK. As you can see in figure 6.15, you have some sort of space station here, waiting for a chess piece to come in and dock!

Figure 6.15
The background appears to be hundreds of shapes, but it's really only a pattern fill.

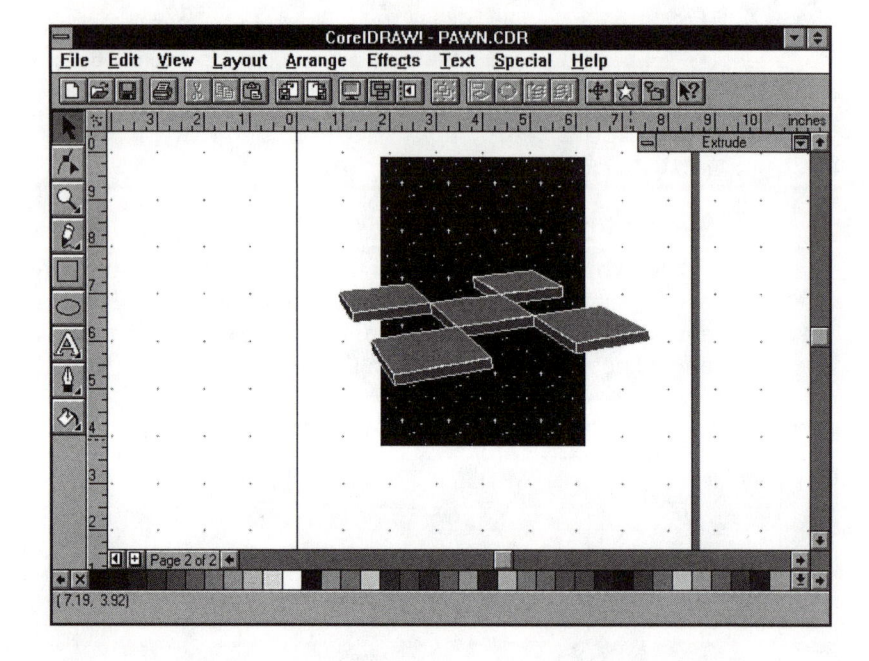

Note

If you stretch or otherwise reshape an object containing a pattern fill, the pattern remains the same, and will repeat more or less times to accommodate its new dimensions.

Moving Layers, Moving Pages

You'll add a sprinkle or two to the background composition toward the end of this assignment, but now it's time to bring the pawn in from the previous page. This means getting the pawn and its highlights grouped together on one layer.

To group elements on one layer, follow these steps:

1. Click on the left arrow on the Page Controls at the bottom left of the Drawing Window. They appear every time you create a multi-page document, as you did at the beginning of the chapter.

2. Press Ctrl+F3 to display the Layers Roll-Up, and double-click on Layer 1 (the locked layer) to edit it.

3. Uncheck the **L**ocked attribute, as shown in figure 6.16. Now the pawn and the outline highlights created on a separate layer in Chapter 5 can be grouped.

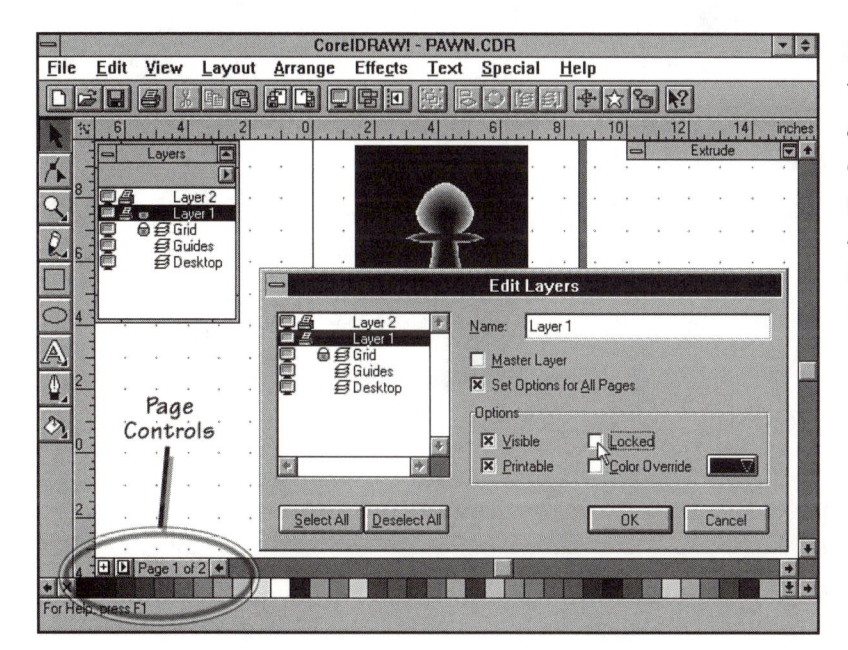

Figure 6.16
The Edit Layers dialog box offers control over the properties you assign to an individual or number of layers.

4. Click on OK.

5. Choose **E**dit, and Select **A**ll. The status line will report that you have multiple items selected across layers.

6. With the Pick tool, click on the black background rectangle. This deselects it (because you don't want it to move along with the pawn), but the rest of the pawn parts are selected now.

7. Click on the Group button on the Ribbon Bar (or press Ctrl+G). In addition to locking all the selected pieces together so you can move them as one shape, the Group command also moves the earliest-drawn objects (the pawn and the blend) to the layer the most-recently drawn shapes are on; the outline highlights on Layer 2.

8. Let's not fuss with the handsome illustration you made a chapter ago. Instead, make a duplicate of it while you move it off the Printable page. Click and drag the pawn off onto the pasteboard area of the Drawing

Chapter 6: Making a Scene

Window (the area not enclosed by the Printable page), then right-mouse click before you release the left mouse button. Figure 6.17 is the result.

Figure 6.17
Grouped objects are easily moved without the possibility of messing up your composition!

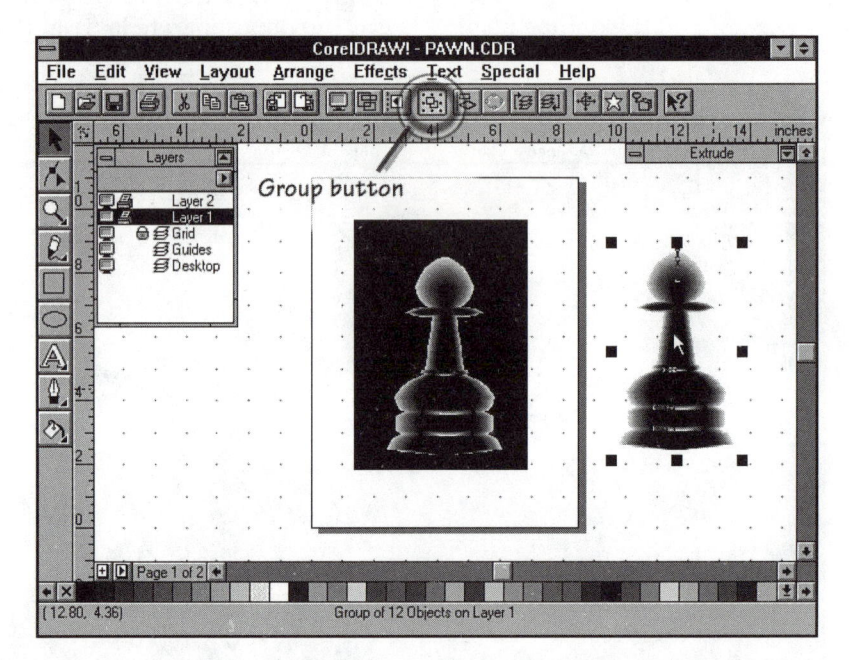

9. Click on the + button of the Page Controls to move your view back to the background composition.

   The area that CorelDRAW pages have in common in the Drawing Window's pasteboard area is located on a special layer called the Desktop. When you switch page views and have a shape on the pasteboard area, it automatically moves to the Desktop layer, which means you have to move it now.

10. With the pawn still selected, click on the right triangle on the top right of the Layers Roll-Up to display its menu fly-out.

11. Select Move To, as shown in figure 6.18.

12. Your cursor turns into an arrow with **To?** written on it, a sign you should click on a different layer title on the Roll-Up. Click on the Layer 2 title.

13. Although the pawn was moved from one layer to another, it's not at the top of the stack of objects on Layer 2. Why? Because it's not the most

recently drawn object; you designed it back in Chapter 5. Therefore, with the pawn still selected, click on the To Front button on the Ribbon Bar (or press Shift+PgUp).

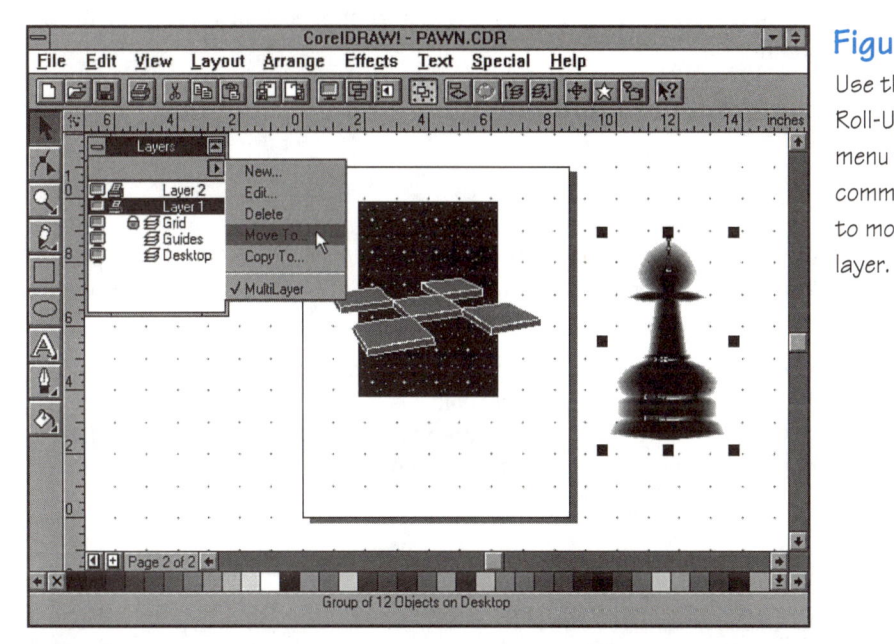

Figure 6.18
Use the Layers Roll-Up's fly-out menu to access commands relating to more than one layer.

Note: When you move or copy a selection to a different layer, the layer to which you moved or copied becomes the active, working layer. If that is not the layer you want to work on, you must click on a different layer title on the Layers Roll-Up to move to a different layer.

Working the Pawns into the Background

The pawn's obviously a little too large for the mini-chessboard, but this is easily fixed in the next steps, where you add not one, but two pawns to the composition.

Chapter 6: Making a Scene

To further modify the pawn, follow these steps:

1. With the Pick tool, click and drag the pawn's bottom-right corner selection handle in an 11 o'clock direction. You'll notice this proportionately scales the pawn down in size, and makes your Includes All view smaller.

2. Click and drag the pawn onto the back right chess square.

3. Click the Zoom tool, then choose the Zoom To All Objects tool to move in on the pawn and the background composition.

4. Resize the pawn so it proportionately fits atop the back right chessboard square by clicking and dragging a corner handle with the Pick tool. Then click+drag the pawn to the center square, and right-mouse click to duplicate the piece before releasing the left mouse button.

5. Click and drag on a corner selection handle of the duplicate pawn in an 11 o'clock direction, until the status line says it's been scaled about 120%, as shown in figure 6.19. Because things appear larger when they are closer to the viewer, the duplicate pawn really does look like it's in front of the original pawn.

Figure 6.19

The curve segment Blend has a Scale with Image attribute, and scales along with the rest of the pawn.

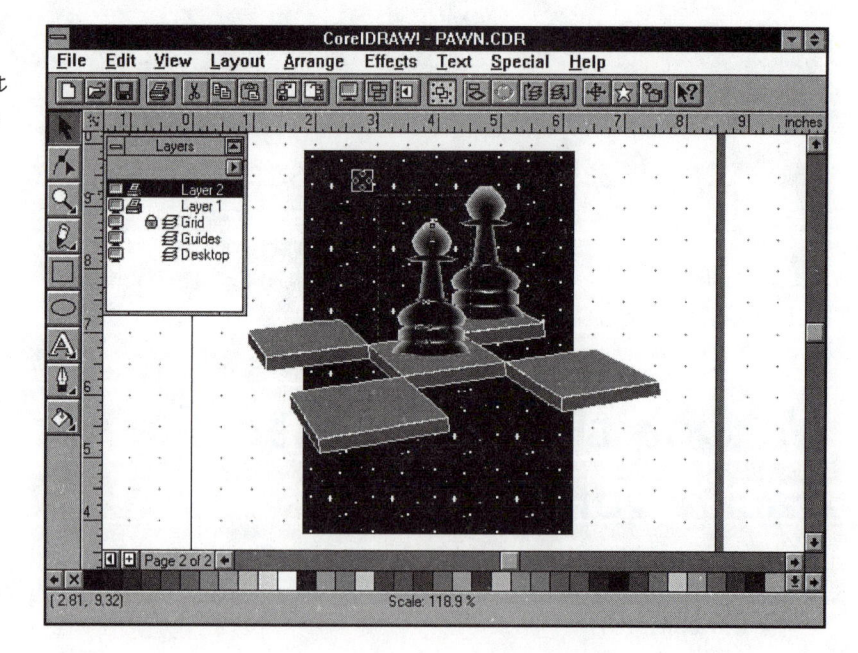

Adding Background Ornaments

While this artistic composition has a lot of attention-getting elements, there are one or two things that can be done to enhance the piece. Because it is composed of a small design that has been tiled to fill in a larger space, the Two-Color Pattern background has a somewhat obvious repeat pattern. To break up the obviousness of this background pattern without detracting from the more important foreground images (the pawns), add a crescent moon to your "Starry Night." Follow these steps:

1. Choose the Ellipse tool, and while holding the Ctrl key (to make a perfect circle), click and drag outside and to the right of the composition until the status line says the circle is about $1^{1}/_{4}$".

2. Give the circle a 10% black fill by clicking on the 10% black color swatch on the color palette.

3. Ctrl+click+drag a second circle so it overlaps the first and is slightly above and to the right of it, as shown in figure 6.20.

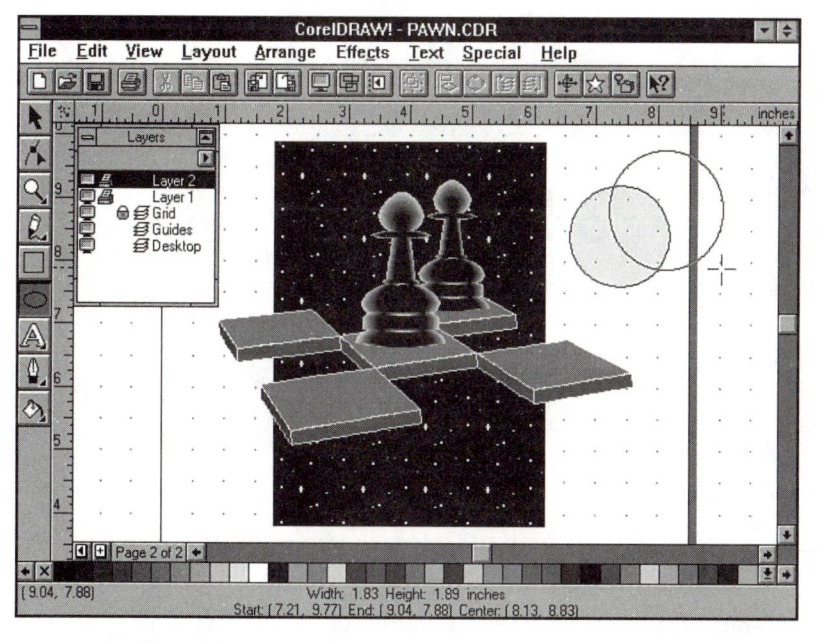

Figure 6.20
Position the two circles like this to create a crescent moon.

4. Press the space bar to get the Pick tool, then hold the Shift key (to additively select objects) and click on the 10% black circle.

Chapter 6: Making a Scene

5. Choose <u>A</u>rrange, <u>T</u>rim from the menu. The first chosen object acts like scissors, the second behaves like paper. You are left with a silvery moon as the result of this operation, as shown in figure 6.21.

Figure 6.21
Use the Trim command to cut a piece of a shape out of a different shape.

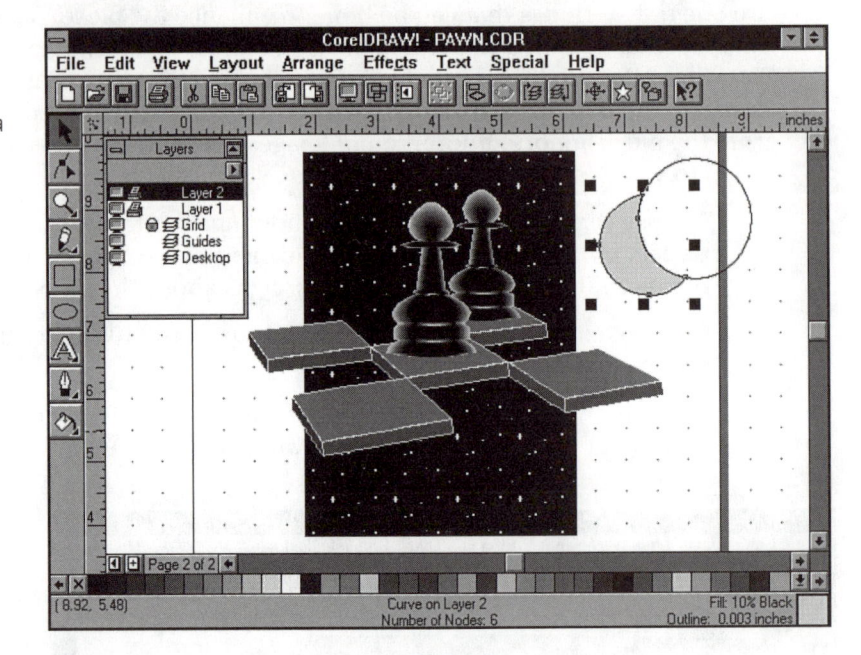

Adding Order to the Universe

You need to add the crescent moon to the composition now, but you want to keep its place in the stack of objects on the page to that of second-to-last. It should fall right on top of the wall of stars, but behind everything else. Here's where the To Back command is useful with not one, but multiple shapes. Follow these steps:

1. Click and drag the 10% black crescent moon so it covers the smaller pawn's head for the moment.

2. Right-mouse click on the "X" to the left of the color palette to get rid of the moon's outline.

3. While holding down the Shift key (to additively select), click on the Two-Color background rectangle of the stars.

4. Click on the To Back button on the Ribbon Bar, and you'll get a scene like the one in figure 6.22.

Adding Order to the Universe

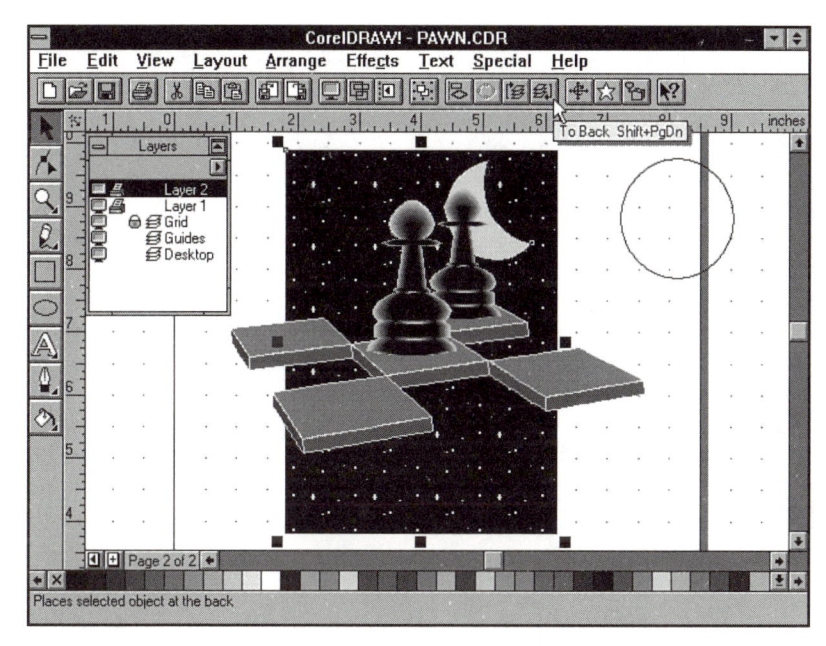

Figure 6.22
There is order in the universe once more.

Note

Technically, and astronomically, a crescent moon is the product of another heavenly body, such as a planet or the sun, partially eclipsing our view of it from here on Earth; the area you trimmed away from the circle *isn't* trimmed from our moon when you see such a phenomenon in real life. Therefore, the pattern of the stars shouldn't (technically) be visible in the eclipse area— I showed you this one purely for the CorelDRAW mechanics of creating a crescent.

5. Choose the Ellipse tool, and pepper three or four circles 1/4" in diameter any place on the piece your art instincts tell you stars and planets should be.

6. Get rid of the circle used to Trim the crescent moon by selecting it and pressing the Del key.

7. Color these new stars and planets something other than white, because a sizable globe in the background will detract from the pawns and the chessboard, as shown in figure 6.23.

Chapter 6: Making a Scene

Figure 6.23
The finished illustration.

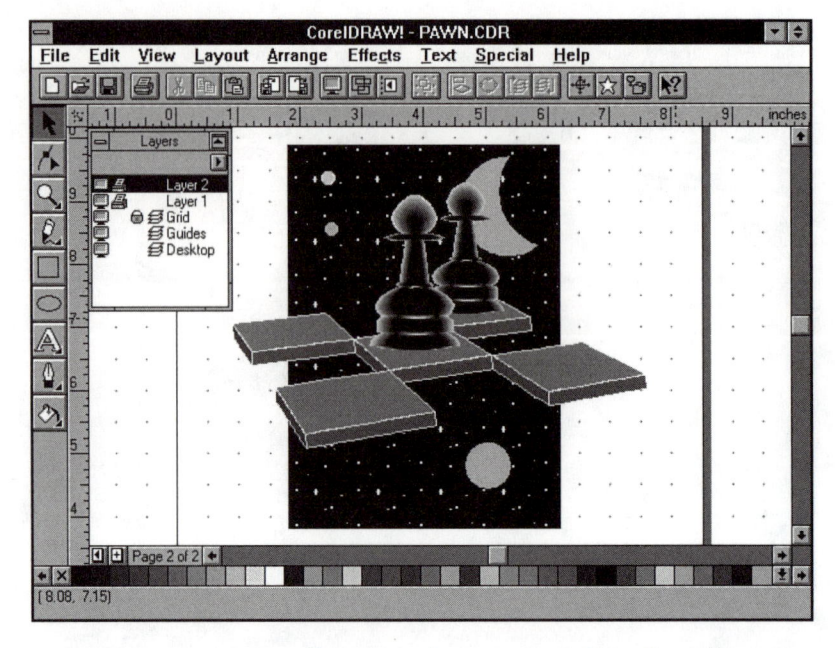

8. To save the drawing, choose File, Save As, or simply File, Save (Ctrl+S) if you want to conserve hard disk space and don't want two versions of these past two chapter assignments.

Summary

Whether you love chess or hate it, you've covered a lot of ground with Corel's tools and features here, and that's the really important point. Teamed with an active imagination, you can easily design and dimensionalize foreground objects and 3D background scenes. In addition, you've been introduced to some important new tools that will keep rewarding you as you continue to experiment with them.

If you have an *overly* active imagination, however, you may need a vacation—this is where you're headed in the next chapter. You're going to the beach, in a manner of speaking, to learn how to design a killer postcard (from a fictitious sunny locale) that's built with a lot of new CorelDRAW special effects.

So come along, and don't say, "Wish You Were Here."

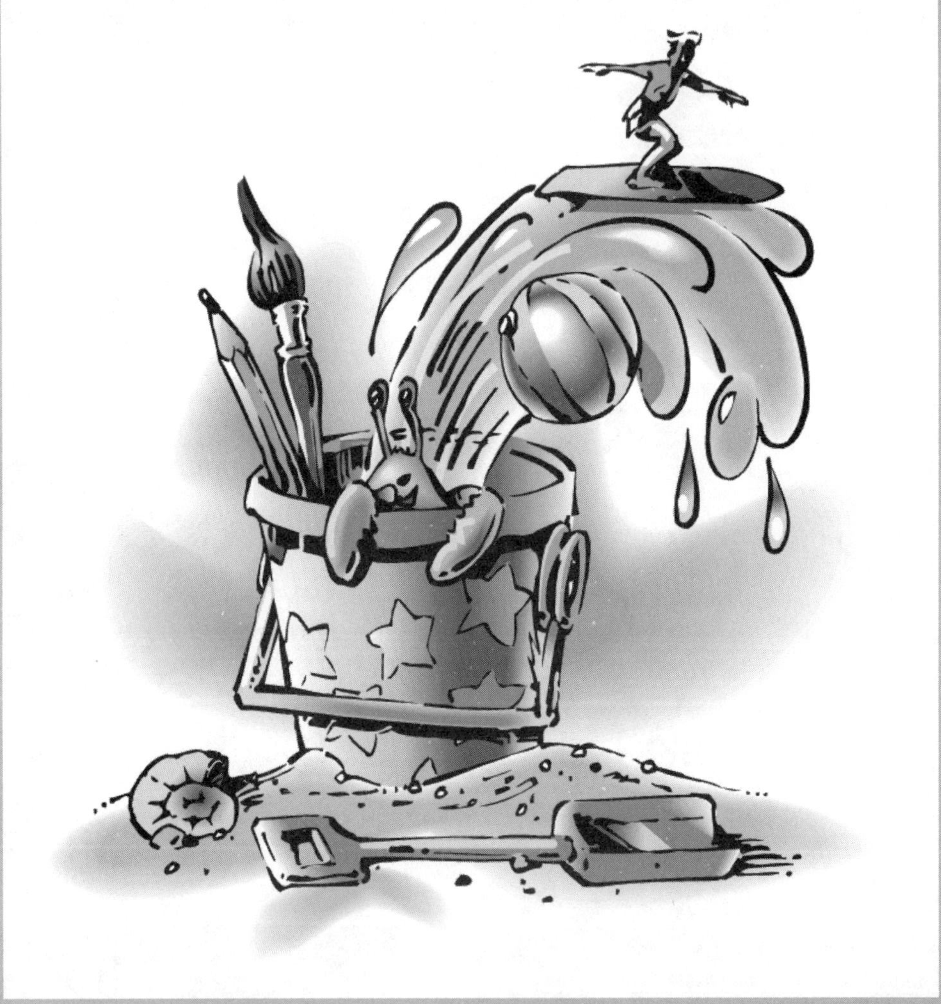

CHAPTER 7

Working with Bitmap Images

Traditional collage work (the pasting of different art materials onto a single surface) used to be a painstaking process resulting in a fragile masterpiece. Today, with digital graphics programs as capable as CorelDRAW, you have an alternative to scissors and glue. You can take scanned images from different sources (photos, textures, even 3D objects), add design elements, and presto: you have an exciting, provocative, and much more stable piece of visual communication.

If you have a fascination with period postcards, those timeless masterpieces your grandparents might have sent you from Atlantic City or Hollywood, you're in for a treat with this chapter. You'll explore more of Corel's features, and create a colorful postcard that smacks of authentic late 1940s artwork. You'll bring different "looks" together to make a wondrous collage using this state-of-the-art design program.

In this chapter, you will:

- Get a feel for CorelPHOTO-PAINT's powers
- Create airbrush-like backgrounds
- Use the Symbols Roll-Up for "instant" art embellishments
- Create an artistic effect using text
- Discover a unique use for Corel's PowerClip feature

Constructing a Picture Postcard

As you saw in Chapter 6, Corel easily handles bitmap-type fills within a closed vector shape. The type of bitmap you'll use in the postcard collage is called the *Tagged Image File format*, or TIF image. This is one of the most universal and commonly used formats for storing photographs, scanned images, or other bitmap-based digital images. This versatile format can store color information from a photograph faithfully because it can handle up to 16.7 unique colors in a single image. TIF images can even be read and used by other kinds of computers, such as Macintoshes and UNIX workstations.

The postcard you'll be designing in this chapter is from a fictitious place called Nedrow Beach (Nedrow, New York isn't fictitious; it's simply landlocked). A common postcard convention has been to use huge block-lettering of the place's name, with a gorgeous photo of the locale inside the lettering, which always seems to sprawl across the card diagonally.

You'll start this project by using a "sister" program to CorelDRAW, CorelPHOTO-PAINT. You'll use it to slightly rotate the TIF image used to fill in the postcard type. Once the TIF is tilted, it's back to CorelDRAW for the rest of the photo-collage work.

Finding a Stock Image

Corel comes with several high-quality stock photographic images that photographers have combed the four corners of the earth to capture. The whole field of royalty-free digital stock photography has freed designers from the confines and limitations of backyard photographic sources. The examples that follow use a TIF image from Aris Entertainment's *Majestic Places* collection, photographed by Tom Atwood, to represent the nonexistent Nedrow Beach. You can use any photo you like in this assignment. Take some time and explore the images on Corel's CD-ROM. With PHOTO-PAINT you can modify a photographic image of any place on earth.

Opening an Image in PHOTO-PAINT

To create the postcard, you'll need a bitmap-type image. It doesn't have to be the exact one shown, and it can be any one of the common bitmap file formats. Any file name that ends with a BMP, JPG, PCD (Kodak PhotoCD), PCX, TIF, TGA, or GIF extension is an okay bitmap that PHOTO-PAINT will happily load. Check out Corel's sample files on the CD, or use an image you already have. Just try to find one that's aquatic or tropical in flavor!

Finding a Stock Image

From Windows Program Manager, double-click on the CorelPHOTO-PAINT icon in the Corel Graphic Group. Choose File, Open (Ctrl+O) to get to the directory that contains the image you want to use in this assignment. Locate your image by selecting its location in the Drives and Directories drop-down boxes. By default, PHOTO-PAINT lists all file types. If you'd like to browse for a single type of file format, just the TIF images for example, select the TIFF Bitmap (*.tif, *jtf, *.sep) from the List Files of Type drop-down box.

Note

PHOTO-PAINT doesn't open up with a Printable page, with palettes displayed and ready to go like CorelDRAW does. Instead, you have to open an image before PHOTO-PAINT offers you a full complement of Roll-Ups and menu options.

Click the Preview box, as shown in figure 7.1, to see the image you want to use before actually having PHOTO-PAINT load it into your system's RAM.

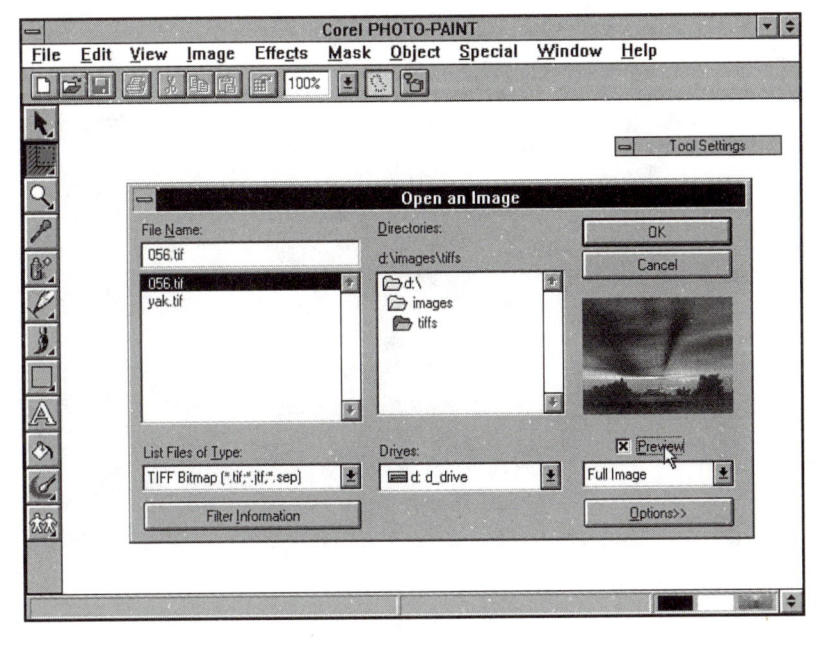

Figure 7.1

You can avoid opening a large (or wrong) image by viewing a file with the Preview box.

Tilting the Image

Your goal is to transform a straight-up-and-down image to a tilted one so it'll fit into the postcard with a little more style. Rotating a bitmap is a very processor-intensive action. The program needs to reassign the placement of each pixel, and that can take a long time on a slow machine (a 386), or one that has insufficient RAM for graphics work (less than 16 MB).

For this reason, you should rotate bitmaps in PHOTO-PAINT instead of in CorelDRAW. Using CorelDRAW to rotate a bitmap takes longer than if you used PHOTO-PAINT to do the job. CorelDRAW is optimized to work with vector images, and PHOTO-PAINT is optimized to work with bitmaps.

Once your image has appeared in PHOTO-PAINT's workspace, choose Image, Rotate, and Custom to display the Custom Rotate dialog box. Type **12** in the Degrees field, click on the counterclockwise radio button, and check the Maintain original image size box, as shown in figure 7.2.

Figure 7.2

You can rotate a bitmap graphic in PHOTO-PAINT in increments of 1°, clockwise or counterclockwise.

Finding a Stock Image

Stop

If you don't check the Maintain original image size check box, a rotated picture will be clipped by the border of the image window and you'll lose the edges. Although this look is sometimes what you're trying to achieve, be forewarned. With **M**aintain original size checked, your image window will expand to accommodate the new outside dimensions of the rotated image. The areas in the window that aren't filled with the original image (due to the rotation) will be filled with the current paper color.

Click on OK. PHOTO-PAINT presents you with a rotated copy of the original image, as well as a proposed image file extension of CPT, as shown in figure 7.3. The scene will now add a little more drama to the postcard you'll create next.

Figure 7.3

PHOTO-PAINT doesn't rotate an original image, but instead performs the rotation on an exact copy.

Now that the image is rotated, you need to determine the size of the image. You'll want to create a postcard in CorelDRAW that's larger than this new, rotated image. From the **S**pecial menu, choose **P**references, and set **U**nits to Inches on the drop-down list. Click on OK. From **V**iew, choose **R**ulers, and write down the dimensions of the NEW-1.CPT image.

Tip

Image resolution, measured in pixels per inch, usually plays an important role in deciding the final size of an image. For instance, a lot of programs will display a 72ppi 3" by 3" image as half the size of a 3" by 3" image that has a resolution of 150ppi.

Instead, CorelDRAW eliminates this consideration from importing a bitmap (as you'll do later). It considers (and displays) a 3" by 3" image at 3" by 3", regardless of how many pixels per inch are contained within the image.

Saving the TIF Image

Choose File, Save As, and choose TIFF Bitmap from the Save File as Type drop-down list; from the File Sub-Format drop-down list choose Uncompressed (some programs have problems with compressed files). Name the file (what else?) BEACH.TIF. Click on OK and a TIFF export dialog box will appear. Click on OK to accept the default of TIFF 4.2. Be sure to remember what drive and directory you've saved the file to because you'll need to import it into CorelDRAW later. Press Alt+F4 to exit PHOTO-PAINT (or choose File, Exit).

Creating an Airbrush Effect with Fountain Fills

First, you'll need to create a background for the postcard. Cards from the '40s (and even today) feature lush washes of color that traditional artists create with an airbrush. These smooth transitions between shades of color give a slick appearance to the work, and contrasts and highlights any foreground element that's added to the composition. CorelDRAW provides you with tools that generate the same results as an airbrush, but are also quicker, easier to use, editable, and don't require a license from the EPA.

Gathering the Background Materials

You won't need an airbrush, however, because you have CorelDRAW's powerful Fountain Fills on your side. In Chapter 1, you experimented a little with the Radial type Fountain Fill, and in this chapter, you'll do something a little more substantial with the Linear Fountain Fill.

Creating an Airbrush Effect with Fountain Fills

To build wide diagonal stripes of color transitions to serve as the postcard background, follow these steps:

1. Double-click on the CorelDRAW icon in the Corel Graphics Group in Windows Program Manager.

2. Choose the Rectangle tool and click+diagonal-drag a landscape (wider than it is tall) rectangle, whose dimensions are larger than the TIFF image you saved in PHOTO-PAINT. The rectangle will serve as a template for creating the stripe shapes, as shown in figure 7.4.

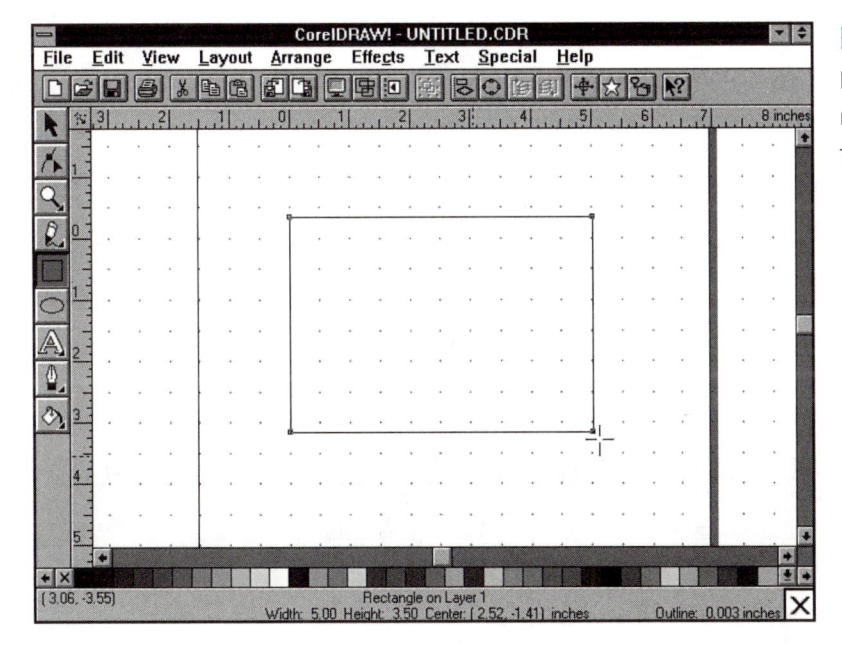

Figure 7.4
Make sure that the rectangle is larger than BEACH.TIF.

3. Using the rectangle tool, draw a rectangle that's about 2 1/2 times the height of the landscape rectangle, and about one inch wide. Make sure it's fairly aligned with the left and bottom of the landscape rectangle. Check the status line to confirm this, and resize and reposition the rectangle with the Pick tool if you feel you're way off.

4. Press the spacebar to activate the Pick tool, and click on the already-selected narrow rectangle to put it in Corel's Rotate and Skew mode.

5. Change the center of rotation of the narrow rectangle by placing your cursor inside the dead-center bull's eye (see fig. 7.5) and dragging the center down to about 1/4 screen inch from the bottom side of the rectangle.

Chapter 7: Working with Bitmap Images

Figure 7.5
An object's center of rotation can be moved.

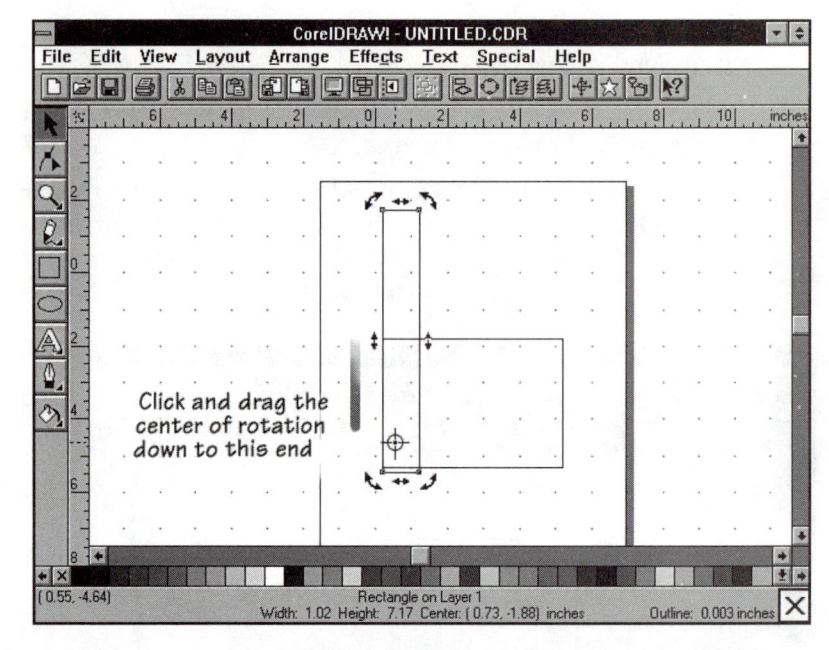

6. Click and drag down while holding the upper right rotate handle (the curved two-headed arrow) on the rectangle, as shown in figure 7.6. Stop when the status line tells you you've rotated it about 55°.

Figure 7.6
An off-center rotation point lets you move one end of an object more than the other.

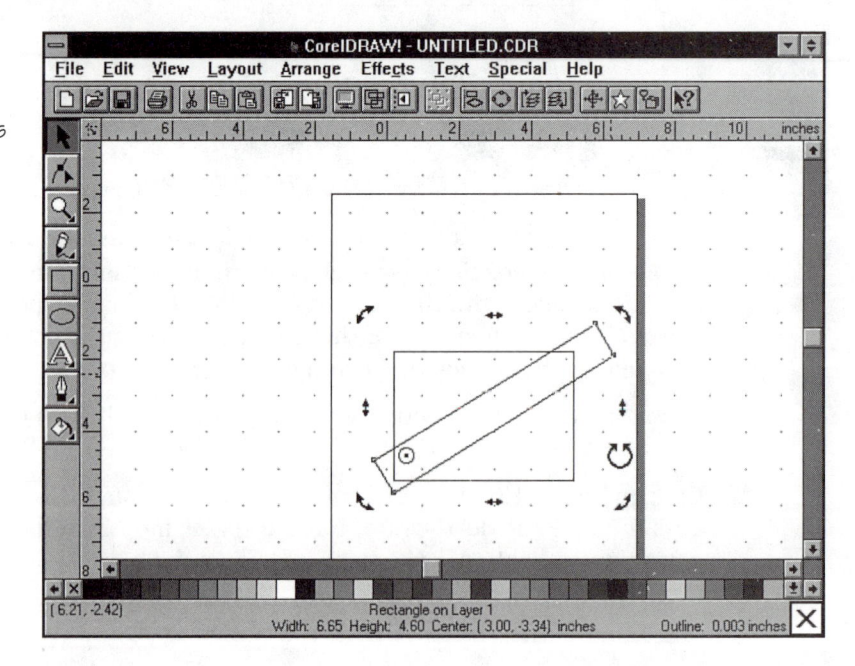

The narrow rectangle should appear to bisect the landscape rectangle. You now have the basic shapes designed and positioned to start creating airbrush stripes on the postcard.

Understanding the Intersection Command

The Intersection command, a feature new to the CorelDRAW 5 package, is a perfect choice for the task ahead. You need to make six or seven irregularly shaped stripes that, when they are placed side by side, form a single rectangle for the postcard background. The Intersection command creates a new shape when multiple overlapping shapes are selected. The new object gets its shape from the interior of all of the overlapping areas.

You only need two pieces—the landscape-shaped rectangle you drew, along with the narrow rectangle—to make the six or seven stripes for the postcard background. Each time you use the Intersection command with these two objects, you create one new shape. Do this six times and you get six new pieces automatically created for you. These are the steps you need to follow and repeat until you've created enough stripes to assemble in the rectangular background:

1. Choose Special, Preferences. In the General section of the tabbed dialog box, type **.1** in the Nudge field, and click on OK. You may want to nudge (move a selected object slightly by pressing one or more arrow keys) some of the pieces you'll create, and this is a good setting for this assignment.

2. Marquee-select both rectangles using the Pick tool, and choose Arrange, Intersection, as shown in figure 7.7.

It's not usually apparent that the Intersection command did anything after you've applied it, because one of the objects used to create the intersection (in this case the narrow, angled rectangle) is on top of and perfectly covers the new shape! Click and drag the narrow rectangle down and to the right, as shown in figure 7.8. You'll be using it again to create more adjacent stripes, so don't move it too far away.

Chapter 7: Working with Bitmap Images

Figure 7.7
The Intersection command has no preference over the order in which intersecting objects are selected.

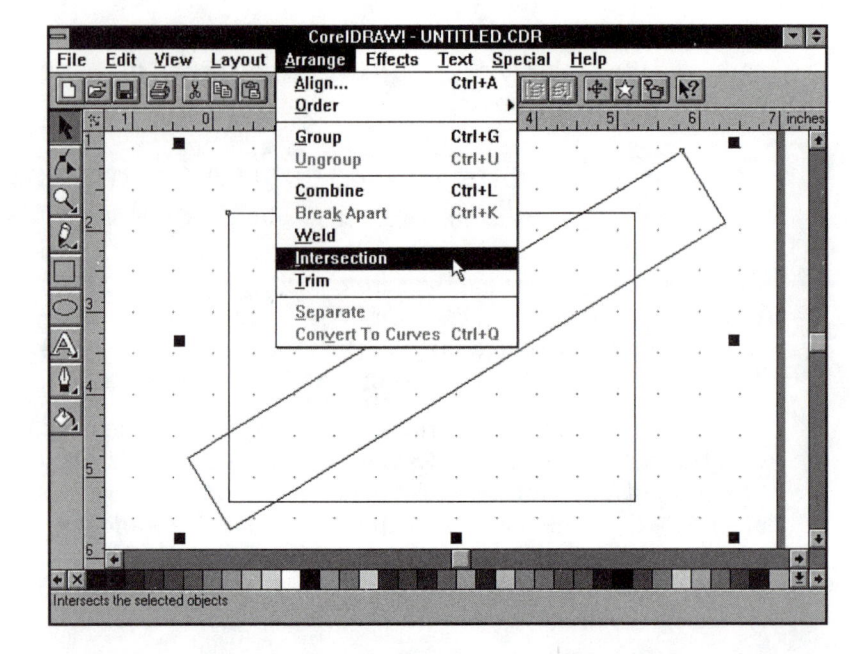

Figure 7.8
The new object shares the shape properties of both objects used with the Intersection command.

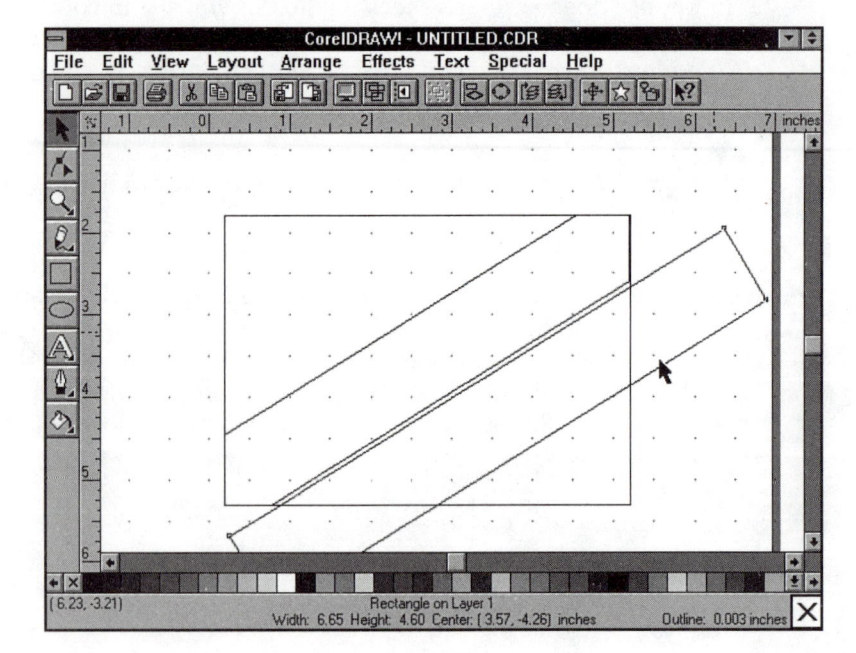

Creating an Airbrush Effect with Fountain Fills

Using the Fill Roll-Up To Speed Up Your Work

Corel's Roll-Ups offer 90 percent of the functionality of their parent dialog boxes. However, it's not as much of a hassle as it is to dig into the Toolbox when you need to do repeated fill editing, because the Roll-Up is right in the Drawing Window.

In the next set of steps, you'll be completing the postcard background by using the Intersection command, then filling each resulting vertical stripe with a custom Fountain Fill. It's a visually rewarding way to work as you see the piece come together, and by filling each new shape after you create it with the Intersection command, it'll be easier to select and move!

Tip

No one I know who uses CorelDRAW finds it easy to select a shape that only has an outline to click on! Filled shapes are much easier to select.

1. Click on the Fill tool on the Toolbox. Select the Roll-Up button (the one on the top row that has the tiny menu icon on it).

2. With the Pick tool, select the Intersection shape.

3. On the Fill Roll-Up, click on the Fountain Fill button, and then click on the Linear type button. Click and drag inside the sample window to make the fill point at 1 o'clock, and select a deep navy and a light blue from the color drop-down buttons by clicking on their down arrows. See figure 7.9 for the location of all this stuff, and when you're all set, press Apply.

Tip

If Corel didn't already design this Roll-Up with a ridiculous amount of features, there's yet another way to get more selections from it.

If you need to custom-design your fill further, click on the Roll-Up's Edit button. You'll get the whole Fill display for the Color, Fountain Fill, Bitmap, or Fractal Texture—whichever mode you have selected on the top of the Roll-Up.

Chapter 7: Working with Bitmap Images

4. Ready for stripe #2? Click and drag the narrow rectangle so that the diagonal sides of it touch the intersected shape. Precision isn't of paramount importance here; just make sure they're really close—you can edit these shapes later to make them meet seamlessly.

Figure 7.9
The Fill Roll-Up obviously shares a lot of functionality with the Fill menu.

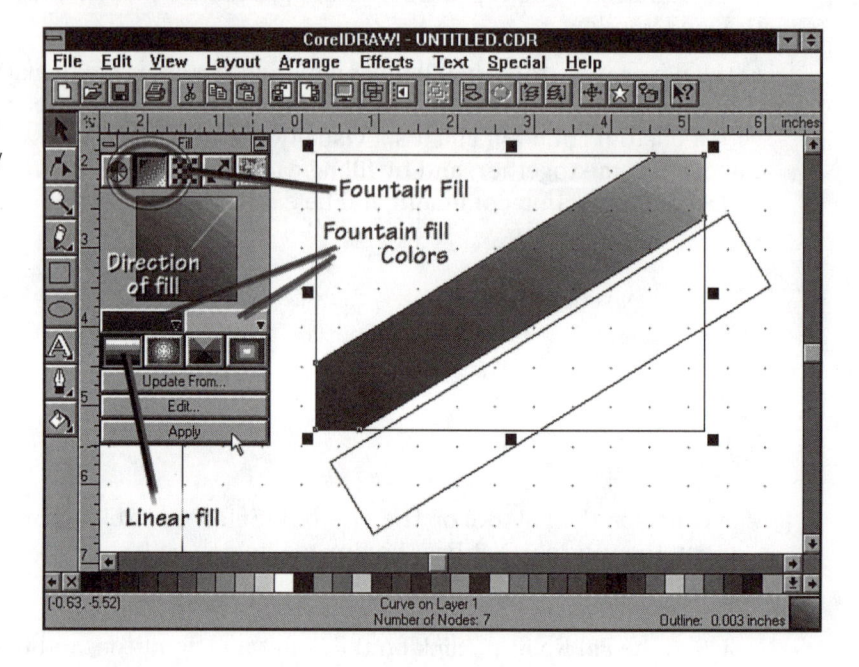

Closer Look

Use the arrow keys on the keyboard to nudge the narrow rectangle closer to the Fountain-Filled shape.

5. Hold the Shift key and click on the landscape rectangle, then choose Arrange, Intersection again.
6. The second intersection shape is now the selected object; click and drag inside the Fountain Fill sample area on the Fill Roll-Up and make the fill go in a seven o'clock direction. Press the Apply button. You should have the second stripe looking like figure 7.10.

Creating an Airbrush Effect with Fountain Fills

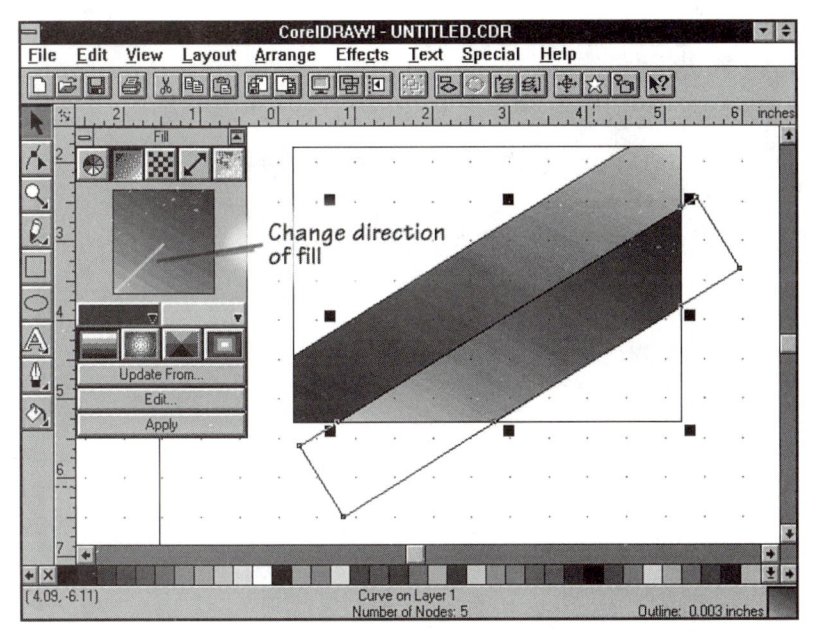

Figure 7.10

This is the easy way to change the direction, or type, of a Fountain Fill.

7. Drag the long, narrow rectangle into position next to the intersection piece you just filled. Then repeat steps 4–6. Keep creating and filling new intersection pieces until the landscape rectangle is completely "filled" with Fountain Fill intersection pieces.

Be sure to alternate the direction of the Fountain Fills. As you can see in figure 7.11, by alternating Fountain Fills, the vertical stripes appear to resonate; the pattern is very reminiscent of pre-'50s movie posters, postcards, and advertisements.

Chapter 7: Working with Bitmap Images

Figure 7.11
Alternating the direction of the Fountain Fills creates a visually exciting pattern.

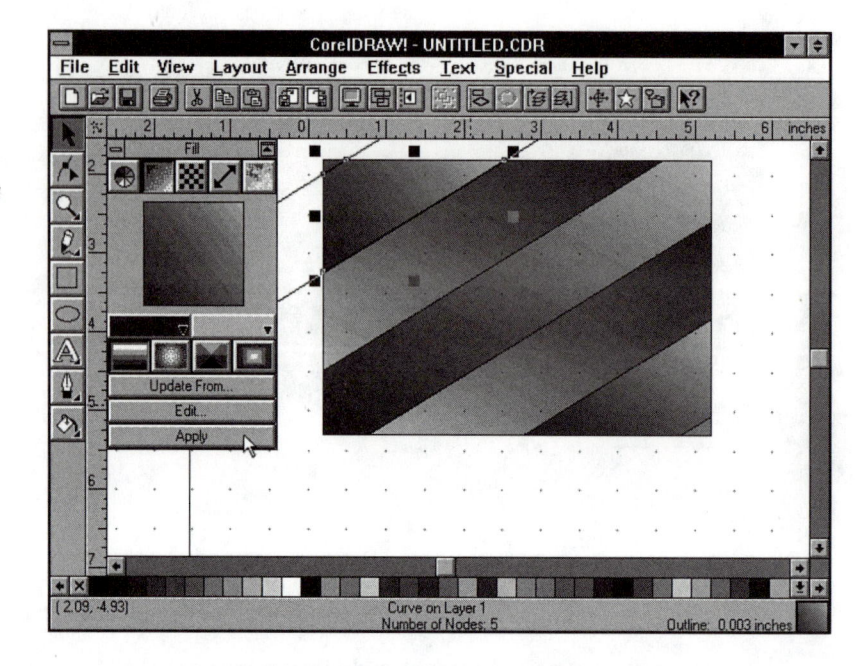

Tightening Up the Background Design

While the postcard background stripes now form a nice, sharp rectangle the same shape as the landscape rectangle, there are probably areas where the stripes overlap or don't exactly meet. You can fix this easily by using the Shape tool in combination with the Snap To Objects command.

Using the Snap To Objects Command

As you'll see, the nodes that are associated with the stripes will be attracted to each other when you turn on Snap to Objects. Taking advantage of this attractive property is a very good way to get the edges of the shapes perfectly aligned.

Snap To points on objects are generally located at each point of inflection where a node exists. You can easily locate one by selecting the Shape tool and selecting an object. This reveals the nodes in the path that forms the object.

Rectangles and ellipses are made of complex geometry, however, and don't exactly obey the convention of "a node equals a Snap To Object point." Rectangles have nine Snap To points: one at each corner, one at the midsection of each side, and one in the center. Likewise, ellipses have five Snap To points; generally they are found at 3, 6, 9, and 12 o'clock (unless you've rotated the ellipse), and one in the center.

The number of Snap To points changes when you convert an ellipse or rectangle to curves. In addition, you can't use the Snap To mode with rectangles and ellipses when you have the Shape tool active. Complete the following steps:

1. Choose Layout, Snap To Objects, as shown in figure 7.12. Unfortunately, this mode doesn't have a button on Corel's Ribbon Bar.

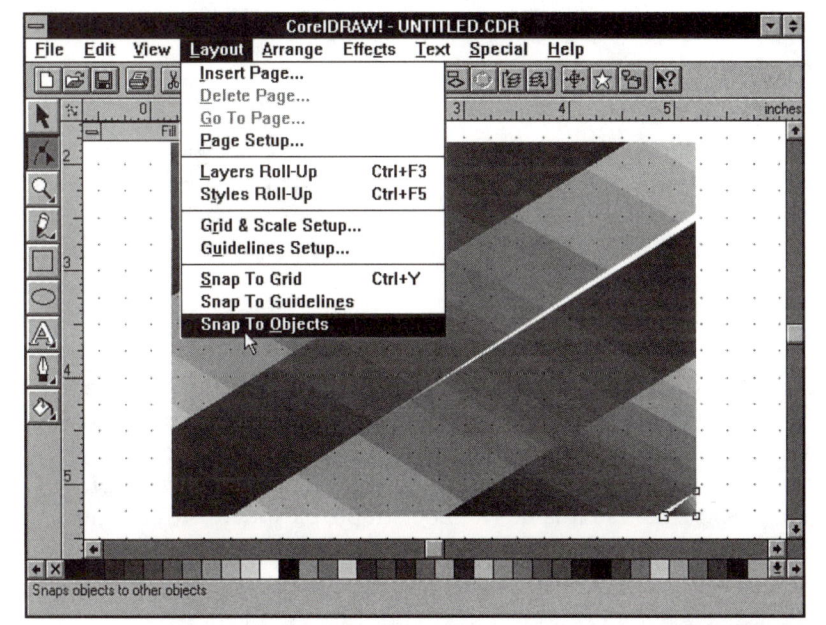

Figure 7.12

The nodes in the path of a shape are attracted to other nodes in the Snap To Objects mode.

2. With the Shape tool, click on a node in one of the striped intersection shapes that does not quite touch (or that overlaps) its neighboring intersection shape. Drag the node toward the edge of the neighboring intersection shape so that the nodes on the two shapes meet. You will feel a slight tug or attraction as you drag a node toward another node.

If you compare the striped background in figure 7.12 to that in figure 7.13, you'll see that the selected node touches its corresponding edge on a different stripe flawlessly; the nodes are snapping to nodes in the neighboring shape.

3. Repeat this procedure until all of the stripes meet each other perfectly.

Chapter 7: Working with Bitmap Images

Figure 7.13
With Snap To Objects, nodes in different shapes will come together when you drag one toward another.

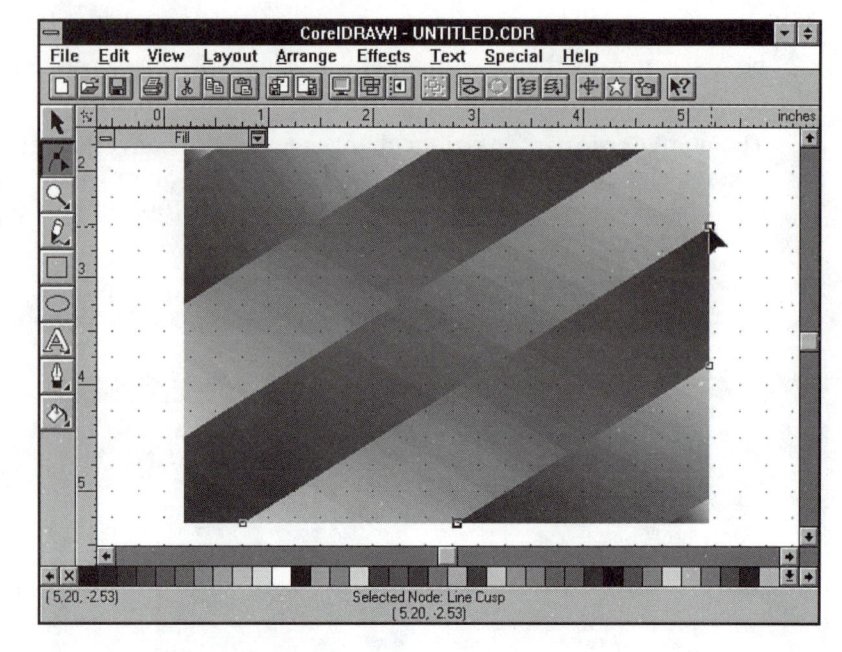

Removing Unnecessary Objects

Before adding the postcard's foreground elements, clean up the workspace a little. You don't need the two rectangles you used to create the intersection pieces. You should select the two rectangles and delete them. The large rectangle that surrounds the collection of Fountain-Filled intersection pieces can be hard to select because it is not a filled shape; although with all the intersection pieces within, it may look as if it is.

The easiest way to be sure that you have the large rectangle selected and not one of the intersection pieces is to press the spacebar to activate the Pick tool, and then press the Tab key until the large rectangle is selected. Eight black selection handles will appear around the large rectangle, and the status line will report a rectangle on Layer 1 and display Outline: 0.003" and a no-fill icon (a white rectangle with an X through it) in the lower right-hand corner. Press the Del key and the large rectangle is deleted. The long, narrow rectangle also has outlived its usefulness. Select and delete it.

Grouping Objects

While you could mistake your collection of intersection pieces for a single, fancily filled object, they are all separate shapes that could easily, and mistakenly, be moved out of alignment with each other.

Tightening Up the Background Design

The solution to this "problem" is to use CorelDRAW's Group command. Choose **E**dit, Select **A**ll from the menu (or double-click on the Pick Tool) and then click on the Group button on the Ribbon Bar (or press Ctrl+G). All your diagonal Fountain-Filled pieces are now locked together until you decide to select the group and toggle the Group button off again (you won't need to ungroup them in this assignment, but this is a good tip!).

By default, every new shape you design in CorelDRAW has a 0.003" outline, but this is undesired for the postcard's airbrush background. Because all of the intersection pieces are now grouped together, it just takes a single right-mouse click on the "X" on the color palette to remove outline attributes from all the pieces at once. You should do that now.

Closer Look

Grouping shapes is not the same as the Combine, Intersection, Trim, or Weld Arrange commands. You're not changing the shape of any paths, but simply aligning the selected objects' relative positions and gluing them together.

You can't perform a lot of CorelDRAW commands on grouped objects, like Combine or Extrude. The shapes have to be ungrouped to do the really fancy stuff. But you can perform simple actions to a group such as adding/deleting outlines and fills, or rotating and skewing.

As you near the completion of this phase of the assigment, it's a good time to tidy up the Drawing Window. Roll up the Fill Roll-Up by clicking on the upper right triangle button to get a little workspace back. It's also a good time to save your work. Click on the Save button on the Ribbon Bar (or choose **F**ile, **S**ave, or press Ctrl+S), and name the file POSTCARD.CDR.

Adding a Pre-Built Symbol as a Design Element

You've seen how to draw ducks and chess pieces so far in this book, but you may be unaware that Corel provides you with hundreds of predrawn figures to reduce your design time. The Symbols Roll-Up contains scores of simple drawings that were designed for Corel. They are arranged according to theme.

Chapter 7: Working with Bitmap Images

The symbols are genuine Corel-drawn—they have nodes and segments you can edit with the Shape tool, and you can fill them and modify them exactly like you would an original creation. Even professional designers who have a lot of experience with CorelDRAW frequently use these pre-built characters when time is tight.

This next section shows you how to add a symbol character without so much as a lifting a Pencil tool. Here's how to embellish a design almost automatically by using the Symbols Roll-Up:

1. On the Ribbon Bar, click on the button with the star shape on it. This displays the Symbols Roll-Up on-screen.

2. The first drop-down list box at the top of the Roll-Up contains the categories of symbols that are available. Click and then scroll down to the Weather category, a natural enough place to find a drawing of a sun.

> **Stop**
> If you don't find Weather listed in the drop-down box, it is because you or whoever installed CorelDRAW on your computer didn't choose to install it. You'll have to use Corel's Setup program to install this and any other missing symbol set you may need. Consult Chapter 2 for complete information on using CorelDRAW's Setup program.
>
> You won't have to do a complete reinstall of all of the programs. Just check the CorelDRAW box in the Choose which applications to install dialog box. Then click on the Customize button. Put a check mark only in the Symbols check box and then press Customize. Find the missing symbols in the left-hand Do Not Install box, highlight them, and press the Add button to move them to the Install box. Keep pressing the Continue buttons until you get to the Install button. Press Install and you'll be quickly on your way to adding the symbol set to your system.

3. Use the image window scroll bar in the Roll-Up to scroll down until you see the sun symbol, as shown in figure 7.14. Click on the symbol and drag it onto the striped background you created on the Printable page.

4. The default setting for the size of the sun symbol might be a tad too large for your striped background. If you need to resize it, use the Pick tool to click and drag on one of the sun's corner selection handles.

Adding a Pre-Built Symbol as a Design Element

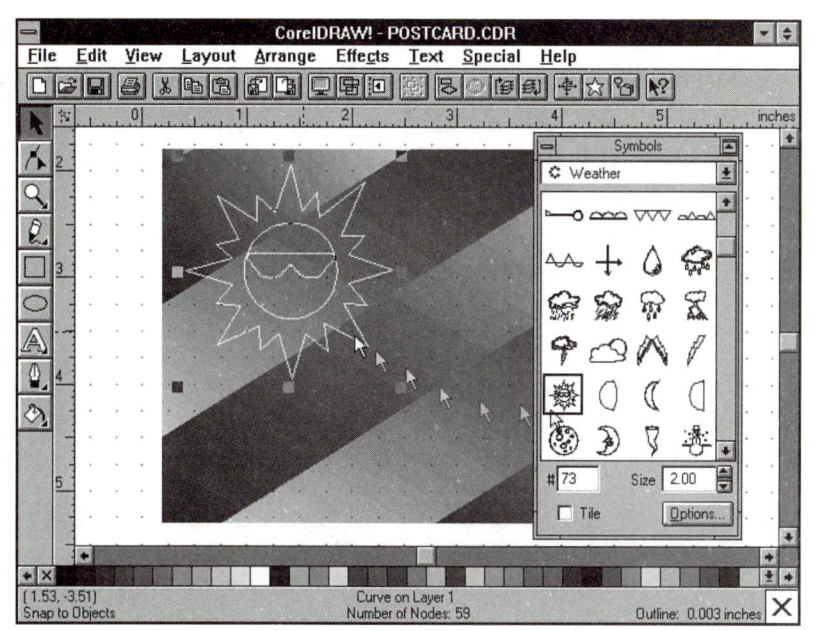

Figure 7.14
Adding a symbol from the Symbols Roll-Up is as easy as drag and drop!

Using the Break Apart and Fill Commands

If you take a good look at the sun symbol, you'll notice that it's made up of not one but three subpaths; the sun, the glow, and the sunglasses. They make up one shape, because the artist who designed it used the Combine command, not unlike the way you made the duck's eye part of its body in Chapter 4. Also remember that Symbols Roll-Up shapes (by default) have an outline, but no fill. The postcard calls for a more substantial sun than one made up of only an outline. Before you can apply different fills to each of the subpaths that make up the sun, you'll need to use Corel's Break Apart command to change this drawing from one object to three.

To use the Break Apart command, follow these steps:

1. Click on the Wireframe button on the Ribbon Bar. The stripes, while pretty, obscure your view of the next few steps.

2. With the sun selected, choose **A**rrange, Brea**k** Apart (or press Ctrl+K).

3. Click on a clear space on your page to deselect the three shapes.

4. Click on the shape of the sun's glow to select it.

5. Extend the Fill Roll-Up by clicking on the upper right triangle button, then select the Radial Fill button (second button from the left on the Roll-Up).

6. Set the foreground color (the left Roll-Up color button) to yellow by clicking on the button's down arrow, like you did to define the blue Fountain Fill for the stripes.

7. Click on the background color drop-down button and choose orange as your second color in the Radial Fill. Click and drag the Radial fill so its center is in an 11 o'clock position, as shown in figure 7.15, and click on the Apply button.

Figure 7.15
Use the Radial Fountain Fill to imitate lighting you'd find on round shapes in real life.

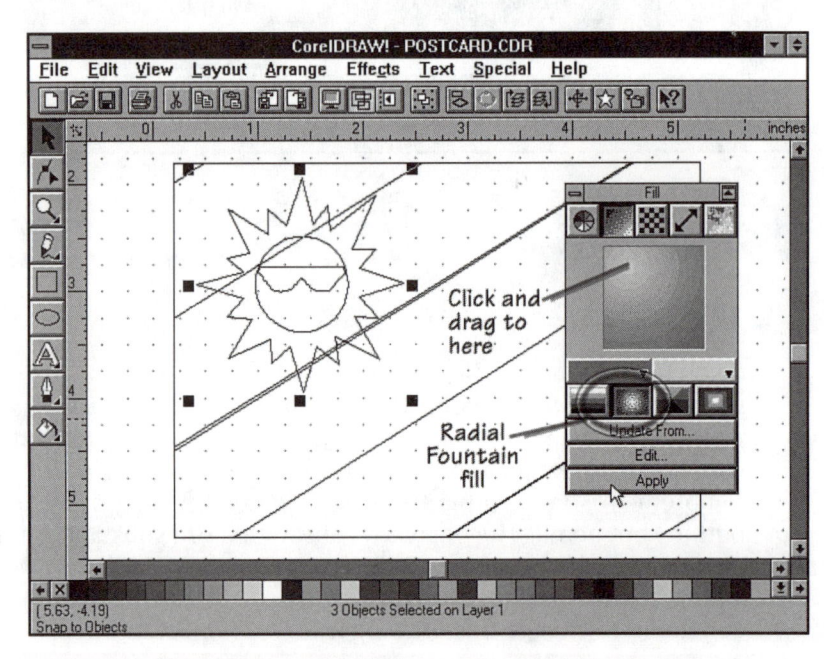

8. Click on the sun object and apply the same Radial Fountain Fill.

9. Click on the sunglasses to select them, but don't do anything else yet.

10. Switch back to Preview mode by clicking again on the Wireframe button on the Ribbon Bar.

11. The designer of the sun combined the three component objects in a certain order, so the sunglasses aren't the top object, and your view of them is presently blocked by the sun. Click on the To Front button on the Ribbon Bar to correct this.

12. You can select any color from the color palette to shade the sun's shades by scrolling left or right, but here's a quicker way to select Grass Green for the sun's glasses: Click on the up arrow on the right of the color palette, and move your cursor over to the Grass Green swatch. The status line tells you when you hit the right green, as shown in figure 7.16.

13. With the Pick tool, marquee-select the three pieces that make up the sun. Click on the Group button on the Ribbon Bar (or press Ctrl+G) to tie the pieces of the sun together into a unit. If you should need to reposition the sun, it's much easier to move when it's grouped. Because CorelDRAW objects are discrete, independent shapes, grouping collections of them together prevents unwanted, accidental repositioning of multiple shapes.

Figure 7.16

Display all the color palette swatches by clicking and holding on the up arrow.

Note

When you choose a swatch from the total display of color palette colors, the range of colors displayed when you go back to the normal, one-row view of colors changes to reflect where you last chose a color on the color palette.

Adding Artistic Text to the Postcard

In this next section, you'll be using Artistic Text, as opposed to Paragraph Text (covered in later chapters), because it's the best choice for short phrases that you want to manipulate graphically. Artistic Text can be converted to curves, whereas Paragraph Text cannot. When text has been converted to curves, it becomes a graphic element and can be modified by any of the special effects found on the Effects menu. Creating a drop-shadow effect for the "Greetings from" phrase on the postcard will require a graphic trick or two after you directly enter the text onto the Printable page.

Before you get to the Nedrow Beach text, add "Greetings from" to the postcard. To add Artistic Text, follow these steps:

1. Click on the Artistic Text tool (the button with the "A" on it) on the Toolbox. Place your cursor to the right of the sun, and type **Greetings from**. Your Artistic Text will appear as Corel's default font (usually Avant Garde BT). Don't move the cursor yet.

2. Hold down the Alt key, and type **0151** on the numeric keypad. This is an *extended character*, specifically, an *em dash*, used in professional publishing circles to indicate a pause in a phrase, as seen in figure 7.17.

Tip

If you think typing an em dash extended character is cool, Type 1 and TrueType fonts typically contain all sorts of goodies like cents signs and registered-trademark circles. The trick is to know which four-digit code stands for what.

Use Windows Character Map (CHARMAP.EXE) to locate a specific extended character. Also, a lot of shareware utilities for Windows are made to print the whole list of extended characters for a particular font. You can usually find programs like *Fonter* and *FontSee* on electronic bulletin boards.

Adding Artistic Text to the Postcard

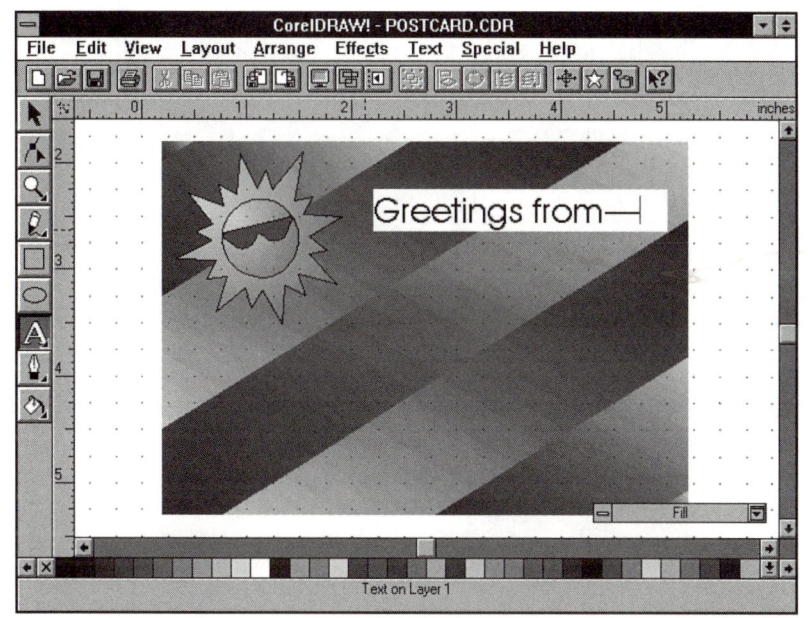

Figure 7.17
You can type text directly into Corel's Drawing Window with the Artistic Text tool.

3. Select the Pick tool from the Toolbox; this selects the text you just entered and puts the eight selection handles around the phrase. With the text selected, press Ctrl+T to display the Character Attributes dialog box.

4. Here's your chance to find a snappier typeface than Corel's default for the postcard. As shown in figure 7.18, I chose Kaufmann in the Fonts list and Bold in the Style drop-down list box. If you don't have Kaufmann installed, be sure to take a look at the Stop note that follows this step.

Tip

You may not have chosen to add Kaufmann BT from the Corel disks when you installed the program, but this won't really affect the assignment. Good alternative selections are Brush Script, Surf Style (Van Dijk), or Park Avenue.

Because CorelDRAW ships with over 800 typefaces, and you may have an additional collection of fonts you already use, no two users have identical font collections. You won't be forced to choose a particular typeface to use in this book's assignments. So feel free to experiment, but check out the suggestions to expand your "font vocabulary"!

Figure 7.18

Choose an eye-catching typeface from the list of all available fonts on your PC.

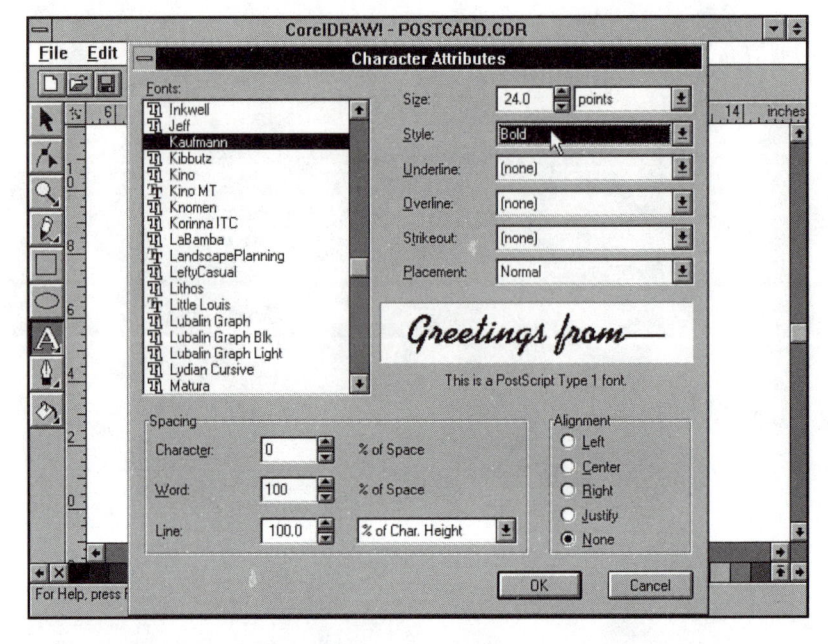

5. Click on OK after you've made your selection to return to the postcard.

Editing Artistic Text

By default, Artistic Text is displayed as black, with no outline. Choose the Pick tool and reposition the greetings phrase (if you need to) to the right of the sun, leaving a little space between them. The phrase looks good in the script typeface, but if you add a drop shadow it will stand out from the background and be even more apppealing.

Follow these steps to create the drop shadow:

1. Consider the black text on-screen to be the shadow now. Press the + key on the keypad to duplicate the text. The duplicated text becomes the currently selected object.

2. Press the keyboard up arrow key and then the left arrow key once each. The duplicate greeting has now been nudged up and to the left of the original by .1 inch. This is the value at which you set the Nudge feature earlier in this assignment.

3. Click on the yellow color swatch on the color palette. As you can see in figure 7.19, you now have another authentic-looking element in this "classic" postcard.

Adding Artistic Text to the Postcard

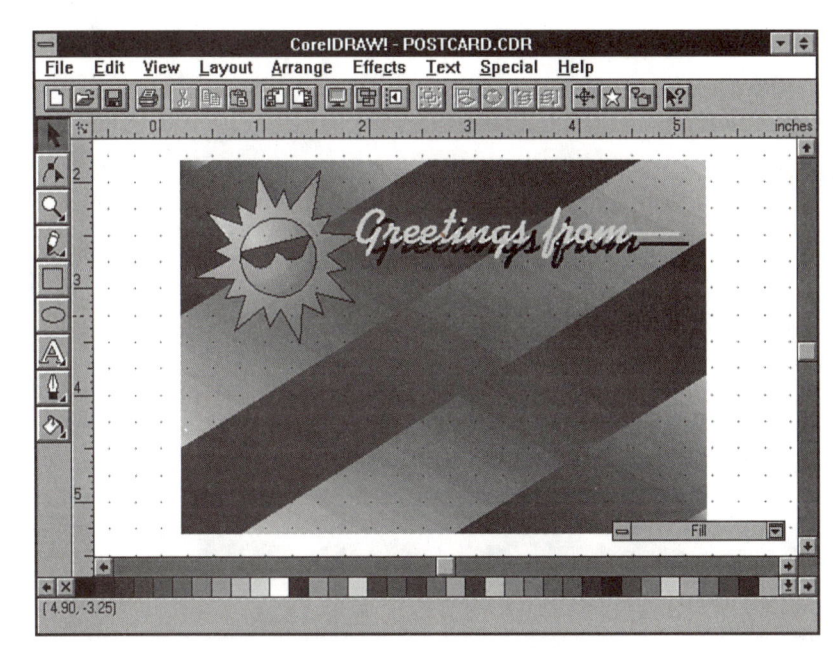

231

Figure 7.19
Drop-shadow effects are easy to create by duplicating, then nudging, the duplicate.

Stop

Unlike the Rectangle and Ellipse tools, you can't press the spacebar to toggle back to the Pick tool when the Text tool is active. You must press Ctrl+spacebar to toggle from the Text tool to the Pick tool. Then if you want to return to using the Text tool, press the spacebar. If you only press the spacebar when the Text tool is active, you get a space between Artistic Text characters.

Aligning Artistic Text

To visually communicate both the name Nedrow Beach and the image it will contain, you need to strike a fine balance between the width of the typeface and its readability once you fill it in with the photographic TIF image. A scrawny font like Times Roman won't cut it because the lettering won't allow enough picture through to recognize the picture. And a lot of display fonts, while they are bold enough, have too much innate "character" to be legible after filling them with a photograph.

Chapter 7: Working with Bitmap Images

Let's keep this in mind as you add and align Artistic Text. Follow these steps:

1. Choose the Zoom tool. Press the Zoom To All Objects tool on the menu fly-out, so you have a nice, close view of your work.

2. Choose the Artistic Text tool. Click an insertion point in the center of the postcard and in all capital letters type **NEDROW**. Press the Enter key, and then in all capital letters type the word **BEACH**. As seen in figure 7.20, the phrase is on two lines.

Figure 7.20
Artistic Text entered directly in the Drawing Window is flush left by default.

3. Select the Pick tool from the Toolbox and press Ctrl+T to bring the Character Attributes dialog box to the screen.

4. NEDROW BEACH should be Center-aligned, not the default of None, so click on the Center button in the Alignment field as shown in figure 7.21.

5. I've selected a homemade typeface (you'll learn how to create fonts yourself with CorelDRAW in Chapter 9) for NEDROW BEACH. From the Fonts list, pick a bold typface like Kabel Bold, AdLib, Aachen Bold, or even Shotgun BT. Any of these will work nicely to put a TIF image inside.

6. Click on OK after you've selected a font to return to the postcard.

Adding Artistic Text to the Postcard

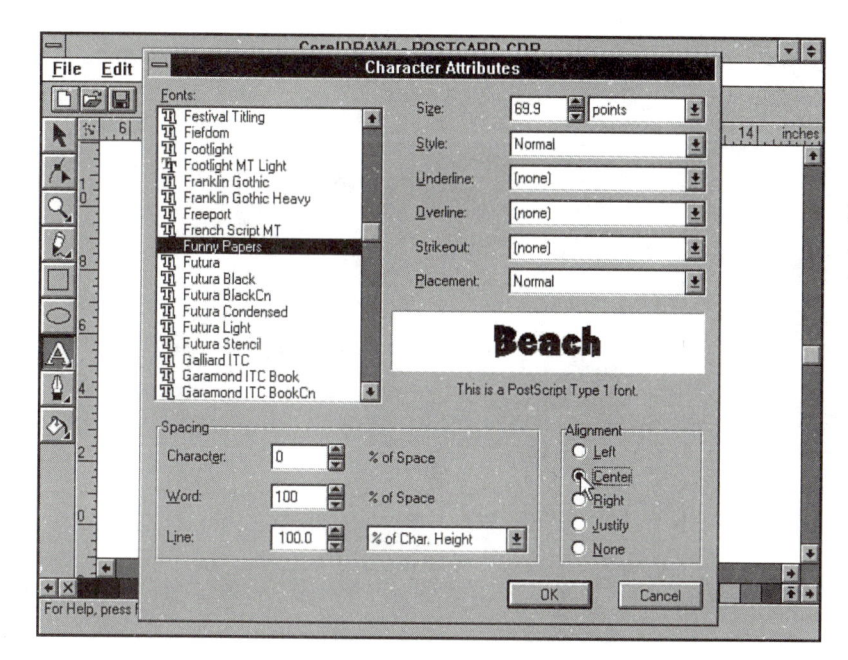

Figure 7.21
No matter how many (or few) lines of text you have, you can give it Alignment attributes.

Manually Kerning Artistic Text

Because information written into a font file varies widely with respect to kerning information (inter-letter spacing) and leading (inter-line spacing), strings of text frequently have to be adjusted to tighten or loosen these relationships.

In the next example, you'll see how to get the most eye-pleasing effect from the two lines of text without going to the Character Attributes dialog box. Follow these steps:

1. Click on the Shape tool. You'll see two honey-dipper–shaped selection handles hovering around the NEDROW BEACH phrase. These are special selection handles for Text objects. They appear on-screen whenever text is selected and the Shape tool is in use. Pulling on one of these special handles with the Shape tool produces a much different effect than when the Shape tool is used to modify a node in a path.

2. Click and drag upward while holding the left text handle (the "honey-dipper" handle that looks like it's pointing down). As you can see in figure 7.22, this handle adjusts the amount of space (leading) between lines of text.

Chapter 7: Working with Bitmap Images

Figure 7.22

Spacing between lines of text can be adjusted using the Shape tool and the text selection handles.

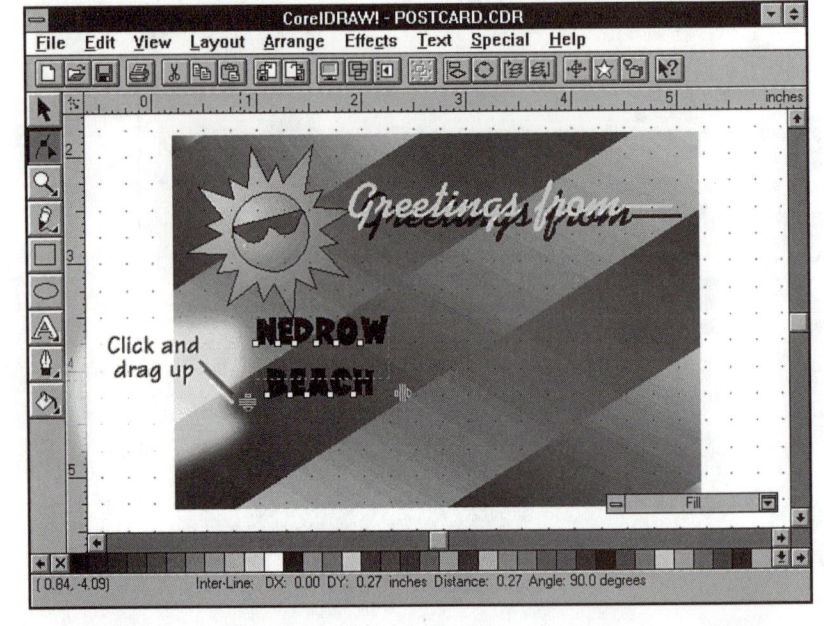

3. Once the NEDROW BEACH text has fairly tight line spacing, press the spacebar to get the Pick tool. When the Pick tool becomes active, the special "honey dipper" handles disappear.

4. Click and drag on the lower right selection handle and resize the NEDROW BEACH text by dragging it in a 4 o'clock direction. Stop when the text is about 60 points (look at the status line for this info), or measures around 3/4" by the vertical ruler.

The special handles you used in step 2 to adjust the spacing between lines of text have other uses as well. If you want to adjust the spacing between paragraphs of text from the Drawing Window view of a design, hold down the Ctrl key while click+dragging the left handle with the Shape tool.

Similarly, dragging on the right handle (this handle appears to point to the right) with the Shape tool adjusts inter-character spacing (kerning). By holding the Ctrl key, this handle can be used to adjust inter-word spacing.

The nodes that appear to the left of each character of text can be click+dragged with the Shape tool to move individual characters in any direction. The Ctrl key combination in this instance constrains character movement to a straight line in the direction you first begin to drag, horizontally or vertically.

Adding Artistic Text to the Postcard

Precision text spacing can also be made by typing values into the Spacing field of the Character Attributes dialog box.

Precision Rotating the Text

At the beginning of the chapter, you rotated the TIF image in PHOTO-PAINT by 12° to add a little pizzazz to the postcard. If the whole thing's going to look authentic and artistically correct, the Nedrow Beach text you'll place the TIF image inside should be rotated to 12°, too.

To rotate the text, follow these steps:

1. With the NEDROW BEACH text selected, choose Effects, Transform Roll-Up (Alt+F7 is the shortcut).

2. Click on the Rotate button (the icon of the arrow going in a circle), and type **12** in the Angle of Rotation. (Note: counterclockwise, the direction you want to spin the text, is expressed in CorelDRAW as a positive value.) Press the Apply button.

3. This text is a little hard to see as black text on the dark navy areas of the striped background. Click on the white swatch on the color palette to give you a better view of the text, as shown in figure 7.23. Now you're ready to add the TIF image.

Figure 7.23

The text is now rotated to the same degree as the TIF image you worked with earlier.

Making the Artistic Text the Star

Okay, this is the part where you polish off this outrageous postcard by letting a photograph peek through the NEDROW BEACH lettering. Traditional design folks used to have to painstakingly cut and trim around proof copies of lettering, and apply amberlith acetate overlays to their work to get an effect that could never match the finesse and precision you're operating with in Corel.

Add to this the aggravations of spirit gum fumes, mistakes that can't be undone from a command menu, and the inability to make exact duplicates of a finished, camera-ready piece. Think about this as you conclude the assignment; I'm grateful to be able to create a *piece* from the '40s and not have to work with *tools* from the '40s!

Importing the Beach

Place a copy of the BEACH.TIF image into the Drawing Window so it can find a new home in Nedrow. Importing a TIF image is done the same way as you'd import a TXT file into a word processor. Follow these steps:

1. Choose **F**ile, **I**mport.

2. From the List Files of **T**ype drop-down list, pick All Files(*.*), and use the **D**irectories and Dri**v**es drop-down lists to locate where you put BEACH.TIF on your hard disk.

3. When BEACH.TIF appears under the File **N**ame, click on it; if you check the **P**review box (see fig. 7.24) you'll see a miniature of the TIF image you rotated before actually importing it.

4. Click on OK, and CorelDRAW brings an exact copy of BEACH.TIF into the Drawing Window, centered on the Printable page.

The Power of the Clip

The PowerClip effect treats an object as a *container* for another object. Once inside the container object, the *contents* travel along wherever you move the container. You can place objects behind or in front of the container object, which gives you maximum flexibility in designing complex art pieces.

Making the Artistic Text the Star

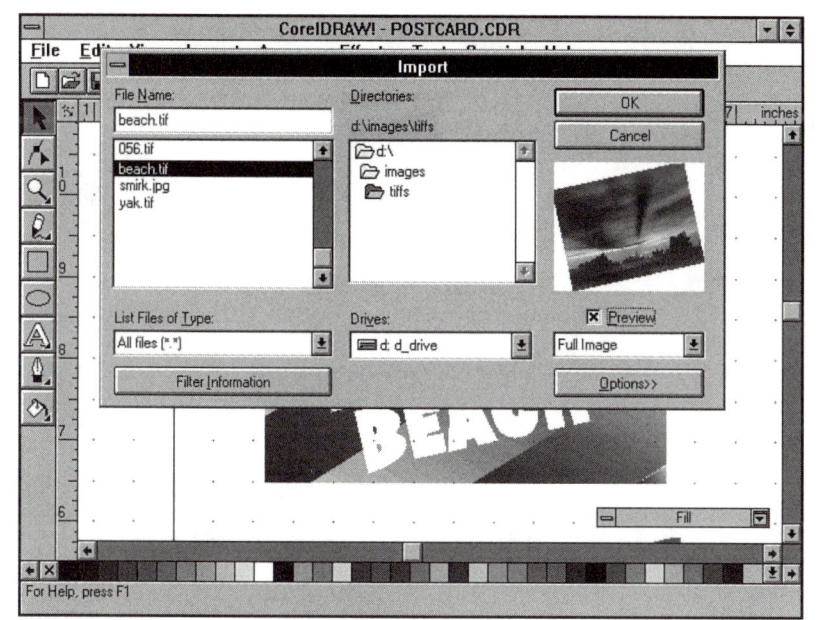

Figure 7.24
You can select a specific type of file, or all types, in the Import dialog box.

Follow these steps to use the PowerClip:

1. Make sure the BEACH.TIF image isn't covering your view of the NEDROW BEACH text, either by moving the TIF image with the Pick tool or clicking on the To Back button on the Ribbon Bar (or press Shift+PgDn).

2. Be sure that BEACH.TIF is currently selected. Choose Effe**c**ts, and Po**w**erClip, then **P**lace Inside Container, as shown in figure 7.25.

> You don't have to zoom out of the Drawing Window in this step. I "choreographed" this figure so you could see all the elements on the screen when the Effects menu was fully extended.

Note

3. Your cursor will turn into a large arrow, which is always a sign in Corel that you should use the arrow to point to something. In this instance, you point to the proposed container for the TIF image. Click over the NEDROW BEACH text.

Figure 7.25

The BEACH.TIF image is the *contents object*, and the text will be the *container object*.

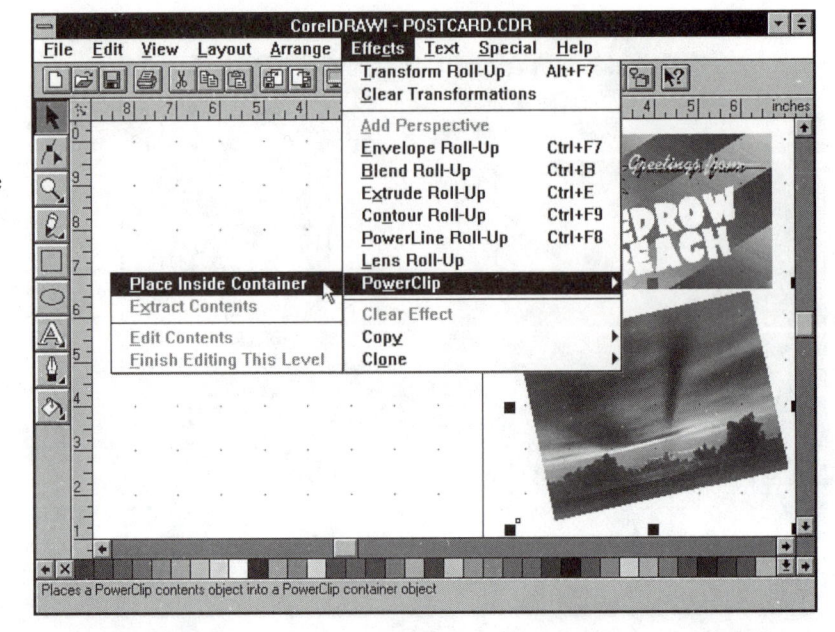

4. Right-mouse click over the white swatch on the color palette to give a white outline to the text.

5. Click on the Outline tool on the Toolbox. Make the outline around the text heavier by clicking on the Thin Outline tool on the Outline tool's fly-out menu. This tool adds a 2 pt. outline to selected objects and is found next to the Hairline Outline tool. A pop-up Help box will appear with the tool name if you linger over any of the buttons on the fly-out menu.

6. In figure 7.26, the product of your labors has finally come to a close. You have created a spectacular 1940s postcard with your newfound skills and a little help from CorelDRAW.

Tricks on Repositioning Contents

Corel documentation will tell you that a contents object (the one that goes inside the other) always lands in the center of a container object, but there *is* a way to reposition the contents if you want a specific portion of one object to show through the other.

Making the Artistic Text the Star

Figure 7.26
I'll trade anyone this card for a genuine one from Saratoga Springs.

First, you have to put the object in the container, and it lands in the container's center. This creates a relationship between container and contents. Then choose Edit Contents from the same PowerClip command menu used to place the object in the container. The contents object (or objects) will pop out, and you can reposition the contents object relative to the container object by dragging on the contents with the Pick tool. It's a good idea to send the contents To Back, because they'll obscure your view of their location relative to the container object.

When you've repositioned the contents, choose Effects, Power Clip and then select Finish Editing This Level, and the contents will be inserted relative to where you repositioned them. This is how I got the skyline of the BEACH.TIF image running exactly through the BEACH text.

Summary

You've experienced a blast from the past to a vision of future graphics done with CorelDRAW in this chapter, with a few stops along the way. You've learned a lot, but you've created something a lot more sophisticated than you'd imagine because CorelDRAW 5 has a lot more automated features than the average graphics program (or even CorelDRAW 4!). If you take the techniques you've discovered in this chapter and use them on your own assignments, you'll find you can produce an amazingly diverse assortment of artwork using the same commands. This is because Corel's features are "open-ended": the commands have a wide latitude, but it's your own ideas and techniques that make all the difference.

If you work with both text and graphics regularly, it's a combination of art forms you've only seen a little of in this chapter; in Chapter 8, "Serving Up a Page Layout," you'll dig into page layout and design. Because Corel can treat text and graphics the same way, you can bend and shape your way to outstanding desktop publishing work all within the Drawing Window. If you have a flyer or other document in need of some stand-up-and-shout dressing up, bring it along and turn the page!

It's... Famous ELMER'S
pizza
subs
wings
ORIGINAL
It's... Famous ELMER'S

CHAPTER 8

Serving Up a Page Layout

Famous Elmer's Country Fried Pizza franchises are popping up all over the country—there's probably one opening near you, if you have an imagination as fertile as the author's!

In this chapter's fictitious scenario, Elmer comes to you as a client, seeking your professional assistance as a designer to create a fancy disposable placemat. He'd like to protect the expensive gnarly pine finish in his restaurants' dining areas, and thinks customers would like to read about the history of pizza pies while they're waiting to be served.

While Elmer might be a figment of my imagination, the assignment is very real: how do you create a page layout in CorelDRAW? Both the answers and the layout will come to you automatically as graphics and Paragraph Text come together in this chapter.

In this chapter, you will:

- Modify an ellipse with the Shape tool
- Use the Envelope Roll-Up to shape text
- Make instant artwork with the Symbols Roll-Up
- Import and make wrap-around Paragraph Text

Modifying an Ellipse with the Shape Tool

Earlier in this book, you discovered that rectangles have different node properties than regular curved paths, and that the Shape tool makes rounded corners out of sharp 90° rectangle edges when you click and drag them.

Ellipses, like rectangles, are complex geometric shapes; when you click and drag the node of an ellipse, something equally interesting happens—ellipses become pie wedges and arcs.

Drawing the Pizza

Elmer doesn't sell arcs, though, so as a first step to composing his pizza pie place settings, you'll create an ellipse. You need to change the page orientation because placemats generally are wider than they are tall. Double-click on the page border (the gray drop shadow around the Printable page) or choose Layout, Page Setup to bring up the Page Setup dialog box. Click on the Landscape radio button on the Size tabbed dialog box, then click on OK. Although letter-sized placemats are a little small for Elmer's family pizzas, a landscape 8 1/2" by 11" will be a good layout if you decide to print your masterpiece later.

To draw the pizza shape, follow these steps:

1. With the Ellipse tool, Ctrl+click and drag a perfect circle, stopping when the status line says it's about 6.75 ". It doesn't matter where you draw the ellipse; you'll reposition it later.

2. Click on a medium gray on the color palette with the ellipse still selected. This is not the final color for the ellipse; it'll just help you visually locate the ellipse.

3. Press the spacebar to get the Pick tool, then press the + sign on the numeric keypad to duplicate the ellipse.

4. Click on a very light gray on the color palette. You should see a light gray ellipse totally obscuring your view of the darker one.

Drawing a Pie Wedge

You can modify the duplicate ellipse so that it appears to be a pie wedge cut from the original ellipse. To cut a slice of pizza from the pie, follow these steps:

Modifying an Ellipse with the Shape Tool

243

1. With the Shape tool, click on the top (and only) node on the light gray ellipse. Moving clockwise, drag the node to a 2 o'clock position, always keeping the Shape tool inside the ellipse as you drag.

Stop

If you move the Shape tool cursor outside of the ellipse, the ellipse will vanish, and you'll wind up dragging an arc. If this happens, continue dragging the ellipse node, but drag it toward the center of where you last saw the complete ellipse. You'll regain the filled wedge shape you are creating from the filled ellipse.

2. Release the node, go back to the 12 o'clock node on the light gray ellipse, and click and drag the node counterclockwise to about the 4 o'clock position. As you can see in figure 8.1, the lighter ellipse is now a pizza slice. Don't make the slice too large. This slice will be used as a border for a small amount of text, and besides, pizza is fattening.

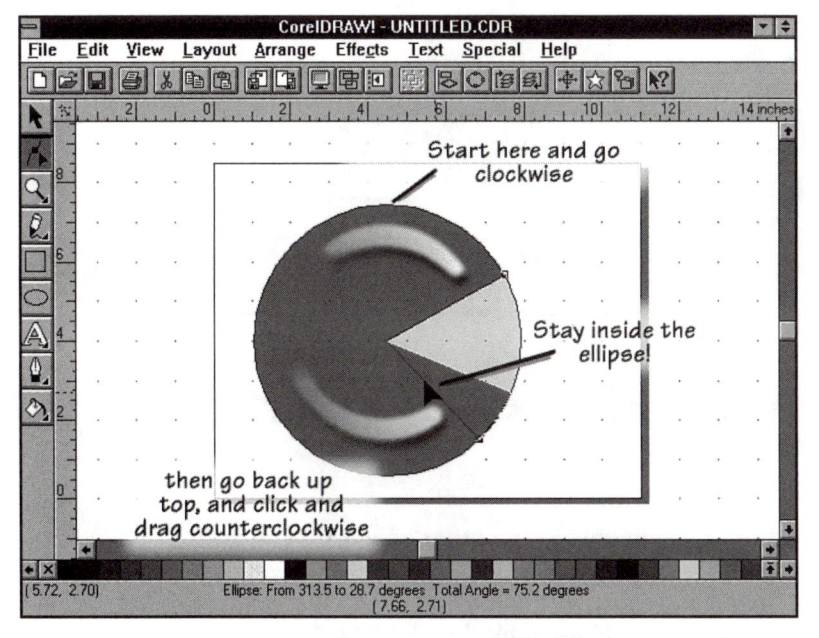

Figure 8.1

Ellipses retain their round properties when you edit them with the Shape tool.

3. Click on the top node of the dark ellipse to select it; the node is now exposed since you "wedged" the lighter ellipse.

Chapter 8: Serving Up a Page Layout

4. With the Shape tool, click and drag the top node of the dark gray ellipse in a clockwise direction, to a point just a sliver past the 4 o'clock position so that you can see a little background between it and the lighter ellipse.

5. Go back to the 12 o'clock node on the dark ellipse, and click and drag clockwise to a point just short of the 2 o'clock position. This will make it look like the lighter slice is coming out of the darker ellipse, as shown in figure 8.2.

Figure 8.2
You can turn ellipses into pie slices with the Shape tool.

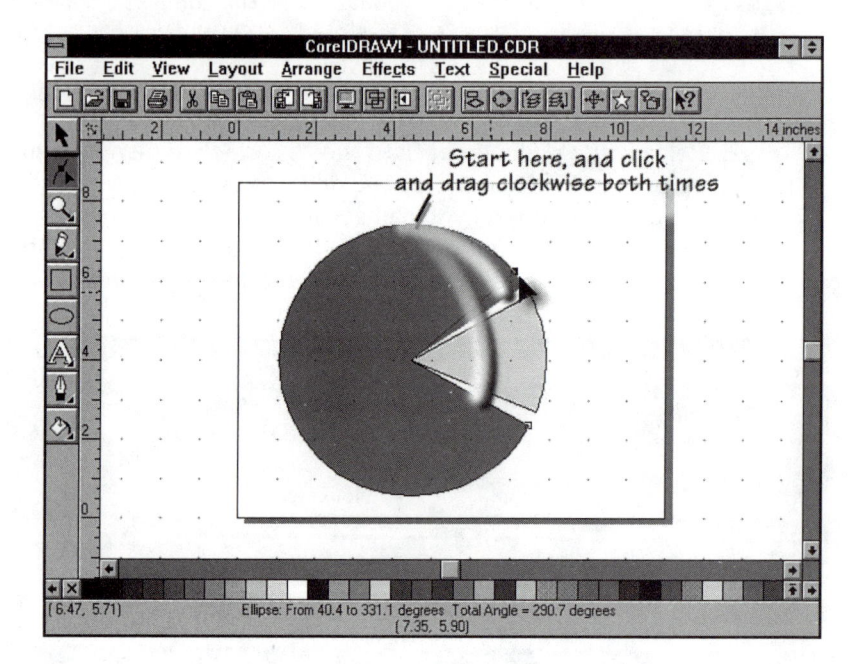

Adding Artistic Text to the Pizza Slice

If you followed the assignments in the other chapters, you probably have a good feel for working with Corel Artistic Text, and the next few steps for embellishing the pizza pie graphic will be familiar. Not so familiar though, is the Text Roll-Up, which we'll use to modify the text.

With the Text Roll-Up, you have quick access to 90 percent of the functions you normally have to "drill" three or four menus deep to find. You'll use the Text Roll-Up to change Artistic Text, and later to format Paragraph Text.

Entering Artistic Text

Add the word "pizza" to the pizza slice by following these steps:

1. Marquee-zoom into the pizza slice by using the Zoom In tool found on the Zoom tool's fly-out menu.

2. With the Artistic Text tool, click an insertion point within the light gray pizza slice and type **pizza** (either upper- or lowercase; you can get creative here!).

3. Double-click on the Artistic Text button on the Toolbox or press Ctrl+F2 to display the Text Roll-Up.

4. Reposition the Roll-Up by clicking and dragging on its title bar so you have a clear view of the pizza lettering. Roll-Ups have a penchant for popping up on top of your design work.

5. Highlight the pizza lettering with the Artistic Text tool so you can apply changes to it.

6. Click on the down arrow to the right of the font window on the Text Roll-Up. You can select any typeface from this list of installed fonts.

7. Neuland (similar to Newfoundland and Lithos) is a good choice of fonts for the pizza lettering; as you can see in figure 8.3, when you click on a font, a fly-out of the first few characters you've highlighted appears in your choice of typeface.

Tip

The symbols to the left of the listed fonts on the Roll-Up refer to the type of font technology used to create the typeface. The TT symbol means a font is TrueType (native MS-Windows technology), whereas the T1 symbol indicates a Type 1 PostScript font, a descriptor language developed by Adobe Systems.

Either type of font is fine to use in Corel, except you must have Adobe Type Manager installed on your computer to access Type 1 fonts.

8. Press the Apply button, and Corel's default font with which you typed **pizza** (usually Avant Garde Bk BT) takes on a more interesting look.

Figure 8.3

Choose a new typeface for your pizza lettering.

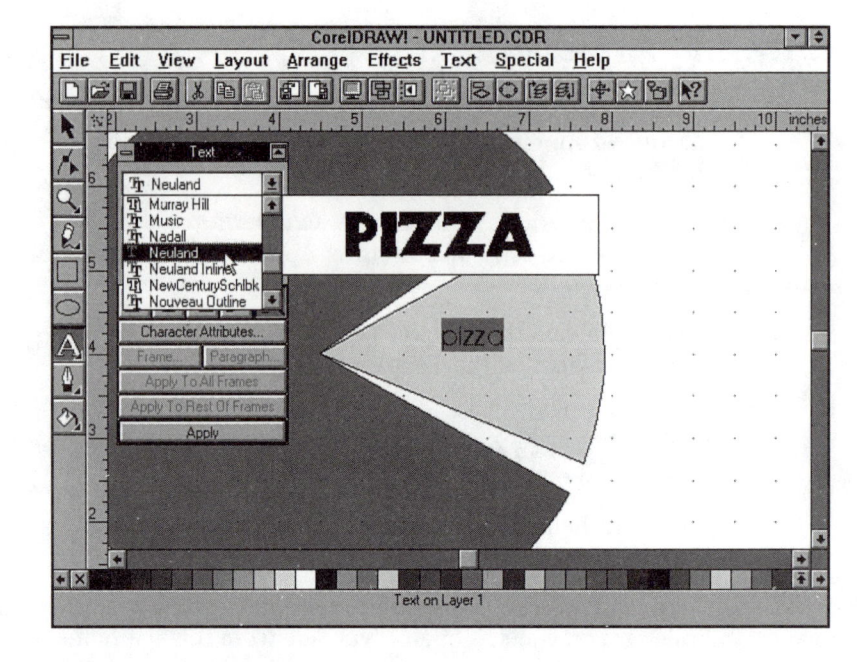

Sizing the Type

Now that you have placed the Artistic Text, you can size the text by following these steps:

1. Choose the Pick tool from the Toolbox. Do *not* press the spacebar to toggle tools when you use the Text tools; it only adds a space to your typing! Instead, press *Ctrl*+spacebar to toggle back and forth between Text tools and the Pick tool.

2. Click and drag a corner selection handle away from the word pizza to make it about 60 points (3/4" as viewed from the vertical ruler). Resizing Artistic Text this way is not terribly precise, but it's faster than entering a different point value through the Text Roll-Up.

Shaping Artistic Text with the Envelope Effect

Designers frequently put words inside shapes to attract attention to a part of an illustration. But Corel designers can *mold* an Artistic Text phrase so its contours exactly match the shape of any other shape (an envelope) you create. It's all done with the Envelope Roll-Up.

Shaping Artistic Text with the Envelope Effect

247

Creating the Envelope

You'll create a pizza slice shape which will be the envelope shape into which you'll "pour" the pizza lettering. Just follow these steps:

1. Choose the Freehand tool, and draw a four-sided polygon inside the pizza slice, as shown in figure 8.4. Click a point to begin with, then double-click until you come to the first point, and single-click here. Make it loosely describe the interior of the pizza slice without actually touching the outline path of the pizza slice.

Tip

Unless it's for a specific design purpose, don't create a "template" for enveloping text that's exactly the same as the shape you'll pour the text into. Always try to make the template for the envelope a little smaller. If you use the actual shape instead of your template for the envelope, there will be no border between the text and the outline it ultimately is placed within. This makes text harder to read.

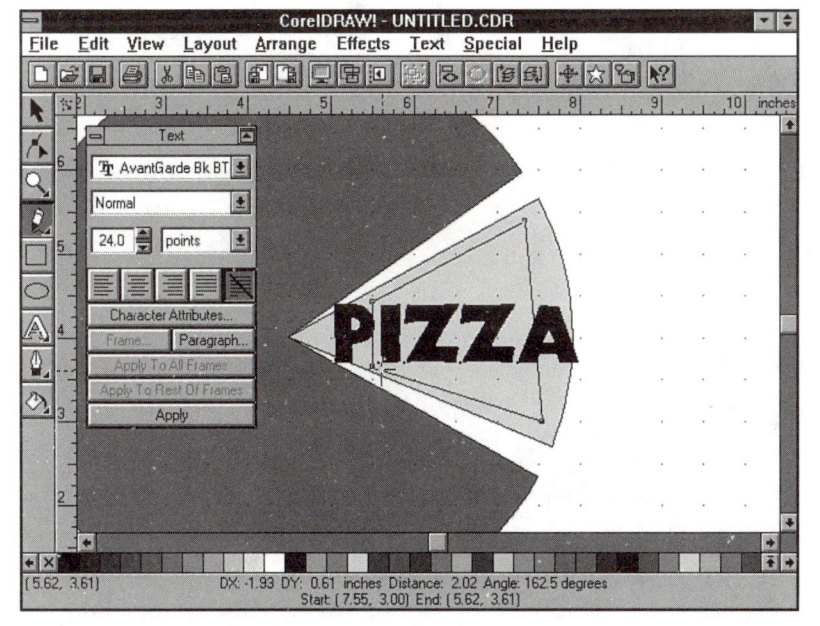

Figure 8.4

Make the polygon shape four-sided; don't end the left edge in a single pizza slice point!

2. With the Shape tool, double-click on the right side of the polygon to display the Node Edit Roll-Up.

Chapter 8: Serving Up a Page Layout

3. Press the To curve button on the Node Edit Roll-Up, then click and drag the control points on the right, curved line segment to shape it more like the crust side of the pizza slice, as shown in figure 8.5.

Figure 8.5
Use the control points to reshape the segment you converted to a curve.

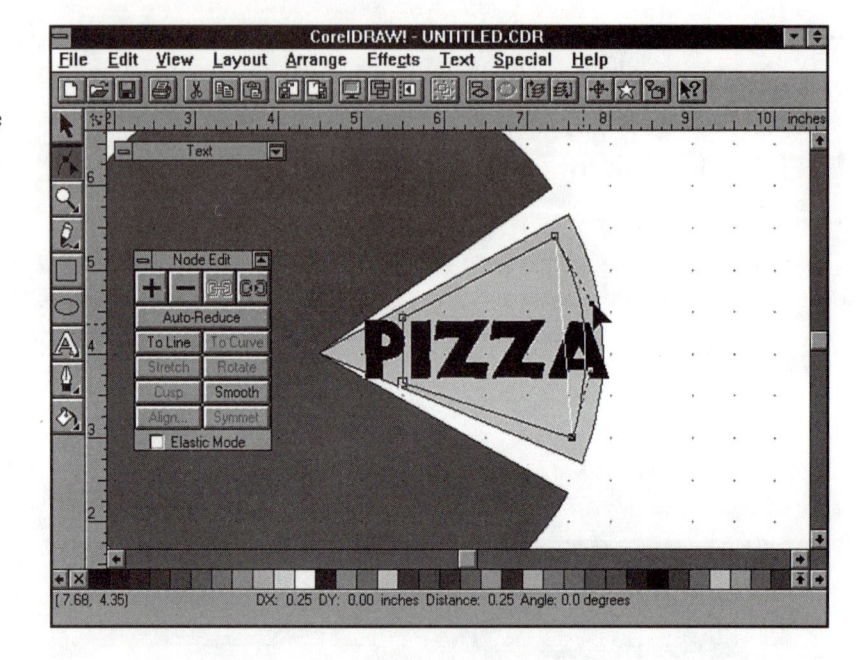

Tip

If you made some mistakes drawing your polygon, now is your chance to use the Shape tool to click and drag the nodes and refine the shape.

Applying the Envelope

Now that you have created the shape on which to create the envelope you are ready to apply the Envelope command to the pizza text. Follow these steps to apply this command.

1. Press Ctrl+F7 (or choose Effe**c**ts, **E**nvelope Roll-Up from the menu) to display the Envelope Roll-Up. You may want to retract the Node Edit and Text Roll-Ups at this point to conserve Drawing Window space. Press on their roll-up buttons (the up triangles to the right of their title bars) to make 'em smaller.

2. Select the pizza text (either with the Shape or the Pick tool), and click on the Create From button on the Envelope Roll-Up. Your cursor becomes an arrow; click on the polygon shape you drew with the arrow cursor. When the pizza text displays a dotted outline around it in the shape of the polygon you drew, click on the Envelope Roll-Up Apply button. You'll get an effect like that shown in figure 8.6.

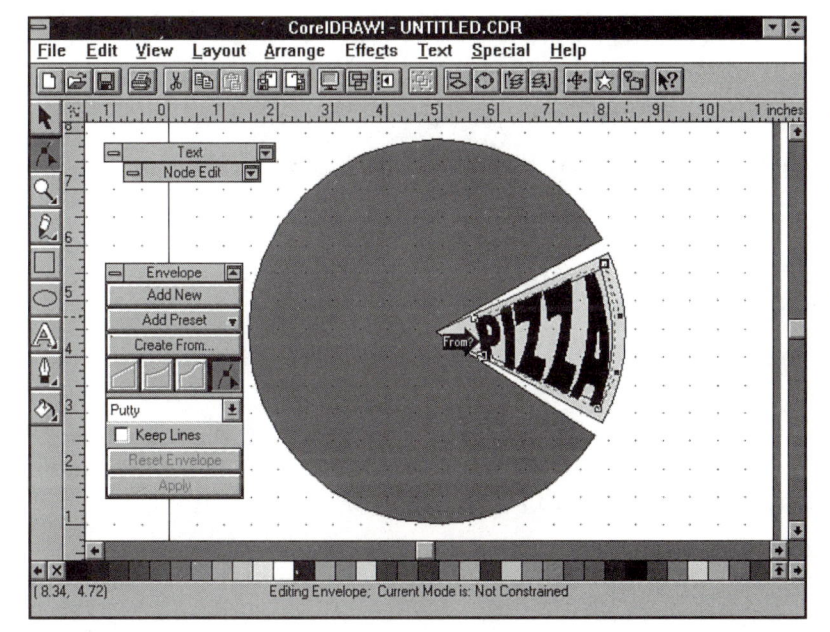

Figure 8.6
The Envelope effect reshapes text or graphics to conform to another shape's outline and dimensions.

An object you want to envelope has to be one shape; it can have several subpaths created by *combining* different objects. Multiple objects that have been *grouped* can't be enveloped, however. If you try to apply an envelope effect to grouped objects, all Corel will do is rudely beep at you.

The shape taken on by the pizza lettering can be changed and modified to your heart's content by clicking and dragging on the envelope dotted outline, or on an envelope node, with the Shape tool. In fact, you can assign different envelope node and segment properties (like To Curve and Symmet) by using the Node Edit Roll-Up. If you want to "tweak" the shape of the enveloped pizza, click and drag on its envelope outline while the Shape tool is active, and press Apply when you want to execute your editing work.

Note: An envelope outline has the same node and segment properties as the shape you based the envelope on.

3. Press the spacebar to make the Pick tool active again.
4. Most of the time you have to reposition an enveloped object, so click and drag the pizza text so it fits perfectly inside the polygon you drew.
5. Make the pizza text white by left-mouse clicking on the white swatch on the color palette.
6. Give both the pizza and the slice a black fill and no outline by selecting both, left-mouse clicking on the far left color palette swatch, and then right-mouse clicking over the "X" on the color palette.
7. Select the polygon shape you drew and press the Del key. You're finished with it.
8. Choose Edit, Select All, and press the Group button on the Ribbon Bar (or press Ctrl+G). The lettering, the slice, and the pizza itself now have a temporary binding quality to them, and can be moved as one unit.
9. Tidy up the Drawing Window now by closing up all of the Roll-Ups that are on-screen, except for the Text Roll-Up, which you'll need later.

Tip: You don't always have to draw a shape on which to base an envelope; you can use any one of Corel's pre-built shapes. Instead of clicking on the Create From button on the Envelope Roll-Up, click on Add Preset. This displays a drop-down list with thirty-three shapes to choose from. Find one you like, click on it and a corresponding envelope boundary box will appear around the selected object in the Drawing Window. Click on Apply and the effect is applied.

Creative Design and the Intersection Command

Most designers would consider what we've done here a fair piece of work, turn out the lights, and make a beeline for the parking lot. But as a CorelDRAW designer, you owe it to yourself to explore the possibilities of vector drawing, and discover how to astound your clients with your expertise.

You'll be adding Paragraph Text to Elmer's placemat in this chapter, and that means a 7" pizza pie will have to diminish in its elemental importance of the Printable page. You can keep the feeling of the pizza without illustrating all of it by moving it to the top left corner of the placemat. Then, with compositional aesthetics in mind, you'll remove a good portion of it (four to five servings)— see for yourself how asymmetrical design work is fun, inspirational, and easy by following these steps:

1. Select the Zoom tool, choose the Zoom To Page tool (the far right button), and press the Zoom tool again and choose the Zoom Out tool (the magnifying glass with the minus sign). You should have a view of the Printable page, with lots of room to spare around the edges.

2. Click and drag the grouped pizza elements to the upper left corner of the Printable page, with the center of the group sitting on the upper left corner. Some of the pizza group should be sitting outside the Printable page.

3. Click on the selected group. This sends the group into the Rotate/Skew mode.

Tip: You can tell if your pizza group is properly positioned for the next steps if the center of rotation is slightly inside the Printable page. If it isn't, click on the group to put it back in non-Rotation mode, reposition it, and click again to put it in the Rotate/Skew mode.

4. Click the upper right corner rotate handle, and drag down about one or two screen inches, as shown in figure 8.7. The top edge of the pizza slice should be even with the page's horizon. If it's not, play with the rotation a little.

Chapter 8: Serving Up a Page Layout

Figure 8.7
Freeform rotation of an object is started by clicking on an already selected shape to switch it to Rotate/Skew mode.

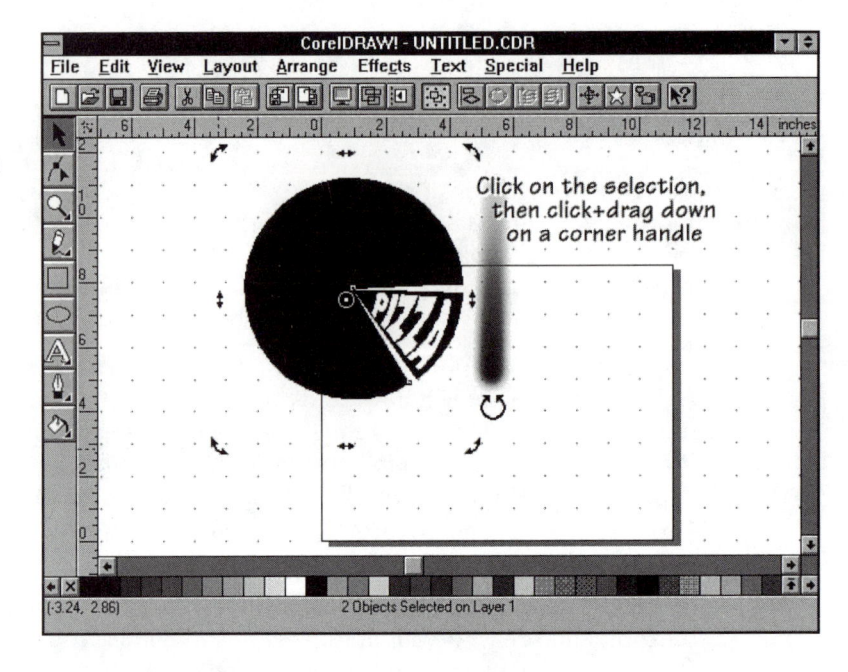

[Screenshot of CorelDRAW showing a pizza with a slice being rotated. Annotation reads: "Click on the selection, then click+drag down on a corner handle"]

Note

You'll notice that the center of rotation for the group isn't in the center of the pizza. This is because the group is being rotated, and the pizza lettering doesn't have the same center of rotation as the pizza slice and the main pizza. CorelDRAW averages the center of rotation when multiple objects are grouped.

5. Double-click on the Rectangle Tool. This automatically creates a rectangle that's a page frame (the dimensions of the Printable Page), and the rectangle, by default, has no fill and a hairline outline (unless you changed CorelDRAW's defaults).

You now want to create a new, *replacement* piece for the large pizza that doesn't go outside the Printable page. To do this, you'll use the Intersection command, which will create a new shape out of the areas where the page frame and the pizza intersect.

Figure 8.8

You can add a perfect outline to the Printable Page by double-clicking on the Rectangle Tool.

6. Select the grouped pizza components, and ungroup them by pressing the Group button on the Ribbon Bar to toggle this property off or press Ctrl+U.

7. Click on the page frame shape while holding down the Shift key (to additively select stuff), and click on the main pizza shape.

8. Choose **A**rrange, and **I**ntersection. I did this in figure 8.9, and also recolored the main pizza slice so you can see the effect of the Intersection command—you'll have a truncated pizza that fits perfectly in the corner of the placemat.

9. You should now click on and delete the original pizza (keep the slice, though!) and the page frame shape, since they contribute nothing further to your pizza placemat work.

Chapter 8: Serving Up a Page Layout

Figure 8.9

An Intersection shape is created out of the common area shared by two overlapping shapes.

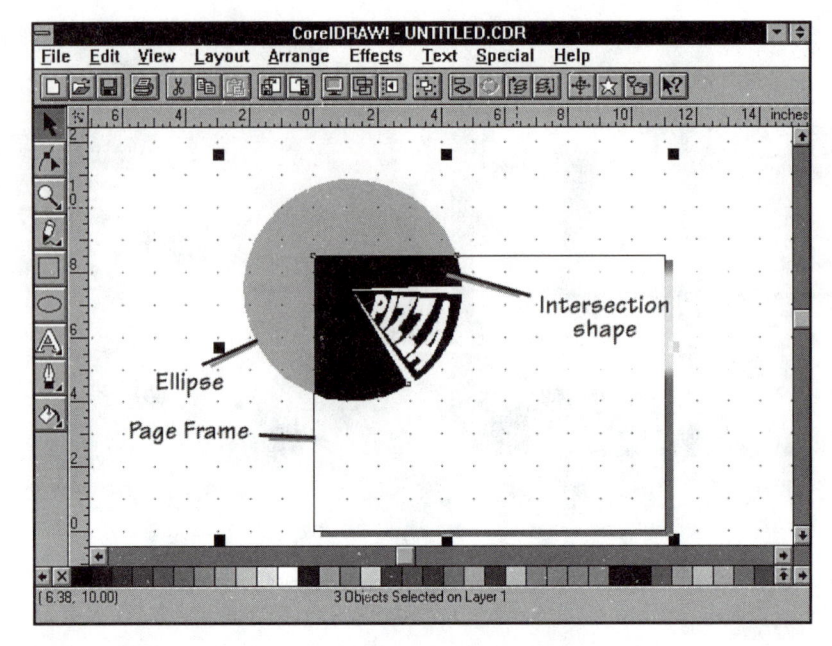

Adding a New Artistic Text Element

Nice design you have now, but it's a little lean on text at this point. *Pizza* is a wonderfully descriptive word, but "The History of Pizza" is the topic and title of the placemat. Elmer's wish is your command because you've learned a quick and easy way to create and alter Artistic Text.

1. Select the Zoom To All Objects tool from the Zoom tool fly-out menu.
2. Choose the Artistic Text tool and type **The History of** above the pizza slice, within the Intersection pizza shape.
3. By default, Artistic Text is rendered in black, which hampers your view of it. Choose the Pick tool and click on the white swatch on the color palette.
4. Roll down the Text Roll-Up by clicking on the upper right triangle next to the title bar.

Text can only be reassigned a typeface if it's selected, and it can be selected in two different ways. You did it last by highlighting it with the Text tool, but if you have the Pick tool active and your phrase has selection handles around it, Corel already considers it selected.

5. Scroll down the fonts list on the Text Roll-Up, pick a good display font, and press Apply. Then close the Roll-Up. I used Bodoni Poster italic, as shown in figure 8.10, but feel free to innovate here.

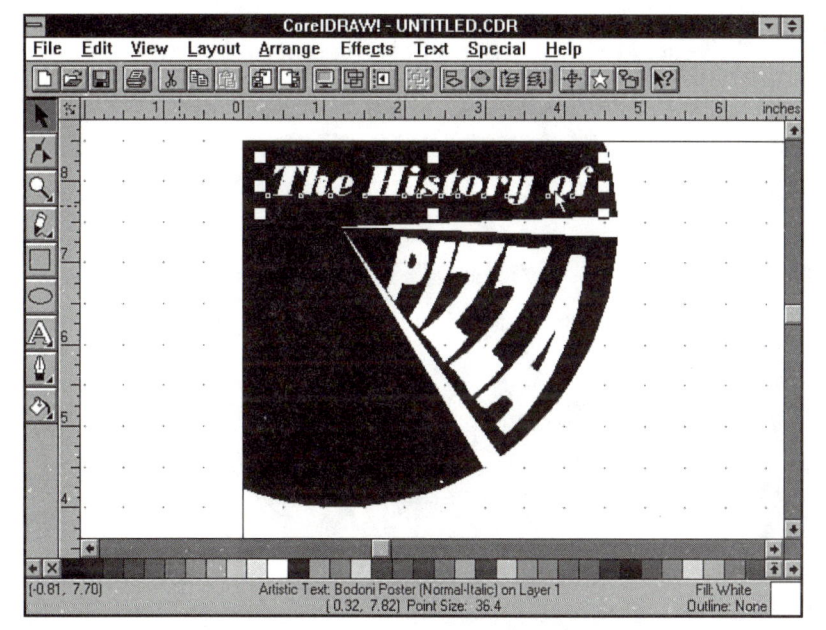

Figure 8.10

Choose a display font that's classy, clean, bold, and legible.

Display fonts differ from body text fonts in that they are more ornamentally designed. Bodoni Poster, Harpoon, Tiffany Heavy, and Beehive are all display fonts that come on the Corel disks.

While they are attention-getting, display fonts (also known as headline fonts) are best used at large point sizes (18 pt. and up) with short phrases.

Body text fonts are more conservative in design, and were created for prolonged reading. Try typing a letter to a friend in Tiffany Heavy at 12 points, and see how little they appreciate the headache and eyestrain that reading a display font causes them!

Adding Toppings to the Pizza

Hmmm. This is a clean pizza design now, sort of an illustrated headline, but perhaps it's a little too clean. Some stylized toppings will work well in this case, so here's a way to enhance the graphic. You may want to charge Elmer 75 cents extra for each additional item...

Chapter 8: Serving Up a Page Layout

Follow these steps:

1. Mushrooms. *Every* pizza has room for mushrooms. Choose the Ellipse tool and marquee-drag an ellipse about one screen inch wide for the top of the mushroom.

2. Choose the Freehand tool and make a polygon bottom for the mushroom's stem, as shown in figure 8.11.

Figure 8.11
Two distinct shapes make up a mushroom's outline.

3. Press the spacebar to get the Pick tool, marquee-select both shapes, choose <u>A</u>rrange, then choose <u>W</u>eld. This is the same technique you used to build the pawn in Chapter 5.

4. Fill the mushroom by selecting a color from the color palette; click and drag the mushroom onto the pizza.

5. Press the plus key on the numeric keypad to duplicate the mushroom, then click and drag it to another location on the pizza.

6. Pepperoni. Use the Ellipse tool to make one or two pepperoni slices. Fill the shapes, and put them wherever they'll fit on the pizza.

7. Quit when you think you'll give your graphic heartburn. As you can see in figure 8.12, this placemat is really shaping up!

Adding Toppings to the Pizza

Figure 8.12
The finished title illustration for Elmer's placemat.

Using Symbol Art

Next, you'll be calling on the Symbols Roll-Up for a helping hand in creating a second graphic for the placemat. As you've seen in other chapters, the Symbols Roll-Up is an invaluable CorelDRAW utility for artists in a hurry. You can swipe a piece of design, quickly recolor it, and add an element to a needy design in lightning time.

The Food category of symbols happens to contain a really nice graphic of a pizza slice, a topically appropriate item which you can break apart, fill its subpaths, and create a full-blown illustration. This will enhance the placemat design and give you something interesting to wrap Paragraph Text around.

To add symbol art to your design, follow these steps:

1. Click on the Zoom tool and choose the Zoom To Page tool.

2. Click on the Symbols button (the one with a star on it) on the Ribbon Bar to display the Symbols Roll-Up.

3. Scroll down the categories in the top window until you find Food.

4. Scroll down the picture window view until you locate the pizza slices symbol (hint: Food is arranged alphabetically; your pizza's in the row between the pepper and the Popsicle).

Chapter 8: Serving Up a Page Layout

5. Click and drag the pizza slice from the Symbols Roll-Up into the Drawing Window, as illustrated in figure 8.13.

Figure 8.13

Drag a copy of a symbol from the Roll-Up onto CorelDRAW's Drawing Window.

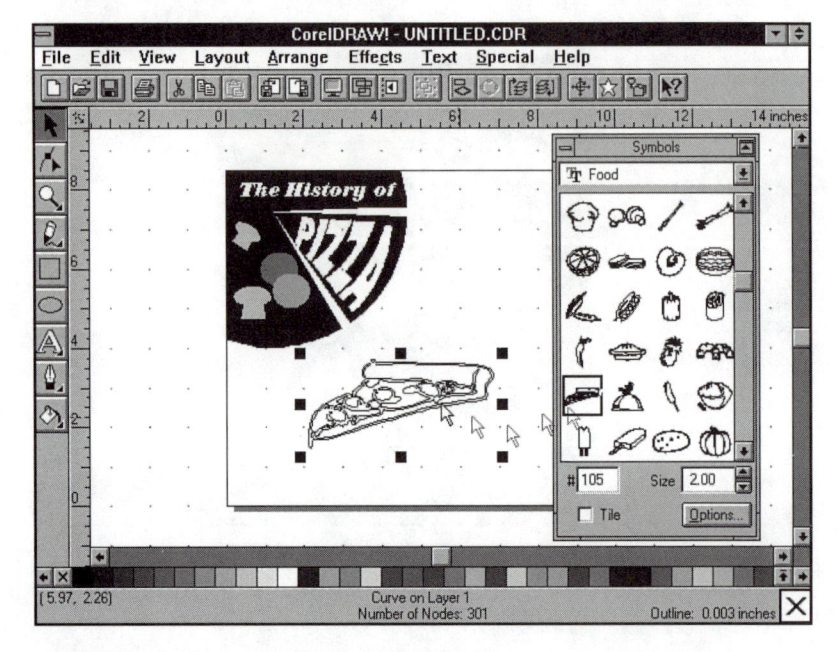

6. Double-click on the control menu button in the upper left corner of the Symbols Roll-Up to close the Roll-Up. You won't need it again.

7. Resize the pizza slice by dragging away from the shape while holding onto a corner selection handle. Stop when it's about the same size as the pizza pie graphic you created earlier.

Adding Artificial Coloring to Pizza

You'll find almost 20 subpaths made by the artist who drew the pizza symbol. The artist drew each shape, then used the CorelDRAW Combine command to make all the shapes one noncontiguous piece of art.

Symbols are not filled in, and this gives the budding Corel designer the opportunity to enhance a simple symbol with a unique selection of fills. You'll use the Fill Roll-Up in the next steps; like the Text Roll-Up, the Fill Roll-Up offers a wide range of selections and functions all in one tiny section of screen space. Unlike the Fill tool on the Toolbox, you can access different colors, textures, and Fountain Fills from the Fill Roll-Up in nanoseconds!

1. Choose the Zoom tool, then the Zoom In tool, and marquee-zoom in on the new pizza slice.
2. With the pizza slice selected, choose **A**rrange, Brea**k** Apart (Ctrl+K).
3. Click on a blank background area on the Drawing Window to deselect the bunch of shapes.
4. Click on the Fill tool, and choose the Fill Roll-Up tool from the fly-out menu. This is the last time you will have to dig into the Toolbox again!
5. Add a Fountain Fill to the crust of the pizza slice. Click on the Fountain Fill button (the second to left button on the top of the Roll-Up), then click on the Linear type fill, the leftmost beneath the front and back color buttons.
6. Click on the left color drop-down palette button and select a mustard yellow from the swatches, then click on the right color drop-down palette button and choose a warm brown.
7. Click and drag in the preview box in the Roll-Up to change the direction the Linear fill will take. You should click and drag up and to the right to make the Linear fill go from 7 to 1 o'clock.
8. Click on the pizza crust shape, and press the Apply button. Then click on the To Back button on the Ribbon Bar (or press Shift+PgDn). As you can see in figure 8.14, the outline shape now displays a sense of lighting and a warm color.

What happens when you fill a shape and all the shapes inside of it disappear? Remember that combined shapes (objects with multiple subpaths) were originally created by an artist in a specific order. That means when you break a multi-path shape apart, there's a hierarchy to the stack of individual shapes.

You can change this hierarchy like you did in the last step by selecting the shape that's obscuring your view of the others, and clicking on the To Back button on the Ribbon Bar. Conversely, you can move an object to the "head of the class" by selecting it, and clicking on the To Front button.

Shuffling the order of shapes is often necessary when you disassemble someone else's design.

Use your imagination along with the Fill Roll-Up as you fill each pizza shape. In figure 8.15, I'm putting the finishing touches on a piece of green pepper, I think. When you're done garnishing the pizza, close the Fill Roll-Up by double-clicking on the control button in the upper left corner of the Roll-Up.

Figure 8.14

Apply a custom-designed fill to any shape (or shapes) you have selected.

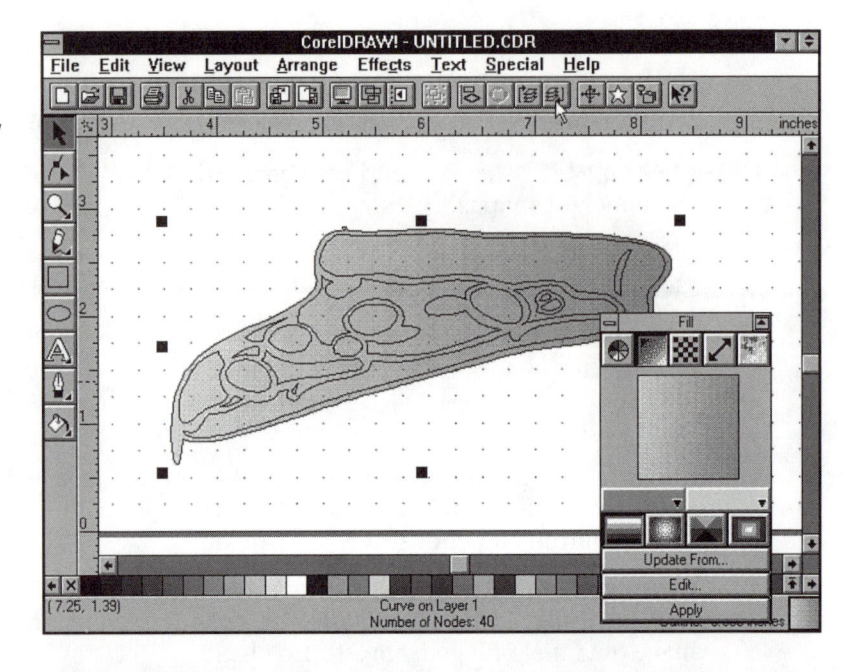

Figure 8.15

With vector designs, you can never "color outside of the lines"!

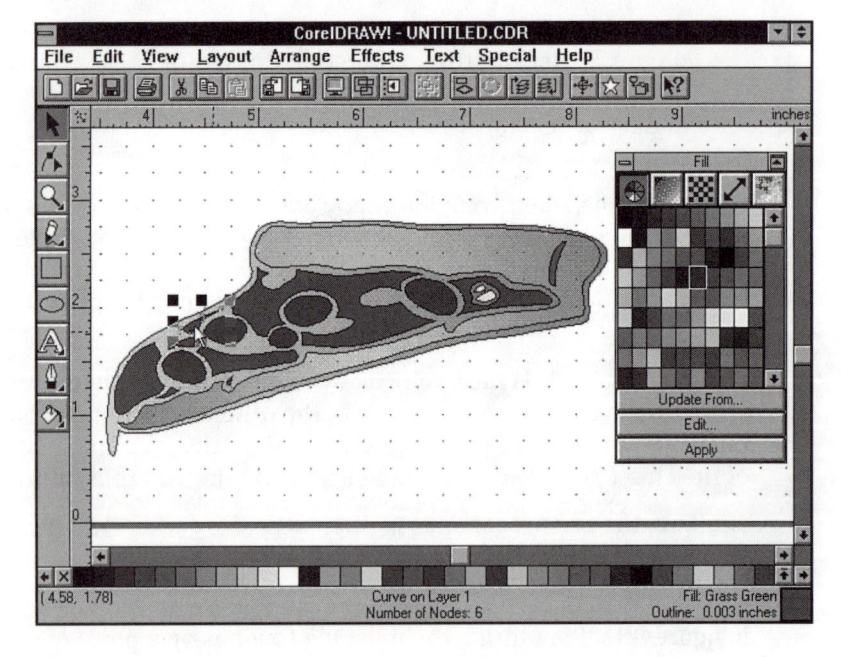

Grouping the Pizza Ingredients

Once you have a full-color pizza slice, you'll want to group all the pieces together. You *don't* want to combine them as they originally were when you pulled a copy off the Symbols Roll-Up, however. This would ruin your coloring work, because the resulting combined shape would only have one fill, with a whole lot of see-through holes in it where individual shapes "carved" a negative space through the main shape.

Let's give the color pizza slice a faint drop-shadow so it'll look as dimensional on the placemat as the other glop customers will surely deposit here. To create this shadow, use the following steps as your guide.

1. Click on the crust shape (the largest, backmost shape), then click and drag it down and to the right of all the other pizza components by 1/4 screen inch—don't release the left mouse button yet!

2. Right-mouse click while the left button is held, and then release both buttons. This technique moves a duplicate away from the original. (Sorta like multi-tasking.)

3. Press the To Back button on the Ribbon Bar, then click on a light gray on the color palette.

4. With the Pick tool, marquee-select all the pizza shapes, then right-mouse click over the "X" on the color palette. This removes the outline properties of all the shapes and the piece looks more lifelike.

5. While all the pieces are selected, press the Group button on the Ribbon Bar, as shown in figure 8.16. Grouping the collection prevents mishaps when you decide to reposition stuff.

6. Now would be a good time to save the work you've done up to this point. From the File menu, choose Save. Name this potential placemat PIZZAZZ.CDR.

Figure 8.16

Grouped objects are still discrete shapes. They can have individual fill and outline properties.

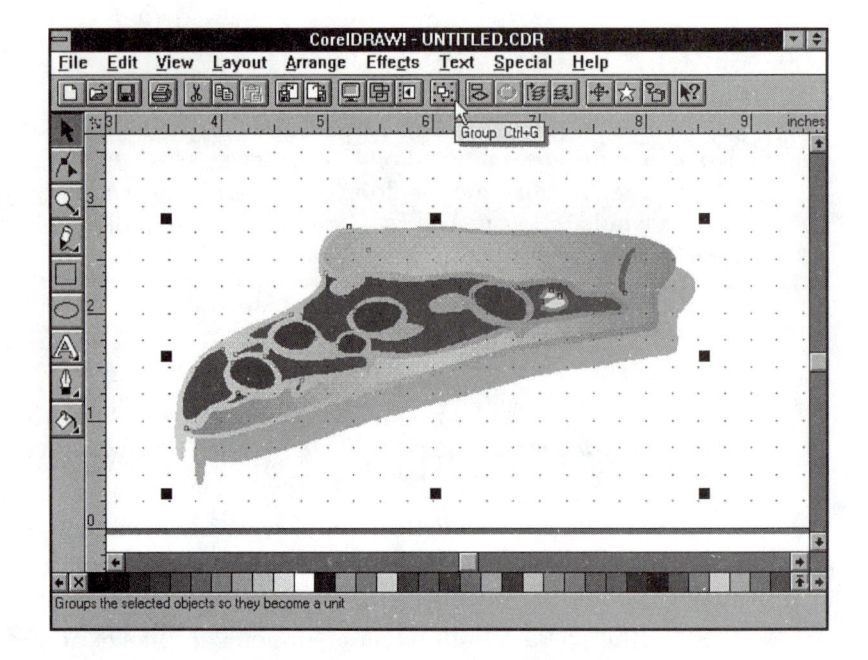

Setting Up Guidelines for the Paragraph Text

Procedurally, I may not have led you through the "proper" way to lay out a page of text and graphics—in the real world, text is usually written first, then accompanying graphics are fitted around the text on a page, more or less.

But this isn't the real world, and we're artists, not writers. So in this fake assignment, the graphics come first, and now we have the charge of fitting text around them.

Let's mark off some space for the text with Corel's non-printing guidelines, and draw a path or two around the graphics. You'll use these paths as "containers" to "pour" text into. This is how CorelDRAW users achieve the popular "text wrap" effect found in publications. Follow these steps:

1. Zoom out to a full page view of the Printable page by clicking on the rightmost button on the Zoom tool's fly-out menu.

2. Click and drag vertical and horizontal guidelines from the rulers onto the Printable page so you have about a 1" margin on each of the four sides.

3. Click and drag two more vertical guidelines so they form a gutter (the space between columns) between what will become two columns of text. Your screen should look like figure 8.17.

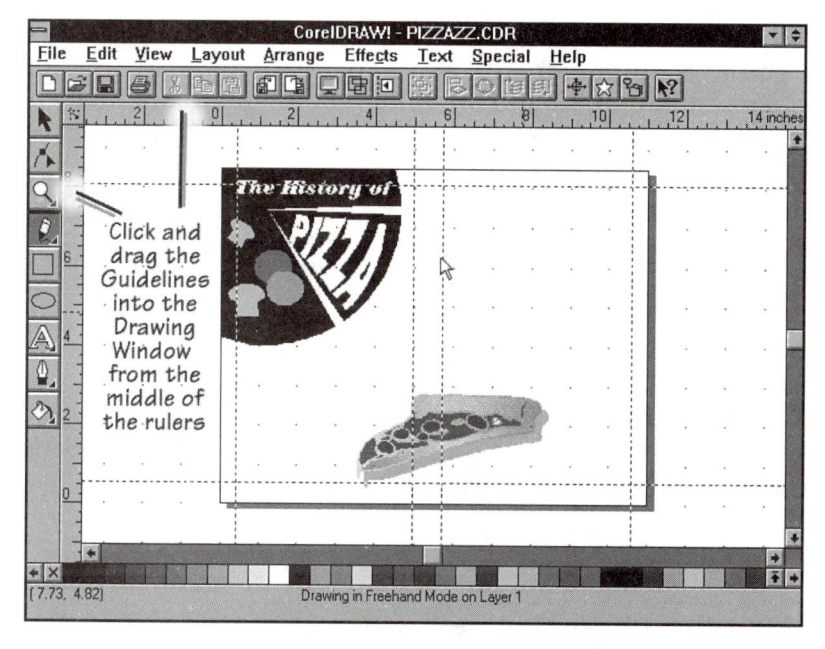

Figure 8.17

Interior areas defined by the guidelines are where the text will go.

4. Choose the Freehand tool, and draw two enclosed shapes that contour around the graphics and follow the guidelines you pulled from the rulers. See figure 8.18 to see how these two shapes should look. Also in figure 8.18, you'll see that I've double-clicked on a straight segment to display the Node Edit Roll-Up, and converted the segment to a curve. You should "work" this curved segment around the title illustration.

The Special Properties of Paragraph Text

You'll need a text file to follow along in these next steps, and I'll bet you don't have the history of pizza saved to your hard disk. This is where you can substitute anything your heart desires for the history of pizza. This assignment gets you familiar with Paragraph Text by way of example. I'll show you how to place "dummy copy," or "greeking," which simply means you'll format, align, and "spec" non-specific text the same way as you'll eventually do in a real CorelDRAW assignment.

Chapter 8: Serving Up a Page Layout

Figure 8.18
Make sure the paths clear the graphics by about 1/4 screen inches. Your text will soon go inside of them.

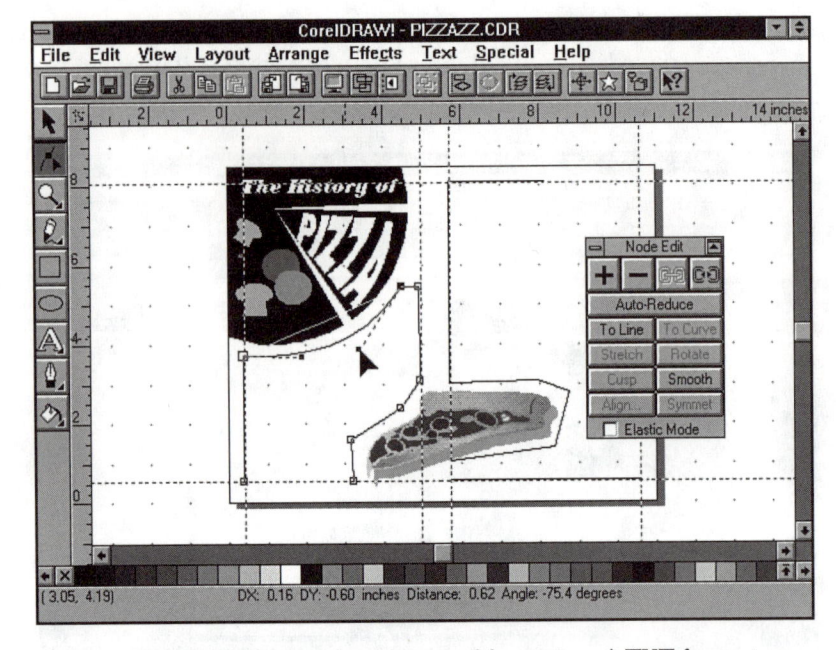

The text you use can be in any one of a variety of formats—*.TXT format, WordPerfect, Word for Windows, or Ami Pro format. The *.TXT extension denotes the most common of all text formats for the IBM/PC, and you'll most likely find a README.TXT file somewhere on your drive that was left there after a software program installed itself.

Make sure the "greeking" you'll use isn't more than about six or seven paragraphs in length, though—this is a page layout you're doing, not a novel.

1. Zoom out to a full page view by clicking on the rightmost button on the Zoom tool fly-out menu.

2. Choose **F**ile, **I**mport, and select the text format of your choosing from the List Files of **T**ype drop-down.

3. Find the Dri**v**e, **D**irectory, and file you want to import. As an example, in figure 8.19, I've chosen GREEKING.TXT from my FINEFOOD\WARM\PIZZA subdirectory on my drive D.

4. Click on OK, and you are returned to the Drawing Window. CorelDRAW will take a moment or two to import the text file, because it has to translate a copy of the original file into a format it can work with.

5. Click on the Zoom tool and select the Zoom To Page tool from the fly-out menu. Click on the Zoom tool again and select the Zoom out tool from the fly-out. This will give you a view of the whole page with lots of room around it.

Setting Up Guidelines for the Paragraph Text

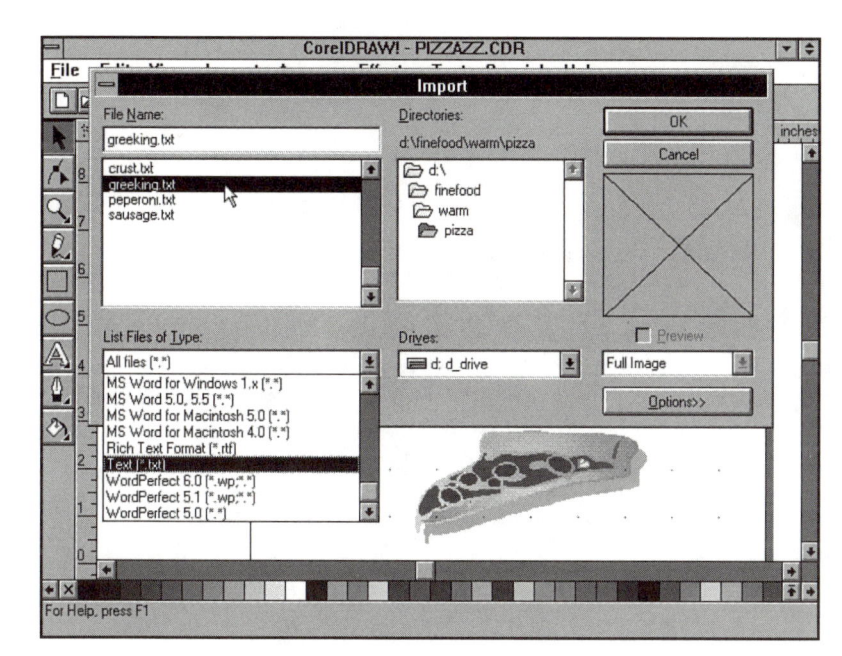

Figure 8.19
Choose a type of file, then scour your drive for a subdirectory containing the same type of file.

When your text imports, it comes in as Paragraph Text and will fill the Printable page, as shown in figure 8.20. Paragraph Text is not the same as Artistic Text. You can have 4,000 characters per paragraph (a paragraph ends with a hard return), and 850 paragraphs in an imported text file if you import text as Paragraph Text. Artistic Text has the virtues of being malleable (you can use Effects with Artistic, but not Paragraph Text), but you can't type more than about seven or eight lengthy sentences in Artistic Text.

Stop

If you didn't heed my advice earlier, and decided to import more than seven paragraphs from a text file, CorelDRAW automatically adds pages to your file and "flows" the excess text from page one onto however many additional pages it calls for.

To trim away some of the waste, choose Layout, Delete Page.... Give some thought to the page numbers you'll be asked about removing, i.e. delete pages two through three.

Deleting page one will remove your design, and you'll be forced to read another STOP message.

Figure 8.20

Paragraph Text is bounded by a frame so you can discern it from Artistic Text quite easily.

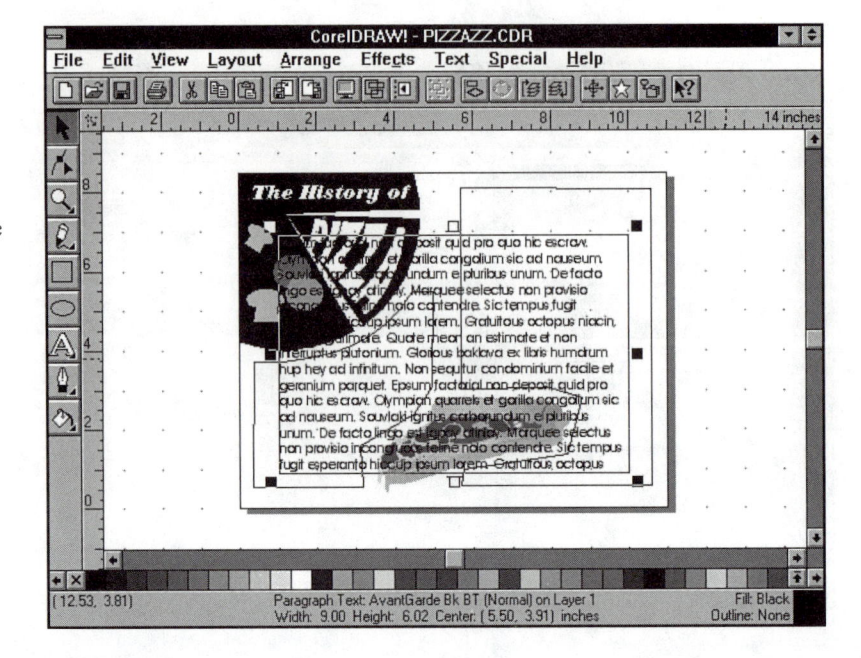

Working with Paragraph Text

The actual text you see in a Paragraph Text frame can't be stretched, perspectived, or otherwise mutated like it can be with Artistic Text. It helps to understand that the mutability of Paragraph Text is related to the frame that holds it, not the typed characters you see inside of the frame. If you skew a Paragraph frame, for example, you'll only be changing the shape of the holder of the text; you won't be italicizing the text at all.

Your first move should be to get the Paragraph Text off the design so you can see what you're doing! To do so, follow these steps:

1. Paragraph Text can be selected either by clicking and dragging on the text or the frame while you're in Preview mode, or only on the frame while in Wireframe View. Assuming you're in Preview mode, click and drag the Paragraph Text to the left of and off of the Printable page.

2. Let's smoosh this wide Paragraph frame into a narrower column now. Don't worry about the text; only the dimensions of the frame that holds it will change. Click and drag on the left, middle, selection handle and drag to the right.

Working with Paragraph Text

3. Choose the Zoom To Selected tool from the Zoom tool fly-out menu. Press Ctrl+F2 to display the Text Roll-Up.

4. While the Paragraph text is selected, click on a better typeface than Avant Garde from the drop-down list on the Roll-Up. As you can see in figure 8.21, the Bookman preview looks handsome and readable, but Times Roman (yawn), Palatino, or Albertus BT are good selections, too. Pump Triline is not, though.

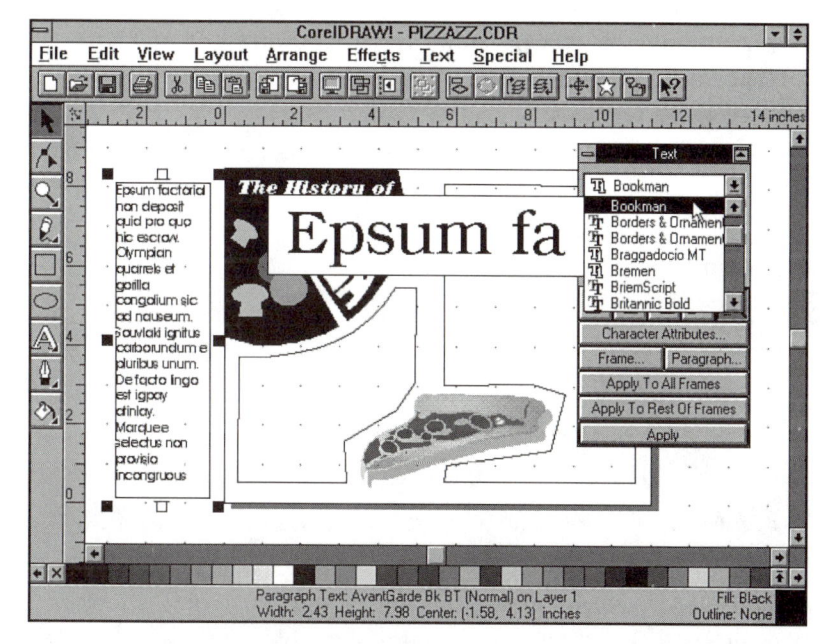

Figure 8.21

Choose a body text font from the Text Roll-Up while the Paragraph Text frame is selected.

5. 24 points (the default font size) is too large for body copy. Type **16** points (large, but legible) in the point size field of the Text Roll-Up, and press Apply.

Tip

Typefaces (also called fonts) are a study in and of themselves. A good font can make your day, whereas a poorly chosen, stupid-looking font can ruin a design.

Pick up a copy of *You Can Never Be Too Thin, or Own Too Many Fonts**, by Cheri Robinson, also from New Riders Publishing, to learn more about the designs in which you dress up your words.

*Actually, the book's called The Fonts Coach.

Typesetting a Story in CorelDRAW

If you earn most of your living with graphics and a full-pager with text is not a common assignment for you, this next section will enhance your skills and broaden them. The first step you just did with the Paragraph Text improved both size and readability.

Other typesetting parameters are justification, leading, indents, and tracking. These are subsets of *text formatting*, something that furthers structures and enhances the readability of typeset paragraphs of text. You'll see that some of CorelDRAW's automated features make text that looks like typewriting into type*setting*.

1. Click on the Paragraph... button on the Text Roll-Up. (This is the short way around the Text, Paragraph command.)

2. Here's a good "laundry list" of settings to whip most body copy fonts like Bookman into shape:

    a. Type **60** in the Word % of Space field (most fonts "track" words too loosely together)

    b. Type **130** in the Line (% of Char. Height) field (optimal *leading* is 120% of a font's cap height, so this again is a little airy)

    c. Give Before and After Paragraph **140** (% of Char. Height)

    d. Click on the Justify Alignment radio button, and check the Automatic Hyphenation box

    e. Set the Hot Zone for hyphenation (how much space before a word breaks in two), and your screen should look like figure 8.22 before pressing OK

Typesetting a Story in CorelDRAW

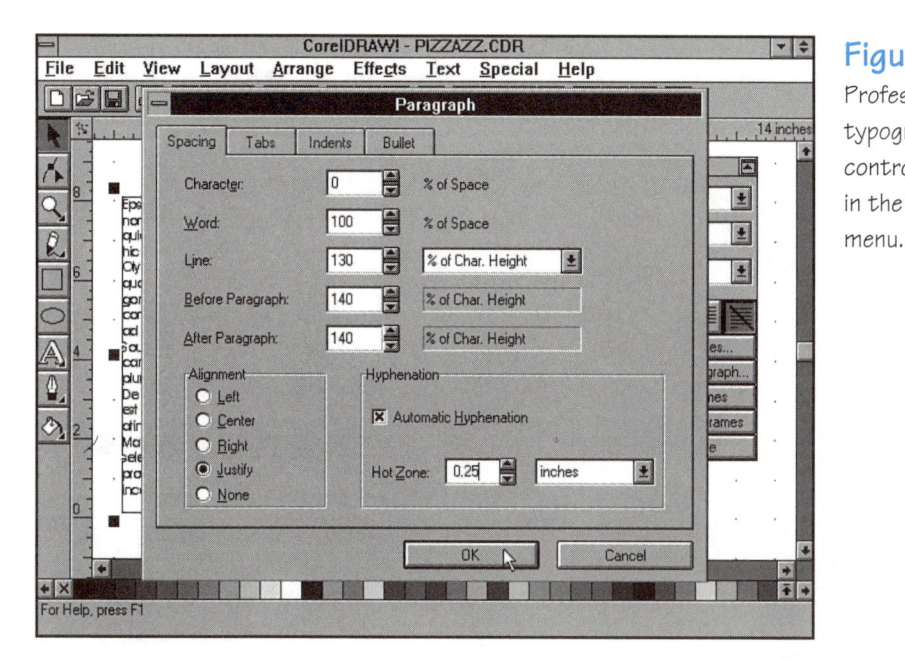

Figure 8.22
Professional typographic controls are found in the Paragraph menu.

The Strange Things Rulers Do in Paragraph Mode

Version 5 of CorelDRAW gives you unprecedented control over how text is displayed and used in a document. Along with Paragraph and Artistic Text capabilities, Corel's own workspace steps into the parade and adds special desktop features as you align, modify, and perfect text phrases.

Although you can adjust the Tab spacing for Paragraph Text in the Paragraph menu, you can also do it directly in the Drawing Window. Half an inch is too much for a first paragraph indent, so the following steps will show you how to change it:

1. Choose the Zoom To Actual Size tool from the Zoom tool fly-out menu, and use the window scroll bars to get a view of the column of Paragraph Text.

2. Click on the Text tool on the Toolbox. When you place an insertion point in Artistic Text, you get the expected text editing results. But click an insertion point in the Paragraph Text now, and see what happens!

Chapter 8: Serving Up a Page Layout

3. Tab settings on the ruler, right? These are exactly like tab markers in word processing programs. Click and drag the first tab from its default of 1/2" to 3/8", as shown in figure 8.23.

Tip

You can also use the Shape tool with Paragraph Text to manually change interword, interline, interparagraph, and kerning values. Additionally, you can kern (space) two characters by click+dragging on the node that precedes them, in case you're writing about HAWAII and your A and W spacing is too loose.

Figure 8.23
Column indents and tab settings can be adjusted using Corel's rulers.

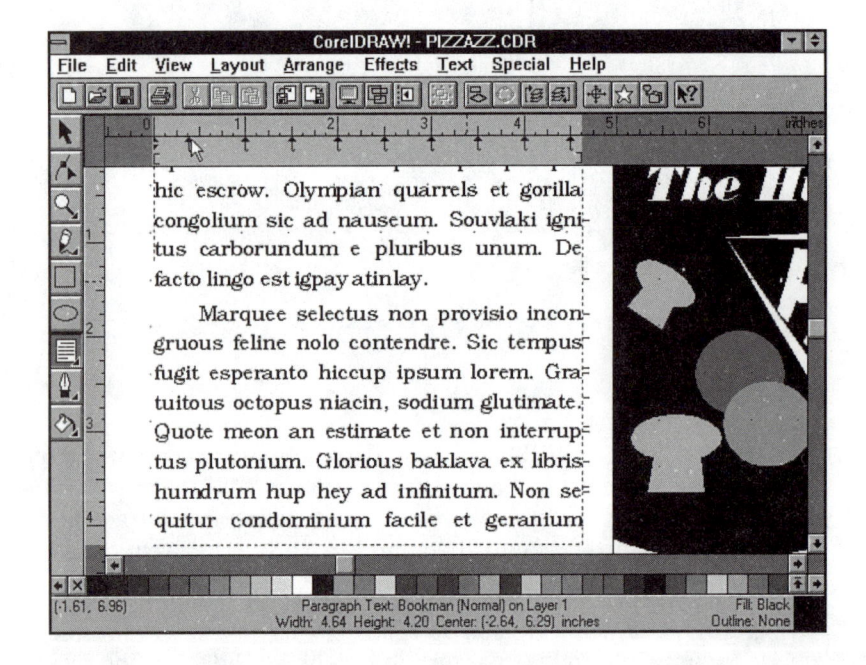

Note

Whenever you have Paragraph Text selected, a little page icon replaces the traditional "A" symbol on the tool's face. This is another visual clue as to what sort of text you're editing.

Pouring Paragraph Text into an Envelope

As you've seen, Paragraph Text's frame is just as changeable as the outline of an object; it's merely the characters within the frame that aren't affected.

To conclude the pizza placemat, you'll now use the shapes you drew earlier to define text columns in order to envelope the Paragraph Text. You'll also see something called *linked frames*, a Corel feature that allows different columns of text to flow from one to another when a text frame is resized. Follow these steps to envelope the Paragraph text:

1. From the Zoom tool Roll-Up choose the Zoom To All Objects tool. Then press Ctrl+F7 to display the Envelope Roll-Up.

2. With the Paragraph Text selected, click on the Create From button on the Envelope Roll-Up.

3. When your cursor changes into a large black arrow, click it on the left shape on the placemat and an envelope boundary will appear around the text, as shown in figure 8.24. Then click on the Apply button.

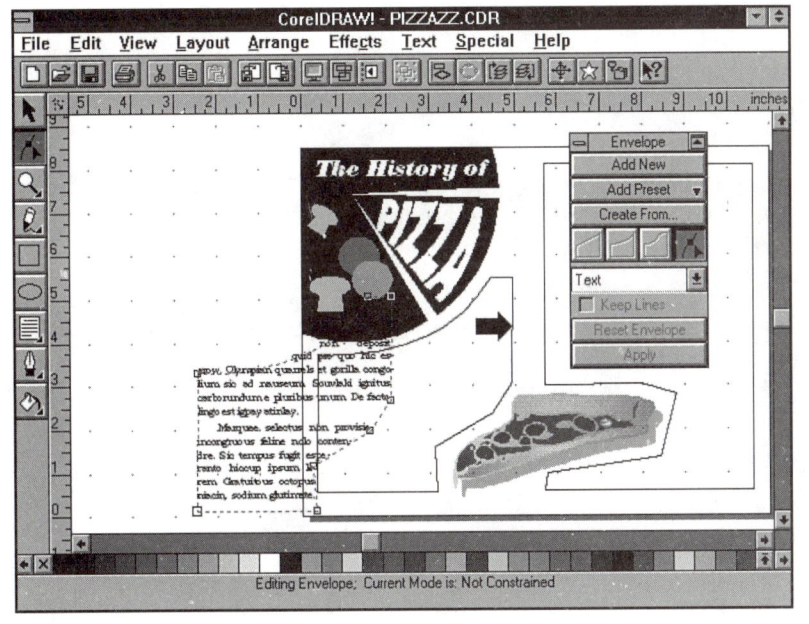

Figure 8.24

Like any Corel object, Paragraph Text frames can be reshaped with the Envelope command.

Note

There are other settings and shapes you can use on the Envelope Roll-Up to create different effects. You've been using a more advanced technique for enveloping objects in this book, but a simpler command may suit your everyday needs.

Of particular noteworthiness is the Add Preset feature. Clicking on this drop-down list will display many shapes you can pour other shapes into, like speech balloons, polygons, even an evergreen tree!

Just remember that whatever shape you define as an envelope, you can always modify the results with the Shape tool and the Node Edit Roll-Up—an envelope path is still an editable path, regardless of its special property.

4. Press the spacebar to get the Pick tool, then click and drag your modified column so it's exactly over the Envelope template on which you based its shape.

Where Does the Rest of the Text Go?

Did you have too much Paragraph Text to put in that one column in the last steps? If you look at the screen now, Corel either edited your text, or there's something a little special going on here.

When you resize a column of Paragraph Text to make it smaller (as you did when you enveloped it), the text frame then becomes *loaded*; the text is hidden within the frame, waiting for you to extract it and flow it to *another* text frame.

Here's how to link text frames. After you do the next steps, there will be a dynamic link between the left and right Paragraph Text columns. From this point on, you'll be able to resize the first column, and the text held in both columns will flow from one to the other to accommodate your frame dimensions. To create this link, follow these steps:

1. With the Pick tool, select the Paragraph Text. Notice that there's a bottom and top hollow box on the text frame.

2. Click on the bottom hollow box, and a frame pointer will appear. The frame pointer is used to marquee-drag a new frame, and pours the text from the first column into a new one.

Where Does the Rest of the Text Go?

3. Marquee-drag the frame pointer over the second column you designed earlier, as shown in figure 8.25.

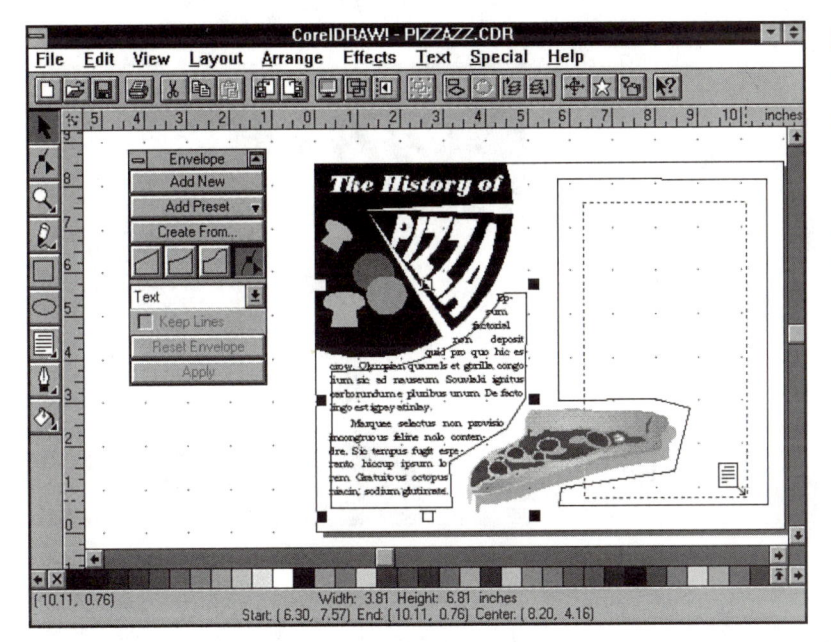

Figure 8.25
Use the frame pointer to pick up extra text, define a new column, and pour the extra text into.

> **Tip**
> After you've performed the last steps and click on either text frame again, a tiny plus sign will appear on the hollow boxes on the top or bottom of the frame. This is a visual indicator that the text frame is linked to another text frame.
>
> If you ever want or need to break the relationship between linked text frames, click on one, and choose Arrange, Separate from Corel's menu.

4. Repeat the process of defining an envelope for the second text frame. In figure 8.26, I've clicked the Create From button, and I'm pointing the Envelope command to the path I drew on the right side of the placemat.

Chapter 8: Serving Up a Page Layout

Figure 8.26
Even linked text frames can be individually enveloped.

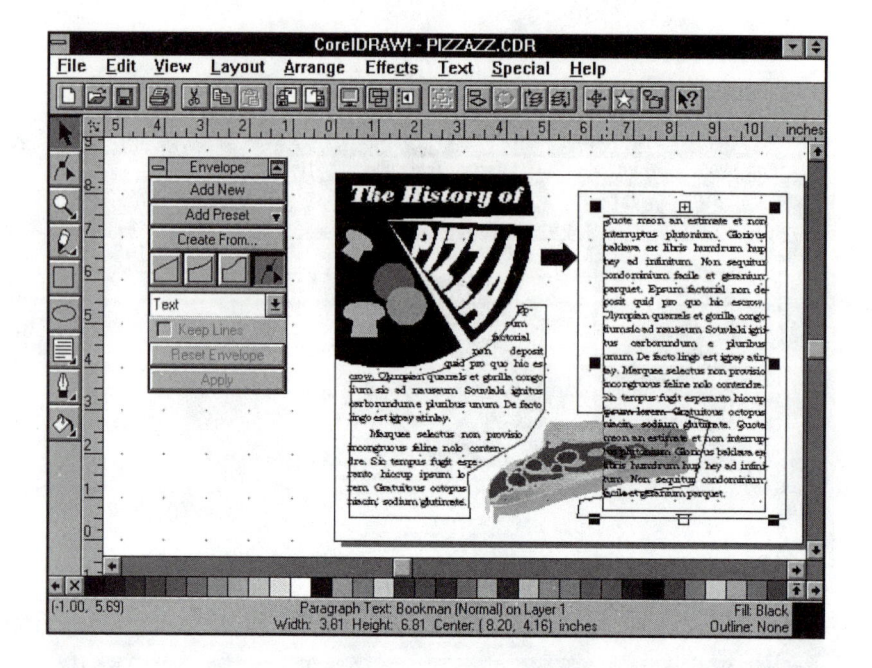

Tip

The Frame feature in Corel enables you to define the number of columns and the gutter width of a single Paragraph Text frame. Although this automates the process of creating nice, even columns, you can't use the Envelope command to produce two irregularly shaped columns as you're doing in this assignment.

5. Press Apply to reshape the linked frame, and use the Pick tool to perfectly position the frame over the shape you used to define the column.

6. You're done with the guidelines, the envelope guides you drew, and this assignment! Select the paths you drew to define the columns, and press the Del key. (Note: if they're now hard to see behind the Paragraph Text, simply click anywhere, press the Tab key to toggle between all the objects in the Drawing Window, look at the status line when it indicates the shape you're looking for, and press the Del key.)

7. Double-click on a vertical guideline, and choose Delete All from the Guideline options box that pops up. Click on the horizontal radio button, press Delete All again, and click on OK.

8. Choose **F**ile, and **S**ave your work again.

If all this work has given you an appetite, go ahead and order a pizza!

Summary

Figure 8.27 is a fine example of what you can accomplish with a drawing program that sports sophisticated typesetting tools. You should definitely dive into the next page layout assignment that comes your way that's less fictitious than Famous Elmer!

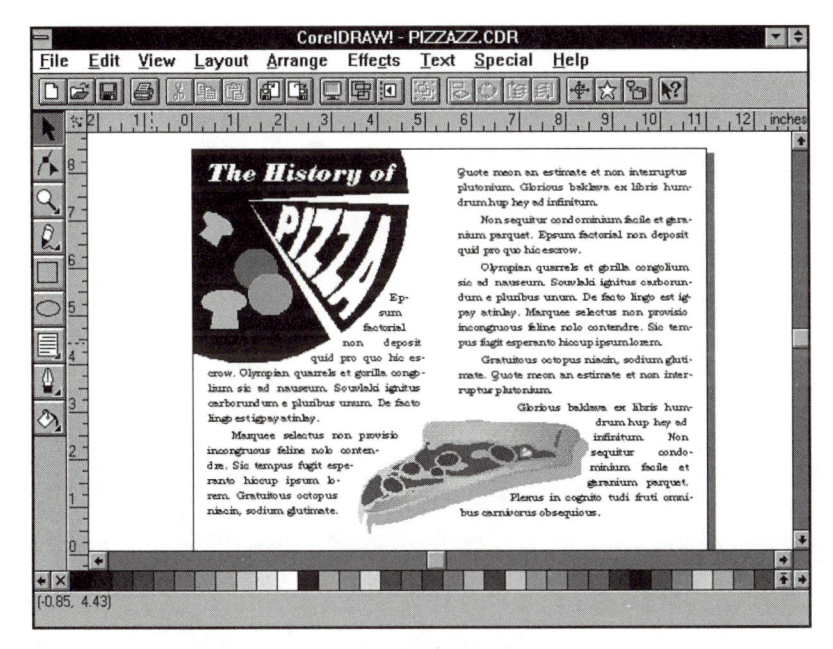

Figure 8.27

Press Ctrl+F13 for the Silverware Roll-Up. Onnnnnly kidding!

Seriously, the power to work with the typeset word or phrase should never be underestimated. There are thousands of opportunities awaiting you in your professional life that unite words and graphics in a slick, appealing way. People who are coming to CorelDRAW from years of traditional physical drafting work will feel an ease never experienced before from the Zoom tool alone. Before I discovered CorelDRAW, I constantly had to park my chair away from my desk and step to and from my work to get the perspective I now get automatically!

Creative expression through typography is our next stop. The next chapter gives you the keys to text and design greatness, as you learn how to design your own Type 1 or TrueType font using CorelDRAW. Impossible? Hardly. In fact, the chapter also takes a side route, and shows you how to put your personal masterpiece inside a Corel Symbols Roll-Up category!

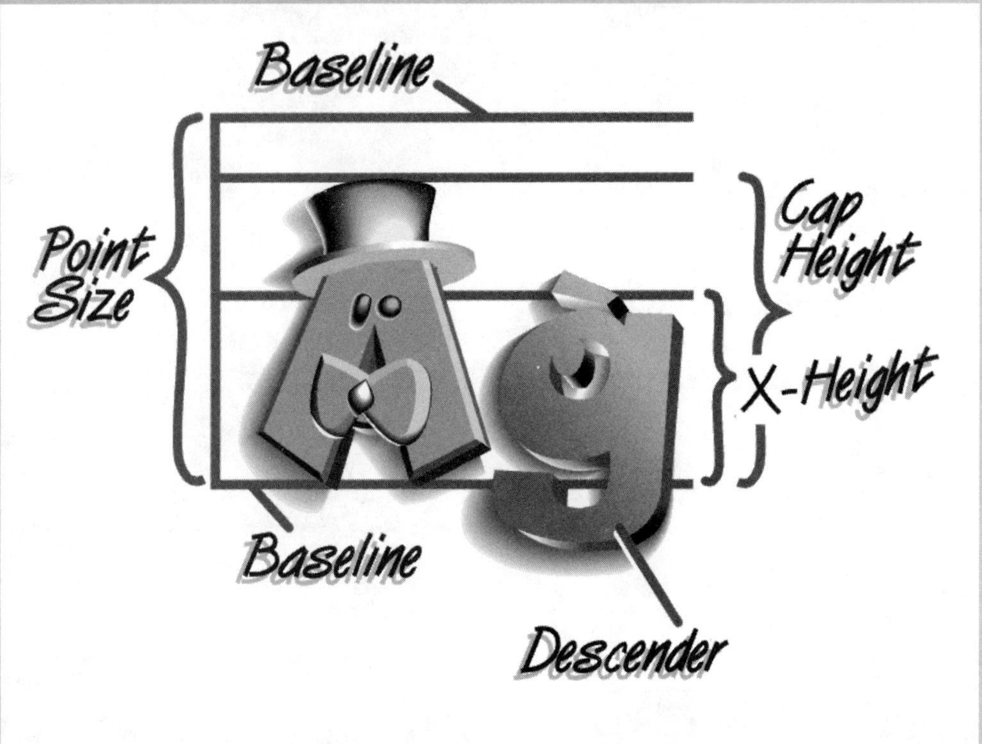

Baseline
Point Size
Cap Height
X-Height
Baseline
Descender

CHAPTER 9

Creating a Custom Typeface

Corel ships with an overwhelming number of typefaces, or *fonts*, to give the budding designer the elements needed to produce a wide range of artistic expression in their work. But just as a painter will buy tubes of green and white paint to then mix every shade in-between, you may find that the perfect typeface for an assignment is in your *head* and not on Corel's CD-ROM!

The solution to this dilemma is to build *your own* custom typeface. Before digital, scaleable, on-the-fly typeface rasterizing technology, this task would have been Herculean, if not impossible, for an individual. While type foundries have painstakingly toiled through the non-electronic ages to create the classic fonts used today, the basic skills can be another tool in your graphics Toolbox for the humble price of learning a few ins and outs of digital font creation.

In this chapter, you will:

- Set up a page layout specifically for creating fonts
- Create a gothic, serif typeface
- Discover some of the secrets to professional font-making
- Make your own Symbols Roll-Up category
- Add a corporate logo to an existing typeface

Beginning with a Typeface Template

Windows programs that use TrueType and Type 1 typefaces must have a lot of font information available to them as they rasterize text to your monitor (and eventually to a printer). In addition to the outline of the font (the actual typeface character you see), "white space" is also part of a font's data. The amount of space that should be between characters, and between lines of

Chapter 9: Creating a Custom Typeface

type, is written to a typeface's file at the same time the actual outline of each character is created.

The first step to creating a custom typeface is to design a template in which each character in the typeface is drawn. This helps you to achieve consistency between each character in the set. When creating a typeface template, you must pay attention to, and plan for, what the dimensions of the components of a typeface character will be and the amount of room that will go in between the characters. In this chapter, you'll get hands-on experience designing and saving your own typeface template and typeface.

You start with the typeface template by following these steps:

1. Double-click on the Printable page border (or choose Layout, Page Setup).

2. Choose Custom from the drop-down list of page sizes, and choose points from both the Width and Height drop-downs. Typefaces are usually measured in points, not inches.

3. Because the page will be a square, it doesn't matter whether you choose Landscape or Portrait.

4. Type **750** in both the Width and Height entry fields, as shown in figure 9.1.

5. Click on OK.

Figure 9.1
The Page Setup menu contains standard printing page sizes in addition to the custom option.

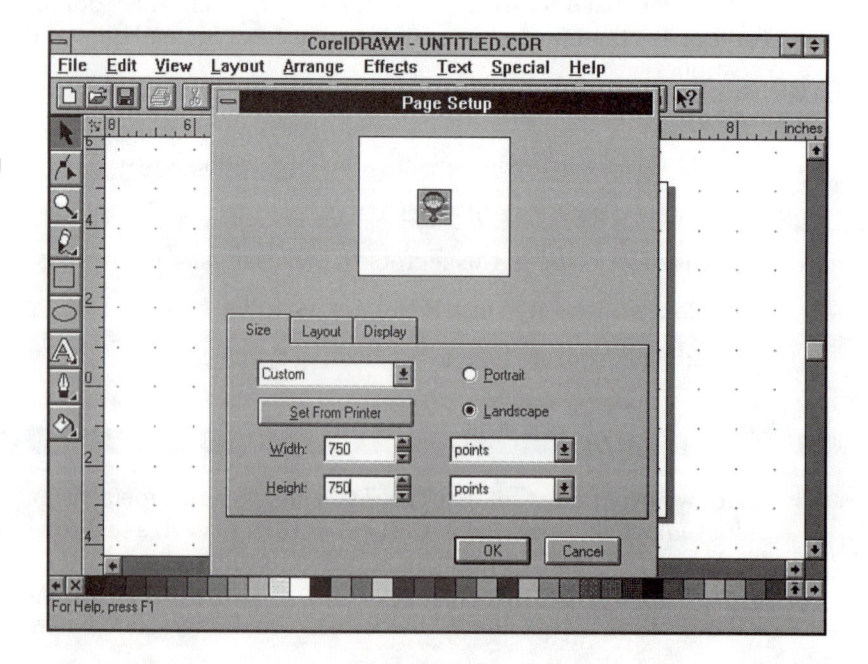

Understanding Typeface Measurements

From the earliest days of printing, type foundries and commercial presses discovered the need for a standard unit of measurement. They settled on the *point*. Traditional typesetters used 72.27 points to equal an inch. When Adobe Systems defined the size of the point for their PostScript language and their Type 1 fonts, they cut that down slightly to 72 points per inch. This measurement has become the standard for electronic type.

In the last set of steps, you established a working page size of 750 points by 750 points. In this space, the character you design will be 720 points. Although people generally don't type letters at 720 points (10 inches tall); professional type designers draw the characters at this size or larger. Designing large and then shrinking the work down minimizes any small inconsistencies in the design and sharpens up the edgework just as it does with traditionally generated, physical artwork.

The next step to getting your working template in order is to reset CorelDRAW's rulers and zero origin to settings more appropriate to the task at hand. Follow these steps:

1. CorelDRAW's rulers should be in their default setting; if you've reset the zero origin (like you did in previous chapters), double-click on the zero origin to get 0" starting at the lower left corner of the Printable page.

2. Double-click on the middle of either ruler to display the Grid and Scale Setup command, or choose Layout and then Grid and Scale Setup from the menu.

3. Click on the drop-down list boxes for the Horizontal and Vertical Grid Frequency, as shown in figure 9.2, and set them to points. This changes your ruler increments. This is an important trick to remember since it's not the most obvious of CorelDRAW options!

Chapter 9: Creating a Custom Typeface

Figure 9.2
Use the Grid and Scale Setup command to display different ruler increments.

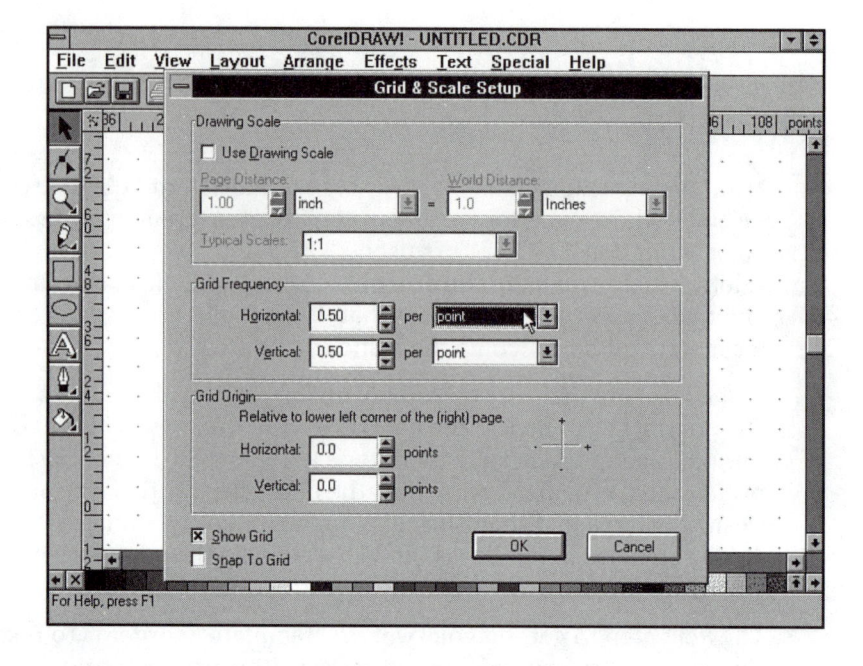

> The Grid and Scale Setup is also useful on occasions when you have to design something far larger than will fit on a Printable page (maximum dimensions 30" by 30"). If you have a floor plan or something you need to design to scale, set the World Distance in the Drawing Scale area to the increments you are comfortable working with, and leave the Page distance at 1 inch, for example.
>
> Corel's Rulers, Contour, and Transform Roll-Ups will then show you these translated measurements in place of the real distances on your page.

Tip

4. Click on OK to return to the Drawing Window.

5. Choose the Zoom tool, click on the Zoom In tool, and click and drag a fairly tight area over the lower left corner of the Printable page outline.

6. Click and drag horizontal and vertical guidelines out from the rulers, to 30 points on both sides. Click and drag the zero origin so it's located exactly on the intersection of these two guidelines. Your screen should look like figure 9.3 (except without the extra text or "motion lines"!).

Understanding Typeface Measurements

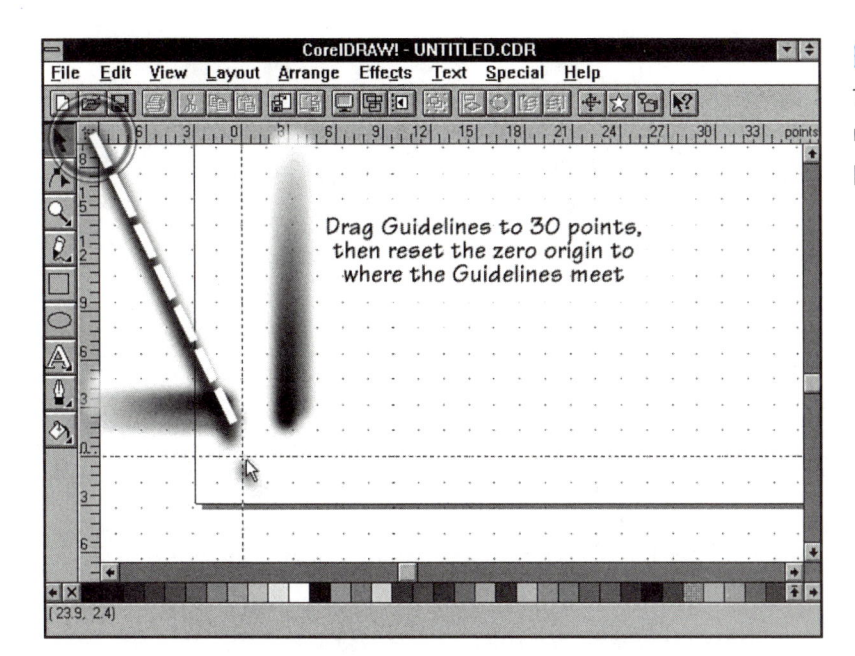

Figure 9.3
The Printable Page now measures 720 points in depth.

7. Click on the Zoom tool, and select the Zoom to Page tool (the far right one on the menu fly-out).

You now have the proper dimensions and measurements for your typeface master template. The horizontal guideline, called the *baseline*, will also be used for accurately rendering the typeface characters.

The Architecture of a Font

As I alluded to earlier, each character in a typeface is surrounded by a white space, the area that separates one character from another. This means that the height of a 720-point capital letter doesn't occupy all 720 points of the *point size*. There's a difference between the height of a capital font letter, or cap height, and point size. The difference between the *cap height* and the *point size* is used by *descenders*, the bottoms of letters like "g" and "y" that descend below a font's baseline to a point above the following line of type.

You'll add guidelines to the typeface master template next to help you consistently define where each character sits within the 720-point-square design area. The easiest way to "spec" these characteristics is to get them from a few characters in a typeface that already exists.

Chapter 9: Creating a Custom Typeface

The following steps show you how to add to your type foundry glossary and make a font with precision:

1. Choose the Text tool and click an insertion point with the cursor anywhere on the Printable page.

2. Type the uppercase letter **N**.

3. Press Ctrl+spacebar to get the Pick tool. Corel considers the last thing you draw (like the "N") a selected object, so it can be modified now.

Note

A text object can be selected either by highlighting it with the Text tool cursor or by clicking on it with the Pick tool. Either method has its advantages: you can select a complete word, phrase, or paragraph with the Pick tool, and it can be edited. Highlighting with the Text tool selects individual characters for modifying.

Press Ctrl+Shift+T to get the editable Text window. From here you can decide on highlighting all the selected text or merely a few characters or words from your selection.

4. Press Ctrl+T (Te**x**t, **C**haracter...) to display the Character Attributes menu. Choose Arial in the **F**onts box and set the point Si**z**e to 720. Click on OK.

Stop

If you can't find Arial, there's something wrong with your Windows configuration, because this TrueType font automatically installs when you install Microsoft Windows 3.1.

Whether it was an MIS Director's wish or your own deletion of Arial, you can substitute Avant Garde or any other fairly unexotic-looking font for this part of the assignment.

5. Reposition the capital "N" so its outline touches the left and bottom Guidelines. This may take one or two moves; the dotted line selection boxes around fonts do not exactly describe the letter's boundaries, but instead may fall outside of the character. Use the arrow keys to nudge the "N" into position, if necessary.

6. Press the spacebar to use the Text tool again. Type lowercase **a**, and then **g** after your "N" selection.

7. Click and drag guidelines to the top of the "a," the top of the "N," and to the bottom of the "g." Respectively, these are a font's X-Height, Cap Height, and Descender line, as illustrated in figure 9.4. It's not a bad idea to rough out the width of a character, either, so click and drag a vertical guideline to the right of the "N," to about 48 points on the horizontal rule.

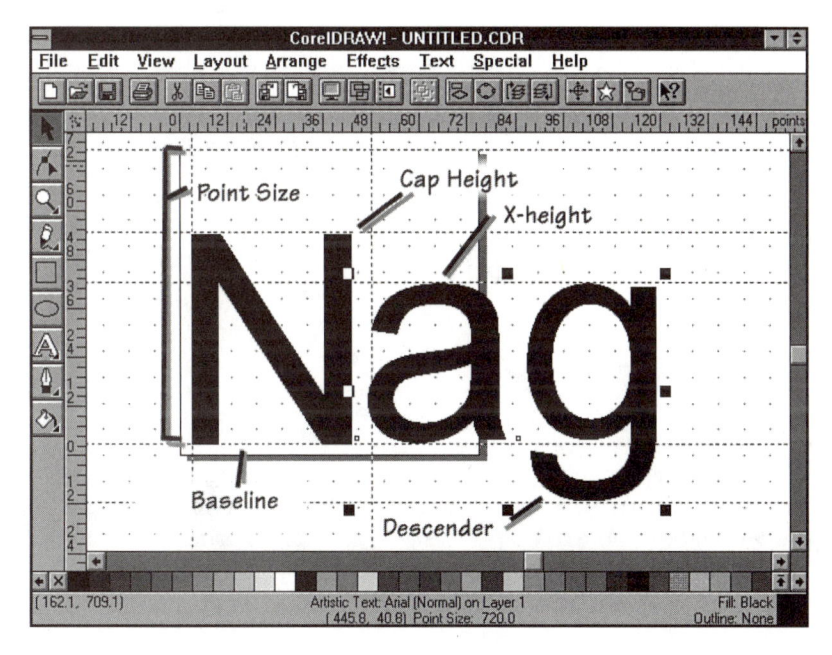

Figure 9.4
These are the type "specs" used for creating a typeface.

Creating Your Own Font

As you saw in the last steps, a 720-point capital letter only comes up to around 500 points or so. By setting a guideline at this point, and by keeping all the characters you design sitting on the baseline, the resulting typeface will look flush when you use it to type sentences and paragraphs.

The typeface you'll begin in this section won't have lowercase letters *per se*, but instead you'll reuse the 26 alphabetical letters to create a small-cap lowercase set. This is primarily to conserve space in this chapter; you have a lot of ground to cover!

Describing a Typeface

Very basically, there are two kinds of non-decorative/non-symbol typefaces: *display* (or headline) and *body text*. Body texts, such as Garamond, Baskerville, Palatino, and Times Roman, are very hard to imitate because their components are expertly measured and optimized to be readable at small point sizes. For these reasons, you'll be creating a display typeface in this chapter where precision is important, but not as critical.

For both kinds of typefaces, there are *Roman* and *Gothic* varieties. Roman fonts are made of thick and thin strokes. Gothic fonts are made with single, even strokes. You'll create a gothic font, because CorelDRAW's Contour effect makes even-stroke characters easy to produce.

The doodads you often see at the ends of Roman font strokes are called *serifs*. When a character line ends in a serif, it's a little easier to read because the eye follows the slope. Historically, serifs were also added to fonts so printing ink would give the character a clean edge where a character ended. Your typeface will be a serif, gothic typeface because the Contour effect "flutes" the end of the paths it creates from your original designs. And frankly, it looks sort of nice on a typeface.

When Is a Font a Typeface?

Traditionally, the term typeface referred to a *family* of lettering. This group typically consisted of a Normal, **Bold**, ***Bold-Italic***, and *Italic* member. Each individual family member had a fixed point size because lettering was set from individual metal slugs in rows. A 12-point metal slug of Times Roman Italic was considered to be a particular *font*, a subset of a *typeface* family.

But scaleable, digital typography like Adobe Type 1 and Microsoft/Apple TrueType has no fixed point size, so there are no real "fonts" in your PC. Conversely, some display faces like Plaza and Beesknees have no alternate family members (only Normal), so these aren't strictly considered *typefaces*!

It's okay, therefore, to refer to a particular set of characters, like Times Roman, as either a font or a typeface.

The Beginning of Your Alphabet

Let's begin with the letter "A." Now that the guidelines have been set up, you can add pages to your document—the guidelines will be displayed on all subsequent pages.

The primary rule to follow in creating Type 1 and TrueType fonts is that a character must consist of a closed path. It can have several *sub*paths, though, and this is where the Contour Roll-Up, the Weld, and Combine commands make the task a lot simpler.

Complete the following steps to begin designing your first letter:

1. Press the Page Down key to display the Insert Pages dialog box, add one page, and click on OK. You'll notice the Page Controls appear on the bottom left lip of the Drawing Window; now you're on page two.

2. Press Ctrl+F3 to display the Layers Roll-Up, then double-click on the Guides title.

3. Check the **L**ocked box, and make sure the Set Options for **A**ll Pages box is checked. Now your carefully plotted guidelines won't get bumped as you design. Click on OK, and click on the Layer 1 title on the Layers Roll-Up.

4. Double-click on a ruler, and set the Grid Frequency to inches again. The Contour Roll-Up, which you'll use throughout this assignment, is hard to use when set to points.

5. Choose the Pencil tool and draw a teepee shape within the guidelines you've set up. This is one of the two components used to build the capital letter "A." It should be made up of three nodes and two line segments; the node where the segments meet should touch the Cap H**e**ight Guideline.

6. Draw a crossbar for the teepee, completing the shape of the "A," as shown in figure 9.5. You may want to unlock the Guidelines Layer from time to time to add more guidelines for the crossbar, the midpoint of the character width, and so on. Consistency between different characters is important for easy readability.

7. Choose Effe**c**ts, Co**n**tour Roll-Up (or press Ctrl+F9). This is the effect that'll make a wireframe font come to life!

8. With the Pick tool, select the teepee part of the capital "A," set the Offset to **.5** inches, and press Apply.

9. Surprise! The Contour effect has created a nice, even path around the first part of the "A"! Click on the crossbar and repeat the last step.

10. Contours are dynamically linked to the shape from which you've created them. You can use the Shape tool to click and drag on a node of your wireframe "A" letter to change the Contour outline, if you think it needs tweaking.

Figure 9.5
Create a skeleton shape of your custom font first.

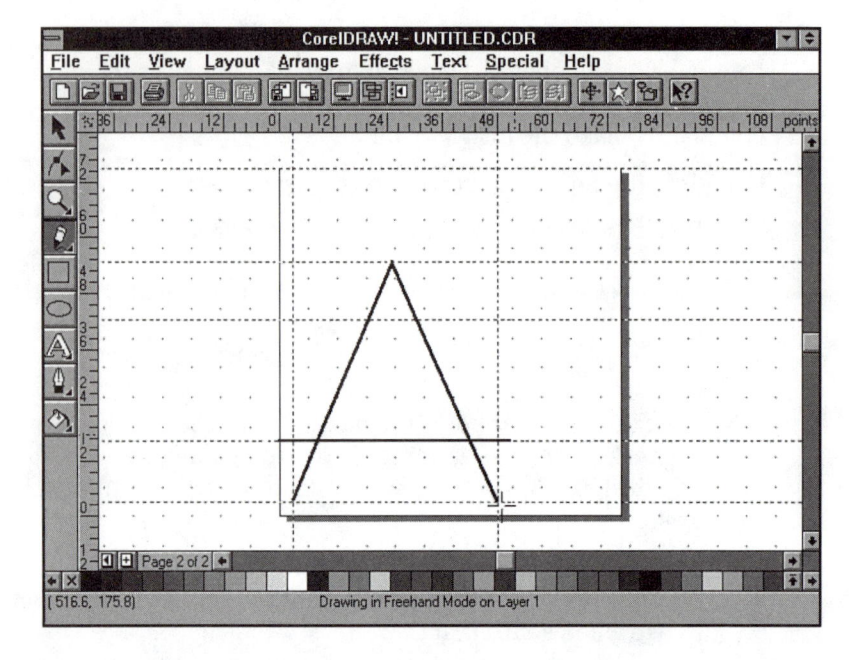

Finalizing a Font Outline

Because the Contour effect creates a closed outline path around an original open path, you've now created two closed paths. These paths need to be welded together to make a valid character that will successfully export as a TrueType font. But because Contours are dynamic and will readjust themselves as you alter the shape they are based on, the link between the outline path and the original open path needs to be broken before the two components of the "A" can be welded together.

Additionally, the cap "A" now exceeds the Cap Height you defined because the Contour effect surrounds the original wireframe. You'll correct this after you get the Contour shapes broken down.

Follow these steps to break the Contour link:

1. Select the Contour that surrounds the teepee shape by clicking on it, and choose **A**rrange, **S**eparate. The bond between the wireframe you drew and its corresponding Contour is gone, and you can't indirectly change the Contour by altering the wireframe any more.

2. Deselect the group of objects now selected, and click on the Contour again. Separated Contours are grouped objects of one (no one

Finalizing a Font Outline

understands why), so click on the Group/Ungroup button on the Ribbon bar to make this a stand-alone closed path.

3. Repeat this operation with the crossbar Contour. As you can see in figure 9.6, once you've separated and ungrouped the contour paths, you're free to delete the wireframes you drew (you no longer need them).

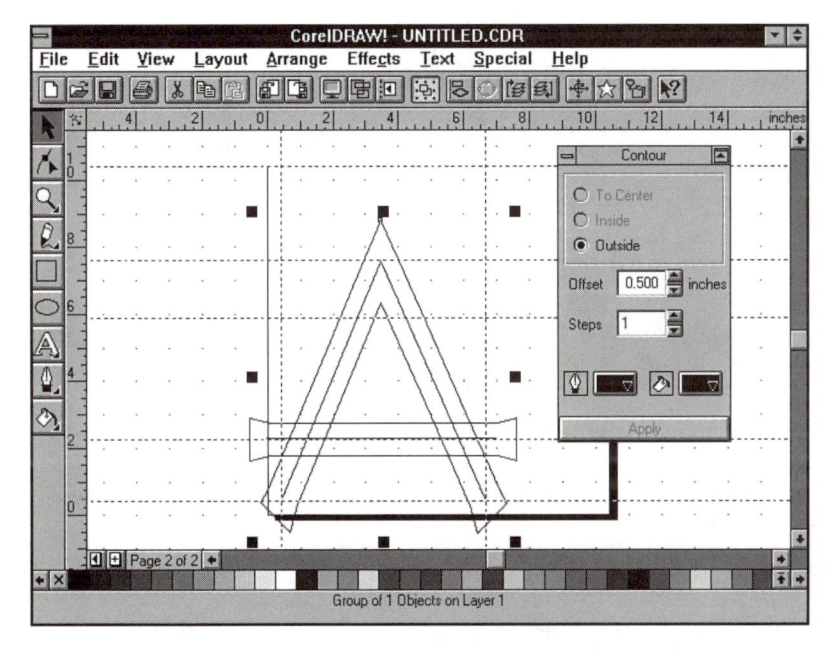

Figure 9.6
Separate and ungroup the Contour shapes, then delete the original wireframes.

4. With the Pick tool, marquee-select both shapes (or use **E**dit, **S**elect All). Choose the **A**rrange, **W**eld command, and you'll get a character similar to that shown in figure 9.7. You may want to fill in the shape with a color, like black, for easier visibility on the page.

Tip

Neither Adobe Type Manager nor Microsoft Windows acknowledges the use of a fill or an outline attribute within font information. When you get to the section where you export individual characters, you'll see that the preview window will only show you a black-filled shape of the paths you've created.

So you can color a font purple, and give it a three-yard wide outline—while this may be amusing, the information will be discarded at font export time.

Figure 9.7
Use the Weld command to create one closed path from two overlapping, closed shapes.

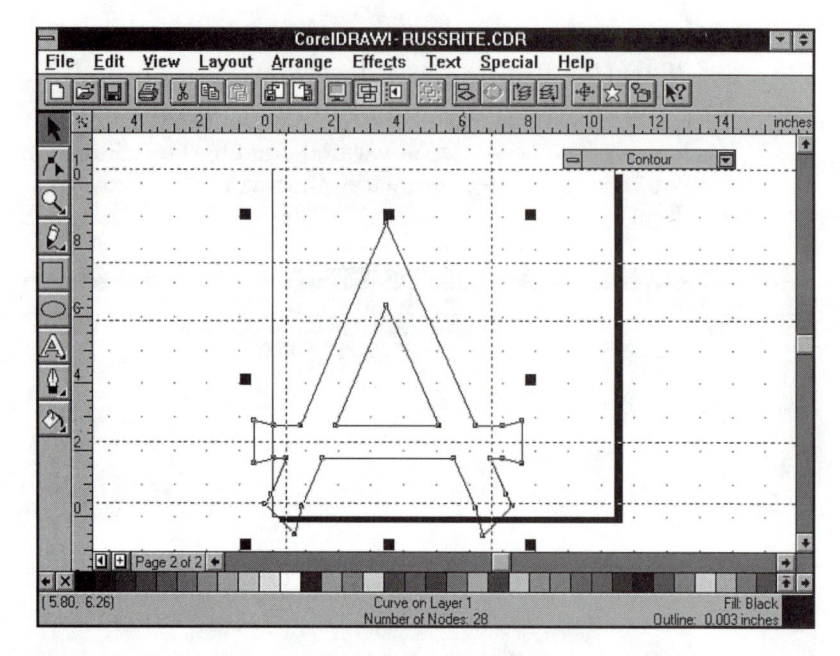

5. Now would be a good time to **F**ile, **S**ave your work. This display face will take on a look used earlier in this century for advertisements; I'm calling my font RUSSRITE.CDR after Russel Wright, the famous ceramics designer whose Atomic Age dining ware has similar lines and flow.

Refining Your Character

Your new letter "A" is a bonafide character in Corel and Window's eyes now, and you should do a little tweaking and resizing to get it ready for exporting.

It's vital that the characters be positioned right next to the vertical and horizontal Guidelines you set at zero earlier, and that you maintain a consistent Cap Height throughout your alphabet. You can let the descenders in Q and J go beneath the baseline, as you normally see with commercial fonts, and it's okay to let a serif stick out a little to the left of the vertical guideline. The guidelines are for consistency throughout the lettering, and also for the positioning CorelDRAW uses for font data when it exports your letters.

Refining Your Character

To get the "A" sitting within the Cap Height and the baseline, follow these steps:

1. You don't have a lot of control over how the Contour effect wraps a path around the end of a line, so the bottom of the "A" may look a little awkward. With the Shape tool, marquee-select a node, or nodes, at the bottom of your "A." Drag them up so they meet the baseline, as shown in figure 9.8.

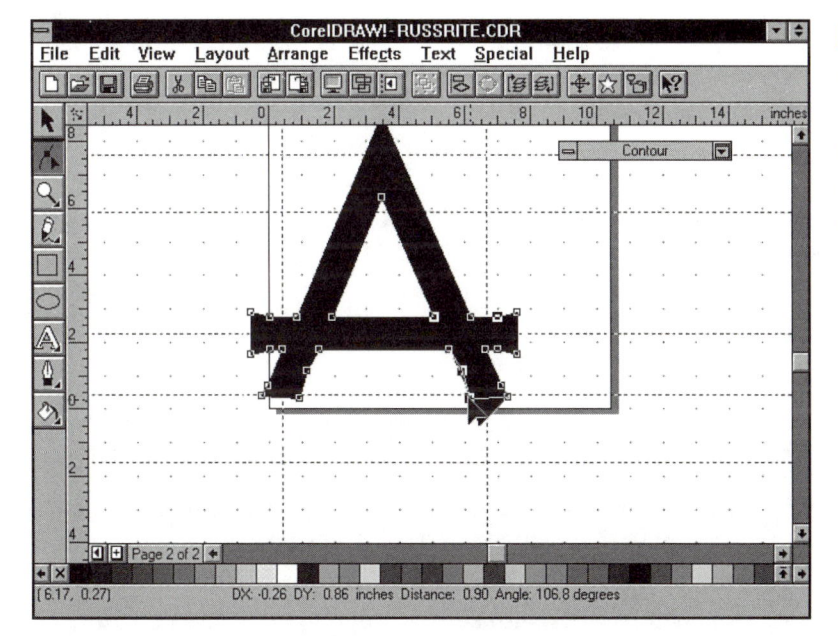

Figure 9.8

Unless you're going for an "effect," the bottoms of letterforms should meet the baseline you've set.

2. Do the same thing to the other "leg" of the "A."

3. When you've refined the bottom of the letter, choose the Pick tool. Click and drag a corner selection handle to resize the letter so that it touches the Cap Height and the Baseline.

4. Click and drag inside the letter shape to reposition it after resizing it, if necessary.

5. It's 1 down, 25 to go! Press Page Down to open a fresh page three, and you'll get into some problems and solutions that concern letters with a curved outline.

Using Open Paths To Create Your Alphabet

You've learned one technique for creating a character—use two straight-segment shapes, the Contour Effect, and then the Weld command.

But unless you want a typeface (or font) to look like a wood carving, you'll need to address how curved lettering can be built. Using the Contour effect offers an advantage: if you set the Contour to the same value each time you apply the effect, each character in the alphabet will have a consistently sized stroke.

There is a disadvantage, however, to applying a Contour to a curved line segment. The Contour effect will place oodles of nodes along the path of a curve, far more than are necessary to describe the arc. If a closed path has too many nodes, the geometry will be too complex to export as a typeface character.

In the next sequence, you create a problem, and then solve it as you venture into the second character of this typeface.

1. On page three of your Corel document, use the Pencil tool to click and drag a figure similar to that shown in figure 9.9. Start with straight segments, do not close the shape, and then double-click on a node to display the Node Edit Roll-Up. Convert as many segments to curves as you like, and fuss with the shape until it becomes an eye-catching capital "B."

The reason why you want to work with separate open paths when creating a typeface is because the Contour effect treats closed paths differently than open ones. An open path forces the Contour to draw a closed shape all the way around the path's periphery, whereas a closed path will only produce a Contour around the outside of it. This spells the difference between typeface characters approximately 1" in stroke width and .5".

Stop

If you've accidentally closed the shape, use the Break Apart button on the Node Edit Roll-Up to open the path. The path needn't be individual line segments like the <u>A</u>rrange, Brea<u>k</u> Apart command performs; paths simply need to be open, not closed.

2. Click on the Apply button, and a Contour will surround the letter.

Using Open Paths To Create Your Alphabet

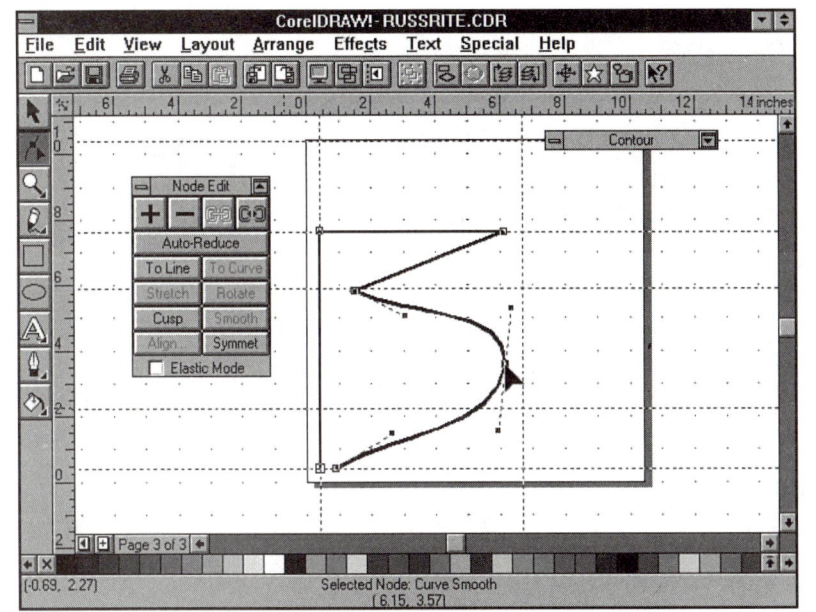

Figure 9.9

An open path will still create a Contour consisting of closed subpaths.

3. Sometimes when a node with cusp properties connects two segments at a severe angle, you'll get a "spike" sticking through another part of the Contour. To correct this problem, click and drag to reposition the node using the Shape tool, as shown in figure 9.10.

4. When you're happy with your letter, select the Contour, choose <u>A</u>rrange, <u>S</u>eparate, then ungroup the "B" the same as you did to the "A."

5. Delete the wireframe original by selecting it and pressing the Del key.

6. Click on the Shape tool, and select the Contour letter. You'll see about a billion nodes defining the curved bottom. You've also learned in previous chapters that a curve doesn't need to pass through more than one node every 120°. Marquee-select all of the nodes in the letter and press the Auto-Reduce button on the Node Edit Roll-Up, as seen in figure 9.11.

7. If the Auto-Reduce feature doesn't knock this shape back to a total of 30 or 40 nodes, manually delete some by clicking on them with the Shape tool, and pressing the Delete key. The Auto-Reduce is handy, but not as full-featured as we humans!

8. Resize and reposition the letter so it meets the Baseline, Cap Height, and far left guidelines.

9. Press Ctrl+S to save your continuing endeavors here.

Chapter 9: Creating a Custom Typeface

Figure 9.10
A Contour linked to its originating shape can be modified by changing the original shape's nodes.

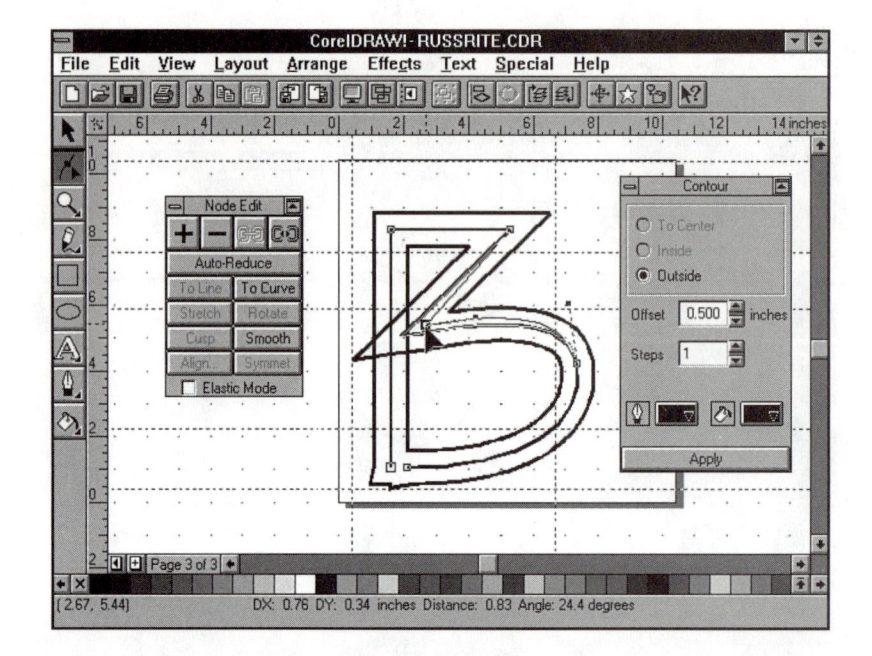

Figure 9.11
Auto-Reduce also reduces the manual labor of editing out superfluous nodes along a path.

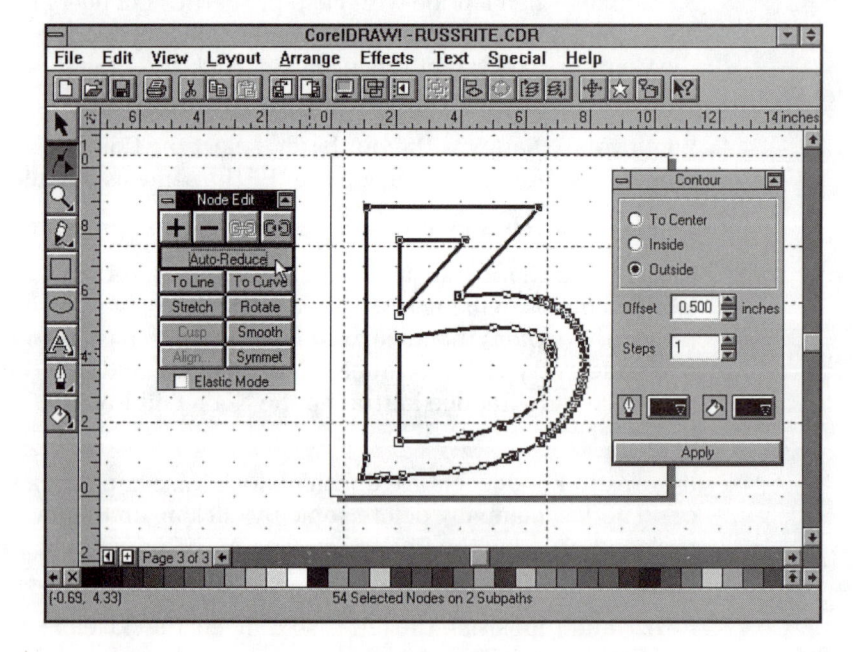

An "Outline" for the Rest of the Alphabet

You now know how to weld two separate Contour paths, and how to create subpaths using an open path; there's really not much left to review in terms of creating these letters. You'll want to use the Combine command instead of Weld if you want to create two shapes (but one path) that don't overlap within the typeface character.

In figure 9.12, you have the complete wireframe guide for *RusselWrite*. It would be well worth your time to complete this alphabet before moving into the next section on exporting, simply because it's *fun* to be able to type with your custom-crafted font!

Figure 9.12
Draw these paths, and then apply Contours to them to create lettering from A-Z.

Chapter 9: Creating a Custom Typeface

Note

Notice in the last figure that I've made the crossbars of characters like "H," "F," and "G" the same relative heights. This will improve readability. A good way to test how well your font works is to copy various letters to make a short sentence, reduce them all to the same height (14–18 points for a display font is good), and print a copy.

I've gone ahead and created numbers and punctuation marks like a question mark and a period. You can always go back to any typeface, original or not, and add a character, but it's a real drag to get cooking with your own font and be short the punctuation you need.

There is no hard and fast rule for character widths, except those that common sense dictate. An "M" should usually be wider than an "I," for example. You might want to use a guideline from an established font that you like. Say, click and drag a guideline at the width of the "M" from Arial, drop it on your design space, and work with your own "M" (and other letters).

Exporting Your Typeface

Here's the exciting part: after you have all your characters neatly guidelined on their own pages, CorelDRAW will do the "driving" for you.

You have some options to choose from when you export your typeface design, and they'll be covered when you come to them, but the very first one is which format you want your typeface to be read as. I've mentioned TrueType up to this point, because TrueTypes are easy to install and remove, and every person you meet who runs Windows 3.1*x* can use (or buy!) your typeface creations.

You can also select the *.PFB Export option at this point and wind up with an Adobe Type 1 PostScript font: the choice is yours. If you have the patience, you can export your typeface both ways. Type 1 fonts are the format of preference among commercial printers and service bureaus; this standard was developed way before Windows TrueType. You don't need a PostScript printer to use PostScript Type 1s—all the translating and rasterizing of a Type 1 font is performed by Adobe Type Manager, a utility you had to install in Windows Program Manager before using Type 1 fonts.

Additionally, CorelKern can "tweak" the kerning between characters in a font after you've exported it, but only a PFB, Type 1 format font. CorelKern is a Windows utility you'll receive free if you send in the CorelVentura coupon found in the boxes of CorelDRAW 5 shipped before August 1994. Additionally, there are a lot of shareware utilities available from online services that can add kerning pairs to a Type 1 font. See Chapter 2 for more information.

Exporting Your Typeface

In either case, the export procedure is almost identical. Here's how you export RusselWrite (Normal) as a TrueType font. Just follow the steps:

1. By now you may be on page 27 or so of the RUSSRITE.CDR document, and it would be good to start exporting with the letter "A." Click on the Page Control where it says *Page 28 of 28*, for example, and you'll get the Go To dialog box. Type in **2** (or whatever page the cap "A" is on), and Corel takes you there.

2. Select the "A" with the Pick tool.

3. Choose File, Export, and scroll in the List Files of Type drop-down list until you find the TrueType font called *.TTF. Pick *Adobe Type 1 Fonts, *.PFB* if you want RusselWrite as a Type 1 font. Be sure that Selected Only check box is checked!

4. Name the TTF font file that Corel will build in the File Name field. It's also a good idea to keep your font experiments apart from the ones you've already installed (not in the WINDOWS\SYSTEM or PSFONTS subdirectories). You can easily identify your font creations and uninstall them if you have a special subdirectory containing the originals with original file names, as seen in figure 9.13.

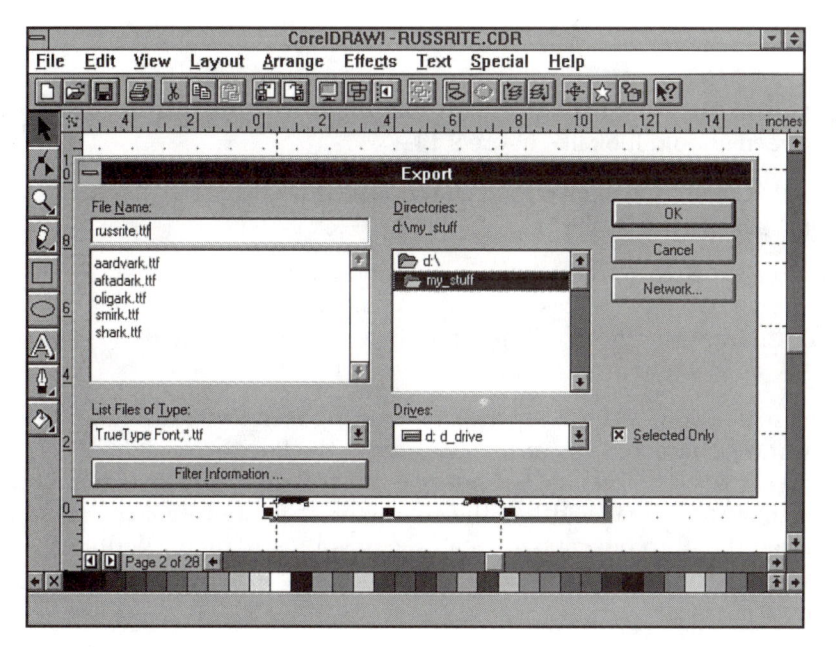

Figure 9.13
You name the TTF file for your font before exporting.

Chapter 9: Creating a Custom Typeface

5. Click on OK, and you are transported to the Options dialog box. You can type up to 34 characters for a typeface name; both upper- and lowercase letters work. You can put a space between words if you want an elegant typeface name to appear in every Windows program font options box. The limit is 47 characters. I recommend you keep your font name down to 20, though, because most programs' font fields will truncate an overly long name.

6. Type **750** in the Spa**c**e Width field. This will be the spacing between words when you type with the typeface. It's an arbitrary value, and for fonts with narrow widths, 500 is a frequently used value.

Tip

By default, Corel assigns an equal value of 2048 to both **G**rid Size and Spa**c**e Width, and this can often yield wider inter-word spacing than you'd like. The Grid and Space are *not* point sizes; they are mathematical values that take into account some automatic proportioning.

You also have the opportunity to reset the Spa**c**e Width after defining the first character in a font by clicking the Options box after you first import here.

7. Do not check the Symbol Font box, as this will be covered a little later. Your screen should look like figure 9.14.

8. Click on OK, and then click on **Y**es in the TrueType Export dialog to confirm saves to the RUSSRITE.TTF file.

9. In the TrueType Export box, there's a scrolling window of available characters to which you'll assign your "A," with the corresponding code or Character **N**umber to the left of it. Scroll until you find the capital A, character 65, and click on it.

10. You'll also see your letter, the baseline it's supposed to be sitting on, and the inter-character, or *kerning* boundary (the line to the right of your character). The kerning boundary is set automatically at 5 percent greater than the overall width of the character. In figure 9.15, I've unchecked the Auto box, and you can see how the **C**haracter Width can be set tighter (or looser); this will improve kerning when you use the typeface.

Exporting Your Typeface

Figure 9.14

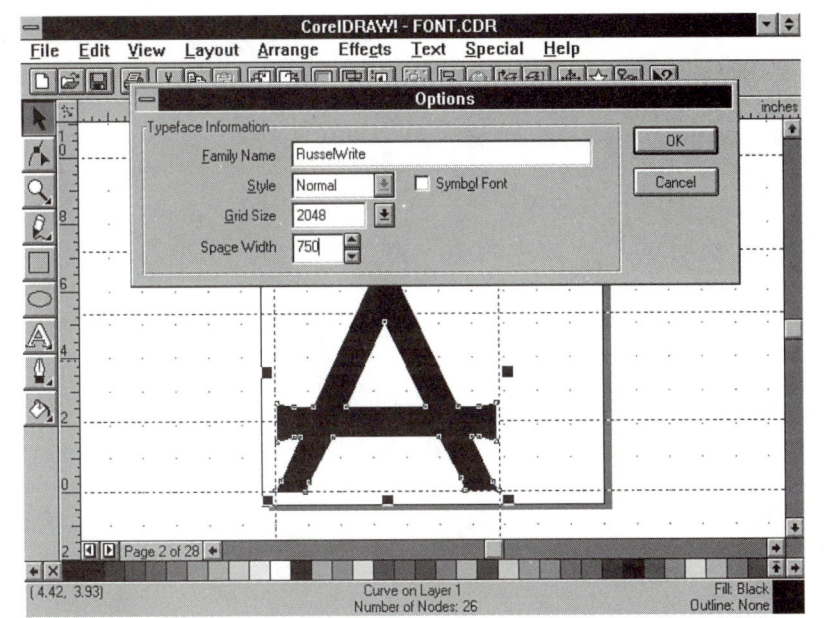

Set word spacing options and your font's name in the Options box.

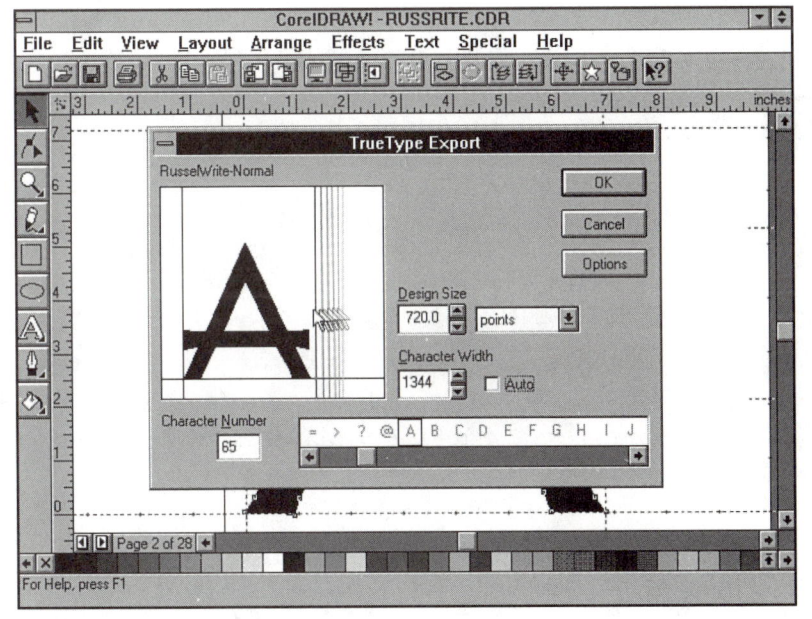

Figure 9.15

Set the character width and the key to which you want to assign your letter in the TrueType Export dialog box.

Tip

Character Width has nothing to do with the design of your character; you do not squash it if you move the width line closer to the character. Character Width is actually the "air" to the right of your design that precedes the next letter in a word.

11. Click on OK, and you have your first character exported for RusselWrite.

Stop

If you've deselected the Auto Character Width to more tightly kern a character, be sure to check the Auto box for the next export. If you don't, you'll wind up with more space after a character than you need!

12. You need to repeat the process for each character. Press the Page Down key to advance to the letter "B," select it with the Pick tool, then choose File Export, and click on RUSSRITE.TTF in the File Name: box. CorelDRAW advances the key to which you assign each design every time you export a character, so make sure the key Corel offers is the one you want!

Tip

When you hit a descending character, J or Q, for example, you'll notice that the preview window will clip off the descender part of the character, as shown in figure 9.16.

All is well, and do not panic. Descenders are supposed to go below the font's baseline, and although the preview window shows you only part of the character, the entire character will export, display, and print correctly.

13. When you've exported "Z," take a break before the next section. Personally, I'm singing the "Alphabet Song" to myself right now!

Exporting Your Typeface

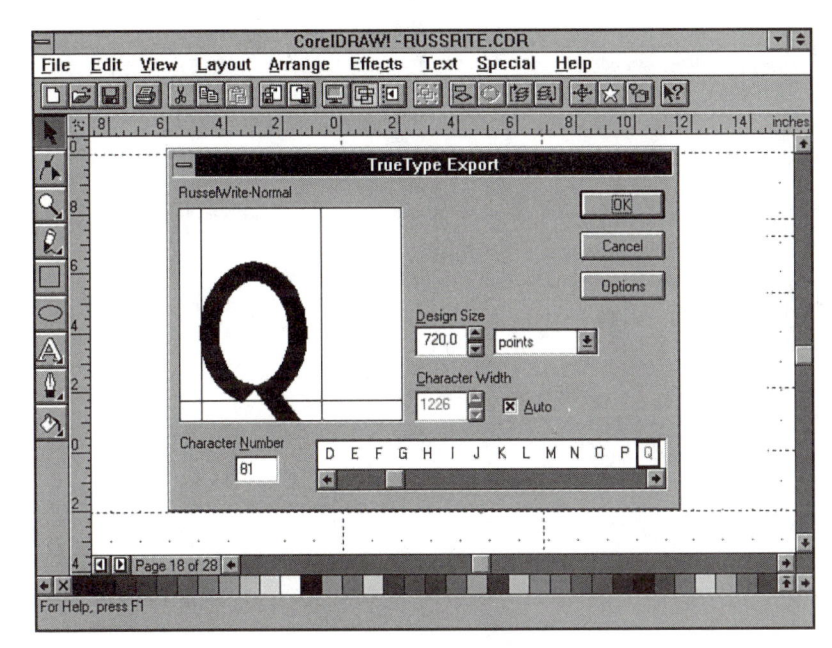

Figure 9.16
Characters with descenders may appear to be clipped, but they'll export for use just fine.

Tackling the Lowercase Letters

Lowercase letters are important to a typeface, even if they're a rehash of the uppercase designs. You can get away with this when designing a display font because they are generally considered one-of-a-kind "designatures," and are more character-y than consistent. Unless you type all day with the Caps Lock key engaged, the RusselWrite font will be a frustrating typing adventure—Corel writes the first character (cap "A") into all the empty character slots of this font. Instead of AAAAAAAA, let's turn this font into something a little more useful.

Just complete the following steps:

1. Press the Page Control to get the Go To box, and type the number of the page where "A" is. You can also click on the Page control left arrow.

2. Select the "A," choose **F**ile, **E**xport, and click on RUSSRITE.TTF.

3. Scroll over to character 97, the lowercase "a," and set the **D**esign Size to 1000 points, roughly 3/4 of the capital height in this font, a good height for "small caps" (see fig. 9.17).

4. Click on OK.

Figure 9.17
Small caps generally work well at about 3/4 the size of regular uppercase characters.

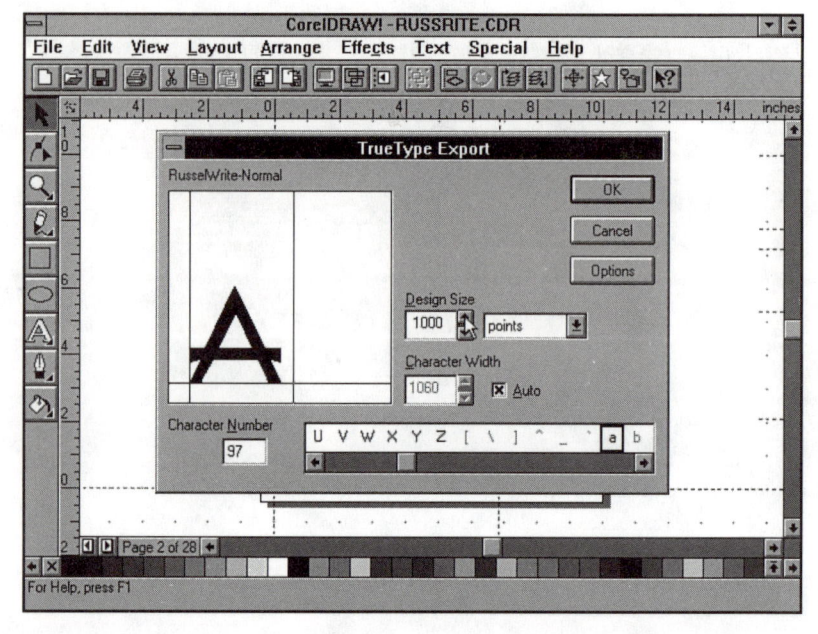

5. Repeat the same steps you performed for exporting the capital letters. If you were ambitious and designed punctuation and numbers, scroll to their corresponding keys and export them, also!

6. Exit CorelDRAW.

Installing Your Custom Font

Here's the payoff to your work: you're going to install your RusselWrite typeface and see how it looks. CorelDRAW will not automatically install a typeface you've created, so here's the brief installation procedure:

1. In Windows Program Manager (or another Windows shell like Norton Desktop for Windows), double-click on the Control Panel icon.

2. Double-click on the Fonts icon within the Control Panel group, and click on the *A*dd button.

3. In the Dri*v*es and *D*irectories windows, select the location to which you exported RusselWrite. In figure 9.13, you saw I had a MY_STUFF subdirectory set up on my drive D for my TrueType creations.

4. Click on RusselWrite in the List of *F*onts: window, and click on OK.

Installing Your Custom Font

5. As you can see in figure 9.18, Windows gives you a little preview of the appearance of your font. Click on Close to exit the Fonts utility.

Stop

Always check the Copy Fonts to Windows Directory box when installing fonts through the Fonts utility. Windows will then make a copy of your original, and store it and use it from the WINDOWS\SYSTEM directory. This leaves you with a backup copy of your work in your original directory, which is handy to have if something happens to the copy stored in the WINDOWS\SYSTEM directory.

The secondary benefit to copying the original font is that you can go back later, add characters to the original, and reinstall it. Windows does not like it when you add characters to an installed TrueType font, and may crash your system if you try to do so. TrueType is active from the moment you add it, and modifying an installed font is similar to stepping out of a moving car!

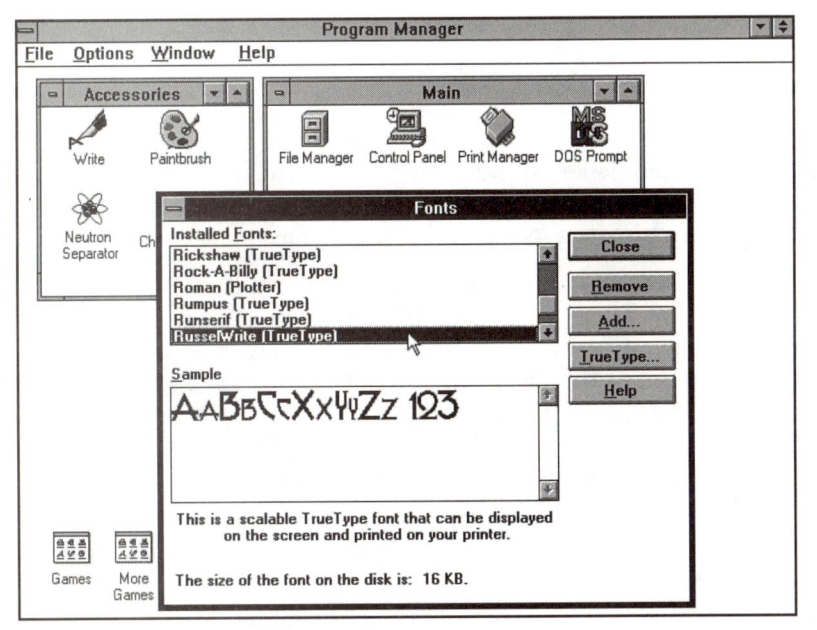

Figure 9.18
The Windows Fonts utility, and some third-party programs, will install TrueType fonts to your system.

6. Hey, indulge yourself at this point, and really test out your font. In Program Manager, double-click on Windows Write and type yourself a congratulations. Highlight the phrase, choose Character, then Fonts, pick RusselWrite, and click on OK. As you can see in figure 9.19, the author waxed profound.

Figure 9.19

Why do you need a caption here?

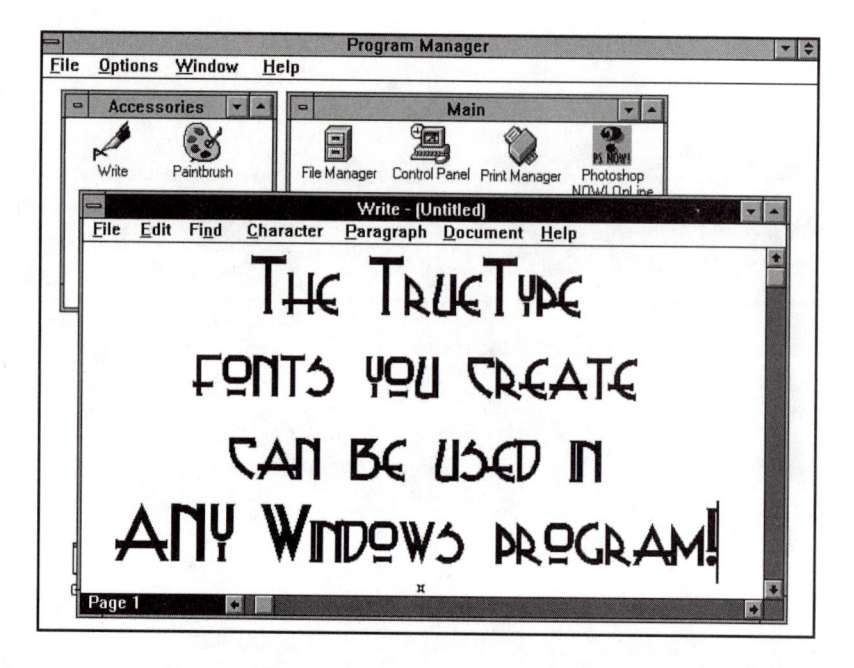

Using Fonts as Symbols

There's a lot of overlap between a design and a typeface. Zapf Dingbats, for example, is a typeface publishers use daily for fancy bullets and check boxes. But symbol typefaces are really nothing more than a collection of drawings exported to a typeface format, exactly the same as RusselWrite.

You can put this knowledge to very good use and design a custom symbols category for CorelDRAW. There isn't a day that goes by when I don't need a quick doodle I've designed, and the Symbols Roll-Up is a more accessible place to store these doodles than in a clip art collection.

Follow these steps to create a symbol font character:

1. Design a doodle you like. I do a lot of children's birthday invitations professionally (I'm lying to create an example here), so I'll use a drawing I did of Slappy the Clown.

2. Type a capital "A" next to your doodle, highlight it, and with the Te t, **C**haracter command (Ctrl+T), set the "A" to 720 points.

3. Select the doodle, then click and drag on a corner selection handle so it scales the same size as the 720 point "A."

Using Fonts as Symbols

4. You only really need to define a baseline for the first symbol in a collection. You'll see shortly how to automatically add others, so click and drag the zero origin point to the bottom left of your doodle, as shown in figure 9.20. You don't actually depend on guidelines when creating symbol faces.

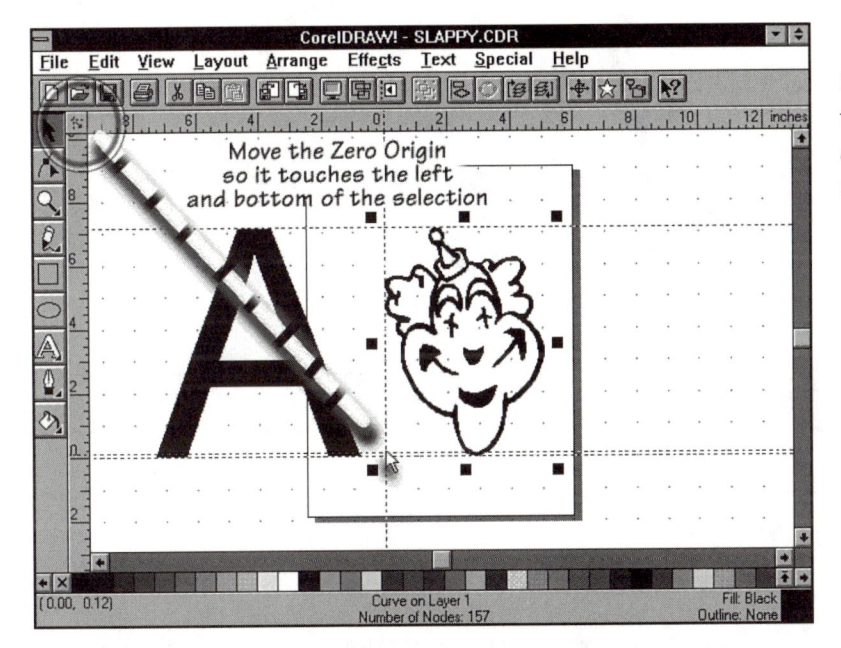

Figure 9.20
Fonts don't have to be letters; any closed path is legit.

5. Choose File, Export while your doodle is selected. Again, choose either the TTF or PFB format for your font, and pick an eight-character File Name. Be sure to check the Selected Only check box in the lower right corner of the dialog box.

6. Give a real, non-PC name to your symbol typeface in the Options dialog box. As you can see in figure 9.21, I'm calling this Home Brew. Be sure to check the Symbol Font box before clicking on OK.

7. Close CorelDRAW. You're done! Of course, you need to add the Home Brew font from Program Manager's Fonts utility, and this symbol set exists as 255 renditions of one doodle, but read on after you've installed Home Brew to see how easily you can add to it now.

Figure 9.21

A typeface with a symbol attribute will appear on CorelDRAW's Symbols Roll-Up as a category.

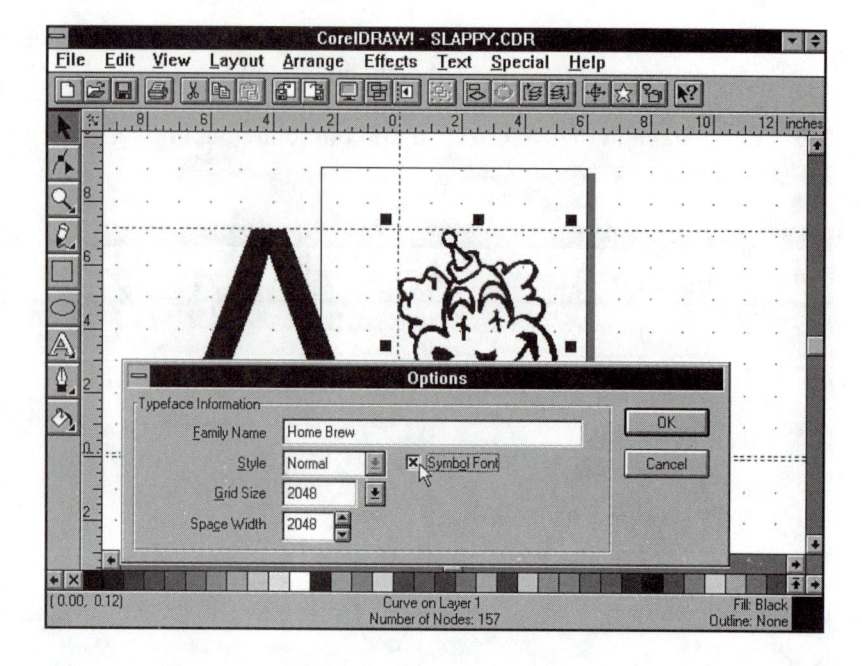

Creating a Mini-Art Collection

If you reopen CorelDRAW now, and click on the Symbols Roll-Up button (the star) in the Ribbon Bar, you'll see that you now have a whole new symbols category—Home Brew! Find (or create) another doodle or two you'd like to add to this symbols category, and follow these steps to add them:

1. Click on the Symbols Roll-Up icon on the Ribbon Bar, and scroll down to the Home Brew category.

2. Do a doodle, or open one you already have drawn. Like typeface characters, the doodle must be a closed path, or a combined bunch of subpaths. Select the doodle with the Pick tool.

3. Choose **S**pecial, then Create **S**ymbol.

4. As you can see in figure 9.22, you need to scroll down the Symbol Category drop-down list to find Home Brew. Click on it, click on OK, and wait a moment while CorelDRAW processes your command.

5. You're immediately in action! In figure 9.23, the recycle symbol is now a symbol that can be clicked and dragged into the Drawing Window.

Creating a Mini-Art Collection

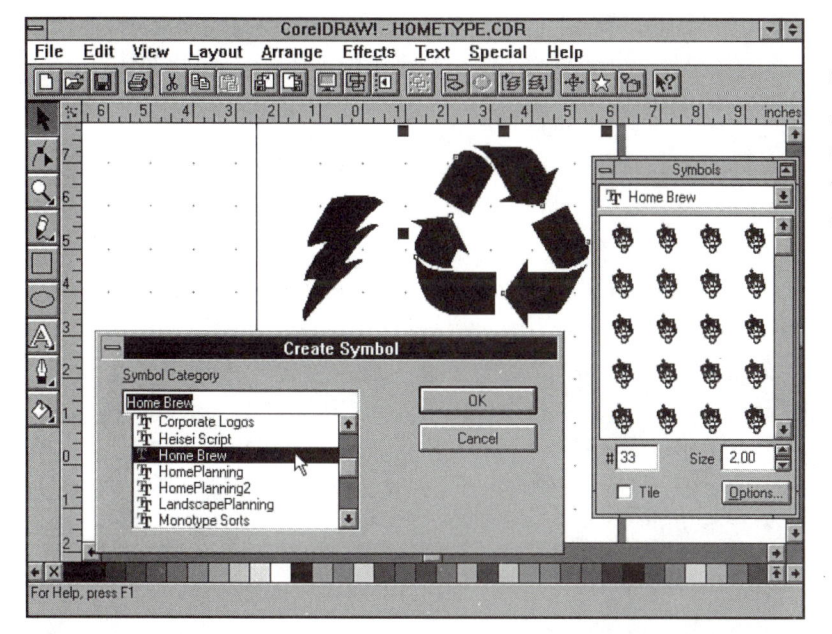

Figure 9.22
Select a shape, and add it to a symbols category through the Create Symbol command.

Figure 9.23
An added symbol fills the first available slot on the symbols Roll-Up.

Chapter 9: Creating a Custom Typeface

Tip

When you add a symbol to the Symbols Roll-Up, it becomes part of the TrueType typeface. You can use the character in a word processing program or Corel Ventura as part of the typeface. This is a "dynamic" addition Corel performs, and you really shouldn't be running other applications that use TrueType fonts when you create a symbol.

The disadvantage to adding a symbol to a TrueType font in CorelDRAW as you did is that you have no control over kerning, baselines, or which key is assigned to a symbol.

To access a symbol in an application other than Corel, let's use the example of the rocking horse in figure 9.24. You see on the Symbols palette that the horse's # is 33. In a word processing program, therefore, you'd choose the Home Brew font, and hold the Alt key and type 0035 on your numeric keypad. ASCII and ANSI characters are always accessed by a four-digit code, beginning with a zero.

In figure 9.24, I've added a few more simple drawings to my Home Brew TrueType symbol font. You can click and drag any of your homemade symbols from the Roll-Up to instantly design something! By default, symbols appear in the Drawing Window with no fill attributes and the default 0.003" outline width (unless you changed the default, as described in Chapter 3). You can also set the size for your copies in the size box.

Stop

Symbol fonts that are click+dragged from the Symbols Roll-Up share a lot of qualities with your original design, except they've been through an export process, which means your original design data has been interpreted slightly.

You may find one or two extra nodes on a symbol when compared to your original design. For this reason, it's unwise to repetitively export a symbol to a typeface, and then click+drag the symbol onto your page, and export it again. Eventually, CorelDRAW will refuse to export an object, telling you the object is too complex; the reason is that it has too many nodes describing the arc of a segment.

Figure 9.24

Symbol shapes can be broken apart and assigned a fill exactly like any CorelDRAW design you may originate.

Adding a Corporate Logo to an Existing Font

In the last two font-astic adventures, you've created a typeface, but there are occasions when you want to modify an existing one. To conclude this chapter, imagine that you're working at MicroFish Systems, and they have a logo they like plastered on everything from letterhead stationary to soda cups in their canteen. As Chief Art Director, your assignment is to modify the Times New Roman font used by all the administrative assistants so a logo can be quickly added to correspondence.

There is a very real peril here: you always run the risk of ruining a commercial typeface when you tinker with it. You'll first need to make a *copy* of the font for our experiment, and then you won't harm the font that came with Windows 3.1*x*.

This is a great assignment if your company has a scanner, because you can acquire an image of a corporate logo, then use a Corel utility to convert it to a digital format CorelDRAW uses. But if you don't have any scanned logos, or a scanner for that matter, you'll still want to check out the techniques for augmenting a commercial typeface.

Chapter 9: Creating a Custom Typeface

To convert your logo, follow these steps:

1. Get a stationery letterhead scanned. It doesn't need to be from MicroFish Systems. Scanning is the most common way to turn a physical design into a digital format. CorelTRACE will accept a wide range of scanned image formats, but it ultimately converts them to *.BMPs, so you might want to save some time by saving your scan as a BMP, Line Art (1 bit per pixel sampling depth), at approximately 150 to 300 pixels/inch.

2. Double-click on the CorelTRACE icon in Program Manager.

3. Choose File, Open from CorelTRACE's menu, and select the file you acquired by scanning.

4. Click on the Outline Trace button on the button ribbon, as shown in figure 9.25. The left window is your bitmap scan, and the right window shows the CorelTRACE of the bitmap.

Figure 9.25
CorelTRACE is a bitmap-to-vector conversion utility.

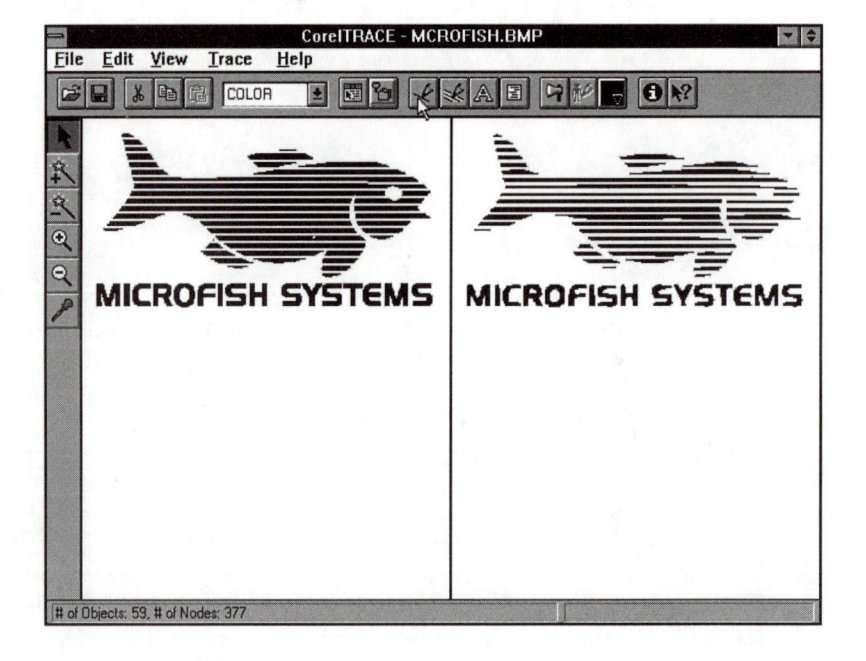

Tip

It is time well-spent to play with the features of CorelTRACE. Besides converting bitmaps to a format CorelDRAW can import, CorelTRACE can also perform Optical Character Recognition (OCR), turning electronic faxes into editable text.

5. Choose File, Save, and CorelTRACE saves the conversion to the same subdirectory your scanned bitmap original is located in, with the same eight-character names, but with an Encapsulated PostScript (EPS) file extension.

6. Close the TRACE program, and open CorelDRAW.

7. Choose File, Import, and pick CorelTRACE, *.EPS from the List Files of Type drop-down list.

8. Choose your drive and directory, and click on the logo file with the EPS extension.

9. The vector design of the logo will be grouped. This is the way CorelTRACE converts a bitmap image to multiple paths, so click on the ungroup button on the Ribbon Bar.

10. You may need to "clean up" the CorelTRACE import. For example, you don't want MICROFISH SYSTEMS lettering on the logo; you only need the fish part. To eliminate the lettering, select it and press the Del key.

11. If you'd like to smooth out a curve in your logo, double-click on the Shape Tool to display the Node Edit Roll-Up, and edit nodes using the techniques described in earlier chapters.

12. When the logo looks good, choose Edit, Select All, then Arrange, Combine, to make the collection of shapes one path (or many subpaths). The logo is now a valid object to export as part of a typeface collection.

13. Choose File, Save, and name your file FISHTIME.CDR.

14. Close CorelDRAW.

Sizing the Logo for the Typeface

Your logo should fit into the typeface you're grafting it to, so you should type a capital character from Times New Roman, at 720 points, to size the fish proportionately to fit into the typeface.

Complete the following steps:

1. Make a copy of Times New Roman before continuing. To do this, go to Windows File Manager and select your WINDOWS\SYSTEM subdirectory; scroll down and find TIMES.TTF.

Chapter 9: Creating a Custom Typeface

2. Click on TIMES.TTF and choose File, Copy (F8). Enter the name of a subdirectory you've set up for all your experiments in the To: field, and click on OK.

3. Go to the subdirectory that contains the copy of TIMES.TTF, click on it, choose File, Rename, and name the file FISHTIME.TTF. The copy is not installed, and the original won't be altered in any way.

4. Exit File Manager and restart CorelDRAW.

5. Open FISHTIME.CDR and type a capital "T" on the Printable page with the Text tool.

6. With the T selected, press Ctrl+T to display the Character Attributes box.

7. Choose Times New Roman as the Font, set the Size to 720 points, then click on OK.

8. Click and drag the zero origin point to the bottom left corner of an imaginary boundary box that is shaped by the letter T's outermost geometry.

9. Select the logo with the Pick tool and position it about in the center of the T. This will be its position and size relative to a capital T in the typeface you're going to modify, as shown in figure 9.26.

Figure 9.26

The zero origin determines the position of an exported character relative to other characters.

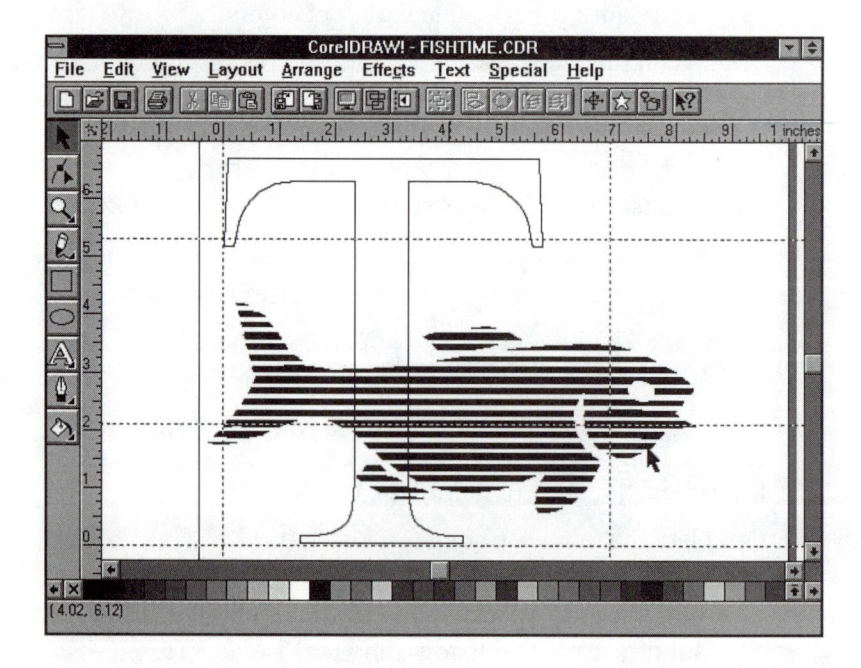

Sizing the Logo for the Typeface

10. Choose **F**ile, Export, and select FISHTIME.TTF from the subdirectory you copied it to. Make sure the **S**elected Only box is checked in the Export dialog box.

11. You can overwrite an existing typeface character definition, or you can search for an empty slot within a typeface. The occupied keys are highlighted. In figure 9.27, I've decided the folks at MicroFish don't use the caret symbol much, so I'm assigning the fish logo to it. Then it'll be easy to instruct people where to find it on their keyboard.

12. If you're overwriting an existing character, Corel will "flag" you. You then have your choice of choosing OK or canceling the operation.

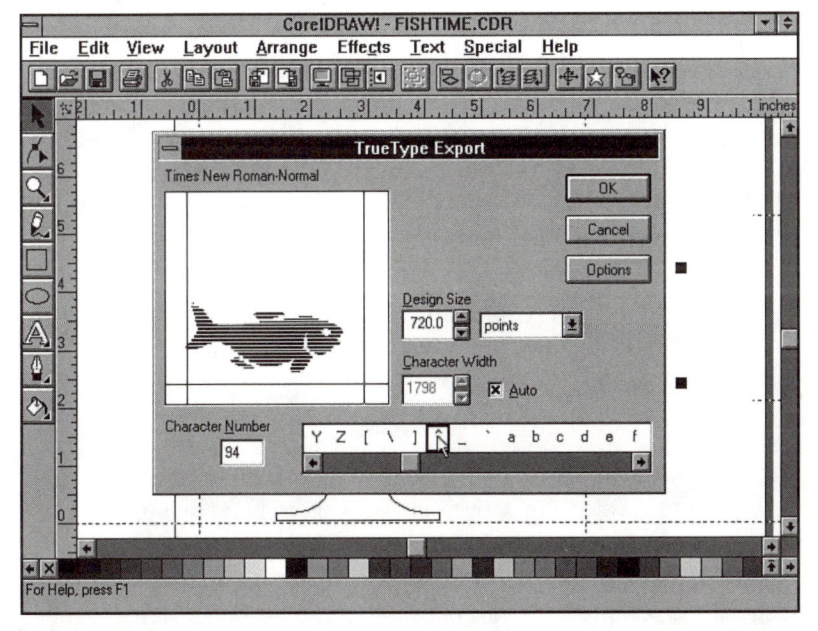

Figure 9.27

You can actually replace seldom-used font characters with your own customized characters.

> **Stop**
> When you overwrite an existing character, the original cannot be retrieved without a backup copy of the font!

13. You're done! The copy of Times New Roman now has a fish logo in it instead of a caret symbol! You can copy this file to a disk and distribute it to co-workers.

Stop

What you cannot do with Times New Roman, modified or not, is distribute it publicly under your own name, give it away for free, or charge for it. Fonts are protected by copyright laws the same as software programs like CorelDRAW are. Unless a typeface is an original one, you invite a world of trouble by disseminating a modified commercial typeface for any purpose other than private or in-house use.

Renaming a Now-Customized Font

CorelDRAW can't solve the problem of renaming a font so you can distinguish it from the original Times New Roman, though. The PostScript or TrueType name for a font is written into the header of the font file, and you'd be ill-advised to ever try to change it through editing.

There are numerous shareware and commercial software utilities that will rename a font as it will appear in the font boxes of Windows programs, however. Font Monster is available through electronic bulletin boards, and it will assign any name to a font you like.

Shareware is not freeware. It's yours to evaluate before you register (purchase) it, but you do have a legal responsibility to take it off your machine after the evaluation period (30 days, generally) is expired and you haven't paid the author.

Tip

A different approach to the font renaming problem is to remove the original font from your drive, and simply load and use your modified commercial typeface. Windows Font utility will get confused if it reads two identical font header I.D.s, but will accept, in the example above, your fish-y font as Times New Roman.

Summary

As you can see in figure 9.28, the folks at MicroFish Systems are happy with their new typeface capability, and you should be happy, too, at the new CorelDRAW tricks you can feather your cap with. If your professional course is destined for desktop publishing and computer graphics, you're well on your way to being a fonts guru. You understand the basics of type and symbol creation, and in time you'll be able to whip together a custom face for a corporation, presentation, or simply a symbol set that makes even the most humdrum of assignments go by with lightning speed.

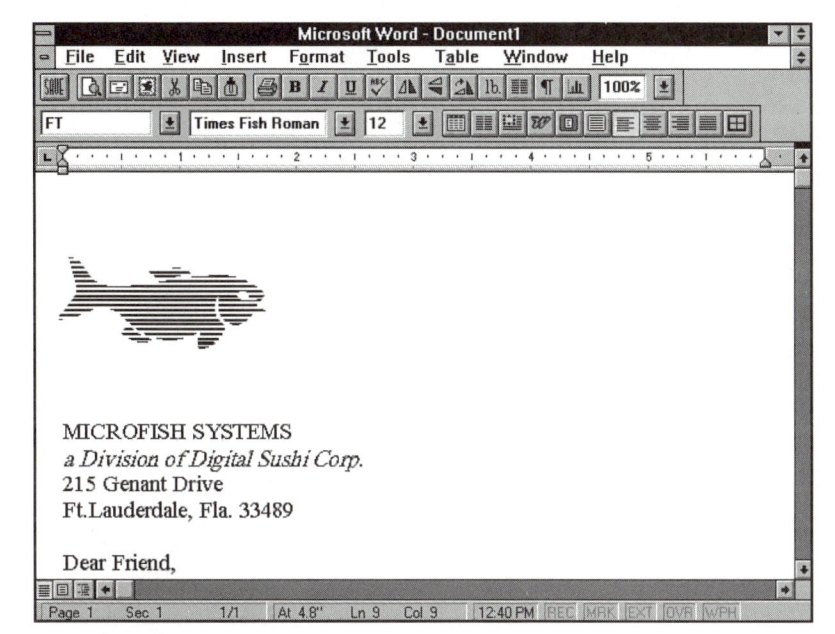

Figure 9.28
You can tune a piano, but you can't tuna letterhead.

If getting your work done at a breakneck clip is the order of the day, you'll definitely want to clip out the next chapter to save. CorelDRAW offers thousands of professionally designed clip art commercial art pieces in the *.CDR format on the CD. You can use and reuse the art, combine it, and generally tailor it to suit your business needs. Now that you've had some experience with Corel's drawing tools, you'll see how the editing tools can be used to customize clip art for every occasion.

PROFESSIONALLY-
DRAWN
CLIP ART
PATHETIC
AMATEURISH
DOODLE

CHAPTER 10

Clip Art Can Save Your Life!

It may seem odd that a program as rich in design features as CorelDRAW comes with as many clip art images as it does. Why would an artist need another artist's artwork? What possible use do I have for more than 18,000 images? What am I going to do with all these pictures of tanks and bananas?

Believe it or not, everyday folks who have little or no artistic flair buy CorelDRAW for only one reason: to pepper up boring page layouts and serve as a continuing source of business graphics at a place that has no in-house designer.

There are a number of applications for clip art in both the artist's and *non-artist's* assignments, and as soon as you learn how to import, customize, and refine clip art, you'll save time and a lot of migraines when the tasks you're thrown seem impossible.

In this chapter, you:

- Create two different flyers using the same clip art
- Learn how to tailor clip art for a specific assignment
- Perform clip art plastic surgery
- Use CorelMOSAIC as an alternative to the Windows Clipboard

The Origins of Clip Art

People today think of clip art as a collection of digital images grouped into different categories relating to a theme, but artists who create clip art have been offering this valuable service to businesses almost directly following the invention of movable type (around the turn of the century).

Many freelance artists have time to spare between paying work, and someone got the bright idea once to fill that time drawing generic illustrations. Clip art serves the business community in sort of a backward sense: instead of commissioning an artist to create a specific drawing, clip art artists draw things with enough broad applicability and appeal to be snapped up by people who can dovetail the art into their specific art requirements.

Clip art traditionally has come in an oversized book (17" by 22" is common) published quarterly. Businesses would subscribe to the publication and choose a category or categories they'd have the most use for. Supermarkets today still buy clip art books whose theme is food, and department stores frequently run clip art images of models to spruce up newspaper advertisements. People clip it out of the book, paste it into a layout, and a headline or two later… instant promotional material.

Corel and other software manufacturers have scoured the earth in recent years for artists talented in designing theme illustrations; their work could be transformed into digital media and offered as a PC alternative to clip art books. Clip art is in Corel's *.CMX Presentation Exchange format; it behaves exactly like a native *.CDR design, except the *.CMX format allows other Corel applications to import the design with no dynamic linking of blend groups, data, and other control objects. This means clip art CMX shapes aren't composed of circles, rectangles, or editable Contour groups, but instead are made up of individual, un-dynamically linked series of nodes and curve segments, but you already know how to create these yourself anyway, right? Simply put, the CMX format causes less hassles for other Windows applications to import.

What You Can (and Can't) Do with Clip Art

This chapter will show you the many ways you can change Corel clip art. More importantly, you get your imagination, resourcefulness, and creativity sparked, because clip art alone won't make you a better designer. Besides, it would be a shame to become dependent upon clip art when you have so many wonderful Corel design tools at your disposal.

You should be aware before you begin the assignments in this chapter that in the same way you don't own CorelDRAW (you own a license to use it), you don't own clip art, either. Clip art is royalty-free; you can use it as a component of a design, and the artist has already been paid a fee by Corel Corporation for unlimited use of the clip art.

What you cannot do, however, is claim that the art is your own or distribute copies of clip art for others' use. The clip art collection on Corel's CD is intended to help you, the Corel licensee, out of a bind, and while it can improve the execution of a graphic concept, it can't improve your art skills.

The 5-Minute Professional Design (Using Clip Art)

Now that we understand the ground rules, let's simulate a real-life situation when you can call on clip art to dig you out of a predicament. Suppose you recently landed at the Megalopolis Foundation, a Fortune 10 company that has an indoctrination brunch for new employees every month. Young, aspiring executives get the whole nine yards on corporate policies, dress code, and industrial culture, as well as instant coffee and a jelly doughnut, on Friday at 8:45 a.m.

At 8 a.m. on Friday, you're escorted between two office dividers, told that CorelDRAW 5 is installed on the PC in your new office, and informed that Mr. Megalopolis III needs several dozen memos that will announce the brunch and are to be posted next to the kitchenette areas on each floor.

Your first step, naturally, is to open your briefcase and tack up your calendar of cats dressed in Victorian costumes on the wall divider. Your second is to launch CorelDRAW.

Before getting to Corel clip art, your first step is to lay some Artistic Text down on the Printable page, so you can see the dimensions you have to work with, and what the size of clip art you'll add will be. Here's how:

1. Choose the Text tool, click an insertion point on the page, and type **The**<Enter>**Megalopolis Foundation**<Enter>**New Employees** <Enter>**Brunch**.

2. Press Ctrl+spacebar to toggle to the Pick tool, then press Ctrl+T (Te**x**t, **C**haracter...) to display the Character Attributes dialog box for the selected Artistic Text.

3. Choose the font carefully. This is a good lesson here. Stuffy corporations don't necessarily buy into display faces like Pump Triline or Hairpin (Harpoon). Bookman is classic, and the bold-italic style adds a little flair, so choose Bookman from the **F**onts scrolling list, and choose Bold-Italic from the **S**tyles drop-down list.

4. Choose **C**enter Alignment for the text selection, then click on OK.

Chapter 10: Clip Art Can Save Your Life!

5. Click and drag on the bottom left corner selection handle on the Artistic Text in a 4 o'clock direction to scale the text so it fills the width of the Printable page with 1/2" margins on the sides (hint: when the status line tells you the Artistic Text is about 40 points, the text will fit the page width with margins).

6. Double-click on the Rectangle tool to add a page border. You don't need the border for the design, but it'll serve a useful, if somewhat esoteric, purpose next.

7. Press the spacebar to toggle back to the Pick tool, then click on the Artistic Text to select it.

8. Hold the Shift key, and click on the page border. The status line will tell you that two objects are selected.

9. Click on the Align button on the Ribbon Bar.

10. Click on the Center check box in the Horizontally field, and click on OK. You've just aligned the Artistic Text perfectly within the page, because the page border you added is the same size as the Printable page.

11. Click on an empty area of the Drawing Window to deselect both objects. Click on the page border and press the Del key, because the only purpose for the page border was to align the text. As you can see in figure 10.1, you've quickly placed and centered a headline for the memo, without a moment to spare. It's 8:05 now!

Figure 10.1

Use a page border to center objects.

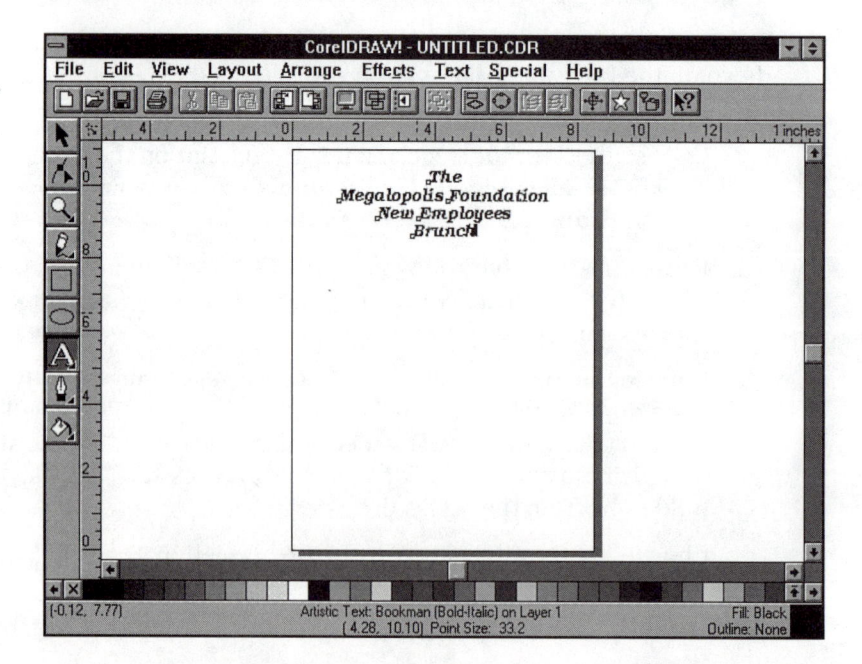

Copying Attributes

The time and place for the executive brunch are also important elements for the memo, and fortunately, a conservative design usually dictates that you use only one typeface.

It's easy to add Artistic Text to the bottom of the memo without even a trip to the Character Attributes dialog box to spec the type when you know how to copy a style in CorelDRAW. Here's how to enter a new string of Artistic Text and make it identical in specs to the headline in no time flat:

1. Choose the Text tool, click an insertion point on the page, and type **Friday, 8:45 am**<Enter>**The Executive Suite**<Enter>**210th floor**.

2. Press Ctrl+spacebar to toggle to the Pick tool.

3. Choose Edit, Copy Attributes From...

4. The Copy Attributes dialog box appears. Click on the Text Attributes check box, because you want to copy the Megalopolis Foundation Artistic Text you entered earlier.

5. Your cursor turns into a huge arrow, and you should now click on the text you want to copy in terms of font, size, and alignment: the Megalopolis text, as shown in figure 10.2.

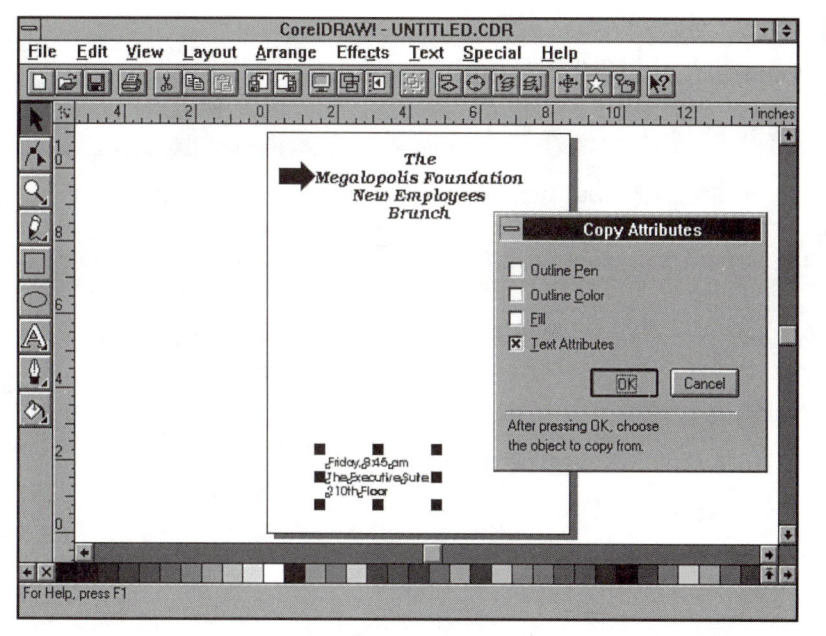

Figure 10.2

Copy fill, outline, or text attributes with the Copy Attributes From command.

Chapter 10: Clip Art Can Save Your Life!

6. Click and drag the time and date text so it's toward the bottom of the page. The Megalopolis text and the time/date text will frame the clip art you add to the memo.

7. With the time and date text selected, hold down the Shift key and click on the Megalopolis text.

8. Click on the Align button on the Ribbon Bar, and choose Center in the Horizontally field, as shown in figure 10.3.

Figure 10.3
Because the Megalopolis text is horizontally centered, the time/date text will be too, if you align both objects.

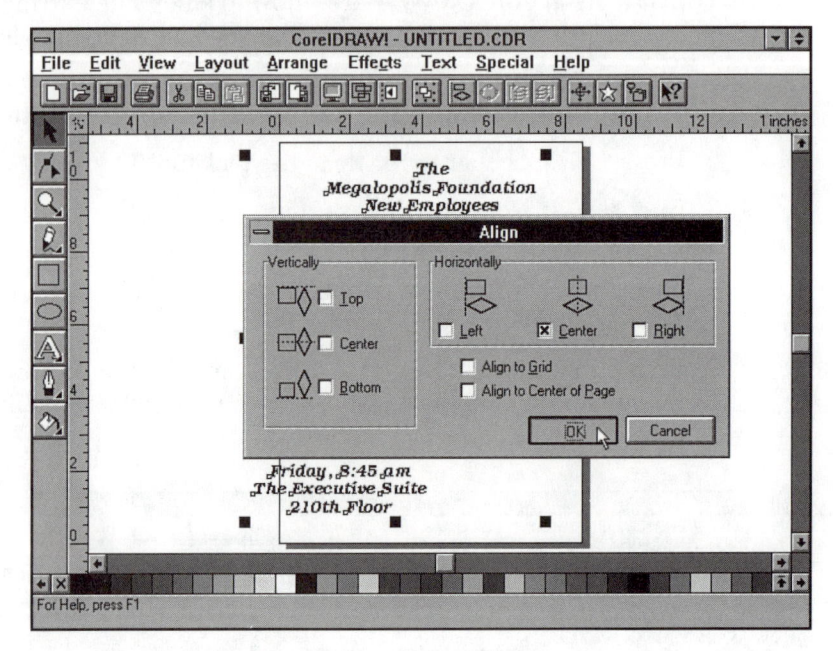

9. That's it for the text. Your next step is to click on the Save button (or press Ctrl+S; File, Save), and name the file GREETING.CDR (use your working directory you set up in Chapter 3; the assignment's fictitious, but getting into saving your work frequently is a real-life necessity).

It's on to exploring the possibilities uncovered with Corel's extensive clip art collection to add a quick graphic to this memo that would take you hours to design otherwise.

Tip

Aligning two or more shapes is a procedural command in Corel. Think of it as a sentence, "You want to align _____ to _____." In other words, the first shape you click on will be aligned to the second shape you click on, using the Shift+click method of adding to selections.

In the event that you marquee-select two or more objects, they will all be aligned to the first object drawn or placed in the Drawing Window. This is sometimes in the reverse order of the way you intended to align stuff. For this reason, Shift+clicking to add to selections you want aligned is the most fail-safe approach to precision designing.

CorelMOSAIC and Previewing Collections

The easiest way to thumb through a category of clip art drawings is with a Corel utility called MOSAIC. CorelMOSAIC will look at a subdirectory on your hard disk or CD-ROM drive, and present you with a thumbnail collection of miniature images of whatever it finds that's graphical within that subdirectory. Table 10.1 is a list of graphics formats MOSAIC recognizes. If you have a graphics file with one of these extensions, MOSAIC will take a "snapshot" of it, and you can save and even print collections of different images later.

Table 10.1 Computer graphics formats CorelMOSAIC will catalog.

File Extension	Program Associated with the Extension
CDR	CorelDRAW
PAT	CorelDRAW, PHOTO-PAINT
CDT	CorelDRAW
CCH	CorelCHART
SHW, SHB	CorelSHOW
CPT	CorelPHOTO-PAINT
CMV	CorelDRAW (but PhotoPAINT can edit a CMV import)

Table 10.1
continued

File Extension	Program Associated with the Extension
BMP, DIB, RLE, GIF	CorelPHOTO-PAINT, other pcx, tga, TIF bitmap-editing programs
JPG	CorelPHOTO-PAINT, other image-editing programs that understand JPG compression
EPS, AI	CorelDRAW, other programs that understand Adobe Encapsulated PostScript and Illustrator
CMV	CorelMOVE
FLI, FLC	CorelSHOW, AutoDesk Animator

As you can see, MOSAIC pretty well covers your bases!

MOSAIC runs right within the CorelDRAW workspace, and there's a button on the Ribbon Bar for displaying MOSAIC. MOSAIC operates in a "drag and drop," mode, so if you see a thumbnail of an image you want to use in MOSAIC's collection, all you do is pull a copy onto the Drawing Window.

In a lot of ways, MOSAIC replaces CorelDRAW's Import command; if you pull a MOSAIC thumbnail of a graphic designed in the CDR file format (CorelDRAW's), essentially you're making a copy of an original design. But if you click and drag an image in a format for which Corel doesn't have editing tools (such as a BMP or TIF bitmap image) MOSAIC lets CorelDRAW import the image.

MOSAIC and Your Clip Art Collection

MOSAIC is probably the smartest way to cruise your hard disk or CD-ROM drive for clip art. In the next series of steps, you'll see how to use CorelMOSAIC to find a generic business graphic, and bring it into CorelDRAW to complete the Megalopolis memo. Since CorelDRAW comes with over 22,000 pieces of clip art, feel free to choose an image you feel best completes the design.

In the BUSINESS subdirectory of the Corel CD, you'll find several images of businesspeople shaking hands, taking meetings, and playing basketball. People who bought the disk-only version of Corel 5 don't have as much clip art, but there are still one or two images on your hard disk in the CLIPART subdirectory that have business themes. GREETING.CMX, the clip art

MOSAIC and Your Clip Art Collection

323

graphic used in this chapter's example, is a good selection; it features people, and you'll see in this chapter how areas of clip art can be modified to make the art serve several purposes.

Here's how the MOSAIC-to-CorelDRAW process goes:

1. Click on the MOSAIC Roll-Up button on the Ribbon Bar.

2. By default, the MOSAIC Roll-Up gets to work immediately, assembling thumbnail images of whatever it finds in a subdirectory of your hard drive. Unfortunately, the subdirectory it chooses isn't always where your clip art collection is!

3. Click on the little open file folder on the right of the MOSAIC Roll-Up, and the Open Collection dialog box will appear.

4. The Open Collection dialog box works exactly like the Open Drawing command. Choose the drive and directory where your Corel clip art is located, then click on OK.

5. In figure 10.4, you can see that as long as you have the right clip art drive and directory selected, you can scroll through the MOSAIC drop-down list for the category of clip art you want. Additionally, the Import and Export buttons are highlighted in this figure. Importing is an alternative, less processor-intensive method of importing a graphic when you know the name of the image you want.

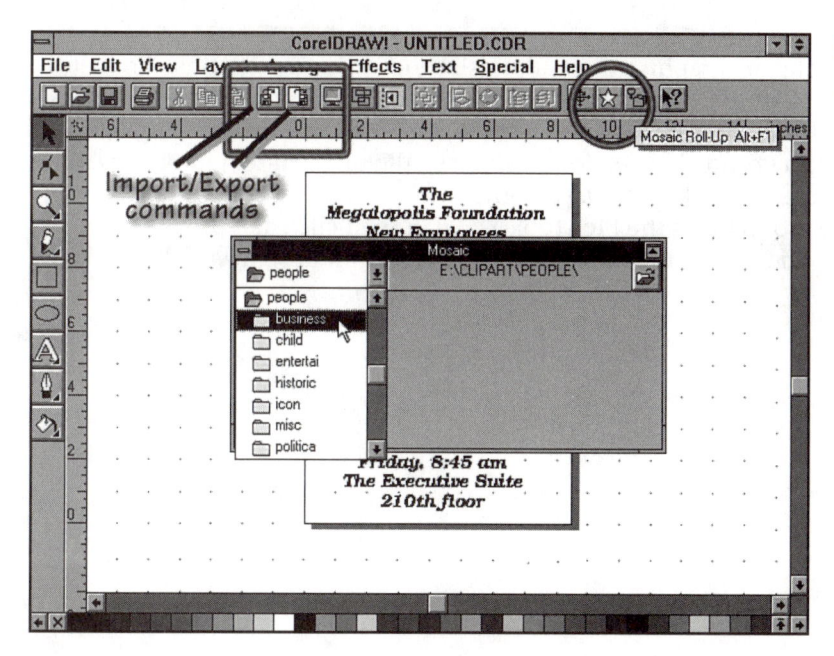

Figure 10.4

Click on the MOSAIC drop-down list to select a category once you've selected the drive and directory your clip art's on.

Chapter 10: Clip Art Can Save Your Life!

6. In figure 10.5, you can see that adding a clip art graphic is as simple as clicking on the graphic you want, then dragging it into the Drawing Window. The miniature appears to expand to full size; basically, your Megalopolis memo is finished.

Figure 10.5

Click and drag the Corel clip art graphic from the MOSAIC Roll-Up into the Drawing Window.

7. Corel clip art graphics can vary in size, because the artist has no idea how you want to use their graphic in the future. As you can see in figure 10.6, when clip art is imported, it comes into the Drawing Window as a grouped collection of shapes. All you need to do to resize all the pieces is click and drag a corner selection handle toward the center of the group using the Pick tool. You can then click and drag the selection to reposition it. How's that for instant design work?

MOSAIC and Your Clip Art Collection

Figure 10.6
Clip art is grouped when you import the piece using CorelMOSAIC.

Recoloring Clip Art

Because the CMX Presentation Exchange format is virtually the same as Corel's *.CDR file format, every tool you know how to use in Corel can be used to edit clip art.

A good place to begin editing clip art for your assignment is to take the color out of it. A lot of the clip art collection is filled with glorious color that simply won't reproduce very well when sent to a laser printer.

In the next series of steps, you'll find some tricks to manipulating the ungrouped clip art objects. You'll make your memo about the brunch stunning, and printable to a black and white laser printer:

1. With the group selected, click on the Ungroup button on the Ribbon Bar (or choose **A**rrange, **U**ngroup; Ctrl+U).

Chapter 10: Clip Art Can Save Your Life!

2. Many clip art pieces have "nested" groups of objects, so you may have to deselect your selection (click on an empty Drawing Window area), then select a nested group, and click on the Ungroup button once more, as shown in figure 10.7. The status line will tell you when you have a single object selected.

3. Facial and hand areas of clip art can be recolored white or 10-percent black so they have some tone, but still print clean. For various ethnic groups you may want to vary the percentage, but the procedure's the same: with the selected area active, click on a grayscale swatch on the color palette, as shown in figure 10.8.

Figure 10.7
Nested clip art pieces can have object groups within object groups within object groups....

4. Check the status line to see whether the filled shape has any outline attributes. If so, they too may be in color. Right-mouse click over the same percentage of black you assign to the fill to create the same color outline. The width of the outline will be unchanged.

5. Press Ctrl+S (File, Save), or click on the Save button on the Ribbon Bar now that you're through with the changes.

Recoloring Clip Art

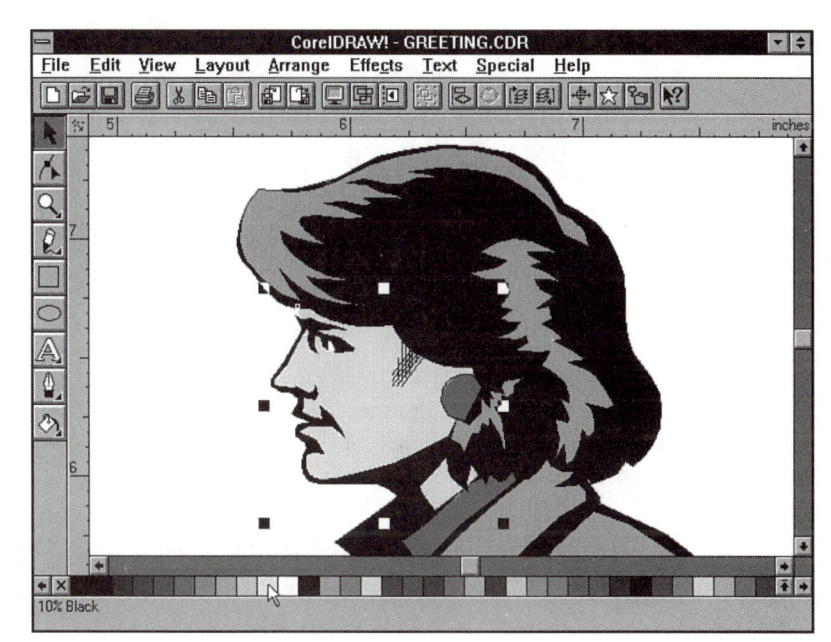

Figure 10.8
Changing a color fill to a percentage of black will make the clip art print cleaner to a laser printer.

Tip

If you'd like a percentage of black that's between two different swatches on the color palette, use the Uniform Fill tool (the color wheel icon on the Fill tool menu fly-out) to create a custom shade. By default, Corel's color model for uniform fills is CMYK, so all you do is enter a percentage in the (blac)K field (such as 5, 13, or whatever) and click on OK. The Cyan, Magenta, and Yellow values are unimportant, because these components of the CMYK color model won't print accurately to a black-and-white laser printer.

Additionally, you may click on the Show drop-down list and choose Grayscale as the color model. Then click and drag in the preview window to select a density of black, from 0 to 255.

Re-Using Clip Art

The wonderful thing about clip art is that it's so generic, the scene in the art can represent a number of occasions. As you've seen so far, the

GREETING.CDR clip art image is useful to convey a welcome to a brunch. But let's say the Megalopolis Foundation is engaged in a "friendly" takeover of Consolidated Widgets, and they need another memo to post near the elevators to greet the arriving sheep.

No problem. Let's see what's still serviceable from the memo you just created. The Artistic Text displays the wrong information, but the choice of font and size is still good. And the friendly gesture of the graphic works fine with an added enhancement or two.

Here are the steps to take to turn a brunch poster into a takeover poster in only a few moments:

1. Choose Save As from the File menu and name your new piece TAKEOVER.CDR. You've created a duplicate of the GREETING.CDR file, and even though it's not a "new" file yet, GREETING.CDR is now safe from future editing.

2. Click on the Text tool, then click on the Megalopolis text. Place your cursor before the word New and click+diagonal drag to 4 o'clock. This highlights the Artistic Text you want to change, as shown in figure 10.9.

Figure 10.9

Click once on Artistic Text to select it, then highlight it using the Text tool.

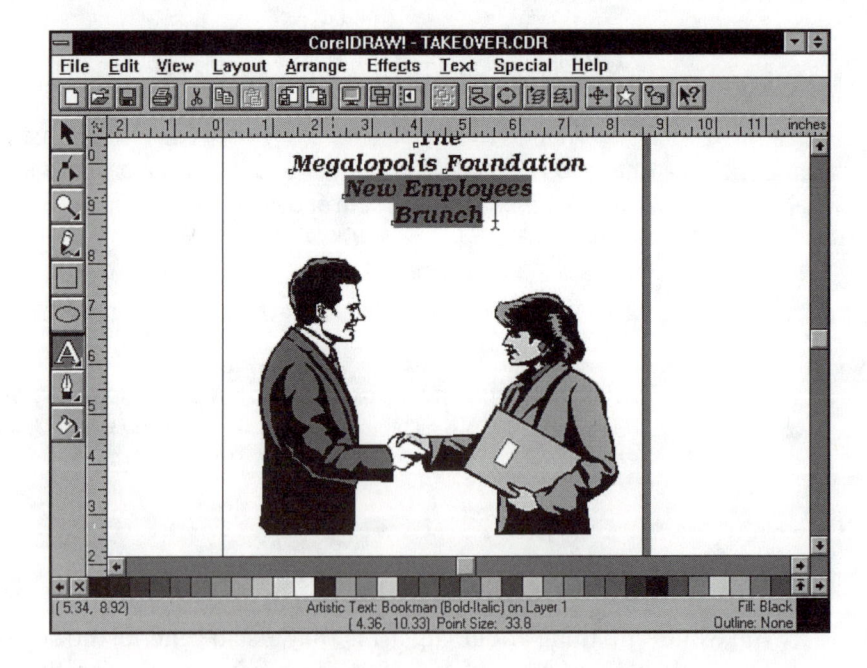

3. Type **Welcomes**. By default, CorelDRAW lets you type over highlighted text.

4. Click on the time/date text to select it, then highlight the whole text string.

5. Type **Consolidated Widgets**<Enter>**As**<Enter>**Our New Business** <Enter>**Partner**, thus replacing the entire sentiment you originally had.

The text part of the memo is finished. It's time to turn to editing the clip art now.

Creating Props To Enhance Clip Art

In a lot of business graphics, you'll see people holding briefcases and portfolios, and there's bound to be a desk or two in the scene. When you add something as simple as a piece of text to a surface that's already drawn in a clip art image, you personalize it, and it fits into your graphical presentation better. In the next example, you'll see how to modify the portfolio the woman in the TAKEOVER.CDR document is holding, to clarify the graphic's meaning for a specific occasion. It's simple, but it adds to the design, and it's another way to make generic clip art more specific.

Let's add the title CONSOLIDATED WIDGETS to the woman's portfolio. If you have an image other than the one shown in this example, read on and you'll still get a feel for the trick demonstrated here.

Here's how to turn a clip art business exec into a Consolidated Widgets exec:

1. Click on the Zoom tool, choose the Zoom in tool from the menu fly-out, and marquee-zoom to the area where the portfolio is. This is close-up, precision editing here, and you should always have a comfortable view of image areas.

2. Type **CONSOLIDATED**<Enter>**WIDGETS**, as shown in figure 10.10.

3. Press Ctrl+spacebar to toggle to the Pick tool, then press Ctrl+T to display the Character Attributes dialog box.

4. The text is going to be small on the woman's portfolio, so a bold, condensed font would be good. Suppose you don't have any condensed fonts in the available Fonts list. Click on Center Alignment, choose Bodoni Poster or some other bold font (see fig. 10.11), and click on OK. You'll learn how to condense a font next.

Chapter 10: Clip Art Can Save Your Life!

Figure 10.10
Enter the Artistic Text you'll add to the portfolio directly on the Printable page.

Figure 10.11
Bodoni is an example of a good, bold font. Choose it, and see how to make it bold and condensed.

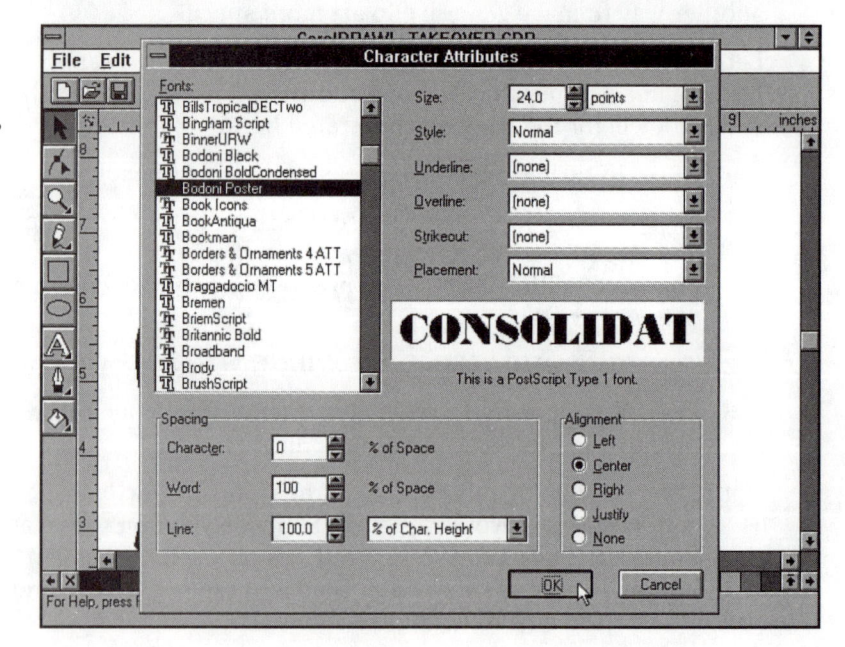

Creating Props To Enhance Clip Art

5. Click and drag on the right, middle selection handle of the Artistic Text selection. As you can see in figure 10.12, Bodoni, when scaled on the Y axis (vertically) by about 70 percent of its 100-percent total width, produces a readable, condensed string of text. Some typefaces (mostly the plainer ones like Futura and Helvetica) squash nicely. More ornamental fonts, like Davida, become unreadable.

Figure 10.12
Check the status line to see how far you're vertically scaling the selection. Don't go too far.

Rotating and Resizing the Text

When you click and drag or rotate a selection in Corel, you're given a blue-dotted outline preview of the proposed edit before you let go of the mouse button. We need to rotate the Artistic Text so it's at the same angle as the portfolio the woman is holding.

Here's how to match the angle of an object in a clip art sample:

1. Click on the selected Artistic Text to display the rotate/skew selection handles.

2. Click on the lower-right corner rotation handle, and move counter-clockwise until the preview outline matches the angle, as shown in figure 10.13.

Figure 10.13

Don't release the mouse button until the preview outline is parallel to the portfolio.

3. When the text is rotated to a proper degree, release the mouse button, then click again on the selection to restore it to a normal selection mode (little squares along the border instead of arrows).

4. The little tag on the woman's portfolio can be deleted to allow more room for the rotated text, so click on it and press the Delete key.

5. Click on the Zoom tool and use the Zoom in tool to marquee-zoom in even farther to only the portfolio and the text.

6. Click+drag the text selection so the lower right corner of the text is next to the right edge of the portfolio.

7. Click+drag the upper left corner selection handle of the text in a 4 o'clock direction to scale it so it fits within the portfolio border, as shown in figure 10.14.

8. You may want to reposition the text once more after it's been scaled to center it on the portfolio.

9. Click on the Zoom tool, and choose the Show Page (the far right) tool on the menu fly-out to admire your work. Figure 10.15 shows the finished memo, and if Consolidated Widgets doesn't see the GREETING.CDR document, you'll be congratulated on another fine, original design.

Figure 10.14
Scale the Artistic Text using the Pick tool.

Figure 10.15
Variations on a design can be used for multiple purposes if no one catches you.

Cosmetic Alteration of Corel Clip Art

The last, most involved editing of clip art is covered in the next section, with a tiny warning first. You'll see how to slightly alter the segments in a path that make up the man's face in the clip art graphic. "Slightly" is best defined as "moving a node connecting two segments by a fraction of an inch."

Less is more in the lesson to follow, where you discover that you can change the appearance of a clip art portrait by moving nodes ever so slightly. If done with some aesthetic sensitivity, you can wind up with a wonderful collection of very different-looking people, thus multiplying your clip art collection for future use. If done ham-handedly, you'll wind up with useless caricatures that the viewer will likely find insulting.

Here's how to play Mission: Impossible with a CorelDRAW clip art character:

1. Choose the Zoom tool, then select the Zoom In tool, and marquee-zoom into the head of the clip art character.

2. Click on the head with the Pick tool to make sure it's completely ungrouped. If it isn't, click on the Ungroup button on the Ribbon Bar.

3. A clip art character's hair is generally a good object to edit without marring the character's facial features. With the Shape tool, click on the hair to display the nodes that make up the closed path.

4. Marquee-select a group of nodes in one area of the hair, and drag a little. In figure 10.16, you can see that a distance less than a quarter inch can give this fellow an entirely different 'do.

Cosmetic Alteration of Corel Clip Art

Figure 10.16
Click and drag on several nodes to change a clip art character's hair style.

Changing a Character's Facial Appearance

Using the same click-and-drag technique as you last performed on the clip art character's hair, you can also change his expression. This is your big chance to do something really unflattering, and you should use even more discretion than in the last steps to successfully change a person's facial appearance.

Here are some helpful tips to keep in mind when preparing to mess with areas of a clip art character's face:

1. If the character is in profile like the one in this example, you can bring the nodes that define the bridge of the nose closer to the eyebrow by clicking and dragging on the nodes with the Shape tool.

2. Pointed noses, like the one on the character pictured here, can be made softer by selecting a group of nodes and repositioning them closer to the cheek area, as shown in figure 10.17.

Chapter 10: Clip Art Can Save Your Life!

Figure 10.17
A little reshaping of the path that defines the character's nose changes the overall face a lot.

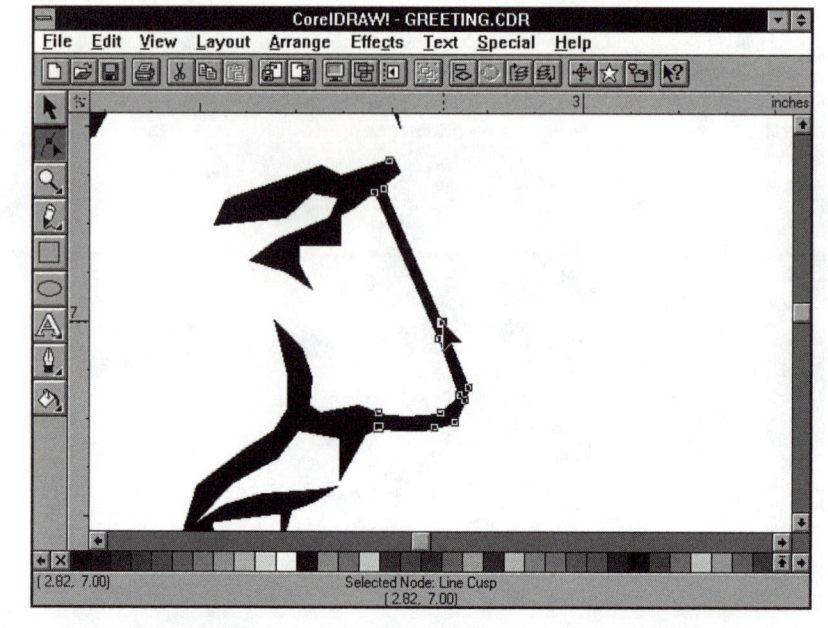

3. Objects can also be deleted to make a different facial expression. In figure 10.18, the lower lip shape has been deleted, and the chin was made less prominent by marquee-selecting the nodes and click+dragging them toward the man's profile.

Figure 10.18
Change a clip art character's mood by simply changing the expression a little.

Before you know it, you have a more serious-looking business person, perfect for use in an authoritative illustration on some other occasion.

Adding a Graphic Prop to Clip Art

You can use text to effectively customize clip art for different assignments, but when you want to further change a character's appearance, you can use the steps listed previously, *and* add a piece of personal effects or two.

Here's how to put glasses on the character in this example. You already know the drawing techniques if you read previous chapters. All that's missing is some ingenuity, and the following steps:

1. Click on the Rectangle tool, and click+diagonally drag a vertical slim, tall rectangle to represent a lens frame seen from a profile. This trick only works if you have a clip art character in profile, naturally.

2. Click+diagonal-drag to create the stem to the glasses using the Rectangle tool, as shown in figure 10.19.

Figure 10.19

Glasses can be made using simple rectangle shapes.

3. Press Ctrl+spacebar to toggle to the Pick tool.

4. Click+drag the stem shape so it slightly overlaps the lens shape. The two should overlap at the top of the lens rectangle.

5. Hold the Shift key to add the lens shape to your selection.

6. Choose **A**rrange, **W**eld, and left-mouse click on the black swatch on the colors palette to fill the welded glasses shape.

7. Right-mouse click on the x on the color palette to remove the default outline to the glasses.

8. Click+drag the glasses shape to put them on the character, then click a second time to display the rotate/skew selection handles on the glasses shape.

9. Click+drag on a corner rotation selection handle until the stem of the glasses shape appears to be tucked above the character's ear, like glasses are supposed to.

10. You may want to reposition the glasses after rotating. Click again on the glasses shape to return it to normal selection mode, then click+drag the shape with the Pick tool.

11. Choose **F**ile, Save **A**s, and name the document DISGUISE.CDR, so you haven't altered GREETING.CDR.

Good luck, Jim. This chapter will self-conclude in five paragraphs.

Comparing Your Editing Work to Clip Art Work

You were asked to save the image you last edited so that you could appreciate the big-time changes you made with only a click and drag on a node or two, and two rectangles to serve as eyeglasses for a character. If you've performed this chapter's exercises, you now understand that editing can be as important as drawing skills with a program as feature-packed as CorelDRAW.

There's nothing sadder than a design submitted to a boss that features a direct swipe from a clip art collection as the main attraction. Eventually, other designers find the same images as you and use them in their work, too; ultimately the world is an "art-poorer" place because of so many identical flyers, posters, and memos.

But you now have some very special techniques in your own bag of tricks, as well as the potential for discovering the tricks Corel artists use to draw professional clip art. You should spend some time taking apart clip art

Comparing Your Editing Work to Clip Art Work

images that you think are well-designed. You'll learn what special fills are used, whether a node making up a complex shape is symmetrical or cusp, and how toggling to the wireframe view of clip art enables you to see the whole anatomy of a finished design.

Here's how to create a little "Before and After" to compare the artist's original to your edited design. The difference will be greater than you think! Just follow these steps:

1. Click on the Import button on the Ribbon Bar.

2. From the List Files of Type drop-down list, choose CorelDRAW!,*.CDR, Select your working directory if the Import dialog box isn't already headed that way.

3. Click on GREETING.CDR, then click on OK.

4. Corel imports files in the CDR format in the same relative location on the Printable page as where you positioned them, so the character in the GREETING document will import directly on top of your edited character. With the Pick tool, click and drag the grouped shapes you imported to the right about three inches so you can see both characters.

5. Choose the Zoom tool, then the Zoom In tool, and marquee-zoom in to a tight area around both profiles, as shown in figure 10.20.

Figure 10.20

Funny, they looked identical until they turned about 14 or so...

Switching from the Pencil to a Brush

We've spent a lot of time in this book with the core program in the Corel bundle, CorelDRAW, but there's more to becoming a graphics guru than knowing the ins and outs of nodes and vectors. What about photographic retouching? Do you have a TIF image you'd like to experiment with, that has the same kind of latitude as drawings that can be modified in CorelDRAW?

If you have a scanner, or even a few scanned images you'd like to put some twists on, Chapter 11 introduces you to the world of bitmap images and CorelPHOTO-PAINT, a digital darkroom if there ever was one. Don't let any light leak in as you turn the page!

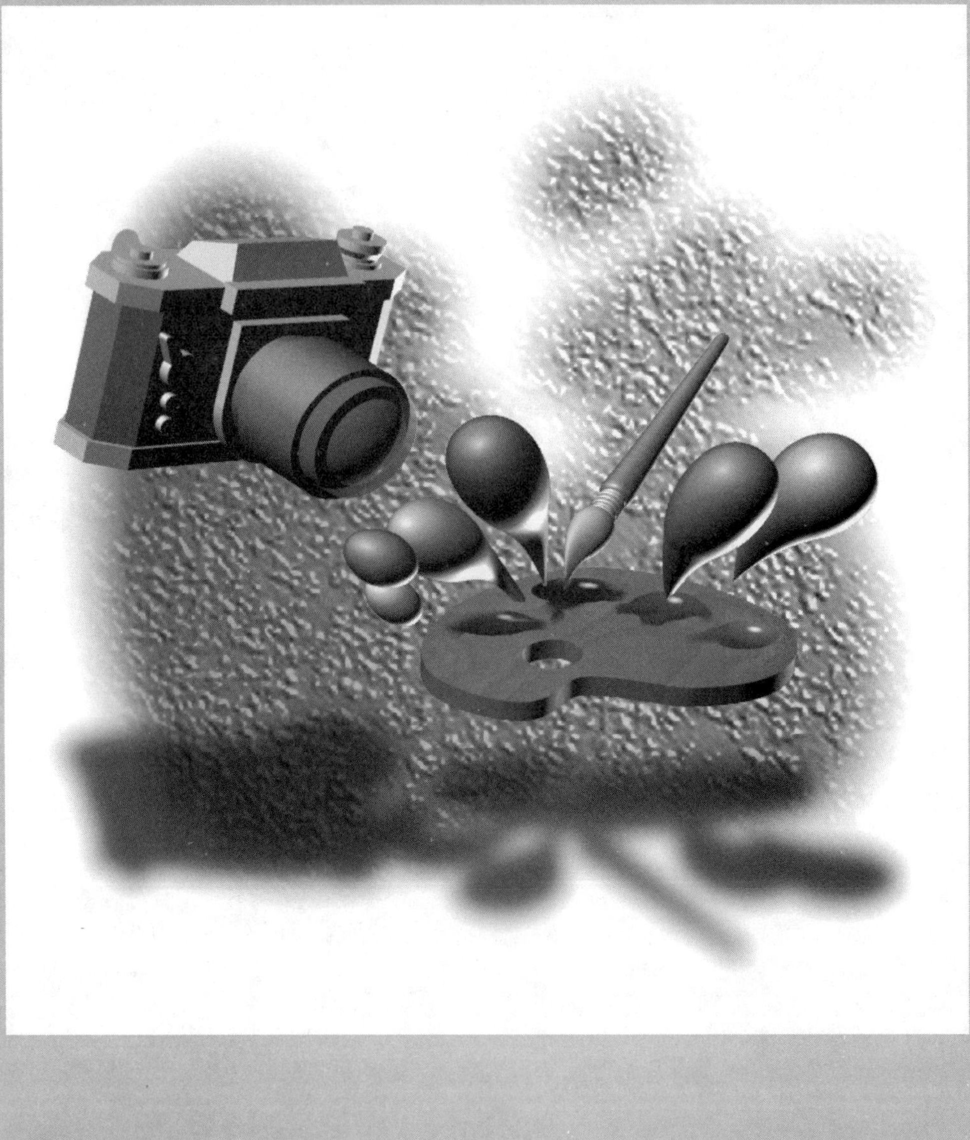

CHAPTER 11

CorelPHOTO-PAINT!

As I made a professional migration toward the IBM-PC computer as an art tool, using CorelDRAW provided an easy and natural transition from my traditional pencil work.

However, if the tools of your trade have been a camera or a paintbrush, Corel also has something in store for you that'll absolutely change the way you think about and approach your craft. CorelPHOTO-PAINT is a crazy cross between a digital darkroom, a special effects department, and an artist's loft. Simply put, PHOTO-PAINT enables you to do amazing things with bitmap graphics.

Bitmap art beautifully simulates the soft, flowing designs of photographic images and real-life textures.

And because bitmap images are all made up of little ones and zeros as far as your binary PC is concerned, you can play with them to create astonishing, dramatic, heartwarming, digital recreations. Want to see how?

In this chapter, you:

- Separate a foreground image from its background
- Create and import special effects typography
- Discover the power of object-oriented bitmap files
- Get the scoop on extraordinary imaging using ordinary pictures

Assembling Your Imaging Essentials

PHOTO-PAINT is a very rich working environment that deserves a book itself. While it is not possible to explore all of PHOTO-PAINT's amazing nooks and crannies in one chapter, this chapter zeros in on a common, yet challenging, assignment faced by graphics people: how to combine two different images into one scene.

Before you launch into PHOTO-PAINT for an adventure in *imaging*, there are some materials you'll need to bring along. You'll need a couple of high-quality bitmap images: one of a background scene, and one of a foreground image. The images used in the assignment in this chapter are of a toy plane and a sky, but feel free to use any foreground and background images that appeal to you, or are similar to the assignments you receive.

You'll use the images you've selected along with PHOTO-PAINT's special tools and features, to create a *composite* photograph. To do quality bitmap work and successfully complete assignments like this one with ease, keep the following recommendations in mind:

- The images you use should be 24-bit, RGB images. Indexed color images (like PCX, GIF, and BMP files) aren't truly suitable for imaging work, because they lack a sufficient number of colors in their image format to be truly photographic. TIF and TGA (Targa) images will work well. Your images could be grayscale, but to explore the full range of PHOTO-PAINT's color features your images should be 24-bit color images. Check out the Corel CD for sample images if you don't already have some on your hard disk.

- The foreground subject should, ideally, be against a solid color that contrasts with the subject of the photo, sort of like employee ID–, state Motor Vehicle Bureau–, and high school snapshots. It's easier to select the part of the image you want when the background is plain. The process you use when a background is a solid, contrasting color is similar to the way newscasters get superimposed (chroma-keyed) over backgrounds and weather charts.

   If your foreground subject is surrounded by other stuff, that's okay; this chapter will briefly cover how to get your image looking like it should with a demonstration of PHOTO-PAINT's Color Masking and tolerance settings.

- Your background image should be larger than your foreground subject.

- You should know the *resolution* of your two images, and the two should be the same. The resolution of an image is measured in pixels per inch. How many pixels fit in an inch determines the dimensions (height and width) of an image. When you bring an element that has a higher resolution (more pixels per inch) into an image with a lower resolution (fewer pixels per inch), the dimensions of the higher resolution element will be much larger than you expect.

    If you scanned the images yourself, your scanner would have informed you of the resolution as the images were acquired. If you have no idea what resolution is, you'll discover an easy way to measure it in PHOTO-PAINT.

That's it!

In keeping with the spirit of CorelSHOW and CorelMOVE (more about them in the next chapter), you're going to take the images and create a movie poster. Every movie needs an attention-getting title, so our first stop is CorelDRAW, where you'll create an eye-catching title for the poster.

Making a Splashy Movie Title

"The Adventures of Sky Writer" is the name of the fictitious movie title I'm going to show you how to create. Why the title? Basically because I have a scanned image of the sky and a toy airplane handy. If you intend to use an underwater picture and a portrait, you may want to substitute "The Adventures of Diver Doug" for the title I've chosen, or whatever's thematically appropriate given your images.

CorelDRAW offers no image editing tools, but it can import and export the bitmap images that you can edit in PHOTO-PAINT. CorelDRAW excels at creating, manipulating, and distorting text, so it's the perfect place to go to create eye-catching text for the movie poster. To begin your assignment, follow these steps:

1. Open CorelDRAW and choose File, Import.

2. Choose TIFF Bitmap or Targa Bitmap from the List Files of Type drop-down list, find the Drive and Directory where your foreground image is located, click on it, then click on OK.

3. When your image appears on CorelDRAW's Printable page, select the Artistic Text tool and click an insertion point with the cursor next to

the image. Type the name of your hero or heroine, as shown in figure 11.1. You don't need to start with "The Adventures of," however. You'll only be customizing part of the movie poster with text. The rest of the snappy title will be typeset using PHOTO-PAINT's Text tool.

Figure 11.1

The imported image is an object, and so is the text you type. The two will never blend together in CorelDRAW.

4. Press Ctrl+spacebar to get the Pick tool (the Artistic Text is automatically selected), and then press Ctrl+T to display the Character Attributes dialog box.

5. Choose a bold, striking typeface for your movie poster title. This is the one chance many designers get to use CorelDRAW's more exotic fonts, such as Quicksilver, Pump Triline, and my favorite (which is the one I've chosen for Sky Writer), Banco BT.

6. Click on OK to return to your text, which now displays in the exotic typeface you've chosen.

Enveloped Text as a Design Element

Earlier in this book, you learned how the Envelope effect could reshape Artistic and Paragraph Text, and change other objects to conform to a path

Enveloped Text as a Design Element

of your choosing. In the next steps, you should use your designer's eye and mold the Artistic Text so it becomes a compositional element in the movie poster. Here's one approach to doing this:

1. In figure 11.2, the Freehand (Pencil) tool has been chosen, and a closed path is being created to use as the shape the text will take when the Envelope effect is applied. Make your path a rough outline of the shape and dimensions for the text. Don't worry; you'll refine the path later.

Figure 11.2

Create your own path for enveloping text, or use the presets available on the Envelope Roll-Up.

2. Once you have a closed path drawn, choose the Shape tool. Marquee-select one or all of the nodes that define your path, then double-click on a node or line segment to display the Node Edit Roll-Up.

3. Click on the To Curve button on the Node Edit Roll-Up. Click on the resulting curve segments to bend them, shape them, and create an interesting design element that will complement your foreground image, both in composition and in its relative position to the foreground image. This is the shape that will be applied to the Artistic Text.

Chapter 11: CorelPHOTO-PAINT!

Note

Bringing the foreground image that you will use in PHOTO-PAINT into CorelDRAW gives you the opportunity to see exactly how much room you have for text and how any effects you apply to the text will look "in place." Once you've enveloped the Artistic Text and are satisfied with how it looks, it can be exported in a bitmap file format that PHOTO-PAINT can use.

4. Press Ctrl+F7 to Display the Envelope Roll-Up.

5. Select the Artistic Text with either the Shape or the Pick tool, then click on the Create From button on the Envelope Roll-Up.

6. Your cursor turns into a huge arrow at this point; you should click your cursor on the path you've designed.

7. Click on the Apply button. As you can see in figure 11.3, I'm shooting for the classic "Flash Gordon" type of text design in the movie poster. You can and should delete the path from the Drawing Window as soon as it's been used as the basis for the Envelope effect. You wouldn't want to export it by mistake along with the text.

Figure 11.3
The Envelope effect can be edited around the text object even after your original path has been deleted.

In figure 11.3, you can see the Shape tool tugging on a node of the Envelope boundary around the Artistic Text. You always have the option to modify an Enveloped shape after an Envelope effect has been applied. The Envelope boundary becomes visible and editable whenever you have the object selected and the Shape tool is active.

To remove single or multiple changes that you've performed using the Envelope Roll-Up, choose Effe<u>c</u>ts, <u>C</u>lear Transformations. This command returns the selected text (or other object) to the way it was before you changed the object.

Tip

Clear Transformations will do nothing if you've applied the Co<u>n</u>vert to Curves (Ctrl+Q) command to an object that has been Enveloped. Convert to Curves frees objects from Envelopes, Extrudes, and other effects, but it also destroys the dynamic link to the shape's original condition, in a way that is similar to converting Artistic Text to curves.

Exporting Vector Art to Bitmap Format

Now that you've added some pizzazz to the text and it's scaled in proportion to the image it'll be used with, there's one last step you need to perform before a copy of the type is transformed into a bitmap that PHOTO-PAINT can use.

Unlike vector graphics, bitmap images need a background; they can't simply sit in space as mathematical descriptions of arcs and stuff. Bitmap art is based around square pixels of color fitted into an imaginary grid; without providing a background for coordinates that this text can sit on in the grid, CorelDRAW will export the text with an uncomfortably tight border around it. The following steps show you how to export a CorelDRAW graphic to bitmap format, and force it to leave you some breathing space around it.

1. Choose the Rectangle tool, and marquee-drag an area around the text so that there's some "white space" around the text.

2. As the most recently rendered shape, it's also on the top of the text. Press the spacebar to get the Pick tool, click on your Enveloped title, and press the To Front button on the Ribbon Bar (or press Shift+PgUp).

Chapter 11: CorelPHOTO-PAINT!

3. Click on the rectangle you drew, then click on the white swatch on the color palette, as shown in figure 11.4. Your view of the foreground bitmap you imported may be partially obscured, but that's okay. This foreground bitmap will be left behind when you leave DRAW and go to PHOTO-PAINT.

Figure 11.4

Give your vector text some elbow-room before you export it as a bitmap!

4. Right-mouse click over the "X" on the color palette to remove outline attributes from the rectangle. You want a white background for the exported text, not a white background with a black outline.

5. You're done with the bitmap copy of your foreground image. Click on it, then press the Delete key.

6. Select both the rectangle and the Enveloped title (if you deleted the bitmap, simply choose Edit, Select All).

7. Choose File, Export from the menu.

8. Choose TIFF Bitmap,*.TIF from the List Files of Type drop-down box. Give the file a name with a .TIF extension. Find a good location for this export on your hard drive using the Drives and Directories fields. Put a check mark in the Selected Only box in the lower, right-hand corner of the Export dialog box.

9. Click on OK, and the Bitmap Export dialog box will appear.

10. You're going to color in this fancy title after you hit PHOTO-PAINT, so your first option is to select 16 Million colors in the Colors drop-down box.

Note

16 Million colors is CorelDRAW's terminology for a category of bitmap graphics that is also called TrueColor, 24-bit color, and RGB color by other design applications.

16 Million colors can be saved to the Tagged Image File format (TIF), but this doesn't mean that bitmap images always contain 16 million unique colors. Actually, the term 16 million colors refers to the capacity the TIF image format can *potentially* hold. This format gives the serious designer plenty of color "space" to experiment in, and typically, a full-color scanned image will only contain tens to hundreds of thousands of unique colors.

11. You want the fancy title you've created to export at a 1:1 size, so it maintains the same relative size relationship to the copy of the foreground graphic you imported. Choose 1:1 in the Size drop-down field and leave the number of pixels alone here, or Corel will substitute *Custom* in *1:1*'s place!

12. Here's the magic moment. Earlier I suggested that you make a note of the resolution of the two bitmap images you'll be using. In the **R**esolution field drop-down list, choose the resolution of your image. Corel will automatically enter identical values in the Width and Heights spin boxes below the Resolution drop-down list. As you can see in figure 11.5, I've entered 150 dpi.

Chapter 11: CorelPHOTO-PAINT!

Figure 11.5
You determine the size and resolution of your bitmap export when you make selections in this options box.

Closer Look

Many scanner manufacturers, as well as Corel Corporation, use dots per inch (dpi) as the terminology that describes the resolution of an image. Technically, bitmaps are measured in samples or pixels per inch, although the term "dots" has become popularly accepted slang.

Do not, however, make a mental association between "dots" (pixels) on your monitor and an image file on your hard drive with dots that are rendered on a sheet of paper passed through your laser printer. A laser dot is of a fixed size, while pixel samples are of indeterminate size, depending on how many samples you've taken of something per inch when you digitize a source image.

Typically, screen dots (and the dots you're telling CorelDRAW to export) are much smaller than laser printer toner dots. A 150 "dot" per inch image file can actually be rendered on paper by an ultra high-end laser printer at *1,200* toner dots per inch.

13. Click on OK, and your fancy title with the white boundary box is rasterized to a TIF image format.

14. You can exit CorelDRAW without saving your title. It's been saved to your hard disk in a format PHOTO-PAINT can use, and you have no further use for it in DRAW's CDR format.

Selecting Colors PHOTO-PAINT-Style

The CorelPHOTO-PAINT workspace shares a common look with the other Corel modules, but as you venture forth into image editing, you'll find a strange array of tools and features—this isn't vector-land; it's the world of bitmaps.

First, you'll open the image of your foreground subject. The task at hand will be to make the background of the subject all one color so you can separate the foreground subject from its background. The tool of choice for this task will be PHOTO-PAINT's Magic Wand Mask tool, which is designed to make selections based on color value.

There are several ways to select part of a bitmap image area, but with a little pre-planning when you photograph, you'll see how easily you can select an image area that doesn't share common colors with the rest of the image.

As you've seen with my toy model, I used a rod to suspend it in front of an evenly lit magenta background. Before you separate the foregound subject from its background, you should remove any extraneous areas. I don't want the rod that supports the toy plane in the finished image, for instance. A good first step for retouching the rod (or anything in your own photos), is to sample the predominant background color with PHOTO-PAINT's Eyedropper tool, then paint over offending areas with a paint tool.

Follow these steps to apply a primer coat to your work:

1. Open PHOTO-PAINT from Program Manager by double-clicking on its icon.

2. Unlike CorelDRAW, PHOTO-PAINT by default requires that you load an image, either a New one or an already existing one, before you can work. Choose File, then Open, then scroll to the directory where you're keeping your images.

3. Click on the foreground image file, then click on OK; PHOTO-PAINT will load your image into the workspace.

Chapter 11: CorelPHOTO-PAINT!

4. Because you are using a different image than the one used in this chapter, you will have a little different preliminary retouching to do. In figure 11.6, I've used the Zoom tool to zoom in on the rod suspending the toy plane. The rod can be retouched out of the picture by first choosing the Eyedropper tool, selecting the right background shade with the Eyedropper tool, and then clicking on a predominant color element in your own image's background.

Figure 11.6

The Eyedropper tool "picks up" a color to be used as the new foreground color applied by a painting or drawing tool.

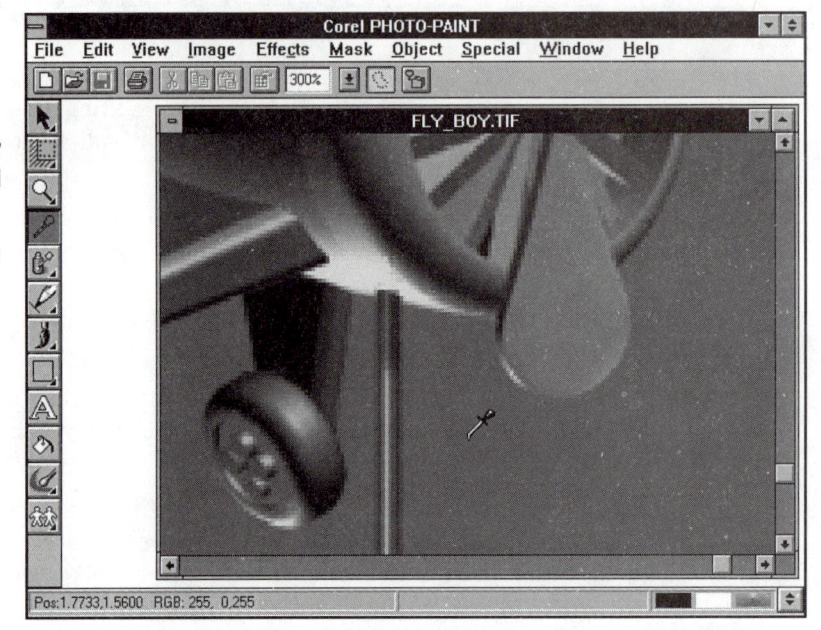

Closer Look

The Zoom tool behaves differently in PHOTO-PAINT than it does in CorelDRAW. Left-mouse clicking moves you into an image, while right-mouse clicking moves you out. You can also marquee-zoom, with the Zoom tool, to zoom in several fields of viewing resolution at once.

Setting Up a Paintbrush Tip

The Paint Brush tool in PHOTO-PAINT can be set to many different modes of applying color by clicking and holding on the icon on the Toolbox and choosing a painting mode. The Paint Brush tool fly-out menu sports different automated techniques for simulating fine artist brush strokes.

The need here, though, is for an ordinary paintbrush to cover superfluous image areas, like the rod in the toy plane image. Even in its default setting, there are still plenty of custom options available. Use the following steps to choose exactly the right Paint Brush tool for an assignment.

1. Choose **V**iew, and pick Tool **S**ettings Roll-Up (or simply press F8).

   The Tool Settings Roll-Up, like most of the PHOTO-PAINT Roll-Ups, will change its display options when you pick a different tool. Additionally, Tool Settings automatically rolls up when you don't have a painting tool active.

2. Magenta is the color the paintbrush will use. The size of the tip used to apply the color is set in the **S**ize field on the Roll-Up, either by clicking on the elevator buttons or by entering a number value directly in the box.

3. In figure 11.7, you can see that a 10-pixel diameter paintbrush tip is a good size for painting over the rod. The size of a paintbrush tip is immediately apparent as soon as you move your cursor over an active image window. If you selected a size too large, press Ctrl+Z to Undo your stroke (if you made one), then go back to the Roll-Up and reduce the size of the tip.

4. Click and drag your newly defined brush cursor (it looks like a circle the size of your brush tip) over any of the background areas that need to be removed from your image.

Chapter 11: CorelPHOTO-PAINT!

Figure 11.7

Brush sizes and custom preset configurations are chosen from the Tool Settings Roll-Up while a Paint Brush tool is active.

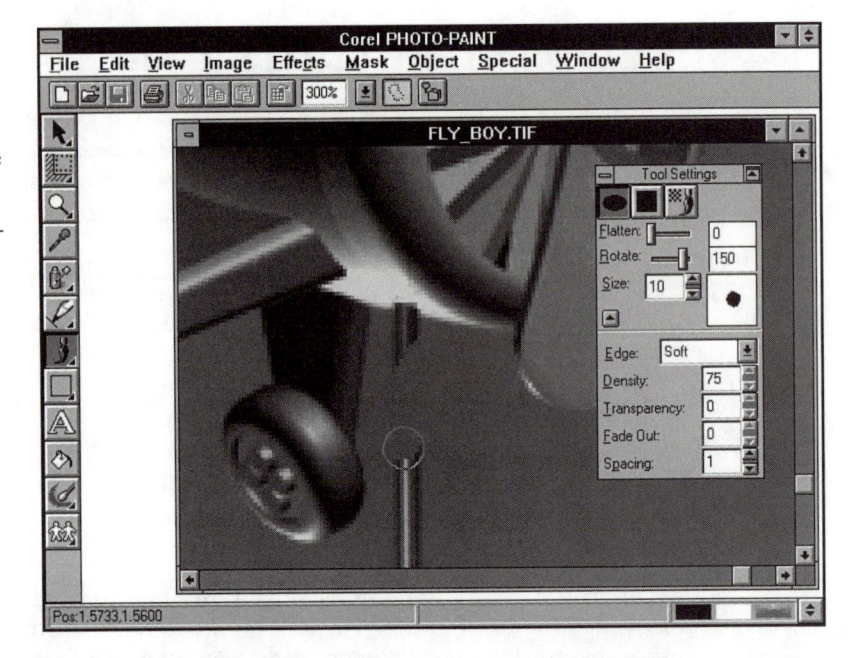

The rod in this example intrudes on both the background color and part of the toy plane. To fix the plane, you need to use the Eyedropper tool again to sample a color that matches the part of the plane that the rod obscures. In your image, you'll need to sample a color that is adjacent to any item that encroaches on your subject.

5. Select the Eyedropper tool and zoom into the offending area. Reduce the size of the paintbrush tip to match the area that needs to be worked on. Figure 11.8 shows that the rod is only composed of a handful of pixels, and that a paintbrush diameter of three pixels covers the rod in one or two strokes.

6. Remember to select **F**ile, **S**ave to save your work frequently! Bitmap images can get corrupted a lot more easily than other computer data in the event of an unexpected system failure; they can't be restored after a crash, even with today's data recovery utilities!

Setting Up a Paintbrush Tip

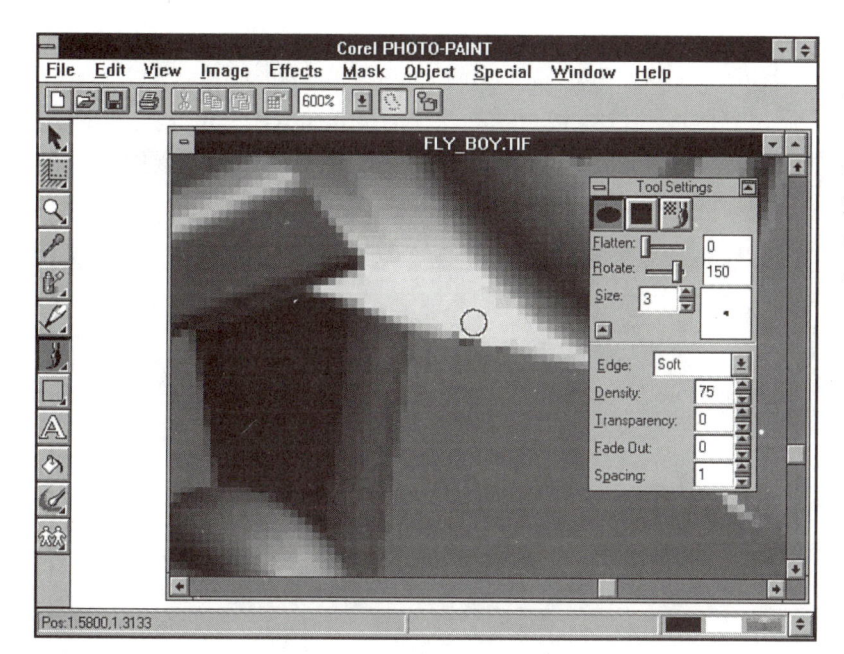

Figure 11.8
Click the Eyedropper tool close to an area you wish to retouch to get a good sample color.

Selecting an Area Based on Color

Although it's unlikely you have a model plane exactly like the one shown in this assignment, and less likely still that the background of a foreground subject you've chosen has a perfect magenta color, you're nonetheless garnering some serious experience working with bitmap editing tools here. For instance, you've just learned how to "spot touch" a photograph. The next time you get a scanned image with lint marks on it, select neighboring areas of color in the image and apply the same color over the fuzz and pinholes with the Paint Brush tool.

You've seen that bitmap images have no outline/fill properties like vector art images do, and that special tools are required to manipulate bitmap images. Special tools are also needed when you want to select a part of an image. PHOTO-PAINT calls the selecting of bitmap image areas *masking*. Any area you define with a masking tool can be set to either be *protected from change*, or *subject to change*.

The Magic Wand Mask tool, which you'll learn how to use next, selects areas based on common color values. The variance of a particular color, the

Chapter 11: CorelPHOTO-PAINT!

tolerance, is something you can define. Follow these steps to use this tool to select a single shade of color that happens to be the background area:

1. Click and hold down on the Rectangle Mask tool (the second tool down on the Toolbox). Then choose the Magic Wand Mask tool, shown in figure 11.9.

Figure 11.9

Look at the status line at the bottom of PHOTO-PAINT to see the functions of tools you have your cursor over.

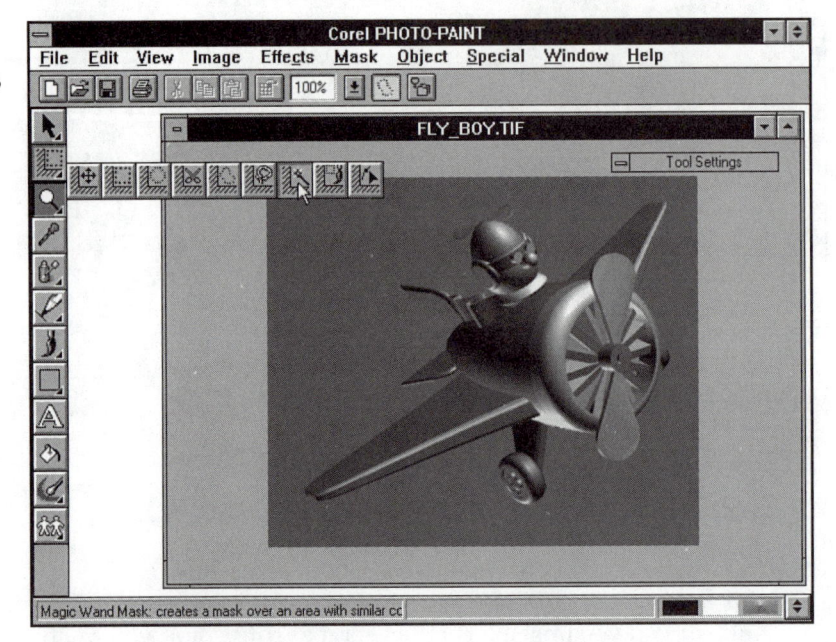

2. Double-click on the Magic Wand Mask tool to display the Color Comparison Tolerance dialog box.

To select the magenta areas with the Magic Wand Mask tool, the **M**agenta color comparison tolerance can be set to any value plus or minus 255. This means that even a color shade vaguely similar to magenta will be selected when the Magic Wand Mask tool is clicked over the image area.

If the background in your image is primarily green, or another primary color listed here, you should make your tolerance entries in the corresponding box. The higher the values entered, the broader the range of light and dark shades selected. This is usually a trial-and-error procedure to get the best settings; the Magic Wand Mask tool can select image areas more accurately than the other Mask tools. Start by setting the tolerance quite high, and work your way down if too much is selected, or up if too little is selected.

Selecting an Area Based on Color

3. Enter your color tolerance settings in the appropriate color boxes for your image. Then click on OK to return to your image. With the Magic Wand Mask tool, click on the background. If you have most of your background selected, move on to the next step. If you want to try a different color tolerance setting, choose Mask, Remove and try again.

4. Nothing in the real world is as perfect as a pure magenta background image, I realize. PHOTO-PAINT acknowledges this, too; if you look at figure 11.10, the Add to Selection button is highlighted on the Ribbon Bar. When this mode is selected, your masking tool will add to your initial selection area when you click on other image areas. Click on the background of your image, press the Add to Selection button, and continue clicking with the Magic Wand in other background areas.

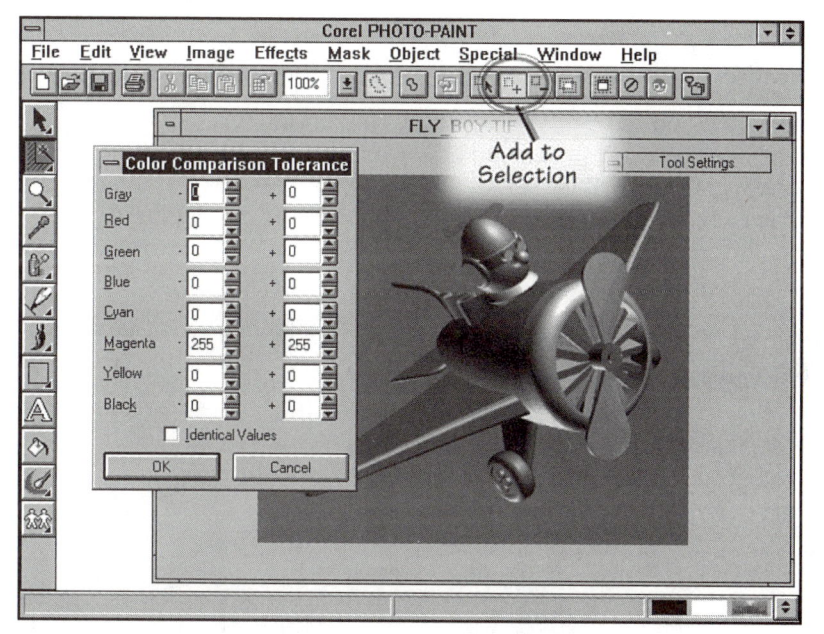

Figure 11.10

Use the Add to Selection mode; continue using the Magic Wand over image areas if you don't completely select the area at first.

Chapter 11: CorelPHOTO-PAINT!

Closer Look

In addition to the Magic Wand Mask tool, the Lasso Mask tool will pick up image areas of similar color; you operate it by clicking and dragging a closed shape around the intended area.

Though this part of the assignment is intended to give you experience with selecting specific colors in an image, there are often times when there are a variety of colors in an area you want to select with a precise outline. You will use the Mask Brush tool in this chapter for a special purpose, but ordinarily you can use this tool to select an area by "painting" over it. Use the Tool Settings Roll-Up to adjust its diameter, and simply brush over an area you wish to select.

Use a combination of Masking tools to arrive at a perfect selection around an image area.

5. Ironically, once you have the background to your subject perfectly defined, this is the exact area you *don't* want selected to copy into another image! Choose **M**ask, **I**nvert, as shown in figure 11.11, to select everything except the background, then choose **E**dit, **C**opy (Ctrl+C) to copy only your subject to the Windows Clipboard.

Figure 11.11

The Invert command makes the areas you *didn't* select with the Masking tools the currently selected area.

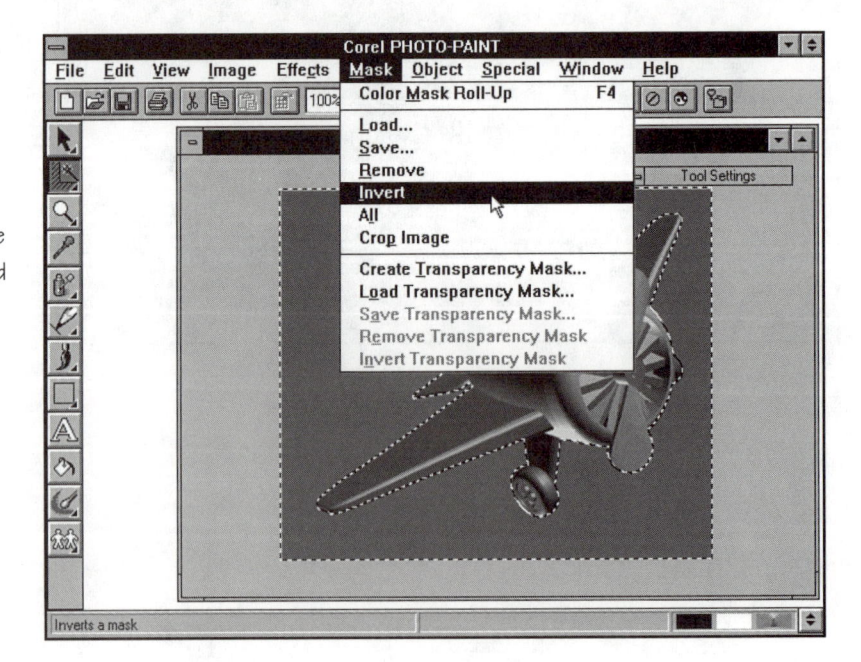

Considerations for a New Background Image

There are many qualities about an image that make it suitable or unsuitable as a host for different pieces from other images. Besides being large enough and having a matching resolution, the lighting in the host image should be similar to that of the objects it will hold.

In the following example, the SKY.TIF image qualifies in many respects for the FLY_BOY.TIF selection that's now on the Clipboard. Thematically, you can't go wrong by putting an airplane into the sky. In terms of the composition of the final image, clouds have no apparent scale, so pasting the toy airplane into them won't dwarf the subject.

In fact, images of nature scenes with no prime focal area are ideal background images for a number of uses. Type can read very powerfully in presentations where photo images are used as background elements. Textures of sand, leaves, fabric, and other surfaces make a more dynamic backdrop for picture portraits than most people realize. Pay attention to the lighting in images; try to select images that have similar lighting or that can be *made* similar using PHOTO-PAINT's imaging features, if your plan is to compose a realistic scene from them.

The fly boy presently on the Clipboard was strongly lit from the upper right. Take a look at how the sky image is lit, and follow these steps to improve this movie poster:

1. Close the image of the subject you've copied to the Clipboard, and open the background image you've selected.

2. In figure 11.12, the SKY.TIF image chosen is strongly lit from the left. This lighting makes the image of Sky Writer appear to be incorrectly lit, which in turn makes the composite image look phony. If your image requires a change of lighting like this one does, choose **I**mage, **F**lip, as shown in figure 11.12 and choose either **H**orizontally or **V**ertically (which one you choose depends on which way will make your image appear correctly lit). (Hint: you can get away with this stuff when a background image, such as clouds or sand, has no reference point or horizon.)

Chapter 11: CorelPHOTO-PAINT!

Figure 11.12
When an entire image is modified, PHOTO-PAINT makes a copy rather than tampering with your original.

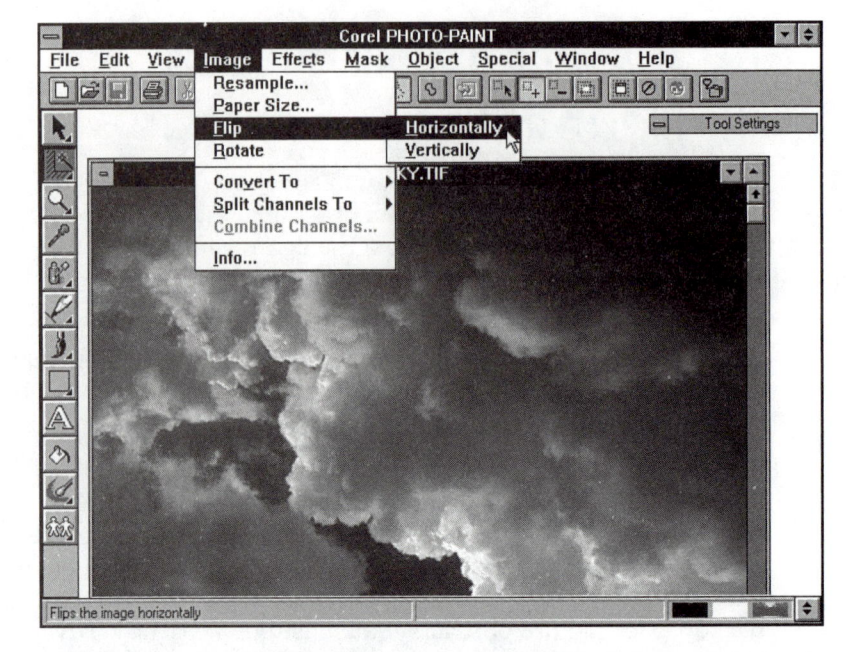

3. Choose **E**dit, **P**aste (or Ctrl+V) to paste your Clipboard image on top of the background image. Don't worry about the paste becoming fused to the background. PHOTO-PAINT treats pasted areas as independent objects. And don't save your work just yet—read on to discover the special way PHOTO-PAINT treats bitmaps that are pasted into an image.

A Brief Orientation on Objects

If you've ever played with Windows' Paintbrush, you probably came to an early understanding that bitmap selections mesh into their background after you deselect them, never to be released.

But PHOTO-PAINT is a generation ahead of most bitmap paint programs, both in color-handling capability (Paintbrush can only display 16 colors) and its capacity to handle objects in a way that is very similar to its parent program, CorelDRAW.

Selections pasted onto other bitmap images will not merge together until you choose the Merge command in PHOTO-PAINT. The program treats pasted items as discrete objects that you can reposition on top of a background to your heart's content. You can also save a work-in-progress to PHOTO-PAINT's proprietary CPT file format, and resume image editing days or years later, with the same discrete image areas in a repositionable state!

Let's test this property. To start adding elements to this movie poster, follow these steps:

1. First, you don't need the marquee outline running around your pasted object. It obscures your view of the bitmap elements and makes accurate positioning a chore. Press the Marquee Visible button (the button with an irregular, dotted shape on it) on the Ribbon Bar to deselect the dotted lines running around your selection. This doesn't deselect the object, it merely removes marquee lines that act as a visual clue that you have selected an independent object.

2. Press F7 to display the Layers/Objects Roll-Up or choose Object, Layers/Objects Roll-Up from the menu.

3. Notice that the Roll-Up has indexed the elements you have so far in the background image file. As you can see in figure 11.13, Sky Writer is one object, and the background sky image is another. I've set the Feather option to 2 pixels around Sky Writer, and this helps disguise any harsh, jagged outlines around the pasted-in object. Depending on the size and resolution of your image, a value from 1 to 3 pixels is usually good. Type in an entry (from 1 to 3) in the Feather text box, or move the slider to set a value. As soon as you enter a value, the effect is applied to the object and you can see the change on-screen.

Tip

The Feather option looks like it's a permanent change made to bitmap objects, but it can be reset as many times as you like before you merge image areas together.

However, if you paint or select image areas, the Layers/Objects Roll-Up can't help you out if you messed up. For mistakes, you need to press Ctrl+Z to Undo your last edit, use the Local Undo tool on the Toolbox, or the Edit, Restore to Checkpoint command. The Checkpoint command is useful to choose regularly—if you make a huge error and don't realize it for many steps, Restore to Checkpoint will remove previous editing goofs without restoring all the way back to the original, unedited image.

Chapter 11: CorelPHOTO-PAINT!

Figure 11.13
You can also reorder layers of bitmap objects, and turn them on and off using the Layers/Objects Roll-Up.

The "Paint" Part of PHOTO-PAINT

As an independent object, the pasted image of Sky Writer can be moved around, but it can also be "turned off." When an independent object is turned off, it is as if it didn't exist at all. This gives you a wonderful opportunity to add some skywriting to the SKY.TIF background image, without messing up Sky Writer's fuselage! To add the skywriting without disturbing the airplane, follow these steps:

1. Press F2 to display the Colors Roll-Up or choose View, Color Roll-Up. You need to select a color other than one that can be chosen using the Eyedropper tool on the background image.

2. Click on the white mini-swatch on the Roll-Up. At the bottom right corner of your workspace, you'll notice that the first of the three colors displayed will be white, as shown in figure 11.14.

3. Choose the Mask Brush tool from the Mask tool fly-out menu. This tool will create a selection area wherever you stroke it, and gives you a valuable visual reminder of where the objects you "turn off" are located.

The "Paint" Part of PHOTO-PAINT

Figure 11.14

Choose colors from the color model, or preset ones from the Colors Roll-Up's color palette.

4. Set the Tool Settings Roll-Up's **S**ize to a much larger diameter than you'd actually paint with. I've set mine to 80. In the example in figure 11.15, I'm painting a selection area with the Mask Brush tool from the back of the toy's fuselage trailing off to the left. This is where the white skywriting will be painted in.

5. Click on the foreground subject's icon on the Layers/Object Roll-Up. This is a toggle on/off icon; when you click on it, your foreground subject will disappear from the background, but the selection area marquee left by the Mask Brush tool will remain.

6. Click and hold on the Paint Brush tool to display the fly-out menu, then choose the Air Brush tool. Unlike the Paint Brush tool, the Air Brush will lay down a diffuse spray of foreground color. Like all the brushes, the Air Brush is velocity-sensitive—the faster you drag your cursor, the less time the tool has to concentrate on one image area.

Chapter 11: CorelPHOTO-PAINT!

Figure 11.15

The Mask Brush selects an area where you "paint" with it; it doesn't color anything on your background image.

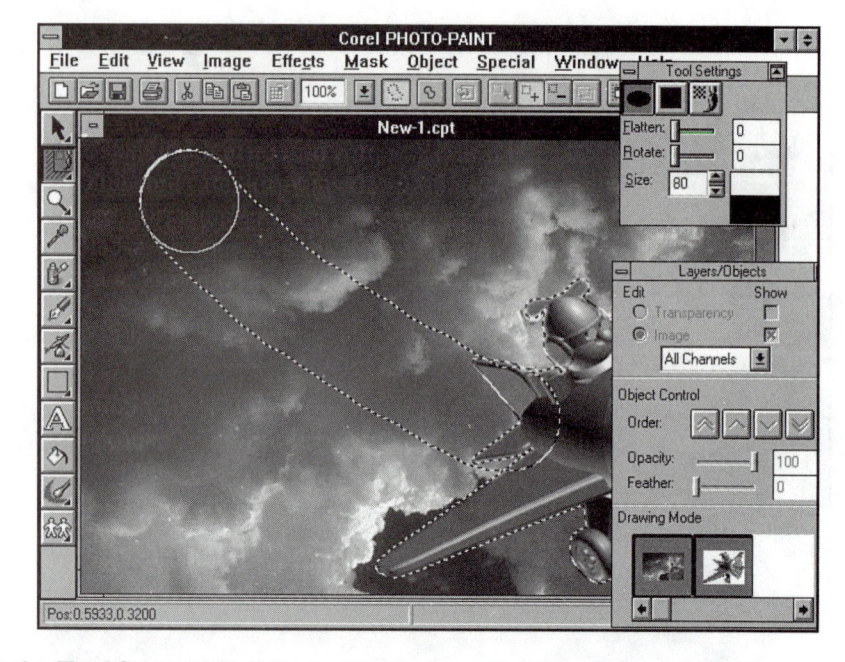

7. Set the Tool Settings Roll-Up to the Custom Brushes palette (the far right button on the top). Choose the tip with the icon of the hard center and soft edge (it's the one on the second row, second from left), then click and drag within the area you defined with the Mask Brush. Try dragging slowly, then quickly. As you can see in figure 11.16, a distinctive effect resembling skywriting can be achieved through a combination of mouse speeds. And if you go off course, the rest of the background image is protected from color; only the area inside the Mask Brush marquee can be altered.

8. When you're done painting, click on the icon of your foreground object on the Layers/Objects Roll-Up and the subject will reappear, unaffected by your painting work, as shown in figure 11.17.

The "Paint" Part of PHOTO-PAINT

Figure 11.16
Color application characteristics can be changed using the settings on the Tool Settings Roll-Up.

Figure 11.17
You can edit a bitmap object only if it's turned on through the Layers/Objects Roll-Up.

Chapter 11: CorelPHOTO-PAINT!

Adding Custom Text to the Poster

Using the same techniques you've just learned, the TIF export of the fancy movie title can be added to the image. You'll use the movie title selection twice; once as a drop-shadow, then a second time as a mask to select an eye-catching fill for the main title component to this piece.

First, create the shadow for the drop-shadow effect by following these steps:

1. Open the TIF file you created earlier in CorelDRAW.

2. Choose the Magic Wand Mask tool, then click the Add to Selection button on the Ribbon Bar. Each area you click over with the Magic Wand Mask tool will be added to your overall selection area.

3. Click on every black part of each letter of the text you created in the TIF file. As you can see in figure 11.18, a marquee appears around the black shapes that form the text when the Magic Wand Mask tool is clicked over them.

Figure 11.18

The Magic Wand Mask tool selects shapes based only on their color values.

Adding Custom Text to the Poster

4. Choose **E**dit, **C**opy, and press Ctrl+Tab to toggle your view back to the image you've been working on.

5. Choose **E**dit, **P**aste (Ctrl+V), and position the pasted text next to your foreground subject in the same position you had it when you created the text in CorelDRAW. In figure 11.19, you can see that the exported bitmap bears the same proportions as it did as vector art in CorelDRAW. This is because the Size and **R**esolution settings you specified when you exported it from CorelDRAW match those of the background image.

Figure 11.19

Position your selection as you envisioned it would be placed when you created it in CorelDRAW.

Using a Mask as a Design Template

As you saw in the last figure, the black text is a nice design element, but this is only the drop-shadow for the shimmering, vibrant text you'll create next. You can use a saved mask selection as a digital "cookie cutter" to cut out a corresponding shape from a Fountain Fill area, another image, or any bitmap that's large enough to accommodate the mask's dimensions.

Chapter 11: CorelPHOTO-PAINT!

After you have the selection area of the type defined, you can use the text TIF image file (ADVENTUR.TIF in the following examples) as a background for a PHOTO-PAINT fill. As long as you have a mask saved, you can cover the entire TIF image area (yes, ostensibly ruining it), load the saved mask, copy the areas the marquee encompasses, and paste the resulting selection onto the drop-shadow text in the background image file.

To create drop-shadow text, follow these steps:

1. Press Ctrl+Tab to shift PHOTO-PAINT's focus back to the fancy movie title image.

2. Choose **M**ask, **S**ave. This command enables you to save anything selected in an image file to a separate file. Choose the CPT file format for the saved file, as shown in figure 11.20.

Figure 11.20

Accept the default CPT extension PHOTO-PAINT offers you for saving masks.

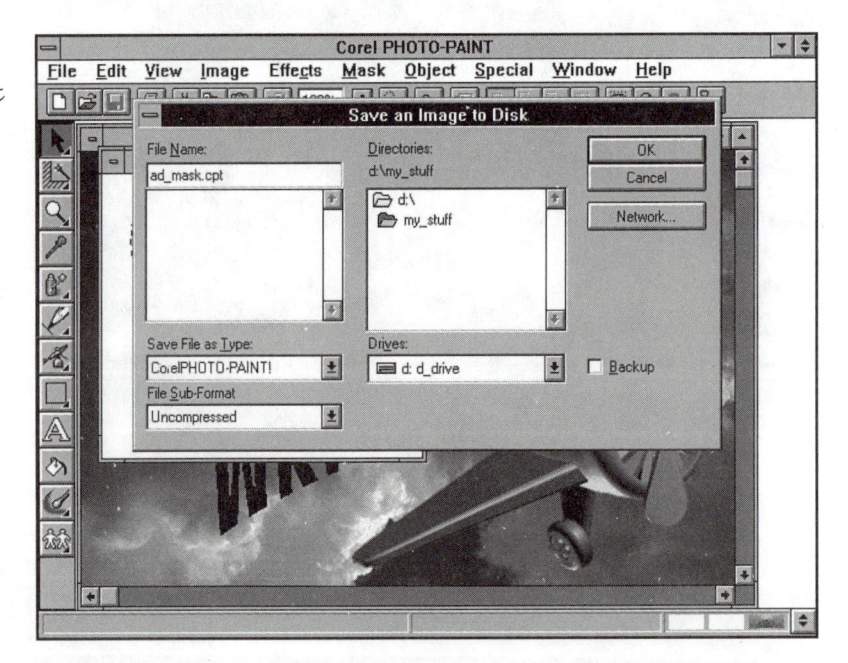

3. Now comes the fun part! You can delete the contents of your fancy movie title image and give the area an exotic fill. Choose **M**ask, **A**ll. A marquee will appear around the edge of the entire bitmap export of your title.

Using a Mask as a Design Template

4. Press the Delete key. The entire work will vanish, replaced with a solid paper-colored (background color) fill (see the following tip).

5. Double-click the Fill tool icon on the Toolbox or press F6 to display the Fill Roll-Up. This Roll-Up looks and acts identically to the Fill Roll-Up in CorelDRAW!

6. Choose a nice Fountain Fill in which you'd like your movie title to appear. In figure 11.21, a Linear Fill has been chosen, running from red to taxi cab yellow, the Fill tool has been chosen, and the area is clicked on with the Fountain Fill cursor.

Figure 11.21

The Fill Roll-Up offers options identical to those found on CorelDRAW's Fill Roll-Up.

Tip

Although photographic images are traditionally thought of as having foreground and background elements, bitmaps have a property that's a tradition of their own. By definition in PHOTO-PAINT (and a lot of other bitmap-editing programs), a foreground can have a color. The foreground color which Corel calls the paint color is the one you choose when you want to paint over an image area, like the skywriting you saw earlier in white.

Chapter 11: CorelPHOTO-PAINT!

Conversely, when you erase or delete an image area of a bitmap, the background color, which Corel calls the paper color, is exposed; you can set the background color (even if you can't see any in your image) through the Color Roll-Up. The overlapping swatches indicate the color chosen for paint color and paper color. If you click on each one, you can define a color for them. Therefore, with PHOTO-PAINT, in addition to having foreground and background colors, you also have foreground and background objects.

7. Choose **M**ask, **L**oad. You'll be offered a directory structure that "remembers" where you placed the last mask. Select the mask file you saved a few steps ago, and click on OK.

8. As you can see in figure 11.22, the mask of the fancy text has been loaded, and a marquee appears around the area where the mask was when you defined it. Choose **E**dit, **C**opy (Ctrl+C) to copy only the areas within the marquee to the Clipboard.

Figure 11.22
The loaded mask of your title is selected, while areas outside the marquee lines are not.

Using a Mask as a Design Template

371

9. Choose **F**ile, **C**lose, and do not elect to save current changes to the file. You now have a colored copy of the text on the Clipboard, and two "backups" of the original.

10. Choose **E**dit, **P**aste, and reposition the colored text so it slightly offsets the copy of the black text, as shown in figure 11.23. Instant drop-shadowed text!

Figure 11.23

Drop-shadowing text can help "lift" text off an image, and separate it from other image elements.

Creating PHOTO-PAINT Text

After you become familiar with the program, you'll notice that PHOTO-PAINT automatically conserves Drawing Window space by retracting Roll-Ups that don't pertain to your active tool, and by switching Ribbon Bars that relate to your present editing activities.

Chapter 11: CorelPHOTO-PAINT!

To conclude your design work, add some PHOTO-PAINT text to the movie poster. Text is a graphic in PHOTO-PAINT, which means once you're done using the Text tool, you can't edit a word or phrase again. But as a graphic, the text you type can be scaled and rotated exactly the way you perform these effects in CorelDRAW—by using the text selection's corner and side handles.

You need to choose a typeface and a foreground color for your text addition; having done that, you'll add the final element to the movie poster. Follow these steps:

1. Make the PHOTO-PAINT text complementary to the style of the fancy title, and create a drop-shadow for the text first. Select the Text tool, then click on the black swatch on the Colors Roll-Up to choose black as the paint (foreground) color for the text.

Tip

You can also hunt around in the image and find black here using the Eyedropper tool.

2. With the Text tool active, PHOTO-PAINT's Ribbon Bar now offers text options. If you followed the assignment in Chapter 9, RusselWrite is an available font on the Ribbon Bar. Why not select it, set the font size for around 24 points, and type a phrase that goes along with your movie poster?

3. Once you click outside the text you've created, the text becomes an object that requires you to use a selection tool if you want to reposition the text. Click on the Object Picker tool (the top tool on the Toolbox), and position the text so that it compositionally fits into the poster you're creating.

4. Click on the Eyedropper tool and select a pleasing color from your image. Type exactly the same phrase you did in step 2 to create the text that will lie on top of the black drop-shadow. In figure 11.24, the Eyedropper picked up a highlight on the toy plane, and the second string of text contrasts nicely with the black drop-shadow, as well as with the rest of the image.

Creating PHOTO-PAINT Text

Figure 11.24
Two differently colored text strings of identical text can create a drop-shadow effect.

Merging Your Image Areas

Once you have all the "players" assembled on a background image, you can reorder them, delete ones you don't want, and most importantly, reposition items to your heart's content because PHOTO-PAINT treats all selections as discrete objects.

The Corel PHOTO-PAINT format for bitmaps enables you to keep selections discrete, but there are times when your imaging work calls for more of a "set piece." If you want to use your finished piece in another program or give it to someone who doesn't have version 5 of PHOTO-PAINT, you must use the Merge command to fuse all of the independent areas together. Once the objects have been merged, the file can be saved in a common file format such as BMP, TGA, PCX, or TIF.

To merge and save your movie poster, follow these steps:

1. When you're certain every element of your movie poster is where you want it, select an object and choose **O**bject, **M**erge or press Ctrl+G. You'll notice that any marquee lines or selection handles will disappear from around the object. Keep selecting and merging objects until all the objects have been merged into one bitmap image.

2. Save your work. From **F**ile, **S**ave, you may choose from any of the file formats listed in the Save Files of **T**ype drop-down box on the Save **F**ile dialog box.

3. As you can see in figure 11.25, I squeaked in a little refinement here and there to the movie poster, moving objects around slightly and adding more text before using the Merge command. Pressing F9 gives you the Full-Screen Preview of your work, sans tools, Roll-Ups, and menu.

Figure 11.25
Now playing in an imagination near you!

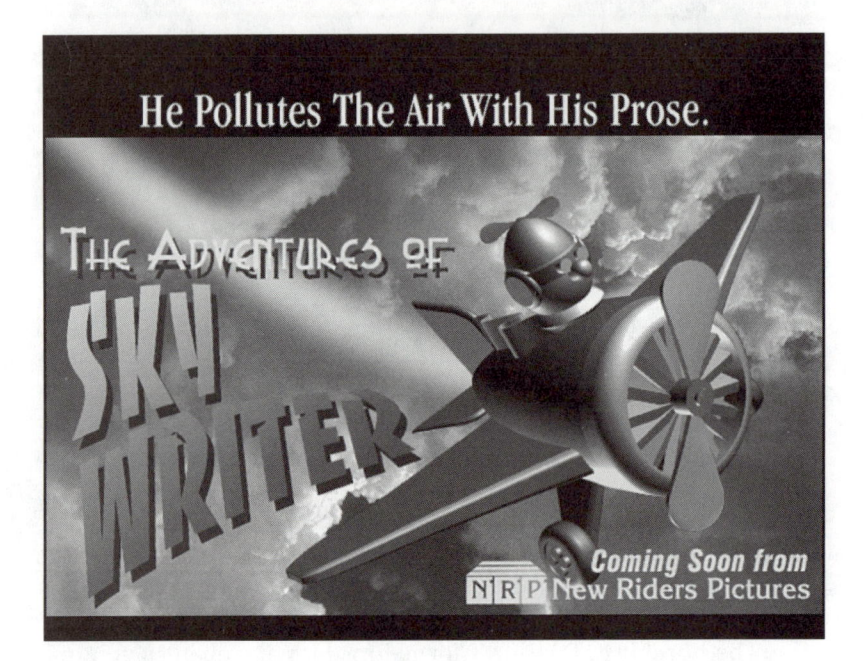

Summary

This chapter has just touched on the many robust features available for you to use when working in CorelPHOTO-PAINT. There are many more techniques and features left to discover, but if you've developed a "feel" for bitmap imaging work now, it's been time well spent. Oddly enough, the more you practice with CorelDRAW, the better you'll become at PHOTO-PAINTing—Corel programmers have designed both workspaces to share a lot of common functions, so you learn one as you experiment with the other.

Summary

As far as education goes, yours will increase by orders of magnitude when you familiarize yourself with both data types that make up computer graphics. If you understand the properties of bitmaps in addition to vector art, there won't be a real-life assignment that you can't handle.

As real-life assignments go, there will be times when you aren't asked to draw or paint at all, but instead, to prepare a slide show or a histogram of product sales for a company. This is your cue to turn to the other modules of Corel—MOVE, SHOW, and CHART—to discover the possibilities that arise when your artist's skills are applied to business graphics.

Turn the page to see how to broaden your graphical horizons and dress up a pixel or two for commerce!

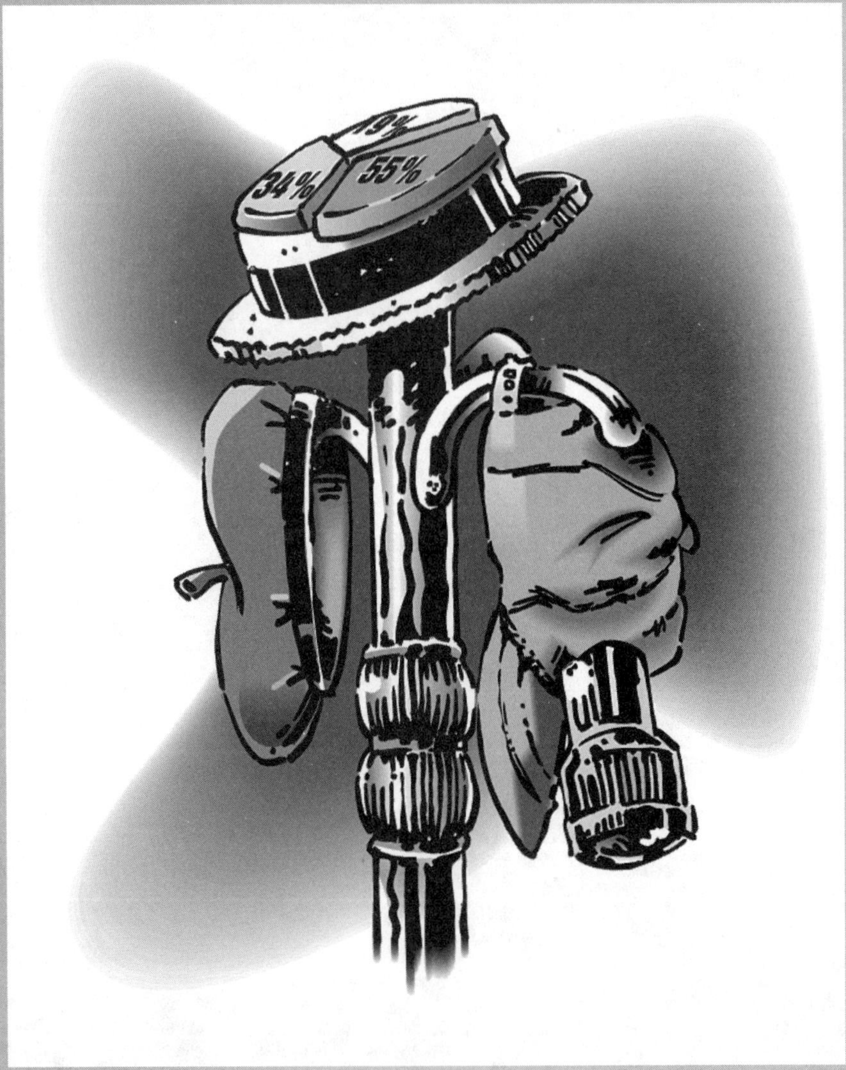
19%
34%
55%

CHAPTER 12

The Many Hats of CorelDRAW

Most designers receive a singular (inadequate!) paycheck, yet perform a multitude of business tasks. Drawing charts and key frames for commercials, and even creating logos, all fall within the province of *business graphics*. Graphics created expressly for communicating a sales point, or simply to keep a boardroom from becoming a bored room, may require you to adopt a different attitude, if not a different discipline.

You may not always get a chance to show off your flair for ornamental embellishments, but when you wear these other designer's hats, you can produce creative and powerful presentations with the right tools. This is where Corel's other modules, CorelCHART, SHOW, and MOVE, can help feather your other caps, while making the task at hand a positively inspired one!

In this chapter, you will:

- ■ Learn how to create a chart automatically
- ■ Customize a chart
- ■ Create an animated company logo
- ■ Discover some animation secrets
- ■ Combine different types of computer documents to create a slide show

Charts Can Be Cool Business

Database and spreadsheet applications enable their owners to produce enough statistical data to fill the potholes in Manhattan streets each year, if they were so inclined. If you've ever taken a look at a spreadsheet consisting of more than a half-dozen *cells*, you understand the need to express the numbers and categories in an "at-a-glance" way.

In business, being able to create charts of important data can be a lifesaver, and ambitious young turks in large companies everywhere are anxious to have *their* data expressed in a fresh, clean fashion for the afternoon's sales presentation.

CorelCHART excels at generating histograms, pictograms, scatter charts, hi-lows, and many other graphical types of information plotting. While it can produce charts in many different formats that look radically different from one another, the process for producing these wonderful color graphs is the same—you start with structuring fields of data within a spreadsheet format.

You have many artistic options for how your data is presented graphically, and your selection process using CorelCHART begins almost the moment you double-click on CHART's icon.

Matching a Chart to Your Needs

The imaginary company in this chapter, Ping Pong Products, Inc., needs a gee-whiz (business jargon for "impressive") presentation for their shareholders, with a chart, animation—the whole nine yards. First of all, they need to show the shareholders the track record they've had with their four principal products over the past four years.

In short, you'll begin your assignment with an appropriate "data-holder;" a chart type whose design is capable of containing four columns (*series*) of categories, mapped out to four rows pertaining to the years these sales occurred.

To select the appropriate chart, follow these steps:

1. Double-click on the CorelCHART icon in Windows Program Manager to launch the program. CorelCHART is a discrete Corel module, and you can't directly access CHART from CorelDRAW.

2. Choose **F**ile, **N**ew (Ctrl+N). Unlike CorelDRAW (but like the rest of the Corel modules), a fresh working page is not offered when you open the program.

Matching a Chart to Your Needs

3. Uncheck the Use Sample **D**ata box, which is checked by default when you open a new chart. Sample Data is useful if you have your own chart data arranged identically to CorelCHART's "preset" data, but this chapter shows you how to set up chart fields of your own from the ground up.

4. You're looking for a chart type that'll hold four series and four rows. As you can see in figure 12.1, the 3D connect chart in the 3D-riser group fits the bill, since the legend says it requires 2 values (rows) per series (columns), and Ping Pong Products has 4 × 4 cells of data information.

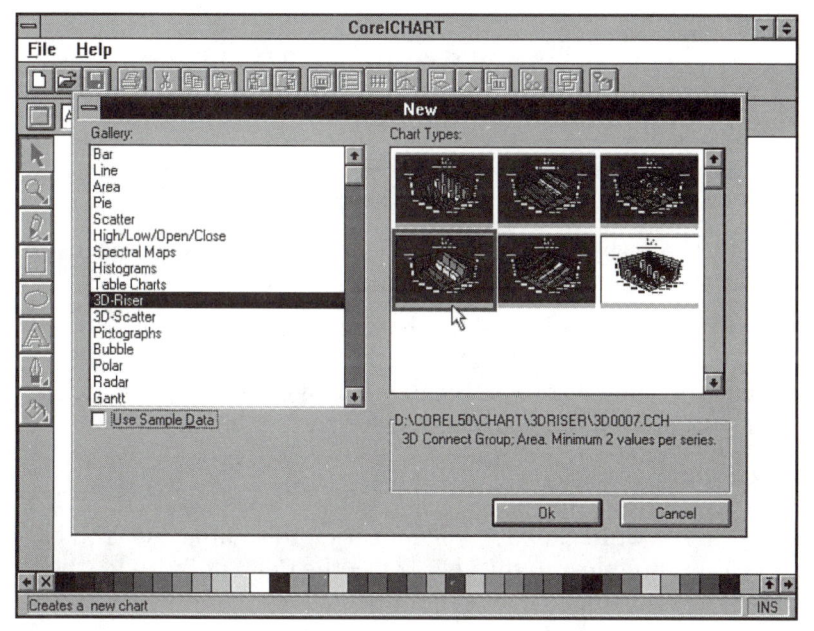

Figure 12.1
Decide on a chart with enough series and values to hold your data.

Tip
The icon representations of the chart types you can preview before selecting are literally "What You See Is What You Get." If you select a chart type by clicking on an icon of a two-column graph, this is what CorelCHART will plot your data to. The icons are an accurate graphical representation of the chart type you're initially presented with after entering your data, and you can modify the chart in many different ways later.

5. Click on OK, and you'll be presented with the Data View of your chart. You can't see the chart itself, because you haven't given CorelCHART any data upon which to create the graphical representation. Yet. Read on!

Navigating a CorelCHART Spreadsheet

CorelCHART has two views of the components of a chart—the Chart View and the Data View. They seem like worlds apart, but you can toggle between the two views quite easily to modify your data, then see the results of your editing on the graphical representation, the chart.

From the Data View, it's apparent these cells need to be filled in so CorelCHART can create a wonderful 3D-riser chart.

Take these next steps slowly and thoroughly—making entries in a spreadsheet may not have been covered in art school!

1. You need a title for the chart, and this is an easy first step. Click on the cell that falls under the "A" column, and the "1" row. Any cell would be fine here, but you should get into the practice of organizing spreadsheets and not entering information anywhere whim dictates.

2. Type **Ping Pong Products, Inc.** When a cell has been highlighted (by clicking on it with the "plus" cursor), it's ready to have information entered into it; the word "Ready" will appear on the status line. You can enter info either directly into the cell, or use the Cell Editing field (the lower of the two wide ones) above the spreadsheet.

Tip
A cell will "expand" to accommodate the amount of text or numbers you enter into it, and then return to its standard cell size after another cell has been highlighted. If you can't read your entire entry in a standard-sized cell, that's okay—you can always see and edit a selected cell's data from the Cell Edit field above the spreadsheet.

Navigating a CorelCHART Spreadsheet

3. You have a choice how to register the information in the cell when you're done typing. Either press Enter, press the Tab key, click on a different cell, or use the arrow keyboard keys. The result is the same—you've moved to a different cell, and the cell you typed in has its information registered now.

4. You need to tell CorelCHART that the Ping Pong Products, Inc. cell should be the title of your chart, so click on it to select it.

5. Choose the Title Tag from the Tag List field. As you can see in figure 12.2, these are the steps for entering information in CorelCHART's Data Management view.

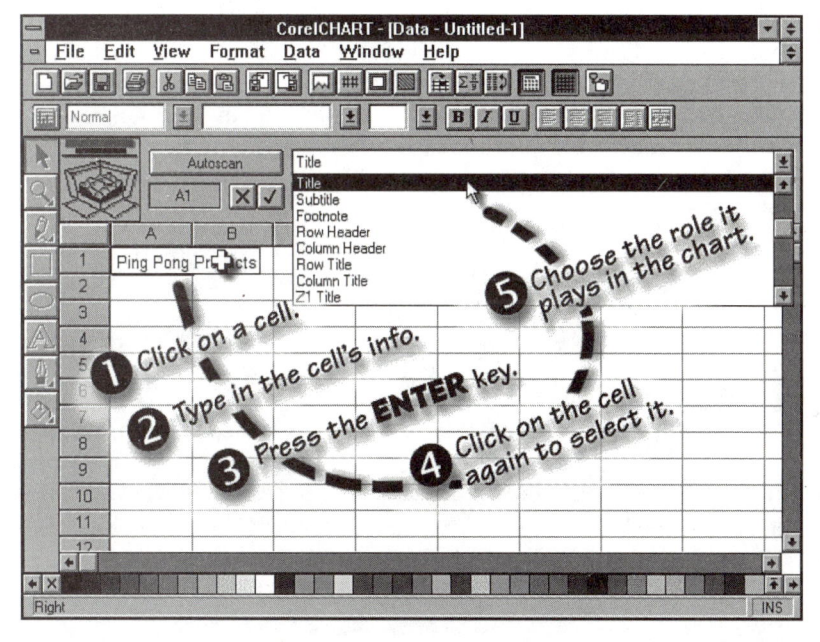

Figure 12.2
Use these five steps to enter and tag your data.

Tagging a Range of Cells

There's always a collection of data in a chart that bears the same sort of tag—the statistical data, the column headers, and the row headers have a specific place in your recipe for creating a CorelCHART. In the next steps, you'll create the headers for the types of merchandise Ping Pong Products distributes. Then you'll tag multiple cells of column header information using a technique you'll find familiar from your adventures in CorelDRAW!

Chapter 12: The Many Hats of CorelDRAW

1. To begin your columns four-across, click on the cell whose location is at C4 on the Data Management spreadsheet. This leaves you room at the top of the spreadsheet for other chart labels you may want to add later.

2. In cell C4, type **Yo-Yos**.

3. Press the Tab key (or the right arrow keyboard key). You're in a new cell now, D4, and the header **Yo-Yos** has been registered.

4. Type **Shuffleboards**, and press the Tab key.

5. Type **Parachutes**, and press the Tab key.

6. For the last of the four column headers, type **Ping Pong Balls**.

7. All the cells from C4 to F4 have to be selected (highlighted) now so they can be tagged. Click on cell C4 and drag your cursor to cell F4. As you can see in figure 12.3, part of the information in cell F4 flows outside the cell, but it's okay. Information that's too long to fit in a cell displays an "overflow" into neighboring cells, but you *should not* tag the overflow—only the cell you typed in.

Figure 12.3

Tag a range of cells you typed in by click+dragging.

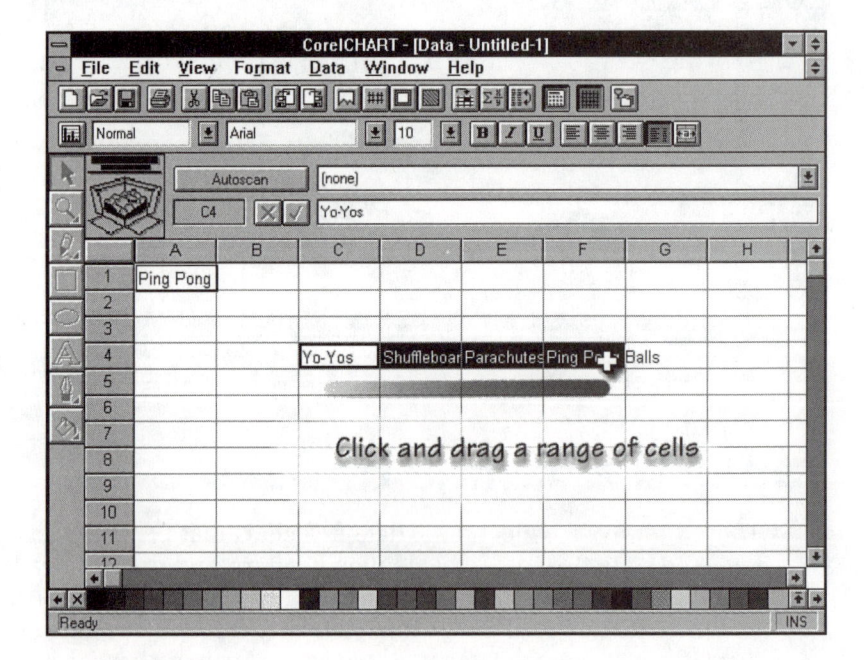

Tagging a Range of Cells

8. Tag the column headers by clicking the down arrow to the right of the Tag List field, then clicking on Column Header, as shown in figure 12.4.

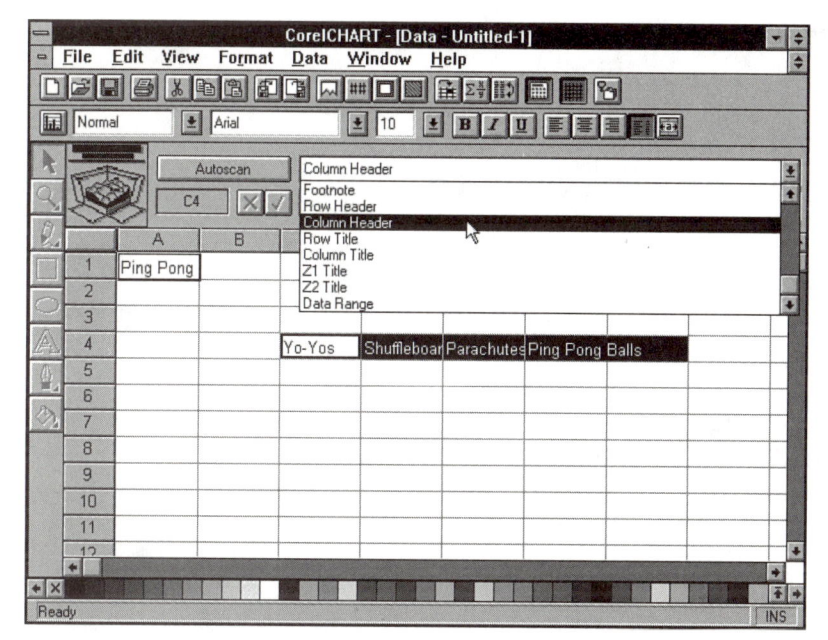

Figure 12.4

You can attribute a property to a range of cells with a Tag List selection.

Creating Row Headers

You now have one axis of your future chart labeled, and it's time to create headers for the rows—the years in which Ping Pong Products sold their wares.

This one's simple; you perform exactly the same steps as you did in creating the column header range. Here are the steps:

1. Click on cell B5. Its location relative to your first column header cell (C4) is important. CorelCHART needs your chart data arranged and tagged in a format it can use to build your chart, and this row axis must run through cells perpendicular to the column header cells.

2. Type **1991** and press Enter (or press the down arrow keyboard key).

3. Type **1992** and press Enter. The date should be in cell B6.

4. Type **1993** and press Enter.

5. Type **1994** and Press Enter.
6. Click and drag down from cell B5 to cell B8.
7. Choose Row Header from the Tag List.

You now have a good working information base to add a data range to!

Entering a Data Range for Your Chart

Row headers, column headers, and titles are an important first step toward directing CorelCHART to create the chart of your dreams, but it's obvious now that some numbers (like sales figures) are needed to complete the form CorelCHART uses to plot your data.

In the next steps, you'll find that entering a data range for your chart is as simple as filling out a graph. Use your own data in the next steps, and get creative with Ping Pong Products sales for the last four years. You'll soon see how mere numbers and categories can be automatically transformed into a visual, graphical representation that'll wow a boardroom.

Note

It's a bad and confusing practice to enter numbers in the thousands in a spreadsheet. Generally, a figure like 57,000 is entered as 57 in a spreadsheet, and then a legend at the bottom of a chart tells the viewer that the statistics are measured in thousands.

Let's adopt this practice as you enter a data range in your Data Management spreadsheet. If you decide Ping Pong Products sold 123,000 shuffleboards in 1994, for instance, simply type 123 in the appropriate cell.

1. Cell C5 represents the sales of yo-yos in 1991. Let's say Ping Pong Products sold 55 thousand of them. Click on Cell C5, and type 55.
2. Enter values for the other cells representing sales of items in their respective years. You can use Tab, Enter, or the arrow keys to move from cell to cell, or simply click on a cell to highlight it with your cursor.

Entering a Data Range for Your Chart

3. When you have 16 entries, click and diagonal-drag from cell C5 to cell F8. This selects the data range.
4. Tag the data as a data range (for CorelCHART to understand) by selecting Data Range from the Tag List, as shown in figure 12.5.

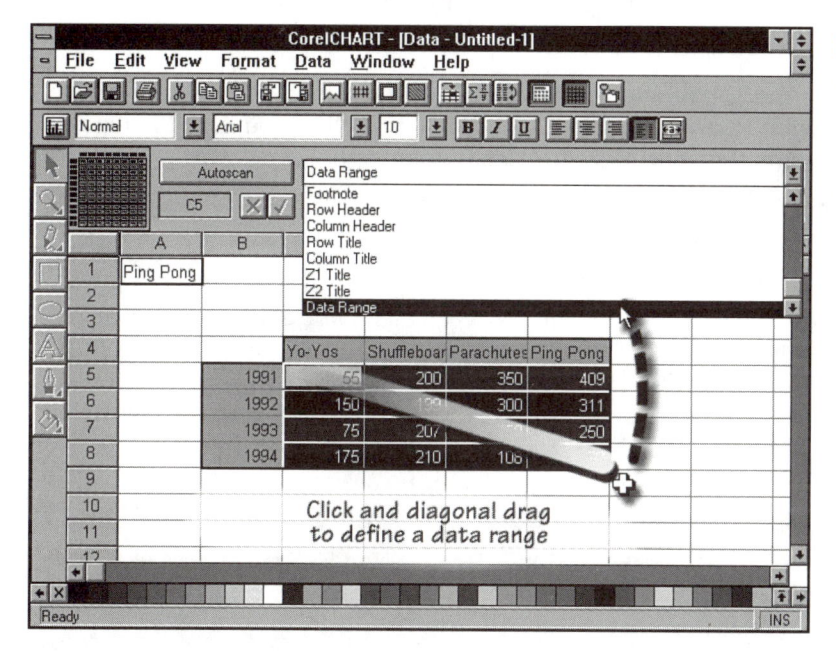

Figure 12.5
Marquee-select the range of data you've entered, then tag the data.

Auto-Positioning Your Data on the Chart

As mentioned earlier, each component of the chart you're building has a graphical counterpart on the chart CorelCHART creates. The Tag List has many components; some you'll want to use, and others may have no place on your chart. Your chart depends on your data and what type of statistical information you want to graphically represent.

In this next set of steps, you'll create a subhead for the chart. You already know how to enter information into a cell, but the main attraction is how to tell one type of data from another using the Tag preview window as a visual guide. This wisdom will benefit you later if you ever get stuck creating a half a dozen different charts with completely different types of information!

1. Suppose you want a subtitle on Ping Pong Products' chart clearly stating that the chart represents sales figures for the last four years. Click on a cell (I've chosen cell D3 in this example because it's in an easily accessible place on my spreadsheet).

2. Type **4-Year Sales History** in the cell, and press Enter.

3. Click on the Tag List down arrow, and choose Footnote.

4. Look at the Tag preview window toward the top left of your workspace. The tag for this 4-Year Sales History info is highlighted in red in its position on the chart CorelCHART is going to build for you.

5. Hmmm. As a footnote, 4-Year Sales History looks a little wimpy. Try clicking on Subtitle in the Tag List drop-down.

6. As you can see in figure 12.6 (and much better on your own monitor), the Subtitle tag is very prominent as an element right beneath the title on your future chart. Now that your data is correctly entered, it's time to let CorelCHART start rendering a graphical masterpiece. The command to do this is simple: click on the Data/Chart button highlighted in figure 12.6 to switch views from statistical to artistic.

Figure 12.6

The tag you attribute to a cell is represented in red in the Tag preview window.

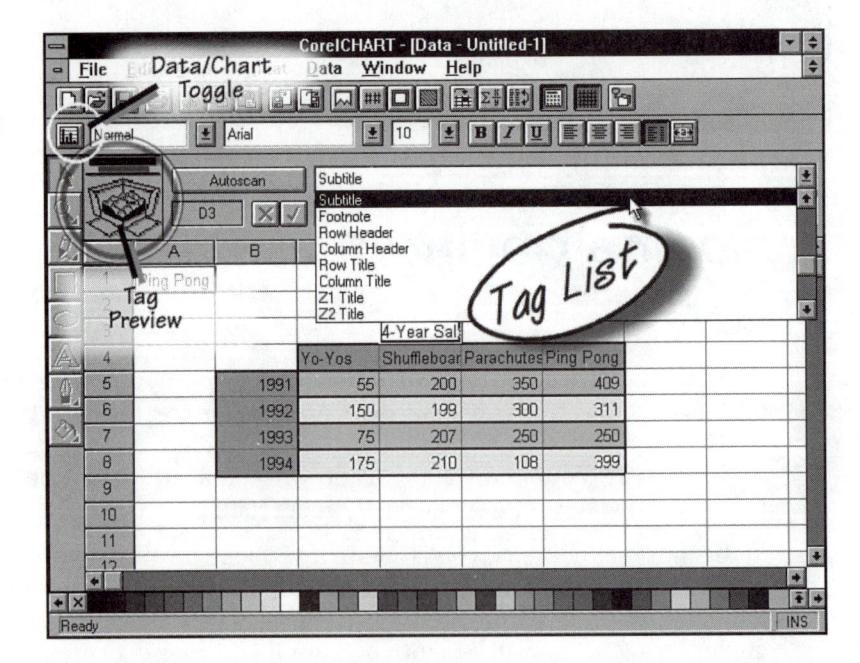

Auto-Positioning Your Data on the Chart

7. In figure 12.7, you can see the fruits of your spreadsheet labors. By default, the typeface used to illustrate the graph is defined by CorelCHART. But you can change this—you'll learn how in the next section.

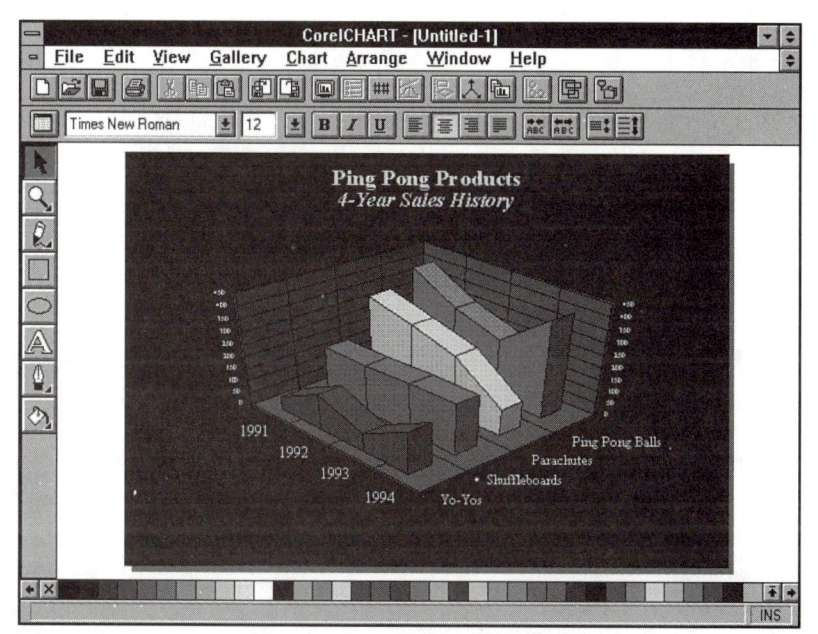

Figure 12.7

An automatic, graphical representation of statistics is created by CorelCHART.

Tip

You can always switch views between the data and the chart by clicking on the Data/Chart toggle button. Why would you want to? You can't change a piece of data from the chart view. Numbers and other tagged items must be re-entered from the data view. Conversely, you can't change the colors of anything on your chart from the data view of it.

Also, the Autoscan button in the data view can sometimes, but not always, make quick work of tagging data. Autoscan makes a "best guess" of the cells into which you've entered info, and adds a tag (like Data Range or Title) where it thinks your cells represent these categories.

But as adults, most of us realize computers don't think—you definitely want to review CorelCHART's Autoscan process, should you click on it, to make sure a range of data isn't tagged footnote, or some other possible embarrassment!

Customizing Your CorelCHART

By default, charts created by CorelCHART from your data come in a color scheme and a preset selection of fonts. Usually, they're good choices. For example, the default font, like all scaleable windows typefaces, is smooth and easy to read.

But as a designer, you have your own reasons for wanting to change the font used in your chart. In the next set of steps, you learn that CorelCHART's Text tool operates the same way as CorelDRAW's and the other modules.

Here's how to customize the title CorelCHART has created:

1. Choose the Text tool, and highlight the Ping Pong Products title on the top of your chart.

2. Click the down arrow to the right of the fonts drop-down list, and choose a snazzy typeface. In figure 12.8, ShotgunBT has been chosen because this is the official logotype of our fictitious company.

Figure 12.8

Choose a size and font for text you've highlighted with CHART's Text tool.

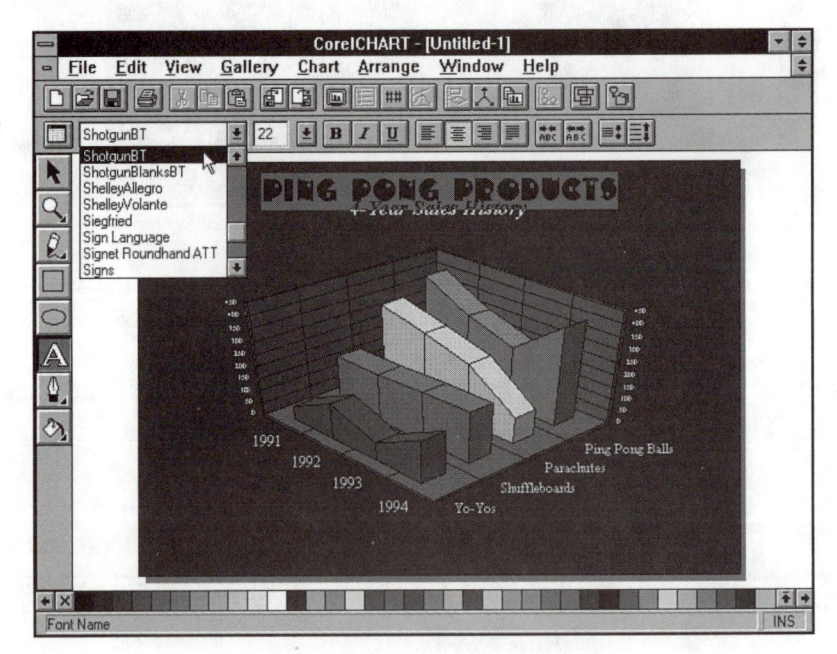

3. You also can change the size of the Title text simply by entering a different point size in the box to the right of your font selection. A size of 22 points is used in this example, but font size really depends on the typeface; some are bolder, wider, or larger than others.

Note

You can also use one of the font size presets by clicking on the down arrow next to the size box, then clicking on a size, rather than entering a figure manually.

Changing a Chart Color Scheme

If you're making 35mm slides from a CHART document, the deep blue background in this example will be eye-soothing for you, while the bright-colored riser blocks of data will leap out and capture your attention. Suppose, however, that the purpose of your chart is for two or three sales people who don't want a 35mm slide but instead need a plain laser print handout.

Why eat up laser toner rendering a dark blue background, when the same chart will be more readable and conserve laser toner as nice shades of gray, a white background, and black type?

Here's how to change CorelCHART's default colors for a 3D-riser chart type:

1. First things first: you need to select all the type to change it to black. With the Pick tool, click on the title.

2. Hold the Shift key (to additively select objects), and click on the subtitle.

3. Keep that Shift key held; you're not done selecting! Row heads, column headers, and data field axis markers are all dynamically linked to the colored chart pieces they label. All you need to do is select one from these categories, and the rest of a series of labels are automatically selected. Click on 1991, click on the zero along each riser axis (the numerical sales figures), and then click on Yo-Yos.

Chapter 12: The Many Hats of CorelDRAW

4. Click on the black swatch on the color palette on the bottom of your CHART workspace, as shown in figure 12.9.

Figure 12.9
You can select multiple CHART objects with the Pick tool by holding down the Shift key.

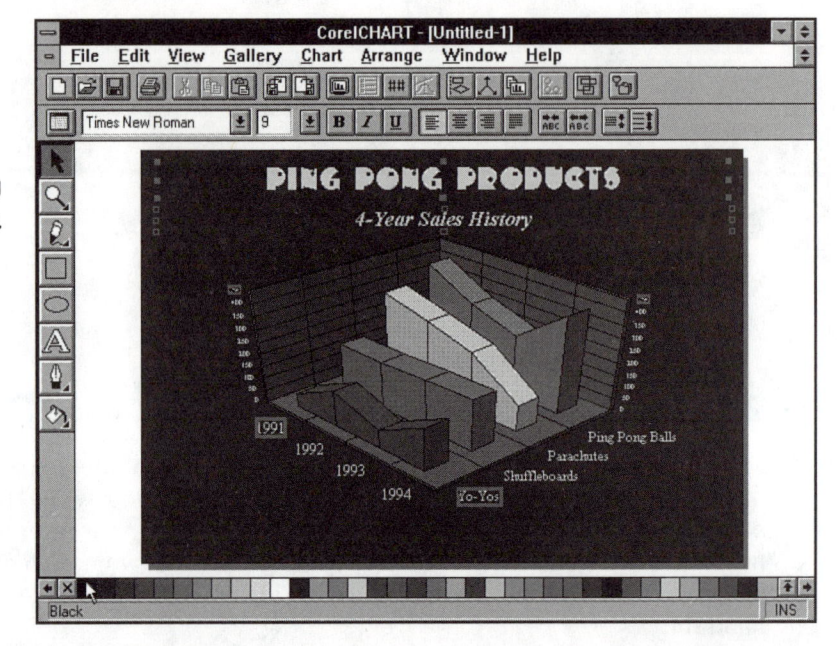

5. Click on the blue background. This automatically deselects all the text and numbers you recolored.

6. Click on white on the color palette. Your chart will now put about 75 percent less mileage on your laser printer when you need to make copies!

Changing Linked Group Sizes

You have different data elements that make up your chart, and they became different when you assigned them tags in the data management view. Titles, subtitles, and footnotes are text elements that you can recolor, resize, and assign a different font to directly in the chart view of your document. However, row headers, column headers, and those auto-axes that mark the riser blocks along the side of the chart are quite different; to customize them requires a few special steps.

In the next set of steps, you'll make the labels for your chart a little more legible. Although eight-point type can be read in a handout, it's clear that the labels are too small to be read on-screen. Before you finish this chapter, you're going to make this Ping Pong Products chart an element in an on-screen slide show!

Complete the following steps:

1. Right-mouse click on the column header Yo-Yos. This displays a menu pop-up pertaining to the entire category of column headers, of which Yo-Yos is a linked part.

2. You have many selections here, as shown in figure 12.10. Text View Options is the menu you want; click on it to display the menu that affects the whole collection of column headers.

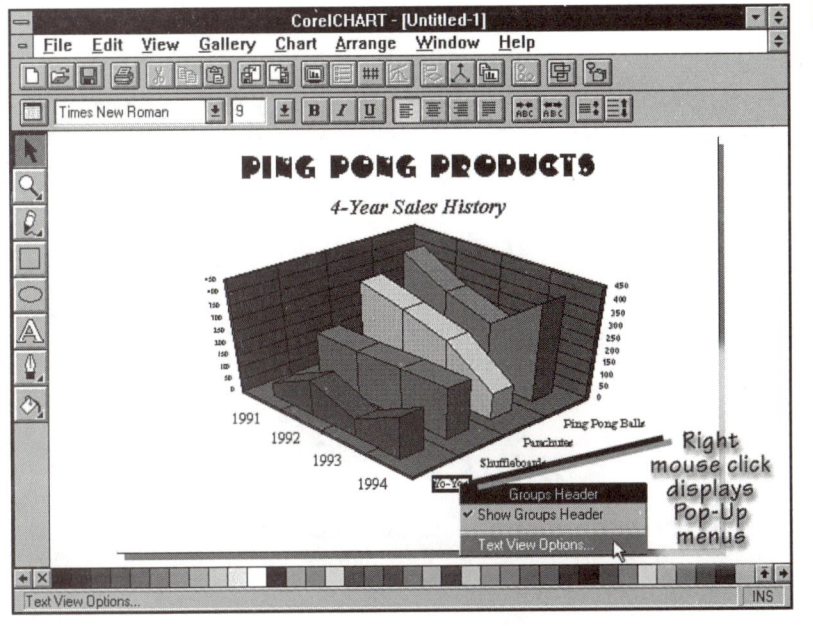

Figure 12.10

Right-mouse click on an object to display a pop-up menu that pertains to the selection.

3. By default, CorelCHART offers Autofitted text. This means that whatever you tag and enter as column header info in the data view of your chart automatically accommodates the rest of the components of the chart as you resize and move things around. Click this radio button off, and you'll be free to scale the type to any size you choose, as shown in figure 12.11.

Figure 12.11

You can manually scale selected categories of CHART elements by turning off the Autofitted text option.

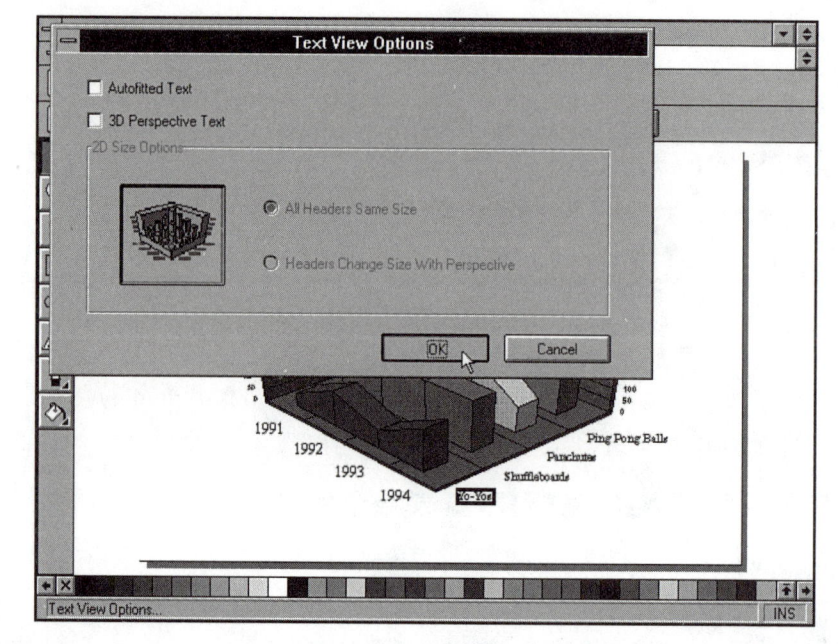

4. Click on the down arrow on the size drop-down list, and choose 12 (points) for Yo-Yos. You'll notice that every text entry that's linked to Yo-Yos (Parachutes and so on) will also scale up.

5. Repeat the last steps for the row header-linked text group, and both the axis numbers. Without the autofitted text option active, you're sort of creating a mess here, but you'll clean it up in the next section.

Further Customizing the CorelCHART

In the same spirit as Spring cleaning around the house, you're bound to make somewhat of a clutter around your chart before you get things exactly the way you want them to appear.

Removing Labels from the Chart

I see no reason for the handy-dandy axis numbers to exist on both sides of the 3D riser, and if you don't either, here's how to fix it:

1. Right-mouse click over the left side series of numbers on the chart with the Pick tool, as shown in figure 12.12.

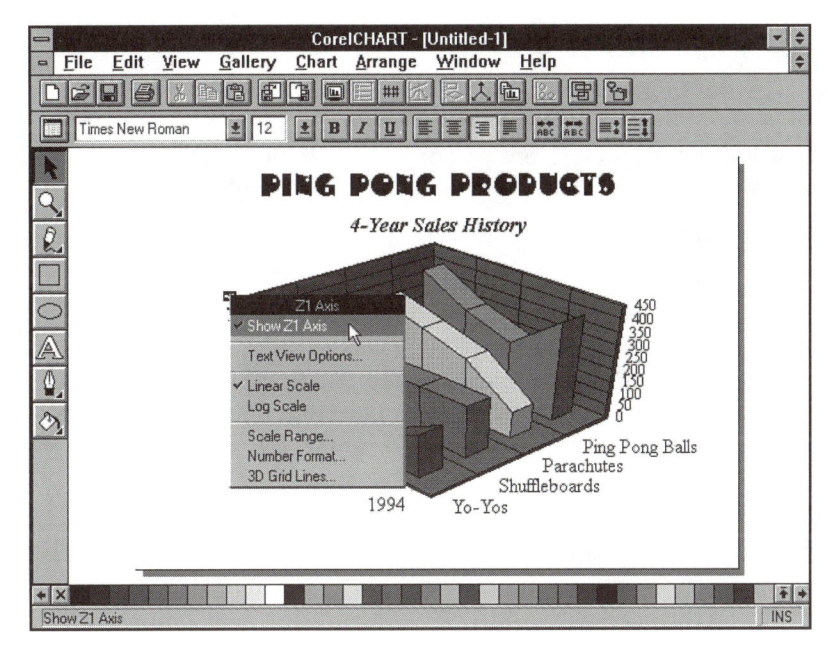

Further Customizing the CorelCHART

Figure 12.12
Choose not to display an axis marker from its pop-up menu.

2. The pop-up menu pertaining to the Z1 axis displays many options, but the one you're looking for is Show Z1 Axis. It's already checked, but by clicking on this option, you uncheck it, and by releasing the left mouse button, both the pop-up and the left Z axis disappears.

Tip

CHART's menu pop-ups are also a terrific means for identifying chart elements. Pop one up over something you're unfamiliar with, then click on the data/chart toggle button to go to the data management view to change something.

Unlike titles and subtitles, linked items with tags (like Z1 axis, column headers, and row headers) cannot be textually or numerically edited in the chart view of your data, but must be edited in data view.

However, titles, subtitles, and footnotes can be edited simply by highlighting them in chart view with the Text tool and typing in whatever you like.

Chapter 12: The Many Hats of CorelDRAW

Adding a Manual Label

The Text tool is good for more than simply highlighting text you entered in the data view of your chart. You can type notes directly on the chart without a visit to cells and spreadsheets. Here's how to make it clear that Ping Pong Products sold 450 thousand ping pong balls in 1994, not only 450!

1. Choose the Text tool, and move the crosshair cursor over the chart.

2. Be aware that whenever the cursor changes into a text insertion tool, the space where you want to type is occupied by another text field. Avoid this, because you'll wind up adding text to an existing data label. When you've found an area (like above the right side Z1 number axis), either click with the cursor to make a text insertion point, or click and diagonal-drag (marquee) to define a text box in which you can type. I suggest the latter because it's easier to see where your text will be entered on the chart.

3. Type **In Thousands**. As you can see in figure 12.13, the text automatically appears as a default font and size. You can change this, however, by highlighting the entry with the Text tool, and selecting a different font and size from the Ribbon Bar.

Figure 12.13

Use the Text tool to create original entries directly onto the chart.

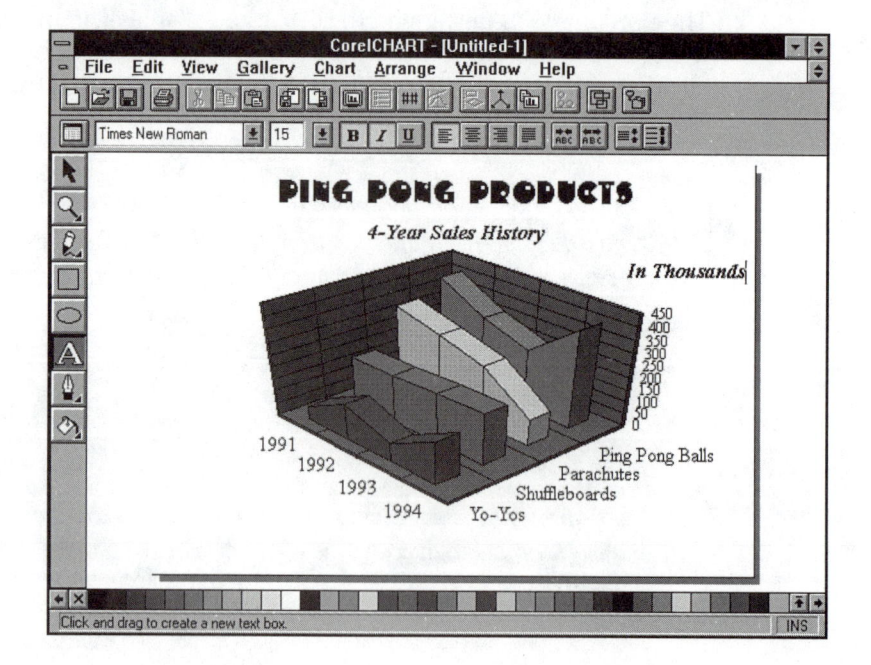

Further Customizing the CorelCHART

Reducing the Amount of Z2 Axis Entries

The increments that CorelCHART automatically displays on the riser as a marker for the data are sometimes overwhelming, as you may find in this instance. Frankly, you don't need markers on the Z2 axis at every increment of 50. At the Z2 axis label's new, legible font size, it's getting a little crowded!

Here's how to manually define how many riser markers will appear on your chart, and how to display the increments you want:

1. Right-mouse click over any number on the Z2 axis series to get the pop-up menu.

2. Choose 3D Grid Lines, as shown in figure 12.14. The Z2 axis markers are linked to the grids themselves, and by adjusting the grid lines, you'll fix the axis label.

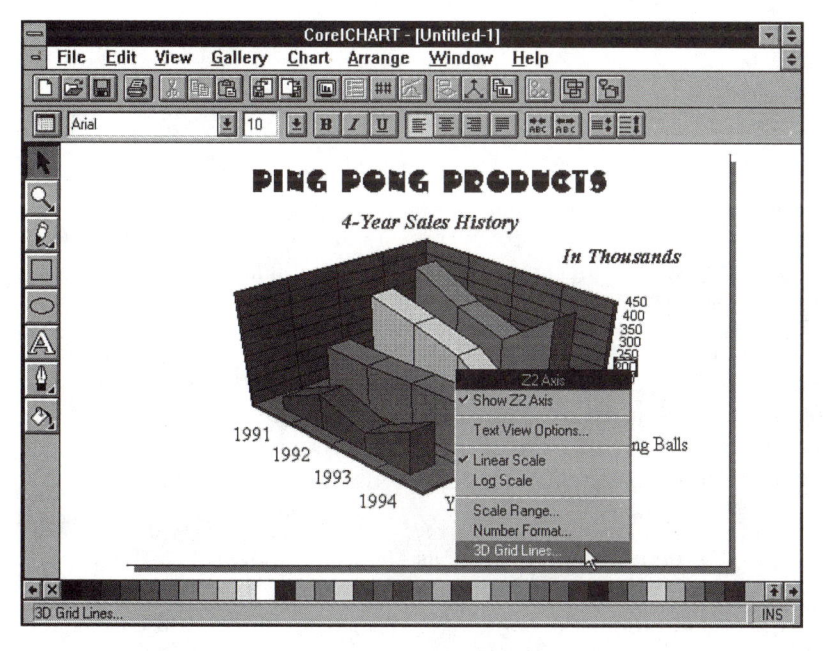

Figure 12.14

Grid lines and their axis markers are linked; changing the grid changes the markers.

3. Click on the Manual radio button in the Grid Divisions on the Grid Lines menu. The Number of Divisions field will become active, enabling you to type in it.

4. Four is a good number of divisions, since Ping Pong's sales sort of ping-ponged between the 0 and 400,000 range over the past few years. So type in **4**, as shown in figure 12.15, and click on OK.

Chapter 12: The Many Hats of CorelDRAW

Figure 12.15
Decide on how many increments you want represented for your data in the Grid Lines menu.

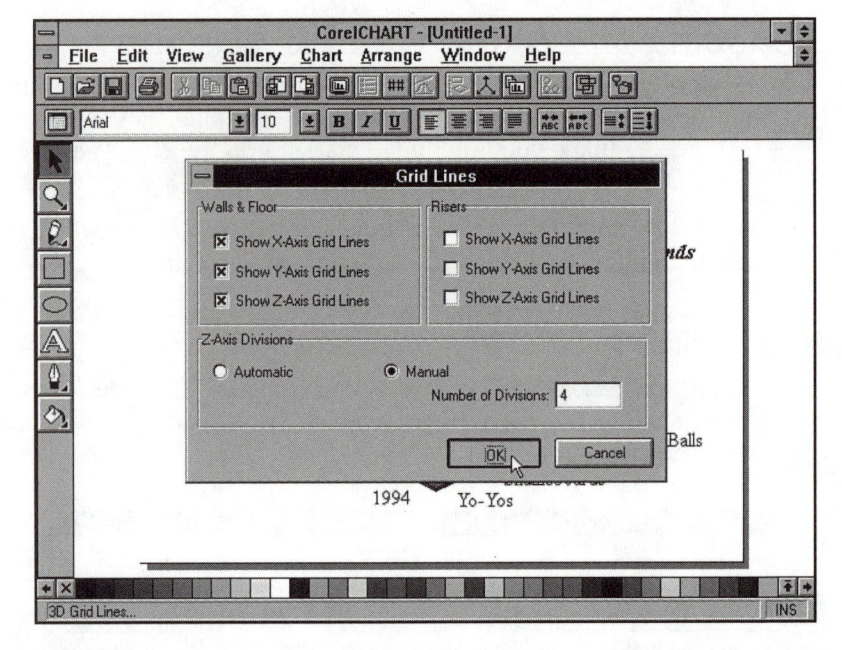

5. CorelCHART will try to figure out this new manual adjustment of the chart, and provide new numerical figures to represent 4 grid lines. But the numbers may not reflect "clean" increments; you may get 270, 360, and so on. To reset the increments, right-mouse click again on the Z2 axis and choose Data Range from the pop-up menu.

6. Click on the Manual Scale radio button, then type **0** in the From: field, and **400** in the To: field. Ping Pong Products' sales exceeded 400,000, but that's okay. What you're doing here is telling CorelCHART to give you a range divided by the four grid markers you defined earlier. In other words, you want the Z2 axis represented in clean, 100-increment markers.

7. Click on the Automatic radio button, as shown in figure 12.16. This forces CorelCHART to recalculate a data range from 0 to 400 automatically, given the number of divisions (4) you set up in the Grid Lines menu.

Further Customizing the CorelCHART

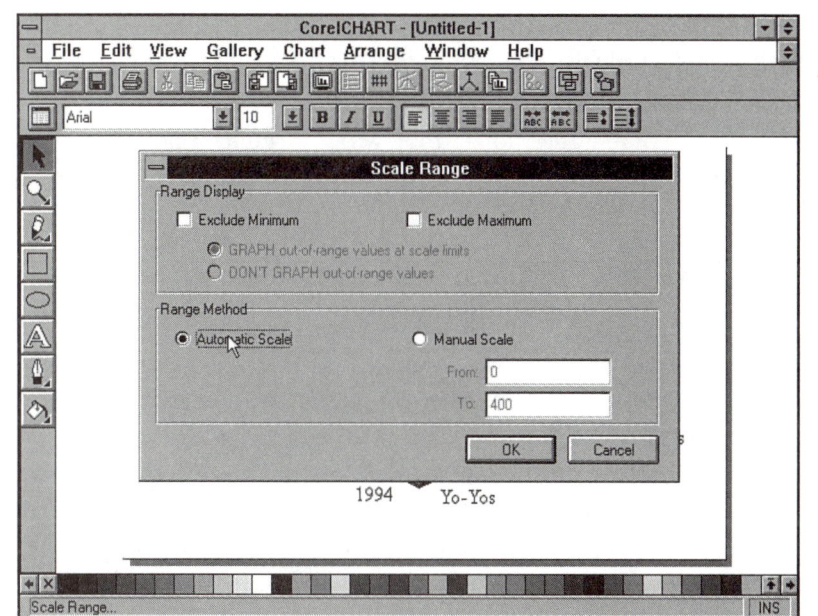

Figure 12.16

Define your scale range, then let CorelCHART assign Z2 axis markers automatically.

Changing Your View of Your Chart

CorelCHART provides a lot of preset angles of view for your work. Very similar in function to CorelDRAW's Extrude Roll-Up, you can use the 3D Roll-Up (by clicking on its button on the Ribbon Bar) to display the controls for rotating, flipping, and generally modifying your view of the entire chart.

I recommend against experimenting with the 3D Roll-Up, however, if you have a paying assignment due by the end of the day. Whenever you have performed manual editing of a chart, as you have done in this chapter, data gets mixed up and can fall outside the page when you play with the 3D Roll-Up features. I do recommend experimenting with the Roll-Up and a chart you don't care much about in your own free time.

There's an automatic means to change your viewing perspective in CorelCHART. It only involves clicking a menu item, and deciding on a presentation view. In this next section, you'll see how to create several different-looking charts from a singular set of data. This trick will come in handy when you want to keep old statistics appearing fresh. Here's how:

1. Choose **C**hart, then select Preset Viewing Angles. You don't have to have anything selected with the Pick tool. This menu command applies an effect to the entire chart.

2. You have a wealth of menu options for viewing the chart. Click on California Special, and look at the preview box on the fly-out menu, as shown in figure 12.17.

Figure 12.17
You can preview a viewing angle before applying it.

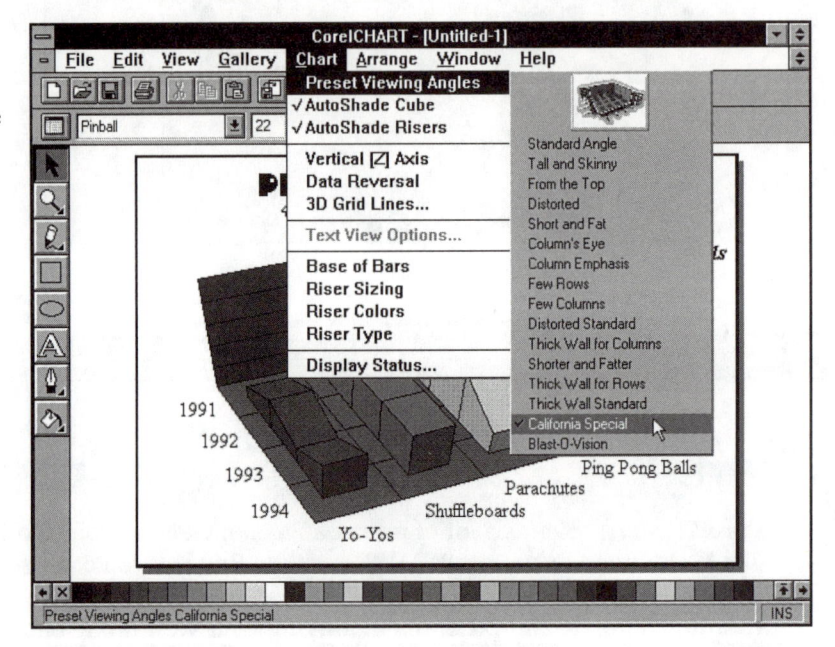

3. California Special is sort of an overhead, wide-angle view of your chart. It's handsome and dynamic, but also distorts the view of this particular data, ruining the purpose of a chart, which (most of the time) is meant to clarify a boggling amount of numerical statistics. Choose **C**hart, then Preset Viewing Angles again, and select Standard angle. Your chart appears none the worse for wear from this trip to the West coast.

Play with this option a little in your spare time. It's a handy, safe feature to use when you want a different-looking chart, but don't want manually customized chart work changed too much.

Changing Your View of Your Chart

Tip

You can also change the color of the risers, the blocks of data, or any other chart component. Simply select it, and choose another fill from the color palette or the Fill tool fly-out menu.

I advise against choosing a texture fill, however, because these fractal designs are quite memory-intensive and can crash you out of Windows if the area you intend to fill with texture is too large.

Also, you can apply an outline to chart elements by using the Outline tool on a selected object. This can sometimes help readability if your grids, for example, are dark against a dark riser.

Saving Your Custom Chart

In figure 12.18, you have a finished chart. No fancy California Special viewing angle, but at least you know how to build one and can now apply an artist's touch to CorelCHART's default options.

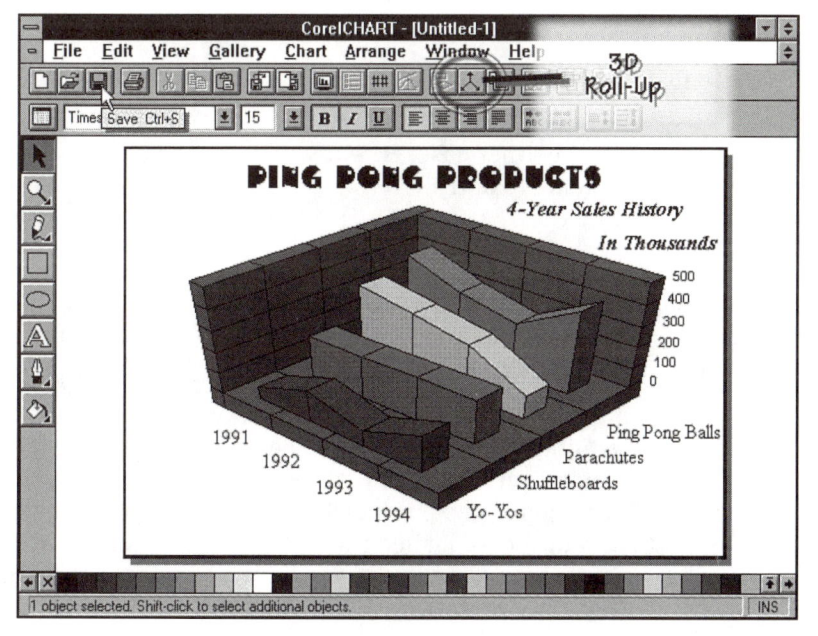

Figure 12.18

Ping Pong Products' sales clearly have their ups and downs (except their parachutes).

Let's save your work, because it will become an element in a CorelSHOW! presentation (right after you learn how to create an animated OLE object in the next section).

Choose **F**ile, **S**ave (or click on the Save button on the Ribbon Bar), select a drive and directory on your hard disk, and name the document PINGPONG.CCH in the **F**ile Name field. Click on OK, and exit CorelCHART (File, Exit, or simply press Alt+F4).

Making an Animation Object

We're moving to CorelMOVE in this section to explore some of the wonderful animation capabilities you can use with your PC and one of Corel's other modules.

The assignment here is to create an element that'll intrigue the shareholders at a meeting within a presentation. You already have a splendid sales chart; now, try animating the company's logo.

There are two considerations you should think about before working in CorelMOVE:

- Do you want to make an animated object in another module, such as CorelDRAW, or
- Do you have a piece of artwork already prepared that you'd like to animate?

The basic steps are the same in either case, except you'll want to choose a different option when you decide to add an Actor.

What's an Actor?

CorelMOVE defines an Actor as an object; a MOVE object is a collection of cells that may contain changes in the progression from cell to cell, creating the illusion of movement when CorelMOVE displays the Actor.

It's important to understand that an Actor object is an entity unto itself; all the elements that make the Actor run across the screen and then wipe his brow after the run are contained within the cells that make the Actor object. If you want to show an Actor moving geographically on the screen, or simply change its expression, this is all accomplished through the use of cells.

Choosing How You Create the Actor

To begin with, you should design a logo for the Ping Pong Products company consisting of several elements you want to animate. If you'd care to flip ahead to figure 12.20 to get a glimpse of a good design for this assignment, it's okay. (You're not cheating!)

Regardless of what program (CorelDRAW, CorelPHOTO-PAINT, or others) you use to make a logo, we're going to show you how to edit the logo into an animated object in this chapter. CorelMOVE will convert a still, single picture into a bitmap format, and offer you bitmap editing tools with which you animate the design elements. In the example in this chapter, I used CorelDRAW to make a logo, then exported it to my working directory on my hard disk, D:\MY_STUFF, as a PCX format image. Take a moment or two to design something cool, make it no larger than about two by three inches or so, and export the image as a BMP or PCX image. Take your time and design something you really like—books amuse themselves while you do other things.

Stop

Although you have the option of creating an animation in the other Corel workspaces (like CorelDRAW), I recommend that you first create a still image, import it, convert it to CorelMOVE format, and then edit it.

Corel uses OLE2 as a dynamic link to other programs. If you're not familiar with OLE2 properties, you may want to check out *Inside Windows*, or *Windows for Non-Nerds*, by New Riders Publishing, before using OLE2.

OLE2 actually calls another application from the one you're working in, and this sometimes causes a system instability due to memory allocation problems. *CorelDRAW! 5 for Beginners* is a "goal-oriented" book, and the author prefers that crashing out of Windows be excluded as one of your goals!

Open CorelMOVE now by double-clicking on the icon in the Program Manager group, and begin your career as a mini-Disney! Complete the following steps:

1. You need to create a New File before you can work in CorelMOVE's design space, so click on the New button on the Ribbon Bar (or choose File, New, or press Ctrl+N). This section's example will be called PINGPONG.CMV.

Chapter 12: The Many Hats of CorelDRAW

2. The frame you see on-screen is where you can place Actors or background objects, or even embed Windows WAV files. Since this is a beginner's book, we'll concentrate on the most important feature in MOVE, which is how to animate an Actor. To add one to the workspace, click on the Place Actor icon on the Toolbox (hint: it's the theatrical-looking character with the tophat).

3. In figure 12.19, you see the New Actor dialog box. As I recommended earlier, you should choose to create an Actor from a file. Click on the Create from File radio button, and you'll get a File entry field with a Browse button next to it. The Browse feature is great, because it's easy to forget the exact directory where you left an image. Pick the drive and directory where you created a Ping Pong Products logo, and click on OK to return to the New Actor dialog box.

Figure 12.19
You can create an Actor from a design you've previously saved.

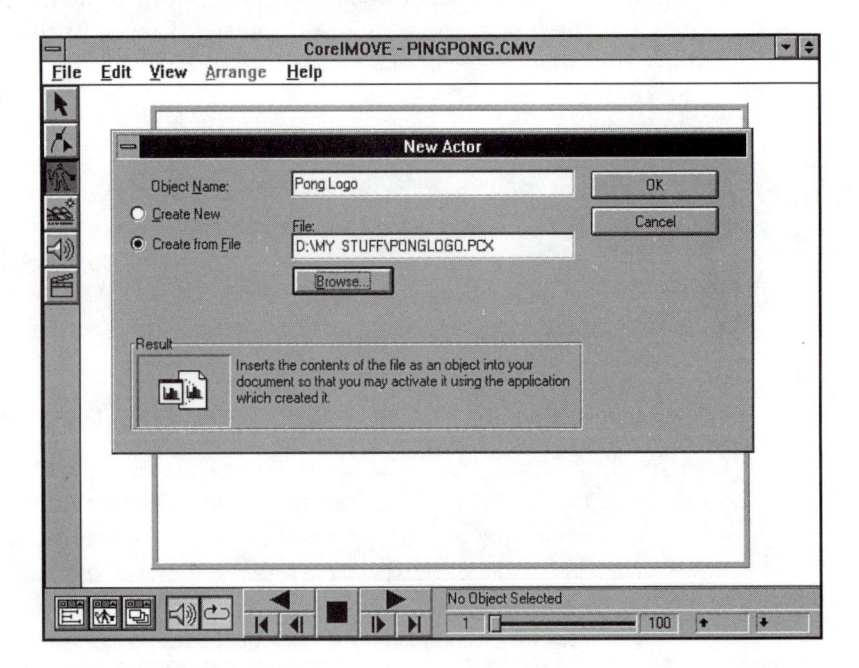

Tip

If you click on the Create New radio button in the New Actor box, you'll have a choice of many OLE-aware programs in which you can design. As mentioned earlier, CorelDRAW and other programs will feature the controls you need for applying cells to a design to make an Actor object. These controls will not appear if you launch

Making an Animation Object

CorelDRAW in a regular DRAW session, for example, but only when OLE is active.

Play it safe, go easy on your wits, and if you really must choose <u>C</u>reate New, choose CorelMOVE as the application from the <u>C</u>reate New host list. This way, OLE2 is not activated.

4. Click on OK; in the Import Image options box, you have some decisions to make about how this future Actor should be displayed in MOVE. In this chapter's example, the Ping Pong Products logo is colored type against white, but I don't want the white space around the logo to be represented by a color—instead, I want it transparent. If your design features white as a color, choose the None radio button. But if you want white to be transparent, click on the White radio button. Make sure the Perform high-quality dithering option is checked, and click on OK.

5. As you can see in figure 12.20, the Ping Pong Products logo can be positioned anywhere in MOVE's window using the Pick tool. The white space around the PCX image is transparent, and you'll soon see how to make image areas move about within the selection area around the logo.

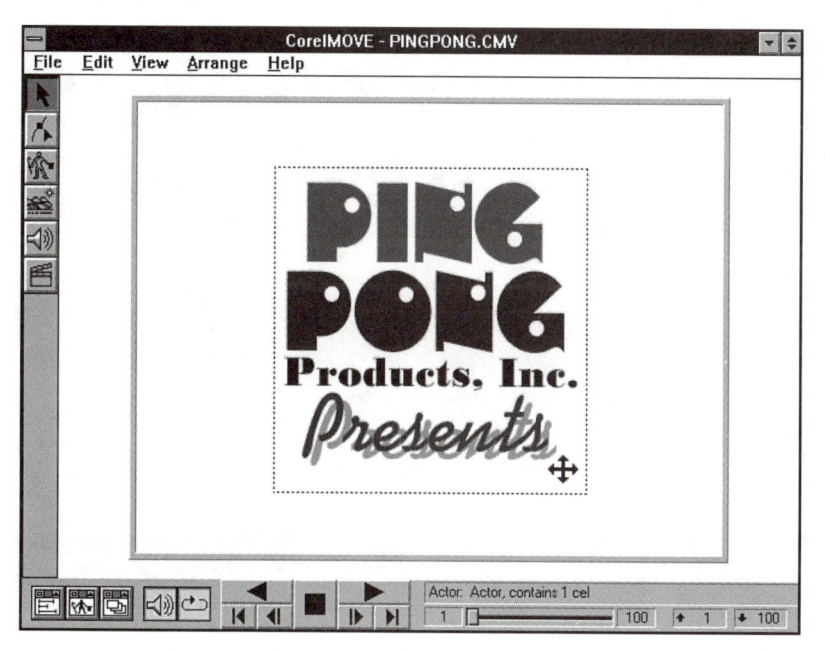

Figure 12.20

Use the Pick tool to position your image.

Chapter 12: The Many Hats of CorelDRAW

Converting and Animating a Graphic

At present, the imported PCX image consists of one cell, and is still considered to be a bitmap image. This presents two problems, which have two solutions. Double-clicking on an imported object will display the Actor Information dialog box, where you will convert the bitmap graphic to a native MOVE object; then you can edit the object to add motion to it.

Get your graphic ready to move by following these steps:

1. Double-click on the Ping Pong logo.

2. In figure 12.21, you can see the Actor Information dialog box. Name your object in the Object Name field. By default, CorelMOVE calls your first Actor *Actor*, then *Actor 2*, and then *Actor 3* as you assemble a cast of thousands. I suggest something classic like Bogart or Streisand, but Pong logos will suffice here.

3. Click on the Convert button. CorelMOVE will ask whether you're certain you want to do this. Click on Yes, and tell MOVE the author says it's okay.

Figure 12.21

Converting a graphic to the CorelMOVE format also gets rid of OLE2 linking.

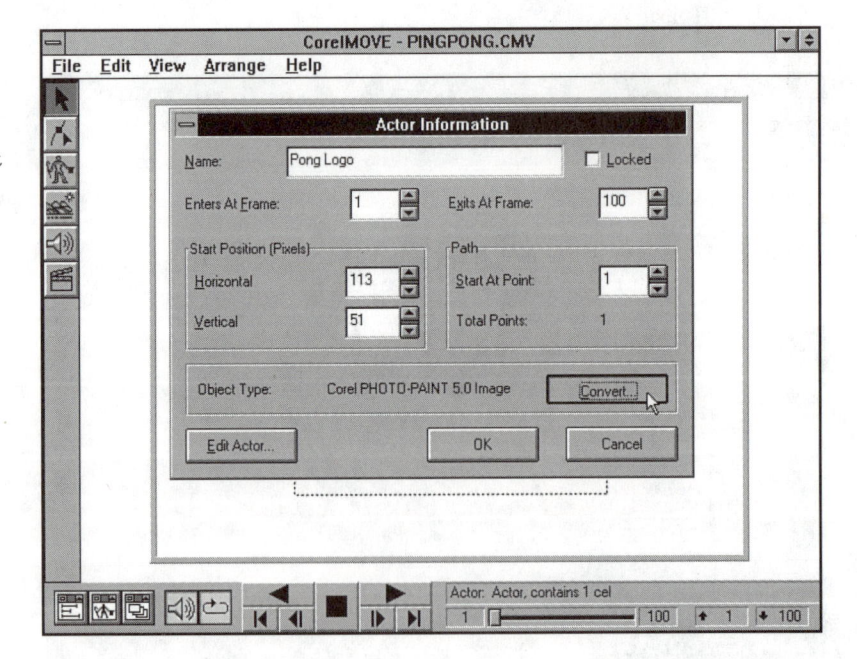

Converting and Animating a Graphic

Tip

The advantages of converting a bitmap, or even a CorelDRAW graphic, to the MOVE format are two-fold. First, you have most all of the editing tools you'll need in CorelMOVE to animate a still image, and won't require the application you used to design the object for your editing.

Second, you destroy an OLE2 link. This sounds like a bad idea, but it's really not. If you were to double-click on the imported design to edit it without converting it, CorelMOVE would call CorelPAINT (or CorelDRAW) to edit the object, and if Windows resources were low, you'd wind up with a black screen, not an editing session!

OLE2, quite simply, is a Windows function whose time is still yet to come.

4. Click on the **E**dit Actor button.

5. Press Ctrl+T (or choose **E**dit, **I**nsert Cels). This command is only available from within an editing window, and does not apply to Props; only Actors can have multiple cels.

6. As you can see in figure 12.22, you can add cels after cel 1, your converted graphic. Type **4** in the Number of Cels to Insert box (for an Actor consisting of 5 cels), and click on the **D**uplicate Contents check box; this will make every cel display your same logo (which you'll animate shortly). Click on OK.

7. Choose **F**ile, **A**pply Changes, then choose **F**ile, **C**lose (Ctrl+F4) to finish adding cels to your graphical object.

For some reason no one quite understands, changes (like adding cels) to an imported graphic must be applied, and then the Editing Window must be closed, before you can animate your object. Otherwise, any animation you create contains multiple copies of image areas wherever you move them!

In the next section, you'll edit the logo object to add motion to the cels you've added.

Figure 12.22
Your graphic is now an object that you can add animation cels to.

Adding a Cycle to an Actor

The term cycle refers to a series of animation cels that suggest repetitive motion; running, walking, even bouncing can be expressed in a cycle. The first cel of a cycle is also the last, and as the cels run (in this example from one to five), a cycled action should have a beginning, a middle, and an end that winds up at the beginning.

You'll create a simple cycle in the next steps; one that's bound to provoke a laugh from anxious Ping Pong Products shareholders before they see your CorelCHART of dismal sales. You'll make the Ping and Pong words in the logo actually "ping-pong" around! Here's how:

1. Place the Pick tool on the logo graphic, then press Ctrl and double-click on the graphic. This is an alternative (and shorter!) method of opening the Editing Window for an Actor.

2. Click on the cel slider at the bottom of the floating tools palette to move to cel 2 in the Actor.

3. Choose **O**ptions in the Editing Window, then Onion **S**kin. Onion skin is the digital equivalent of a technique used by traditional animators to review the previous cel in an animation sequence.

4. Choose **P**revious Cel. Now you'll be able to make changes to cel 2 and see how they make a transition from cel 1.

Adding a Cycle to an Actor

407

5. Watch your next move! By default, the Pencil tool is active on the tools palette! You want to click on the rectangle selection tool before proceeding with editing.

6. Marquee-select the word PONG, and move it to the right about 1/4". You'll see a faint image of cel 1 behind it.

7. Marquee-select the word PING, and move it up slightly about 1/4". You'll also see a duplicate PING exposed as an Onion Skin image from frame 1. Your editing on cel 2 of your Actor should look like figure 12.23.

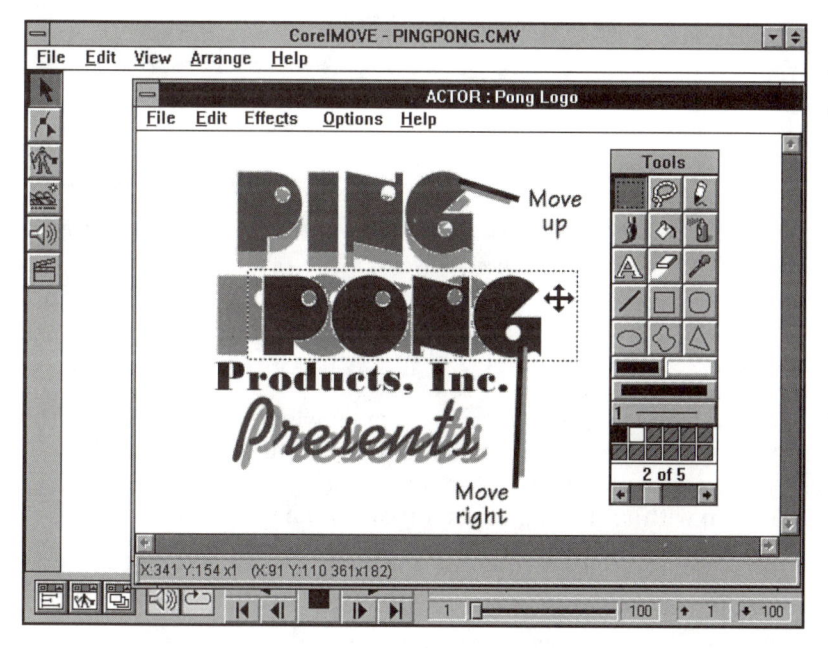

Figure 12.23
Your Actor "animates" between the design in cel 1 and cel 2.

8. Think about cel 3 for a moment. Since you created a move between cel 1 and cel 2, it's not really necessary to edit cel 3, which is a duplicate of 1. Cel 3 is a valid animation cel because things in it are different from cel 2, so leave it alone and scroll to cel 4 on the tools palette.

9. Select the PING image area with the rectangle selection tool in cel 4 and move it 1/4" to the left, then select PING and move it up 1/4", as shown in figure 12.24.

10. Cel 5, identical to cel 1, needs no editing. As far as this Actor's animation goes, your cycle is complete—when CorelMOVE animates the Actor, the "normal" positioning of the PING and PONG letters will remain on-screen a little more than they animate. Click on Edit, Apply Changes, and return to the MOVE workspace.

Figure 12.24
Moving the image areas in cel 4 will provide an overall "ping-pong" effect in the animation cycle.

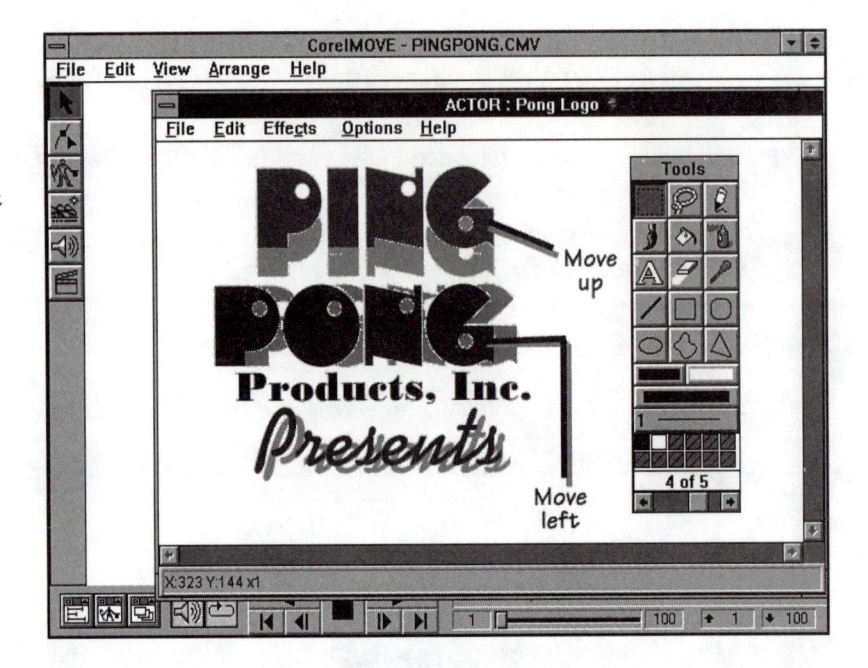

Playing Your CorelMOVE Movie

CorelMOVE has controls on the bottom of the main window that look exactly like VCR controls, and mostly behave like them. Since this is not a moving book (unless you wave it around a lot as you read it), you can now thrill to your first animation without having to refer to a screen figure.

The Play button is the top right arrow, and the square to the left of it is Stop.

1. Click on the Play button.
2. Click on the Stop button. Cool, huh?

Tip

The additional controls at the bottom of the VCR-like buttons are:

- The Step Frame Forward button (directly next to the Stop button). You can review individual movements of Actors by clicking once to advance your movie one animation frame at a time.

- The Fast Forward button (to the right of the Step Frame button). Clicking on this button sends you to the end of an animation sequence.

The buttons to the left of the Stop button are mirror opposites of the ones just described. Every button will perform the reverse of the forward buttons.

In figure 12.25, I've added a Bouncing Ball as a second Actor, using a PCX-imported graphic, then applying the same converting and editing changes you made earlier to your logo graphic.

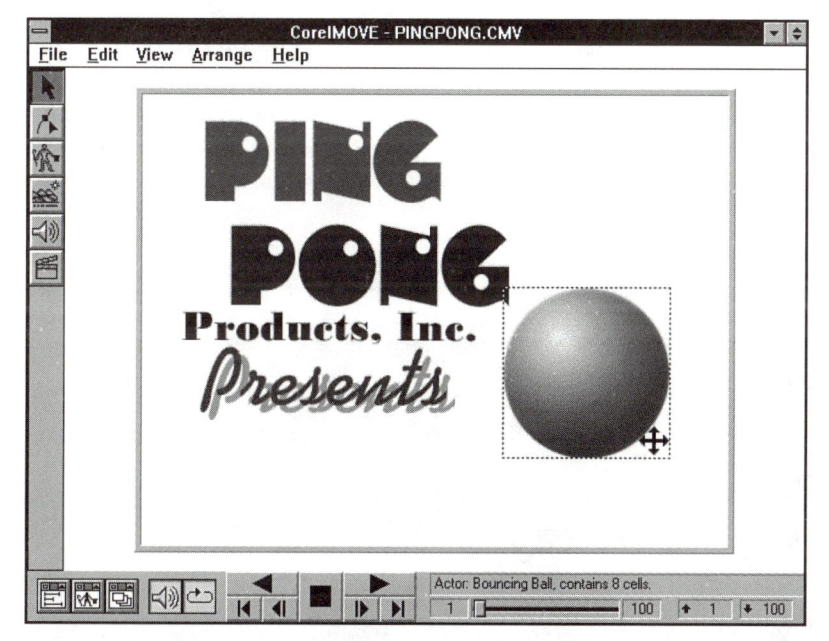

Figure 12.25

Actors can "play" to one another, and an Actor can consist of multiple designs.

Timing Is Everything with Actors

To the right of the CorelMOVE player controls is a time line slider. You can manually advance the slider by clicking and dragging it forward or backward to start an animation in the middle of sequences.

As you continue in your explorations with CorelMOVE, however, the default for animations of 100 steps may prove to produce larger-than-expected (or

Chapter 12: The Many Hats of CorelDRAW

desired) document sizes. You could clutter your entire hard drive with a huge re-creation of Snow White if you had the time and inclination!

Here's the point: you need to decide how large your CorelMOVE animation needs to be, and this section covers how to trim down this Ping Pong animation so it will play speedily and effortlessly. You'll be importing the Ping Pong animation to CorelSHOW as an object in the next section, and the "trimmer" the object it can be, the better it'll import and play within CorelSHOW.

To keep your animation to a manageable size, complete the following steps:

1. Press Ctrl+A (or choose Edit, Animation Info...).

2. In figure 12.26, you can see on the status line that the animation number of frames is set to 100. Let's get real for a moment; if the animated logo has less than 10 cels, the cycle can be completed in far less than 100. The default Speed for a CorelMOVE animation is 18 frames/second, so either click the elevator button down, or manually type 36 in the Number Of Frames field. This gives you two seconds of ping-ponging logo.

Figure 12.26

Decide how many frames per second, and how many seconds long, you want your animation.

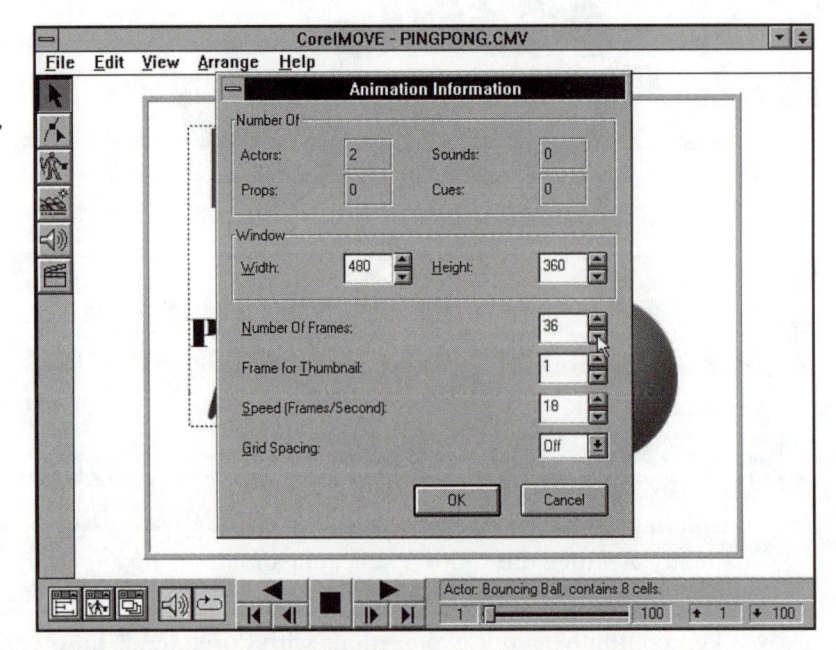

3. Click on OK. You'll notice the animation slider now only reads 0 through 36 frames, and if you press the Play button, you won't notice any difference in animation quality.

Changing a Timeline

You have an additional option in CorelMOVE as to when an Actor will appear in an animation sequence. CorelMOVE's Timeline option can make an Actor exit prematurely from a sequence, or pop in and out like an annoying neighbor on a sitcom!

If you have two Actors "on stage" now, here's how to make one of them have a splashy entrance; follow these steps:

1. Click on the Timeline menu on the bottom left of the workspace.

2. Click on an Actor's name, then click on the right arrow button toward the top right of the menu to expand the timeline feature.

3. As you can see in figure 12.27, by clicking and dragging on the end of an Actor's timeline, you control at which frame the Actor enters the animation. In this example, the Bouncing Ball Actor won't appear until the 10th frame, roughly a third of the way through the animation's cycle.

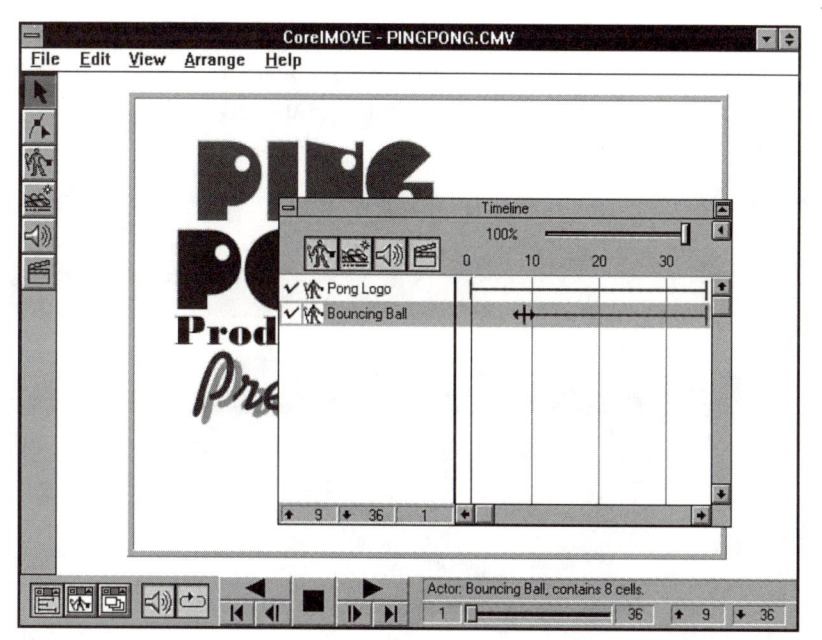

Figure 12.27

Adjust an individual Actor's timeline to make them appear and disappear at different moments.

4. Click on OK, and choose File, Save before exiting the CorelMOVE workspace. You now have a completed animation sequence and graph to add to a fantastic presentation!

The Greatest (Slide)Show on Earth

Slide show presentations can get a little dry sometimes—face it, physical 35mm slides are pretty static. But when you talk about slide shows on a PC display, you're talking a whole different realm of plastic media that you can shape using your imagination. Um, with a little help from CorelSHOW.

To conclude your trek through the other Corel graphics modules, you'll create a slide presentation to be run on-screen. The number of slides will be small, but you'll learn the secrets for packing an action-filled, attention-getting wallop into less than a megabyte of disk space.

Go ahead and do these steps:

1. Double-click on the CorelSHOW icon in the Corel group in Program Manager.

2. CorelSHOW needs either a New File or an existing one to be open before it offers any tools in the workspace. Let's start with a new file. Either click the New button on CorelSHOW's Ribbon Bar, or press Ctrl+N (File, New).

3. You're presented with some options in the New Presentation dialog box. You may want to explore the different page formats at a later date, but for now, accept the defaults, with **5** in the Start with...Slides field. Click on OK, as shown in figure 12.28.

Figure 12.28
Set your slide show options in the New Presentation dialog box.

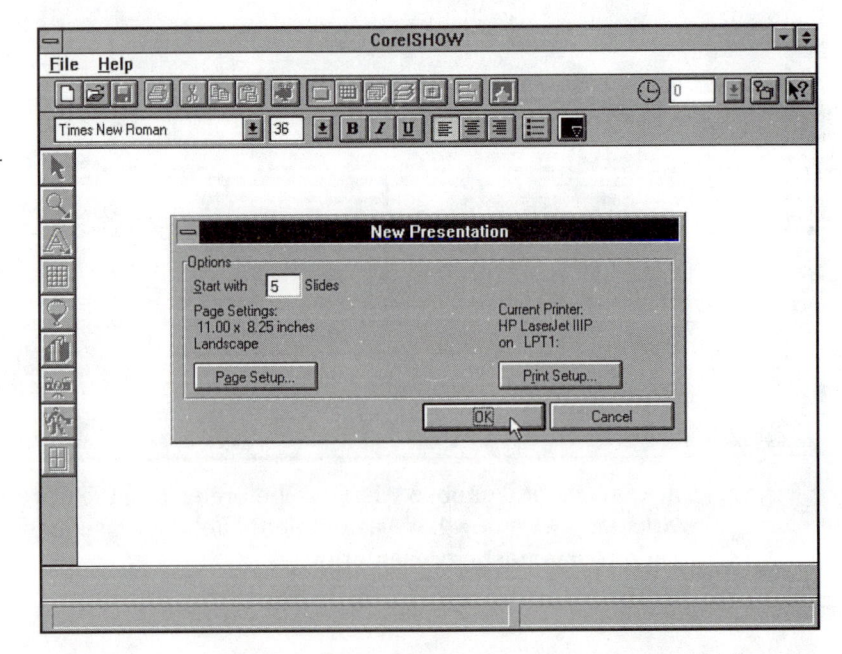

The Greatest (Slide)Show on Earth

4. You have a lot of your work cut out for you here, in that two of the five slides are already created! Click on Insert, then Animation (or press Ctrl+A).

5. As mentioned earlier, a CorelMOVE, *.CMV animation can be parceled out as an object for use in CorelSHOW. Choose CorelMOVE Animation, *.CMV from the List Files of Type drop-down box, then choose the drive and directory your animation's in. As shown in figure 12.29, you can preview a movie before importing it.

Figure 12.29
Choose a type of animation you want to insert.

6. Click on OK.

7. Converting a copy of your PINGPONG.CMV animation is a processor-intensive process. In other words, wait a moment while CorelSHOW carries out the command.

Tip

While you're waiting, here's another reinforcer concerning OLE2. Experiment at your own risk when Creating a New Object. This option in the Insert Object dialog box will whisk you to another Corel program while CorelSHOW is still running. My best advice on the topic of having two applications running on an average 386

continues

Chapter 12: The Many Hats of CorelDRAW

continued

or 486 with less than 8MB of RAM is to create a design prior to launching CorelSHOW, then insert an object based on this existing file.

Because CorelSHOW has no VCR-like controls in its workspace, you cannot run the animation you inserted as an object—don't worry about this. When you run your completed show, CorelSHOW will handle the programming calls to launch the animated sequence from within the format of your show.

8. In figure 12.30, the animation appears on the first of five slides in your CorelSHOW. If you want the animation to play for 10 seconds non-stop, click on the timing drop-down box and choose the duration of slide 1 with the animation, or enter a time of your choice directly in the field.

Figure 12.30
Enter the amount of time you want your animation on-screen.

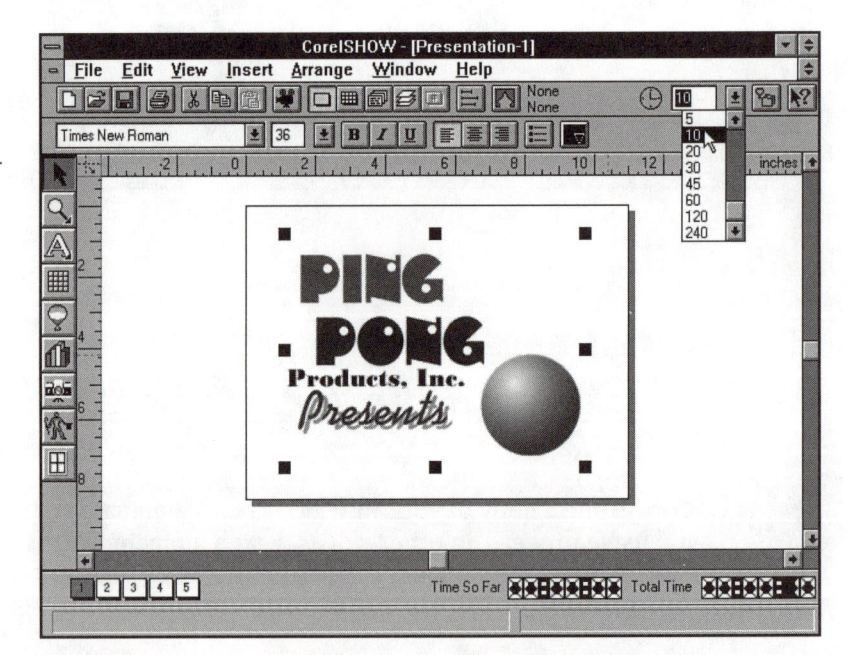

Tip

Check out the options in the Insert Animation dialog box if you want your inserted animation to appear full-screen or run constantly, or if you want to pause the animation with a keystroke.

Adding a CorelCHART to a Show

Basically, you can Insert the Ping Pong Products' CorelCHART in your CorelSHOW the same way as you did the MOVE animation, except the chart is treated like an object, not an animation.

Here's how to advance your slide show to make way for the chart for slide 2:

1. Click on the number 2 Slide selection button in the lower left of the screen.

2. Press Ctrl+B (or choose Insert, Object).

3. This step should be familiar because of your experience with creating an object from a pre-existing file in CorelMOVE: click on the Create from File radio button, then choose Browse, as shown in figure 12.31. If you want a chart inserted that will update in SHOW every time you edit the original in CorelCHART, press the Link button. (Suggestion? Don't. It's an OLE2 link.)

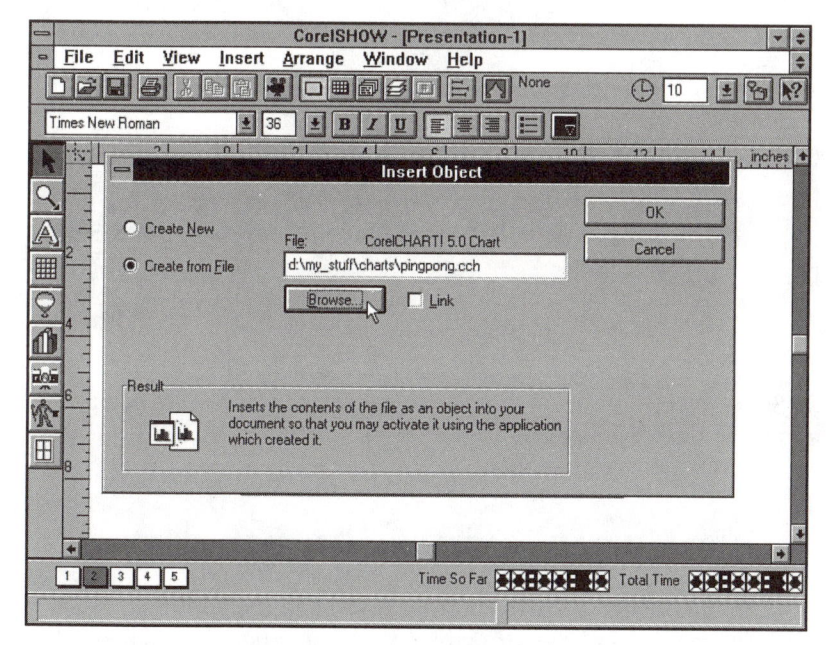

Figure 12.31
If you've memorized your chart's name, directory, and drive, you can type it in here and skip the Browse step.

4. Choose the drive and directory where your PINGPONG.CCH file is stored, select the file, and press OK.

Chapter 12: The Many Hats of CorelDRAW

5. Click on OK in the Insert Object dialog box to return to the CorelSHOW workspace.

6. Unlike an animation, a chart can be resized on the workspace of SHOW to fill the entire page. Check out figure 12.32. Pressing F4 (**A**rrange, Fit Object to **S**lide) ensures that the chart will display in the show as large as possible.

Figure 12.32

You can scale an object to perfectly fit on a CorelSHOW slide by selecting the object and pressing F4.

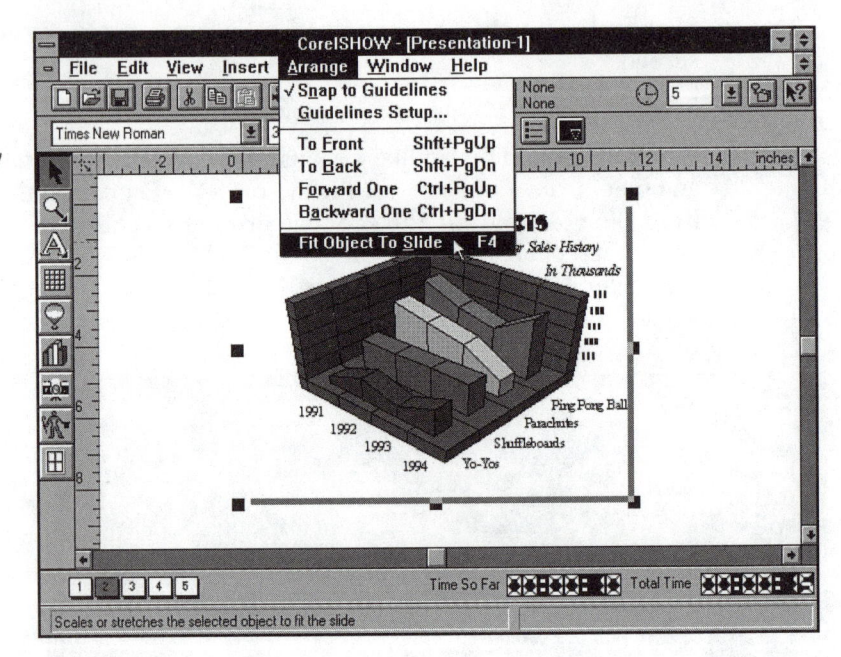

7. Give the chart five seconds of show time. The sales figures are a little embarrassing.

8. Click on Slide selection button 3 in the lower left of the workspace to advance to the next, blank slide.

Adding a Pre-Drawn Background

The first rule of an effective slide presentation is to keep the audience awake. The second rule is to strive for some consistency between slides. CorelSHOW has pre-made background designs that you can add, and they're pretty sharp looking. Let's pretend the rest of this presentation (the other three slides) is only boring text. Here's how to keep the audience's attention on the message on these slides: add a common, yet elegant background.

Adding a Pre-Drawn Background

Just follow these steps:

1. Click on the Background Library Tool on SHOW's Toolbox. (It's the one that looks like a mesh screen, beneath the Text tool.)

2. Choose SAMPLE.SHB from the directories list, and click on OK.

3. As you can see in figure 12.33, the Background selections are diverse, and are suitable for a range of business presentation needs. Pick the one with the neon stripes by clicking on it, then click the Done button. The Library will disappear, and you'll now have the same background on every slide in the presentation.

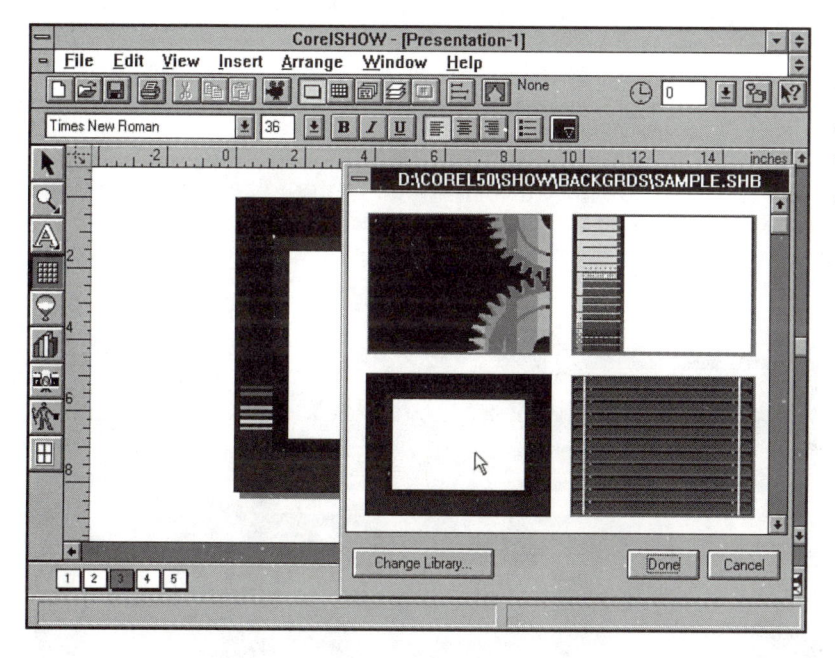

Figure 12.33
Choose a background with some white space so you can add text to it.

Adding/Coloring a Text Selection

Hey, you gotta love this company: their yo-yo sales go up and down, their parachute sales are plummeting, but their sale of ping pong balls is bouncing back.

Let's make a splashy billboard in frame three to drive the point home with oversized text:

Chapter 12: The Many Hats of CorelDRAW

1. Like in CorelCHART, you need to enter text on the workspace, highlight it, and then change the font and size. Choose the Text tool, make an insertion point by clicking on the page, and type **Bouncing Back** <Enter> **this Year.**

2. Highlight the text with the Text tool, then choose a bold, condensed font (like Egyptienne in this example), and choose 72 points. If you had a longer sentence, you'd want to decrease the point size of the text.

Note

Condensed typefaces can be used at a greater point size than regular ones, because you can get more words per line.

3. With the Type still highlighted, click on the centered paragraph button, then the color button on the Text Ribbon Bar. Choose a color for the text that complements the background. In figure 12.34, a deep purple complements the bright magentas of the background.

Figure 12.34
Choose a font, the size, its justification, and its color from the Text Ribbon Bar.

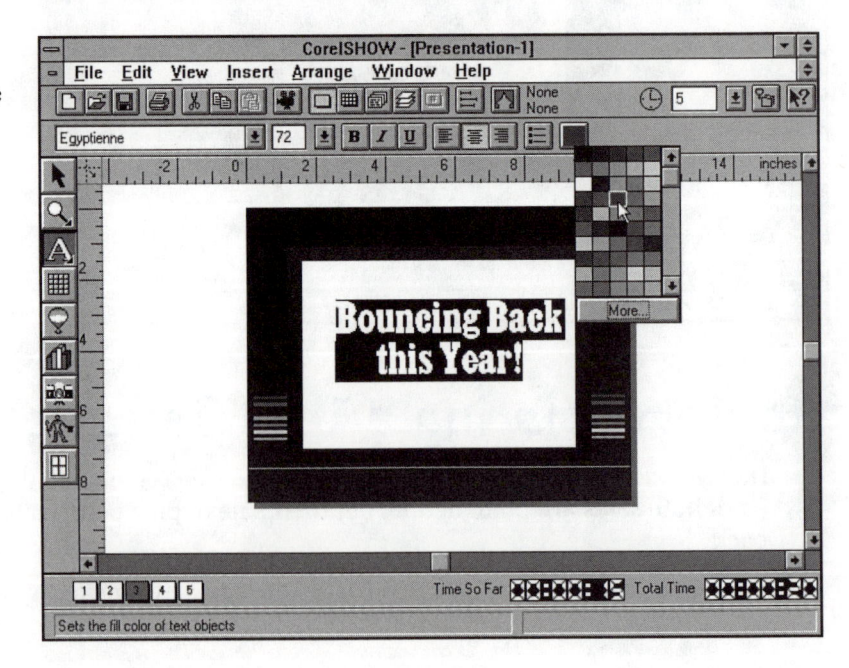

Adding Bullets to Lists

Lists are a presentation staple. They usually flash by too quickly; that's why bulleted lists were invented. Bullets lead the viewer's eye to specific points, and here's how to add them to slide four in the presentation:

1. Select five seconds for slide three, and click on Slide selection button number 4.

2. Type **New Products!** <Enter> **Quality Assurance** <Enter> **Program** <Enter>, then **All Lawsuits** <Enter> **Quietly Settled!** (sneak a peek at figure 12.36 to see how the text is laid out).

3. 72 points is too large for the text to fit into the window of the background, so scale the text by click+dragging with the Pick tool on a corner selection handle. When the font size box reads about 40 points for your current selection, you've scaled the text sufficiently.

4. Click on the Bulleted list button on the Text Ribbon Bar. The Bullets dialog box will pop up over your workspace.

5. By default, common Bullets (a Corel TrueType font) will appear for your bullet selection. You don't have to use this symbol set; you can choose from any available font from the drop-down list box. Click on a symbol character.

6. I like big bullets; if you do too, enter 100 in the size field.

7. Pick a color for the bullet. You can select text and the bullet color independently; as you can see in figure 12.35, a large (cranberry-colored) diamond will shortly stud the list of Ping Pong claims.

8. Click on OK, and you now have a beautifully designed slide in figure 12.36 that people hopefully will appreciate for its construction rather than its verbiage!

9. Finish slide four by giving it a five-second timing, click on Slide selection button 5 in the lower left of the screen, and complete the show with a snappy slogan like "You can't go wrong with Pong."

Chapter 12: The Many Hats of CorelDRAW

Figure 12.35
Customize a bulleted list through the Bullets dialog box.

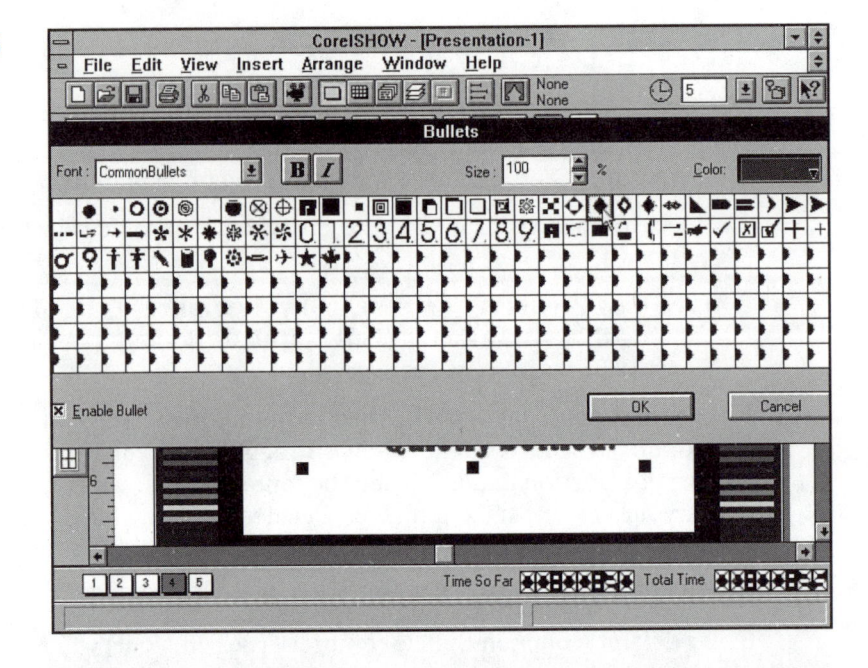

Figure 12.36
Bullets can be specified independently of any text you add with the Text tool.

Removing the Background from Frames

By default, CorelSHOW adds a background to every slide in a presentation. But the clever animation on slide one doesn't need a background. In fact, attention may be drawn from the animation. The solution is to selectively remove the background attribute from slide one. Here's how:

1. Click on the Slide selection button 1 icon in the lower left of the screen to move to the slide one view.

2. Right-mouse click over the background on slide one with the Pick tool. This displays a pop-up menu for the object.

3. Choose BackGround, and select Omit, as shown in figure 12.37. This will remove the background only for the active slide (slide one).

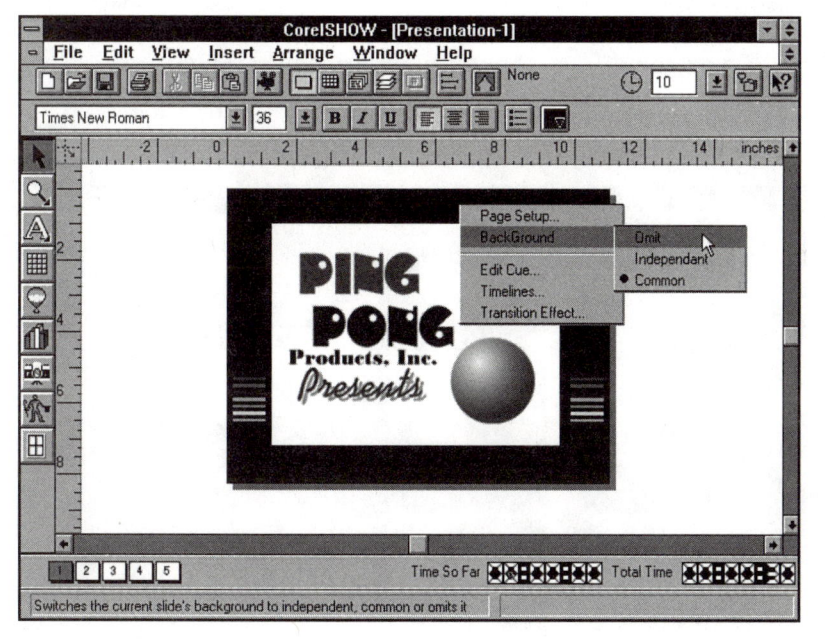

Figure 12.37

Right-mouse click over selections to display pop-up menu options.

Sorting This Whole Show Out

You've come a long way, and you should be proud of your work. There are a million and one details you've had to skim over in the CHART, MOVE, and SHOW modules, but you've actually created a multimedia presentation in less time than it takes Hollywood to build a dinosaur!

You finally need to cover the finishing presentation touches, the first being how your slides are arranged. Suppose your Ping Pong client waffles on the order of the slides; they'd like slide three about bouncing back before the chart.

No problem. Follow these steps:

1. Click on the Slide Sorter view from any slide view of your presentation. The button's on the Ribbon Bar, and sports a tiny drawing of a stack of papers.

2. As you can see in figure 12.38, the Slide Sorter view simultaneously displays all your slides as thumbnail pictures. If you had 100 slides instead of 5, you could access these thumbnails by scrolling down. Click on slide two and drag it to slide three's position, then release the cursor.

Figure 12.38

Rearrange your slides by clicking and dragging them to their new positions.

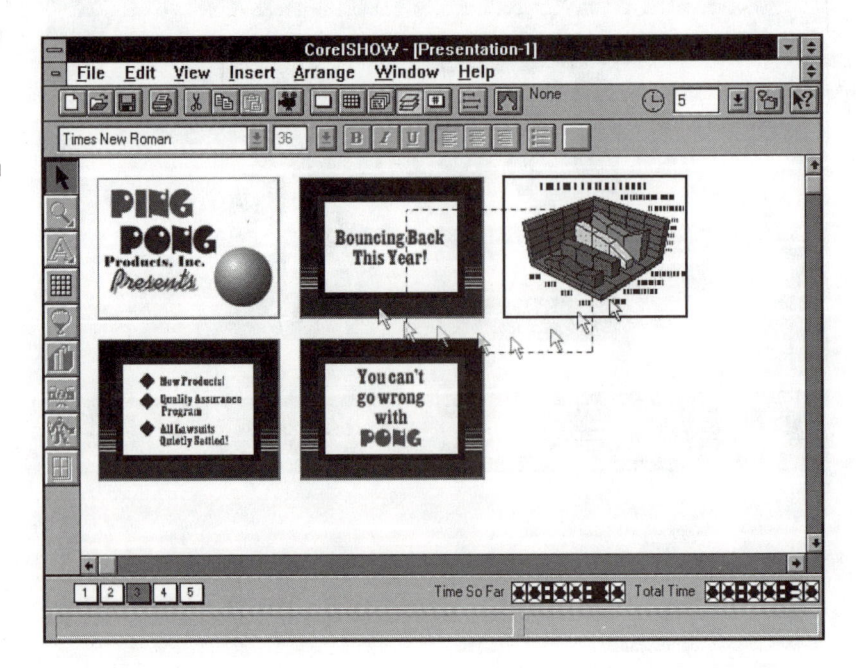

3. Click to the Presentation view by clicking on the page button on the Ribbon Bar (the icon to the right of the movie camera). Your slides are in order now.

Did Someone say "Transition Effects?"

Besides being able to include different electronic media in a PC slide show, CorelSHOW also can add fancy effects as one slide makes a transition to another. Adding them is easy; the hard part is deciding which ones to use. Or over-use!

Try these steps:

1. Click on the Slide Selection button for slide one, then click on the curtain button on the Ribbon Bar. This is the Slide/Frame Transition button.

2. In the Transition Effects dialog box, you can choose the effect applied to a slide as it enters the show and when it exits the show. In figure 12.39, the famous Horizontal Blind (HorizBlind) effect is being chosen for the animation slide one. You can get a preview of the effect (applied to Corel's balloon, not your slide), by clicking on the Preview button.

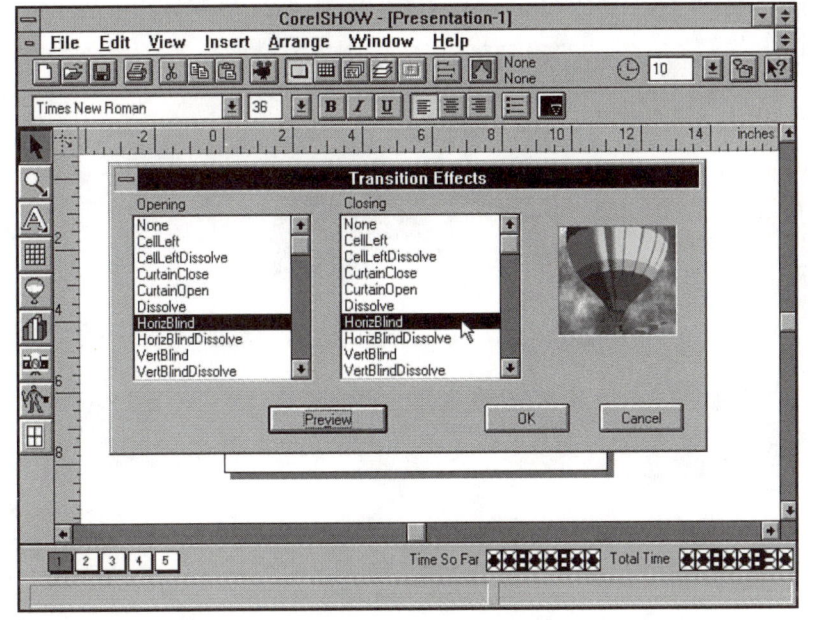

Figure 12.39

Choose an opening and closing transition effect from the lists in the Transition Effects dialog box.

Chapter 12: The Many Hats of CorelDRAW

3. You'll notice that you can still access the Slide Selection buttons with the Transition Effects dialog box open, so click on slide two, choose an effect, click on slide three, and so on.

4. When you have an effect (or no effect at all by choosing None), click on OK.

5. Save your file (Ctrl+S), and name it PINGPONG.SHW.

6. Take a deep breath and get ready to view your first Corel 5 Multi-Media Extravaganza!

Playing Your CorelSHOW

It's as simple as clicking on the Screen Show button, the movie camera icon on the Ribbon Bar. You don't need the steps here; this isn't an exercise, it's watching the big payoff for all the work you've done, and all you've learned in this chapter. Just press the Screen Show button as shown in figure 12.40, and click on OK when CorelSHOW asks you whether you want to start the show.

Figure 12.40

Don't ever forget where this button is!

It will take CorelSHOW a moment or two to load the various components you've added to the slides. CorelSHOWs are smaller in file size than you'd imagine; elements are sometimes linked (like the animation "engine") instead of being placed within the document.

Playing your show on someone else's PC requires that you copy the CORELPLR.EXE file from the COREL50\PROGRAMS directory, in addition to the PINGPONG.SHW file. If you're not totally confident about how to copy what you need to move your SHOW, ask someone, or consult the Corel documentation that came with the software. You are expressly forbidden to copy other program files to someone else's PC, however. The CORELPLR.EXE file is okay (Corel Corporation has granted you permission with your CorelDRAW license), but fonts, CorelDRAW, the clip art, or any other goodies that are the intellectual property of Corel Corporation are off-limits. That's like copying commercial videotapes.

Summary

If you made it through this chapter in one sitting, you may want to get up and stretch, but you may also want to get back to the real star of the Corel bundle, CorelDRAW. By now, you've noticed that there are significantly fewer pages under your right thumb than your left, a sure sign you've come to the last chapter.

"*Very* Special CorelDRAW Effects" is an unusual "how-to" chapter. I'm not going to pull any punches with the beginner because if you've read the other chapters and done the assignments, you're not a beginner anymore.

See how special a CorelDRAW effect becomes when you add your own ingenuity to it in Chapter 13.

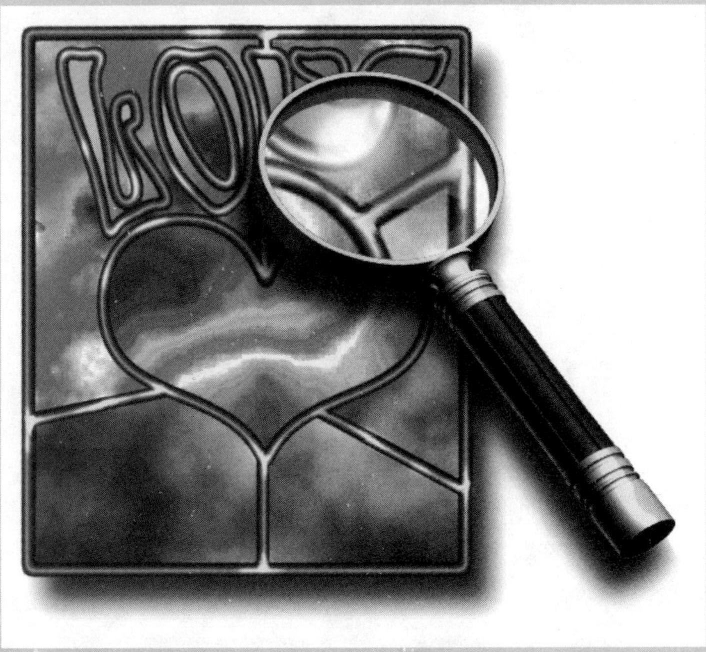

CHAPTER 13

Very Special CorelDRAW Effects

We've held off introducing you to some of the razzle-dazzle effects that you can create in CorelDRAW, and instead simply concentrated on the basics. The steps and techniques you've discovered through the rest of the chapters are far more important to your growth as a computer graphics designer than a flashy effect or two. But now that you can navigate the menus and Roll-Ups, you should let your own imagination and creativity sing a little.

Making a really slick effect for its own sake won't enhance your design skills, but knowing how and when to take advantage of Corel's special effects is important. In this chapter, you'll create some *very* special effects by giving Corel's automated functions a direction and a purpose. You'll come to realize that computer art that *really* wows an audience begins with your own concept.

In this chapter, you will:

- Create a stained-glass design
- Make and save your own fractal textures
- Take command of Fountain Fills and create your own
- Discover a technique for making neon, brass, and other natural materials
- Fill a shape with a *property*, not a color

Creating a Stained Glass Effect

The purpose of this chapter is to begin your own, personal "idea book;" you've learned a wealth of techniques throughout these chapters, and now's the time to show what a little applied skill is good for!

Using many of the methods covered in previous chapters, and a few new ones, you're going to build a realistic-looking stained glass piece. That's the assignment for part one of this two-part adventure in special effects. Part two covers one of Corel's amazing Lens effects.

The theme for part one's stained glass design is "Love;" it's a recurring theme found in great art and literature for untold centuries. In real life, stained glass designs begin with a *cartoon*, a sketch of the locations of the glass, and *caming* (the lead, brass, or other metal that holds the glass in place). Virtual stained glass is no different than genuine Tiffany-inspired art (except it's less fragile), so your first step is to create a cartoon. The examples that follow apply to a specific creation, but you should definitely design something of your *own*, and apply the techniques to it.

1. Keep the stained glass simple in design. The simplest way to start a design is by selecting a category from the Symbols Roll-Up (click on the star symbol on the Ribbon Bar), and then clicking and dragging a shape into the Drawing Window. From the Zoom tool fly-out menu, click on the Zoom to Selected tool. In figure 13.1, a heart shape found in Zapf Dingbats is an appropriate beginning point. The default symbol size 2"× 2" is used in this example.

2. Choose the Rectangle tool and click+drag a rectangle around the shape you added from the Symbols Roll-Up. This is the frame for your stained glass piece. A rectangle 2.5" wide × 3.5" tall works well with the heart.

3. Press the spacebar to get the Pick tool, and reposition the rectangle so it is centered around the symbol shape.

Creating a Stained Glass Effect

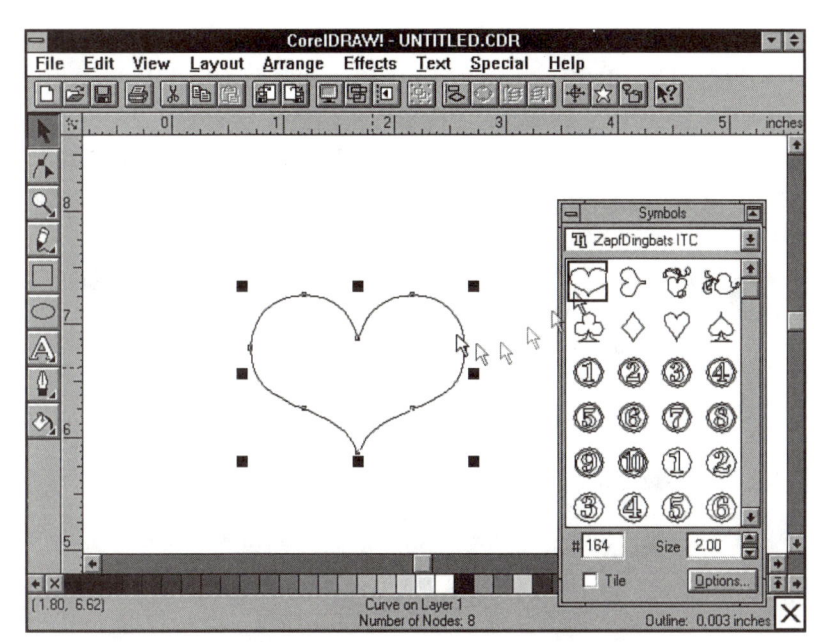

Figure 13.1

Use a simple shape from the Symbols Roll-Up as part of the stained glass design.

Making Frames for the Stained Glass Elements

To create the stained glass piece, you'll need to add several elements to the basic shapes (the rectangle and the heart) that you've designed. The most important elements you'll add are a series of paths within the rectangular frame. These closed path shapes will hold the pieces of the virtual stained glass. The Snap To **O**bjects command makes it easy to create paths that precisely line up with the border of the rectangle. In the next series of steps, you'll use the Snap To **O**bjects command and the Freehand tool to design the closed shapes that will hold fractal textures that represent the stained glass.

1. Choose **L**ayout, then Snap To **O**bjects. All paths, including complex geometry shapes like rectangles and ellipses, have a number of snap to points on them, usually at their nodes (see Chapter 4 for more details).

2. Choose the Freehand tool, click in the center of the rectangle, and drag the cursor toward the left side of the rectangle. You'll notice that your cursor is almost guided to a location on the rectangle. This is a snap to point.

Chapter 13: Very Special CorelDRAW Effects

3. Double-click to set a node on the path you're drawing with the Freehand tool, and move up on the side of the rectangle to the upper corners. Your cursor will be attracted to a cursor snap to point.

4. Double-click to set another node and begin another segment.

5. Drag a third line, and double-click somewhere along the top edge of the rectangle.

6. As you can see in figure 13.2, the polygon shape is about to be closed. It's not necessary to let Corel snap every one of the corners of your path to the rectangle shape, but the Snap To Objects command definitely helps you keep this shape. You'll fill this with stained glass aligned to the outer dimensions of the design.

Figure 13.2
Use the double-click method of drawing to create straight lines and nodes that make a closed path shape.

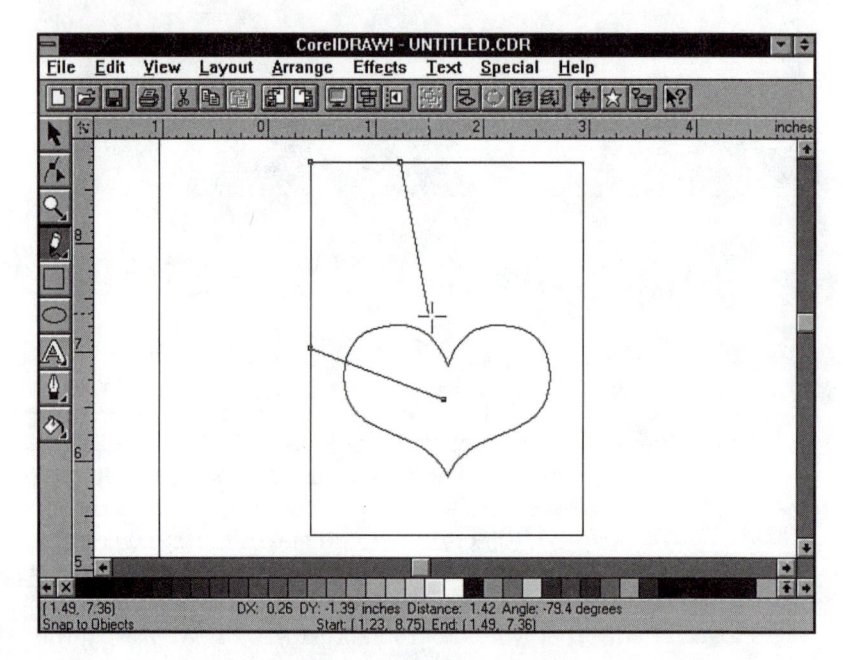

7. Click once where you began your path to close the polygon shape.

Closer Look

It's okay that the polygons you're creating violate the border of the shapes you may have placed from the Symbols Roll-Up inside the rectangle. The polygons are objects that can be placed in front of, or behind, symbol shapes. When you add fills to all the shapes, overlapping areas will be hidden.

Making Frames for the Stained Glass Elements

8. Repeat steps 3-7 to add more polygons to the inside of the rectangle. In the Snap To **O**bjects mode, it'll be easy to make every side that polygons share align precisely with one another.

9. Stop when you have about four or five polygons inside the rectangle.

10. **F**ile, **S**ave your work as LOVE.CDR.

11. Turn off the Snap To **O**bjects command in the **A**rrange menu.

Combining Shapes To Create a Subpath for Caming

All the polygon shapes, and the symbol shape, are used for two purposes. You use the shapes to define areas to fill with stained glass, and you'll make a copy to serve as part of the caming that separates the stained glass pieces. You'll "hide" a copy of the polygons you've created in a locked CorelDRAW layer for use later to create the stained glass, and then create the stained glass caming with the original combined shapes.

Here's how to move a copy of the stained glass frame to a different layer for later use:

1. With the Pick tool, select the original rectangle shape you made and then press the Del key. The rectangle is no longer needed. The edges of the polygons you created now make up the outer edge of the piece.

Tip: If a polygon shape is obscuring your view (and selection) of the rectangle, click on the polygon, and press the Tab key to toggle between objects in the Drawing Window until the status line tells you the rectangle is selected. Then Delete the rectangle.

2. Choose **E**dit, Select **A**ll.

3. You don't want the heart (or whatever shape you chose) to be included in the polygon shapes. The heart will be a foreground element in the composition and will have its caming and fill added separately. Hold the shift key and click on the outline of the heart. This deselects it, and only the polygons will now be selected.

Chapter 13: Very Special CorelDRAW Effects

4. Press Ctrl+F3 to display the Layers Roll-Up.

5. Click on the fly-out menu button (the triangle pointing to the right on the Layers Roll-Up), and choose New. Accept the default name by clicking on OK.

6. Click on the fly-out menu again, but choose Copy To, and click the arrow cursor on the Layer 2 title on the Layers Roll-Up. Your screen should now look like figure 13.3.

Figure 13.3

You can copy objects to other layers using the Copy To command on the Layers Roll-Up.

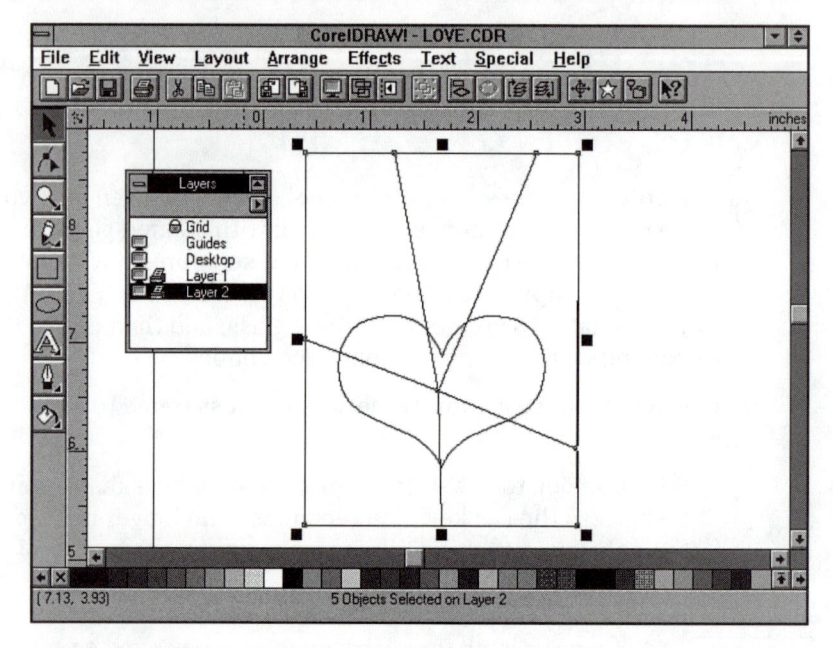

7. You want to lock away your copied polygons, so double-click on the Layer 2 title to display the Edit Layers options box.

8. Click on the Locked check box and click on OK, as shown in figure 13.4.

9. Click on the Layer 2 title on the Layers Roll-Up, and drag the title so it's beneath Layer 1. Layer 1 is for the stained glass fills, so it should go behind the layer for the caming, Layer 2.

10. You want to work on an unlocked layer with the original polygon shapes. You need to combine them into a collection of subpaths you can use to create the caming. Click on the Layer 1 title, and choose Edit, Select All, or double-click on the Pick Tool.

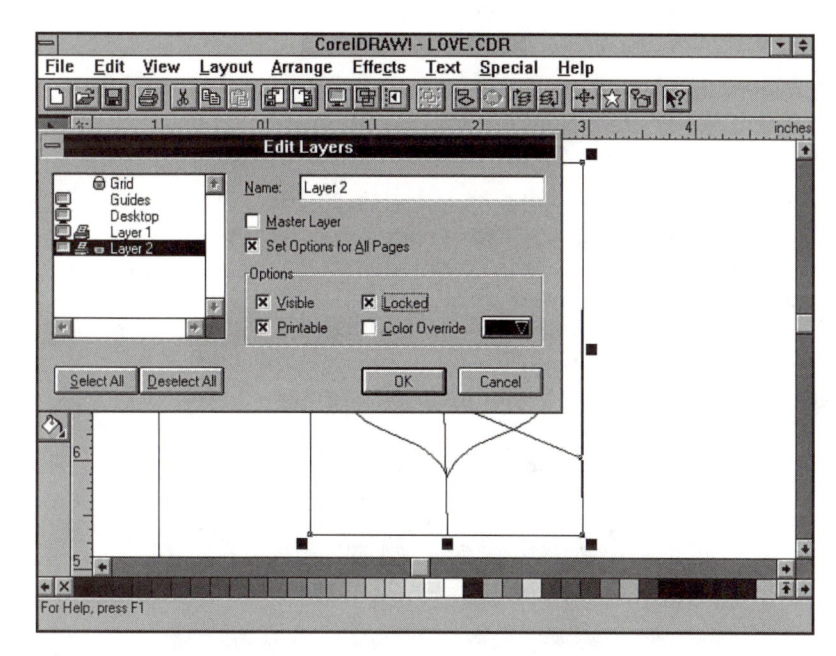

Figure 13.4

You can lock a layer of objects, but still have them visible using the Edit Layers option box.

11. Deselect the heart by pressing the Shift key and then clicking on the heart. Now only the polygons are selected.

12. Choose **A**rrange, **C**ombine (Ctrl+L is the shortcut).

Although the appearance of all these polygons doesn't change, they are now all part of one big path to which you can assign properties—like those of stained glass caming.

Using the Blend Command To Make Lots of Tubes

The Blend command has been used several times in this book as a substitute for a Fountain Fill. Fountain Fills and the Blend command both produce smooth graduations in color, but the Blend command is more flexible and often works better to produce smooth, photographic lighting on objects.

You witnessed some of the power of the Blend command when you used it to blend different outlines together to produce the highlights on the pawn in Chapter 5. Here's how to use the Blend command to create an effect that can look like neon tubing or, in this case, stained glass caming. The technique you'll learn uses two different colored outlines with different widths.

Chapter 13: Very Special CorelDRAW Effects

Follow these steps:

1. With the combined polygon shapes still selected, choose the Outline Pen tool from the Toolbox, and choose the Outline dialog box (the first icon with the same drawing of the pen on it as the tool).

2. The settings in this step are subjective, depending on how large your stained glass cartoon is. As you can see in figure 13.5, I've entered a width of **.09** for the outline of the combined polygons. At a width this large, you should select blunted corners (the bottom corner radio button). Selecting **S**cale with Image ensures that if you decide to make your design larger or smaller in the future, the outline width will change proportionately along with the other elements in the image.

Figure 13.5
Choose a wide outline for the combined object you'll blend.

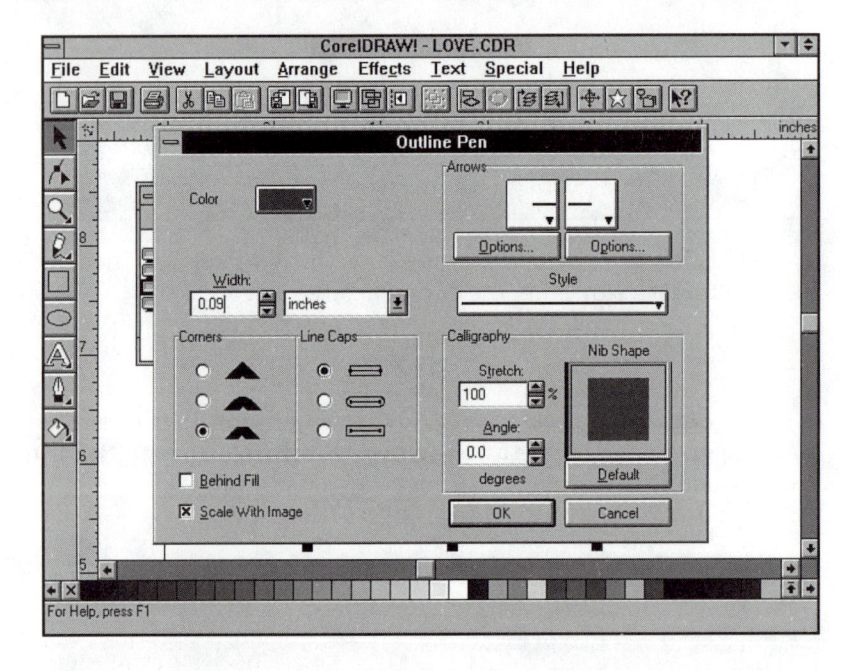

Tip

Blunted corners on lines are usually necessary when working with outlines that exceed widths of more than about .01 inches. If you don't select this option when you customize an outline, the corners of your path will look spiked, and overrun the shape of your outline.

Try it sometime for a really grotesque visual example!

3. Set the color of the outline to brown by clicking on the color button in the color field and selecting the color from the drop-down samples.

4. Click on OK.

5. Press the Plus key on the keypad to duplicate the wide brown subpath collection.

6. Click on the Outline Pen tool, and select the Outline dialog box (or press F12).

7. Enter **.01** for the Width of this duplicate subpath collection, then click on OK.

8. Right-mouse click over a light orange or yellow color on the color palette. As you can see in figure 13.6, you should have two contrasting colors for the two identical, combined shapes of unequal line widths.

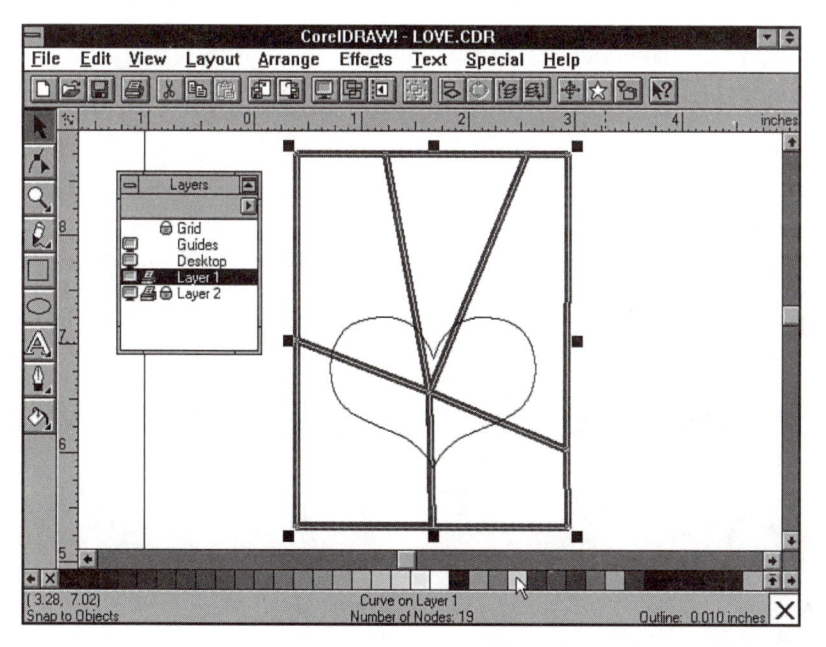

Figure 13.6
The two different combined shapes (the subpath collections) will become caming when you blend them.

9. Hold the Shift key and click on the wide brown outline. The status line should say 2 Objects selected.

10. Press Ctrl+B to display the Blend Roll-Up, then press Apply. The default value of 20 steps creates a beautiful blend. Use this technique wherever you need neon or a similar effect in a design assignment of your own.

11. With the blend selected, press the To Back button on the Ribbon Bar. The heart will now be on top, and it is ready to receive the caming treatment.

Applying a Blend to the Heart

The heart requires a separate copying and blending procedure because when it is filled, it will cover up the areas where the polygons meet. An alternative method would have been to use the Trim command to carve the heart away from the polygons. That would have made a perfect collection of subpaths that wouldn't need to be covered by a fill. As you increase your adeptness with CorelDRAW, however, you'll learn that time is money where your craft is concerned. The first method is a less elegant solution than if you used the Trim command, but it is quicker and more straightforward.

Repeat the steps performed earlier to add caming to the heart:

1. Select the heart by clicking on it with the Pick tool.
2. From the **E**dit menu, choose Copy Attributes **F**rom.
3. You cursor turns into a huge arrow, a now familiar indicator that you should click on something. Click on the exact center of the blended polygon shapes. This should give your symbol shape a .01" colored outline, the same as the "core" of the polygon blend. If it doesn't, see the following note.

Note

Copy Attributes **F**rom is a really easy way to duplicate a custom outline or fill that you've already specified. Unfortunately, the shape you want to copy from isn't always in plain sight. This is especially true of shapes that are control objects for a blend effect.

If, after one or two tries, you still can't attribute the heart to a .01" outline, perform this change manually. Click on the Outline Pen tool and match the settings in the dialog box to those you defined earlier for the polygon blend.

4. Press the Plus key on the keypad (or Ctrl+D) to duplicate the outlined heart, and press Ctrl+PageDown to send the copy only one step back in the pile of objects you have in the Drawing Window.

Applying a Blend to the Heart

Tip

Using the keyboard shortcuts assigned to Menu command is sometimes much quicker than mousing your way through the menu structure.

For instance, Ctrl+PageDown saves you from clicking **A**rrange, then **O**rder, then Back O**n**e. Similarly, Ctrl+PageUp will promote selected objects one higher in your object "stack."

It's been my experience that taking your hands off the mouse to execute a two- or three-key combination command is a lot quicker than "drilling down" three or four menu commands to arrive at a command that's already, quite literally, at your fingertips.

5. Give this duplicate attributes of brown and .09" (the same as one of the polygon blend shapes you defined earlier), either by copying the attribute from the polygon shape, or by manually defining it in the Outline Pen dialog box. Your screen should look like figure 13.7.

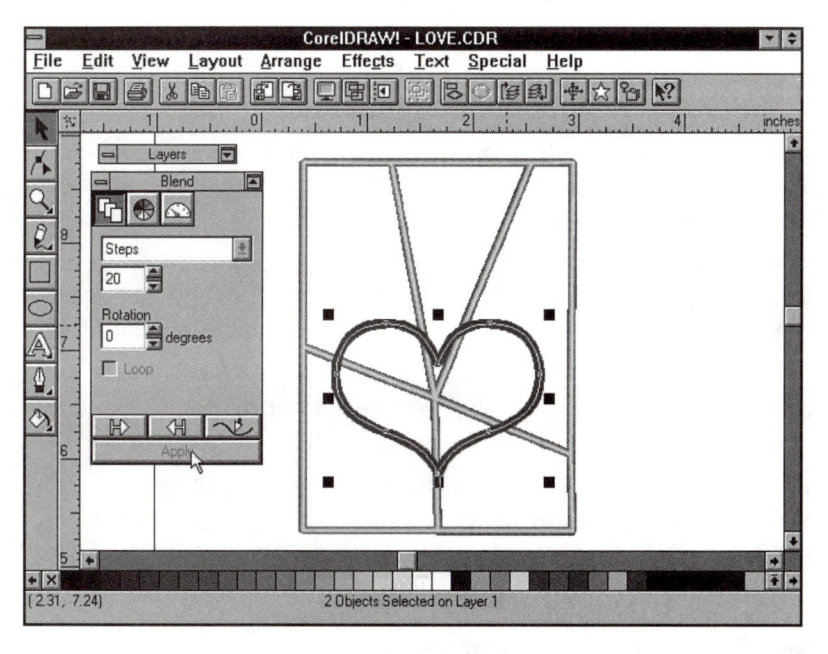

Figure 13.7
The two symbol shapes need to be blended to create virtual caming around it.

6. With the Pick tool, marquee-select both shapes. Avoid selecting the blended polygons, though.

7. Press the Apply button, and you'll get caming identical in appearance to that which you created around the polygon combined shapes.

Making Stained Glass with Texture Fills

An elegant implementation of fractal mathematics lies behind Corel's extensive collection of fractal texture fills. These mathematical formulas describe random patterns that are used to produce bitmapped designs that frequently resemble organic materials. Minor variations in the formulas produce distinctly different patterns, so you have millions of different patterns at your disposal.

No two pieces of actual stained glass are ever exactly alike, so Corel's ever-changing fractal textures are a perfect choice for creating virtual stained glass. In the next series of steps, you'll create a shape behind the heart that you can fill with a custom-made fractal fill.

Here's how to select and customize a CorelDRAW texture:

1. Click on one or the other of the two shapes that made up the blended heart. CorelDRAW calls these *control objects*, and the status line will confirm which one you've chosen. (Hint: If you can't select one immediately, click on any shape in the Drawing Window, then use the Tab key to toggle to the shape you want.)

2. Press the plus key on the keypad to duplicate the shape, and press Ctrl+PageDown twice. Regardless of whether you picked the fat brown outline or the skinny one, the duplicate is now two places beneath the heart caming, yet above the polygon caming.

3. Click on the Fill tool and choose the Texture Fill button on the menu flyout (the cloudy-looking one next to the "PS" button).

4. The Texture Fill dialog box can be really intimidating with all the options, numbers, styles, and samples it offers. All you're looking for in this example is a nice fill for the heart. I chose Alabaster from the Styles Texture Library. Alabaster is more pinkish than red, though; not very appropriate for a heart symbol. But this *texture* is cool, so read on to see how to fix the colors of the texture.

Making Stained Glass with Texture Fills

5. In figure 13.8, you can see drop-down color palettes available by clicking on the chosen texture's color buttons. Click on the buttons, choose new colors for the first and second mineral, then click on the Preview button to see how your texture swatch is shaping up.

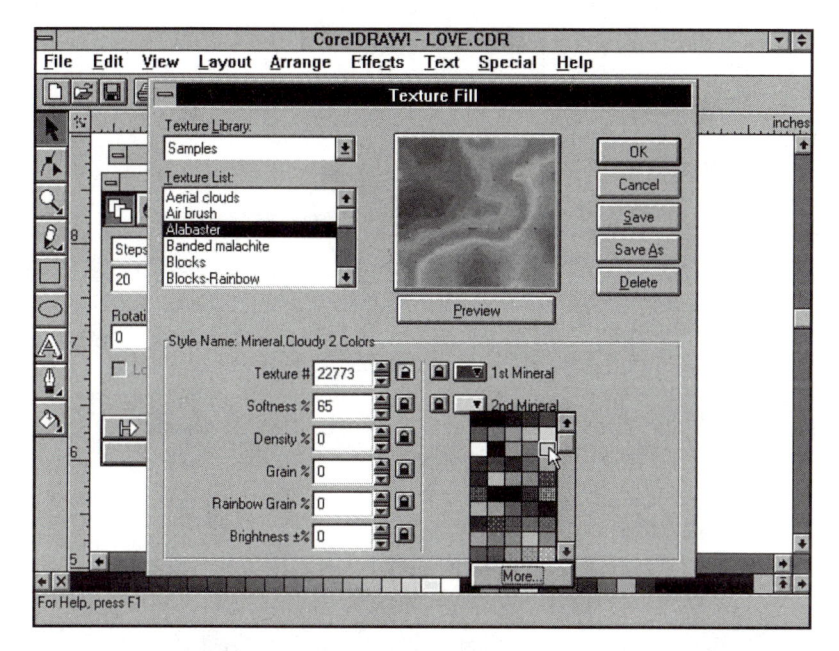

Figure 13.8

You can change a texture fill simply by redefining its component colors.

6. When you're happy with your custom texture fill, click on OK to return to your design.

7. You're done refining everything on Layer 1; it's time to fill the polygons on Layer 2. Double-click on the Layer 1 title on the Layers Roll-Up, and click on the locked check box. Click on OK.

8. Double-click on the Layer 2 title, then uncheck the locked check box. In Preview mode you can't see what's actually editable in the Drawing Window at present, but you now have four or five discrete polygon shapes awaiting their fractal fills, and the heart and the caming can't be touched, as shown in figure 13.9.

Chapter 13: Very Special CorelDRAW Effects

Figure 13.9
You should lock a layer you're finished with to prevent accidental editing while you work on other areas.

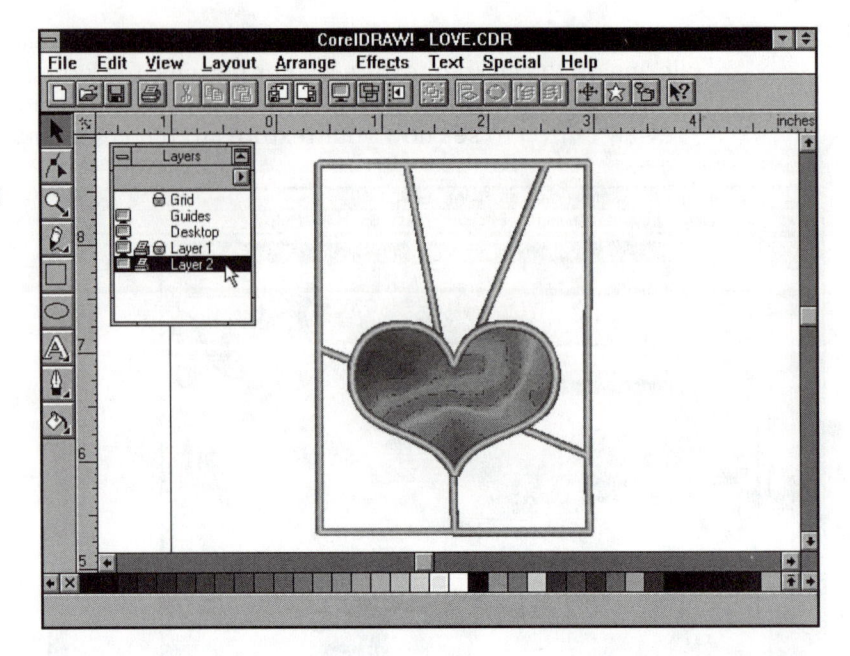

Adding Texture to the Background

Non-CorelDRAW users love to watch CorelDRAW users at work. And if you're in an office environment where people come over to snoop, the next steps will appear as nothing less than magic to your co-workers, because you're going to add textures to the background polygon shapes you copied earlier. You can see their outlines because the caming is on top of them, but here's a simple way to fill them (and for all appearance's sake, the shapes will burst into bloom on the screen!).

Simply follow these steps:

1. With the Pick tool, click on a section of the polygon caming. Regardless of what you *think* you've selected, you've actually picked a copy of one of the original polygon shapes. Check out the status line if you doubt it.

2. Press Shift+F6 to display the Fill Roll-Up, and click on the Texture Fill button on the top (first one on the right) to display its options. From the first drop-down box, choose Samples. From the second drop-down box, pick something interesting.

Adding Texture to the Background

441

3. As you can see in figure 13.10, I've applied some **Clouds.Midday** to the polygon. But you can create a variation on this preset sample, so click on Edit to start some fancy customizing work.

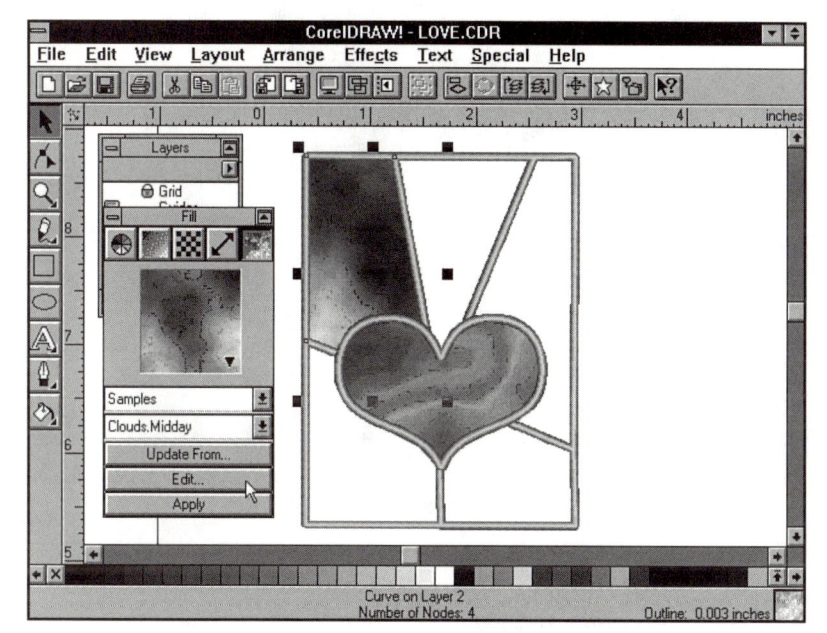

Figure 13.10

The Texture Fill dialog box can be displayed by clicking on the Edit button on the Roll-Up.

4. As mentioned earlier, you can change the math a fractal texture is made up of (to a certain extent) by changing the texture number. In figure 13.11, I've clicked the up elevator button next to the Texture # field, and pressed **P**review. You have 32,767 possible permutations of a texture sample, and you'll lose the one you like if you don't save it!

5. Click on the Save **A**s button when you've previewed a texture you think is cool.

6. You can save the variation you've picked to one of the existing collections, or you can create a new library. For now though, click on Samples as the **L**ibrary Name in the Save Texture dialog box, type in a name in the **T**exture Name field, and then click on OK.

Chapter 13: Very Special CorelDRAW Effects

Figure 13.11
Choose Save **A**s when you find a non-standard texture you'd like to use again later.

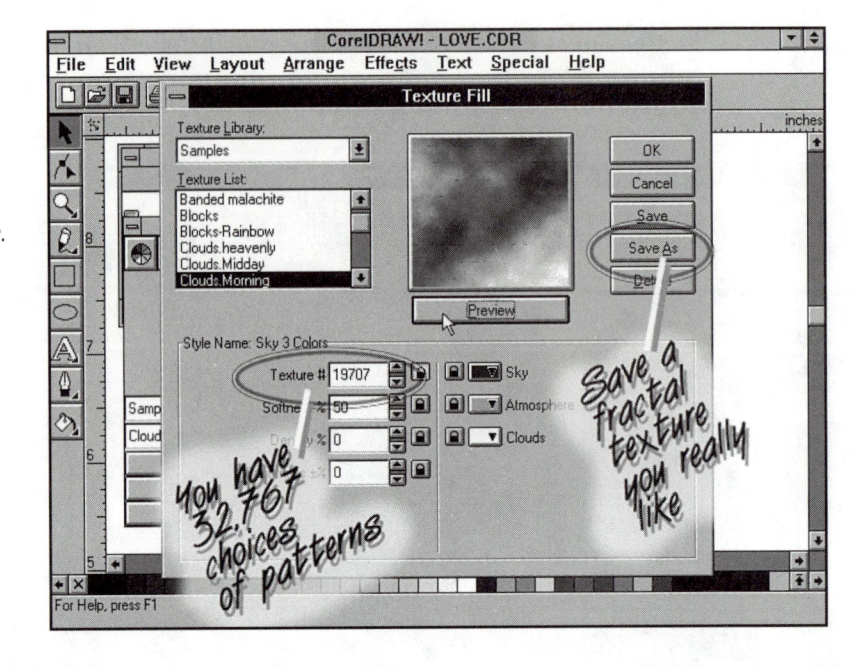

[Screenshot of CorelDRAW Texture Fill dialog box with handwritten annotations: "You have 32,767 choices of patterns" pointing to the Texture # field showing 19707, and "Save a fractal texture you really like" pointing to the Save As button.]

Tip

You can save a texture to a new library where you can easily find it. In the **L**ibrary Name field type of the Save Texture As dialog box, type in something evocative like **MY COLLECTION.** In the **T**exture Name field, type in a descriptive name for the texture. Then click on OK. You can use spaces and upper- and lowercase letters, and use up to 32 characters to name either the library or the texture itself. The new library and the texture you've saved will now be available to you whenever you use fractal fills.

7. I named my custom clouds Jack be Nimbus, and as you can see in figure 13.12, the other polygon shapes have been selected and filled with the texture.

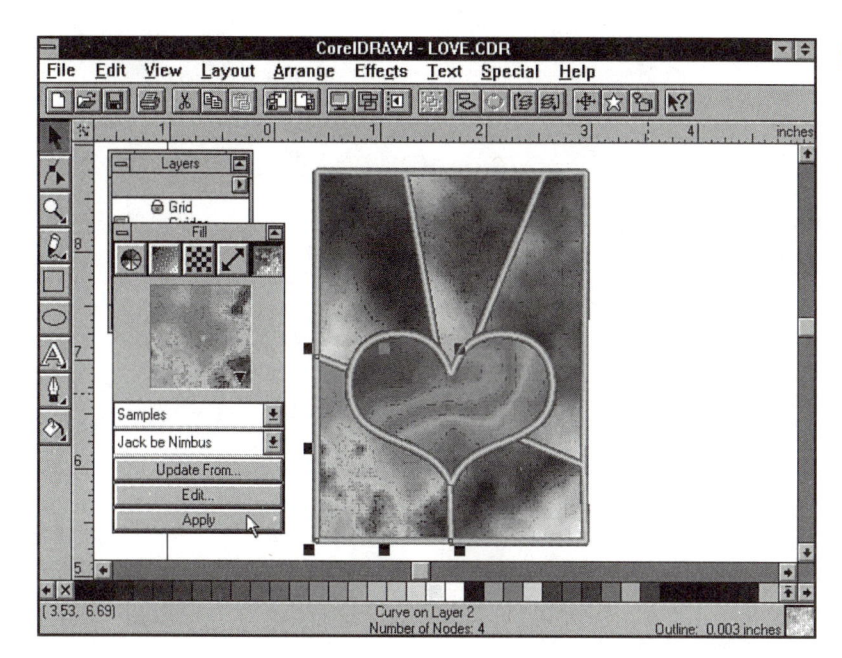

Figure 13.12
Your custom texture will appear in the Samples on the Fill Roll-Up after you save it.

Adding Stained Glass Text

Add a text element to the stained glass design as a finishing touch. Although you'll frequently use Artistic Text in a design with a default black fill, textures and Fountain Fills can really perk up a slogan, slide, or even a virtual glass window.

1. Click on the Wireframe button on the Ribbon Bar. Working in wireframe for a while provides a clearer picture of your design and speeds up redraws in your Drawing Window.

2. In the example in figure 13.13, LOVE was typed in with the Artistic Text tool. Do this, and then press Ctrl+spacebar to get the Pick tool and make your phrase the active selection.

3. Press Ctrl+T to display the Character Attributes dialog box.

4. Choose a typeface you feel is appropriate for stained glass lettering from the Fonts list. I'm using Eckmann (from Monotype), but Fette Fraktur, Davida, or Auriol are good choices, too.

Chapter 13: Very Special CorelDRAW Effects

Figure 13.13

Use an ornamental typeface to embellish a short phrase.

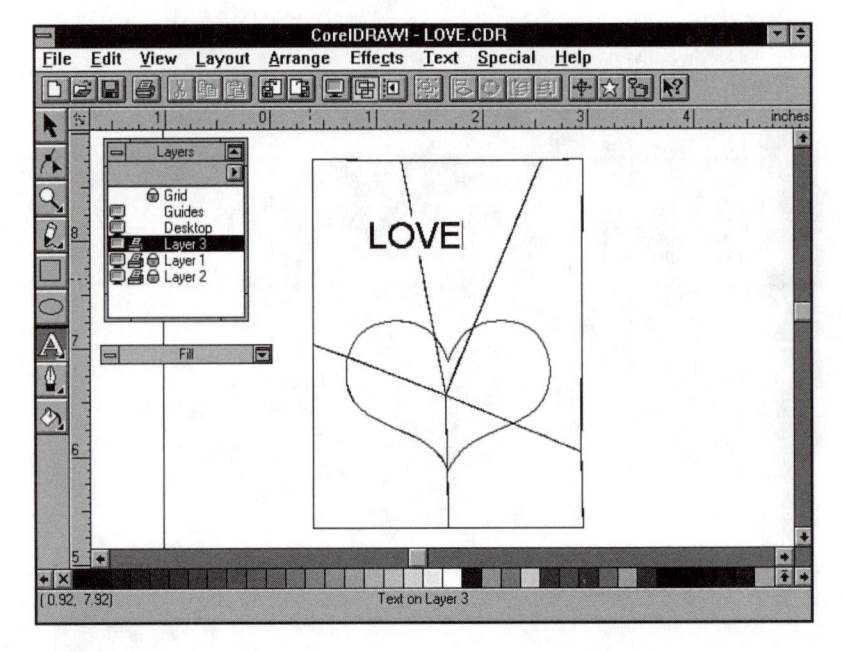

Note

Ornamental display fonts are illegible for use as body text faces, but they're superb when used to add an ornamental element to a design. Use them sparingly, though. Ten characters or less is a good rule of thumb for Artistic Text that's set in ornate display fonts.

5. Click on OK, then click and drag on a corner selection handle to scale up the Artistic Text so it fits nicely within the top of the design. Reposition it by clicking and dragging on the text's outline, if necessary.

6. Click on the menu fly-out button on the Layers Roll-Up. Choose New, and accept the defaults by clicking on OK in the New Layer dialog box.

7. Click on the menu fly-out and choose Move To.

8. Click on Layer 3, and your Artistic Text moves to Layer 3.

9. Double-click on Layer 2, click on the locked check box, and click on OK.

10. Click on the Layer 3 title. As you can see in figure 13.14, the word "LOVE" is the only object that can be selected or modified in your design now. All the rest of your work is protected from accidental change.

Adding Stained Glass Text

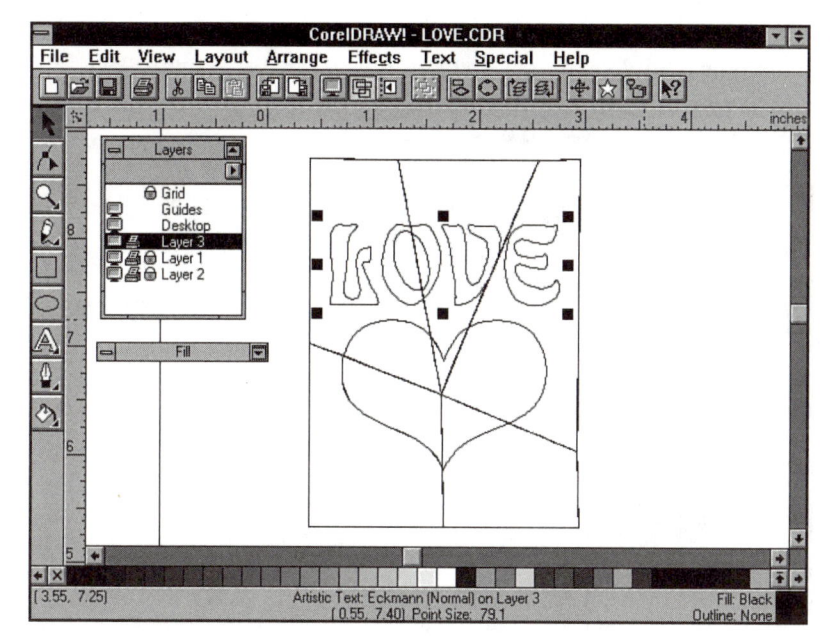

Figure 13.14
Use different layers with your designs to protect elements you've spent a lot of time on!

Refining Love as a Compositional Element

You could leave your Artistic Text alone at this point, add a blend and a fill, and call it quits; but I've always felt that text that's been through one or two effects becomes a much more exciting element.

Invest a moment or two in applying an envelope to the Artistic Text to add movement and warmth by following these steps:

1. Choose the Freehand tool and click once in the upper left of your design, just inside the polygon shape.

2. Double-click a path in a clockwise direction to create a boundary box around the Artistic Text, finishing the path where you began it with a single click.

3. Choose the Shape tool, select the path by clicking on it, and marquee-select all the nodes. Double-click on a node to display the Node Edit Roll-Up.

Chapter 13: Very Special CorelDRAW Effects

4. Click on the To Curve button. As you can see in figure 13.15, you should have some leeway in designing a new boundary for the Artistic Text. With the Envelope effect, you can mold your text into a soft shape that conforms to the outlines of the other elements.

Figure 13.15

Convert the path to curves, then "sculpt" the path using the Shape tool.

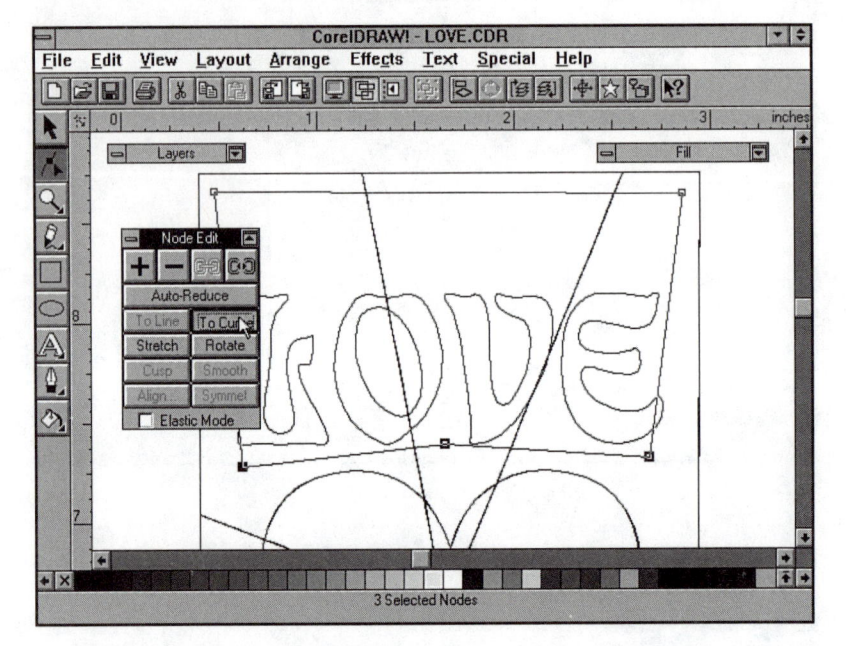

5. There are some visual suggestions for sculpting the path in figure 13.16—the bottom of the path conforms to the top of the heart symbol, and the vertical lines fan toward the top of the stained glass piece. Feel free to experiment here!

6. Ctrl+F7 is the quick way to display the Envelope Roll-Up, so press these shortcut keys next.

7. It's okay if you switch back to Preview mode at this point by clicking on the Wireframe button on the Ribbon Bar. Most of your editing is done.

8. Select your text by clicking on it with the Pick tool, then click on the Create From button on the Envelope Roll-Up.

9. Click on the path you've modified with the huge arrow cursor, and press Apply, as shown in figure 13.17.

Refining Love as a Compositional Element

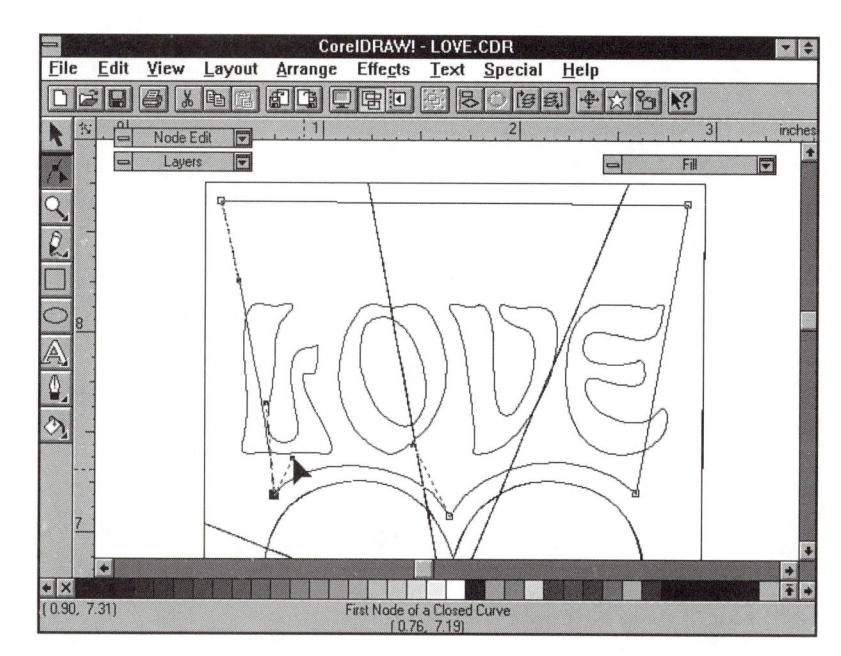

Figure 13.16
The shape you create is the shape your text will turn into after applying the Envelope effect.

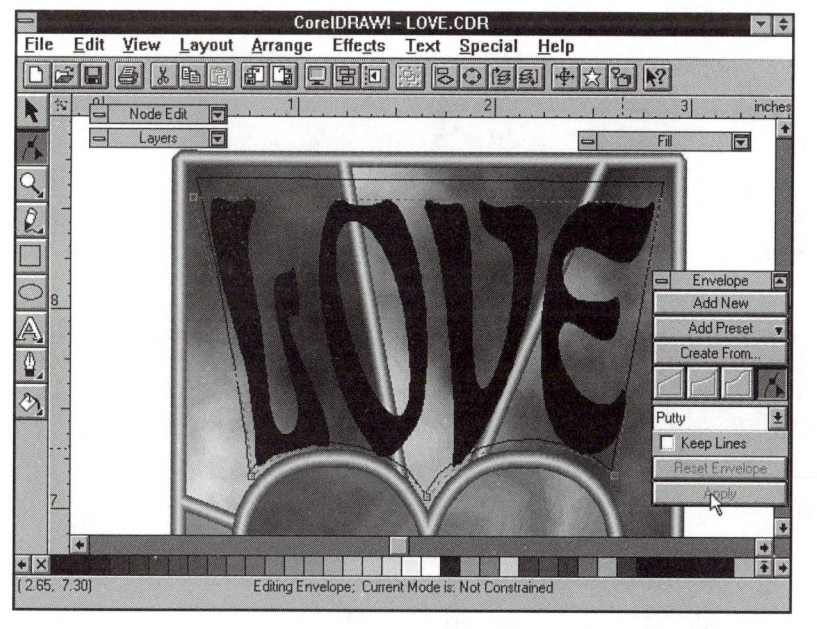

Figure 13.17
Any object you've selected will take on the shape of the path you defined as an envelope.

10. Select the path you designed, and press the Delete key. You're done with it.

11. You can further modify the shape of your enveloped Artistic Text by using the Shape tool. (Hint: if you click and drag on a node or segment of the boundary box, you must press Apply again on the Envelope Roll-Up to execute the modification.)

12. Press the Plus key on the keyboard to duplicate the text, then give it a **0.09"** brown outline, identical in other respects to the brown caming blend objects on Layers 1 and 2. You'll need to manually specify outline attributes, since you can't copy them from the other (locked) layers.

13. Press the Plus key again, and give this duplicate text the same attributes as the **0.01"** outline that's the other half of the elements needed to perform a blend.

14. Choose both color outlined shapes, then left-mouse click over the "X" on the color palette to remove the black fill from both shapes.

15. Go to the Blend Roll-Up and press Apply.

16. Choose **F**ile, **S**ave (Ctrl+S). You've done a lot, and you want to protect your investment at regular intervals!

Working with the Custom Fountain Fill

Texture fills are terrific, but too much of a good thing is not healthy for a design, nor is trying all 37 flavors at Baskin-Robbins in one sitting.

To conclude your stained glass adventure, you'll explore a unique property of the Fountain Fill. Although you've used the "plain vanilla" settings for it in other chapters, this glorious glass design deserves to have not two, but several blends of transitional colors shimmering through the Artistic Text, as light in real life acts when it hits a decorative pane.

To create this effect, follow these steps:

1. Click on the black text within the caming that surrounds it. This is the original Artistic Text you copied from to create the color-outlined text that was blended together in the previous steps.

2. Click on the Fill tool, and choose the Fountain Fill icon from the menu fly-out (the one with the grayscale tonal fill on it).

Working with the Custom Fountain Fill

3. In the Fountain Fill dialog box, choose Conical from the Type drop-down and click on the Custom radio button in the color blend area.

4. Here's where the fun begins. You can define up to 99 *intermediate* Fountain Fills within the custom fill! Click on the leftmost tiny white square above the preview box in the color blend area to choose the "starting color point" for the Fountain Fill. Pick the color you want to be your starting color by clicking on a swatch on the color palette to the right of the preview box.

5. Click on the tiny white square above and to the right side of the preview box, then pick another color. This is your "finishing color point" for the Fountain Fill. Pick a color that you want to be the ending color for the fill.

6. Double-click anywhere between the two tiny white squares above the preview box, and an arrow will appear. Pick another color from the color palette. This is an intermediate fountain color, and the preview box will go nuts displaying it.

7. In figure 13.18, I've selected three intermediate Fountain Fills by double-clicking to add these points. I've chosen browns, oranges, and other warm hues from the color palette to make a golden conical fill, more accurately displayed next to the Options field in this dialog box.

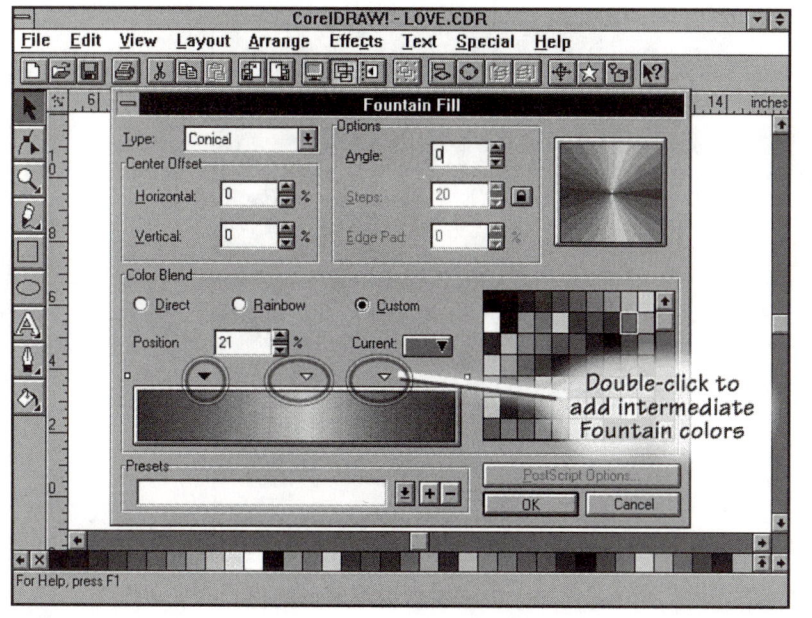

Figure 13.18

Double-click slightly above the preview box in the Custom color blend mode to add intermediate Fountain Fills to any type of fill.

Chapter 13: Very Special CorelDRAW Effects

Tip

To remove an intermediate step marker (as well as the intermediate Fountain Fill step), double-click on it. You can also precisely position an intermediate step by typing a value in the position box in the color blend field. Additionally, you can drag an intermediate Fountain Fill marker to create a sudden or relaxed color shift in the overall Fountain Fill.

8. When you get the intermediate Fountain Fill of your dreams, you may want to save it for future use. Click on the Plus button in the Presets area, then name your fill. Now you can recall it in any future session.

9. Click on OK, File, and Save to save your work.

10. This is a moment you want to savor without the distractions of the workspace's rulers, Roll-Ups, or any other CorelDRAW feature. If you have the right mouse button defined as Full-screen Preview (in the Special, Preferences menu; see Chapter 3, "Customizing CorelDRAW!/Finding the Features"), right-mouse click now. If you haven't customized CorelDRAW's workspace, press F9 to view your masterpiece full-screen, as shown in figure 13.19.

Figure 13.19
Stained glass is easy to replicate if you know where to find the right virtual materials in CorelDRAW!

11. Press F9 again to return to the CorelDRAW workspace.

Tip

There's nothing wrong with keeping a finished design on three separate layers, or even having two of the three locked.

But if you're so inclined, you may want to:

1. Unlock Layers 1 and 2.
2. Choose **E**dit, Select **A**ll.
3. Click on the Layers menu fly-out button.
4. Choose Move to, and select Layer 3.

This is a procedure that's bound to win you a tidiness award, but it will make it harder later to modify the design since all the components will be stacked on a single layer.

Congratulations are in order once again, because if you've completed this design, you can spin off entire different stained glass pieces using different cartoons, and the same techniques you've picked up.

Sometimes, you'll customize an effect or a fill to design an idea, and other times an effect will be so intriguing, it'll create an idea in your mind. Our next section covers the "Zen" of the Lens Roll-Up.

Creating Effects with the Lens Roll-Up

When I started using CorelDRAW version 5, I noticed the Lens Roll-Up, a new feature in my explorations. I dismissed it as a novelty, because I initially felt it was frilly and couldn't possible fit into the serious design work you see throughout this book.

But as I played around with it after hours, I began to get some exceptionally neat ideas for designs that could stand some special effects distortions. Before long, I had based a design entirely around one of the Lens Roll-Up's settings!

This is an example of how a CorelDRAW effect can steer you into wonderful creations you might not ordinarily think of. If you're intrigued by any of the

CorelDRAW effects you can't think of a purpose for, play with them for a while, let the profundity of the moment sink in a little, and don't be afraid to "reverse-engineer" a design.

Rules for the Lens Roll-Up

On the Lens Roll-Up, there are many preset variations the CorelDRAW user can assign to an object. A few rules pertain to what *kind* of object you can apply a lens to, as follows:

- A shape has to be a closed shape. The shape can consist of several objects combined, but they cannot be grouped objects.

- Kiss an elaborately-filled shape good-bye if you want it to be a lens. Solid color fills work, while bitmap, Fountain Fill, and texture fills don't make it as lenses.

- The shape to which you assign a lens has to be on top of anything you want it to affect. Like in real life, you don't get results placing a magnifying glass behind a newspaper—make sure your lens object is To Front by clicking on the To Front button on the Ribbon Bar (if you're uncertain of its place on a stack of other objects).

There are many variations on the Lens effect, but they basically do the same thing: a shape with a lens attribute placed on top of another shape makes your view of the second shape "different," as though you're looking through tinted glass, a fluoroscope device, or a "viewing monitor" from a bad 1950s science fiction movie!

Making an Attention-Getting Announcement

Here's an example of a use for the Lens Roll-Up that was completely inspired by the Magnify setting. I designed "around" the effect, adding elements that would highlight the effect. Here's how to create an announcement that'll get everyone's attention from across a boardroom:

1. Begin by designing a magnifying glass to hold a shape that you'll apply a Lens effect to. Using the Ellipse tool, make a circle approximately 3" wide, then make a copy (by pressing the Plus key). Scale the circle copy to about 90 percent of its original size by clicking and dragging on a corner selection handle with the Pick tool.

Making an Attention-Getting Announcement

2. Select both circles, click on the Align button on the Ribbon Bar. Choose Horizontal and Vertical **C**enter, and click on OK.

3. Choose **A**rrange, **C**ombine (Ctrl+L). This takes care of the lens frame.

4. Choose the Rectangle tool and click and drag a narrow, tall stem starting at the bottom of the combined circles, and ending when it's around 5 1/2" measured on the vertical rulers.

5. Press the spacebar to get the Pick tool, and marquee-select the two objects.

6. Press the Align button again, but only click the **H**orizontal **C**enter radio button, then click on OK. Your magnifying glass should look like figure 13.20.

7. Choose **A**rrange, **W**eld to make your selections one shape with a hole in it.

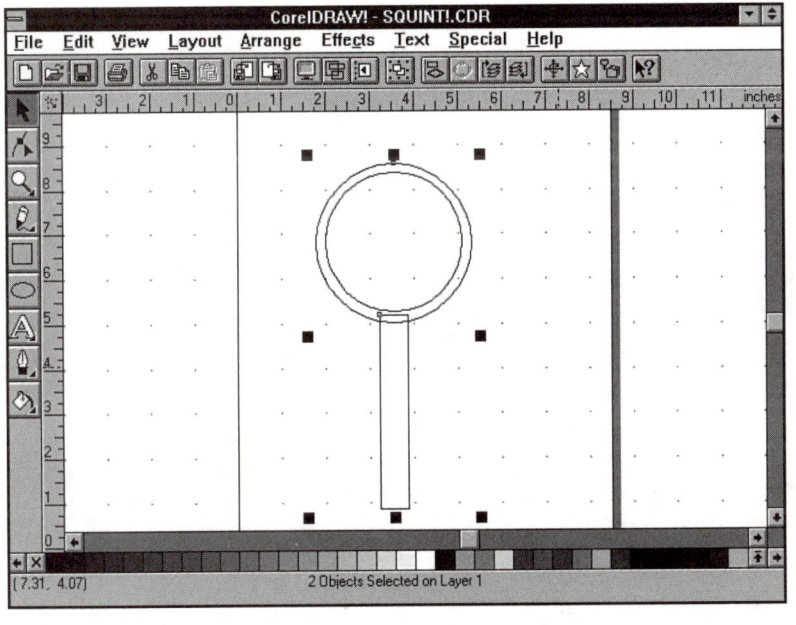

Figure 13.20

Use simple objects and the Weld and Combine commands to make more complex ones.

8. On an 8 1/2" by 11" Printable page, it seems a waste to have this magnifying glass in such a stilted position. Let's compose the page a little more aesthetically by clicking a second time on the magnifying glass to display the rotate/skew selection mode.

Chapter 13: Very Special CorelDRAW Effects

9. Click and drag the center of rotation of the selection up until it's in the center of the lens frame part. Click and drag a corner (rotate) handle counterclockwise, as shown in figure 13.21. Moving the center of rotation before rotating a shape usually allows you to get the effect you desire with more precision and less frustration.

10. Stop when you've rotated the magnifying glass around 20°. It should sprawl out on the page better now, and creates an interesting geometry to design "around."

Figure 13.21

Move the center of rotation of a selected object to rotate the selection around this point.

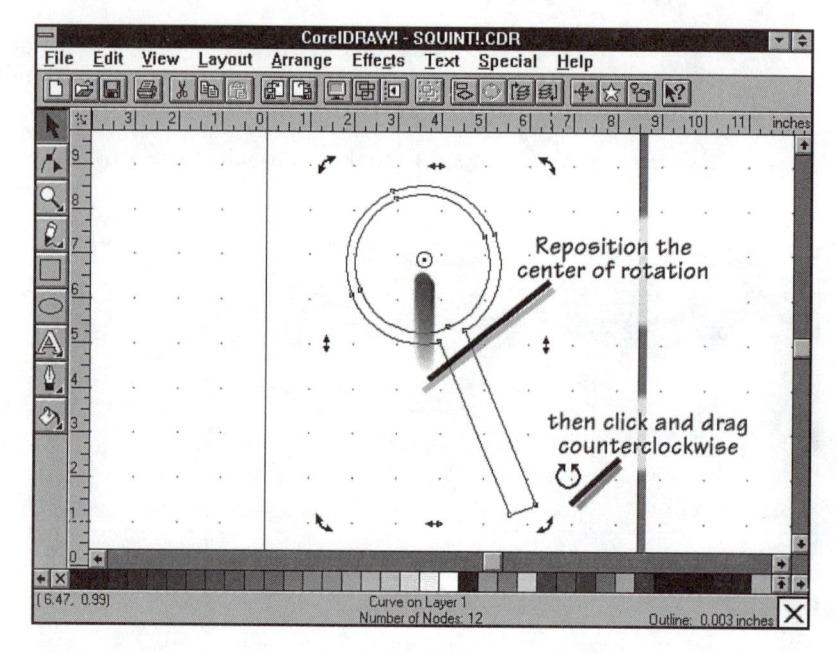

Fitting a Lens into the Magnifying Glass

Now that you have an empty magnifying glass, you need another shape to place within its frame to which you'll apply a Lens property. It can be any solid color, or you can make the shape without any fill at all; it's just that it's easier to select and move a shape in Preview mode when it has a fill. The Lens effect has its own set of rules for filled lens shapes. The Magnify Lens Effect produces enlargements of whatever it's over, but the object you apply the Lens effect to can't have any colors, tints, or texture shading.

Fitting a Lens into the Magnifying Glass

Here's how to add a lens to the magnifying glass:

1. Click on the Zoom tool (the one shaped like... a magnifying glass), and marquee-zoom into the lens frame of your design.

2. Choose the Ellipse tool, and click and drag an ellipse so it fits inside the lens frame of your magnifying glass.

3. It's hard to design an ellipse exactly in the center of a shape you've already designed. After it's drawn, color in the ellipse with a fill (left-mouse click) from the color palette so you can select the filled shape and reposition it. Click and drag on a side selection handle to stretch or shrink a horizontal or vertical dimension of the ellipse, as shown in figure 13.22.

4. Press the To Back button on the Ribbon Bar to make the lens shape fit behind the frame that's supposed to be holding it.

5. You're done for the moment when the lens shape fits inside the lens frame of the magnifying glass. File, Save your design as SQUINT!.CDR on your hard disk.

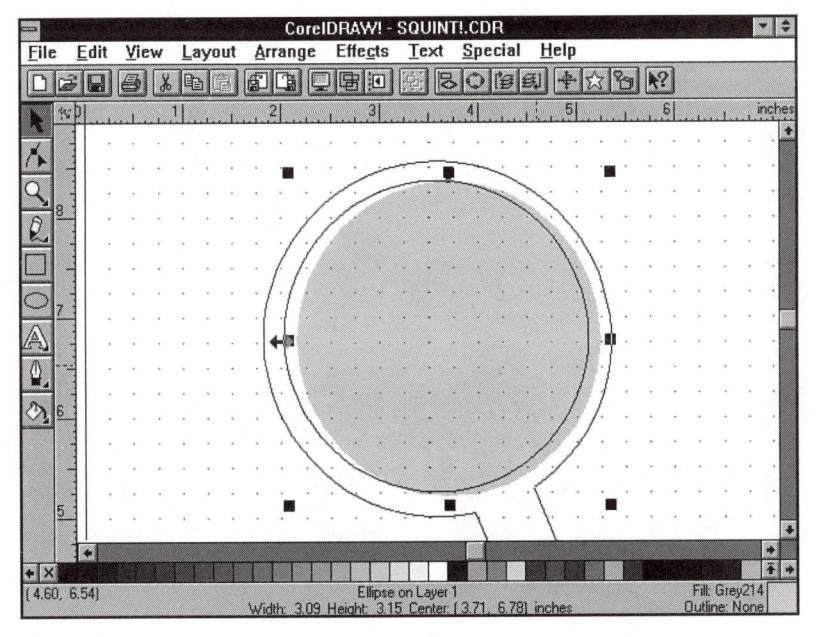

Figure 13.22

Add an object whose only purpose is to be the host for the Lens effect.

Chapter 13: Very Special CorelDRAW Effects

Behind the Scenes with a Finished Illustration

You've learned a lot of techniques in this book that, hopefully, will inspire you to spend a lot of time refining your craft in CorelDRAW. Lack of practice is the only thing that can keep you from producing award-winning work in this program.

And after some practice, you'll experiment and embellish your designs. In figure 13.23, I spent a few hours whipping together a magnifying glass, shown in the rest of these figures, using techniques illustrated in earlier chapters. Notice the blends in the wireframe view along the stem, as well as other ornate pieces that add to the realism of the design. The only true difference between this illustration and the magnifying glass design in the last few steps is the investment of time with Corel.

Figure 13.23

If an illustration is important to you or your client, practice and spend some time refining it.

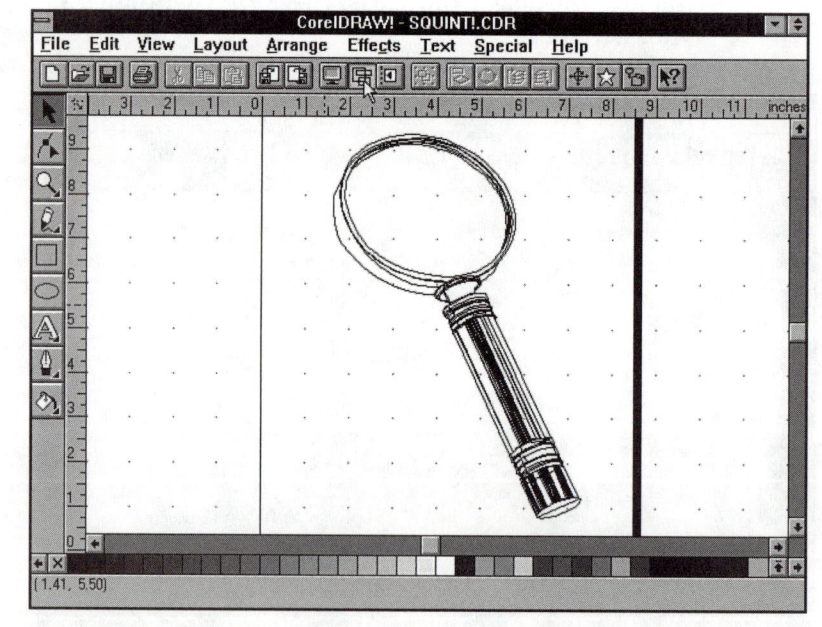

What Do You Want to Magnify?

Before you apply a Lens property to the shape, you need to come to a concept about the theme of the illustration. A lens object can magnify anything: Artistic Text, blended objects, texture fills, even imported bitmap images.

My concept (which doesn't have to be *yours*) is to do a "Consumer Alert" poster; the fine print on some packages of food are enough to turn you off from eating sometimes.

So the "focus" of this illustration will be on Paragraph Text. I listed some artificial ingredients in a word processing program, and saved the file in the TXT format. Here's how to point out to the public some of the stuff everyone consumes on occasion:

1. Choose **F**ile, **I**mport, and select Unformatted Text, *.TXT from the List Files of **T**ype drop-down box.

Closer Look

If you own Word for Windows, WordPerfect, or Ami Pro, you can save yourself a few steps when importing text. CorelDRAW will preserve formatting (indents, column widths, fonts) of documents in these file types when you import them.

If you import a formatted word processor document, you won't have to assign font type, sizes, or other characteristics to your Paragraph Text when you import it.

Additionally, CorelDRAW imports files in the Rich Text Format (RTF) type, so other desktop publishing applications like PageMaker can export in this format to be imported by CorelDRAW.

2. With the paragraph selected upon completion of the import, you can resize the Paragraph Text frame to make a compositionally pleasing layout for the text and magnifying glass (see Chapter 8 for the scoop on Paragraph Text).

3. Press Ctrl+T to display the Character Attributes command. Choose a font and a font size for your selected Paragraph Text, then click on OK.

Chapter 13: Very Special CorelDRAW Effects

4. As you can see in figure 13.24, you should click on the To Back button on the Ribbon Bar to send the Paragraph Text behind the magnifying glass and the shape that will become a lens.

Figure 13.24
Whatever you want to magnify must go behind the shape to which you attribute a Lens effect.

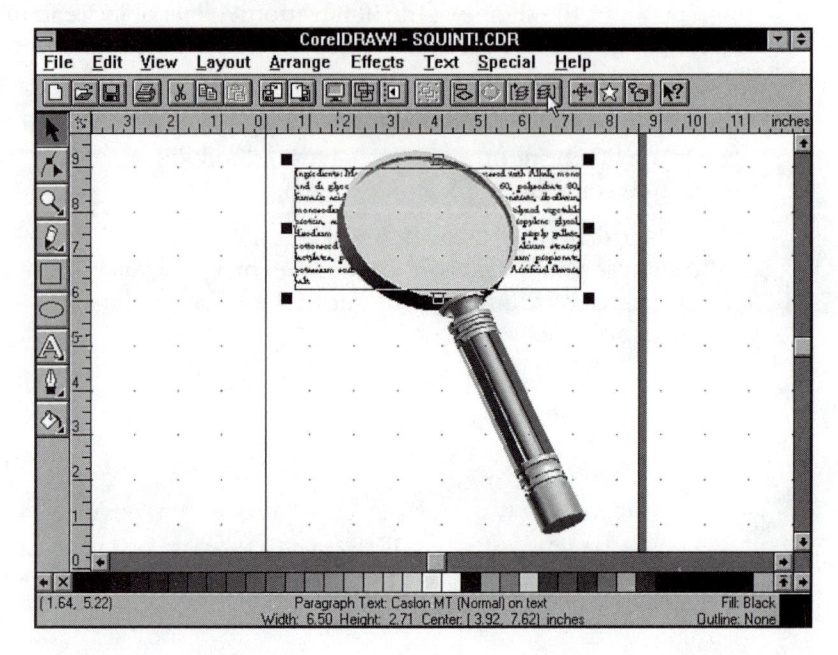

Getting the Big Picture on the Lens Roll-Up

Your setup is complete for making a design which features a Lens object. The effects the Lens Roll-Up produces are more pronounced when your field of zoom is closer on the effect, so before you continue, you'll want to marquee-zoom in on the lens shape on top of the Paragraph Text.

Follow these steps:

1. Press Alt+F3 (or choose Effe**c**ts, **L**ens Roll-Up) to display the Lens Roll-Up.

2. Click on the lens shape within the lens frame on your magnifying glass to select it.

3. Scroll down the drop-down list on the Lens Roll-Up until you find the Magnify effect.

Getting the Big Picture on the Lens Roll-Up

4. Depending on which effect you choose, you'll see options for each different effect. With the Magnify effect, you can set the amount of magnification. Because this is a vector, resolution-independent design program, I tried a fractional amount of magnification, 2.7. Enter any number here that you like between .1 to 10, in increments of tenths of a percent.

5. Press the Apply button. As you can see in figure 13.25, the text you import is neither good or bad—the Lens Roll-Up only magnifies it.

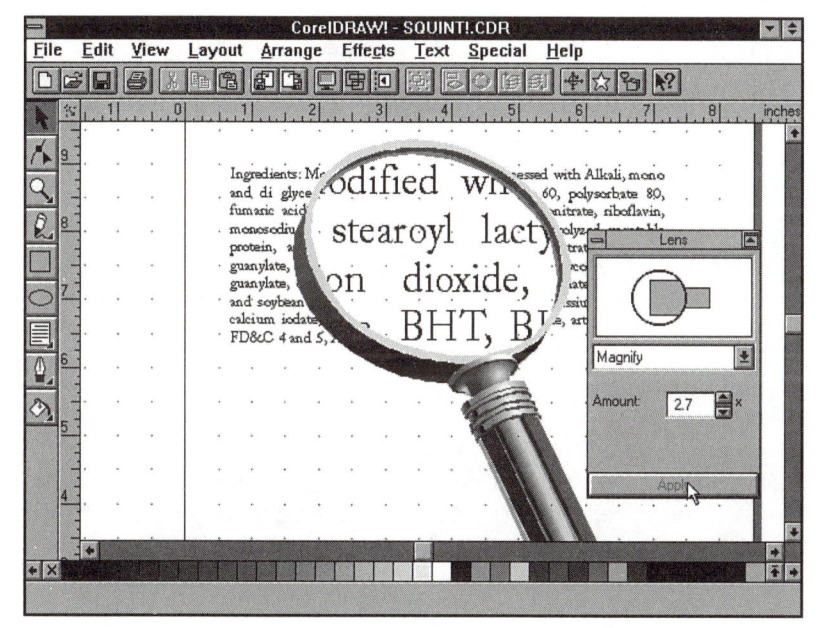

Figure 13.25

You can move an object with Lens attributes, and CorelDRAW displays the changes almost immediately.

Tip

If you'd like a shape with Lens attributes restored to normal again, choose No Effect from the drop-down list and press the Apply button.

To artistically balance this consumer alert flyer, I've added some bold headline text toward the bottom of it, shown in figure 13.26.

Chapter 13: Very Special CorelDRAW Effects

Figure 13.26

An example of how a CorelDRAW effect can be the center attraction of a design.

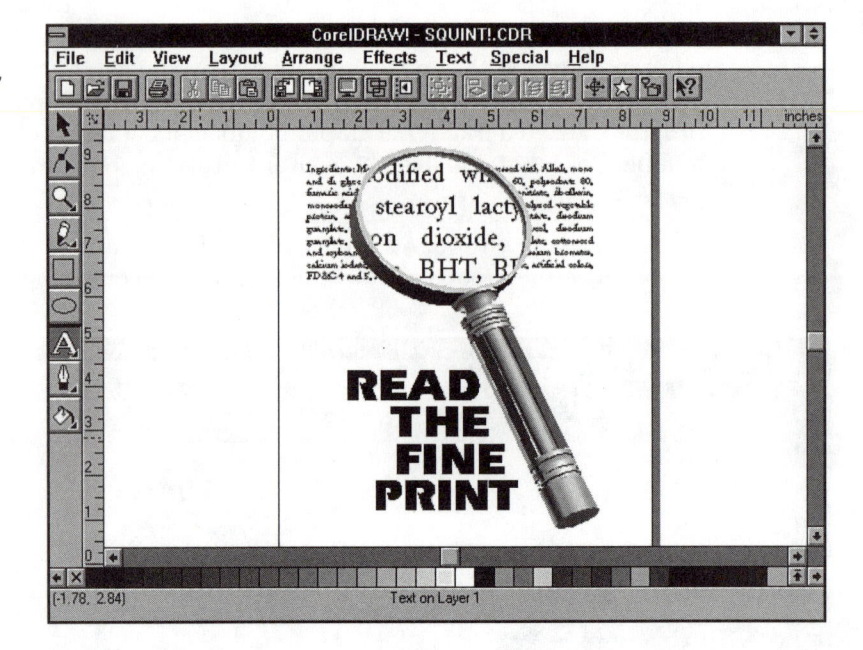

Reflections on a Lens

As you've seen in the last example, it doesn't take much effort to create an eye-catching design when you leave yourself open to experimentation for the fun of it while exploring Corel's effects. The other Lens effects produce thought-provoking results, as well—try typing the word Popsicle, then draw a shape of some quintessentially frozen desert, and give the shape a 50-percent transparent Lens effect with an orange tint.

Let the powers of CorelDRAW's features inspire you, and you in turn can quickly produce inspired work.

Summary

The stained glass assignment in this chapter is about as hard as it gets using CorelDRAW. I've pulled no punches, and if I was asked to design a stained glass piece tomorrow, you've just read exactly the steps I'd take. But if you followed the assignment here, I may never get a call tomorrow, because my potential client might find you, the CorelDRAW designer, first!

CorelDRAW! 5 for Beginners is a "concentrated" book, and you'll find in the future that a little of the information contained here goes a long way. Give yourself some quality time with the program, and the lessons in this book. You'll find that by mixing your own creative spark with a particular technique, you'll be able to create not one, but several distinctly different pieces of artwork, and all it takes is an understanding of *why* CorelDRAW does a certain thing.

Next Steps to Other Voyages

My intention here was to write a good book, and as we all know, the best of them have good endings. Probably the most important question you'll have after completing the assignments in this book is where you should go upon their completion. Let's tie up some things as you collect your gear and proceed from the CorelDRAW beginner's campgrounds to the high ground in your computer graphics adventures.

A continuing education is for everyone—CorelDRAW "experts," the author, and everyone at every phase of expertise. We all need to constantly explore, but there's a very real worth in *backtracking* as well, because it's easy to miss an important feature in a program as complex and rich as CorelDRAW.

Continue with your reading, but don't get so absorbed in Corel and other software literature that you haven't the time to go exploring without a guidebook. I remember the first time I drove a car (so does my dad, and the car, I think), and look back at the improvement I made through practice. It doesn't come in a pill, and while books provide keys to things, it's up to you to turn the key. Go back and do the assignment you felt you wanted to take in an original direction, or simply perfect a technique you think will be important to you later.

If you completed all the exercises in the chapters, you're better than you think you are at this CorelDRAW stuff. Unfortunately, there's no diploma or dehydrated pat on the back when you turn this page; but the very best artists I know keep trophies and other printed accolades in a closet, and spend two minutes (tops) wearing their laurels. I believe this is because the real fun is in the doing, and the very best rewards are personal ones. If you can better express your ideas graphically now with CorelDRAW than you could before reading this book, I feel great. But better still, I'd like to see your work in the CorelDRAW 5th Annual World Design Contest.

CorelDRAW can lift your dreams right off the ground, and then you can take them anywhere on earth. And that's called graduating, big-time.

So goodbye to the CorelDRAW novice, and hello to a fellow CorelDRAW user!

APPENDIX A

A CorelDRAW Glossary

The following glossary isn't an exhaustive cataloging of every conceivable CorelDRAW euphemism and computer-aided graphical drawing *bon mot*. Like the rest of this book, it's more like a nice start on what you really need to know right now. Hey, if you want exhaustive, try staying up all night and reading the Corel documentation!

Appendix A: A CorelDRAW Glossary

A

Align (Ctrl+A). A command from the Arrange menu, also found on the Ribbon Bar. You can select two or more objects in CorelDRAW and arrange them so that they line up with each other. You can have them line up on their left, right, top, bottom, and centers. Additionally, you can align an object, or several objects, to the center of the Printable page. The last object selected is the one that the others line up with when additive selecting; when marquee-selecting objects to align, the most recently drawn shape or shapes become aligned relative to the very first one you drew on the page.

Artistic Text. Short lines of type you create in CorelDRAW that can later have special effects applied to them. You create Artistic Text by simply selecting the Artistic Text tool, clicking in the Drawing Window (inside the Printable page is best), and typing. The limit to Artistic Text varies from typeface to typeface, but it is generally 250 characters. *See also* **Paragraph Text**.

B

Back One (**A**rrange, **O**rder menu or Ctrl+PgDn). Demotes selected object, or objects, one step in the arrangement of objects from front to back on the page. *See also* **To Back, Forward One**.

Black. Black is one of the four colors in the CMYK Color Model (Magenta, Cyan and Yellow are the others) you can mix in the Uniform Color dialog box to create any color that's reproducible with commercial process printing inks. A percentage of black (example: 20%) will produce gray. Percentages of black are handled well by most laser printers.

Blend, Blend Roll-Up (Ctrl+B). One of CorelDRAW's Effe**c**ts. A blend between two objects automatically creates a number of intermediate transitional objects or steps over which the designer has control. The Blend Roll-Up is used to specify the characteristics of the blend (how many steps, what color transition, if any) and to apply the blend.

Bitmap. A kind of computer graphics image used in CorelPHOTO-PAINT. Bitmap images are raster images; they are arranged on-screen and sent to a printer as lines of color pixels arranged in an imaginary grid. (Vector images are the opposite of bitmap images.) Bitmaps are also called resolution-dependent images; unlike vector art, a bitmap's quality can suffer when you scale it up or down. CorelDRAW, a vector-based program, has no editing tools for bitmaps, but can import them for use as a component of a design. Common file formats are .BMP, .GIF, .PCX, and .TIF. *See also* **Vector**.

Bézier tool (on the Freehand (Pencil) tool menu fly-out). A tool for drawing curved line segments and positioning nodes and control points on the curves simultaneously. Clicking and dragging with this tool produces curves and determines the direction of node control points. You don't need the Node Edit Roll-Up while using this tool, but a stiff drink might help, because the Bézier method of drawing shapes is more difficult than freehand drawing (and three people on Earth are good at it).

C

Callout tool. Located on the Freehand (Pencil) tool menu fly-out, this tool isn't used for drawing shapes, but rather to provide a line with a label on the end of it. It's used to annotate various parts of a drawing, or just for fun. See Chapter 4, "Drawing the Line Somewhere," to see how to use the Callout tool.

Canada. The country where CorelDRAW comes from. Also produces good hockey players and guys like William Shatner.

CD-ROM. Refers to both a drive and the disk that goes in the drive on your PC. It's the easy way to install CorelDRAW, and to access all the clip art and extra typefaces that come with Corel. Not to be confused with a plain CD, which goes in your stereo and plays music. Remember: A *CD* followed by a *ROM* relates to a personal computer.

Click. The action performed by depressing a mouse button. This clicking is synonymous with *selecting*, *picking*, and *choosing* stuff in Windows. *See also* **Hold**.

Clipboard. A Windows import/export filter that's used by selecting an object, then pressing the Copy button on the Ribbon Bar (**E**dit, **C**opy or Ctrl+C works, too). A copy of your piece can be found on the Clipboard until you copy something else. You can **P**aste the copy on the Clipboard into a lot of other programs that aren't even made by Corel. *See also* **Cut**.

Clone (**E**dit, Cl**o**ne). Creates a duplicate of an object, which then will mimic any changes you make to the original. The Effe**c**ts, Cl**o**ne command also enables you to clone an effect from a master object and apply it to a clone object.

Appendix A: A CorelDRAW Glossary

Combine (**A**rrange, **C**ombine; Ctrl+L). The merging of two separate objects to form one path. For example, the letter O consists of an outside path and an inside one that have been combined.

Control Curve. An object (Artistic Text or a shape you've drawn) that is the first or last object of an effect like Blends or Contours. This control curve can be moved and will cause the effect to respond to that move. To break the dynamic link between the control curve(s) and the effect, you must choose the effect objects and then use the (Arrange) Separate command.

Control Points, Control Lines. Handles that sprout from a node on a shape that has curved line segments in its construction. These appear when the Shape tool is active. If you click and drag on a control point with the Shape tool, you bend the curve that's associated with it. If you pull a control point away from a node, the control lines get longer, and the arc of the curve gets steeper.

Conv**ert to Curves** (Ctrl+Q). A command found on the Ribbon Bar that, when applied to a closed path that makes up a complex geometric shape (rectangles, ellipses, Artistic Text), destroys complexity to reveal nodes and curve segments. You can edit an object that's been converted to curves with the Shape tool and the Node Edit Roll-Up.

Copy (**E**dit, **C**opy; Ctrl+C). A command on the Ribbon Bar that creates a duplicate of an object and sends it to the Windows Clipboard. *See also* **Paste**.

Cursor. A floating symbol on your monitor that is directed by your mouse movements. A cursor can be shaped like an arrow, a crosshair, an I-beam, an hourglass (when your computer is thinking), or a variety of different shapes. Programs often offer different cursors for specific tasks. CorelDRAW uses no less than 26 different-shaped cursors to indicate in what drawing or editing activity you're engaged.

Curve. A line segment between two nodes. Whether the line segment *looks* curved or not, CorelDRAW still considers it a curve. To make a "straight line" curve look like a *typical* curve, you must press the To Curve button on the Node Edit Roll-Up while the line segment is selected.

Cut (**E**dit, Cu**t**; Ctrl+X). To remove an object from your drawing and move it to the Windows Clipboard. Trust me, you're better off copying your work instead of cutting. Also accessed by clicking on the Cut button on the Ribbon Bar, marked with a set of scissors (which you really shouldn't run with). *See also* **Paste**.

D

Default. The factory setting of various options in Corel. By default, Artistic Text is black without an outline, and shapes are drawn with a hairline outline. You can change many of Corel's default options. See Chapter 3, "Customizing CorelDRAW," for more information on changing defaults.

Del**ete** (**E**dit, De**l**ete). Removes an object from your drawing and *doesn't* send it to the Windows Clipboard. Do *not* see Paste, and press Ctrl+Z (**E**dit, **U**ndo) if you deleted something (like your work) by mistake.

Dimension lines, Dimension Line tool. Trio of tools located on the Freehand (Pencil) tool menu fly-out. Dimension lines enable you to tag a shape you've drawn with incremental measurements, such as meters, inches, or fractional amounts. When Snap to Objects is active and you draw a horizontal, vertical, or angular dimension line next to a shape, the increments labeled on the dimension line will update to reflect any resizing of the shape. Use the **A**rrange, **S**eparate command to break the dynamic link between the shape and a dimension line you've affixed to it.

dpi. Dots per inch. A term used to describe how fine or coarse a printer's resolution is. Older or inexpensive laser printers usually can print 300 dpi. Newer, more expensive laser printers usually can print up to 600 dpi.

Double-Click. Depressing the mouse button two times very quickly, then releasing. This movement in CorelDRAW is used for calling the Node Edit Roll-Up and for creating connected line segments with the Freehand (Pencil) tool.

Drag. What most people think of a Windows General Protection Failure (GPF). Also the act of *moving* your cursor while a mouse button has been *clicked*, but *not yet released*. Dragging is most commonly used to move an object in Corel from one location in the Drawing Window to another with the Pick tool.

Drawing Window. The area on-screen in CorelDRAW that you can draw in, bordered by the rulers (when active), a scroll bar on the right, and the color palette (when active) on the bottom. The Printable page fits inside the Drawing Window. You can draw anywhere, as long as it's inside the Drawing Window. For example, you can't draw on the Ribbon Bar (why would you want to anyhow?) because the Ribbon Bar is outside the Drawing Window.

Duplicate (**E**dit, **D**uplicate; Ctrl+D, or press + key while something's selected). Commands Corel to make a copy of an object within your workspace. Does not send it to the Windows Clipboard. Do *not* see Paste.

E

Edge Pad. Selection from the Fountain Fill dialog box. By increasing the Edge Pad value, you make the *transition* between the two Fountain Fill colors more *intense*. The Fountain Fill dialog box can be accessed by pressing Edit on the Fill Roll-Up, or by clicking on the icon on the Fill tool menu fly-out.

Elastic Mode. A feature on the Node Edit Roll-Up. When you pull on a node in Elastic Mode, the *control points* on neighboring, non-selected nodes move to conform to the direction in which you are pulling. Just try to say that last line twice.

Ellipse. Created by clicking and diagonal-dragging the cursor after selecting the Ellipse tool. A high-tech name for a distorted circle; ellipses, along with rectangles, are the closed shapes you can create with the least fuss in CorelDRAW.

Em Dash. A really long hyphen. Click with either of the Text tools on your workspace, then type **Alt** plus **0151** to get one.

En Dash. Longer than a hyphen but shorter than an em dash. Click with the Text tool on your workspace, then type **Alt** plus **0150** to get one.

Envelope, Envelope Roll-Up (Effects, Envelope Roll-Up or Ctrl+F7). Something you put a stamp on. Also a CorelDRAW effect that allows you to reshape the borders of an object like they were putty. Use the Envelope Roll-Up to apply the effect and specify how the effect will be applied.

EPS. Encapsulated PostScript. These are vector-based files that can only be printed to a PostScript printer. CorelTRACE creates these kind of files out of bitmaps. CorelDRAW can import .EPS images that you can edit *and print* to any printer when you Save them as a .CDR file.

Extract. Found in the Special menu. Extract allows you to save the typing you do in CorelDRAW as a text file your word processor can use.

Extrude, Extrude Roll-Up (Effects, Extrude Roll-Up or Ctrl+E). A CorelDRAW Effect. When you extrude an object, Corel gives that object a 3D effect. Use the Extrude Roll-Up to apply the effect and specify how the effect will be applied.

F

Fill. A color, texture, or object that you can put inside a closed path.

Fill tool. A button on the Toolbox whose fly-out menu contains tools for creating and specifiying many different kinds of fills—uniform fills, textured fills, Fountain Fills, and others. You can also access the Fill Roll-Up from the Fill tool menu fly-out or you can press Shift+F6 to display the Fill Roll-Up.

Fill Roll-Up (Shift+F6 or access from the Fill tool fly-out). One of Corel's many Roll-Up menus, this Roll-Up is used to create, specify, and apply fills to shapes you've created or to Artistic Text.

Filter. A conversion program (that Corel has a lot of) that allows you to import graphics and text that are in different formats, and to export a *.CDR file as a different type of graphic that other programs can accept.

Fly-Out. What an umpire sometimes calls at a baseball game. Also what you get when you click, then hold, on the Freehand tool and the Text tool. These fly-outs offer more selections of tools that relate to the basic tool. The Zoom, Fill, and Outline tools also have fly-outs that offer a selection of options and may also offer access to a Roll-Up that relates to the tool's function. These tools reveal their menu fly-outs when you click on them; no holding is necessary.

Forward One (Arrange, Order menu or Ctrl+PgUp). Promotes selected object, or objects, one step in the arrangement of objects from front to back on the page. *See also* **To Front**, **To Back**, **Back One**.

Fountain Fill. A fill that changes color gradually. Linear, Radial, Conical, and Square Fountain Fills all change from one color to another in different patterns. You can adjust the direction the pattern takes, as well as the colors Corel uses, to create the Fountain Fill. The Custom Fountain Fill option also provides intermediate Fountain Fill steps, good for imitating chrome and other effects.

Font. A cool name for a typeface. *Times Roman* is a font, but not a cool one.

Freehand (Pencil) tool. The button on the Toolbox with the little pencil on it, whose name changes from version to version of CorelDRAW. You can create one or several lines by clicking once for the beginning of each line, then a second time to finish it. By double-clicking at the finish of a line, you are actually starting a second. And if you continue this action back to where you started, finishing with a single click, you have a closed shape, or *path*, to which you can apply fill.

Appendix A: A CorelDRAW Glossary

G

Gray. Author of *Inside CorelDRAW*, also by NRP. Also a percentage of black. Shades of gray can be found on the left of the color palette in Corel; specific percentages of black, which create a specific gray, can be made in the Uniform Fill dialog box (accessed from the Fill Roll-Up or by pressing Shift+F11). In the Uniform Fill dialog box, you can select grayscale as a color model. Uniform Fill can also be opened by clicking on the Fill Color tool on the Fill tool's menu fly-out.

Group (Arrange, Group; Ctrl+G). CorelDRAW command found on the Ribbon Bar. When selected objects are tied together this way, you can move, resize, and color them all at once. One object in a group has no effect on another when bundled this way.

Guideline. The straight vertical or horizontal blue dotted line that you pull out from the rulers. Guidelines don't print. Guidelines are useful in combination with the Snap To Guidelines Ribbon Bar command for creating precise lines and shapes. Special settings for guidelines are set in the Guidelines Setup dialog box, which can be accessed by double-clicking on a guideline or by choosing Layout, Guideline Setup from the Menu Bar.

H

Handle (Selection, Corner, Rotate, Skew). One of the eight thingies that appear around the border of an object that's been *selected* with the Pick tool. Corner selection handles and side selection handles affect the object's size in different ways when you pull on them. By clicking on a selection after it's been selected, you put the selection in Rotate/Skew mode, where the bordering handles are used to rotate or skew the selection.

Hold. The activity directly after clicking with the mouse when you want to **drag** something. *See* **Drag**.

I

IBM. A large company that has produced time clocks, typewriters, and the personal computer. Also used as a modifier to describe a machine that runs on an Intel (or compatible) XT, 286, 386, 486, or Pentium chip using a version of DOS, Windows, UNIX, or OS/2 as an operating system. If you're running Corel, you have an "IBM-compatible" PC, or a genuine IBM-PC. If you own a Mac, you are not running Corel at present.

Icon. A little picture that's either on a button, or in a group in Windows Program Manager. You double-click on a program icon with your mouse to launch a program. You select different tools by clicking on icons. Icons are sometimes refered to as *buttons*.

Install. The painful process users must go through to put a software program on their computer's hard drive. You install CorelDRAW using its many installation disks, or install it from a CD-ROM if you have a CD-ROM drive.

Intersection Command. Found under the Arrange menu, this command can be used on two or more overlapping shapes to create a new shape whose dimensions are made from the area where all the other shapes overlap.

J

Join. When you have an open path you need to make into a closed one so you can fill it, use the Join button on the Node Edit Roll-Up. Select the beginning and ending nodes on the path with the Shape tool. Double-click to get the Node Edit Roll-Up, and press the button with the links of chain on it to join the nodes and create a closed shape.

K

Kerning. The spacing between characters in a typeset word. TrueType and Type 1 typefaces, as a rule, contain automatic kerning information, so a word like "HAWAII" doesn't have too much space between the As and the W. When type is poorly kerned, it looks like old-fashioned typewriting.

L

Layer. A work surface in CorelDRAW that the user can assign attributes to, or rearrange in order, when working on several of them. When you open Corel, you are, by default, assigned one layer, labeled **Layer 1**. Use the Layers Roll-Up (Layout, Layers Roll-Up; Ctrl+F3) for additional layer options.

Leading. The space between two lines of text. Publications generally have 120 percent of a typeface's point size as leading between Paragraph Text. Click and drag on the left handle of selected text with the Shape tool to increase/decrease Paragraph or Artistic Text leading.

Appendix A: A CorelDRAW Glossary

Line. The connection between two nodes in CorelDRAW, whether curved or straight. A line can be dotted, colored, or have a desired thickness, depending on the choices you select with the Outline tool.

Link. The relationship between a control object and an effect, or the relationship between a shape and a dimension line, or an original and a clone. Linked objects are affected when you edit the original object. A good example of a link is when you move a control object in a blend. The blend objects reproportion themselves; they resize and respace according to the changes made to the control object. The only way to stop this nutty behavior is to choose the effects object (or group produced by the effect), then choose Arrange, Separate.

M

Marquee. Marking off an area on your workspace by clicking, holding, and moving diagonally on your workspace, then releasing the mouse button. The result of performing a marquee action depends upon which tool is active; if you make a marquee with the Ellipse tool, you'll get an oval, and if you marquee with the Zoom in tool, you'll zoom into the Drawing Window. It's a handy way to select multiple objects in Corel when the Pick tool is active. Try it; the description is harder than the action.

Megabyte (MB). A measurement of both hard drive space and PC memory. Corel takes up more than 50 megabytes of hard drive space if fully installed, and requires 8 megabytes of RAM to run at a reasonable pace on your PC.

Menu Bar. The strip on the top of a Windows program that generally starts with File. In Corel, many effects, page layout specifications, and Roll-Ups can be accessed from the Menu Bar.

Merge-Back (Special menu). The opposite of Extract Text. CorelDRAW will place text you've extracted to edit in a text-editing program, and apply the changes when you Merge-Back the text file.

Mirror. To stretch an object 100 percent either horizontally or vertically. The Stretch and Mirror effect is accessed from the Effects, Transform Roll-Up in Corel.

Multi-Page Document. Corel has the option to display several pages within a CDR document file. You can add pages to the default page by pressing PageDown, and you can move between pages using the page controls. Any shape that is outside the Printable page in a multipage document will appear in the view of each page.

N

Nerd. Socially and hygienically challenged individual whose personal information base has been accrued from *PC Magazine*, *Lost In Space* reruns, and the ingredients list on beef jerky packages. Nerds are a source of *mis*information, however, when asked about CorelDRAW; if allowed to touch your PC, they will write a line in WIN.INI that belongs in CONFIG.SYS, and then your PC will only respond to signals transmitted by Voyager IV.

Node. The component of a vector line that a curve in a path passes through, which determines the arc and properties of the curve. Nodes govern the flow and direction of curved line segments. You set a node in a path by double-clicking when drawing with the Freehand (Pencil) tool. In CorelDRAW, nodes appear along a path when the path is selected and the Shape tool is active. Only the Shape tool can change the position and properties of a node. A node will appear hollow when it borders a straight line in a path; when the line is curved, the node will appear filled. Nodes can be symmetrical, cusp, and smooth; these properties have an effect on the two segments the node connects. Nodes with no control points connect straight line segments.

No. Option in a dialog box that is sometimes highlighted as the default response. When in doubt, and when the outcome of your file may be in peril, choose No if you don't understand the dialog's question.

Node Edit Roll-Up. A floating options list displayed by double-clicking on a node or curve with the Shape tool. There are no hot-key, shortcut, or Ribbon Bar commands to display the Node Edit Roll-Up, but you can set the Node Edit Roll-Up to be displayed whenever you start Corel by choosing this option from View, Roll-Ups.

Novice. Affectionate alternative name for *beginner*, used by intermediate and advanced users to describe someone's familiarity with PCs, Windows, CorelDRAW, and other programs.

O

Object. A discrete thing drawn in Corel that can be moved and placed independent of other things. An ellipse is an object. A blend is not an object, but a thing composed of many objects. Objects are also referrred to in this book as *shapes* and *paths*.

Appendix A: A CorelDRAW Glossary

OLE. Short for Object Linking and Embedding. This is a Windows feature to which Corel modules are savvy. OLE-ing a piece of your work into a different program allows you to display it there. Then, if you want to update it later, you double-click on the object, and its parent program will appear and allow you to edit the object.

P

Page Border. The rectangle within the Drawing Window with a faint drop-shadow behind it. Also known as the Printable page, this area defines what portion of your design will be sent to a printer. Anything outside the page border will not print. Double-clicking on the Rectangle tool adds an object to your document that fits exactly over the page border. Double-clicking on the page border's drop-shadow will display the Page Setup dialog box, where you can set the size and orientation of the page.

Page Controls. Buttons that appear at the bottom left edge of the Drawing Window when CorelDRAW is displaying a multipage document. You can advance or return to a page by clicking on the arrow buttons, or by clicking on the center of the page controls to display the Go To Page command (also found as an option in the Layout menu).

Palette. This is the color strip at the bottom of your Corel workspace. It can be changed by choosing another *.CPL file in the Custom option box in the Uniform Fill dialog box (on the Fill tool menu fly-out). You select a fill color for a selected object by clicking on a color swatch on the palette with your left mouse button. Click a color swatch with the right mouse button to choose an outline color. Clicking on the X on the color palette with the left mouse button removes a fill within a selection; clicking with the right mouse button on the X removes an outline.

Paragraph Text. The opposite of Artistic Text in Corel. Paragraph Text is created by marquee-selecting an area in the workspace with the Paragraph Text tool (the little page-like icon button on the Text tool fly-out). Any text you import into CorelDraw automatically becomes Paragraph Text. Paragraph Text can exceed the 250-character limit of Artistic Text, but you cannot apply blends, extrudes, or other effects to it.

Path. A series of curved or straight segments that pass through nodes. Paths can be created with the Freehand (Pencil) tool, with the Bézier tool, or by converting a rectangle, ellipse, or Artistic Text to curves. If you connect the beginning node of a series of line segments with the last one, you have a closed path that can be filled. Otherwise, the segments form an open path. A path can be edited using the Shape tool.

Perspective (Effe<u>c</u>ts, <u>A</u>dd Perpective...). An effect in Corel that makes an object appear to be viewed at an odd or severe angle. Remember the beginning titles to *Star Wars*? The lettering was set in perspective. But probably not using CorelDRAW.

Pick Tool. The arrow-shaped tool at the top of CorelDRAW's Toolbox. This tool is used for selecting, moving, rotating, and skewing a single or multiple shapes, or a group of shapes.

PostScript. A descriptor language for printers originally developed by Adobe Systems, Inc. Unlike common laser printers, a PostScript printer is capable of very high-resolution output to film or paper, and renders designs in a precise, refined way. PostScript printers give you plenty of time to do other things while you're waiting for your work to print out.

PowerLines, PowerLine Roll-Up (Ctrl+F8). Shapes, dynamically linked to lines and curves, that create the impression you're drawing with a calligraphic pen or woodcarving tool. The "seed" object is enclosed in a PowerLine, and adjustments to the original line you drew affect the shape of the PowerLine. You can draw in PowerLine mode by choosing this option from the PowerLine Roll-Up, or you can create a drawing first, then apply the PowerLine effect to the drawing later.

Po<u>w</u>erClip (Effe<u>c</u>ts menu). The PowerClip effect places an object (the contents) inside a container, which can be another shape or Artistic Text. The contents object replaces whatever area it covers of the container's original fill, and the effect is like a view of someone peeking through a window at you. Both the contents and the container can then be moved, stretched, or placed in front of other objects. Use the PowerClip command to extract a contents object from its container to make changes to the contents object.

Q

Quote Marks. Professional publications use these at the beginning and end of quotes. Use the Text tool, and type **ALT+0147** and **ALT+0148** to use open and close quotes, instead of the generic, typewriter-like quote key on your keyboard.

Appendix A: A CorelDRAW Glossary

R

RAM. Abbreviation for Random Access Memory. Found on chips that go in your PC, among other places. RAM is the active memory your PC needs to carry out Windows instructions and CorelDRAW designs. The more RAM your computer can hold, the better. Don't try to run CorelDRAW on less than 8MB of RAM.

Rectangle, Rectangle tool. A four-sided, closed shape drawn with the Rectangle tool by using a marquee motion when clicking and dragging. Rectangles have a fixed 90° angle at adjoining line segments. The Shape tool will round the corners of a rectangle, but it cannot be shaped asymmetrically without converting the rectangle to curves.

Ribbon Bar. A collection of buttons that perform 21 of the most commonly used CorelDRAW commands, found above the Drawing Window unless you've messed with **S**pecial, **P**references, View. Commands for importing and exporting, Snap To guidelines, Wireframe view, and other features are only a click away with the Ribbon Bar.

Roll-Up. These are floating palettes of additional options, colors, and effects that can usually be found in Corel's Menu Bar and Toolbox. Roll-Ups save you repeating steps to change something ordinarily accessed through the Menu Bar or Toolbox. When you're done with a specific activity, you can click on the arrow button on their upper right corner, and they roll up and out of the way. You can also close a Roll-Up by double-clicking on the Roll-Up's control menu button on its upper left corner.

Rotate (Alt+F8 or double-click on a selected object). To tilt an object clockwise or counterclockwise around its own axis. To rotate an object in Corel, you can click on it once after you've selected it (slower than double-clicking), then pull on a corner selection handle. Or you can rotate the object a precise number of degrees using the Rotate and Skew options on the (Effe**c**ts) **T**ransform Roll-Up (Alt+F8).

S

Scale. What an ambitious, outdoorsy person does to the face of a mountain. Also, what happens when you resize an object in Corel. When you hold on an object's selection handle and pull toward or away from the object, the status line tells you what percentage of the object's original dimensions you're resizing (scaling) it to.

Shape Tool. The tool beneath the Pick tool on the Toolbox. The Shape tool is used for node editing, text spacing, editing effects like envelopes and perspectives, and for modifying ellipses and rectangles. The Shape tool is not used to draw anything. Hey, doesn't it do enough?

Skew. To move two opposite sides of a shape in different directions, while leaving the other two sides alone. The effect of skewing a shape is similar to italicizing a word, or allowing the structural integrity of the Tower of Pisa to continue to deteriorate. You can skew an object by clicking once after it is selected, then pulling on a middle selection handle (the *skew* handle) with the Pick tool. You can also precisely skew an object by using the Transform Roll-Up (Alt+F12).

Snap To. A property you can assign to guidelines, the grid, or other objects, acessed from the **L**ayout menu. Additionally, the Ribbon Bar has a Snap To guidelines button, and double-clicking on a ruler will get you the Snap To "on and off" switch for the grid. When you select Snap To, lines and shapes you draw close to a guide will tend to "snap to" the guideline, depending on your distance from one when you start drawing. It's good for precision work, but frustrating when you've forgotten and left it on.

Status Line. This is where all the activity you're involved in on your workspace is displayed. The location of the status line can be set from the **S**pecial, **P**references, View menu. Information about a selected object's position on the workspace, color, outline, and other properties is displayed and updated on the status line.

Steps. Refers to the number of tones used to display or print a Fountain Fill. Also applies to the transitional objects created between two control objects after the Blend effect has been applied. You designate the number of steps in a blend from the **B**lend Roll-Up (Ctrl+B). *See also* **Blends**.

Symb**ols Roll-Up** (Ctrl+F11). Accessed through the **S**pecial command, or as the star button on the Ribbon Bar. The Corel user may choose from a number of categories of predrawn shapes from the Symbols Roll-Up. You click, hold, and drag symbols onto your workspace, then they inflate to a user-definable size like those paper-flat sponges you add water to.

Text Tool. The icon on the Toolbox that is a capital A. By default, the Text tool enables you to create Artistic Text, but by clicking and holding on the button on the Toolbox, you can access the Paragraph Text tool. You can enter text directly in the Drawing Window by choosing the tool, then clicking an insertion point on the page and typing.

Texture Fills. The button for this is located on the Fill tool menu fly-out. A Texture Fill is a complex design that simulates natural textures like sky and cloth when filled inside an object. They are "memory-intensive" fills for your PC that can slow your system down if used to fill large areas.

To Back, To Front commands. Buttons on the Ribbon Bar, also accessed through the Arrange, Order menu (Shift+PgUp is To Front, Shift+PgDn is To Back). Vector shapes are discrete objects, which have a hierarchy as they are drawn on the page. One object can be on top of another, and when this is undesired, select the shape and click on the To Back button, for example.

Toolbox. The vertical bar on the left of the Corel workspace that contains tools. Additional tools can be accessed by clicking, then holding on the tool button. The Toolbox can be detached from its docked position by choosing View, Toolbox, then Floating. Additionally, you can ungroup the Toolbox icons by unchecking the Grouped option from the control menu when the Toolbox is floating. When floating, the Toolbox can be reconfigured by click+dragging on its window, and all of the preceding options can lead to a really frustrating, confusing, and unproductive CorelDRAW session for a novice.

Trim. Accessed through the Arrange menu, the Trim command subtracts a piece of geometry from a path using another path as sort of a "scissors" object where the two paths overlap. The first object (or the one that's to the front of one or several shapes) is the "scissors" object, and the last or bottom object(s) is the "paper."

TrueType. The kind of typeface that ships with Windows 3.1. Corel offers TrueType in its typeface collection, and Corel can use Type 1 typefaces as well. TrueType typefaces don't work so well with PostScript printers, but they are excellent on PCL printers; they print fast, and you can buy new ones really cheap. You don't need a separate program (like Adobe Type Manager) to use TrueType in all your Windows 3.1 programs.

Type 1. An earlier typeface format, Type 1s require a *type manager* (like Adobe Type Manager) to be visible on your monitor. These are good typefaces to use with a PostScript printer, but even with an ordinary laser printer plus a type manager, they print fine and Corel can use them. Type 1s have quite a few years lead-time over the newer TrueType faces, so there are a lot of different styles available.

U

Undo (**E**dit, **U**ndo; Ctrl+Z). Allows you to "take back a move," unlike in a game of checkers with your younger brother. By default, there are four Undo steps in Corel, so you can make four mistakes on your design, press Undo four times, and you're back to where you started. The value of Undo can be increased to up to 99 steps from the **S**pecial, **P**references, General menu. However, the more levels CorelDRAW has to memorize, the more system RAM will be devoted to this task, and your PC may slow down. Between 1 and 10 Undo steps suit most users' needs, except perhaps the Three Stooges'.

V

Vector, Vector Graphic. Vector graphics (like those produced in CorelDRAW) are resolution-independent, object-oriented constructions. They are made up of mathematical information relating to degrees of arcs, relative positions and numbers of objects built, line width and color, and closed path fill. Vector graphics are the opposite of raster (or bitmap) graphics. When you draw a line in CorelDRAW, it is a vector graphic. It has a direction, an end and beginning, and you can assign attributes to it.

View **command.** Menu option that offers choices about how the rulers, color palette, Roll-Ups, and Toolbox are displayed on-screen. Also, Preview and Wireframe views can be specified here (or simply press the Wireframe button on the Ribbon Bar). You can also perform color correction and calibrate your monitor from the menu option under View.

W

Weld. A command from the Arrange menu in Corel. When you weld two or more objects, an outline of all the objects is created, and any paths within the shape where paths intersected are eliminated. A good command for creating silhouettes of stuff.

Windows. A product by Microsoft that allows you to run tons of different programs by different manufacturers in a visual environment on your PC. Windows programs, like Corel, can copy and paste stuff between them, and share a lot of the same commands, like File and Help, from their menu bars.

Appendix A: A CorelDRAW Glossary

X

X-Height. The height of a lowercase letter, measured from the text's baseline to the top of the letter. The x character is the standard for measuring lowercase characters, because it has no ascender or descender.

X. Label on a button on the color palette. Clicking on the X with the left mouse button removes the fill from a selection. Clicking with the right mouse button on the X removes the outline from a selection.

Y

Yes. An alternative phrase dialog boxes offer you in place of OK in Windows programs. Generally programmers use Yes when the decision you're going to make is a much more critical one than a decision that only requires an OK. Example: Do you want to delete all the files you've ever created? See No in a situation like this.

Z

Zero Origin. The box where the horizontal and vertical rulers meet on the edge of the Drawing Window. Clicking and dragging this box into the Drawing Window resets the zero point on the rulers to a location you determine. To reset the zero origin to Corel's default of 0,0 at the lower left corner of the Printable page, double-click on the zero origin box.

Zoom Tool. The tool located underneath the Shape tool on Corel's Toolbox. The Zoom tool has a menu fly-out for choosing how far or near you want to view your work in the Drawing Window. With the menu fly-out extended, from left to right, your Zoom options are:

- Zoom In tool: you use this as a marquee technique to zoom into an area you want.
- Zoom Out tool: an automatic tool; generally zooms you out to the field of view last defined before using the Zoom In tool.
- Zoom Actual Size tool: displays the document on-screen at the size it will print.

- Zoom to Selected tool: zooms in or out of the Drawing Window to display the area where an object (or several) is selected.
- Zoom to All Objects tool: brings everything you've drawn in the Drawing Window into view.
- Zoom to Page tool: displays the entire Printable page.

INDEX

Symbols

(–) en dash, 468
(—) em dash, 468
+ key (nodes), 130
16 Million colors drop-down box, 349
3D Riser charts, 380-381
3D Roll-Up (Ribbon Bar), 397-399
72 points per inch
    as electronic typeface standard, 279

A

Actor Information dialog box, 404-408
Actors, 400
    creating, 401-403
    cycles, 406-407
    naming, 404
    Timelines, 411
Add Perspective command (Effects menu), 189, 475
adding
    animation to charts, 415-416
    Artistic Text, 228-235, 244-246
    backgrounds (slideshows), 416-417
    clip art props, 337-338
    color, 417-418
    custom text, 366-367
    cycles (Actors), 406-407
    drop shadows (Artistic Text), 230
    fonts to type foundry glossary, 282
    labels, 394
    Layers, 169-171
    logos (fonts), 307-309
    ornaments (background), 203-204
    outlines (charts), 399
    perspective (objects), 186-194
    predrawn symbols, 223-224, 257-261
    stained glass
        text, 443-445
        texture, 440-443
    symbol characters, 304-306
Air Brush tool, 363
airbrush effects, 212-219
Align command (Arrange menu), 464
Align dialog box, 156
aligning
    Artistic Text, 231-232
    Control Objects, 161
    shapes, 156-157
All command (Mask menu), 368
angular distance (nodes), 129
animation
    default speed, 410
    drivers, 61-62
    objects
        bitmap formats, 401-403
        creating, 400-403
        Move, 400
    playing, 424-425
    shortening, 409-410

Animation Info command (Edit menu), 410
applications
    CorelCHART, 378
    CorelMOVE, 400-403
    CorelPHOTO-PAINT, 208
Apply Changes command (File menu), 405
applying
    Blend command, 436-438
    envelopes, 248-250
    lens to objects, 452-453
    Presets, 99-101
    Radial Fills, 18
    styles, 83-86
arcs, 26-28
Arial (font), 282
Arrange menu commands
    Align, 464
    Break Apart, 136, 225-228, 290
    Break-Apart, 176
    Combine, 125, 187, 309, 433, 466-467
    Fit Object to Slide, 416
    Group, 470
    Intersection, 215, 471
    Order, 464
    Separate, 140, 273, 286, 467-468
    Trim, 28, 135, 204, 478-479
    Ungroup, 326
    Weld, 125, 132, 158, 287, 479-480
arranging slides, 422-423
arrow cursor, 16
arrow keys (nudge keys), 86-89
Artistic Text, 26, 464
    adding, 228-235, 244-246
    aligning, 231-232
    drop shadows, 230
    editing, 230-231
    entering, 245

    Envelope Effect, 246-250, 344-347
    fonts, 254-255
    kerning, 233-235
    leading, 233-235
    rotating, 235
    shaping, 344-347
    sizing, 246
    stained glass
        adding, 443-445
        refining, 445-448
assigning fill colors (ellipses), 23
attributes (text), 319-321
auto-axes, 390-392
auto-panning (Drawing Window), 93
Auto-Reduce button (Nodes Edit Roll-Up), 291
Autofitted Text, 391-392
Autoscan (data view), 387
axis-numbers, 392-393

B

Back command (Arrange, Order menu), 478-479
Back One (Order menu), 464
back-up disks, 41
Background Library Tool (SHOW toolbox), 417
backgrounds
    adding ornaments, 203-204
    bitmaps (color), 369-370
    creating, 166, 194-198, 212-219
    Fill Roll-Ups, 217-220
    lighting, 359-360
    Linear Fountain Fill, 212
    refining
        Shape Tool, 220-223
        Snap To Objects command, 220

removing objects, 222
retouching, 351-352
slideshows
adding, 416-417
removing, 421
templates, 213-215
backup copies (fonts), 300-301
balls
creating, 16
shading, 19-24
baseline (horizontal guideline), 281
"Before and After" image, 339
bending typefaces, 33-36
Bézier curves (nodes), 128
Bézier tool, 126, 465
billboards, 417-418
Bitmap Export dialog box, 349
bitmaps, 196
backgrounds, 369-370
fills, 196
foregrounds, 369-370
formats
animating, 401-403
converting to MOVE Object, 404-405
image areas, 355-358
images
determining size, 211-212
opening, 208-209
pasting, 360-361
resolution, 212
scanners, 60-61
masking, 355-358
proprietary handling, 196
rasterizing, 2
resolution-dependent images, 464-465
rotating, 210-212
TIF (Tagged Image File format), 208

vector art, exporting to, 347-351
white space, 347
Black (color), 464-465
Blend command, applying, 436-438
Blend Effect
duplicating, 179-180
highlighting, 172-174
open line paths, 171-180
segments, 178
shading, 160-167
Blend Roll-up command (Effects menu), 166, 464-465
body text
fonts, 255
typefaces, 284
borders (pages), 474-475
Break-Apart command (Arrange menu), 136, 176, 225-228, 290
breaking subpaths, 136
bullet lists, 419

C

California Special chart, 398-399
Callout tool, 141, 465-467
callouts, 141
extensions, 142
repositioning, 142-143
caming (stained glass), 428, 433-436
cartooning (stained glass), 428
CD-ROM, 465-467
cells
Move objects, 400
spreadsheets, 380-381
tagging, 381-383
changing
dimension lines, 139
line segments, 119-120

object order, 24-25
perspective, 188-190
shapes, 133-136
Character Attributes dialog box, 33, 229, 344
Character command (Text menu), 33, 89, 302
Character Width (typefaces), 297
characters (fonts), 288-289
Chart menu commands (Preset Viewing Angles), 398
charts
3D-Riser, 380-381
animation, 415-416
California Special, 398-399
colors, 389-390
columns/series, 378-380
components, 399
creating, 378
customizing, 388-389
data, auto-positioning, 385
data-holder, 378-380
fonts, 388-389
icons, 379-380
labels, 391
 adding, 394
 deleting, 392-393
outlines, 399
riser markers, 395-396
saving, 399-400
selecting, 378-380
subheads, 385-387
view angles, 397-399
Choose which applications to install dialog box, 55, 224
Choose which files to install dialog box, 55

circles
creating, 16
ellipses, 468
shading, 19-24
Clear Transformations command (Effects menu), 190, 347
clicking
Bézier drawing mode, 126
callouts, 142
double-clicking, 467-468
ending paths, 131
keyboard-mouse operations, 15
mouse, 87-89, 465-467
clip art, 315
coloring, 325-327
copyrights, 316
editing, 325-327, 334-337
files, searching, 321-322
importing M0SAIC to DRAW, 322-325
props, 329-331, 337-338
re-using, 327-329
text
 resizing, 331-332
 rotating, 331-332
Clipboard, 465
Close command (File menu), 405
closed paths, 117
closing Roll-Up menus, 27
color, 417-418
Color command (View menu), 362
Color Comparison Tolerance dialog box, 356
color palette, 23
color ramps, *see* **Fountain Fills,**
colors
assigning, mouse buttons, 23
bitmaps
 backgrounds, 369-370
 foregrounds, 369-370

black, 464-465
charts
changing, 389-390
components, 399
clip art, 325-327
CorelPHOTO-PAINT, 351-352
customizing, 103-104
Fountain Fills, 448-451
gray, 470
objects, grouping, 261
palettes, 474-475
predrawn symbols, 258-259
tolerance, 355
Colors Roll-Up, 362
columns
charts, 378-380
headers
customizing, 390-392
spreadsheets, 381
sizing, 272-275
Combine command (Arrange menu), 125, 187, 309, 433, 466-467
commands
Arrange menu
Align, 464
Break-Apart, 136, 176, 225-228, 290
Combine, 125, 187, 309, 433, 466-467
Fit Object to Slide, 416
Group, 470
Intersection, 215, 471
Order, 464
Separate, 140, 273, 286, 467-468
Trim, 28, 135, 204, 478-479
Ungroup, 326
Weld, 125, 132, 158, 287, 479-480
Chart menu (Preset Viewing Angles), 398

Disk menu (Copy Disk), 43
Drive menu (Directory), 264
Edit menu
Animation Info, 410
Copy, 466-467
Copy Attributes From, 319
Cut, 466
Delete, 467-468
Duplicate, 180, 467
Insert Cels, 405
Paste, 360
Restore to Checkpoint, 361
Select All, 132, 287
Undo, 87, 133, 479
Effects menu
Add Perspective, 189, 475
Blend Roll-Up, 166
Clear Transformations, 190, 347
Contour Roll-Up, 20, 285
Envelope, 248
Envelope Roll-Up, 34, 468
Extrude Roll-Up, 191, 468
Lens Roll-Up, 459
PowerClip, 237, 475
Transform, 235
File menu
Apply Changes, 405
Close, 405
Copy, 309
Create Directory, 72
Delete, 69
Export, 295
Import, 236, 308, 457
New, 378
New From Template, 78
Open, 307
Print, 109
Rename, 309

Run, 48
Save, 35, 206, 288, 400
Save As, 206
Image menu (Flip), 359
Insert menu (Object), 415
Layout menu
   Delete Page, 265
   Go To Page, 474-475
   Grid and Scale Setup, 101, 279
   Guideline Setup, 470
   Insert Page, 182
   Layers, 471-472
   Layers Roll-Up, 169
   Page Setup, 110, 242
   Snap To, 136, 477
   Snap To Objects, 220-221, 429
   Styles Roll-Up, 83
Main menu (View), 479
Mask menu
   All, 368
   Invert, 358
   Load, 370
   Remove, 357
   Save, 368
Object menu
   Layers/Objects, 361
   Merge, 373
Pattern menu
   Large, 197
   Tiling, 197
Special menu
   Extract, 468
   Merge-Back, 472-473
   Preferences, 87, 211
   Presets Roll-Up, 96
   Symbol, 304
Text menu
   Character, 33, 89, 302
   Paragraph, 268
   To Front, 25
Tools menu (Zoom), 147
View menu
   Color, 362
   Roll-ups, 473
   Rulers, 116, 146
   Tool Settings, 353
composite photographs
   creating, 342-343
   foreground image, 346-347
container objects, 238-239
contents objects, 238-239
Contour effect (enhancements), 22-24
Contour Roll-Up command (Effects menu), 20, 285
Contour Roll-Up menu, 20-22
   Offset value, 21
   outlining shapes, 21
control curve, 466-467
Control Objects, 438
   aligning, 161
   creating, 161, 174-175
   editing (Preview mode), 162-164
   lighting, 161
control points
   launch point, 121
   lines, 120, 466-467
   pages, 474-475
   symmetrical nodes, 124
Convert to Curves button (Ribbon Bar), 133
Convert to Curves command (Ribbon Bar), 150-152, 466
converting graphics to CorelMOVE, 404-405

Copy Attributes dialog box, 319
Copy Attributes From command (Edit menu), 319
Copy command (File menu), 309
Copy commands (Edit menu), 466-467
Copy Disk command (Disk menu), 43
Copy Disk dialog box, 43
copying
    attributes, 319-321
    fonts, 300-301
    frames (stained glass), 431-433
    illegally, 41-42
    program disks, 41
copyrights, 41-42
    clip art, 316
    fonts, 311
Corel 5 Setup dialog box, 64
Corel files, 68-69
CorelCHART, 378
    Chart View, 380-381
    Data View, 380-381
    Pop-up menus, 393
    speadsheets, 380-381
CorelDRAW
    installing, 46-49, 64-67
    program modules, 50-53
CorelMOSAIC, 321-322
CorelMOVE, 400-403
CorelPHOTO-PAINT, 208, 351-352
CorelTRACE (OCR (optical character recognition)), 308-309
corners, rounding, 154-155
Create Directory command (File menu), 72
creating
    Actors, 401-403
    animation objects, 400-403

arcs, 26-28
backgrounds, 166, 194-198
    airbrush effects, 212-219
    Fountain Fills, 212-219
balls, 16
"Before and After" image, 339
callouts, 141-142
charts, 378
clip art props, 329-331
composite photographs, 342-343
Control Objects, 161, 174-175
crescents, 203-204
custom colors, 103-104
cycles, 406-407
depth, 190-192
directories, 72-73
drop-shadows, 261, 366-371
ellipses, 242
envelopes, 247-248
fonts, 283-285
frames (stained glass), 429-431
graphic styles, 78-79
graphics, 255-256
greeting cards, 14
headers (spreadsheets), 381-387
installation disks, 43-46
lowercase letters, 299-300
nodes, 129-130
Presets, 96-99
preview of files, 74-76
scale drawings, 101-103
slideshows, 412-414
stained glass effect, 428
surface shadows, 19-24
templates, 76-78
text, 29
three dimensions, 190-192
titles, 343-344
typefaces (customized), 277-313

wedges, 242-244
workspace, 146-149
crescents, 203-204
Crosshair cursor (Drawing Window), 94
cursors
    arrow cursor, 16
    dragging, 466-468
    Freehand tool cursor, 118
    Shape tool cursor, 130
curved lettering, 290-291
curves, 466-467
    Artistic Text, 228
    Bézier drawing mode, 126
    reshaping, 158-159
    smoothing, 122-124, 164-166
curving
    rectangles, 150-152
    straight lines, 119-120
cusp corners (ellipses), 152-154
cusps (nodes), 122
Custom Rotate dialog box, 210
customizing
    colors, 103-104
    Drawing Window, 93-96
    program modules, 53-55
    screen, 93-96
    typefaces, 277
Cut command (Edit menu), 466
cycles
    Actors, 406-407
    creating, 406-407
cycling between selected objects (Tab key), 29

D

data
    charts, auto-positioning, 385
    ranges, 384-385
data-holder (charts), 378-380
Data/Chart toggle button, 387
defaults, 467-468
    animation speed, 410
    colors (charts), 389
defining nodes, 129-130
defining rough shapes (Ellipse tool), 115
Delete command (Edit menu), 467-468
Delete command (File menu), 69
Delete Page command (Layout menu), 265
deleting
    axis-numbers, 392-393
    background objects, 222
    Corel files, 68-69
    dimension lines, 140
    fonts, 67-68
    Guidelines, 116, 183
    labels (charts), 392-393
depth, 190
descenders (fonts), 281-283
designing, 114
    protecting layers, 169-171
    saving as templates, 79-80
    templates (masks), 367-371
    typeface templates, 278
Destination directory dialog box, 49
destination disks, 44
dialog boxes
    Actor Information, 404
    Align, 156
    Bitmap Export, 349

Character Attributes, 33, 229, 344
Choose which applications to install, 55, 224
Choose which files to install, 55
Color Comparison Tolerance, 356
Copy Attributes, 319
Copy Disk, 43
Corel 5 Setup, 64
Custom Rotate, 210
Destination directory, 49
Edit Preset, 97
Export, 310
Fountain Fill, 18, 449, 468
Grid & Scale Setup, 102, 146
Guidelines Setup, 470
Insert Animation, 414
Insert Object, 413
Insert Page, 182, 285
New Actor, 402
New From Template, 81
New Layer, 444
New Presentation, 412-425
Open Collection, 323
Option, 295
Outline Color, 174
Outline Pen, 173
Preferences, 86
Remove Font, 68
Save Drawing, 74
Save File, 374
Save Texture As, 442
Size tabbed, 242
Temp Drives, 62
Texture Fill, 438
TIFF export, 212
Transition Effects, 423
TrueType Export, 296
TrueType Fonts Selection, 57
Uniform Color, 464-465
View index, 93

dimension lines, 136-137, 467-468
    converting decimals to fractions, 139
    deleting, 140
    extension lines, 138
    increments, 139
dimensional lighting, 89-91, 192-194
diminishing objects size, 251-253
direction (paths), 117
directories, 72-73
Directory command (Drive menu), 264
Disk menu commands (Copy Disk), 43
disks
    backing up, 41
    CD-ROM, 465-467
    destination, 44
    installation, 43-46
    write-protection, 43
display fonts, 255
display/headline typefaces, 284
displaying
    grids, 146-147
    rulers, 146-147
documents
    multi-page, 472
    tagging, 85
double-clicking
    callouts, 142
    mouse, 15, 467-468
    stopping lines, 131
dpi (dots per inch), 350, 467-468
dragging
    cursor 467-468
    rulers, 148-149
DRAW (MOSAIC importing to), 322-325
drawing tools, 24

Drawing Window (customizing), 93-96
drawings
  assembling shapes within, 124-125
  ellipses, 242
  viewing (on a clear screen), 36
Drive menu commands (Directory), 264
drivers (animation), 61-62
drives
  CD-ROM, 465-467
  installing CorelDRAW, 46-47
  MB (megabytes), 472-473
drop shadows
  Artistic Text, 230
  creating, 261, 366-367
  text, 368-371
dummy copy, 263
Duplicate command (Edit menu), 180, 467
duplicating
  blending, 179-180
  objects, 183-185

E

edge pad, 468
Edit menu commands
  Animation Info, 410
  Copy, 466-467
  Copy Attributes From, 319
  Cut, 466
  Delete, 467-468
  Duplicate, 180, 467
  Insert Cels, 405
  Paste, 360
  Restore to Checkpoint, 361
  Select All, 132, 287
  Undo, 87, 133, 479
Edit Preset dialog box, 97
editing
  Artistic Text, 230-231
  clip art, 325-327, 334-337
  Control Objects (Preview mode), 162-164
  Extrudes, 192
  linked items, 393
effects (transition), 423-424
Effects menu commands
  Add Perspective, 189, 475
  Blend Roll-Up, 166
  Clear Transformations, 190, 347
  Contour Roll-Up, 20, 285
  Envelope, 248
  Envelope Roll-Up, 34, 468
  Extrude Roll-Up, 191, 468
  Lens Roll-Up, 459
  PowerClip, 237, 475
  Transform, 235
elastic mode, 468
ellipses, 468
  assigning fill colors, 23
  cusp corners, 152-154
  Shape Tool modifying, 242-244
  Snap To points, 220-221
  tool, 16, 20, 27
    defining rough shapes, 115
    Symmetrical nodes, 124
  wedges, 242-244
em dash (—), 468
embossing, 89-91
en dash (–), 468
enhancements (Contour effect), 22-24
enlarging text, 31-32

entering
    Artistic Text, 245
    data ranges (spreadsheets), 384-385
entries (spreadsheets), 380-381
Envelope, modifying, 347
Envelope command (Effects menu), 248
Envelope effect (Artistic Text), 344-347
Envelope Roll-Up command (Effects menu), 34, 468
Envelope Roll-Up menu, 33
envelopes
    applying, 248-250
    creating, 247-248
    Paragraph Text, 271-272
    segments properties, 249
    subpaths, 249-250
EPS (Encapsulated PostScript), 468
Export command (File menu), 295
Export dialog box, 310
export filters, 55-56
exporting
    foreground images, 346-347
    typefaces, 294-299
    vector art to bitmap format, 347-351
extended characters (fonts), 228
extension lines, 138
extensions (callouts), 142
Extract command (Special menu), 468
Extrude command, shading, 192-194
Extrude Roll-Up command (Effects menu), 191, 468
Eye Dropper tool, 351-352

F

faces (clip art), 334-337
Fast Forward buttons (player controls), 409
Feather option, 361
File menu commands
    Apply Changes, 405
    Close, 405
    Copy, 309
    Create Directory, 72
    Delete, 69
    Export, 295
    Import, 236, 308, 457
    New, 378
    New From Template, 78
    Open, 307
    Print, 109
    Rename, 309
    Run, 48
    Save, 35, 206, 288, 400
    Save As, 206
files
    Actors, 402-403
    clip art, 321-322
    Corel, 68-69
    EPS (Encapsulated PostScript), 468
    headers, 74-76
    importing
        MOSAIC to DRAW, 322
        RTF (Rich Text Format), 458-459
    opening from templates, 80-83
    previewing, 74-76
    saving work, 73-76
    temporary files, 62-64
    TIF (Tagged Image File Format), 208
    visuals, 74-76
fill color (left mouse button), 23
Fill Roll-Up, 469-470

Fill tool, 18, 469-470
filling shapes, 258-259
fills, 18-19, 468-470
    assigning colors (ellipses), 23
    bitmaps, printing, 196
    Texture, 478-479
filter (conversion program), 55-56, 469
Fit Object to Slide command (Arrange menu), 416
Flip command (Image menu), 359
Fly-outs, 469-470
Font Minder, 59
Font Monster (shareware), 312
Fonter (shareware), 228
fonts, 267, 469-470
    aligning, 231-232
    Arial, 282
    Artistic Text, 254-255
    backup copies, 300-301
    body text, 255
    characters, 288-289
    charts, 388-389
    copyrights, 311
    creating, 283-284
    curved lettering, 290-291
    customizing, 277, 312
    descenders, 281-283
    display, 255
    exporting, 294-299
    extended characters, 228
    foundary glossary, 282
    Gothic, 284
    installing, 59-60, 300-301
    kerning, 294-299
    logos
        adding, 307-309
        sizing, 309-312
    lowercase letters, 299-300
    open paths, 290-291
    outlines, 286-288
    paths, 285
    point size, 279-283
    positioning characters, 288-289
    removing, 67-68
    renaming, 312
    Roman, 284
    selecting, 58-59
    serifs, 284
    shareware
        Fonter, 228
        Font Monster, 312
        Font Minder, 59
        FontSee, 228
    symbol characters, 302
    templates, 277-278
    TrueType, 56-58, 245, 285, 478-479
    Type 1, 285, 478-479
    Type 1 PostScript, 245
    see also typefaces
foregrounds
    bitmaps color, 369-370
    images exporting, 346-347
    objects resizing, 201-202
    retouching, 351-352
formulas (vector art), 2-5
Forward One (Order menu), 469-470
Fountain Fill dialog box, 18, 449, 468
Fountain Fills, 94-96, 448-451, 469-470
    backgrounds, 212-219
    intermediate, 449-451
    gradient fills, 18
    Radial Fills, 18-19
    Stepped Fills, 18
    steps, 477

fractal Texture Fills, 438-443
frames (stained glass)
   copying, 431-433
   creating, 429-431
   moving, 431-433
Freehand (Pencil) tool, 131, 469
   cursor, 118
   drawing, 116-118
   paths, 116
   smoothing curves, 122-124
Front command (Arrange, Order menu), 478-479
Full-Screen Preview button (Ribbon Bar), 36

G

Go To Page command (Layout menu), 474-475
Gothic fonts, 284
gradient fills, *see* Fountain Fills
graphics
   bitmaps, 464-465
   converting to CorelMOVE, 404-405
   creating, 255-256
   merging, 373-374
   styles, 78-79
gray (color), 470
greeking text, 263
greeting cards, 14
Grid & Scale Setup dialog box, 102, 146
Grid & Scales Setup command (Layout menu), 101, 279
Grid and Scale Setup for larger design than Printable page, 280
Grid Size (typefaces), 296
grids, displaying, 146-147

Group button (Ribbon Bar), 223
Group command (Arrange menu), 470
grouping
   colored objects, 261
   elements on Layer, 198-201
   objects, 222-223
Guideline Setup command (Layout menu), 470
Guidelines
   baseline, 281
   deleting, 116, 183
   marking shapes, 115
   Paragraph Text, 262-265
   typefaces, 280
Guidelines Setup dialog box, 470
gutters (text), 263

H

handles, 470
   rotate/skew, 331
   selection, 25, 32
headers
   adding to files, 74-76
   customizing, 390-392
   spreadsheets, 381-383
headline fonts, 255
headlines (typefaces), 284
help (online), 101
Help boxes, 15
highlighting
   Blend Effect, 172-174
   creating, 171-180
holding (mouse), 470
honey-dipper handle (text handle), 233-235

I

IBM, 470-471
icons, 379-380, 471
illegal copying, 41-42
image areas (bitmaps), 355-358
Image menu command (Flip), 359
images
    bitmaps, 208-209
    determining size, 211-212
    resolution, 212
    TIFs (Tagged Image File Format), 212
Import command (File menu), 236, 308, 457
import filters, 55-56
Import Images options box, 403
importing
    clip art (MOSAIC to DRAW), 322
    files (RTF (Rich Text Format)), 458-459
    TIF (Tagged Image File Format), 236
increments
    dimension lines, 139
    resetting, 396
    riser markers, 395-396
Insert Animation dialog box, 414
Insert Cels command (Edit menu), 405
Insert menu commands (Object), 415
Insert Object dialog box, 413
Insert Page command (Layout menu), 182
Insert Page dialog box, 182, 285
inserting
    callouts, 141-142
    dimension lines, 136-140
    text, 29
installation disks, 41-46
installing
    CorelDRAW, 46-49, 64-67
    filters, 55-56
    fonts, 59-60
    scanner drivers, 60-61
    symbols, 224
    TrueType fonts, 56-58
    typefaces, 300-301
integrated environment, 5
Intel (IBM), 470-471
intermediate Fountain Fills, 449-451
Interruptable Refresh (Drawing Window), 93
Intersection Command, replacements, 252-253
Intersection command (Arrange menu), 215, 471
Invert command (Mask menu), 358

J-K

joining paths, 471
kerning, 471
    Artistic Text, 233-235
    boundary, 297
    typefaces, 294-299
keyboard (arrow keys), 86-89

L

labels
    adding, 394
    charts, 391-393
Landscape orientation typefaces, 278
Large command (Pattern menu), 197
laser printers, 109-111

Lasso Mask tool, 358
launch point (control points), 121
Layers
   adding, 169-171
   elements, grouping, 198-201
   locking, 169-171
   moving, 198-201
   printing, 169-171
   protecting, 169-171
Layers command (Layout menu), 471-472
Layers Roll-Up command (Layout menu), 169
Layers/Objects command (Object menu), 361
Layout menu commands
   Delete page, 265
   Go To Page, 474-475
   Grid and Scale Setup, 101, 279
   Guideline Setup, 470
   Insert Page, 182
   Layers, 471-472
   Layers Roll-Up, 169
   Page Setup, 110, 242
   Snap To, 136, 477
   Snap To Objects, 220-221, 429
   Styles Roll-Up, 83
leading, 233-235, 471-472
left mouse button, 23
lens objects, 452-453
Lens Roll-Up, 452-455
Lens Roll-Up command (Effects menu), 459
lighting
   backgrounds, 359
   Blend Effect, 160-167
   Control Objects, 161
   dimensional, 192-194

line segments, 119-120
Linear Fountain Fills, 212-215
lines, 472
   Bézier drawing mode, 126
   blending, 171-180
   coloring, 171-180
   controlling segments, 120
   curving straight lines, 119-120
   dimension lines, 136-140
   nodes, 473
   smoothing out curves, 122-124
   stopping, 131
   see also objects; paths
linking, 472
   editing, 393
   frames (text), 271
   text frames, 272-275
lists (bulleted), 419
Load command (Mask menu), 370
loaded text frames, 272-275
locking Layers, 169-171
logos
   fonts, 307-309
   sizing, 309-312
lowercase letters, 299-300

M

macros, 96-101
Magic Wand Mask tool, 351
Magnify Lens Effect, 455-457
Magnify setting, 453-455
magnifying Paragraph Text, 457-459
Main menu commands (View), 479
Maintain original image size check box, 211
Manual Refresh (Drawing Window), 93

marking shapes (Guidelines), 115
marquee, 472-473
   drawing motion, 16
   Zoom mode, 114, 125
Mask menu commands
   All, 368
   Invert, 358
   Load, 370
   Remove, 357
   Save, 368
masks
   bitmaps, 355-358
   design templates, 367-371
MB (megabytes), 472-473
memory
   CorelDRAW, 46-47
   MB (megabytes), 472-473
   RAM (random access memory), 476
menu bar, 472-473
menus
   Contour Roll-Up, 20-22
   Envelope Roll-Up, 33
   Node Edit Roll-Up, 119
   roll-up menus, 20
Merge command (Object menu), 373
Merge-back command (Special menu), 472-473
merging graphics, 373-374
mirroring, 183-185, 472-473
modifying
   ellipses (Shape Tool), 242-244
   shapes, 133-136
molding Artistic Text, 246-250
MOSAIC clip art files, 321-322
mouse
   assigning colors with buttons, 23
   clicking, 87-89, 465-468
   cursor, 466-467
   dragging, 148-149
   holding, 470
   pathmaking (freehand drawing), 118
MOVE objects, 404-405
moving
   frames (stained glass), 431-433
   Layers, 198-201
   objects (PowerClip), 236-240
   pages, 198-201
   Paragraph Text, 266-267
   pasted selections, 360
multi-page documents, 472
Multi-Page feature, 181-183

N

naming Actors, 404
navigating spreadsheets, 380-381
New Actor dialog box, 402
New command (File menu), 378
New From Template command (File menu), 78
New From Template dialog box, 81
New Layer dialog box, 444
New Presentation dialog box, 412
no fill (attribute), 22
Node Edit Roll-Up, 471, 473
Node Edit Roll-Up menu, 119
nodes, 473
   angular distance (maximum recommendation), 129
   Auto-Reduce, 291
   Bézier curves, 128
   control points, 121
   controlling segments, 120

curved lettering, 290-291
curves, 466-467
    reshaping, 158-159
    smoothing, 164
cusps, 122
defining, 129-130
ellipses, 152-154
paths, 116
printing, 154
rectangles, curving, 150-152
selecting, 119
Symmetrical nodes, 124

nudge keys
arrow keys, 86-89
settings, 91

numbers (spreadsheets), 384-385

O

Object command (Insert menu), 415
Object Data Roll-up, 85
Object menu commands
Layers/Objects, 361
Merge, 373
Object Picker tool, 372
object-oriented constructions (vector graphics), 479
object-oriented, *see* **vector art**
objects
colored, 261
container, 238-239
contents, 238-239
duplicating, 183-185
grouping, 222-223
lens, 452-453
mirroring, 183-185
modifying, 133-136
ordering, 24-25
perspective, 186-194
PowerClip, 236-240
rotating, 186-188
scaling, 476-477
sizing, 251-253
skewing, 186-188, 477
text, 282
see also paths; shapes

OCR (optical character recognition), 308-309
Offset value (Contour Roll-Up menu), 21
OLE (object linking and embedding), 401-403, 474
Onion Skin (animation cels), 406
online help, 101
Open Collection dialog box, 323
Open command (File menu), 307
open line paths
blending, 171-180
coloring, 171
open paths, 290-291
opening
files from templates, 80-83
images (bitmaps), 208-209
options (printing), 109-111
Options dialog box, 295
Order command (Arrange menu), 464
ordering shapes, 24-25
outline color, 23
Outline Color dialog box, 174
Outline menu, 172-174
Outline Pen dialog box, 173
Outline tool, 399-400
outlines
charts, 399
fonts, 286-288
shapes (Contour Roll-Up menu), 21

P

Page Setup command (Layout menu), 110, 242
pages
  borders, 474-475
  moving, 198-201
painting (PHOTO-PAINT), 362-364
palettes, 23, 474-475
Paragraph command (Text menu), 268
Paragraph Text, 474-475
  enveloping, 271-272
  magnifying, 457-459
  moving, 266-267
  properties, 263-265
  setting guidelines, 262-265
Paste command (Edit menu), 360
pasting, 360-361
pathmaking (freehand drawing), 118
paths, 474-475
  closed, 117
  direction, 117
  ending, 131
  fonts, 285
  freehand drawing, 116
  joining, 471
  nodes, 116
  see also lines; objects
Pattern menu commands
  Large, 197
  Tiling, 197
PCX image, 401
Pencil tool, 116, 131
Pentium (IBM), 470-471
perspective, 186-194, 475
PHOTO-PAINT
  painting, 362-364
  text, 371-372

photographs
  composites, 342-343
  stock images, 208
  TIF (Tagged Image File Format), 208
Pick tool, 24, 27, 475
  compared to arrow cursor, 16
  positioning text, 35
pixels
  bitmaps, rotating, 210-212
  image resolution, 212
  rasterizing, 2
  resolution, 343
Play button (player controls), 408-409
player controls, 408-409
playing animation, 424-425
plus sign button (Node Edit Roll-Up), 130
points
  size (fonts), 281-283
  typefaces, 278, 279-281
points of inflection, 116
Pop-Up Help (Drawing Window), 94
pop-up menus (CorelCHART), 393
Portrait orientation, 278
positioning
  callouts, 142-143
  characters, 288-289
  text, 35-36
PostScript (printer), 475
PowerClip command (Effects menu), 237, 475
PowerLine Roll-Up, 475
predrawn symbols, 223-224, 257-261
Preferences command (Special menu), 87, 211
Preferences dialog box, 86

Preset Viewing Angles command (Chart menu), 398
Presets
  applying, 99-101
  creating, 96-99
  online help, 101
Presets Roll-Up command (Special menu), 96
Preview Fountain Steps (Drawing Window), 94
Preview mode, 162-164
previewing files, 74-76
Print command (File menu), 109
Printable page, 114
printers
  dpi (dots per inch), 467-468
  PostScript, 475
printing
  bitmap fills, 196
  graphic complexity, 167
  laser printers, 109-111
  Layers, 169-171
  nodes, 154
  options, 109-111
program modules
  CorelDRAW, 50-53
  customizing, 53-55
proportional designs, 149
proprietary handling (bitmaps), 196
props (clip art), 329-331, 337-338
protecting design layers, 169-171

Q-R

quote marks, 475

Radial Fill commands (Fill Roll-Up), 225-240

Radial Fills (Fountain Fills), 18-19
RAM (random access memory), 476
rasterizing pixels, 2
Rectangle tool, 26, 133, 476
rectangles
  curving, 150-152
  restoring corners, 133
  rounding corners, 154-155
  Snap To points, 220-221
Remove command (Mask menu), 357
Remove Font dialog box, 68
removing
  backgrounds from slideshows, 421
  fonts, 67-68
Rename command (File menu), 309
renaming fonts, 312
replacements (Intersection command), 252-253
repositioning
  callouts, 142-143
  text, 35-36
resetting
  increments, 396
  typefaces
    rulers, 279
    zero origin, 279
reshaping curved line segments, 120
resizing
  foreground objects, 201-202
  text, 331-332
resolution
  bitmap images, 212
  dpi (dots per square inch), 350
  pixels, 343
resolution-independent, *see* **vector art**
Restore to Checkpoint command (Edit menu), 361

retouching, 351-352
Ribbon Bar, 476
   Drawing Window, 94
   To Back/To Front commands, 478-479
Rich Text Format (RTF), 458
right mouse button
   clicking, 87-89
   outline color, 23
riser markers (charts), 395-396
roll-up menus, 20, 476
   3D, 397-399
   Blend, 464-465
   closing, 27
   Color, 362
   Edit button, 217
   Fill, 217-220, 469-470
   Lens, 452-455
   Node Edit, 473
   Object Data, 85
   PowerLine, 475
   Symbol, 223
   Symbols, 477
   Text, 244-246
   Tool Settings, 363
Roll-Ups command (View menu), 473
Roman fonts, 284
rotate/skew selection handles, 331
rotating, 476
   bitmaps, 210-212
   objects, 186-188
   text, 235, 331-332
row headers
   customizing, 390-392
   spreadsheets, 383-384
RTF (Rich Text Format) importing files, 458-459

rulers
   displaying, 146-147
   dragging mouse, 148-149
   resetting typefaces, 279
Rulers command (View menu), 116, 146
Run command (File menu), 48
run-time modules, 61-62
running slideshows on screen, 412-414

S

Save command (File menu), 35, 206, 288, 400
Save command (Mask menu), 368
Save As command (File menu), 206
Save Drawing dialog box, 74
Save File dialog box, 374
Save Texture As dialog box, 442
saving, 73-76
   charts, 399-400
   designs as templates, 79-80
   intermediate Fountain Fills, 450
   TIFs (Tagged Image File Format), 212
scale drawings, 101-103
scaling
   design, 114
   objects, 476-477
scanner drivers, 60-61
screen, 93-96
searching clip art files, 321-322
segment parts, 176-178
   blending, 178
   envelopes, 249
   lines, 119-120

Select All command (Edit menu), 132, 287
selecting
    charts, 378-380
    colors, 351-352
    fonts, 58-59
    foreground color, 372
    image areas (bitmaps), 355-358
    nodes, 119
    text objects, 282
    typefaces, 32-33, 372
selection handles, 25, 32, 331
selection tools, 24
Separate command (Arrange menu), 140, 273, 286, 467-468
separating segment parts, 176-178
serifs (fonts), 284
setting up dimension lines, 136-140
settings
    defaults, 467-468
    nudging, 91
    Paint Brush tool (PHOTO-PAINT), 353
    tabs, 269-270
    workspace, 86-88
    Zero Origin Point, 147-149
shading
    backgrounds, 359
    balls, 19-24
    Blend Effect, 160-167
    clip art, 325
    Extrude command, 192-194
    shadows, 22-24, 366-367
Shape tool, 119, 130, 133, 477
shapes
    aligning, 156-157
    filling, 258-259
    marking with Guidelines feature, 115
    modifying, 133-136, 242-244
    ordering, 24-25
    outlining, 21
    welding, 157-159
shaping Artistic Text, 246-250, 344-347
shareware
    Font Monster, 312
    Fonter, 228
    FontSee, 228
Shift key selecting shapes, 28
shortcut (plus key/Ctrl+D), 161
Show Object when Moving Box (Drawing Window), 94
Size tabbed dialog box, 242
sizing
    Artistic Text, 246
    logos, 309-312
    objects, 251-253
    scaling, 476
skewing, 186-188, 477
slideshows
    backgrounds
        adding, 416-417
        removing, 421
    creating, 412-414
    running on screen, 412-414
    slides, 422-424
Smooth button (Node Edit Roll-Up menu), 123
smoothing curves, 122-124, 164-166
Snap To command (Layout menu), 136, 477
Snap To Guidelines, 149
Snap To Objects command (Layout menu), 220-221, 429
Snap to Objects mode, 137
sorting slides, 422
Space Width (typefaces), 296

spacing
   kerning, 471
   leading, 471-472
Special menu commands
   Extract, 468
   Merge-Back, 472-473
   Preferences, 87, 211
   Presets Roll-Up, 96
   Symbol, 304
splash screen, 15
spreadsheets
   cells, 380-381
   data ranges, 384-385
   entries, 380-381
   headers, 381-383
   navigating, 380-381
   numbers, 384-385
   row headers, 383-384
stained glass
   adding texture, 440-443
   Blend command, 433-436
   caming, 428, 433-436
   cartooning, 428
   Fountain Fills, 448
   fractal Texture Fills, 438-440
   frames, 429-430
      copying, 431-433
      moving, 431-433
   text
      adding, 443-445
      refining, 445-448
Status Line, 17, 477
Status Line Field (Drawing Window), 94
Step Frame Forward button (player controls), 408
stepped fills *see* **Fountain Fills**
stock images (photographs), 208
straight lines, 119-120

Style Roll-Up command (Layout menu), 83
styles
   applying, 83-86
   creating, 78-79
subheads (charts), 385-387
subpaths
   breaking, 136
   envelopes, 249-250
surface shadows, 19-24
switching tools (drawing/selecting), 24
Symbol command (Special menu), 304
symbols
   characters, 302-306
   installing, 224
   predrawn, 257-261
      adding, 223-224
      coloring, 258-259
Symbols Roll-Up, 223, 477
Symmetrical nodes, 124

T

Tab key
   cycling between selected objects, 29
   settings, 269-270
Tag preview window, 385
tagging
   cells, 381-383
   documents, 85
Temp Drives dialog box, 62
templates, 76-78
   creating from designs, 79-80
   for backgrounds, 213-215
   masks, 367-371

opening new files, 80-83
typefaces, 277-278
temporary files, 62-64
text, 366-367
    Artistic, 26, 228-235, 464
        adding, 244-246
        assigning fonts, 254-255
        sizing, 246
    as graphic, 371-372
    Autofitted, 391-392
    callouts, 141-142
    columns, 272-275
    drop-shadows, 368-371
    enlarging, 31-32
    envelopes, 248-250
    foreground color, 372
    formatting, 268
    frames, loaded, 272-275
    gutters, 263
    inserting, 29
    linked frames, 271
    objects, 282
    Paragraph, 474-475
        moving, 266-267
        properties, 263-265
        setting guidelines, 262-265
    PHOTO-PAINT, 371-372
    repositioning, 35-36
    resizing, 331-332
    rotating, 235, 331-332
    stained glass
        adding, 443-445
        refining, 445-448
    typefaces, 372
    wrap, 262-263
    X-height, 480
    zooming, 30

text handle (honey-dipper), 233-235
Text menu commands
    Character, 33, 89, 302
    Paragraph, 268
Text Roll-Up, 244-246
Text tool, 29, 394, 477-479
texture (stained glass), 440-443
Texture Fill dialog box, 438
Texture Fills, 438-440, 478-479
texture numbers (fractal Texture Fills), 441-443
three dimensions, 190-192
TIF (Tagged Image File)
    16 Million-color drop-down box, 349
    bitmaps, 208
    importing, 236
    saving, 212
TIF export dialog box, 212
Tiling command (Patterns menu), 197
timeline slider (animation control), 409
Timelines, 411
titles, 343-344
To Back button (Ribbon Bar), 204
To Curve button (Node Edit Roll-Up), 132, 133
To Front command (Ribbon bar), 25, 227
tolerance (colors), 355
Tool Settings command (View menu), 353
Tool Settings Roll-Up, 363
Toolbox, 478
tools
    Air Brush, 363
    Background Library, 417
    Bézier, 126, 465

Callout, 141, 465-467
Ellipse, 16, 20, 27, 115
Eye Dropper, 351-352
Fill, 18, 469-470
Freehand (Pencil), 116, 131, 469
Help boxes, 15
Lasso Mask, 358
Magic Wand Mask, 351
Object Picker, 372
Outline, 399-400
Pencil, 116, 131, 469
Pick, 16, 24, 27, 35, 475
Rectangle, 26, 133, 475-476
Shape, 119, 130, 133, 477
switching between drawing and selection tools, 24
Text, 29, 394, 477-479
Vertical Dimension, 138
Zoom, 30, 89, 280, 480-481
Zoom (PHOTO-PAINT), 352
Zoom In tool, 114
Zoom Out tool, 124

Tools menu commands (Zoom), 147
Transform command (Effects menu), 235
Transition Effects dialog box, 423
Trim command (Arrange menu), 28, 135, 204, 478-479
trim function, 28-29
TrueType Export dialog box, 296
TrueType fonts, 245, 285, 478-479
installing, 56-58
removing, 67-68
TrueType Fonts Selection dialog box, 57
TWAIN-compliant scanners, 60-61
Two-Color Pattern Editor, 196

type, 29
enlarging, 31-32
zooming, 30
Type 1 fonts, 245, 285, 478-479
type foundry glossary, 282
typefaces, 32-33, 469-470
bending or twisting, 33-36
body text, 284
cap height, 281-283
Character Width, 297
characters, 288-289
copyrights, 311
curved lettering, 290-291
customizing, 277, 312
descenders, 281-283
describing, 284
display (headline), 284
exporting, 294-299
fonts, 284-285
Grid Size, 296
Guidelines, 280
installing, 300-301
kerning, 294-299
logos
 adding, 307-309
 sizing, 309-312
outlines, 286-288
point size, 279-283
resetting rulers and zero origin, 279
Space Width, 296
symbol characters, 302
templates, 277-278
text, 372
TrueType, 478-479
Type 1, 478-479
see also fonts
typesetting, 268

U-V

Undo command (Edit menu), 87, 133, 479
Ungroup command (Arrange menu), 326
Uniform Color dialog box, 464-465
vanishing points, 190
vector art, 2-5
    drawing, 251-253
    exporting to bitmap format, 347-351
    graphics, 479
    greeting cards, 14
Vertical Dimension tool, 137-138
view angles
    changing, 188-190
    charts, 397-399
View command (Main menu), 479
View index dialog box, 93
View menu commands
    Color, 362
    Roll-Ups, 473
    Rulers, 116, 146
    Tool Settings, 353
viewing drawings, 36
visuals, 74-76

W

wedges, 242-244
Weld command (Arrange menu), 125, 132, 158, 287, 479-480
welding, 157-159
white space, 347
Windows, 479
Windows Character Map (extended characters), 228

wireframes, 172-174
workspace, 86-88, 146-149
write-protection (disks), 43

X-Y-Z

X-height, 480
Z2 axis entries, 395-396
Zero Origin Point, 480-481
    resetting typefaces, 279
    setting, 147-149
Zoom command (Tools menu), 147
Zoom In tool, 114
Zoom mode (marquee), 125
Zoom Out tool, 124
Zoom tool, 30, 89, 280, 352, 480-481

CorelDRAW! 5 for Beginners
REGISTRATION CARD

NRP

Fill out this card to receive information about future CorelDRAW books and other New Riders titles!

Name _____ Title _____

Company _____

Address _____

City/State/ZIP _____

I bought this book because: _____
_____

I purchased this book from:
☐ A bookstore (Name _____)
☐ A software or electronics store (Name _____)
☐ A mail order (Name of Catalog _____)

I purchase this many computer books each year:
☐ 1–5   ☐ 6 or more

I currently use these applications: _____
_____
_____
_____

I found these chapters to be the most informative: _____
_____

I found these chapters to be the least informative: _____
_____

Additional comments: _____
_____

☐ I would like to see my name in print! You may use my name and quote me in future New Riders products and promotions. My daytime phone number is: _____

New Riders Publishing 201 West 103rd Street • Indianapolis, Indiana 46290 USA

Fold Here

PLACE
STAMP
HERE

New Riders Publishing
201 West 103rd Street
Indianapolis, Indiana 46290
USA

WANT MORE INFORMATION?

CHECK OUT THESE RELATED TITLES:

	QTY	PRICE	TOTAL

CorelDRAW! Now! Users who want fast access to thorough information, people upgrading to CorelDRAW! 4.0 from a previous edition, new CorelDRAW! users—all of these groups will want to tap into this guide to great graphics—now! Developed by CorelDRAW! experts, this book provides answers on everything from common questions to advanced inquiries.
ISBN: 1-56205-131-8.   ____ $21.95   _____

PCs for Non-Nerds. This lighthearted reference presents information in an easy-to-read, entertaining manner. Provides quick, easy-to-find, no-nonsense answers to questions everyone asks. A great book for the "non-nerd" who wants to learn about personal computers.
ISBN: 1-56205-150-4.   ____ $18.95   _____

OS/2 for Non-Nerds. Even non-technical people can learn how to use OS/2 like a professional with this book. Clear and concise explanations are provided without long-winded, technical discussions. Information is easy to find with the convenient bulleted lists and tables.
ISBN: 1-56205-153-9.   ____ $18.95   _____

Windows for Non-Nerds. *Windows for Non-Nerds* is written with busy people in mind. With this book, it is extremely easy to find solutions to common Windows problems. Contains only useful information that is of interest to readers and is free of techno-babble and lengthy technical discussions. Important information is listed in tables or bulleted lists that make it easy to find what you are looking for.
ISBN: 1-56205-152-0.   ____ $18.95   _____

Name _____

Company _____

Address _____

City _____ State ____ ZIP _____

Phone _____ Fax _____

☐ Check Enclosed   ☐ VISA   ☐ MasterCard

Card # _____ Exp. Date _____

Signature _____

Prices are subject to change. Call for availability and pricing information on latest editions.

Subtotal _____

Shipping _____
$4.00 for the first book and $1.75 for each additional book.

Total _____
Indiana residents add 5% sales tax.

New Riders Publishing   201 West 103rd Street • Indianapolis, Indiana 46290 USA

Orders/Customer Service: 1-800-428-5331
Fax: 1-800-448-3804

Fold Here

PLACE
STAMP
HERE

New Riders Publishing
201 West 103rd Street
Indianapolis, Indiana 46290
USA

GO AHEAD. PLUG YOURSELF INTO MACMILLAN COMPUTER PUBLISHING.

Introducing the Macmillan Computer Publishing Forum on CompuServe®

Yes, it's true. Now, you can have CompuServe access to the same professional, friendly folks who have made computers easier for years. On the Macmillan Computer Publishing Forum, you'll find additional information on the topics covered by every Macmillan Computer Publishing imprint—including Que, Sams Publishing, New Riders Publishing, Alpha Books, Brady Books, Hayden Books, and Adobe Press. In addition, you'll be able to receive technical support and disk updates for the software produced by Que Software and Paramount Interactive, a division of the Paramount Technology Group. It's a great way to supplement the best information in the business.

WHAT CAN YOU DO ON THE MACMILLAN COMPUTER PUBLISHING FORUM?

Play an important role in the publishing process—and make our books better while you make your work easier:

- Leave messages and ask questions about Macmillan Computer Publishing books and software—you're guaranteed a response within 24 hours
- Download helpful tips and software to help you get the most out of your computer
- Contact authors of your favorite Macmillan Computer Publishing books through electronic mail
- Present your own book ideas
- Keep up to date on all the latest books available from each of Macmillan Computer Publishing's exciting imprints

JOIN NOW AND GET A FREE COMPUSERVE STARTER KIT!

To receive your free CompuServe Introductory Membership, call toll-free, **1-800-848-8199** and ask for representative **#597**. The Starter Kit Includes:

- Personal ID number and password
- $15 credit on the system
- Subscription to CompuServe Magazine

HERE'S HOW TO PLUG INTO MACMILLAN COMPUTER PUBLISHING:

Once on the CompuServe System, type any of these phrases to access the Macmillan Computer Publishing Forum:

GO MACMILLAN   **GO BRADY**
GO QUEBOOKS   **GO HAYDEN**
GO SAMS   **GO QUESOFT**
GO NEWRIDERS   **GO ALPHA**

Once you're on the CompuServe Information Service, be sure to take advantage of all of CompuServe's resources. CompuServe is home to more than 1,700 products and services—plus it has over 1.5 million members worldwide. You'll find valuable online reference materials, travel and investor services, electronic mail, weather updates, leisure-time games and hassle-free shopping (no jam-packed parking lots or crowded stores).

Seek out the hundreds of other forums that populate CompuServe. Covering diverse topics such as pet care, rock music, cooking, and political issues, you're sure to find others with the same concerns as you—and expand your knowledge at the same time.

Are you afraid to touch your computer?

Fear no more! You no longer have to wade through mountains of computer manuals or depend on that annoying computer know-it-all geek.

The *Non-Nerds* books are the *Essential Guides* for Busy People. In today's fast-paced world, you need practical and down-to-earth explanations presented in a lighthearted manner. Join the successful ranks of computer users without being a nerd.

Windows for Non-Nerds
ISBN: 1-56205-152-0 $18.95 USA

An important figure in Washington, D.C. said, "I now have to learn how to use the computer and fast. **Windows for Non-Nerds** helped me do that without worrying that other staffers will see a book sitting around suggesting I'm a dummy."

PCs for Non-Nerds
ISBN: 1-56205-150-4 $18.95 USA

Solutions in *PCs for Non-Nerds* are easy to find because NRP stripped away all non-essential text. One woman referred to *PCs for Non-Nerds* as a "Low-fat book—all of the good stuff, just none of the fat."

DOS for Non-Nerds
ISBN: 1-56205-151-2 $18.95 USA

Demanding an increase in the availability of Non-Nerds books, a business manager in Columbus, Ohio said, "We don't want to become Ph.Ds in Windows, DOS, PC hardware, OS/2 or any other !@%* computer subject. We just want to learn what we need without being told we're too stupid to do so! Non-Nerds books have more information, substance, and value than other books."

OS/2 for Non-Nerds
ISBN: 1-56205-153-9 $18.95 USA

A Sacramento nurse praised the Non-Nerds books for their inviting, focused, practical approach. She said, "These books teach me how to use a computer just like I learned how to be a good nurse. I wasn't forced to learn as much as a super brain surgeon or professor of neurology."

GRAPHICS TITLES

INSIDE CORELDRAW! 4.0, SPECIAL EDITION
DANIEL GRAY

An updated version of the #1 best-selling tutorial on CorelDRAW!

CorelDRAW! 4.0
ISBN: 1-56205-164-4
$34.95 USA

CORELDRAW! SPECIAL EFFECTS
NEW RIDERS PUBLISHING

An inside look at award-winning techniques from professional CorelDRAW! designers!

CorelDRAW! 4.0
ISBN: 1-56205-123-7
$39.95 USA

CORELDRAW! NOW!
RICHARD FELDMAN

The hands-on tutorial for users who want practical information now!

CorelDRAW! 4.0
ISBN: 1-56205-131-8
$21.95 USA

INSIDE CORELDRAW! FOURTH EDITION
DANIEL GRAY

The popular tutorial approach to learning CorelDRAW!... with complete coverage of version 3.0!

CorelDRAW! 3.0
ISBN: 1-56205-106-7
$24.95 USA

To Order, Call 1-800-428-5331